Linguistica Extranea, Studia 12

MORPHONOLOGY:
the dynamics
of derivation

MORPHONOLOGY:
the dynamics
of derivation

WOLFGANG U. DRESSLER

EDITED BY KENNETH C. HILL

1985

KAROMA PUBLISHERS, INC.   ANN ARBOR

Cover design by Lilian E. Stafford

ISBN 0-89720-034-9 (Paperback Only)
Published and Printed in the United States of America

CONTENTS

PREFACE

Speaking very grossly, linguists tend to approach language with one or the other of two opposed attitudes: that what is most interesting about language is its GRAMMATICAL aspect, its organization according to principles that are specifically linguistic; or that what is most interesting about language is its FUNCTIONAL aspect, the way in which it is embedded in, and serves the purposes of, human cognitive and social organization. American structuralists and generative grammarians most often favor the first view, while European structuralists, anthropological linguists, and sociolinguists incline toward the second.

Again speaking very grossly, theories of grammar point in one or the other of two directions: toward the HOMOGENIST assumption, that a grammar is basically a single object, subject to the same conditions and restrictions throughout; or toward the assumption that that a grammar is a complex object, composed of a number of heterogenous subparts (at least syntax, morphology, and phonology -- for some writers semantics and phonetics as well). The second, or MODULARIST, attitude is currently dominant among generative grammarians, though there is considerable disagreement about which modules are required by a universal theory of grammar, what their characteristics are, and how one decides when a rule belongs in one module and when in another; see Sadock (1983) and Zwicky (1984) for some general discussion of the issues.

In this monograph Dressler generally assumes a modularist position and asks where the domain of morpho(pho)nology fits in a universal theory of grammar. The issue is the nature of the principles that specify how morphemes are realized phonologically. D argues that some of these principles are phonological rules (PRs), belonging in the phonology module; that others are allomorphic morphological rules (AMRs), located in the morphology module; and that morphonological rules (MPRs), in a third set, share some properties with PRs and others with AMRs. But, he maintains, MPRs have no characteristic properties of their own and so fail to constitute a grammatical module comparable to the phonology and morphology modules. (I will use the term QUASI-MODULE to refer to a set of rules that is distinguishable from other sets on various criteria but nevertheless lacks characteristic properties of its own.)

D's treatment of the quasi-moduld of MPRs in fact attempts a resolution of

the homogenist and modularist positions. On the modularist side, he observes
that a great many criteria distinguish PRs from AMRs and that on these criteria
MPRs are intermediate between PRs and AMRs. But on the homogenist side, he
maintains that the boundaries between PRs and MPRs (on the one hand) and between
MPRs and AMRs (on the other) are somewhat 'fuzzy'. Finally, on the modularist
side again, he proposes that the transitions between (quasi-)modules, though not
sharp, are steep; most rules clearly belong in one module or the other.

D also attempts to accommodate both the functional and the grammatical attitudes within a single framework. Most of this book is taken up with an issue
in grammatical theory, the status of MPRs --D refers to these chapters as 'descriptive'-- but Chapter 10 examines morphonology from the functional viewpoint,
sketching, in D's words, an 'explanatory model' based on semiotic considerations
and uniting the concerns of Natural Morphology and Natural Phonology.

In the more narrowly grammatical chapters, D discusses virtually every issue in phonological theory, some in detail, others in capsule summary. He enu-
merates the criteria (which he treats as scalar) distinguishing PRs, MPRs, and
AMRs; provides considerable critical revision of existing lists of tests; and
relates his distinctions to the allophonic/morphophonemic distinction of structuralist approaches, the process/rule distinction of Natural Phonology, and the
postlexical/lexical distinction of Lexical Phonology. Two case studies, in
Italian and Polish, illustrate D's proposals in detail. Along the way D examines a long list of theoretical proposals in phonology: among them, directionality in phonological relationships, domains of rule application (prosodic or
morphosystactic), morpheme structure rules, abstractness, opacity, rule interaction, cyclicity, and rule strata.

Though these topics appear under headings familiar from the generative literature, D's impressive scholarship is far from parochial. Covering about a
century of writing (in a dozen languages, often in obscure publications) on morphonological matters, his references and data are drawn from a wide spectrum of
theoretical frameworks.

Integrating research in phonostylistics and the sociolinguistic aspects of
phonological variability with theoretical proposals, D critically examines the
distinctions between slow/fast, formal/casual, and attentive/inattentive speech
and relates them to various modularist schemes. In addition to drawing (fuzzy)
lines between PRs, MPRs, and AMRs, D's own framework stresses a distinction be-

tween FOREGROUNDING and BACKGROUNDING processes and crucially uses the notion of
DEFAULT.

Finally, this book touches on many topics external to grammar in the narrow
sense -- extensively on acquisition (with a separate chapter of its own), diachronic change (in almost every chapter), and typology (in the semiotic chapter), but also on aphasia, language games, poetic conventions, language death,
and pidginization.

This diversity of subject matter in a book on morphonology is not an affec-
tation on D's part. Morphonology cust across several modules of grammar (phonology, morphology, and syntax) and the lexicon; describing a morphonological
system requires appeals to many sorts of evidence, both internal and external;
and explaining why morphonological systems are the way they are takes us still
further afield. We are in D's debt for this attempt both to embrace the whole
enterprise and to supply explicit proposals for the details.

Arnold M. Zwicky
Ohio State University

0. INTRODUCTION

0.1.1. Any conceivable definition of morphonology must be derivative: Whereas semantics, syntax, morphology, phonology can be defined within their own respective domains without referring to one another, a definition of morphonology must be derived from previously defined morphology and phonology. And as we will see in the descriptive chapters 1-9, all morphonological phenomena can be derived from morphological and/or phonological phenomena. And the explanatory chapter 10 will show that morphonology cannot be explained without explaining morphology and phonology.

It is my contention that this derivation of morphonology from morphology and phonology must be of a dynamic nature: The dynamic interaction of morphology and phonology creates and constrains morphonology. A consistent static conception of morphonology results in the negation of its existence (as in Martinet 1965). The dynamics of derivation embodied in our approach can both isolate morphonological phenomena in synchrony, diachrony, language acquisition and disturbance as in many other types of substantive evidence, and derive them from more basic concepts.

0.1.2. This chapter will be brief,[1] and this is for two reasons:

(1) An introduction to the approach of this book is successively developed from 1 through 4 for the descriptive part and in the beginning of 10 for the explanatory part.

(2) An ample history of research is unnecessary because this has been done by Kilbury (1976).[2] Therefore what can easily be found there will be outlined very briefly here (0.5); however, important lacunae in Kilbury's account will be filled and research of the last ten years will be briefly surveyed (with cross references to sections of this book).

0.2. According to Trubetzkoy (1931:161ff), the discipline of morphonology (a haplological variant of morphophonology) consists of three parts:

0.2.1. Its first task is 'the study of the phonological structure of morphemes'. This is the area of intramorphemic phonotactics or morpheme structure rules/con-

straints (see 8), e.g., no English morpheme (affix or monomorphemic word) may
end in */md/ (but cf. bimorphemic *scream-ed*).   Extremely few linguists have accepted this view.[3] Since I follow Trubetzkoy by including this task into our
discussion, I also use his term 'morphonology' rather than the competing terms
morphophonology or morphophonemics. But Trubetzkoy's view must be modified:
In 8 I will argue that also within morpheme structure rules (MSRs) morphonology
must be separated from both phonology and morphology.

0.2.2. The second task of morphonology is 'the study of the combinatory phonic
modifications which morphemes undergo in morpheme combinations'. Here morphonology is viewed from the angle of morphology: Morphonological modifications
are deviations from transparent morphology, e.g., in the plural variant *roov-es*
of *roof-s*. Note that only phonemic modifications qualify, not allophonic ones
(but still more has to be excluded, cf. 0.3.2). All those who regard morphonology as part of morphology (0.4.1) tend to reduce morphonology to this part.

0.2.3. The third task of morphonology is 'the study of the alternation series
which serve a morphological function'. Here morphonology is viewed from the angle of phonology, e.g., English velar softening applies only before certain suffixes as in *electri*[s]-*ity, scepti*[s]-*ism, criti*[s]-*ize*. One must stress 'alternation SERIES' (G. 'LautwechselREIHEN') because isolated phonemic changes
such as the synchronically unparalleled vowel and consonant change in E. *was* vs.
were does not qualify for morphology but for suppletion (1.9, 5.4.8).

0.3. Trubetzkoy's second and third task (0.2.2f) correspond largely to what has
been called 'morphophonemics' in American linguistics,[4] and I will use 'morpho-
phonemic(s)' in this sense. I will call morphonology a subject both larger (0.
3.1) and smaller (0.3.2) than morphophonemics:

0.3.1. Morphophonemics deals with phonemic modifications in morphologically derived words and word forms,[5] i.e., these need not necessarily be polymorphemic,
cf. *(to) hou*[z]*e* derived from basic *hou*[s]*e* with morphophonemic voicing: In a
static account one speaks of an alternation between the phonemes /s/ and /z/;
in a dynamic account [z] is derived from /s/ by rule (cf. 1).

But there are also morphonological phenomena in isolated, non-derived morphemes (0.2.1, 8), and one may legitimately speak of phrase or sentence morpho-

nology (2.4.2). This is usually excluded from morphophonemics, in spite of the Indian tradition of grouping word morphology and phonology (as far as phonemic changes are concerned) under the heading 'internal sandhi' and phrase/sentence morphology/phonology under the heading 'external sandhi' (called syntactophonemics by Nida 1946:200).

0.3.2. Morphophonemics includes two types of alternations which must be excluded from morphonology: (1) automatic, exceptionless phonemic alternations which are clearly phonological, e.g., devoicing of the plural /z/ → [s] in E. *beat-s* in contrast to *bead-s*, (2) purely allomorphic alternations such as voicing in E. *to house* (0.3.1), umlaut in E. *foot* → *feet*, and suppletions such as *were* vs. *was*.

0.3.3. However there are gradual transitions between phonological and morphonological alternations, between morphonological and allomorphic ones (5).[6] My view is then that there are prototypical morphonological rules (MPRs) with fuzzy boundaries to phonological rules (PRs) and allomorphic morphological rules (AMRs). Only prototypical MPRs (including 0.3.1) are the object of morphonology in its narrow sense. If morphonology is derived from the interaction of morphology and phonology (0.1.1), then the outcome of this interaction can also be phonological or morphological rather than only morphonological in the narrow sense.

0.4. Where does morphonology belong?[7]

0.4.1. Many linguists assign it to morphology, either as a separate subpart of not. Within structural linguistics we may cite van Wijk (1939:126ff) and in the Trubetzkoyan lineage Martinet (1965) who negates the very existence of morphonology, Kuryłowicz (1968), Stankiewicz (1955 through 1979), Andersen (1969), Buyssens (1980:40ff); presumably earlier Baudouin de Courtenay (1985), more recently Mel'čuk (e.g., 1973), and in America, Pike (1947) and tagmemics

0.4.2. Many other linguists assign morphonology to phonology, generally as a separate subpart, such as at least partially Trubetzkoy (1929, 1931, 1934, omitted in Trubetzkoy as topic for a successor volume), clearly Sapir (1933/1963), Whorf (1956:126), and adherents of generative phonology where --a lacuna in Kil-

bury's (1976) survey-- much energy has been devoted to a differentiation of
rules corresponding to morphonological rules within 'phonology',[8] starting with
the contrast between 'natural rules' ($\approx$ PRs) and 'crazy rules' (Bach & Harms
1972, roughly corresponding to AMRs and, often, MPRs).

0.4.3. Part of morphonological phenomena is assigned to morphology, part to
phonology by adherents of the Prague School such as Ďurovič (1967) and sometimes
by Kuryłowicz (1967), cf. Ford & Singh (1983b).

0.4.4. Morphonology is seen as a separate component/level of the language system by many Russian scholars such as Akhmanova (1971), Reformatskij (1975), Kubrjakova & Pankrac (1983:3f), whereas earlier Prague School writings (e.g., Trubetzkoy 1929, 1934) wavered between this position and the inclusion of morphonology into phonology (0.4.2f). Bloomfield (1939) differentiates morpholexical
variations ($\approx$ MRs, AMRs) and morphophonemic alternations ($\approx$ MPRs and phonemic
PRs) whose input are morphophonemes (cf. 5); he distinguishes these in turn
from phonemes and their phonetic forms: Thus it seems that he set morphophonemics apart from both phonology and morphology.[9]

Hockett (1958:142) defines 'the morphophonemic system' as 'the code which
ties together the grammatical and the phonological systems', and this 'tie' is
elaborated in the format of an item-and-process grammar (cf. 1). Similar views
are expressed by Reformatskij (1979b). For a discussion of stratificational
morphophonemics, see Matthews (1972:200ff).

0.4.5. My own view can be understood as a modification of the last position (0.
4.4): Morphonology belongs neither to morphology nor to phonology; it mediates
between both components without being itself a basic component like morphology
or phonology (cf. Reformatskij 1979b:47).

0.5. If different schools of thought cannot even agree about where morphonology
belongs (0.4), the title of Laskowski's (1981) paper 'Which morphology shall we
choose?' becomes a very pertinent question. The following chapters will give my
answer; here we must briefly review the development of morphonology (and morphophonemics):

0.5.1. For the prehistory of morphonology since Ancient Indian and Ancient

Greek grammarians I can refer to Kilbury (1976) as well as for the Kazan School; the question whether its founder Baudouin de Courtenay (e.g., 1895) or his pupil Kruszewski (e.g., 1881) has to be given more credit for creating the study of morphonology has been amply discussed by Stankiewicz (1972) and Klausenberger (1978, 1979:14ff).

I only want to mention that many ideas of this book have some correspondence in Baudouin's writings, e.g., the emphasis on deduction and explanation (see Stankiewicz 1972:64, 72) and on substantive/external evidence (Baudouin de Courtenay 1895:106ff, Stankiewicz 1972:31), the acknowledgement of covert universals (see Stankiewicz 1972:276f) and of functionalism (see Stankiewicz 1972: 24, 27, 29f, 139, 152, 200, 283), the insistence on the gradual synchronic and diachronic transition from phonetic divergence all the way through to morphological alternations, the first presenting absolute constraints on pronounceability (Baudouin de Courtenay 1895:45, 49); but all divergences/alternations may be productive (see Stankiewicz 1972:109).

0.5.2.   The Prague School, the founding father of systematic morphonology Trubetzkoy, his critics,[10] and many of his followers are well represented in Kilbury (1976), with the exception of certain Russian works he fails to mention, such as Reformatskij (1976), Desnickaja (1967), Tolstaja (1971), Mel'čuk (1973, 1974), and the pertinent contributions in Jarceva (1969). Fortunately these contributions do not present viewpoints fundamentally different from those Kilbury cites; this is also true for more recent studies such as the contributions in Popova et al. (1981) and in Avanesov (1979 with the exception of Kasevič 1979 and Maslov 1979, cf. 5.8). In his process model, Kodzasov (1976 and in Kibrik et al. 1977) distinguishes MPRs and PRs along lines similar to those cited for Generative Phonology in 0.4.2 and for Natural Phonology in 0.5.6.

Of work done in Central and Western Europe that Kilbury (1976) does not mention, I want to cite four articles (Heger 1968, Issatschenko 1974, 1975, Ruijgh 1975-1976) which construct abstract input morphonemes, e.g., Issatschenko inputs /*/ or /#/ for German [ə] that alternates with zero as in *Regen* ['reːgən] 'rain' vs. *regn-en* 'to rain' and for Russian v/ø-alternations; these studies show which tricks a model may resort to unless it is detailed enough and properly constrained.[11] Similar abstract constructions have been possible in American structuralist phonemics (cf. Kilbury 1976:86ff), but not in any system of Generative Phonology (at least since Postal 1968) nor in Natural Phonology, where the inputs to rules are always sound-intentions (cf. 4.1.1, 5.6, 10.7.1).

Another lacuna in Kilbury's (1976) coverage of European structuralist morphonology is the role of morphonology in language typology, as in Skalička (1935
etc., cf. 1979), Sgall (1971), Krámský (1956), Korhonen (1969, and now 1980),
cf. 10.9.

What is also missing in Kilbury (1976) is a discussion of the diachronic
problems of analogy and the synchronic ones of the paradigm (cf. 5.18.7f, 10.8.
3.4.4, 10.9.3.6, 10.10.2). For quantitative phonology, cf. 0.2.1 note 3.

0.5.3. The various schools of American structural morphophonemics are amply described in Kilbury (1976). Therefore I simply want to repeat three useful dichotomies well illustrated in Hockett (1958:279ff):

(1) Automatic alternations as in the English plural *beat*-[s] vs. *bead*-[z]
correspond to PRs in our model (cf. 5.12), non-automatic alternations as in
electri[k] vs. *electri*[s]-*ity*, *foot* vs. *feet* to MPRs and AMRs (5.12).

(2) The difference between regular and irregular alternations ('a matter
of degree', p. 280) will be treated within our criterion of generality (5.12).

(3) The differentiation of phonemically and morphemically conditioned, a
major problem of this book, will be dealt with in 5.8f.

0.5.4. Generative Phonology is less adequately treated in Kilbury (1976), as we
have already seen for rule differentiation (0.4.2).[12] Or Kilbury does not mention the problem of opacity[13] that MPRs typically have.

In fact the explicit and implicit contributions of Generative Phonology to
morphonology are so many[14] that our chapter 5 will abound in references to them.
For Cyclical and Lexical Phonology, see 5.17.1.5f, for Derivational Phonology,
5.17.1.3.

0.5.5. Kilbury (1976) did not notice emerging Natural Generative Phonology,[15]
where --in reaction to Generative Phonology-- morphonology is extirpated from
phonology without being provided a detailed model of its own.

0.5.6. Most adherents of Natural Phonology (cf. 4, 10.7) --also neglected by
Kilbury (1976)-- did exactly the same, but with two exceptions: (1) Darden

(e.g., 1971, 1977, 1979, 1981) concentrated his research on morphonology. (2) When W. Mayerthaler (1977, 1980a, 1981, etc.), Wurzel (1980a, 1980b, 1980c, etc.), and Dressler (1977e, 1977a, 1980a, 1980b, 1980d, etc.) started to develop Natural Morphology (cf. 10.8-10), morphonology soon became understood as the area of interaction between phonology and morphology (see Dressler 1977a, 1980b, 1981b, Wurzel 1980c, 1981a). This will be dealt with in chapter 10.

0.5.7. Another type of studies in morphonology that Kilbury (1976) did not report are psycholinguistic investigations[16] on, and research in substantive/external evidence[17] for or against the psychological reality of MPRs.

0.5.8. One trend already noticed by Kilbury (1976) has continued to grow: the use of functional and semiotic principles, cf. Andersen 1973, 1980, Shapiro 1969, 1974, 1980b, 1983, Maslov 1979, Laskowski 1980, 1981, Roberge 1980, Dressler 1977a, 1980b, 1981b, here 10.3ff.

0.5.9. Kilbury (1976) surveyed synchronic models, but rather neglected diachronic theory: One recurrent topic of morphonological theory is the change from phonological alternations/rules via morphonological ones to morphological ones[18] and thus also a recurrent topic of this book (5.2.7, 5.6.6, 5.9.7f, 5.12. 5ff, 5.18.6ff, 5.19.5, 6.2, 7.2, 10.3.5, 10.3.10f, 10.3.15f, 10.7.11.4, 10.8.4. 7, 10.8.3.5.2f, 10.8.6.2ff, 10.10.5).

0.5.10. Theoretical problems of morphonology have lost nothing of their appeal, notice the sections devoted to them at the International Phonology Meetings of 1980 and 1984 (published in Phonologica 1980, 1984) and at the 11. colloquium of the Société Internationale de Linguistique Fonctionelle (Bologna 1984) and pertinent contributions to Interplay 1983.

0.5.11. In spite of this great interest there are few systematic monographs on morphonology: The Norwegian introduction by Haslev (1972) is rather elementary and outdated. Moessner's (1978) brief German introduction is short on theory and only on English. Kubrjakova & Pankrac's (1983) Russian monograph consists of a very short theoretical introduction[19] and of a longer survey of morphonological phenomena in German. My own rather short German[20] monograph (Dressler 1977a) has been criticized --correctly-- for its sketchiness by Carstairs (1980).

However there exist several morphonological descriptions of particular languages[21] and there are the monographs on diachronic morphonology by Klausenberger (1979) and Roberge (1980) and the historiographical monograph by Kilbury (1976).

This book is intended to remedy this rather odd situation and to reveal morphonology as a show-case of dynamic derivation in linguistics.

Notes

1. In order to signal its brevity, I have assigned it 0 instead of 1.

2. Cf. also Kubrjakova & Pankrac 1983:8ff.

3. And Kilbury (1976) even neglects most who did research in this area, cf. 8.1 and later. In Kilbury (1976) studies in quantitative phonology (as in Altmann 1968, etc., Krupa 1967, cf. 8.3.10) are totally neglected, pertinent generative studies on morpheme structure neglected to a large extent.

4. Cf. Kilbury 1976, Haslev 1972, Moessner 1978, Koutsoudas 1964, Hooper 1976.

5. Cf. Stankiewicz (1979:135): 'the morphophonemic system of a language is ... the ways in which the morphemes of a given language are variously represented by phoneme shapes', cf. Matthews (1972:54f).

6. Cf. Angenot & Dillinger (1981) and Matthews' (1974:196) conclusion 'no simple boundary between levels'.

7. Title of Kloster-Jensen (1975), cf. Haslev 1972:12ff, Dressler 1977g, Moessner 1978:6ff, Kubrjakova & Pankrac 1983:8ff.

8. See S. Anderson 1974, 1975, Cearly 1974 (and other contributions in the same volume NatPhon), Rischel 1974, Hyman 1975:153ff, cf. Karlsson 1974, Dressler 1977g (with more references); later Koutsoudas 1977, Sommerstein 1977:225ff, Comrie 1979, Field 1981, Pullum 1983, etc.

9. For its importance as foreshadowing concepts of generative phonology, cf. Miner 1981.

10. Note the particular sharpness of Čurganova's (1973:224ff) critique, played down in Kilbury (1976:36), cf. also Stankiewicz 1976.

11. Cf. Matthews 1972:365ff; chapters 5, 10.

12. For later developments, see Houlihan & Iverson 1977, 1979, Iverson & Sanders 1978, Koutsoudas 1977; for Lexical Phonology, see below.

13. Kiparsky 1971=1982:57-80, Barkai 1975, Dudas 1974, Kaye 1974a etc.; see Kiparsky 1982a, cf. 5.20.

14. Cf. Kenstowicz & Kisseberth 1979, Dinnsen 1979a and its review by Zwicky 1982; critical: Hooper 1976, 1979b, Wojcik 1981, Istre 1983.

15. Vennemann 1972c, 1974b, Hooper 1975, 1976, Hudson 1974 etc., cf. 1.9, 5.12. 3, 5.20.8.5.2.

16. E.g., B. Myerson 1973, cf. later R. Myerson 1976, Derwing & Baker 1977, MacWhinney 1978, Bolocky 1978, Derwing 1979, Krohn & Steinberg 1979, Baker & Derwing 1982, Bybee & Pardo 1981, cf. 5.13.4.

17. Stampe 1969, Linell 1974, Campbell 1974; see later MacWhinney 1978, Linell 1979b, Campbell 1981b, Field 1981, Manaster-Ramer 1984, Dressler 1977a, 1977c, 1977d, 1979, 1981a etc., cf. chapter 5.

18. From Baudouin de Courtenay (1895) onwards through Klausenburger (1979), Roberge (1980), and Hellberg (1983).

19. They cite a monograph by E. S. Kubrjakova, Osnovy morfonologičeskogo analiza (Moscow 1974), which neither I nor anybody else cited in this section 0.5.11 have seen.

20. Cf. the English reviews by Krámský 1981, Carstairs 1980, Flier 1979, Fox 1980.

21. E.g., Martin (1952, 1954) of Japanese and Korean, Čurganova (1973) of Russian, Laskowski (1975) of Polish, not to speak of Trubetzkoy (1934) on Russian, Chomsky (1951) on Hebrew, and many 'generative phonologies' of languages that are rather morphonologies.

1. PHONOLOGICAL, MORPHONOLOGICAL, AND PHONOLOGICAL RULES

1.0.1. A basic claim of this book is that morphonology is constituted by the interaction of phonology and morphology. Another is the assumption of phonological and morphological processes which the linguist models with the format of phonological rules (PRs) and morphological rules (MRs) respectively. From this follows the essential question of this book: If, in analogy to PRs and MRs, we assume morphonological rules (MPRs), what should their status and their properties be?[1] Possible and actual answers to this question have been adumbrated in the Introduction.

1.0.2. First, a brief justification is in order as to why we speak of PRs, MRs, and MPRs instead of using another approach, i.e., the model of alternations between actually occurring forms. Rules and alternations are interchangeable at least to a certain extent: Take, e.g., the well-known case of German final devoicing,[2] observable in alternations such as:

[hʊnt]	'dog'	pl.	['hʊndə]
[braːf]	'excellent, worthy'	pl.	['braːvə]
[maos]	'mouse'	pl.	['mɔøzə]

These alternations between final unvoiced tense and non-final voiced lax obstruent phonemes, i.e., /p/ ∿ /b/, /t/ ∿ /d/, /k/ ∿ /g/, /f/ ∿ /v/, /s/ ∿ /z/, hold also for syllable-final vs. non-final position,[3] cf. the diminutives of 'mouse': ['mɔøs$çən, 'mɔøs$laen].

These alternations can be represented in the rule-format

$$A \rightarrow B \ / \ C \_\_ D^4$$

as a PR (rather than a MPR):

$$[+obstruent] \rightarrow [-voice] \ / \ \_\_^\$$$

And, of course, allophones can be easily derived from phonemes by rules, i.e., by allophonic PRs (cf. Pilch 1964:81).

1.0.3. Similarly in inflectional morphology (cf. Matthews 1974), alternations can be represented by MRs, e.g., number in English as:

$\emptyset \quad \sim \quad /z/ \qquad \text{or} \qquad \text{noun} \sim \text{noun} + /z/$

or with a rule notation as the spell-out rule[5]

$$[\text{pl.}] \rightarrow /z/ \quad / \quad [X]_N \_\_$$

Likewise in word-formation, e.g., negative *un*-prefixation can be represented as:

adj. $\sim$ un + adj.

or by the MR (spell-out rule)

$$[X]_{\text{Neg.Adj.}} \quad \rightarrow \quad [\text{un} \# [X]_{\text{Adj.}}]_{\text{Adj.}} \quad (\text{cf. Aronoff 1976:63})^{[6]}$$

In addition we must assume allomorphic MRs (AMRs), i.e., MRs that govern morphologically and/or lexically conditioned allomorphy, such as between E. *ox-en, childr-en, brethr-en* on the one hand, and *car-s, cat-s, kiss-es* on the other. However, the alternation among [z], [s], [ɨz, əz, ɪz] in *car-s, cat-s, kiss-es* is effected by two PRs, one changing /z/ into [s], the other inserting a vowel between two sibilants.[7]

1.0.4. Whereas morphological spell-out rules mediate between morphological meaning and form, AMRs, MPRs, and PRs rewrite morphological forms. The most homogeneous description of these changes is achieved if the input of AMRs, MPRs, PRs is pronounceable in principle: e.g., *cat-s, kiss-es* [kæts, ˈkɪsəz] are derived from /kæt+z, kɪs+z/ by PRs, *wives* [waivz] from /waif+z/ by a MPR, *ox-en* from /ɔks+z/ by an AMR, i.e., a primary suffix (e.g., pl. /z/) is assumed to be the input for all suffixal allomorphs. The plural forms *feet* and *sheep* are, however, suffixless: No morphological spell-out rule is assumed to supply the sg. forms *foot, sheep* with a suffix, but an AMR of umlaut changes *foot* into *feet*, similarly *brothr-en* into *brethr-en*, i.e., the AMR of umlaut must be specified to apply to a very small set of diacritically marked nouns. Although plurality is signalled by a suffix and by umlaut in *brethr-en*, but only by umlaut in *feet*, both instances may be analyzed as displaying an AMR of umlaut.

There is an alternative: Umlaut in *brethren* would appertain to an AMR (or would be suppletive), whereas umlaut in *feet* would be due to a morphological spell-out rule of modification (vs. suffixation in *cat-s*). The decision between the two analyses clearly pertains to morphology only, and does not touch the proper characterization and delimitation of morphonology. In choosing the first alternative we allow more possibilities for contrasting MPRs with AMRs, viz. our task becomes at least slightly more difficult (more in Dressler, in prep.).

On the other hand, I reject the third alternative of deriving *feet* from underlying *foot-s,* because then *feet* would have to be treated as a suffixed form on the morphological level, which would not only be needlessly abstract, but would have quite undesirable consequences for morphological analysis (cf. Dressler, Mayerthaler, Panagl & Wurzel, to appear).

1.0.5. Research in phonology, morphology, and morphonology past and present not only has used various formats of alternations and rules, but some models mix rules and alternations: Whereas Baudouin de Courtenay (1895) used alternations for all three fields of inquiry as do structuralists and now Hudson (1980), generativists use only rules; Skousen (1975) and others (e.g., Rischel 1974:229f) prefer rules for phonology, alternations for the rest. Other conceivable combinations of rules and alternations have been scarcely advanced.

Since phonological, morphological, and morphonological phenomena are not always easy to distinguish and even seem to share many properties, a uniform format (either rules or alternations) seems to be preferable. In the following I present a brief argumentation as to why the rule format is better, without insisting on any particular approach.

1.1. First, an argument which pertains to economy of description: Any theory which works with different levels of description (e.g., phonology and morphology, with possible sub-levels) and wants to relate levels to each other, does it best via transduction from one level to another with rules rather than alternations, e.g., 'generative' grammars of various kinds as described by Sgall et al. (1975).[8]

1.2. In general, rules capture generalizations in a more precise and economical way than do corresponding alternations, and I think it is not accidental that process descriptions have accumulated many new findings beyond those gathered by structural descriptions (either word-and-paradigm or item-and-arrangement types), cf. Kenstowicz & Kisseberth (1979) for generative phonology, Dinnsen (1979) also for other process phonologies; a similar development can be observed in word-formation studies in the wake of Aronoff (1976). Even if generative studies are criticized for excessive concentration on descriptive machinery, such machinery of rule description still serves to cover new facts and is used (with variations in notation, formalism, and scope) within other processual frameworks, and an excess of such descriptivism can be turned to better account than a total lack of it.

Hooper (1976:51f) and Hudson (1980:118) deplore the excessive power of MPRs in generative studies, and this argument could be directed against the rule approach proposed here. However, when comparing models, it must first be ascertained whether a less powerful theory which works with alternations can account for the same observable facts, hierarchies, and universals that a theory working with rules can account for. Thus I will concentrate on such phenomena.

1.3. Cases where a given input is subject to more than one rule application are often not easily translatable into an alternation format.

1.3.1. An example of two PRs applying to one input is the singular present conjugation of German *lieb-en* ['liːbən] 'to love': 1.sg. ['liːbə], 2.sg. [liːpstʰ], 3.sg. [liːpʰtʰ]. /b/ is realized as [b] before a vowel (1.sg.); but before an obstruent, an assimilation PR of devoicing applies, but the allophonic PR of tense stop aspiration applies only before a stop (3.sg.), not before a fricative (2.sg.). The ordered application of these two PRs (called feeding order) describes this phenomenon much less clumsily than alternations do.

1.3.2. Another case is recursive application of a rule as in word formation. E.g., one meaning of the German prefix *ur-* is 'one stage earlier', as in *Ur-enkel* 'great-grandson' vs. *Enkel* 'grandson'. Now the writer Erich Fried[9] coins the occasionalism *Ur-ur-ur-ur-ur-ur-ur-ur-ur-ur-ur-ur-ur-ur-ur-ur-ur-ur-ur-ur-ur-ur-ur-enkelkinder* 'great[23]-grandchildren', which is grammatically correct, but perceptually and cognitively nearly impossible to process. Or compare the alternative recursive application of the diminutive suffixes *-it(o)* and *-ic(o)* in (Colombian) Spanish *corte* 'court': *cort-ico, cort-iqu-ito, cort-iqu-it-ico,* etc.[10] It is for comparable cases of recursiveness that rules have been found to be very adequate in syntax, and that alternation descriptions have never been tried.

Recursiveness occurs also in phonology, although to a much lesser extent,[11] cf. syllable-final devoicing and tense stop aspiration in two versions of German *ob er lieb-t* 'whether he loves':   slow/formal [ɔpʰ $ eːr $ liːpʰtʰ] vs. fast/ casual [ɔbɛr $ liːpʰtʰ].[12]

For recursiveness in morphonology, cf. multiple (masculine) diminutives in Polish: the suffix *-ek* is changed to *-ecz* [eč] before another diminutive suffix *-ek*, and thus in a conceivable series of multiple diminutives in /ek/, all but the last one come out as [eč], e.g., *kot* 'cat', *kot-ek*, *kot-ecz-ek*, *kot-ecz-ecz-ek*.

1.4.0. Rules allow the description of many domains of 'substantial' or 'external evidence'[13] within the same format:

1.4.1. Synchronic alternations resulting from diachronic change can often be described with identical or very similar rules as the change itself.

1.4.2. Substitutions of children made during various steps of language acquisition can be described with identical/similar rules.[14]

1.4.3. The same is true for substitutions in aphasia (Dressler 1977c, 1978a, 1978b, 1982b).

1.4.5. Synchronic rules can also account for the integration of loanwords.[15] Notice, e.g., the application of German final devoicing in the pronunciation of the French names *Georges* [žɔrš] vs. *Georg-ette* [žɔrˈžɛtʰ]: Since [ž] occurs only in little-integrated loanwords, there is no alternation /ž/ ~ /š/ in German, but final devoicing still applies, even in the speech of those who pronounce [ž] as an unvoiced lax shibilant, it is tensed in final position into [š]; cf. Darden (1979:88) for a similar Russian example.

1.4.6. In sociophonological variation, PRs have been used in a variety of approaches,[16] whereas alternations are useful only in interdialectal input switches,[17] viz. if a speaker switches from one dialect to another.

1.4.7. This list could be continued (cf. Zwicky 1975a). Of course similar-looking rules must not cover up substantial dissimilarities among these different domains,[18] however the rule approach has stimulated and is still promoting research in finding similarities among these domains, and much more than the alternation approach which did not hold what pioneering research such as in Jakobson (1941) promised. Finding interesting differences among domains of evidence is only the second step (logically and historically) after finding interesting similarities.

1.5. After mentioning the use of rules in the typological comparisons of domains (1.4) I must underline the stimulation of typological comparisons of the phonologies and morphologies of languages.[19] Typological comparison is often easier in a rule format than in an alternation format, and the same holds for research in universals (cf. Ferguson 1978b). Here questions of technical devices and underlying 'philosophies' mesh.

1.6. Alternations are basically non-directional (A $\backsim$ B) or bi-directional (A $\leftrightarrow$ B), such as via-rules in Natural Generative Phonology (Hooper 1976). Rules are directional,[20] first in the sense of rules that transduce phonemes to their allophones, or of spell-out rules (cf. 1.1), i.e., from one level to another one. Second, there are PRs and MPRs which operate within the same level, i.e., they substitute a phoneme for another phoneme (e.g., German final devoicing) or a secondary (derived) alternant for a basic alternant, such as in English plural suffixation; in word-formation even in cases of conversion ('zero-derivation') directionality is ascertainable, e.g., E. *to cut → a cut*.[21]

This second type of directionality (as used in all item-and-process grammars, can be compared with the distinction between principal/primary/basic and secondary/derived alternants (or variants) in item-and-arrangement grammars.[22] If no directionality can be ascertained, it seems to turn out that we are always in the face of suppletion (cf. 1.10).

1.7.0. Any mentalistic theory (such as generative grammar) and any theory which lays claims to 'naturalness', must assume psychological (or mental) reality for the processes it models with rules.[23] The extreme claims are (I) that only inputs (A) of processes and the processes themselves (A → B) are stored in the brain, but not the outputs (B) of processes; (II) that only the alternants (A, B) are stored, but not the processes relating the alternants; (III) that inputs (A), outputs (B), and processes (A → B) are stored.

1.7.1. If claim II were correct, then alternations would be learned by rote (i.e., each alternant would be learned and memorized separately), and the learner could form new alternations with the help of surface analogy (by taking specific pairs of words or word-forms as models). MacWhinney (1978) has found evidence for both types of learning (by rote and by analogy); however also for learning by rule (see 9), cf. Darden (1979).

Similarly in the case of diachronic decay and death of alternations, alternations would have to die word by word (lexical fading), as Hudson (1980:117) is consistent enough to claim as a consequence of his alternation theory.[24] However he has overlooked data of rapid decay of alternations which is best interpreted as rapid loss of rule productivity (strikingly different from slow lexical fading) and therefore bestows psychological reality on rules.[25]

As to language pathology, Glozman (1974a, 1974b, cf. Dressler 1978b) has been able to differentiate aphasics who handle polymorphemic words and word forms predominantly with the help of lexical storage, from others who do it predominantly with the help of MRs relating derived forms to base forms.

Also in poetic licence, productive rules, unproductive rules, and analogical operations are distinguishable (cf. Dressler 1981c).

1.7.2. Nor can claim I (of 1.7.0) be true, as shown by facts mentioned in 1.7.1. Moreover, many instances of surface analogy, only explainable by proportional analogy,[26] have been recorded which vouch for lexical storage of at lease some morphologically and/or morphonologically derived forms, e.g., Louisiana French *ils sontaient* [sõ'tɛ] replacing Fr. *ils étaient* [(z)e'tɛ] 'they were' after *ils sont* [sõ] 'they are' (within a highly irregular and suppletive paradigm).

1.7.3. Claim III (of 1.7.0) would entail an enormous redundancy in storage. Therefore I settle for lexical-storage-only (without storage of rules) in cases of suppletion, and for input-and-rule storage (claim I) in all cases of rarely or so far never uttered forms derived by fully productive PRs, MPRs, and/or MRs. In all other cases I assume both lexical storage of alternants and rule relatedness of alternants. In the case of abstract AMRs, MPRs, PRs, as often posited in standard generative grammar,[27] where either the input (e.g., /bœː/ for E. *boy*) or the output is not a surface alternant, additional evidence must be adduced for the hypothetical input/output; theories such as Natural Generative

Grammar (Hooper 1976) disallow abstract inputs/outputs.

1.8. Since relevant facts about cerebral storage (1.7) are hardly accessible, how can we model rule knowledge and lexically stored knowledge? One possibility is the way used in cognitive science, namely with global patterns of knowledge.[28] Thus we can think of a word such as E. *work* as being represented by a frame (in the sense of Minsky 1980).

Now we should not assume that not only *(to) work* would be represented by a frame, but also its inflectional forms *works, worked, working,* and words derived from it such as *worker, workable* by separate and unrelated frames (all phonetic detail differences in the pronunciation of /k/ included); for in frame analysis 'transformations'[29] are assumed (Minsky 1980) which relate shapes (of the same item) which occur under different aspects, to each other, e.g., different views of the same object as looked at from different angles.

If we take the example of Latin inflectional morphology, this means that in declension we would need a maximum of 132 transformations to relate each of the 6 cases of singular and plural to each other. If we assumed distinct storage of all 12 case forms (not counting syncretism) and separate application of 132 transformations for all Latin nouns, then we would end up with a combinatorial explosion (cf. Beaugrande & Dressler 1981:VII.15, III.32) which would render processing of Latin declension forms unmanageable.

And the situation is much worde for polysynthetic languages like Green-landic Eskimo, where often word-forms correspond to whole phrases, clauses, or even sentences of inflectional languages: How could all these alternants and their relations be stored? Or take a morphology-rich language like Arči where one million morphological forms can be derived from a single verbal root (Kibrik et al. 1977:I.4).

1.9. Hudson's (1980, 1982) claim that all PRs, MPRs, and MRs should be replaced by suppletions, is not only vastly uneconomic and unrealistic,[30] but also sug-gests that all these suppletions have a similar status and that there should be a gradual and steady continuum from phonetic to morphological alternations, notably from weak suppletions (alternations of single segments) to strong sup-pletions (alternations of whole stems).

1.9.1. Let us inspect an instance of (rarely studied) suppletion in word formation,[31] namely French ethnic formation. On the one hand we have completely isolated idiosyncratic suppletions such as:

Le Puy	*Anicien* 'inhabitant of Le Puy'
St. Dizier	*Bragard*
Saint-Étienne	*Stéphan+ois*
Meaux [mo]	*Meld+ois*
Le Puy	*Ponot*
Bourges [buʀž]	*Berruy+er*
Saint-Omer	*Audomar+ois* [odɔmaʀwa]
Saint-Denis	*Dyonis+ien*
Château-Thierry	*Théodoric+ien*
Saint-Paul-Trois-Châteaux	*Tricast+in*
Saint-Dié	*Déodat+ien*
Fontainebleau	*Bellifont(+)ain*

but also:

Reims [ʀɛ̃s]	*Rém+ois* [ʀemwa]
Besançon [bɛzãsõ]	*Bisont+in* [bizõtɛ̃]
Blois [blwa]	*Blés+ois* [blezwa]
Poitiers [pwatĭe]	*Poitev+in* [pwatəvɛ̃]
Arras [aʀa]	*Artés+ien*
Saint-Lô	*Laudin+ien* [lodinĭɛ̃]
Angoulême	*Angoum+ois*
Limoges [limož]	*Limous+in* [limuzɛ̃]
Saintes [sɛ̃t]	*Santon* [sãtõ]
Épinal [epinal]	*Spinal+ien* [spinalĭɛ̃]

1.9.2. On the other hand we have a whole series of ethnics following the relation:

Orléans [ɔʀleã]	*Orléan+ais* [ɔʀleanɛ]	'inhabitant of O.'
Avignon [aviɲõ]	*Avignonn+ais* [aviɲonɛ]	
cf. *cancan* [kãkã] 'gossip'	*cancann+er* [kãkane] 'to gossip'	

i.e., they follow the quite general MPR /õ/ → /on/, /ã/ → /an/ before vowel and
glide.[32] A smaller set of ethnics follows the less general (and as we will see:

less natural) MPR /ɛ̃/ → /in/, /œ̃/ → /yn/, e.g.:

> Saint-Florentin [-ɛ̃]   Saint-Florentin+ois [-inwa]
>
> Autun [otœ̃]   Autun+ois [otynwa]

Less general also is the rule of adding /t/, /d/, or /z/ to an oral vowel before vowel or glide[33] as in:

> Paris [paʀi]   Paris+ien [paʀizĭɛ̃]
>
> Saint-Cloud [-u]   Saint-Clout+ien [-tĭɛ̃]
>
> Châteaurenault [-o]   Renaud+ien [-odĭɛ̃]

The second set of ethnics (1.9.2) follows AMRs or MPRs which occur in word formation of common adjectives, verbs, and nouns and display a certain degree of naturalness (1.9.3), whereas the first set (1.9.1) has no correspondence.

1.9.3. How should we measure the putative continuum between weak (1.9.2) and strong (1.9.1) suppletion? The number of segments changed (or added or deleted) would be a totally misleading criterion: If we followed it, Sant+on, Spinal+ien (1.9.1) would be instances of weak suppletion (1 segment changed), whereas Orléan+ais, Autun+ois (1.9.2) would be instances of slightly stronger suppletion (2 segments changed or added), just the opposite of the assignment we are led to by comparing French adjective (etc.) formation and by using naturalness criteria (cf. 5). If we followed Schane's (1968) more abstract analysis by positing rules such as /an/ → /ã/ in the syllable coda, we would work with rules of an opposite direction, but the clear distinction between the regular (or rather: sub-regular) set (1.9.2) and the batch of disparate and idiosyncratic suppletions (1.9.1) would remain.

Moreover, if the all-suppletion analysis were correct, there should be many intermediate cases whose assignment to 1.9.1 or 1.9.2 would remain doubtful or, at least, would not be clear-cut. Take:

> Saint-Malo [-o]   Malou+in [malwɛ̃]
>
> Boulogne [-oɲ]   Boulonn+ais [-onɛ]
>
> Dax [daks]   Dacqu+ois [dakwa]
>
> Bordeaux [-o]   Bordel+ais [-əlɛ]

In these examples only one segment is changed (or added or deleted), but these changes are idiosyncratic.

In contrast, take:

Saint-Rémy [-i]	*Saint-Rém+ois*
Saint-Bonnet [-ne]	*Saint-Bonn+itain* [-nitε]
Strasbourg [-uʀ]	*Strasbourge+ois* [-uʀžwa]
Cherbourg [-uʀ]	*Cherbourge+ois* [-uʀžwa]

Deletion of final stem vowel before vowel-initial suffix is not 'unnatural' and
is attested in several ethnics and in word-formation (e.g., *oiseau* [wazo] 'bird',
diminutive *ois-illon*); all placenames in *-bourg* display /ž/ epenthesis coming
from *bourgeois* [buʀžwa] 'citizen', derived from *bourg* [buʀ] 'village'.[34]

We might waver with the assignment of

Albi	*Albige+ois* [albižwa]
Arras [aʀa]	*Arrage+ois* [aʀažwa]

Should we assign these rare cases of /ž/ insertion (beyond instances of *-bourg*)
to the MR subset of 1.9.2? I think we should, in view of the big difference to
the isolation of suppletions within the other set (1.9.1). Furthermore, all
consonant insertions can be compared with similar rules in other languages (cf.
4.4.1.4).

Of course we can discern differences in the first set (1.9.1) as well:
metathesis occurs in *Fontainebleau* ∿ *Bellifontain;* the words *Saint* or *Château*
can be truncated in derivation or not; *Laudinien* keeps the stem of *(Saint-)Lô*
and adds a submorph *-in-;* *Anicien* does not retain anything of *Le Puy* whereas
its variant *Ponot* keeps one segment (/p/), etc. However, even instances of
weakest suppletion in 1.9.1 are fairly distant from cases of 1.9.2.

If there are cases of a continuum between suppletion and rule-governed alternation, then they are rare, i.e., similar to lexical diffusion (cf. Wang
1977) and lexical fading; such a continuum cannot be represented by a steady
slope (on the left) but by a curve (on the right):

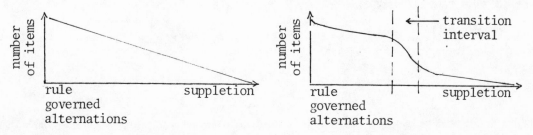

The transition interval (both in synchrony and in diachrony) is rather abrupt.

1.10.   French ethnic formation (1.9) fits well to the classic understanding of suppletion, of which I give the definition by Mel'čuk (1976:50) as 'the relationship between any two linguistic units A and B which meet the following condition: the semantic distinction between A and B is regular, while the formal distinction between them is not regular.' Formal regularity can be defined as following a spell-out MR and either an AMR or a MPR or a PR of the same language. Thus E. *father-ly, mother-ly, brother-ly* are regular derivations from *father, mother, brother*, whereas *paternal, maternal, fraternal* are suppletive (cf. Schwartze 1970:9ff). However, if even the semantic relationship is weak, then the native speaker might still be unaware of it (in the sense of a 'synchronic etymology') or not, e.g., he may or may not relate *-ham* in placenames such as *Nottingham* to E. *hamlet* and *home*.

If one wants to formalize suppletive relationships, then one might think of bidirectional via-rules (as proposed by Vennemann 1974 and Hooper 1976).[35] However, there is usually a semantic direction from a semantic base to a semantically derived item, but there is no formal regularity which allows the establishment of a rule. AMRs and MPRs are unidirectional.

1.11.   Since this book is on morphonology, we will deal with clear MRs of realization (spell-out rules such as suffixation in the E. plural *car-s*) and clear PRs (e.g., allophonic aspiration of English stops) only briefly and insofar as it is needed for the discussion we have to concentrate on: putative MPRs and their discrete and gradual differentiation from putative PRs such as /z/ → /s/ as in *cat-s* and from putative AMRs such as umlaut in *foot* → *feet*, and from suppletions (1.9f, 5.4.8) such as indef. article *a ∿ an*.

There is a typical and unidirectional development of PRs to MPRs and of MPRs to AMRs (5.9.7, 5.18.6-8). This unidirectional evolution suggests that the nature of MPRs cannot be understood without understanding PRs. Therefore we must study the properties of PRs in detail.

Notes

1. Cf. Kubrjakova & Pankrac 1983.

2. In the dialects and sociolects where it exists in the form of collapsing unvoiced tense (fortes) and voiced lax (lenes) obstruents.

3. See Vennemann (1972d, 1978), Wurzel in Heidolph et al. 1981:151, 851f.

4. To be read as: For the input A, the output B is substituted immediately after C and immediately before D.

5. To be read as: Plural is represented by the formative (and phoneme) /z/ immediately after a noun.

6. For the rule format of word formation rules (WFRs), cf. Dressler 1977d.

7. See Zwicky 1975b, Skousen 1981:62ff, Keyser & O'Neil 1980, Ford & Singh 1983b.

8. I cannot follow Linell's (1981) critique of transduction models.

9. In his story 'Genug getan' in the collection 'Alles Möglich' (Berlin, Wagenbach 1975:42.3).

10. Fontanella 1962, cited by Ettinger 1974:105f. Less dramatic cases are cited in Chapin (1970) and Neuhaus (1973, 1975).

11. For recursive application in very fast/casual speech, cf. Donegan & Stampe 1979b:149f, Rudes 1977:12ff. For cyclic application in Cyclic and Lexical Phonologies, see 5.17.1.5f.

12. $\overset{\$}{b}$ means that [b] is ambisyllabic, i.e., the syllable boundary lies within the stretch of articulation of the stop.

13. See Zwicky 1975a, Skousen 1975, Kenstowicz & Kisseberth 1979:154ff; cf. Jakobson 1941, Stampe 1969, Chomsky 1956:241, E. Moravcsik 1977c.

14. E.g., Stampe 1969, Smith 1973, Ferguson 1978a for phonology; Panagl 1977 for morphology.

15. For PRs and MPRs, see, e.g., Dressler 1977a:35ff, Farrar 1977 (also MRs of ablaut), Linell 1979:195ff.

16. E.g., Labov 1972, Bailey 1973, Wodak & Dressler 1978, Dressler & Wodak 1982.

17. *Pace* Hasegawa 1979; cf. Trudgill 1974, Wodak & Dressler 1978:38f, 42, Dressler & Wodak 1982.

18. E.g., Drachman 1978, Dressler 1978a, Ferguson 1978a, Hudson 1980:120f (with exaggerations).

19. Cf., e.g., Interplay 1983. For phonology, see Donegan 1978, Ferguson 1978a; for morphology, Moravcsik 1980, Dressler 1980a.

20. Akhmanova (1971:73) tries to cover directionality within her alternation approach by introducing the term 'irreversible alternation'.

21. See Marchand 1964, Aronoff 1976:115ff, Pennanen 1960.

22. Cf. Matthews 1972, 1974, and Kuryłovicz's (1949) distinction between 'formes de fonement' (= A) and 'forme fondée' (= B).

23. On the problem of what status linguistic rules have, cf. Itkonen 1974, Gumb 1972, Roberge 1980:211.

24. Cf. already Robinson 1972:119ff, Laferrière 1974:194.

25. See Schindler 1972, Neuhaus 1973, Dressler 1977d.

26. E.g., Morpurgo-Davies 1976, 1978a, 1978b; cf. Dressler 1977e:20ff.

27. Cf. Kiparsky 1982a (*sub voce* abstractness), Kisseberth & Kenstowicz 1977, Gussmann 1978a.

28. Cf. Minsky 1980, Beaugrande & Dressler 1981:V.16, VII.18.2, IX.37.2.

29. Not to be confused with transformations as used in Transformational Grammar or other linguistic models.

30. Cf. 1.8. Cf. the critique by Bybee & Pardo (1981:961), who work within Natural Generative Phonology, like Hudson.

31. Some linguists even deny the existence of suppletion in word formation, e.g., Werner 1977.

32. See Kaye & Morin 1978, Tranel 1978, 1981.

33. Cf., e.g., *clou* 'nail' → 'to nail'; see Kaye & Morin 1978, Morin & Kaye 1982:316ff.

34. *faubourg* [fobuʀ] 'suburb' does not contain *-bourg* any longer synchronically; therefore its derivative is *faubour+ien* [fobuʀĭɛ̃] 'suburban', not **faubour-geois*.

35. For the directionality of AMRs and PRs, see 1.6, 1.10; for MPRs, see below 5.2, 5.2.7.3, 5.6, 5.7, 5.13, 5.17, 5.19. This sense of bidirectionality must not be confused with bidirectionality in the sense of mutual interference (see 5.20).

2. PHONOLOGICAL RULES: word and sentence phonology and morphonology

2.0. Phonological rules (PRs), modelling phonological processes, serve various purposes.

2.1.1. PRs model the transduction[1] from the input of the phonological component, i.e., from the phonological representation or underlying phonological forms (often called phonemes) into the phonetic output or phonetic representation, i.e., into the audible phonetic surface forms (often called phones or allophones). There is never a direct transduction from the underlying phonological form to the final output, i.e., by a single PR, e.g., if we take the first phoneme of E. *can* /kæn/, the initial /k/ is first changed to [kʰ] by the English aspiration PR, and then detail PRs specify the exact position of the front and the back part of the tongue (cf. Ladefoged 1980a:495) or predict the acoustic effect. However, usually such detail PRs are not written,[2] and phonologists content themselves with a less concrete output such as [kʰ], the output of the aspiration rule. We will follow this practice, since real detail PRs never have a chance of being mistaken for MPRs or vice versa. Thus the phonetic representations in this book (signalled by square brackets, e.g., [kʰæ̃n]) correspond to phonetic representations in generative and other process phonologies[3] and to the (allo)phonic level of structural phonematics.[4] But even then, more than one PR is needed to achieve transduction, e.g., in one German standard, underlying /hʊnd/ 'dog' is transducted into [hʊntʰ] by final devoicing and aspiration of voiceless stops (similar to English).

2.1.1. The format of these PRs is usually[5] A → B / C __ D, i.e., phoneme/class of phonemes A is replaced by B after C and before D; e.g., German devoicing:

[+obstruent] → [-voiced] / __ $\left\{ \begin{matrix} \# \\ \text{[+obstruent]} \end{matrix} \right\}$, (cf. 1.0.2), i.e., it consists of distinctive features (2.3) and of prosodic features (3), whereas it is already a matter of considerable dispute whether true PRs may contain morphological features (cf. 5.9). Rarer versions are the formats AA → A / C __ D and AB → C / D __ E in the case of contraction or monophthongization (cf. 4.5.4), A → BC / D __ E in the case of split (e.g., diphthongization, cf. 4.4.3), AB → BA / C __ D in the case of metathesis (cf. 4.4.1.2).[6]

2.2. Another purpose is served by those PRs which govern underlying representations themselves and which I call 'prelexical rules' and which are similar to morpheme structure rules/constraints or redundancy rules in classical generative phonology.[7] They fall into two subdivisions (Kenstowicz & Kisseberth 1977: 131ff).[8]

2.2.1. Segment-structure rules state (a) which phonemes occur in underlying phonological representations of a language, (b) which of their features are redundant. Their main purpose in generative phonology is to simplify the economy of description; e.g., E. V → [-nasal] states that English has no underlying nasal vowel phonemes and that they need not be specified as [-nasal].

In Natural Phonology such PRs also describe phonemic neutralizations that occur, e.g., (a) in child language acquisition, as when a young child produces all adult stops as one single stop (either /p/ or /t/), (b) in loanword phonology, as when English speakers render French nasal vowels as oral vowels (cf. Lovins 1973). These PRs have no correspondence in structural phonematics.

2.2.2. Sequential-structure rules restrict the positions where phonemes may occur (without showing up in morphophonemic alternations); e.g., of the two nasal phonemes of Ancient Greek, /n, m/, only /n/ may occur word-finally, thus: [+nasal] → [+coronal] / __ ##. These PRs correspond to phonotactics in phonemics.

2.2.3. Despite the different purposes PRs of 2.1 and 2.2 serve, all are PRs (cf. 8) and all of these two or three types of PRs are related to corresponding MPRs (cf. 5, 8) and, in diachronic development, can be morphologized to MPRs.

2.3. PRs operate within the dimension of distinctive (phonetic or phonological)[9] features, i.e., the continuously varying sound wave produced by the continuous movements of the speech apparatus and the input of the PRs cannot only be represented by discrete segments (phonemes and (allo)phones)[10] but these segments can also be broken up into largely simultaneous features.[11] The temporal duration of these features either coincides with that of a single phoneme or it may stretch over the expanse of several phonemes (e.g., [+voiced] over the whole word *wave*) or it may be restricted to part of a phoneme (see S. Anderson 1976, J. Anderson 1980), e.g., [+low] and [-low] in a diphthong [ae] (e.g.,

E. *eye*), if it counts as one phoneme.

2.3.1. The choice of a particular set of features[12] rests on several lines of
evidence: evidence of synchronic and diachronic PRs, but only of true PRs
(which cannot be considered MPRs), cf., e.g., Donegan (1978:24ff) vs. Sommerstein (1977:97); various external/substantive evidence, as from slips of the
tongue or misperception (e.g., van der Broecke & Goldstein 1980) or from aphasia
(e.g., Blumstein 1973), etc.; and --most direct-- phonetic evidence from acoustic measurements and especially from investigations into articulation (cf.,
e.g., Lindner 1975, Lindau 1978, Ladefoged 1980b, Redenberger 1981) and perception (cf., e.g., Terbeek 1973, Javkin 1979). Since there are often no one-to-
one relationships between these phonetic levels, i.e., acoustics, articulation,
perception, (more abstract) cover features are used, which are then interpreted
on the acoustic, articulatory, and perceptual levels (cf. Ladefoged 1980a, S.
Anderson 1981:497ff, 503ff); for better understandability, articulatory features are privileged here. However, no existing system of features does jus-
tice to all distinctive sound differences in the languages of the world (cf.
Ladefoged 1980b).

2.3.2. Since distinctive features are primarily established for PRs, not for
MPRs or AMRs, the choice of a homogeneous set is less important, so that the
distinctive features of publications cited have been largely taken over. The
features which distinguish consonants (C) and vowels (V) in this book are in alphabetical order (as binary features, cf. 2.3.3):

[+anterior]   = C produced in front of the palato-alveolar region ([š])

[+aspirated]   = C produced with audible breath after release of the ar-
                   ticulation

[+back]   = opposite of [+front]

[+continuant]   = all Vs and those Cs in which the constriction in the oral
                   cavity is not narrow enough to block the air flow

[+coronal]   = C produced with raised blade of the tongue

[+delayed release] = affricates, not produced with instantaneous release
                   of the closure

[+front] or [+palatal] = V or C produced in front of the neutral position
                   of the tongue

[+high]   = V or C produced with raised body of the tongue

[+labial]   = either round V, or C articulated at least as much at the
                   lips as elsewhere in the vocal tract

[+lateral]	= C produced with air flow over one or both lowered sides of the tongue
[+low]	= V or C produced with lowered body of the tongue
[+nasal]	= V or C produced with lowered velum
[+obstruent]	= opposite of [+sonorant]
[+palatal]	= [+front]
[+round]	= labial vowel
[+sonorant]	= all Vs and resonant Cs (which have a regular formant structure
[+strident]	= fricative or affricate C which is acoustically marked by greater noisiness than its non-strident counterpart
[+syllabic]	= all Vs and those Cs which represent the syllable peak/nucleus
[+tense]	= V or C produced with relatively greater 'muscular tension' (which is debatable) than its lax counterpart
[+voiced]	= all non-whispered Vs and those Cs produced with vocal vibration

I used the alphabetical order because there is no undisputed, universal hierarchy of distinctive features. Moreover, H. Andersen (1975) and M. Shapiro (1983) claim that different languages (including different diachronic stages of the 'same language') may differ in language-specific feature hierarchies.

2.3.3. Distinctive features often must be n-ary (i.e., have more than 2 values) on the level of phonetic representation, cf., e.g., the various degrees of aspiration of stops (according to distributional position) in the Breton dialect of Groix (Ternes 1970:11f). For the phonological representation, e.g., Jakobsonian phonemics (cf. Jakobson & Halle 1956) and Standard Generative Phonology (cf. Chomsky & Halle 1968) use only binary features, whereas others[13] use n-ary feature values also for the specification of phonemes, e.g., [1 high] for /a/, [2 high] for /e, o/, instead of +low and [-low, -high] respectively in a 5 vowel system /i, e, a, o, u/. In this book I will use binary feature values only for the sake of descriptive simplification, and if they permit a reasonable rival account of the same phenomenon to an account with n-ary features.

2.4.1. Phonological analysis can be divided into analysis of word phonology and of sentence phonology.[14] Word phonology, the classical object of structural and process phonologies, lies within the domain of a morphological word (as defined by MRs of inflectional morphology and word formation, which produce word-forms such as *black-marketeers*, *cornerstones*, *foreknew*, etc. Sentence phonology is the domain of PRs concatenating morphological words into phonological (see 2.4.2) words, phrases, and sentences, i.e., of sandhi rules (external sandhi) and of traditional sentence phonetics or liaison.[15]

In this book, sentence phonology will be rather neglected, less so for the traditional restriction of phonology to word phonology than for the traditional restriction of morphology to stretches within the morphological word, and thence of morphonology to the same domain.[16]

2.4.2. There exist, however, morphonological alternations of MPRs which are restricted to phrases, such as with clitics, not only suppletions such as the suppletive alternation of *a (name)* and *an (aim)*, the insertion of *e* in It. *glielo*, i.e., the sequence of the clitics *gli* (indirect object pronoun) and *lo* (masculine direct object pronoun singular); but also MPRs of phrase/sentence phonology, e.g., the elision of word final *e* in It. *signore* 'Mr.', *professore* 'professor', *ingegnere* 'engineer', if they occur in titles, e.g., *isgnor/professor/ingegner Baldo* 'Mr./Prof./Engineer Baldo', a similar MPR in Spanish, or the fusion of German prepositions with the dative sg. article *dem*, as in *im ← in dem* 'in the', etc. (cf. Hartmann 1980), or Maltese article morphonology (cf. Comrie 1980). Such phenomena demand a specific treatment.[17]

Other alternations occur within and between words, and thus must be dealt with here at least marginally, e.g., *t*-insertion from F. *petit* [pəti] 'small' (in sentence final position) in *petit ami* [pətit ami] 'small friend', adverb *petitement* [pətitmã] 'to a small extent', noun *petitesse* [pətitɛs] 'smallness'.[18] Celtic mutations split into remnants of word-internal mutations (cf. 5.12.5) and grammatically conditioned mutations at the sentence domain.[19]

2.4.3. Many phonologists relegate PRs of casual or fast speech (which turn, e.g., the auxiliary *have* into [həv, əv, v], cf. 5.11) from the study of word phonology, and Booij (1981) assigns them explicitly to sentence phonology.[20] The decision would be unobjectionable if casual speech rules occurred only in connected speech, but even isolated words may be spoken more or less casually, e.g., Viennese G. *fein* [faĕn] 'fine' with less or more monophthongization (e.g., [fæːn]). Moreover, PRs of casual speech must not be totally disconnected from (antagonistic) PRs of slow, careful, hyperarticulate speech (cf. Linell 1979:

54f, 169f, R. Smith 1980:IV) as in Viennese G. *fein!* [fařːn] (with extra diphthongization and lengthening). And if one claims that PRs of fast (etc.) and
slow (etc.) speech apply only after a word is put into a syntactic construction,
whereas PRs of word phonology apply before, then this presupposes the definition
of one basic (and homogeneous) level of careful phonology within the scale of
phonological forms between the slowest and fastest pronunciations, whish is more
difficult than most phonologists assume implicitly or (seldom) explicitly (e.g.,
Linell 1979:54-57).

Finally, often the same PRs apply obligatorily within a word and optionally
beyond the word, i.e., they apply beyond the word in specific styles of casual
speech (cf. 5.8 on domains) and this is a property of interest for the classification of PRs and MPRs (see 5.11). Thus PRs of casual/fast speech fall into the
scope of this book.

Notes

1. Transduction or translation models as used in all generative and structural theories are attacked by adherents of action theory, cf. MacNeilage (1979: 26ff), Linell (1981). But semiotics, our meta-theory, demands the assumption of chains of signs (10.4.3), and transduction rules constitute such chains of signs.

2. In fact, most phonologists attribute such detail phenomena to phonetics, e.g., Vennemann 1981.

3. Hyman 1975, Sommerstein 1977, Kenstowicz & Kisseberth 1979, Dinnsen 1979a, Kiparsky 1982b, Monahan 1982b.

4. Trubetzkoy 1939, Hockett 1955, Martinet 1949, 1955, Fischer-Jørgensen 1975.

5. Cf. Hyman 1975:115ff, Sommerstein 1977:138ff, Kenstowicz & Kisseberth 1979: 339ff; here 1.0.2.

6. Cf. Sommerstein 1977:136f, Hyman 1975:116, Kenstowicz & Kisseberth 1979: 369ff.

7. Hyman 1975:105ff. In Lexical Phonology (Kiparsky 1982b) these are rules like other PRs (and MPRs) [similar to Natural Phonology], but apply at different levels.

8. Kenstowicz & Kisseberth 1977:131ff, 1979:424ff, Sommerstein 1977:167f, 169ff.

9. My assumption is that phonological and phonetic features should be identical (Donegan 1978:24ff), but see below 2.3.1.

10. Evidence for the psychological reality of segmentation is manyfold, e.g., invention of alphabets, speech errors (e.g., Fromkin 1973:15, 18, etc., 218ff, 243ff), test procedures (e.g., Jaeger 1980a, 1980b). Linear segmentation of the sound continuum is seen as a prerequisite of phonology (as opposed to phonetics) by most phonologists.

11. Evidence for the psychological reality of distinctive features comes again from speech errors (e.g., Fromkin 1973:17f, 223ff), aphasia (e.g., Blumstein 1973), child language (e.g., Blache 1978, Edwards & Schribner 1982), test procedures (Jaeger 1980b, who insists that features are secondary in relation to phonemes as primary psychological entities), cf. 2.3.1.

12. On the history of research, see, e.g., Fischer-Jørgensen (1975:144ff, 218ff, 335, 355f, 379ff, 1981), Hyman (1975:26ff), Baltaxe (1978), Donegan (1978:24ff), Kenstowicz & Kisseberth (1979:241ff), Brakel (1981), Halle (1983), Kodzasov (1976).

13. E.g., Ladefoged 1971, Donegan 1978, Lindau 1978, J. Anderson 1980:201ff; cf. Hyman 1975:55ff, Fischer-Jørgensen 1975 (s.v. binary), Angenot 1981.

14. Hyman 1978, Booij 1981, Vennemann 1981; this distinction is definitional, cf. Clayton 1981. In Lexical Phonology there is the partial correspondence of the strata of lexical vs. postlexical rules (see Kiparsky 1982b, Monahan 1982).

15. Phonology of the sentence meant for Praguian phonologists mostly the study of boundary signals, which is more relevant for word phonology anyway, and of prosody.

16. However often PRs of word and sentence phonology are identical, particular-
    ly in 'close-juncture' languages where syllables are treated alike without
    respect for word boundaries, cf. 2.4.3, 3.3.2.

17. Cf. Zwicky 1983, Zwicky & Pullum to appear, Kaisse 1983, Klavans 1983.

18. Kaye & Morin 1978 and Morin & Kaye 1982 show why an insertion analysis
    should be preferred to a (mor)phonological truncation analysis (which would
    start from the putative underlying masculine form /pətit/). There is an-
    other, morphologically unrealistic possibility, i.e., to derive *petitesse*
    and *petitement* from feminine *petite* [pətit], which is rendered difficult by
    the 'male chauvinism' also of French grammar ('masculine = neutral') and by
    the assumption of a subtractive morphonological rule (fem. /pətit/ → masc.
    /pəti/), which rules are extremely rare in languages of the world (cf.
    Dressler & Acson forthcoming).

19. Cf., e.g., for Breton, Jackson 1953, 1967:308ff. The most detailed des-
    cription of a dialect is Ternes 1970:134ff. For language decay, cf.
    Dressler 1972b.

20. Similarly, proponents of Lexical Phonology (Kiparsky 1982b, Mohanan 1982)
    include them among postlexical rules.

3. PROSODIC PHONOLOGY AND MORPHONOLOGY

3.0. Prosodic phonology is the system of organizing time (duration), the relative tone height (pitch), and prominence (stress) of articulatory and perceptual units.[1] It interacts[2] with (segmental) sentence phonology very much, less so with (segmental) word phonology; e.g., it is unclear (see Dvončova 1972) whether and how prosodic phonology is connected with the segmental basis of articulation, which is important for (segmental) phonological processes (see 4).

3.1.1. Pitch does not seem to be directly relevant to word phonology and its differentiation from morphonology. This is not the case with stress, which is produced with increased muscular effort and subglottal pressure and is frequently accompanied by greater duration and change in pitch. With regard to segmental processes, a stressed vowel or syllable is strong as opposed to an unstressed one.

3.1.2. Organization of time in languages is either syllable-times or rather more stress-timed,[3] i.e., intervals between stresses are approximately regular and/or there is a rhythmic array of syllables (both in articulation and perception). There have been various claims[4] how this distinction is reflected in segmental (word) phonology. An old, often implicit view[5] restricts vowel reduction processes (weakening, deletion, cf. 4.5.2.1) to stress-timed languages, i.e., syllable-timed languages do not reduce unstressed syllables in perception and articulation. Recently McCormick (1981) has maintained that umlaut processes occur only in stress-timed languages. Or in stress-timed languages, such as English, Russian, German, unstressed vowels tend to be laxed, whereas in syllable-timed languages, e.g., Portuguese and Italian,[6] they are tensed, because in unstressed (= weak) position, perception is more difficult and therefore vowels are tensed in order to counteract perceptual reduction (Tonelli 1981).

3.1.3. Isochrony, i.e., approximately equal duration, does not hold only for the intervals between strong syllables or stressed vowels, but also for smaller spans such as two adjacent phonemes. Its effect can be seen in the result of assimilatory processes such as that of total assimilation (e.g., /d+s/ → [s:]) where the duration of the initial segments is approximately maintained. Other examples are compensatory lengthening (cf. Ingria 1980) and metathesis of quantity, as in /V:C/ → [VC:].

3.1.4. The hierarchy of prosodic units is probably:[7] phonological phrase, phonological word, foot, syllable.

3.1.4.1. The phonological phrase (e.g., *a great old man*) is irrelevant for word phonology (and thus for morphonology), and so is the phonological word (e.g., *an aim*), if we exclude clitics from our study of morphonology (see 2.4); we restrict word phonology and morphonology to the domain of (or within) the morphological word (2.4.1).

However, if one claims[8] that in true phonology only phonological domains (including prosody), but no morphological domains may play a role (cf. 5.8), then the phonological word must be a unit of word phonology. In this case, the PRs governing the French alternations between [žə - tə - ɛm], [žətɛm], and [štɛm] *je t'aime* 'I love you' belong to word phonology (or perhaps morphonology); if the domain is the morphological word (cf. 2.4.1), then this is only the case if one regards *je* 'I' and *te* 'thee' as prefixes rather than as proclitics (cf. Dell 1973:236f). One way out is to first equate th phonological word with the morphological word, but then to increase its domain cyclically (most so in rapid speech), e.g., It. *dare* 'to give', *dar # mi* 'to give me', *dar # me # lo* 'to give it to me', where the enclitic pronouns are successively attached to the infinitive; however, according to our definition, the loss of final /e/ in the infinitive falls into the realm of sentence morphonology, the vowel change in *mi* → *me* to sentence morphology (allomorphy).

3.1.4.2. It is still unclear whether the level of the metrical foot[9] is really important for MPRs or even for PRs of word phonology, or whether the definition of strong and weak syllables or vowels suffices. E.g., McCormick (1981) has claimed that the metrical foot is the domain of umlaut (cf. 3.1.2), e.g., in OIcld. *roa* 'to row', 3.pl.past *rǫru*, i.e., the conditioning vowel is always in a weak syllable (here: *ru*) which immediately follows the affected strong syllable (here: *ro*) within the same foot. However, if one limits the notion of foot to sequences of a strong and one or more weak syllables, then iterative (or distant) umlaut falls outside the domain of one foot, cf. double affection (G. 'Doppelumlaut') in Breton, e.g., MBret. *eneff* 'souls', OBret. *menech* 'monks',

Mod.Bret. *nedeleg* 'Christmas', which come from Brythonic **anamī*, Latin *monachi* and *natalicius* respectively; thus /i/ of the third syllable (afterwards lost or lowered) has affected not only the preceding syllable (changing /a/ to /e/), but also the first, unstressed syllable, which does not belong to the same foot.[10] Problems of proper foot delimitation would occur with the possibly foot-internal process of Tamil gemination (cf. Vijaykrishnan 1981:104f).

3.2. The most important prosodic unit for word phonology and morphonology is the syllable:

3.2.1. The syllable can be divided into three parts: (1) non-vocalic onset, (2) nucleus or peak (most frequently a vowel), (3) non-vocalic offset or coda. The nucleus is obligatory, the other two parts optional, e.g., in an open syllable, there is either no offest (type CV) or neither onset nor offset (type V).

3.2.1.1. The usual analysis[11] asserts a symmetric structure of the syllable that can be diagrammed as:

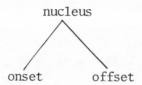

3.2.1.2. The slopes of the diagram correspond to the sonority hierarchy (or to the antagonistic hierarchy of consonantal strength),[12] where the nucleus is highest in the sonority hierarchy (either a vowel, as in E. *pit*, or a sonorant, as in Czech *prst* 'finger', or a fricative, as in *pst*) and the syllable margins (beginning of the onset and end of the offset) lowest, e.g., the stops in E. *print* (with the well-known problems of initial and final clusters, as in E. *stop* and Russ. *rta*, and Fr. *libre* respectively).

A branching[13] diagram of the sonority hierarchy is:

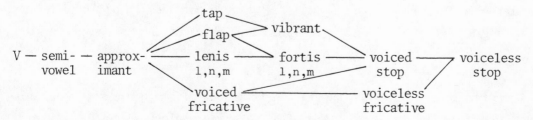

The property of branching shown on this diagram reflects the observation that language-specific relations within the sonority hierarchy are binary between positions connected by a dash, but they are not always strictly linear and relations between positions not connected by a dash are often undecidable,[14] e.g., voiced stops and voiced fricatives are more sonorous than voiceless stops, but their own respective reciprocal position is much less clear.

3.2.2.   Elaborating on an analysis proposed by Hockett,[15] proponents of Metrical Phonology (3.1.4.2) assert the following syllable structure (left diagram), which corresponds to the hierarchical structure of strong (s) and weak (w) positions (right diagram):

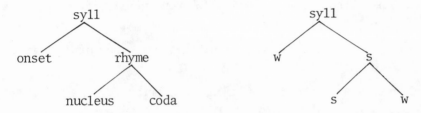

This analysis fits well with observations that CV is the optimal syllable and that the onset is stronger (and phonetically more salient) than the coda (offset),[16] and it is corroborated by much substantial evidence, e.g., poetry (alliteration of onsets vs. rhyming of rhymes), the most frequent type of contaminations, where the onset of one source word is conjoined with the rhyme of the other source word (e.g., *sm/oke* & *f/og* → *sm/og*), etc.[17]

3.2.3.   A major problem for the assignment of a consonant to the strong onset vs. the weak offset of syllables is possibly ambisyllabic consonants, i.e., consonants belonging both to the offest of the preceding and to the onset of the following syllable,[18] such as the second, flapped *t* in E. *entity* (probable in certain speech styles at least). Consonants difficult or impossible to assign to one syllable only, i.e., probable ambisyllabic consonants, seem to occur only in stress-timed languages[19] and --in reference to general language types-- particularly in fusional languages, whereas they do not seem to occur in isolating and agglutinative languages. Thus, ambisyllabic consonants seem to be connected with the opacity of morphonology (cf. 10).

3.3.   When formulating MPRs and PRs in the framework of a process phonology/morphology, often boundary symbols[20] are used, i.e., morphological boundaries such as # (simple morphological word boundary, as in *black#bird*), + (morpheme boundary, as in *electric+ity*), = (pseudo-morpheme boundary, as in *pre=cede*), and prosodic boundaries such as $^{\$}$ (syllable boundary, as in *en$^{\$}$tity*, if the second *t* is ambisyllabic), and ## (phonological word boundary, as in *we've ## done*).[21]

Such symbols have been used in generative phonology for two purposes:

3.3.1. They show that a segment in the formula of a PR or MPR is in a determinate distance (e.g., adjacent) to a boundary, as in German final devoicing, either

$$[\text{+obstruent}] \rightarrow [\text{-voiced}] \ / \ \underline{\quad} \ \#\#$$
$$\text{or} \qquad\qquad\qquad\qquad / \ \underline{\quad} \ \$$$

i.e., at the end of the phonological word or in syllable-final position (according to the dialect).

3.3.2. Boundary symbols may show the domains within which a PR or MPR is allowed to operate, e.g., in Viennese German,[22] the PR

$$n \rightarrow [\alpha \text{ place}] \ / \ \underline{\quad} \ \begin{bmatrix} \text{- continuant} \\ \alpha \text{ place} \end{bmatrix}$$

i.e., an /n/ assimilates to the place of a following stop or nasal, and this PR holds in very formal speech only in morpheme internal position (domain of the morpheme); the more casual the speech style gets, this PR applies, successively, beyond =, +, #,[23] e.g., in *In=fékt* 'infection', *Ún+fall* 'accident', *Móhn# blume* 'poppy flower', and *an # Gérda* 'to Gerda'.

It seems preferable to state these conditions of rule application directly by stating the respective domain than by stating it via boundary symbols.[24]

3.4. Also, prosodic PRs can be morphologized (become MRs) or 'morphologized' (become MPRs), e.g., very often stress assignment has morphological conditions,[25] tone rules may be grammaticalized (e.g., Schuh 1978:252ff). And in many languages stress and tone of morphemes is lexically represented and/or conditioned (i.e., lexicalized).[26] And if one includes rhythmic length alternation of long and short vowels into prosodic phonology, then Slovak rhythmic alternation of long and short vowels is clearly morphologically restricted due to paradigmatic coherence (in inflection) and to lexical coherence (in compounds;[27] codetermination of syllabification is evident in many languages (cf. Cairns 1982:216ff).

These phenomena are not dealt with in this book which is devoted to segmental morphonology, the usual understanding or morphonology.

Notes

1. Cf. Lehiste 1970, Hyman 1975:186ff, Symposium on 'Temporal Relations within Speech Segments': PICPhS 9 (1979) II.240-311.

2. Autosegmental Phonology (Goldsmith 1976) treats segmental phonology and prosodic phonology as separate, though associated layers. I cannot go here into discussing the multiplication of layers ('tiers') in recent work inspired by Autosegmental Theory.

3. Lehiste 1982, Bertinetto 1977, Bailey 1978, Donegan & Stampe 1979a §8, Thomas 1979, E. Mayerthaler 1981, Major 1981, critically Dauer 1983.

4. E.g., Bailey 1978 and Abaurre Gnerre 1981 have proposed that stress-timing becomes more important in faster/more casual styles of English and Brazilian Portuguese respectively. That the importance of stress-timing is a matter of degree is reflected in the terminological distinction of dominant and non-dominant prominence (van Coetsem et al. 1981).

5. Cf. recently Bertinetto 1977 and van Coetsem et al. 1981.

6. See Delattre 1969, Bertinetto 1979, Tonelli 1981, Major 1981.

7. E.g., Selkirk 1980b; for a different terminology, see Pulgram 1970. For the isomorphy of these hierarchical levels, cf. Muysken 1982.

8. As in Natural Generative Phonology, cf. 5.6, 5.8.

9. As in Metrical Phonology, see Kiparsky 1981, Selkirk 1980a, 1980b, Hayes 1981, Basbøll 1981b, McCormick 1981, Prince 1983, and Harris 1983 with references. For a combination with Natural Phonology, see Dogil 1980.

10. Cf. Fleuriot (1964:190ff) and the cautions in Jackson (1953:591f). The Old English 'Doppelumlaut' (Luick 1914:183f), e.g., in ꝫædelinꝫ 'relative' < gaduling (still preserved in Old Saxon), with umlaut of *u* and *a*, poses less of a problem, because *a* is stressed and thus belongs to the same foot as *u* and, presumably, *i*.

11. Explicitly, e.g., Pulgram 1970, Hooper 1976:196ff, Bailey 1978, Donegan & Stampe 1979a.

12. Cf. recently Lass 1971, Vennemann 1972d, 1978, 1981:VI, Hooper 1976:196ff, Escure 1977, Drachman 1977, Bell & Hooper 1979:10ff, Brakel 1979b, 1981, Kiparsky 1981, Cairns 1982.

13. Branching typologies are common in typological theory, cf. Hempel & Oppenheim 1936.

14. Cf. Goman 1981, Drachman 1977.

15. Hockett 1955:51ff, 150ff; cf. Bell & Hooper 1979:21f.

16. Cf. Malmberg 1962, MacKay 1973:176ff, Langdon 1975:232, 280, Hooper 1976:199f, Terbeek 1977, Escure 1977, Dressler & Drachman 1977:288f, Bailey 1978, Donegan & Stampe 1979b:142, Stephens & Justeson 1980, Devine & Stephens 1980:74f, Cairns 1982, Murray & Vennemann 1983.

17. Clements & Keyser 1983 claim to capture these and more generalizations within a multi-tiered analysis. On extrasyllabic appendices, see Booij 1984 with references.

18. Hockett 1955, Pulgram 1970:78ff, Jones 1976, Kahn 1976, 1980:97ff, Rudes 1977, Ingria 1980:467, Vennemann 1981:399. Selkirk (1980) accepts ambisyllabic consonants only within the same foot.

19. E.g., not in syllable-timing Italian, cf. Vincent 1976; even geminate consonants are syllable-initial, not ambisyllabic, see Hurch & Tonelli 1982.

20. Cf. Sommerstein 1977:143ff, Houlihan 1977, Hyman 1978, Basbøll 1978; more discussion in Aronoff & Kean 1980.

21. Mardirussian (1975) has pointed out that the 'sentence word' of incorporating/polysynthetic languages corresponds to the domain of the phonological word. Here it is maintained that such sentence words equal morphological words. A separate boundary '=' can be avoided in morphological analysis (e.g., by lexical marking or by rule ordering), but is still a practical signal.

22. Dressler 1976a, Wodak & Dressler 1978, Dressler & Wodak 1982.

23. If one wants to describe this in terms of the syllable boundary ($^\$$), one would have to say that n must become ambisyllabic for the PR to apply, i.e., successive resyllabifications occur the more casual the speech style gets. This expansion cannot be restricted to the domain of the foot.

24. See Basbøll 1978, 1981b, Dressler 1976a, Donegan & Stampe 1979a §4, Selkirk 1980a.

25. Garde 1968:105ff, Hint 1971, Kenstowicz & Kisseberth 1979:401ff, Warburton 1977, Nicole 1979:165ff, Wurzel 1980, Dogil 1980:13f, Nikolaeva 1983. Cf. cyclic stress assignment in Harris 1983:91ff.

26. Interestingly early generative phonology has underrated morphological conditioning both in segmental and in prosodic PRs.

27. See Horecký 1975, Kenstowicz & Kisseberth 1977:118f, 1979:104f, 155, 393.

4. PHONOLOGICAL PROCESS TYPES

4.0. Many PRs, such as vowel reduction, umlaut, vowel laxing and tensing (mentioned in 3.1.2), resur in very many languages in identical or very similar forms and seem to correspond to general phonetic tendencies. Attempts at classifying such plausible PRs have soon concentrated in the investigation of naturalness of phonological processes.[1] The underlying assumption is that PRs representing general phonological processes are frequent all over the world, whereas idiosyncratic, language specific PRs are rather to be classified as MPRs and non-general. In order to measure phonological naturalness and to identify or compare PRs, 'universal' process types must be established.

4.1.1. Phonological process types, as I call them, have a clear theoretical status in Stampean Natural Phonology as (a) 'universal phonetic processes', or 'language innocent' (= universal) processes, and (b) the residual phonological processes derived from them in natural languages (see Donegan & Stampe 1978), i.e., they are seen as mental substitutions which respond to physical phonetic difficulties.[2]

4.1.2. This corresponds, in Atomic Phonology,[3] to (a) universal 'atomic rules' (e.g., of devoicing of word final stops) and their less restricted variations (dependent rules, 4.5.3.1) governed by universal principles, (b) their language-specific representants.

4.1.3. There are problems with both views[5] and there exist many substantially similar viewpoints, even if they don't assign a theoretical status to these 'phonological processes' or 'natural (phonological) processes/rules'.[6] Therefore we must try to approach a common denominator for these explicit and implicit assumptions.

4.2.1. First, 'phonological process types' to be established by deductively and inductively oriented research in phonological universals and typology[7] must be strictly distinguished from 'phonological processes' (to be modelled by PRs) corresponding to them in individual languages, e.g., aspiration of stops has different conditions in German and English, but both PRs belong to the same

process type in languages with appropriate input or output segments (cf. Goldsmith 1980:414). E.g., the process type of vowel reduction (cf. 4.5.2.1) should
occur in most languages unless its restriction to a subset of languages (e.g.,
stress-timed languages, see 3.1.2) can be motivated. However, process types ap-
pertaining to injective consonants can be found, at least overtly, only in the
rather few languages having injective consonants (Blust 1980), although Natural
Phonology claims that such processes should exist, covertly, in all other languages, where they may be observed when speakers receive or try to pronounce
clicks.

4.2.2. Phonological process types must be separate and distinguishable from
each other (as explicitly stated in Natural and Atomic Phonology), i.e., their
input-output relationship (A → B) must be specific for each type. If the same
relationship A → B is attributable to two different process types, then the hierarchies[8] of either possible inputs and/or possible outputs and/or possible
favoring/disfavoring contexts (environments: / C __ D) must differ, e.g., vowel raising $e → i$ may be either a 'strengthening' or a 'weakening' process type,
but the hierarchies of conditions differ (e.g., 'strengthening' is often context
-free or occurs particularly with long or tense e vs. 'weakening' as typical for
unstressed syllables only, etc.).[9]

4.2.3. Phonological process types must be phonetically plausible and motivated,[10]
i.e., the PRs in question should 'dramatize or enhance minor phonetic effects
that are inconsequential in many other languages' (Goldsmith 1980:414).

4.2.4. Typological evidence should be restricted only to 'true', 'natural' PRs
of individual languages, phonological substitutions which may be rather MPRs
must be excluded in a first step, until doubtful cases are cleared. Therefore
I'm going to stick to (a) allophonic PRs and (b), in the spirit of Natural Phonology and Jakobsonian implications[11] to exceptionless substitutions predicting
or implying existing phonemic systems; e.g., many languages have only unvoiced
obstruent phonemes, apparently no language only voiced obstruent phonemes, thus
for, e.g., Terena, which has the unvoiced obstruent phonemes /p, t, k, s, š, ç/
without voiced counterparts, we can write the PR, a segment structure rule or
MSR: [+obstruent] → [-voiced].

4.2.5. External/substantive evidence, especially from linguistic research in
performance, acquisition, aphasia, etc., may[12] bear, under certain caveats (cf.
5.3) on process types for which 'internal' evidence from 4.2.4 is unclear or incomplete.

4.3.1. The establishment of phonological process types presupposes a uniform
set of typological principles. Uniformity is absent in the classification into
four categories of process types in Schane (1973:49ff, cf. Sommerstein 1977:
227ff): (1) 'Assimilation processes' refers to context-sensitive feature
changes, (2) 'syllable structure processes' to the distribution of consonants
and vowels within the prosodic unit 'syllable', (3) 'weakening and strengthening
processes' to strength hierarchies,[13] (4) 'neutralization processes' to language
specific mergers of segments.

4.3.2. Formal classifications are homogeneous, but they often produce splits of
processes which belong to the same process type. E.g., the distinction of allophonic and phonemic processes (according to whether the output is an allophone
or a phoneme) is useful (cf. 5.18, 5.20), but consider the well-known case of
nasal assimilation before consonant, e.g., in English and in many languages /n/
changes to /m/ before labials (= phonemic), but to [ŋ] before labiodentals (=
allophonic); both changes clearly belong to the same process type, i.e., nasal
assimilation.[14]

The division into context-free (or paradigmatic) processes (formula: A →
B) and context-sensitive (or syntagmatic) processes (formula: A → B / C __ D),
earlier made in Stampean Natural Phonology runs into the following difficulties
(cf. Dressler & Drachman 1977:290f): In diachrony, context-sensitive processes,
such as vowel raising, vowel shortening, etc., often are first context-sensitive
(e.g., favored by certain adjacent consonants or prosodic factors), but later
become context-free. And, more generally, th hierarchies of certain process
types range from restricted applications in limited contexts to generalized,
context-free application.[15] Finally, even context-free processes have a prosodic context (in the sense of figure vs. ground, cf. 10.7.1).

4.3.3.1. Following the age-old distinction between clarity (optimization of
perception)[16] and ease of articulation, Stampe (see Donegan & Stampe 1979b) has
initiated a process typology based on which of these two functions is served by

a process: Processes optimizing perception are called fortition or dissimilatory ($\approx$ strengthening) processes; those contributing to ease of articulation
are called lenition or assimilatory ($\approx$ weakening) processes. This bipartition
ties up with what is widely held to be the main function of phonology in language: to make language pronounceable and perceivable (or more precisely: the
outputs/elements of lexicon and grammar). The bipartition of processes can be
refined in the following way:

4.3.3.2. Processes serving optimal perception should be better named foregrounding processes,[17] e.g., vowel lengthening. The antagonistic function is
backgrounding,[18] e.g., vowel shortening. This is a secondary function; e.g.,
in the case of foregrounding of stressed syllables by vowel lengthening, foregrounding can be made more effective if simultaneously vowel shortening back-
grounds unstressed syllables of the same foot (cf. 3.1.4.2). At the same time,
vowel shortening contributes to ease of articulation, and it seems, in general,
that processes serving backgrounding always serve ease of articulation as well.
However, it is not impossible to combine foregrounding and ease of articulation[19]
(see 4.6[20]). Nonetheless, foregrounding and backgrounding processes are antagonistic (Donegan & Stampe 1979b).

4.3.3.3. How can a process type be classified as a foregrounding or a backgrounding one? Donegan's (1978) and Donegan & Stampe's (1979b) criteria are often too theory-specific and they may lead to absurd results, as in Goman (1981),
who classifies processes such as g → γ → ɦ or xt → jt as fortitions, i.e.,
foregrounding processes (in our terminology). The criteria used in this book
are:

4.3.3.3.1. Foregrounding is typical for, and preferred in prosodically strong
positions (syllable onset, strong syllable), backgrounding in weak positions
(syllable offset/coda, weak syllable);[21] e.g., sounds in strong positions are
more liable to be realized as more audible than in weak position. One result is
that consonant clusters are better preserved in onsets than in offsets; cf.
Georgian monosyllabic words with maximal onsets (e.g., *pt̫konis, brdɣvnis*) and
the much shorter maximal offsets (e.g., *hparavs, ɣmerts*).

4.3.3.3.2. Foregrounding processes (e.g., vowel lengthening) are often general-

ized/maximized in slow or formal or hyperarticulate speech, in emphasized or
loudly shouted syllables; backgrounding processes (e.g., vowel shortening) in
rapid or casual speech; i.e., better or worse perception is called for by socio-psychological reasons (cf. 5.11.1). Notice that in sound symbolism as well,
emphasis (and potency) is connected with perceptual foregrounding.[22]

4.3.3.3.3. In aphasic disturbances, foregrounding processes are largely limited
to non-fluent aphasia, where patients speak haltingly and with much awareness of
their performance.[23]

4.3.3.3.4. Segment structure rules (MSRs, 2.2.7) model processes which generate
the underlying phonemic system of a language (Donegan 1978:133ff, Goman 1981:
108), or of developing phonemic systems in first language acquisition,[24] e.g.,
when a child or a language[25] has only two vowel phonemes, i.e., /a, ɨ/, then
vowel raising, centralization, and --especially-- lowering apply (cf. Donegan
1978:68ff); and when the system consists of /a, i, u/, then also vowel fronting
(palatalization), backing, and labialization.[26] Such context-free processes
are, in general, foregrounding processes. Other criteria can be used for specific process types.[27]

4.4.0. A further sub-division of foregrounding and backgrounding processes can
be made according to the articulatory gestures used to perform them (Dressler &
Drachman 1977) until we come down to the specific process types of our typology.
According to the criteria of 4.2, 4.3.3, we can outline the following typology,[28]
first of foregrounding process types:

4.4.1.1. One process type corresponds to simple realization rules, such as /b/
→ [b], which do not allow any backgrounding process to reduce the phonological
intention.[29] In fact, any phonetic realization involves introducing feature
specifications (phonetic detail) absent in the phonological input.

4.4.1.2. Another process type is metathesis (cf. 5.18.4.2). By transposition
of a segment A, its reduction (deletion, assimilation, or fusion) in the neigh-
borhood of a segment B is avoided;[30] thus AB → BA, CAB → ABC, etc.; often
metathesis results in syllable structures better to pronounce and to perceive.[31]

4.4.1.3. At least many cases of dissimilation belong here.[32] E.g., the change *tl* > *kl* (as in Latin) in strong positions (Nyman 1979, 1984, Dressler 1980c:110) is antagonistic to the assimilation *tl* > *ll* in weak positions, or dissimilation of *ea, oa* > *ia, ua* is a prophylaxis against assimilatory contraction to *a* (Andriotis 1974).

4.4.1.4. As a last sub-class of structure-preserving process types I want to mention epenthesis (insertion).[33] Vowel epenthesis in Spanish *Estanford* 'Stanford'[34] preserves the non-permitted word-initial cluster *st*, which would otherwise be reduced. In addition, this type, as well as insertion of glides or approximants, or sonorants between vowels, makes phoneme sequences better pronounceable at the same time or fits sequences into the rhythmic structure of prosodic feet (cf. Broselow 1982).

4.4.2. A very straightforward and widespread articulatory method of foregrounding is vowel/consonant lengthening, preferred in strong positions and in slow/hyperarticulated speech; it is less evident why vowel lengthening is favored before voiced obstruents.[35] Aspiration of voiceless stops presumably belongs here, as time allotted to the consonant is extended,[36] especially in strong positions.[37]

4.4.3. Many process types are comprehended by the category of polarization or diphthongization, i.e., linear sequencing of the features of one segment into two segments and differentiation of these segments, similar to dissimilation (cf. 4.4.1.3).[38] Beyond diphthongization proper (e.g., /iː/ → /rĭ/ → /eĭ/, etc.), we have to mention change of fricatives to affricates (including glides to affricates via fricatives, e.g., /ĭ/ → /dj/,[39] separation of secondary features such as Ṽ → Ṽn, Ṽŋ; kʷ → kw, etc., i.e., biphonemic groups resulting from splits.

4.4.4. Foregrounding by means of articulatory strengthening (intensification of the articulatory gesture)[40] occurs in many process types, e.g.:

4.4.4.1. One sub-class is the vowel processes of tensing, raising, lowering, and coloring, i.e., palatalization (fronting) and labialization, amply dealt with by Donegan (1978).[41]

4.4.4.2. Obstruent tensing is another clear process type of foregrounding (see Goman 1981:136ff), as well as laxing of sonorant consonants.

4.4.4.3. Strengthening of the consonantal charcter of non-vowels according to the sonority hierarchy (3.2.1.2) is typically preferred in strong positions.[42] Two examples are: stopping of fricatives[43] and fricativization of approximants (stronger/more general in emphasis).[44]

4.4.5. Foregrounding by means of more articulatory effort (cf. Lindner 2975) achieves perceptual clarification; e.g., perceptual and articulatory similarity cannot be expressed on a general parameter encompassing large natural classes of inputs and outputs such has been the case so far in 4. E.g., strident frica-tives[45] such as /s, f/ are perceptually better than mellow fricatives[45] such as /θ, ɸ/ respectively. Many phonemic systems contain /s/ but no */θ/, or /f/ but no */ɸ/; in Ruhlen's (1975) samples of phonemic systems, only Witato has /ɸ, θ/ but neither */f/ nor */s/; only two other languages have /θ/ without having */s/. Some 20 languages have /ɸ/, but no */f/; but notice that all these lan-guages (with the exception of Witoto) contain /ɸ, s/, but no */θ/, so that this constellation could be described as an opposition between mellow /θ/ and stri-dent /s/. In any event, this overall distribution fits with the claim (4.3.3. 3.4) that underlying phonemic systems are, in general, generated by foreground-ing processes, e.g., $\begin{matrix} \text{fricative} \\ \text{[-strident]} \end{matrix}$ → [+strident].[46] More articulatory effort means that /s/ and /f/ are produced with additional 'essential' (Lindner 1975) movements than /θ/ and /ɸ/ respectively.

4.4.6. Foregrounding of primary features at the expense (and eventually loss) of secondary features is also typical for underlying systems, e.g., denasaliza-tion of nasal vowels so that the overwhelming majority of vowel systems have no underlying nasal vowels (cf. Donegan & Stampe 1979b:163f). Another process type is delabialization of labiopalatal vowels (e.g., $y → i$, where palatality is strengthened). Another type is depalatalization of palatalized, fronted stops. This is the origin of palatal stops /c, ɟ/ in languages such as Albanian. No-tice that this type eases articulation as well (cf. 4.3.3.2, 4.6.1).

4.5.0. Processes which are antagonistic to the processes of 4.4 serve the sec-ondary function of backgrounding[47] and the primary function of achieving (more) ease of articulation. In the literature one finds frequently complaints that relative ease of articulation is neither theoretically nor operationally defined. However, it is possible to measure articulatory effort.[48] Moreover, Lindner's (1975) theory of articulatory movements allows a gradual definition according to the degrees of precision and richness of articulatory movements (Lindner 1975:175ff), at least within the same language, and these definitions have been proven useful in speech-therapy and in the assessment of fast/casual speech reductions. Of course extrapolations from German, the main object of Linder's (1975) theory, to other languages is dangerous, especially if they have a different basis of articulation. Therefore the following definition of weakening (reported by Hyman 1975:165) remains useful: 'a segment X is said to be weaker than a segment Y if Y goes through an X stage on its way to zero,' and clearly this means reduction of articulatory effort. All of the following process types can be seen as 'weakening' processes in the sense of Y → X.

4.5.1. Shortening of the articulatory gesture (antagonistic to lengthening 4.4.2) obviously contributes to ease of articulation and to perceptual backgrounding, e.g., vowel shortening maximized in weak positions and in casual/fast speech as in English and many other languages.[49] The same holds for degemination or shortening of consonants not adjacent to a strong vowel; this includes deaspiration of aspirated stops (cf. Houlihan 1977:221f).

4.5.2.1. Weakening of the articulatory gesture in the sense of using less articulatory effort (antagonistic to strengthening 4.4.4) is common for many process types: Vowels can be weakened by being centralized (bleached), laxed, and, finally, deleted,[50] or vowels can be first devoiced (cf. Dressler 1977, Ogawa 1981). Consonants are deleted in consonant clusters, especially in casual/fast speech and in syllable final position.[51] Also dissimilatory loss belongs here (e.g., G. *Pfenning* → *Pfennig* 'penny').[52]

4.5.2.2. Consonants are weakened (lenited) according to the strength hierarchy, which is (roughly) the reverse of the sonority hierarchy.[53] These process-types always have a vocalic (or only sonorant) environment, so that lenitions can be understood as assimilatory processes (4.5.3, cf. Goman 1981:156f), particularly since they are maximized in intervocalic position.[54] E.g., unvoiced, tense stops are voiced/laxed or spirantized in vocalic environments,[55] unvoiced/tense

fricatives are voiced/laxed (e.g., Coetsem et al. 1981:306), aspirated tense
stops are deaspirated (Keating et al. 1983). Voiced (lax) stops are either (1)
spirantized (= classical lenition)[56] --if appropriate clusters exist, even between sonorant consonants as in Koromfe [bilɣmdi] with /g/ → [ɣ],[57] or (2)
changed to nasals (without nasal environment) as in Russian and Nguna fast
speech (cf. Bařinova 1981:122 and Schütz 1969:18 respectively), or (3) /d, n, l/
can be flapped[58] or changed into an apical tap.[59] Affricates become fricatives.[60]
Voiced/lax fricatives are changed to approximants[61] (z also to a tap), as well
as vibrants,[62] fricatives are replaced by [h] and stops by [ʔ],[63] and the end-
point is deletion.

4.5.3. Assimilation processes (antagonistic to dissimilations 4.4.1.3): The
assimilation of features of a neighboring segment eases articulatory effort by
allowing inertia to prevail and smoothing transition from one segment to another
one.[64] Assimilation processes are very often generalized in casual/fast speech.[65]
Of course if a comparatively 'weaker' segment is assimilated to a comparatively
'stronger' one, e.g., /t#ǐ/ → /tš/ in *got you*, then the assimilation (output)
segment may be produced with more articulatory effort than it would have been
without assimilation; but what counts is that the articulatory transition is
rendered easier.[66]

4.5.3.1. In the literature many assimilation process-types have been described
with phonetic details and hierarchies (cf. 4.5.2.2, Vennemann 1972), e.g., vowel
nasalization,[67] complete consonantal assimilation,[68] final devoicing as assimilation to voiceless pause. Its hierarchy pertains to (a) stops, (b) all obstruents, (c) all consonants, (α) word-finally, (β) syllable-finally (naturally including word-final position).[69] A more important role will be played in this
book by another assimilatory rule:

4.5.3.2. Velar palatalization before front vowels (cf. 6.7), e.g., k, g → k′,
g′ / __ i, e. This process type has been dealt with very often;[70] however, it
must be clearly distinguished from similar process types: (1) from palatalization of dentals and other consonants;[71] (2) from change of palatalized to palatal stops (cf. 4.4.5) or to affricates/sibilants (4.6.2). The basic property of
this process type is either (a) assimilatory fronting of velars to prevelars
and/or (b) that velars take on palatality as a secondary feature by anticipation

or, less likely, perseveration from an adjacent palatal semivowel or vowel.[72]
Both variants can occur together in the same PR. Palatalization can be generalized in fast speech.[73] It is due to its assimilatory nature that palatalization
is classed with backgrounding processes, although articulatory effort may be
higher in producing palatalized than non-palatalized consonants.[74] As to its
hierarchy, (1) palatalization is the more likely the more palatal the adjacent
agent of palatalization (/ C __ D) is, e.g., rather before tense/long/stressed
vowels than the reverse,[75] (2) before more fronted (not necessarily higher) vowels than before less fronted ones,[76] e.g., rather before /i/ than /y/, /e/ than
/ɛ/, and /i/ than /e/, if /i/ (as usual) is more front than /e/ in the respective language,[77] and (3) the subtype (b), i.e., palatality taken over as a secondary feature rather before/after higher segments (with narrower articulation)
than the reverse, i.e., most adjacent to semivocalic /ĭ/ or palatal approximant
/j/.[78]

4.5.3.3. The best-known process-types of distant assimilations are vowel harmony[79] and umlaut.[80]

4.5.4. A phonemic sequence can be shortened either by deletion of a phoneme[81]
or by fusion (coalescence) of two segments into one; fusion process-types can
be considered as a special case of (often reciprocal) assimilation.[82] This type
of processes is antagonistic to polarization (4.4.3).

4.5.4.1. One subtype is monophthongization (antagonistic to diphthongization),
which often looks like reciprocal assimilation, e.g., $ai \rightarrow e$, in the diachrony
or in the synchrony (fast/casual speech) of many languages.

4.5.4.2. Contraction processes such as /ae/ → /aː, a/[83] may be fusional or assimilatory or involve deletion (the last one, e.g., in French alcool [alˈkɔl]).
As for consonants, e.g., the fusion of stops and fricatives to affricates[84] belongs here.

4.5.4.3. As Schane (1973:68) has proposed, the reduction of a second segment to
a secondary articulation feature of the first segment can be understood as fusion, e.g., $kw \rightarrow k^w$, or the genesis of prenasalized consonants such as [ⁿd] ←
/nd/ (Herbert 1977b). If the acquisition of secondary features obscures the

perceptual effect of primary ones, then it is antagonistic to loss of secondary features (4.4.6).

4.6. The classical dichotomy of 'optimization of perception' vs. 'ease of articulation' is vitiated by process-types which serve both ends (4.3.3.2, 4.4.6).

4.6.1. There are several types of substitutions of perceptually similar but more effective sounds which at the same time are easier to articulate. A well-known example is the frequent unilateral[85] diachronic change $k^w > p$, a change which increases audibility and eliminates a secondary articulation (cf. 4.4.6).[86] However, this process type does not seem ever to occur as a synchronic process of a language and may be primarily due to misperception in diachronic change.[87] But a similar process type, /ł/ → [w], is also a synchronic process, as in many American English dialects, e.g., *all* [ɒːw] vs. *law* [łɒː], or in Zyrian dialects.[88]

4.6.2. The last process-type I want to mention is the substitution of palatal or alveolar affricates for palatal stops (4.4.6) or palatalized velar stops (4.5.3.2)[89] (and of palatal/alveolar fricatives for palatalized fricatives), as in many Slavic and Romance languages;[90] Quechua (Cerrón-Palomino 1974:48) and Albanian dialects;[91] and Scandinavian (Ralph 1981), Yuman (Wares 1968:57), Caucasian,[92] and Mayan (Kaufman 1969:158f) languages. The output of this substitution involves less articulatory effort[93] and perceptual foregrounding.[94]

Notes

1. Cf. Hyman 1975:153ff, Sommerstein 1977:225ff, Basbøll 1979 for overviews. On markedness, see Basbøll 1981c, Kean 1981, van Lessen-Kloeke 1982:54ff.

2. Donegan & Stampe 1979b:136, cf. already Stampe 1969, 1980. Cf. Humboldt's (1835:459 = VII,82) dictum: 'Man muß die Sprachbildung überhaupt als eine Erzeugung ansehen, in welcher die innere Idee, um sich zu manifestieren, eine Schwierigkeit zu überwinden hat. Diese Schwierigkeit ist der Laut und die Überwindung gelingt nicht immer in gleichem Grade.'

3. Dinnsen 1977b, 1978, 1979b, Dinnsen & Eckman 1978.

4. On earlier views on universal natural rules/rule-schemata/meta-rules as espoused by Chen, Lass, and Schane, cf. Sommerstein 1977:230ff. A subset of universal phonological process types corresponds to markedness rules in generative phonology (Chomsky & Halle 1968, Kiparsky 1982b).

5. For critiques on Natural Phonology, see, e.g., Ohala 1974a, S. Anderson 1981, Dinnsen 1978, Drachman 1978, 1981a, Hooper 1979b, Kodazasov & Krivnova 1981:145ff. These objections will be answered in 4, 5, 8, 10. On Atomic Phonology, see critiques in Donegan & Stampe 1977, Hooper 1979b:148f.

6. E.g., Ferguson 1978a.

7. Although the literature on the phonological and/or phonetic typology of processes is abundant, the resulting characterization of specific process types is far from sufficient.

8. On the intricate problem of whether hierarchies are universal or not, see Donegan & Stampe 1977, 1979b, Dinnsen 1978, 1979b, Drachman 1977, 1981a: 104. Cf. 5.4.3, 10.7.1.4.

9. This has been called the 'rich-get-richer-principle' (Donegan 1978), i.e., relatively 'strong' sounds within a strength hierarchy tend to 'strengthen' in strong position and vice versa. Cf. 5.4.2, 5.4.4.

10. Cf. notes to 4.0-2, work by Ohala (1974a, 1974b, 1980, 1982, etc.), Javkin 1979, Lass 1983, Keating & Linker 1982, etc. Cf. 4.4.2 note 35.

11. See Donegan 1978 and literature in Greenberg 1978:II.

12. 'must bear' in Natural Phonology, cf. Dressler 1979a, Manaster-Ramer 1984. This criterion has been explicitly acknowledged in Chomsky 1957:241.

13. Cf. 4.2.2 note 8, Hyman 1975:161.

14. Cf. Matthews 1974:201ff, Herok & Tonelli 1977, Wojcik 1981.

15. Cf. Goman 1981:108.

16. Which is of course of a more complicated nature than thought earlier on, cf. Terbeek 1977a, 1977b.

17. Or clarification processes (G. Verdeutlichungsprozesse) in Dressler & Drachman 1977, Dressler 1980b:56, 59f.

18. Or obscuration (G. Entdeutlichung). All backgrounding processes are assimilatory (in a broad sense), foregrounding processes are dissimilatory.

19. Cf. Donegan & Stampe 1979b:142.

20. Greater force of articulation hardly seems to be an independent goal, unless one believes that cases of sound-symbolism such as tensing of consonants as a metaphor of aggressiveness primarily have an articulatory motivation, and not a perceptive one; but see Ohala 1982.

21. Cf. 3.1.4.2, 3.2.3f, Hock 1976, Houlihan 1977:222ff. E.g., German obstruents are longer and stronger word-initially than word-finally (Lehiste 1978); cf. Cedergren & Sankoff 1975 and various studies in Nasálfest which show the high cross-linguistic frequency of $VN^\$ \rightarrow \tilde{V}N \rightarrow \tilde{V}$ and the rarity of $^\$NV \rightarrow N\tilde{V} \rightarrow \tilde{V}$.

22. Cf. Kim 1977, Ertel 1969; but cf. Fischer-Jørgensen 1978.

23. Cf. Dressler 1978a, 1982b:10ff, Dressler & Stark to appear.

24. 4.2.4, Donegan 1978:8, 19.

25. Dressler 1975a, Job 1977:52ff, Pike 1964:131, Allen & Hurd 1972, Hoskison 1975, Breen 1977.

26. Donegan 1976:91ff, 134f, Dressler 1975a. Vowel lowering maximizes sonority, vowel raising palatal color; cf. Fischer-Jørgensen 1967, Ertel 1969.

27. But not vowel centralization corresponsible for the two-vowel system /ɨ, a/, cf. 4.5.0.

28. In 5, 6, 7, 9 this typology is used as a convenient frame of reference; in 10.7 it will be justified as a constitutive part of a model of universal phonology.

29. Such PRs are necessary in any transduction model (1.1) where entities of the phonemic level are transduced into entities of the phonetic level. In fact, any phonetic realization involves introducing feature specifications (phonetic detail) absent in the phonological input.

30. Ultan 1978, Hetzron 1980:264ff, Rischel 1975:433f, E. Mayerthaler 1981:193ff; cf. Moravcsik 1977b, Derbyshire 1979:187f, Rood 1975:322f.

31. Ultan 1978, Bailey 1970, Malone 1971, Semiloff-Zelasko 1973, Silva 1973.

32. Donegan 1978:62f, Heine & Reh 1982:8, E. Mayerthaler 1981:156ff, Hjordt-Vetlesen 1981, Vago & Battistella 1982, Manaster-Ramer 1984. Ohala (1979a) accepts neither teleological explanations (cf. 10.2) nor antagonistic processes. His explanation --listeners' misanalysis-- cannot be appropriate for all types of dissimilation; e.g., see Kainz (1956, IV:476f) and Klaus (1968) on 'refractory period'.

33. Daly & Martin 1972, Sanders 1972, Hyman 1975:162f, Dressler 1977f:136ff, Hooper 1976:233ff, Nicole 1979:63f, Dressler & Drachman 1977:290, Broselow 1982. Often only or generalized in slow/hyperarticulate speech, cf. 5.18.4.3, Abaurre 1981.

34. Cf. Hooper 1976:183ff, 234ff. Vowel epenthesis is rare in word/syllable-final (= weak) position, except in loan-word phonology.

35. See Chen 1970, Hyman 1975:172f, Javkin 1979:52ff, Fischer-Jørgensen 1980, Anderson 1981:507ff. Thus phonological process types may be provided with excessive or competing motivations, whereas many MPRs and most AMRs have no phonetic motivation (and hence plausibility) at all.

36. Houlihan 1977, Hurch 1982. Notice that in Korean, aspiration of voiceless stops symbolizes emphasis (Kim 1977). Aspiration increases perceptibility

(Bhatia 1976).

37. Cf. Kahn 1976:41ff, Robins & Waterson 1952:66.

38. Andersen 1972, Stampe 1972, Donegan 1978:106ff, Sasse 1976.

39. Cf. Belgeri 1929:125, 131, Resnick 1975:26f, Allen & Hurd 1972:42. For re-
     strictions to emphatic speech, cf. Kilham 1977:32, for aphasia, cf. Dress-
     ler & Stark, to appear.

40. On kinaesthetic judgements of articulatory effort, see Fischer-Jørgensen
     1972.

41. Whereas loss of secondary features such as context-free denasalization is
     clearly a foregrounding process type, I cannot agree with Donegan (1978:
     67f, 83ff) that laxing and vowel centralization are foregrounding, since
     these process-types behave like other backgrounding process types (general-
     ized in weak positions, in fast/casual speech, in aphasia).

42. Zabrocki 1951, Goman 1981:127ff, Dressler 1980c:111f.

43. Cf., e.g., Ferguson 1978a, Blumenthal 1972, Dressler & Stark, to appear.

44. Dressler 1980c:111; cf. Guile 1973, Stephens & Justeson 1980, Langdon
     1975:230f.

45. See Jakobson & Halle 1956; critiques in Brakel 1981:§3.4.2.

46. For vowels, cf. Terbeek 1977b.

47. 4.3.3.2. For casual/fast speech, see the references in Linell 1979a:172
     note 9 and Dressler & Wodak 1982; cf. 5.11.

48. Catford 1977:117ff, Warren 1976, Slis 1971; cf. the survey by Birkhan
     1979:26ff.

49. E.g., Korhonen 1979:12ff.

50. E. Mayerthaler 1981, Guile 1972, Hooper 1976:233ff, Dressler 1977f:140ff.
     Cf. Bailey 1971, Barinova 1971a, Morin 1971:70ff, Thelin 1971, Dressler
     1972:47ff, Hyman 1975:163f, 170, Drachman 1977:91. Cf. 5.18.4.4.

51. Cf., e.g., Sanders 1979:91, Kim-Renaud 1975.

52. For feature loss of the backgrounding type, cf. Reuse (1981) on deaspira-
     tion in Ofo.

53. 3.2.1.2. Cf. Katamba 1979, Back 1979, Lass 1971, Ewen 1977, Zabrocki 1951.

54. Dinnsen & Eckman 1978:6ff; cf. Ó Dochartaigh 1980.

55. Cf. Katamba 1979, Ultan 1970, Langdon 1975:229ff, Kilham 1977:31, Coetsem
     et al. 1981:311, Keating et al. 1983. In Korean only non-tense stops are
     voiced in intervocalic position (Kim-Renaud 1975).

56. Cf. Ferguson 1978, Keating et al. 1983:280.

57. Rennison, to appear; cf. Resnik 1975:16.

58. Donegan & Stampe 1979b:146ff, Shockey 1973:46ff, Keating et al. 1983:280,
     Sharpe 1972:18, Kilham 1977:31, Pike 1964:130.

59. E.g., Bhat 1974:82f, Droescher 1974:208, Dressler 1965, Nigam 1975:75, 112,
     138.

60. E.g., Mioni 1971:73f; often in diachrony, especially when voiced as in

Slavic and Romance languages.

61. Morin 1971:89, Barinova 1971b:124, 127, Rischel 1974:120, Dressler 1980c: 106ff.

62. Bhat 1974:83, Lindau 1980, Vogt 1971:12, Robins & Waterson 1952:63, Brakel 1974, 1981:§2.4.3.2, 3.5.3.2, 3.6.1f, Angenot & Vandresen 1981, Lass 1983.

63. Lass 1976:163, Shockey 1973:20f, Loos 1969:184, Resnick 1975:1f, 13, 38, Langdon 1975:231f, Hetzron 1977:38, Rubach 1977:104, Tuggy 1979:8, Derbyshire 1979:180, 182.

64. Lindner 1975:151ff, Coates 1980, Batliner 1974, Vennemann 1972, Goman 1981: 155ff, Guerssel 1978, Nicole 1979, Scherfer 1983; cf. Vago & Battistella 1982. For the acoustic counterpart, see Greenlee & Ohala 1980.

65. Lindner 1975:202f, Coates 1980, Shockey 1973:58ff, Barinova 1971b:123, Morin 1971:53ff, Dressler 1972:38ff, Rubach 1977, Herok & Tonelli 1977, Wodak & Dressler 1978:39ff.

66. Lindner 1975:151f, Goman 1981:156f.

67. Chen 1972, 1974, Ruhlen 1978, Dressler 1972:39ff, Greenlee & Ohala 1980: 293f, Cagliari 1983; cf. Nasálfest 1975.

68. Hutcheson 1973, Mascaró 1978:43ff, 51ff.

69. Lass 1971, Anwar 1974, Kim 1972, Janda 1979, Keating et al. 1983; cf. Robins & Waterson 1952:66, Dinnsen 1978, Dinnsen & Eckman 1978, Jakobson 1962:I,107, Kenstowicz 1981:434f, Parker 1981.

70. Bhat 1978, Neeld 1973, Chen 1972, 1974, Belgeri 1929, Lass 1976:185ff.

71. Bhat 1978:51ff, Rood 1975:328; cf. Iverson & Oñederra 1983, Kim-Renaud 1975.

72. Bhat 1978:67f, Mioni 1971:72, 77.

73. Bhat 1978:65, Knudson 1975:57f.

74. Straka 1964.

75. Bhat 1978:55f, Neeld 1973.

76. Bhat 1978:52ff, Neeld 1973:313, Timberlake 1978, Ralph 1981.

77. E.g., in the Romance languages, where there is also good evidence for palatalization before [a], cf. Nicole 1979:23ff.

78. Neeld 1973, Lepschy 1965.

79. Cf. Vago 1981. On the question of autosegmental models, see Clements 1977, Clements & Sezer 1982, Halle & Vergnaud 1981; critically Ringen 1983 and S. Anderson 1982.

80. 3.1.2, 3.1.4.2, 5.8.2, 5.8.5; cf. Basbøll 1982.

81. 4.5.2.1. Of course MPRs, AMRs, and suppletions, as in umlaut and modern Germanic languages (cf. Kubrjakova & Pankrac 1983:34ff), do not qualify as inductive bases for establishing the phonological process type of umlaut.

82. Cf. Rood 1975:325ff, Stahlke 1976, Herbert 1977a, Vennemann 1972, Chene & Anderson 1979 (Anderson 1980:59ff), Sasse 1976, Ewen 1980, Heine & Reh 1982:14f.

83. E.g., Rischel 1974:73ff, Nater 1979:180f.; cf. Drachman 1977:96 on hierar-

chy problems.

84. E.g., Nater 1979:178, Gaprindašvili 1966:241, ts → č in Polish and Albanian fast speech (Dodi 1968:23).

85. Cf. King (1973:573f) against a putative Mohawk counterexample.

86. J. Ohala 1979, 1982, Devine & Stephens 1977, S. Anderson 1981.

87. On this type of change, see Andersen 1973, J. Ohala 1974a, 1974b, 1979, 1980, 1983, Javkin 1979.

88. Jonasson 1971, J. Ohala 1974a:256f, Valle 1977, Dobó 1980, Flier 1983.

89. Belgeri 1929, Melikišvili 1970:70ff, Bhat 1978, Goman 1981:141ff, Luschützky, to appear.

90. Neeld 1973, Belgeri 1929, Ekblom 1935, Stankiewicz 1960; cf. 6, 7.

91. Dodi 1968:41, Desnickaja 1968:83f, 93, 103, 117, 140ff.

92. Klimov 1978:96, Gaprindašvili 1966:245ff.

93. Belgeri 1929:120, 165, 186, 203, Melikišvili 1970:72. Since this substitution is very often context-free, Clements' (1976) classification of this change as assimilatory is of a rather marginal character.

94. Luschützky, to appear, cf. Fry 1979:127. Due to misperception according to J. Ohala 1974a:378.

5. DESCRIPTIVE CRITERIA FOR DIFFERENTIATING MORPHONOLOGICAL, PHONOLOGICAL, AND ALLOMORPHIC MORPHOLOGICAL RULES

5.0.1. I have maintained that morphonology has no unequivocally specific characteristics of its own, but mixes properties of phonology and morphology (cf. 5. 21). If morphonology were a separate or autonomous (sub)component of language, it should have specific (a) inputs (e.g., morphophonemes), (b) principles governing their inventories, (c) principles governing their syntactic combinations, (d) processes relating inputs to outputs, i.e., MPRs. Since I do not assume inputs other than phonemes,[1] which are also possible inputs of PRs and, sometimes superficially, of AMRs, we must concentrate on (d), i.e., the differentiation of MPRs, PRs, and AMRs (cf. 1); (b) and (c) will be dealt with in the subsection on morpheme structure constraints (MSRs), insofar as morphonological properties of the input distribution of phonemes may differ from phonological ones. Now we start with the relative phonologicalness (phonological naturalness) of PRs, MPRs, and allomorphic MRs, because --in striking contrast to morphological characteristics of morphonology-- (1) most of the discussion of morphonology can be dealt with under this heading and (2) very little semiotic metatheory (cf. 10) is needed, but we will include other descriptive criteria as well (including diachronic properties).

5.0.2. In the literature (cf. 1) the following criteria have been the most important, either as the only, single criterion used, or as the most weighty one: (1) neutralization (of phonemes)(= MPRs) vs. allophonic realization (= PRs)(but often the same PR can have both neutralizing (phonemic) and allophonic effects[2]), (2) automaticity (or obligatoriness or generality), a polysemous criterion, (3) phonetic plausibility or motivation (= PRs)(cf. 4.3.3, 5.6)(but also possible with MPRs), (4) productivity (= PRs)(cf. 1.9, 5.13) --however, morphological and phonological productivity must be differentiated-- and there are different domains of productivity, and (5) naturalness of PRs in the sense of phonological universality, plausibility (= 3), productivity (= PRs), and many other meanings. But there is also morphological naturalness. Here we will discuss degrees of phonological naturalness (as a cover term from Natural Phonology) in its various possible meanings and try to calculate the relative importance of the specific criteria of old standing or newly introduced. For this purpose we will try to grade the various relative degrees of naturalness for each criterion on numerical scales.

5.0.3. The discussion of diachronic aspects of morphonology is so enormous[3] that a representative coverage would demand a separate book. Thus I will mention diachronic aspects after having dealt with the synchronic aspects of each criterion; anyway the strict separation of diachronic and synchronic aspects is theoretically unfounded[4] and results in tiresome repetitiveness in any systematic presentation of both aspects. For comprehensive treatments of diachronic morphonology within models of Natural Phonology and Morphology, I refer to Dressler (1977a, 1980b) and Wurzel (1980c, 1981a, 1982).

5.1. Universality

5.1.1. Universality (Linell 1979b:205f), in its weak form, means frequent recurrence of very similar PRs in many/most languages of the world, but in the same sense MRs or morphological principles can have a wide distribution, e.g., suffixation of plural markers.

However, the coincidence of a recurrent morphological technique and a recurrent PR, e.g., distant vowel assimilation, cannot have such a wide distribution. E.g., plural formation by means of umlaut (as a putative instance of distant vowel assimilation), such as in E. *foot → feet* = G. dial. *Fuss → Füss'* (with diachronic loss of the final vowel as in English) is restricted to but a few languages, and the similarity of such plural formation is marred by many idiosyncracies of the respective languages. Thus E. umlaut cannot be a PR, but must be a MPR or (as will be shown in 5.2.4) an AMR. However, there are two problems with the use of this criterion: (a) How should the cross-linguistic identity/similarity of PRs as against MPRs or MRs be established? (b) In how many languages should they recur? A coincidence of phonological and morphological naturalness can occur only in cases of iconicity, i.e., iconic images (e.g., in onomatopoeia, expression of diminution by means of vowel raising/fronting and palatalization); otherwise the relationship of morphology and phonology is arbitrary by definition, i.e., why should plurality be expressed by umlaut rather than by vowel lowering?

5.1.2. In its strong form, universality (Linell 1979b:105f) means that a puta-

tive PR (and not a MPR) should belong or refer to the sort of universal phonological process (as in Natural Phonology; cf. Stampe 1969, Donegan 1978, Donegan & Stampe 1979b). Since (non)universality is not a dichotomous criterion, we
use the procedure of process matching (5.2).

5.2. Process matching

5.2.0. This is a procedure which refers to the universal process types of 4
with their internal hierarchies on the one hand and to a putative PR/MPR/AMR of
a specific language/dialect on the other, insofar as its phonological description is concerned; i.e., we take the formulation of a PR/MPR/AMR in standard
notation (see 1), remove all non-phonological information,[5] and compare it (try
to match it) with a universal process type. The relative ease or difficulty of
this matching results in a scale.

5.2.1. On the scale of process matching, a putative PR (or MPR or AMR) receives
the best score (= value) of phonological naturalness if it can be matched with a
universal process type in one of its hierarchical forms. E.g., final devoicing
in Russian, Polish, Breton, Albanian, etc., can be identified with the hierarchical threshold 'word final position, all obstruents' (4.5.3.1), while in the
Ferrara dialect of Italian, where only word final stops are devoiced, this is
hierarchically more restricted. In Standard German and Turkish, final devoicing
of obstruents (in Turkish, stops and affricates only) occurs in the less restricted hierarchical form 'syllable final position' (cf. 4.5.3.1). Score 1 is
also assigned to ɨ-insertion in English plurala and Saxon genitives and 3.sg.
presents, as in /bʌs≠z/ → /bʌs≠z/ *busses*,[6] or to Albanian ə-deletion:

$$ ə \rightarrow \emptyset \ / \ C_1 \underset{[\text{-stress}]}{\rule{2cm}{0.4pt}} \text{sonorant} + V $$

as in *em*[ə]*r* 'name', *emr-i* 'the name' (Dressler 1977a; cf. 4.5.2.1).

5.2.2. A putative MPR (or PR or AMR) receives the score 2 (= phonologically
less natural) if it must be matched with two process types in such a way that
the output of the first process type is the input of the second process type.
Thus the Cheremis rule (Dressler 1977g:318f) p → b / m ___ #V receives the
score 2 since it corresponds to the two lenition processes (1) p → b and (2)
b → w at the same time.

Lenition (between sonorants) of /d/ results in [ð] in Welsh (score 1), but in [z] in Breton (score 2) with (1) d → ð (lenition process = backgrounding), (2) ð → z (foregrounding, 4.4.5); cf. Welsh, Breton b → [v], corresponding to (1) b → β, (2) β → v. Spanish diphthongization of /o/ to [we] corresponds to two successive foregrounding processes: (1) o → wo (diphthongization, 4.4.3), (2) wo → we (dissimilation, 4.4.1.3).

5.2.3. A putative MPR (or AMR or PR) is given a score of 3 if it corresponds to three successive universal process types.

In Albainia, /k, g/ are changed to palatal /c, ɟ/ (written *q, gj*) after *i* in the verbal paradigm: 2nd pl. indicative *piq-ni*, 1st sg. imperfect *piq-ja* = *piq-sha*, 2nd sg. imperative *piq*, 1st sg. passive *piq-em*, from *pjek* 'I cook'. This corresponds to (1) palatalization k, g → k′, g′ (4.5.3.2 = backgrounding), (2) k′, g′ → [c, ɟ](4.4.5 = foregrounding); in many Albanian dialects, *q, gj* have become affricates [č, ǰ], which corresponds to a third process (4.5.2); for a similar 3 score k → č rule in Faroese, cf. Hellberg (1980:6ff).

In the Vyčegda dialects of Zyrian[7] there is a score 3 (neutralization) rule l → v / __ $, corresponding to the process types: (1) l → ł (velarization, backgrounding), (2) ł → w (perceptual substitution, cf. 4.6.1), (3) w → v / __ $ in the Kudymkar dialect; thus: score 1. Lithuanian[8] has an n-deletion rule

$$Vn \rightarrow V\text{:} \quad / \quad \underline{\quad} \quad \left\{ \begin{matrix} \# \\ \left[\begin{matrix} +\text{obstr.} \\ +\text{contin.} \end{matrix} \right] \end{matrix} \right\}$$ corresponding to (1) Vn → Ṽn (assimilation, cf. 4.5.3.1, = backgrounding), (2) Ṽn → Ṽ: (fusion, 4.5.4, = backgrounding), (3) Ṽ: → V: (loss of secondary feature, 4.4.5, = foregrounding). Latin rhotacism s → r / V __ V should probably be matched with (1) lenition (= backgrounding) s → z (4.5.2.2), (2) lenition z → [ɾ], (3) lengthening (= foregrounding) tap → vibrant (Dressler 1980c:106ff).

5.2.4. So far language specific rules have been matched with universal context-sensitive processes (e.g., final devoicing, vowel insertion, vowel deletion 5.2.1, lenition, diphthongization, dissimilation 5.2.2, palatalization, velarization, vowel nasalization 5.2.3) or context-free processes (e.g., foregrounding of approximants 5.2.2f, palatal stop formation, vowel denasalization 5.2.3). Now if a language specific rule without relevant phonological context can only be matched with a universal context-sensitive process, this relative phonologi-

cal unnaturalness must somehow be expressed. In studying such rules I háve
found that all such rules behave in a phonologically more unnatural way than
rules of score 3 (5.2.3); therefore I assign them score 4.

E.g., among the German (morphologized) umlaut rules, rules (a) u → y /
__ X$Yi as in *Hund* 'dog', adj. *hünd-isch* ['hʏndɪʃ], fem. *Hünd-in* 'bitch' (score
1) and (b) u → y / __ X$Yə as in *Schuss* 'shot', pl. *Schüss-e* ['ʃʏsə] (but *Hund-e*
'dogs' without umlaut)(score 2, corresponding to (1) u → y / __ X   V   and
                                                                    [+palatal]
(2) V → ə / _____) behave less unnaturally than rule (c) u → y / _____
              [-stress]   (morph.
                                                                      contexts)

as in *Bruder* 'brother', pl. *Brüder* ['bryːdər] (corresponding to the same processes as rule (b), but without phonological context). So this rule receives
score 4 as does O.E. umlaut in *mūs, mȳs* 'mouse, mice'; also E. *mouse, mice*
would have score 4.

In Finnish gradation[9] we can contrast the following three types of alternations:

(a) p → v, k → j as in *halpa* 'cheap', *jälki* 'trace', gen./acc. *halvan, jäljen*,
    corresponding to 3 lenition processes (4.5.2.2): (1) p → b, k → g, (2) b →
    β, g → γ, (3) β → v (no lenition), γ → j;
(b) t → d as in *pato* 'dam', gen./acc. *padon*, corresponding to the first lenition
    process only (parallel to p, k → b, g);
(c) pp, tt, kk → p, t, k as in *piippu* 'pipe', gen./acc. *piipun*, corresponding to
    one backgrounding process: shortening (4.5.1).

All three types of alternations have lost their relevant phonological context,
since lengthening of the word form by a suffix does not occur in the context of
the universal process type of lenition. Now all three types of alternation behave in the same way as to their phonological naturalness. Since rules (a) must
be classified as less natural than score 1, 2, and 3 rules, I assign them score
4.

5.2.5. Finally I assign score 5 to rules which cannot be matched plausibly with
any universal process or with a specific sequences of processes rather than with
another sequence one could think of.[10] Two cases in question are:
(a) Latin inverted rhotacism r → s / __ +{s, t} as in *ur-o* 'I burn', perfect *us-*
    s-i, perfect participle *us-t-us*, *heri* 'yesterday', adj. *hes-ternus*;[11]
(b) the Hungarian 2nd person singular present ending is /s/ ([ɛs] etc. in case

of vowel epenthesis) as in vár-[s] 'you wait', küld-[ɛs] 'you send', but /l/
(with epenthetic harmonizing vowel) after fricative sibilants as in kere[š]-
[ɛl] 'you earn', fȫz-[œl] 'you cook'. The function of this substitution of
/l/ for /s/ is clearly dissimilative, however there is no sufficient evidence for constructing a universal dissimilation process s → l. The same
holds for the Old Armenian rule ɾ → r / __ n RANK: (morphological) word
(Dressler 1977g:326) which makes a rhotic better perceivable by changing a
tap to a vibrant before another sonorant.

5.2.6. Evaluation of the five possible scores on the scale of matching language
specific rules with universal phonological processes:

5.2.6.1. A PR must have a score 1 on this scale. Thus Faroese k → č, a score 3
rule (5.2.3) is not a natural PR, not even 'apparently' (Hellberg 1980), nor is
Portuguese (or English) velar softening a 'natural assimilation process' (Araujo
1981). If we allowed rules of score 2 to receive the status of PRs, then we
would no principled way of excluding rules corresponding to processes with vastly different functions, such as Breton d → z, uniting the mutually exclusive
functions of backgrounding and foregrounding (5.2.2).[12] However, we will see
that the inverse implication does not hold: All rules of score 1 are not necessarily PRs; they may be also MPRs and rarely AMRs (see 5.2.6.2).

5.2.6.2. An AMR is to be defined primarily by morphological criteria. MPRs mix
properties of PRs and AMRs. Now since rules of score 5 cannot be matched with
phonological processes, they totally lack this most important criterion of phonologicity. As a consequence, rules of score 5 must be AMRs.

5.2.7. Several mechanisms of diachronic change belong here, in the form of morphologization of PRs > MPRs > AMRs.

5.2.7.1 Rule telescoping,[13] i.e., collapsing of two rules which are in a feeding relation to a single rule. When Breton /ð/ was foregrounded to /z/, this
process applied to the output of the lenition /d/ → [ð] (5.2.2) as well. The
two processes (1) d → ð / sonorant __ sonorant, and (2) ð → z were telescoped to
one rule d → z / son __ son. In this case telescoping was necessary because the
context-free PR /ð/ → /z/ was lost due to restructuring of underlying /ð/ > /z/,

whereas in Cheremis (5.2.2) a sequence of processes might have remained as such for some time, until identical contextual restrictions occurred which vouch for the uniformity of the rule p → w / V __ # v. On the other hand (some of) those English and Brazilian dialects which have to have both PRs l → ł / __ {c, #} and ł → w / __ {c, #} do not seem to have telescoped them, particularly those American dialects where the first PR is obligatory, the second optional, as in *hill* [hɪł] ≈ [hɪw], but *[hɪl]. Notice that no telescoping has occurred in O.E. umlaut ū → ȳ (2.4), but has in Mod.E. /ū/ → [aɪ] with the additional rules ȳ → ī → aɪ; nevertheless both rules have the same synchronic status as an AMR.[14] Thus telescoping is not likely to be a primary force of morphologization.

5.2.7.2. Restructuring of the input of a PR may provoke multiple process matching, without synchronic matching reflecting diachronic change, e.g., Arči (Kodzasov 1976:20) had a PR ä → e / __ c_ii, then /ä/ was restructured to /a/, cf. *naqⁿᵒ* 'earth', ergative *néqⁿᵒi*. The resulting MPR has to be matched with a → æ and æ → e before heterosyllabic *i* (cf. Dressler 1977a:26). For the effect of O.E. *ū* > Mod.E. *au*, see 5.2.4, 5.2.7.1.

5.2.7.3. Rule inversion[14a] as in Latin s → r / V __ +v > r → s / __ +{s, t} (5.2.5, 5.20.8.3.8) may destroy process matching. It is commonly maintained that a PR necessarily changes into a MPR (or AMR) by rule inversion. However if the result of rule inversion is a rule which perfectly corresponds to a universal phonological process type, this needs not be true. A case is the inversion of German x → ç / V __ > ç → x / V __ .[15] Another case is the in-
[-back]   [+back]
version of English ə-loss to ə-insertion in inflectional endings, e.g., pl. z → əz, cf. Keyser & O'Neill (1980). Cf. Magnus (1973) on Aramaic syncope and epenthesis, or Norman & Sanders (1977, criticized by Harris 1978) on the inversion of Spanish diphthongization (e.g., /o/ → [we]) to monophthongization (e.g., /we/ → [o]). On diagrammaticity in rule inversion, see 10.8.3.5.2.

5.2.7.4. Process matching is destroyed if a context-sensitive PR loses its phonological context (cf. 5.2.4) due to another PR:[16] E.g., O.E. umlaut lost its phonological context (palatal vowel or consonant) due to loss of final vowels and assimilation of /j/ respectively, e.g., O.E. *mȳs* 'mice' < reconstructed *mūs-iz*, *fēt*, Angl. *fœt* 'feet' < *fōt-iz*, *fellan*, Angl. *fællan* 'to fell' < *falljan* vs. *fallan* 'to fall'. Such loss of phonological contexts is especially typical for the changes of MPRs > AMRs.

5.2.7.5. All these changes may be subsumed under the heading of rule-interaction.[17] However PRs may morphologize without (previous) rule interaction (cf. Skousen 1975:119ff). On the other hand, rule interaction may improve process matching without ensuring rephonologization, e.g., some German dialects have undergone the change in the umlaut rule a → e > a → æ (Kiparsky 1982a:18).

Thus rule interaction is frequently but not always involved in the morphologization of PRs.

5.3. <u>Phonetic distance between input and output</u>. Our operation of process matching (5.2) resembles the criterion of phonetic distance. Several authors[18] have claimed that PRs show a smaller distance (quantum leap, minimal vs. radical structural change) between their input and output (A → B) than MPRs (or, a fortiori, AMRs).

5.3.1. This criterion is important in diachronic phonologization such as in the change of intrinsic to extrinsic allophones (both are outputs of PRs) and as a prerequisite of phonemization (see 5.18) and of use for signalling morphological distinctions (10.8), i.e., AMRs and MPRs generally involve more radical changes than PRs.

In diachrony it is rather unproblematic to establish whether a PR or MPR of one historical stage involves a greater structural change than the predecessor of this rule at an earlier historical stage, e.g., a rule t → d involves a smaller structural change than a later form of this rule: t → ɗ.

5.3.2. However, in synchrony or panchrony, how should we establish whether a rule of vowel raising (e.g., e → i) involves a greater or smaller structural change than a rule of lenition t → d? An obvious answer is by counting (and weighing) changed features (Comrie 1979). We will have to return to the issue of feature change later on (5.18.3.2ff). Here it suffices to say that it does not supersede process matching, for, in whatever feature system, a PR s → h (e.g., between vowels or before /r/) or a PR of stop deletion (e.g., in cluster reduction) or a PR of total consonant assimilation (e.g., dr → rr) involve more feature changes than a PR of lenition (e.g., b → β); nevertheless they are all equally natural PRs (e.g., of fast speech), and this is correctly stated by matching them with a single universal phonological process (but cf. 5.18.3.2).

5.3.3. The distance between [ɨ] and [w] is as great in the putative rule ɨ → w
(in whatever environment) as in its inverse w → ɨ; but only the first rule can
be matched with a universal phonological process (4.6.1); or Latin s → r / v__v
can be matched with three processes (5.2.3), the inverted rule r → s with none
(5.2.5), etc. In many instances the criterion of phonetic plausibility (5.5)
may help out, but not in the case of matching with several processes (5.2.2 and
5.2.3). Thus an additional criterion 'direction of structural change' would
have to be introduced in order to supplement the criterion 'distance'.

5.4. <u>Regularity</u>. This is another criterion closely related to process matching
(5.2). In order to ease this operation, we have so far neglected the question
whether inputs and outputs of a rule are regular.[19] This is a minor, but in-
omissible criterion.

5.4.1. A universal phonological process type applies to a natural class,[20]
i.e., those phonological segments which share at least one distinctive feature
which is crucial for the operation of the process. E.g., lenition in its subpart of spirantization (4.5.2.2) is limited to stops or (according to the rich-
get-richer principle, 4.2.2) to voiced stops. This has happened in Welsh and
Breton lenitions (b, d, g → β, ð, γ).

5.4.2. If in a language only one segment of such a natural class is present,
then a process can only apply to this isolated sound, e.g., velarization of laterals, if there is only one non-velar lateral.[21]

5.4.3. A process may apply to a natural class differentially, i.e., either not
to all members of the natural class or to some to a greater or more general degree than to others. But this application would follow the rich-get-richer
principle (4.2.2), e.g., in lenition 'weaker' consonants should be prime targets
(cf. 5.4.5.2). Since /g/ is weaker than /d/, lenition of /d/ should not ante-
cede (diachronically) or outdo (synchronically) lenition of /g/. However if /b/
is lenited, but not /d, g/, then lenition is restricted to non-lingual consonants.[22]

5.4.4. We can assign a score of 1 to a rule which follows the principles of 5.4.1-3. A PR must achieve score 1,[23] such as PRs of final devoicing (5.2.1). But also non-PRs may do it, e.g., Welsh (and Breton) lenition and spirantization of /p, t, k/ → [b, d, g] and [f, θ, x] respectively, Welsh nasalization of /b, d, g/ to [m, n, ŋ], Albanian palatalization (5.2.3), Lithuanian nasal deletion (5.2.3), degemination (shortening) as part of Finnish gradation (5.2.4). Even clear AMRs may occasionally be regular in this sense, e.g., the exchange rule as part of plural formation in Luo: [α voiced] → [-α voiced]: *got* 'mountain', *kitabu* 'book', pl. *gode, kitepe*.[24] This means that we have to reckon with morphological regularity as well.

5.4.5. The degree of irregularity could be broken up into several classes (with respective scores), but they would be largely incidental and useless for the differentiation of MPRs and AMRs. So two classes may suffice:

5.4.5.1. Score 2 is assigned to a MPR or AMR if any regularity is left. This holds for Breton spirantization of /p, t, k/ → [f, z, x], German umlaut where (long or short) /u/ → [y], /o/ → [ø], and to a lesser degree /a/ → [ɛ] and /ao/ → [ɔø, ɔe] (according to the variety) can be described as fronting; Spanish diphthongization /o, e/ → [we, ĭe] can be classified as diphthongization (or monophthongization if the direction is inverted, 5.2.7.3), although the change is not strictly parallel, cf. Bulgarian /k, g/ → [c, z] (affricate vs. fricative).

5.4.5.2. Score 3 is assigned to MPRs and AMRs (a) if they change each input segment is a different way, e.g., to Welsh and Breton lenition of voiced stops (5.2.2, e.g., Breton /b/ → [v], /d/ → [z], /g/ is deleted, or changed to [h] in some varieties of Breton), to Finnish gradation of short stops (5.2.4), Greenlandic stop-continuant alternation (Rischel 1974:243ff); (b) if they apply only to one member of a natural class without respect for the rich-get-richer principle (5.4.3), e.g., German velar softening (5.10.3) applies only to /k/ but not to /g/, although /g/ being 'weaker' than /k/ should undergo a 'weakening' process more readily.

5.4.6. Although the criterion of regularity cannot differentiate MPRs and AMRs, we will see that more regular MPRs and AMRs differ in other respects as well

from less regular ones. Due to different degrees of regularity, PRs can conveniently be formulated in terms of distinctive features, MPRs and AMRs often
much more conveniently by enumerating the phonemes of their inputs and outputs,
an observation earlier made in structural linguistics.

5.4.7. In 'diachronic change, first an increase of regularity is involved in
phonologization, i.e., allophonic rules of e.g. palatalization typically change
velars differently both according to whether they are voiced or stops and according to the degree of palatality of the following vowel (cf. 4.5.3.2), but
when the outputs of these PRs become extrinsic allophones or phonemes, the
structural change may be regularized, e.g., may become identical before /i/ and
/e/, etc.[25] However, later on, during the process of morphologization, PRs and
MPRs typically become more irregular (phonologically), cf. Breton mutations (5.
4.3f), Finnish gradation (5.2.4), Bulgarian palatal formation and Spanish diphthongization (5.4.5.1), etc.

5.4.8. The extreme patterns of irregularity are represented by suppletion.[26]
In our context suppletion means allomorphic idiosyncratic alternation, i.e.,
suppletion is distinguished from an allomorphic AMR by the total lack of regularity (in the sense of 5.4); thus they are assigned score 4 on the scale of
irregularity.[27]

5.4.8.1. In weak suppletion either a major part of a monomorphemic word is
still recognizable, e.g., in E. *a* ∿ *an, the* ∿ [ðiǐ] = Hung. *a* ∿ *az* = Ital. *il* ∿
lo (masc.), or major parts of both morphemes of a bimorphemic word (form) are
recognizable, but no AMR can be established for any subclass of alternations
such as for F. *père* ∿ *patern-el* (cf. 1.10) and for most F. ethnics of 1.9, cf.
the Italian adjectives formed from geographical names: *tiber-ino* ← *Tevere*,
londin-ese ← *Londra* or the It. plurals *uomin-i* ← *uomo* 'man', *buo-i* ← *bue* 'bull',
etc.

5.4.8.2. In strong suppletion one morpheme changes completely in alternation,
any resemblance between the two alternants seems to be accidental, as in E.
father ∿ *patern-al*, French ethnics *Anicien, Ponot, Bragard* (1.9.1), It. *luc-ano*
← *Basilicata*, *teat-ino* ← *Chieti*, E. *good* → *bett-er* = Fr. *bon* → *meilleur*, E. *be*
∿ *am* ∿ *are* ∿ *i-s* ∿ *was*. For the historical origin of suppletions, see Meyer-

thaler (1977) and Rudes (1980).

5.4.8.3. I must repeat (1.6ff) that our model of the parameter of regularity
(including suppletion) excludes two concepts of Natural Generative Phonology:
(a) Hudson's (1980, 1982) idea that all alternations involve suppletion,[27a] and
(b) the concept of (bidirectional) via-rules (A ↔ B, cf. Hooper 1976), which
are in adiecto in our system: All MPRs and MRs are unidirectional (A → B),
whereas suppletions are no rules -- whether they are unidirectional or bidirectional is less easy to solve: In meaning there is a direction and thus by default the language learner may assume a diagrammatic relation, i.e., he may expect that a form which is semantically/functionally derived should probably be
formally derived as well; in this expectation he is confirmed by the great majority of semantically derived suppletive forms which are longer than the non-
derived ones and contain affixes, and, due to diagrammaticity, derived (non-sup-
pletive!) forms usually (1) are longer than non-derived ones, and (2) contain
affixation rather than the non-derived ones (cf. 10.4.5.6).

5.5. Phonetic plausibility

5.5.1. This is a criterion often used (cf. 5.0.2), generally in the form of the
weak claim that PRs should be phonetically plausible,[28] rarely in the form of
the strong claim that MPRs and at least AMRs should be phonetically implausible
or arbitrary.[29] This strong claim is simply untrue since they may (diachronically) preserve phonetic plausibility in the process of morphologization.[29a]
This holds also for prosodic conditions: E.g., Wojcik's (1976) claim that only
PRs may depend on stress placement is wrong, cf., e.g., E. trisyllabic shortening, French unrounding œ → ε (Morin 1978:236). Still more dramatic counterexamples to exaggerated claims about the importance of phonetic plausibility are
cases where a MPR has been diachronically restricted in a phonetically plausible
way. E.g., when Swedish palatalization was degeneralized, it remained most stable before /i/ (Ralph 1981:344f). When in the Albanian verb paradigm the MPR of
palatalization lost its original phonological context, it acquired a new one
which is perfectly plausible, i.e., preceding /i/, as in sg. *pjek* 'bake', 1.pl.
pjekim, 2.pl. *piqni*, 3.pl. *pjekin*, imperfect *piqsha*, imperative *piq*, passive
piqem (Dressler 1977a:28).[30] For an Italian example, cf. 6.2.5; for a Serbo-
Croatian one, cf. Thomason (1976:374).

5.5.2. Phonetic (or phonological) plausibility is often used in a rather vague or ambiguous manner. In the meanings of plausibility of the direction of a structural change, of the conditioning/favoring environment (cf. also 5.7), of the distance of the change (cf. also 5.3), it can be subsumed under the operation of process matching (5.2). This has the additional advantage of avoiding the false impression that these criteria are independent of each other.

Sometimes it is understood as phonetic motivation (e.g., Brasington 1976) or causality. We have relegated this concept to the justification of universal natural process types (4.2.3), but cf. also phonological conditioning (5.7.4).

5.6. Constraint on (aid to) pronounceability and perceptibility

5.6.0. Many phonologists hold that a true PR must express a constraint on language specific pronounceability (and perceptibility).[31] And if the main function of phonology is to make language pronounceable and perceivable (4.3.3.1), then a PR should serve this task. Finally, we have matched (5.2) all PRs to universal process types either or foregrounding (serving better perception) or of ease of articulation (mostly backgrounding ones)(cf. 10.7.1).

5.6.1. Those PRs that serve perception better most directly are slow/emphatic speech rules, generalized in slow, hyperarticulate, and emphatic speech, where better perception is called for (see 4.3.3.3.2, 5.11). Conversely, fast/casual speech rules, called for if good perception is of less importance, serve better pronunciation (easier articulation) most directly. Therefore I assign such PRs score 1 of pronounceability/perceptibility.

5.6.2.1. Score 2 can be assigned to those rules which represent constraints on pronounceability and perceptibility (see 5.6.0). These PRs aid better pronounceability and perceptibility only insofar as (1) they can be matched to universal process types which do serve that way, and (2) they are, by making the intended phonemes pronounceable and hence perceivable, a prerequisite for any aspiration towards optimal pronunciation and perception.

5.6.2.2. However such constraints on pronunciation are not absolute. First, they can be violated 'if the speaker makes a special effort';[32] otherwise we could not learn foreign languages or general phonetics. Second, constraints on slow speech forms are often violated in fast/casual and also in hyperarticulate speech.[33]   Third, in perception, foreign sounds which do not exist in language A can be identified and differentiated by native speakers of language A, although with more difficulty than phonemes of language A.

5.6.2.3.   Score 2 is assigned to all allophonic PRs generating obligatory allophones (which cannot be mistaken for MPRs) and to many neutralizing rules (with phonemes as outputs), e.g., (5.2.1) final devoicing in many languages, ǝ-insertion in English (insofar as (5.2.1) *zz, sz, šz are non-permitted sequences in the syllable coda[34]), neutralization of word-initial prevocalic /s, z/ to /s/ in Southern, to /z/ in Northern German dialects (and in Standard German), many neutralizing assimilation rules in many languages (cf. 4.5.3), e.g., devoicing assimilation in E. *cats* /kæt#z/.

5.6.3.   Score 3 is assigned to rules which aid pronounceability or perceptibility even though they represent neither constraints (5.6.2) nor PRs of slow/careful/hyperarticulate/emphatic or fast/casual speech (5.6.1).   E.g., Albanian ǝ-deletion (5.2.1) shortens words thus saving articulatory effort, cf. lenitions (5.2.2, 5.4).   This criterion does not coincide with the criterion whether a rule can be matched with one (or more) process type(s) (5.2), because the Hungarian s → l dissimilation and the Old Armenian change of a tap to a vibrant (5.2.5) aid pronounceability and/or perceptibility, but (at least so far) cannot be matched with a universal process type.   And even if such process types could be established, the points on the scales of 5.6 and 5.2 would not coincide.   MPRs must achieve score 3 or 4, usually they achieve score 3.

5.6.4.   Score 4 is assigned to rules which neither aid nor constrain pronounceability/perceptibility, e.g., English and German umlaut (5.2.5), Classical Latin rhotacism (5.2.3, 5.2.5), English velar softening (5.2.5), as in French from which it has come (cf. F. *électrique* vs. *électricité*).   But some allomorphic MRs and even suppletions may aid pronounceability, e.g., the suppletion of E. *a* and *an*.

5.6.5.   Evaluation: Rules of scores 1 and 2 must be PRs;   score 3 rules are most likely MPRs and vice versa;   score 4 rules are likely to be AMRs and vice versa.[35]

5.6.6. Diachronic evolution proceeds from aid to pronounceability ('optional' PRs of casual/fast speech) or perceptibility ('optional' PRs of hyperformal/emphatic speech) via constraints on pronounceability/perceptibility (obligatory PRs) to aid to pronounceability/perceptibility (MPRs) and finally, if MPRs are not lost, to neither aid nor constraint (most AMRs).

5.7. <u>Phonological conditioning</u>. This term has been understood in many ways.[36]

5.7.1. Rules are conditioned only phonologically (hence PRs) or only morphologically (hence MRs) -- but what about allomorphic MRs which have also a phonological function (e.g., Hungarian 2nd sg. pres. (5.2.5), French hiatus-deleting *t*-insertion after oral vowels in word formation, e.g., *clou* 'nail', *clou-t-er* 'to nail' (1.9.2))? Moreover this criterion would either not characterize MPRs or assign all MPRs to morphology (or to the lexicon)[37] and even some PRs, at least in fast/casual speech.[38] Taken in a large sense, morphological conditioning would include all morphological alternations, so that, in an extreme interpretation, only allophonic PRs which do not occur in alternations would be the only phonologically conditioned ones. Other extreme positions are to consider a rule a PR if all instances of its application contain (also) a phonological condition (e.g., Kalnyn' 1981:206ff), or to disallow any phonological condition for MPRs.[39]

5.7.2. If rules, notably MPRs, (seem to) have both phonological and non-phonological conditions, which ones are more important or 'essential'? (Ward 1972, Roberge 1980). Or should one count the number of conditions?

5.7.3. In a strict sense conditioning means which factors have to be written in the environment of a rule A → B, i.e., whether / C __ D[40] (to take just one notation) are phonological, morphological, lexical, or syntactic entities. However, abstract generative phonologies have been very apt at removing morphological or lexical conditions by devices such as rule ordering. E.g., if one subdivides Welsh and Breton lenition b → v (5.2.2) into two ordered rules (1) b → β with various morphological, lexical, and syntactic conditions, and (2) β → v, then the conditions of (1) are generally not repeated in the formulation of (2), (a) for reasons of descriptive economy (evaluation procedure) and (b) because it captures the true/significant linguistic generalization that neither Welsh nor

Breton has a phoneme */β/.

However this fact must be stated in a (prelexical) redundancy rule (or MSR)[41] which should not be linked to an abstract postlexical rule (1) generating the false intermediary step /β/. For the rejection of such types of abstractions, see Zwicky 1974.

Since the writing of rules is highly theory-specific and since our discussion should be profitable for adherents of more than one single school, we must include apparently redundant morphological, lexical, and semantic conditions in order to see whether this information[42] is relevant.

5.7.4. Often conditioning has been understood implicitly or explicitly in the sense of causality (including causa finalis = teleology or functionalism)[43] such as phonological or phonetic motivation (5.5.2): The phonetic possibilities of the speech and hearing apparatus are only necessary, but not sufficient conditions even for true PRs; thus any direct link between phonetics and the classification of language specific rules should be avoided.[44] In the case of multiconditional rules, causes favoring and disfavoring (restricting) conditions must be distinguished. The identification and characterization of such concepts depends on the theory of language underlying (explicitly or implicitly) the respective theory of grammar or of phonology, and therefore will be discussed in 10.

5.7.5. This chapter (5) concentrates on the level of description and avoids the vague term 'conditioning' (Roberge 1980) by splitting it up into handier terms and operations: process matching (5.2) takes care of 'phonological conditioning' of A → B and, in principle, of the phonological environment / B __ C; the criterion of (non)phonological domains (5.8) has to be added; non-phonological factors, i.e., morphological (5.9) and lexical (5.10)[45] factors, have to be added.

5.8. <u>Phonological vs. non-phonological domains.</u> This criterion can be derived from the criterion of aid to and constraint on pronounceability (5.6), which implies only the relevance of phonological domains. Often it is stated[46] that only phonological domains[47] may play a role in true PRs, i.e., strings consisting of (and confined by) only phonological segments and prosodic phonological units and boundary signs (representing prosodic domains 3.3.2). This concentration may be reduced to the following scale of phonological naturalness:

5.8.1. Score 1 can be assigned to PRs which hold for all ranks of prosodic domains (syllable, foot, phonological word, phonological phrase) and whose environment, in addition, is defined by phonological segments only. E.g., allophonic lenition of consonants (4.5.2.2) applies in many languages in ambisyllabic and intervocalic position both word-internally and, in fast/casual speech, phrase-internally, e.g., spirantization in Viennese colloquial German *Leber* ['leːβɐ] 'liver' and fast speech *leb(e) ich* ['leːβɪç] 'I live' (cf. 1.3.2). According to Linell (1979b:193) this is never the case with neutralizing PRs. However neutralizing German final devoicing (or tensing) applies with some Viennese speakers only syllable- and word-finally: They have [k] e.g. both in *ich flagg'* 'I flag' (after elision of word-final ə) and *flagg' ich* whereas others have it only in the first case, i.e., phrase finally,[48] thus *ich fla*[k###] vs. *fla*[g##] *ich*. Cf. anticipatory assimilation of /n/ to the following point of articulation[49] where in many languages n → m is phonemic (neutralizing, phonotactic), n → ɳ, n → ŋ allophonic; many neutralizing Sanskrit sandhi rules represent absolute phonological constraints.[50]

5.8.2. Score 2 could be assigned to PRs which are confined either to phrase and sentence phonology[50a] or to word phonology, i.e., to the domain of the phonological word. Examples are French ə-insertion (3.2.4.1), certain umlaut rules (before morphologization)(3.1.4.2), a variety of German final devoicing (5.8.1). For vowel harmony cf. 8.3.3. All these PRs hold for any syllable within the phonological word, provided they have the same syllabic position and/or the same environment of phonological segments.

5.8.3. Score 3 (cf. 5.8.4.3) could be assigned to PRs confined to the domain of the foot such as many (non-morphologized) umlaut rules (3.4.4.2) and PRs weakening unstressed vowels, e.g., in Palau (Wilson 1972:39ff, Zonnefeld 1978:228f) to [ə] if between consonants, to Ø in foot-final position, always in the syllable following the stressed vowel; cf. deletion of foot-final high vowels in Northern Greek dialects (e.g., Pontic, Papadopoulos 1955:21f) and Palauan foot-final vowel deletion (Wilson 1972:39); E. flapping may be foot-bounded (Kiparsky 1979:437).

Verner's Law of Proto-Germanic may be stated as intervocalic voicing (= lenition 4.5.2.2) of fricatives (F) unless they have the following (maybe ambisyllabic) position within a foot:

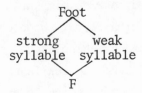

e.g., O.E. *brōþor* 'brother' with (original) first syllable stress vs. *mōdor*
'mother' with (original) second syllable stress.

5.8.4.1. Score 4 could be assigned to PRs confined to the syllable level, i.e.,
to tautosyllabic PRs as they often occur in vowel neutralization (4.5.3.1) or
velarization of syllable final /l/, Spanish syllable final depalatalization of
/ɲ/, as in *don* vs. *doña*. German backing of the palatal fricative ç → x /

 v   __ is problematic: Either it holds for syllable-final and ambisyllab-
[-front]

ic /ç/ as in *Fluch* [fluːx] 'curse', pl. *Flüche* ['flyː$ç$ə], *rauchen* ['raox$ə$n] 'to
smoke', but not in *Frau-chen* ['frao$ç$ən] 'woman' (with diminutive suffix -*chen*
/çɛn/) and in *Bio-chemie* ['biː$o$çe$'$miː] 'biochemistry'. Or, for speakers who
have ambisyllabic /ç/ in *Frau-chen,* etc., as well, morphological word boundary
is decisive.[59] In East Caucasian Arči (Kibrik et al. 1977:I:250ff) pharyngeali-
zation is tautosyllabic but may spread from a stressed syllable into an adjacent
unstressed syllable.

5.8.4.2. PRs are excluded from tautosylabic application in the trivial sense
that distant processes[52] refer to segments in identical position of adjacent
syllables: Thus PRs of distant assimilation and dissimilation cannot apply
within one single syllable (e.g., within a monosyllabic word).

5.8.4.3. PRs restricted to word-final position, i.e., excluded from syllable-
final (and foot-final) position, such as word-final obstruent devoicing in many
languages (4.5.3.1) such as Czech, Sanskrit, or Sanskrit word-final consonant
cluster simplification and stop deaspiration[53] should receive score 3, as well
as foot-level restricted PRs, because they too do not apply in all sub-domains
of the word-domain. Cf. word-final, phrase-medial vowel lengthening in Chi-
Mwiːni (Kenstowicz & Kisseberth 1977:86).

5.8.5. Clearly we must attribute the status of PRs at least to all rules which are assigned to one of these prosodic domains (5.8.1-3) and which have no other condition in their environment than (a) preceding or following phonological segments and (b) position within the syllable (onset, coda, ambisyllabic for consonants; nucleus or non-nucleus for vowels, if glides are non-nucleus vowels). Still it seems justified to assign them different scores of phonological naturalness, because their readiness to be morphologized in diachronic change seems to be different: I suspect (a) that score 1 PRs cannot be morphologized directly,[54] first they must be restricted to score 2 or 3 PRs; (b) that score 2 PRs restricted to phrase and sentence phonology (in the sense of 2.4.2) resist morphologization better than the other score 2 and all the score 3 PRs, cf. umlaut rules and Verner's law (5.8.3) which were morphologized everywhere. On the other hand, allophonic score 4 PRs do not morphologize more easily than score 3 (and even 2) PRs; thus their score assignment is very doubtful.

5.8.6. Score 5 can be assigned to rules whose application depends on morphological/lexical/syntactic factors as well as, at least apparently, on prosodic and segmental-phonological domains, score 6 to those where an otherwise relevant prosodic domain has become irrelevant.

E.g., the phonological process type of umlaut (3.1.4.2, 3.1.?, 4.5.3.3, 5.8.2) has the foot as its first domain, and in some languages the umlaut PR applies to the preceding foot as well. Now, the German WFR of forming adjectives from nouns with the suffix -isch (≈ E. -ish) provokes lexically restricted umlaut within the preceding syllable, e.g., Hund 'dog', adj. hünd-isch (with /u/ → [y]); the morphologically similar suffixation of -lich (≈ E. -ly) does the same in e.g. Tag 'day', täg-lich 'daily' (with /aː/ → [ɛː] or [eː]), but it provokes umlaut also at a distance in Bauer 'peasant', Vater 'father', Bruder 'brother', etc., adj. bäuer-lich, väter-lich, brüder-lich (with /ao/ → [ɔø], /aː/ → [ɛː, eː], /uː/ → [yː]) at a greater distance from /i/ (cf. 5.19.3, 10.7.11.2). Since the process type of umlaut may not reapply after applying vacuously (3.1.4.2), the umlaut rule coupled to the G. -lich WFR does not respect the relevant foot level in bäuer-lich, etc., whose foot structure is:[56]

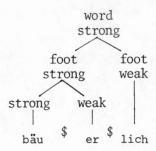

5.8.7. All score 1-4 rules are PRs, score 1-4 rules are PRs, score 6 rules are AMRs, score 5 rules maybe PRs, MPRs or AMRs; if they are PRs, they can morphol-ogize most easily. Rules which do not refer to either prosodic domains (at least syllable position) or to segmental-phonological domains are MRs, e.g., prefixation of negative *un-/in-* or suffixation of plural /z/.[57]

5.8.8. Since Schane (1973), it has often been observed that PRs may adapt a phoneme sequence to canonical syllable shapes (e.g., epenthesis or deletion rules). MPRs and AMRs may still serve this prosodic function, but they do not represent constraints on pronounceability of syllables; thus such phenomena have been handled in 5.6.

5.9. Morphological factors

5.9.0. Morphological factors referred to in (the application of) PRs and MPRs will have to be distributed among various parameters (scales) of morphological naturalness (10.8). Nevertheless a descriptive classification must be[58] given here so that the reader may better appreciate many of the following scales of phonological naturalness. On MSRs, see 8.

5.9.1. A rule may be blocked by certain morphological boundaries.[59] In the process of morphologization, Grassman's law in Vedic was first given up across suffix boundaries (Schindler 1976), presumably # before inflectional suffixes. The prefix boundary # blocks assimilation (velarization) of apical /n/ (Robins & Waterson 1952:60) in the prefix of Georgian *gan-xilva* 'to examine' (Vogt 1971: 12, 177f).. Palauan vowel deletion is blocked by immediately following morpheme boundary (Wilson 1972:49). Old Armenian tap is lengthened to a vibrant (5.2.5), but not beyond internal word boundary (Dressler 1977g:325f); similarly English vowel weakening is blocked by internal word boundary in the semantically trans-

parent compound *wasteland*, but not in the less transparent *mainland* (Allen 1980,
cf. Bolinger 1961:30ff). Polish dialectal palatalization is stronger morpheme-
internally than beyond morphemes (Timberlake 1978). Yuman raising of root-
vowels is blocked by morphological boundaries (Langdon 1975:220ff). Velarization of /n/ to [ŋ] before velar obstruents may be blocked by a suffix boundary
in Moksha-Mordvinian (Hallap 1965:164). Many more examples of PRs restricted to
morpheme internal position in Dressler 1976: §5 (M.H.G. x → k / __ s), §6 (A.Gk.
tĭ > s), §10 (Kabardian monophthongization), §11 (Ubykh a → ɔ / w __), §14
(speech variation in nasal assimilation), §13 (speech variation in Viennese German intervocalic *b*-lenition, cf. Wodak & Dressler 1978:42, cf. Linell 1978b:
193).[60]

As will be seen, most of these rules are PRs (except the Vedic and Armenian
MPRs), not just MPRs as claimed (5.8 note 46f); and the blocking morphological
boundaries cannot be replaced by prosodic ones. But it is true that there too
more MPRs than PRs are blocked by morphological boundaries.

5.9.2. Other rules do not apply morpheme-internally, but only across morpheme
boundaries (cf. derivational or inflectional affixation or word-internal rules
in compounds);[61] the following MPRs (or AMRs?) across inflectional and derivational boundaries only: Albanian ə-deletion (5.2.1), Classical Latin rhotacism
(5.9.8), German umlaut before suffixes (5.9.5.1), Greenlandic stop-continuant
alternation (Rischel 1974:242ff, with various rules); presumably the Quechua[62]
and Pomo rules in Kenstowicz & Kisseberth (1977:88-90, 1978:407ff).

Celtic mutations apply only across certain prefixal, suffixal, internal,
and external word boundaries.[63] Alawa retroflexion (Sharpe 1972:46) applies only across inflectional affix and word boundaries. Thus all these rules may apply only in morphological (or syntactic) alternations.[64]

Whereas all these rules are AMRs or MPRs, Madurese tensing (Stevens 1980)
has a good chance of being a PR, although in one environment (if /s/ intervenes
between the tensing vowel and the tensed vowel) it applies only across morpheme
boundary. Thus this PR is not limited to alternations. Other PRs[65] are hard to
find outside of vowel harmony (cf. 8.3.3). Of course if one separates strictly
a MSR of nasal assimilation which allows E. *timber* but disallows **tinber* from a
PR of casual speech that assimilates *ten pounds* to *te*[mp]*ounds*, then one could
say that such a PR could only apply across word and morpheme boundaries (as in
un-paid).

Unvoiced obstruents are voiced before voiced obstruents (assimilation) only across morpheme or word boundaries in Sanskrit; since stem- or root-internal obstruent clusters are few and always unvoiced (e.g., kṣ, sk, skʰ, stʰ, sp, spʰ, ṣṭ, ps, ts) there is no reason to assume a parallel MSR of obstruent voicing although this PR represents an absolute constraint on pronunciation.

The application of the Hindi PR of ə-deletion depends crucially on the position of a morpheme boundary in the larger environment (M. Ohala 1972:57ff, 212ff, 1977). Still, most rules that apply only across morpheme boundaries are MPRs or AMRs.

5.9.3. In his paper 'Abstractness, opacity, and global rules,' Kiparsky (1973b: 57-86) claims that 'neutralization'[66] processes apply only to derived forms (cf. Kiparsky 1982b, 1982c:152ff). E.g., Sanskrit retroflexion of /s/ after /r, u, k, i/ to /ṣ/ and of /n/ to /ṇ/ applies only either across morpheme- or word-boundary or in otherwise derived environments such as after syncope (in ablaut),[67] e.g., non-application in *busa-* 'vapor', application in the 3.pl. perfect forms *si-ṣicuḥ* from *sic-* 'to pour' and *ja-kṣ-uḥ* from *ghas-* 'to eat'.

In other words, such a PR or MPR applies only to outputs of AMRs or MPRs. Thus this is another candidate for the definition of MPRs: They would be identical with either (phonemic) neutralization rules (as claimed by many, see 5.20) or to non-general neutralization rules,[68] i.e., rules having in addition morphological or lexical exceptions (cf. 5.12).

However, this criterion (cf. Rubach 1981:175) does not exclude PRs: E.g., one can posit a counterpart to Sanskrit voicing (5.9.2), namely devoicing of voiced obstruents before voiceless obstruents. This rule applies not only across boundaries, but to derived forms in general, as in *sad-* 'sit', 3.sg.fut. *sat-syati* or *ja-kṣ-uḥ* from *ghas-* (see above). Yet an identical MSR holds in nonderived forms (e.g., roots with an initial /kṣ/, cf. 5.9.2). Both represent represent an absolute constraint on pronunciation and therefore a PR. If one collapses voicing (5.9.2) and devoicing (5.9.3) into a general PR of voice assimilation (an automatic neutralization rule), then one captures the constraint on pronunciation, but not the difference in the actual instances of application.[69]

Automatic neutralization PRs, which are not identical with MSRs, and thus apply only to derived forms, can be exemplified with word/phrase final devoicing

in many languages (5.2.1, 5.8.1), non-automatic neutralization PRs with fast/
casual speech PRs of vowel or consonant deletion (e.g., German, Breton) or
French glide formation (Morin 1971, Lyche 1979) if the application is restricted
to certain morphological and/or lexical items in slower/more formal styles. For
lexical diffusion, see 5.10.

Thus this criterion is neither good nor independent: It can be derived
from the criteria of neutralization (5.20) and generality (5.12). For rule ordering, see 5.17. A further development of this criterion has led to Cyclic and
Lexical Phonology (5.17.1.5f).

5.9.4. The application of rules can be excluded from certain morphological
classes, i.e., not from all morphological categories defined by a given boundary
preceding or following them; for otherwise this boundary could be identified as
blocking the application of the rule in question (5.9.1).[70] A putative example
is the Saxon genitive of regular English plurals (Zwicky 1975b:165f, Stemberger
1981): This form of *moose* should be /mu:s#z#z/ and become via the PR of ɨ-insertion (5.2.1, 5.6.2.3, 5.9.5.2) */'mu:sɨzɨz/; since the correct form is
/'mu:sɨz/, one could claim that application of this PR is excluded from Saxon
genitive in the plural. But for the reasons given in Zwicky (1975b:165f) and
Stemberger (1981), this is rather an instance of a haplology constraint (Dressler 1976b) or ob ambimorphemicity (Stemberger 1981). In Hindi certain suffixes
block the PR of ə-insertion (M. Ohala 1977). In Greenlandic the rule (AMR) t →
s / i+__ is excluded from three nominal classes, but it is doubtful whether
these are morphological classes in their own right (Darden 1981).

One type of exclusion from morphological categories is the suspension of a
PR within a specific paradigm (cf. 5.10.4), as reported by Kazazis (1969, cf.
Kiparsky 1982:103f) for one stage in language acquisition of his child. Or the
MPR of fleeting vowel deletion in Slavic languages was curtailed in such a way
that inflectional paradigms were more regular (Kisseberth & Kenstowicz 1977:
70ff). On the other hand, Iverson (to appear) has collected instances where
certain forms of a morphological paradigm are simply not used because their production would entail violations of PRs. It is worth noting that good examples
for rules being excluded from specific morphological categories are not easy to
find.[71]

However, it is easier with variable PRs of slow/fast speech: E.g., Labov[72] found that post-consonantal consonants of inflectional endings (as in the verb-forms *step-s*, *stepp-ed*) are deleted much less than the same consonants if they belong to the verb stem, also depending whether deletion results in homophony or not (e.g., *keep-s* and *kep-t* do not become homophonous after final consonant deletion). Or in colloquial Viennese German, word-final ə-deletion is excluded from plural suffixes in -ə except in very fast/casual styles (Wodak & Dressler 1978:37).

5.9.5.1. The application of rules can be restricted to certain morphological categories (vs. only to morphological categories definable by a given boundary, see 5.9.2), e.g., the AMR of umlaut is restricted in English to plural formation (lexically very restricted, cf. 5.10), but in German to specific classes of masculine and neuter plural formation, conjugational forms, and word-formation (cf. 5.9.8); for Old Icelandic umlaut, see Iverson (1978). Such rules belong to the class of minor rules in generative phonology.[73]

Such a restriction (in AMRs and MPRs) may refer to a large morphological category: E.g., the Albanian MPR generating palatal stops (written *q*, *gj*) after *i* is restricted to conjugation, e.g., sg.prs. *pjek* 'to cook', 1.pl. *pjek-im*, 3. pl. *pjek-in*, 2.pl. *piq-ni*, sg. imperfect *piq-ja* or *piq-sha*, sg. imperative *piq*, passive *piq-em*. Cf. Hebrew stop spirantization,[74] Swahili kj → č / __v in nominal class 7 (Goyvaerts 1978:201) and, much more specific, ə → ε / ___ in spe-
$$\overline{\quad\quad}$$ [stem]
cific tenses of the French verb, as in *vous achèteriez* 'you would buy' (Morin 1978), assimilation of West Caucasian prefix consonants in transitive verbs only (Klimov-Alekseev 1980:13, 43f). The specific conditions may be very idiosyncratic and refer to non-natural classes of morphological categories so that several MPRs or AMRs instead of a single one may be posited, as in the case of the Celtic lenitions in prefixations and compounds.[75]

Notice that in sharp contrast to 5.9.4, many examples can be found of MPRs and MPR-like AMRs whose application is restricted to single morphological categories. An AMR however must be restricted to a single morphological category. If there exist similar AMRs (due to rule split, cf. 5.9.8) each of which refers to a different morphological category, then they cannot form a single rule -- this is, of course, a theory-specific criterion.

5.9.5.2. Certain cases of (neutralizing) PRs belong here only apparently, such as English *ɨ*-insertion (or *ə*-insertion) restricted to plural, Saxon genitive, and 3.sg. present suffixes /z/ (5.2.1.5.6.3, 5.9.4). Since syllable final sequences of sibilants never occur elsewhere,[76] we must assume a MSR (cf. 8) which deletes such clusters by consonant deletion or vowel insertion, so that the PR of *ɨ*-insertion applies vacuously outside the aforementioned suffixes.

5.9.5.3. On the other hand, many phonostylistically variable PRs have been found which apply to a very restricted number of morphological categories in slow/formal speech, but are generalized to other, finally to all environments of their structural description the faster and more informal the speech style gets, such as weakening of vowels to [ə] in Breton and Albanian (Dressler 1977g:322f, 3.4.5.1), generation of half-long consonants and ultra-short vowels (easily deleted) in Skolt Lappish (Korhonen 1975:15, 29), lenition of /θ/ to [h] in Yuman languages (Langdon 1975:231f), vowel reduction in Flemish (Prędota 1980).[77]

5.9.6. Morphological factors cannot be evaluated on a unique scale as previous criteria (5.2.5.6, 5.8). And if we take morphological factors as the only or as independent criteria, they cannot differentiate between PRs, MPRs, and MRs. However they will be useful when studied in combination with other criteria, see below 5.11.

5.9.7. As for diachronic change, PRs may start out as optional phonostylistic PRs which are restricted to certain morphological categories (5.9.3, 5.9.6) or to application either within or across boundaries (5.9.1f), but such PRs may hardly be barred from specific morphological categories. When they develop into obligatory PRs, they either have no morphological conditioning whatsoever[78] or, very rarely, are constrained by morphological boundaries (5.9.2). When PRs are morphologized to MPRs, then by definition they comprise morphological domains (either in terms of boundaries or of categories restricted to or barred from).

However, it is extremely unlikely that the same morphological limitations of an optional, phonostylistic PR might reappear as the relevant ones when this rule has gone through the change to a MPR via an obligatory PR, because optional, phonostylistic PRs may not morphologize directly into MPRs (for the reason, see 10.7.11.7, 10.7.12.4). When MPRs change to allomorphic MRs, morphological (and lexical) factors always become more and even all-important.

5.9.8. When a MPR is restricted to/conditioned by different morphological categories, it may split up into several MPRs or AMRs according to these categories,
i.e., the MPR has come under the dominance of morphology.[79] E.g., Latin rhotacism s → r / V__V split at least into the MRs (1) s → r / V__+v in *genus* 'gender', gen. *gener-is*, and (2) r → s / __+{s, t} in *ger-o* 'I lead', perfect *ges-s-
i*, past participle *ges-tus*, frequentative *ges-to*, *ges-tito*;[80] or Albanian velar
palatalization split up into (1) AMR of plural formation, e.g., *mik* 'friend',
pl. *miq* ([mik', mič], palatal stop or affricate according to different dialects);
(2) AMR of aorist formation, e.g., *pjek* 'I cook', aorist *poq-a*; (3) MPR of palatal formation after *i* in the verb paradigm: *pjek*, imperf. *piq*, etc. (cf. 5.9.
5.1, 5.6); (4) AMR(s) before certain derivational suffixes, e.g., in *mik*
'friend', *miq-ësi* (dial. *miq-si*)/*miq-ëri* (archaic) 'friendship', adj. *miq-ësisht*,
miq-ësor, *miq-ësor*, verb *miq-ësohem* 'I become friends'.[81] Other instances of
rule split are: German umlaut,[82] French œ → ε (Morin 1978:230ff), Old Armenian
vibrant/tap alternation (Dressler 1977g:325f), Polish and Slovak syllable lengthening (see Bethyn 1979), Old Armenian *h*-deletion (Dressler 1977g:326f), split
of French denasalization MPRs/AMRs according to morphological categories.[83]

Rule split would mean within the frameworks of Cyclic and Lexical Phonology
(5.17.1.5f) that postcyclic/postlexical PRs would 'climb up' diachronically into
the lexical cycles where, if applying in different cycles, they would apply in
each cycle in different ways.

5.10. Lexical factors[84]

5.10.0. It is primarily for lexical exceptions that generative phonology has
differentiated major rules (quite general rules with a certain number of lexical
exceptions, marked with (negative) minus-rule features) and minor rules (restricted to certain lexical items, marked with positive rule features),[85] which
are either MPRs or AMRs. This bipartition obscures the nature of the conditioning lexical factor, i.e., the general and language-specific stratification of
the lexicon.[86]

5.10.1. One distinct stratum of the lexical stock is that of names.[87] Finnish
gradation (5.2.4) often does not apply to names (Comrie 1979:54 with references).
Old Armenian has MPRs of changing unstressed /e:/ to [i] and a MPR of deleting
unstressed /i/ and /u/,[88] which have a few, irregular exceptions in the lexical

stock (5.10.4), loan words included.   Only in foreign names are there numerous
exceptions[89] such as *Aršéz, Nersés*, gen. *Aršēz-i, Nersēs-i* (MX.II:24);   often
unstressed *ē* is shortened to *e* instead (as in cases of contracted words), e.g.,
Zawén, gen. *Zawin-áy* and rarer *Zawen-áy* (MX.III:40, FB.VI:3), *Basén,* gen. *Basen-*
óy (FB.VI:7), *Databén,* gen. *Databen-áyn* (FB.III:8);   *Artít',* gen. *Artt'-áy,* with
a variant nom. *Artít'és* (Apathangelos 121) instead of **Artt'és.* And *-u-* is never
lost in the declension of *Yisús* 'Jesus', e.g., abl. *Yisus-ḗ.* Whereas one might
make the holiness of the name *Jesus* responsible for the preservation of unstressed /u/,[90] there is no justification available for the other instances other than their status of being names.

5.10.2. Onomatopoetic words are another subset of the lexicon (cf. 8.3.5).
E.g., the Zyrian MPR l → v (5.2.3) does not apply to onomatopoetic words (Rédei
1975:112);   for Finnish, cf. Skousen (1972:57).

5.10.3. More important for morphonology is the differentiation between native
and non-native words, which are either of foreign or of learned origin.[91] Baudouin de Courtenay (1895:75f) differentiated clearly among Russian alternations
(MPRs or AMRs):   truly Russian ones such as *t* ∿ *č, sk* ∿ *šč* as in *svet-it'* 'to
shine', 1.sg.pres. *sveč-u, isk-at'* 'to search', 3.sg.pres. *išč-et;* and Church
Slavonic ones such as *t* ∿ *šč* as in *o-svet-it'* 'to illuminate', imperfective aspect *o-svešč-at',* etc.   English velar softening is restricted to non-native
words (e.g., *electric-ity*),[92] its German counterpart *k* → [t͜s] as well, e.g.,
Fabrik 'factory', *fabriz-ieren* 'to manufacture', *Musik* 'music', *musiz-ieren* 'to
make music'.   Notice that all these verbs have been formed either on the model
of French verbs in /k#e/, such as *fabriqu-er,* or language internally (e.g.,
there is no F. **musiqu-er* as model for G. *musiz-ieren*), and that softening is
restricted to /k/ preceded by a vowel (therefore *Provok-ation* → *provoz-ieren* 'to
provoke', but *Flanke* 'flank' → *flank-ieren, Risiko* 'risk' → *risk-ieren*).   The
source nouns are of Latin or Romance origin, with the exception of *Paprika* 'red
pepper', loaned from Hungarian, with the verb, derived (facetiously) in the 19th
century, *papriz-ieren* 'to spice with p.'.   The same MPR applies to the suffix
-ik before the suffixes *-ismus* '-ism' and *-istisch* 'istic', e.g., *Stoiz-ismus*
'stoicism'.[93]

On the other hand, Turkish intervocalic *k*-deletion does not apply before
non-native suffixes (Sezer 1981:363f, Comrie 1979:57).

5.10.4. The generative concept of major vs. minor rules (5.10.0) fits much better to AMRs and MPRs with random lexical exceptions which cannot be handled by
anything other than ad hoc marking. E.g., the Old Armenian MPRs of 5.10.1 have
regular exceptions (names, phonotactic subregularities) and a few irregular
ones: Thus the gen. of *himn* 'soil' is *himán* instead of **h[ə]mán* -- such examples could be classified as instances of a paradigm constraint[94] or analogical
leveling; but since the coherence of an inflectional paradigm is much more important than that of a derivational one,[95] we are perplexed by examples such as
hing 'five', gen. *hng-íç* (without leveling within the inflectional paradigm),
but with exceptional retention of /i/ in the derivation *hing-erórd* 'fifth', cf.
k'un 'sleep', gen. *k'n-óy* with deletion, but without deletion in the derivation
k'un-én 'I sleep'. Thus the example of Albanian palatalization of *k* being more
productive in inflection (see 5.9.8) than in WF (Dressler 1977a:28f) falls more
in line with the notion of paradigm.

   Another example of a MPR with very few lexical exceptions would be Grass-
mann's law in Sanskrit (Schindler 1976). In Macedonian, $k \rightarrow c$, $g \rightarrow z$, $ch[x] \rightarrow$
s / __*i* are major rules, as in *orech* 'walnut tree', pl. *ores-i*, *miting* 'meet-
ing', pl. *mitinz-i*, *felach* 'fellah', pl. *felas-i*, while at least $g \rightarrow z$, $ch[x] \rightarrow$
s are minor rules in closely related Bulgarian: thus *orech-i*, *miting-i*, *fe-
lach-i*, etc., but applied in only a few words, such as *vlach* 'Romanian', pl.
vlas-i, *ancug* 'suit' (from G. *Anzug*), pl. *ancuz-i*.[96] These words must be marked
with a positive rule feature (e.g., [+ palatal formation] in the lexicon.[97]

5.10.5. However also PRs may be 'minor' or 'major' rules. E.g., in a Northern
Breton dialect (Dressler 1972) the backgrounding process of centralizing vowels
to [ə] applies in formal/slow speech only to two endings: pl. /ed/ and past
participle /ɛt/; the more casual the speech style gets, the more this PR is
generalized to all unstressed vowels (cf. 5.9.5.3 with examples of other phonostylistically variable rules).

   The same holds for (diachronically) very young PRs engaged in the process
of lexical diffusion: First they apply to a few words only, then successively
to more and more words.[98] PRs of phonostylistic variation are allophonic or
phonemic, PRs of lexical diffusion generally phonemic.[99]

5.10.6. Longer words undergo both MPRs (e.g., Turkish *k*-deletion[100] and variable PRs (e.g. Cuna syncope[101]) more easily than shorter words. This is justi-

fied (1) prosodically because longer words are more subject to shortening in
time (due to the tendency of isochrony to allot similar durations to each word),
(2) semiotically, for short words should not become too short.[102] An instance
in sound change is the preservation of Latin final nasals only in monosyllables:
Lat. acc. *rem* 'thing' > Fr. *rien* 'nothing', Lat. *quem* 'whom' > Sp. *quien* 'who',
while in polysyllables Latin final nasals have been lost without leaving any
trace.

5.10.7. Thus (similar to 5.9.6) lexical factors[103] studied in isolation do not
differentiate between PRs, MPRs, AMRs. And only a very crude scale can be constructed. Score 1 would be assigned to 'optimal' PRs (5.10.5), score 2 to obligatory PRs, MPRs, and MRs, score 3 to lexically restricted MPRs and AMRs.

5.10.8. As for diachronic change, we see (similar to 5.9.7) that in lexical
diffusion and in phonostylistic variation (5.10.5) PRs start out with lexical
restrictions, which may be --at least partially-- of a non-categorical, i.e.,
random nature; then either they are lost (due to restructuring of the input) or
they become obligatory PRs with no exceptions[104] or with categorical lexical exceptions in the case of a stratified lexicon (5.10.0, 5.13.2). When PRs become
MPRs --and afterwards often AMRs-- they may acquire both categorical (5.10.1ff)
and random exceptions.[105] This phenomenon may be called lexicalization,[106] a
diachronic process that applies to MRs (especially WFRs) as well. Lexicalization contradicts the inherent productivity of all types of rules, but MPRs and
AMRs lexicalize more easily than PRs. For the subsequent process of lexical
fading or gradual rule loss, see 5.12.5.

What happens if the lexical diffusion of a PR is prematurely stopped before
it reaches completion, i.e., before it applies to all lexical items which meet
its structural description? Either it is lost via input restructuring if there
is no alternation which keeps the rule alive, or it is restricted to these alternating items and thus becomes a MPR. E.g., the Latin change of unstressed
vowels to *i* in open syllables (Janson 1979:47ff) as in *teneo* 'I hold', *contineo*
'I contain' affected only a few items with originally unstressed /u/ and only in
word medial position, as in *caput* 'head', gen. *capit-is*. Later it was rolled
back by analogy in many instances, e.g., in prefixal derivations of *habeo* 'I
have', derived words resisted whose meaning was more opaque (compositionally
less transparent), such as *ad-hibeo* 'I bring/add to', *co-hibeo* 'I contain' (but

co-habito 'I live together'), *in-hibeo* 'I restrain' (but *in-habito* 'I inhabit',
from *habito* 'I live/inhabit'), *per-hibeo* 'I extend', *ex-hibeo* 'I exhibit', *pro-*
hibeo 'I prohibit', *praebeo/praehibeo* 'I offer', *red-hibeo* 'I retain'; *post-*
habeo 'I place after', rare *ante-habeo* 'I prefer', late *de-habeo* 'I lack', *su-*
per-habeo 'I have above'. In Classical Latin this rule has become an AMR, at
least partially because its prosodic condition (unstressed position) has been
lost due to stress shift (*ad-híbeo* < earlier **ád-hibeo*)(cf. 10.8.3.4.1).

5.11. Dependence on speech variation

5.11.0. Speech variation is manifest in various types: diachronic lexical diffusion (5.10.5, 5.10.8) and its converse, lexical fading; dialect switching,
i.e., fluctuation between two or more dialects in the speech of the same speaker
(5.11.8); idiolectal distinctions which do not appear to correlate with any
other factors, i.e., truly free variation,[107] as between word-initial /i/ and
/e/ in E. *economics*, or between [r] and [ʀ] for /r/ in many varieties of German,
or fluctuation between more or less learned variants. This must be sharply distinguished[108] from phonostylistic variation between formal (or even hyperarticulate) and casual speech styles which we will deal with first, according to a
methodology described elsewhere.[109]

This scale of phonostylistic formality is more important than the older
differentiation of lento rules (slow speech rules) and allegro rules (fast
speech rules) because, first, speed is only one trigger of phonological casualness, and second, because fast articulation can be non-casual if much attention
is paid to speech.[110]

5.11.1. In sociolinguistic speech situations calling for great formality, respect for the hearer, and a high level of attention, foregrounding processes are
adequate which ease perception of the hearer(s), while backgrounding processes
are inadequate. On the contrary, in non-formal (casual), especially intimate
and routine speech situations, the details of speech production do not need to
be easily perceived[111] and the speaker may follow ease of articulation and gen-
eralize/maximize backgrounding processes. Thus in hyperarticulate, very formal
or emphatic speech, easy perception takes priority; in casual speech, easy pronounceability.[112] Phonostylistically variable PRs thus present an aid to better
perception or to easier articulation and are therefore assigned score 1 (the

most natural value) on the scale of pronounceability/perceptibility (5.6.1).
Accordingly we may expect that all such phonostylistically variable rules which
occur in (or also in) word phonology are PRs, which seems to be true.[113]

5.11.1. The differentiation of speech styles seems to presuppose that between
hyperarticulate/emphatic/hyper-formal[114] styles on the one hand and casual/slop-
py/informal speech styles on the other, there is a 'normal style' (cf. 8.1.9).
This normal style represents the preferred style of a speaker, i.e., his preference within his style repertory.[115] Hyper-formal and informal styles can then
be contrasted with this preferred style. However, it is very dubious that such
a 'normal style' can be (1) identified with the phonetic representation generated by obligatory PRs of the language in question, (2) regarded as the input to
all (optional, variable) phonostylistic PRs[116] because 'normal styles' differ
greatly from speaker to speaker and there is often no sociolinguistic reason to
prefer one style over another similar style as 'normal' and no phonological justification other than dubious economy of description and the fiat of normative
grammars. In any event, casual speech styles are used much more often than (hy-
per-)formal ones, thus phonostylistic backgrounding PRs are much more important.
'Normal speech style' as uncritically used in the literature is as slippery and
elusive as 'normal style' in stylistic theories that work with the concepts of
styles deviating from 'normality'.[117]

5.11.3. Generalization/maximalization of phonostylistic PRs in casual speech
means that they apply to new inputs, i.e., either to inputs that they are not
allowed to apply to in formal speech or to inputs made available by resyllabification or other phonostylistic backgrounding PRs or because they may apply beyond phonological boundaries (i.e., intrude into greater prosodic domains) which
impede them in formal speech.[118]

5.11.4. It is important to note that among these phonostylistic backgrounding
PRs there are also many neutralizing (5.20.3ff) and phonemic (5.18) ones, e.g.,
processes of total assimilation (not to speak of deletions), partial assimilations such as /n#p/ → [mp] in many languages,[119] Capanahua sr → hr (Loos 1967:
184), cf. vowel gliding in French (Morin 1971, Lynche 1979) and Romanian (Rudes
1977:93), consonant gliding in Russian (Barinova 1971b:123f), Russ. $d → n$ as in
budut 'they become' → bunt (Barinova 1971a:114f). Distant assimilation is rep-

resented in Madurese vowel tensing (Stevens 1970:140, cf. 5.9.2) and in vowel
harmony.

5.11.5. Phonostylistic backgrounding can be excluded from certain morphological
categories in less casual styles, such as Viennese German ə-deletion (5.9.4);
or vowel deletion is excluded from stem morphemes in one Breton dialect (Dressler 1972:55f).

5.11.6. Or they may be restricted to very few morphological categories in formal styles, whereas these restrictions are successively suppressed the more
casual the speech style becomes, e.g., in Albanian and Breton ə-formation, etc.
(5.9.5.3), lax consonant deletion in Russian pronouns (Barinova 1971b). For
Latin, cf. Dressler 1973; thus also sound change may be restricted to specific
morphological categories (e.g., Cerrón-Palomino 1974:45ff).

5.11.7. Phonostylistic PRs may be also lexically governed, e.g., by being excluded from foreign words (non-integrated loanwords, 5.13.2.1) or by being sensitive to word frequency.[120] The rationale for this sensitivity is the following:[121] One incentive to choose a more casual style is greater familiarity/ac-
quaintance with parts of the speech situation; high frequency is one factor of
familiarity; words used by the speaker belong to his speech situation. Thus
clearly the correlation between frequency and phonological casualness is very
indirect (and statistically weak). One example of phonostylistic backgrounding
PRs being generalized with a class of frequent words is Am.E. flapping when restricted to phrase/sentence internal *t* of *to, today, tomorrow*.[122]

5.11.8. Whereas phonostylistic PRs are always very natural PRs, even if they
are morphologically (5.11.5f) or lexically (5.11.7) restrained, this need not be
the case with variable dialect fluctuation (cf. 5.11.0). There are other important differences,[123] e.g., phonostylistic PRs derive variant output forms from
an identical input form while dialect variation is best described in terms of
input switches from one dialect to another. Even if such a switch occurs only
in a very casual speech situation, it need not represent a backgrounding process or even a nutural phonological process at all, etc.

5.11.9. For the implications of phonostylistic variation for diachronic mor-

phonology, cf. 5.10.5, 5.10.8, 5.6.6, 5.9.4, 5.9.5.3, 5.9.7, 5.13.2.1., 5.17.1.
6.2.1.

5.12. Generality and obligatoriness

5.12.1. In the light of previous discussion (especially 5.8-11), generality and
its ideal form, viz. obligatoriness of rules, is not a simple criterion for differentiating types of rules.[124] Traditionally morphophonemic rules are divided
into automatic ones (which apply obligatorily) and non-automatic ones (which
have exceptions).[125] Now it is tempting to consider all automatic morphophonemic rules that are only phonologically conditioned as PRs (e.g., obligatory final devoicing in many languages, obligatory assimilations such as z → s in English plural formation), since this follows from the criterion of the constraint
on pronounceability (5.6).

5.12.2. However this does not allow us to take all non-automatic rules as MPRs,
because phonostylistic PRs are also non-automatic, i.e., (to a certain degree)
optional (5.11) and such variable rules may also have morphological and lexical
exceptions (5.9, 5.10). However other non-variable PRs normally do not have exceptions. Now since variable PRs (especially phonostylictic PRs, but also truly
free variation, PRs of lexical diffusion 5.11.0), as most natural PRs, are easy
to distinguish from MPRs, the criteria (a) of process matching (5.2), (b) of
regularity (5.4), (c) of constraint on/aid to pronunciation (5.6), (d) of phono-
logical/morphological/lexical domains (5.8-10), and (e) of type of variability
(5.11) conjoined can distinguish PRs and MPRs: A non-variable PR must have a
score of 1 in process matching (5.2.1.6), in regularity (5.4.4), score 2 in constraint on pronunciation (5.6.2), and normally no morphological or lexical exceptions (but see 5.9-10), whereas MPRs sledom fulfill any of these criteria and
one and the same MPR may hardly fulfill all these criteria at the same time.

5.12.3. The way general and non-general rules are differentiated is clearly
theory-conditioned.[126] E.g., within the framework of Generative Phonology,
Iverson & Ringen (1978) distinguish: (1) negative focal exceptions if the exceptional item fails to undergo some general rule' (e.g., onomatopoetics 5.10.
2), (2) positive focal exceptions if an 'exceptional item undergoes some special
rule' (e.g., obstruent voicing in E. *wife, wive-s*), (3) negative environmental

exceptions if an 'exceptional item fails to serve as environment for some general rule,' a type which they then reduce to: (4) positive environmental exception if an 'exceptional item serves as environment for some special rule,' e.g., back vowel harmony after a limited number of Hungarian words with final-syllable front vowel. In this way many MPRs are lumped together with a few PRs.

To this contrasts the 'true generalization condition' of Natural Generative Phonology which requires (Hooper 1976:13, 1979b) for PRs 'that all rules express transparent surface generalizations, generalizations that are true for all surface forms.'

This principle would disallow all PRs to have any exceptions and thus wrongly lump some PRs together with all (or most) MPRs.[127]

5.12.4. Kruszewski and Baudouin de Courtenay[128] saw that all types of alternations (thus also rules) can be general or non-general. E.g., most inflectional MRs, a few WFRs, and some allomorphic rules are general. Thus generality in itself is not a good criterion since it is too 'general', especially if it is not distinguished from productivity (5.13). However phonological generality, in its narrow sense, characterizes obligatory PRs which represent a constraint on pronounceability (5.6).

5.12.5. We have already discussed the development of non-general PRs of phonostylistic variation and lexical diffusion to general (obligatory) PRs (5.10.8). The inverse is lexical fading of MPRs and AMRs.[129] Not only new words (including loanwords) are not subject or are rarely subject to a lexically fading rule, but also lexical items and morphological categories which were previously subject to it do not undergo it anymore.

Let us take as an example from Celtic mutations, the fate of Breton lenitions (5.2.2, 2.4.2), i.e., voicing of voiceless obstruents, spirantization of voiced obstruents. After word-internal restructuring it split into (1) MPRs, then AMRs of the syntactic domain, and (2) word-internal lenitions in derivational morphology and composition. In Old Breton, compound name lenition is rarely written but obviously always applied (see Fleuriot 1964:365ff). Later, lenition was restricted in various ways: It is still always applied after the privative prefix *di-*, as in *penn* (Kervella 1947:464, 458ff) 'head' vs. *di-benn* 'headless, end', *kalon* 'heart' vs. *di-galon* 'heartless', *berr* 'short' vs. *di-*

instance is the generalization of the Portuguese plural formations -ão → -ões at the expense of the type -ão → -ãos, as in *irmão* 'brother' → *irmãos/irmões* (even *irmães*).[134] For the spread of Latvian 'palatalization', cf. Andersen 1980:32). Clearly AMRs can spread only within the same category; as a consequence they cannot jump to a different category (cf. Ford & Singh 1983b:67f). For the morphological motivation, see 10.8.6, 10.9.3.7, 10.10.2, 10.10.5.

In Dressler (1977a:25f) I adduced two spurious examples for the claim that MPRs may generalize as well: The first is the change of Old Span. **faço > fago* 'I do', 2.sg. *fazes* after the model of *digo, dizes* 'I say, you say' (Malkiel 1968:41f). But this is rather a case of back-formation, not one of extension of the palatalizing MPR *g → z* to a new *g*-stem. The palatalization rule which has been generalized in Zulu (Herbert 1977a) is also an AMR. Therefore I assume that MPRs cannot spread.

5.13. Productivity[135]

5.13.0. Whereas generality (5.12) means that a rule is applied in all existing words of a language and in the word forms derived from them by existing inflectional MRs, productivity means the degree of application to non-traditional words and word forms. Thus a rule may appear to be fully productive, only very productive or semi-productive, or rather unproductive (slightly productive) or totally unproductive. Productivity of MRs is conditioned by factors we cannot discuss here,[136] but see 10.8.1.3, 10.8.3.3. As for PRs and MPRs, the view seems to be fairly widespread that PRs should be fully productive,[136a] whereas MPRs should be rather/totally unproductive, which is incorrect as we will see. But first of all, the various meanings of productivity must be clearly distinguished.[137]

5.13.1. A first subtype of rule productivity is the application of rules to morphological neologisms of the language in question.[138]

5.13.1.1. A neologism is a possible (grammatical) but hitherto non-existing word of the language, formed by its WFRs. A PR which represents a constraint on pronounceability must apply to neologisms, e.g., German final devoicing, Icelandic preaspiration (Thráinsson 1978:12, 18ff).

verrañ 'to shorten'; but its variant *dis-* lenites only *b-*, as in *blev* 'hair' vs. *dis-vlev* 'hairless', some instances of *gw-*, as in *gwriat* 'to sew' vs. *dis-wriat* 'to unsew', with dialectal variation *diskriet, disgriat* [diz'vruːɟa] (but *gwelout* 'to see' vs. *dis-gwel* 'invisible'), and rarely *m-*, as in /maːla/ 'to masticate' vs. [diz'vaːla] 'to ruminate' (Dressler 1977b:67); i.e., lenition has been fading in derivations with the prefix *dis-*. Extensive fading of lenition has occurred in its application across compound boundary in nominal compounds: lack of lenition more morphotactic transparency, as can be seen in plural formation (Trȇpos 1957:105ff), e.g., the form of 'dolmen' is in the dialects either *t(a)ol-men* or *t(a)ol-ven* (lit. 'table of stone'): the plural is either *t(a)oliou-men* or *t(a)ol-veniou*: If the first element ('table') is pluralizable separately, then there is no lenition; if the compound is pluralizable as whole, then there is lenition.

5.12.6. The end point of lexical fading is rule loss (cf. Miranda 1972), e.g., the often debated case of the loss of final obstruent devoicing in Yiddish and Southern German dialects.[130] The background assumption is that only MPRs or AMRs can be lost, but not PRs.[131] And here morphological factors, particularly analogy, play an important role. Skousen (1975:101, 109f, 125) specifically invokes a tendency towards morphological surface regularity. Of course a PR can be lost if a new PR comes in which renders it vacuous, i.e., when the new PR deletes its input (a bleeding rule) and if no input is left over which would meet its structural description.[132] The collapsing of a PR with a new PR into a more general PR is better understood as generalization of the older PR.

5.12.7. So far, we have seen that PRs may generalize and that MPRs (and PRs on the verge of becoming MPRs) and AMRs may degeneralize in time. However, AMPs may also expand/generalize in time, and I claim that (1) it is just AMRs and not MPRs, and (2) it is for morphological and not for phonological reasons. A well known case is the extension of ablaut in Germanic verbs (Barnes & Esau 1973), i.e., expansion of the morphological category of strong verbs, or the spread of German umlaut plurals[133] just in specific morphological categories such as masculines, e.g., *General-e* > *Generäl-e* 'general-s', *Mops-e* > *Möps-e* 'pug-s'. Note that this specific umlaut rule is an AMR which changes (short or long) *a* to *ä* ([ɛ]), *o* to *ö* ([œ, ø:]), *u* to *ü* ([ʏ, y:]) just before plural [ə] = underlying /ɛ/, i.e., no phonological motivation remains (cf. Wurzel 1980c:448ff). Another

5.13.1.2. Cognate with derivational neologisms are abbreviations and acronyms.[139] Of course allophonic rules apply, e.g., aspiration of voiceless stops in English and German, but not necessarily neutralizing PRs, e.g., the final /g/ in G. *Log*, the mathematical abbreviation for *Logarithm* is not always completely merged with /k/ by final devoicing, i.e., many speakers clearly distinguish it from *Lok*, abbreviation of *Lokomotive*. Comrie & Stone (1978:79) have found a similar fluctuation of final devoicing between [m'id] and [m'it], the acronym for Russian *ministerstvo inostrannyh del* 'ministry of foreign affairs'. In Russian abbreviations as in slow speech and in loanwords the PR of weakening of unstressed vowels can be suspended (Waight 1980:81).

5.13.1.3. A similar phenomenon is represented by novel inflectional word forms, e.g., subtractive vocatives of intimate Russian style.[140] When the final vowel is subtracted, final devoicing does not apply, e.g., *Serëža → Serëž*, *Lida → Lid* (also *bab ← baba*, a variant of *babuška* 'grandmother'). This holds even for foreign names such as *Leva → Lev*, *Ugo → Ug*.

5.13.1.4. Also MPRs and even AMRs may apply to neologisms[141] if they belong to the right lexical stratum of a stratified lexicon. E.g., I asked American informants to derive neologisms from *trochaic*, *iambic*, etc., with the specific meaning given to them: 'to make trochaic, iambic, the fact of being trochaic', etc. They came out as *trochaic-ize*, *iambic-ize*, *trochaic-ity* with velar softening of /k/ → [s]. Moreover, when I proposed forms such as *trochai*[k]*ity* to these informants, all of them found such forms unacceptable. Charles Fillmore invented the term *formulaic-ity* in 1978, which everybody pronounces with [s].[142] If *musicism* is pronounced with [k] (J. Ohala forthc. §IIA), then this may be due to the fact that the above cited bases, *trochaic*, *iambic*, *formulaic*, are synchronically derived words, whereas *music* is not derived (synchronically!) from *muse*. Obviously orthography plays a role,[143] as in the French derivations *bardotisme* from *Brigitte Bardot* [baʀ'doː], *giscardien* from *Giscard* [žis'kaʀ], *mitterandiste* from *Mitterand* [-ʀã] (Blumenthal 1979), where /d, t/ in *-disme*, *-dien*, *-tiste* are available only from orthography; but notice that /d, t/ are common epenthetic consonants in French derivations (1.9). Notice that the aforementioned derivations have been formed and accepted as a matter of fact, but there has been quite a dispute in France how to name a follower of *Pompidou* [põpi'du]; finally French journalists and politicians settled on *pompidolien*.

The reasons for this different treatment seem to be orthography and the fact that there is a productive MPR of dental insertion (1.9), whereas vowel $\sim$ *l* alternation is an unproductive AMR (cf. Mayerthaler 1977).

Literary Breton abounds with neologisms, such as *pell-wel* 'television' formed from *pell* 'far' and *gwel-out* 'to see'. Although most speakers laugh at these neologisms, none would (1) not apply the lenition *gw* → *w* within this compound or (2) not say *e bellwel* 'his television' with obligatory (voicing) lenition after the 3rd sg. masc. possessive.

However, in Swahili (Goyvaerts 1978:201) 'parachute' is *kiangushio* (with class 7 prefix *ki-* from *-angua* 'to drop down', pl. = class 8: *viangushio* and not **ch-angushio* (with *ki* → *kj* → [č]) as one might expect from alternations such as *chakula* 'food', pl. *vyakula*. The reason seems to be that Swahihi palatal formation is lexically restricted, i.e., it is not general in a given morphological category. [114]

5.13.1.5.   The MPR or AMR can also apply only in the correct morphological categories, as velar softening before the Latinate suffixes *-ize*, *-ity*, *-ism*, etc. Cf. for Bulgarian g → z / __i, Bjørnflaten (1981:74f). French *t*-insertion (a MPR of 1.9.2, 5.7.1) is also applied in neologisms, as in *abri* 'shelter' → *abri-t-er* 'to shelter'. Finnish t → s / __i applies in neologisms. [145]

The Austrian author Fritz von Herzmanovsky-Orlando ('Die große Naive') invented an onomatopoetic masculine word for a hesitation noise *Pnof* and pluralized it as *Pnöpfe* with the regular plural umlaut AMR of masculine monosyllables which have an umlautable vowel. Let us call the type *Pnof* a 'fully invented word'. Its status seems to be similar to nonsense words as used in psycholinguistic experiments (5.13.4).

5.13.1.6.   Thus, whereas (lack of) productivity in abbreviations, acronyms, and maybe fully invented words (5.13.1.5) offers no distinctive criterion of MPRs, we may construct a scale for productivity in morphological neologisms: Score 1 is assigned to rules which must apply. All PRs must fulfill this criterion, MPRs or AMRs may fulfill it. Score 2 is assigned to rules which normally apply, but not always. These are MPRs or AMRs. Score 3 is assigned to rules which rarely apply, score 4 to those which never apply: Both may be MPRs or AMRs, but more research is needed.

5.13.1.7. I suspect that in 'inflectional neologisms' all general PRs, MPRs, and AMRs should apply always. 'Inflectional neologisms' are correct and regular inflectional forms (e.g., case forms) of existing words but which a speaker --with high probability-- has never produced nor heard nor read, a phenomenon which Karlsson (to appear) has made probable for Finnish. Such regular word forms must be distinguished from irregular ones, which are awkward for and never used by speakers, but which nevertheless block the use of regular word forms. A case in point is G. *buk*, the strong past of *back-en* 'to bake', which blocks the weak preterit ?*back-te* (cf. the strong perfect participle *ge-back-en*, which shows that *back-en* is a strong verb and thus makes a weak past form awkward). Therefore a fair number of native speakers of German use neither **buk* nor **back-te* and thus have no past form at all.

5.13.2. A second subtype of productivity is the application of rules in the integration of loanwords (LWs).[146]

5.13.2.1. It is often assumed that PRs should apply always, MPRs and AMRs rarely.[147] However, many PRs may be barred in unassimilated citation form (G. *Gastwörter* 'guest words', 'casuals'), e.g., E. *spikes* as G. [spaĭkʰs]. Some (especially MSRs) may be[148] in partially assimilated loanwords (G. *Fremdwörter* 'foreign words'), e.g., Austrian colloquial German [spaĕks, spæːks], with loss of (the supposed) E. stop aspiration and adaptation to mid-glide diphthongs with (optional) monophthongization (PR).

Therefore the aforementioned claim about PRs holds only for totally assimilated loanwords (G. *Lehnwörter* 'loanwords'), as in Austrian colloquial German [špæĕks, špæːks] (dial. even [špɔĕks]), where the MSR s → š / #__c is followed.[149]

An often cited example of gradual application of PRs to loanwords (LWs) is Russian palatalization,[150] especially before /e/. Optional (backgrounding) phonostylistic PRs may apply less in LWs if their use seems to be typical for formal styles (cf. Comrie & Stone 1978:35), e.g., Russian palatalization assimilation c → c' / __c' applies less to LWs such as *portvejn* ([tv', t'v']) 'port (wine)', *atmosfera* ([sf', s'f']) than to native words. Weakening of G. ε → ə (when unstressed) is usual (except in hyperarticulate speech) in *des Ganges* [dəs 'gaŋəs] if it means 'of the corridor', but rare if it means 'of the River Ganges' [dəs 'gaŋgɛs] (cf. Dressler 1981a:447, 452). Phonostylistic foregrounding PRs, however, may apply usually, unless in very casual speech.[151] E.g., G. insertion of glottal stop ($\emptyset \to ?$ / $ _V$) is obligatory in *Antenne* [ʔa-], *Theater* [teʔaːtər], if not pronounced casually (e.g., Austrian G. [tɛɑːtɐ]).

5.13.2.2. On the other hand, productive MPRs and AMRs may always apply to LWs,[152] e.g., the alternation AMR of Hungarian 2nd sg. /s/ → /l/ after sibilants (5.2.5), as in *rokkoz-ol* 'you dance rock-and-roll', *autóz-ol* 'you drive a car'.[153] Cf. Breton initial lenition (Dressler 1977a:36f) and the Albanian AMR (in two morphological categories) i → u / velar + __ in *ring*, def. *ring-u* '(the) ring', *biftek-u* 'the beefsteak' (Mehmeti 1982, cf. 5.13.2.4). As for MPRs, Turkish *k*-deletion is productively applied to contemporary polysyllabic LWs from European languages, e.g., *kartotek*, objective *kartote-i*.[154] Cf. Mangarayi stop nasalization and hardening of *w* in English LWs (Merlan 1982:216f).

5.13.2.3. Obviously those many MPRs that have numerous morphological and lexical exceptions are not very productive in the integration of LWs either, e.g., Albanian palatalization of *k* (Dressler 1977a:28f), Hebrew spirantization of fricatives (Barkai 1975, cf. 5.13.2.8), Russian *k* → *č*, *g* → *ž*,[155] and alternation AMRs such as Yiddish umlaut (Lass 1980:265).

Umlautable LWs typically first do not undergo German umlaut; only (often long) after integration may they be seized by spreading umlaut, e.g., recent *Admiräl-e* for older *Admiral-e* 'admirals'. This time lag apparently does not occur in Icelandic umlaut (Eirickson 1982) and Finnish gradations.[156] But the very fact that they apply at all, contradicts extreme views on productivity. A case of an AMR that never applies is Lithuanian *n*-deletion (5.2.3).

5.13.2.4. Moreover there are MPRs which have exceptions in native words but are totally productive in LWs. One instance is Albanian ə-deletion (Dressler 1977a: 38f), ə → $\emptyset$ / C_1 $\underset{[\text{-stress}]}{\underline{\qquad}}$ [+sonor] + v, which according to Cipo's dictionary (Cipo 1954) has about 10% exceptions in native words, e.g., in *urdhër*, def. *urdhër-i* 'order' in contrast to (much more typical) *emër*, def. *emr-i* 'name'; but in LWs it is exceptionless, e.g., *teatër*, def. *teatr-i* 'theater', *ministër*, def. *ministr-i* 'minister', *marksizëm-leninizëm*, def. *...zm-i* 'Marxism-Leninism', and even in WF such as *ministr-i* 'ministry'.[157] Note that native words and LWs oc-

cur in exactly the same morphological classes, so that Linell's (1979b:196) line
of defense is untenable, i.e., his claim that we seem to be faced with productivity of morphological formation patterns rather than of single MPRs. Cf. Old
Armenian tap strengthening ɾ → r / __n,[158] certain Sanskrit sandhi rules (Haslev
1972:64), Mangarayi stop nasalization, etc. (cf. 5.13.2.2).

The extreme case are rules that apply only in LWs,[159] but these are rather
strategies to make a LW sound still more foreign, cf. anti-vowel harmony in Turkish ʃ[ɨ]vester instead of harmonic *ʃ[i]vester from G. *(Kranken)Schwester* 'hospital nurse', cf. 8.3.3.

5.13.2.5. Of the many factors and conditions that play a role in LW phonology,
a basic one is the influence of orthography. Obviously spelling pronunciations
must be kept apart.[160]

5.13.2.6. Another special subpart is learned nativizations, cf. Field 1981.

5.13.2.7. Lexical stratification must be taken into account (see 5.10.3, 5.13.
2.2 note 154). This may narrow down to a single morpho-lexical field (word-
field), e.g., Bulg. k → c occurs in all names of nationalities derived with the
suffix -ak (Bjørnflaten 1981:74).

5.13.2.8. Here we come to an imported factor: Morphological integration[161] is
often a prerequisite of phonological or morphonological integration. E.g., Issatschenko[162] showed that Russian palatalization and o-lowering and centralization ('akanje'), a phonostylistically sensitive (backgrounding) PR applies less
in [so'te, šo'se] from Fr. *sautée, chaussée* than in their Russian derivations
[sa't'ejnik, ša's'ejnɨj], i.e., when they are morphologically integrated by Russian WFRs (suffixes -nik, -nyj).

Cf. Albanian k-palatalization,[163] Latin rhotacism (Dressler 1977a:37). For
Hebrew stop spirantization Bolotzky (1978:6) states correctly:[164] 'Once a noun
or adjective is verbalized, it behaves like an original verb in every respect,
regardless of its source,' e.g., *hifnil* 'he covered with panels' (ibid.:16),
with p → f.

5.13.2.9. Kiparsky[165] has drawn attention to differential integration of LWs
according to degree of intensity of contacts between the linguistic communities

in question, by contrasting, e.g., casual contacts vs. extensive bilingualism. A classic example of what deformations (popular etymologies) may occur in situations of ignorance of the source language, is Ancient Greek rendering of Old Persian names (cf. Schmitt 1967), e.g., *Smérdis* for *Bṛdiya, Ekbátana* [eg'batana] for Medic *Hagmatāna*.[166] On the other hand, in the East Caucasian language Arči, pretonic vowels are not weakened (centralized) to ə if they are borrowed from Avar, Lak, or Russian, i.e., from languages well-known to Arči speakers (Kodzasov 1976:39).

Another aspect of this contrast is the existence vs. non-existence of (historically grown) routines for dealing with LWs from a given language.[167] As Field (1981) has convincingly demonstrated, Occitan has a routine of applying MPRs to French LWs, such as raising of unstressed *o*, as in *telefuná* 'to telephone' vs. 3.sg.prs. *telefón*.

Similarly, frequent words may be integrated more readily than rare ones, cf. for Bulgarian *k → c, g → z*, Bjørnflaten (1981:78; cf. 5.10.4).

5.13.2.10. That the socio-psychological attitude towards the source language can be an important factor, has been claimed by Thomason & Kaufmann (1976), Lovins (1973:52), Dressler (1977a:39f). A positive attitude should rather impede the application of language specific rules. A counterexample is Bulgarian, where Russian LWs seem to undergo *k → c*, etc., 'palatalization' (cf. 5.10.4) in nominative plurals more easily than other LWs (Bjørnflaten 1981:78, 85). For MSRs, see below 8.3.3, 8.4.2; on loaning of rules, see below 5.13.6.

5.13.2.11. Prague School phonology has always pointed to LWs as (often) being phonologically different from native words.[168] But as 5.3.2 may have shown, this concept in itself is too vague for a comprehensive treatment of the phenomena of LW integration. At least we may say that a rule that never applies to LWs may not be an obligatory PR.

5.13.3. A third type of productivity involves word games.[169] It is often maintained that PRs do apply to the outcomes of such games, whereas MPRs and AMRs do not.[170]

5.13.3.1. Again, allophonic PRs seem to be out of discussion. Phonemic PRs apply, as in G. final devoicing when inverted forms are susceptible to it, e.g.,

Gazelle 'gazelle' → *ellezag* with final [k]. The same is true for Malayalam intervocalic stop voicing and long vowel shortening, which apply to the outputs of
the '*pa*-language' (Mohanan 1982:90f, 103f). For phonemic assimilation PRs and
fast speech rules, see Linell (1979b:201). Again, fluctuation in application of
such rules (cf. 5.13.1.2, 5.13.2.1) occurs,[171] e.g., vowel lengthening does not
apply to outputs of the Kinshingelo word game in Sanga (Coupez 1981:116f). For
sentence PRs, see Campbell (1981:164f, 177). And the Kisela word game (Coupez
1981:117) of Sanga violates 'surface phonetic constraints' (cf. 8.1.9).

5.13.3.2. If certain Finnish diphthongs are derived from underlying long vowels
by a MPR, then we have an example of a MPR applying in word games (Campbell
1981:147ff). In the outputs of word games the conditions for the application of
AMRs are never met.

5.13.3.3. The outputs of a word game are artificial in the sense that a metalinguistic operation has to be carried out which has no counterpart in normal
language. Thus we need not be surprised that sometimes PRs which normally apply, do not apply to such 'artificial outputs' (cf. 5.13.4). E.g., in Kekchi,
vowel copy between consonant and /m/ or /b'/ after the first syllable (Campbell
1974:271, 275f) need not apply in *k'opoxb'apa:nk* from *k'oxob'a:nk* (underlying
/k'oxb'/) and optional *e*-gliding never applies to Campbell's (1974:270, 277)
outputs. Such phenomena restrict the usefulness of word game tests.[172]

5.13.3.4. The term 'word games' may cover also isolated jocular forms. But
such forms should be strictly separated from phenomena of established language
games such as Pig Latin. The difference lies in (1) the quantity of forms produced, (2) the social vs. individual character, and thus (3) the presence vs.
absence of a habitual routine.

Thus the ephemeral past participle *ge-mork-en* instead of *ge-merk-t* from
merk-en 'to notice' in German student jargon of the 18th and 19th century does
not establish productivity of the respective ablaut AMR, nor is multiple umlaut
an AMR of German because of Johann Nestroy's *rökököer* (comparative of *Rokoko*
'rococo' in his play 'Die Anverwandten'). Such isolated forms are due to surface analogy and cannot vouch for properties of MRs (cf. Dressler 1977c:20-22).
Cf. Dryden's isolated coinage *witticism* from *witty* (Ohala forthc. §IIIB).

5.13.4. Much work --and often too much hope-- has been put into psycholinguistic experiments,[173] for evidence for or against the productivity of rules is
often seriously blurred by the more or less artificial situation of subjects
having to perform metalinguistic tasks.[174]

5.13.4.1. E.g., French plural formation of the type *cheval* [š(ə)val] 'horse',
pl. *cheveaux* [š(ə)vo] is an unproductive MR; neologisms and loanwords do not
undergo it, and sometimes old /o/-plurals have been replaced by /al/-plurals
(Mayerthaler 1977:93ff). However, Dispey's (1967:92) adult subjects applied it
90% of the time to nonsense words (and the even less general AMR in *travail*
[tʀavaj], pl. *traveaux*, 85%). Thus this must be an artifact of the specific
test situation and cannot tell us anything about the real degree of productivity
of these MRs.

5.13.4.2. In better controlled experiments, test results varied according to
different conditions such as production vs. concept formation vs. recall vs. decision tests (cf. Anisfeld 1969), use of real forms vs. nonsense words as inputs
to derived forms (summarized in Jaeger 1979, cf. Linell 1979b:201f). In languages with complex non-phonemic orthographies (e.g., English) spelling rules
interfere.[174a] Thus, unfortunately, most tests reported are rather inconclusive
for our inquiry into productivity, especially when errors have been committed
such as using nonsense words or non-Latinate real words as input forms for English WFRs that apply only to Latinate stems, or when incorrect word classes
have been picked as input forms.[175]

5.13.4.3. However, production tests which avoided such experimental artifacts
(5.13.4.2) have shown that subjects do apply MPRs and even AMRs at least sometimes, if not often. A case in point is the Hindi MPR of ə-deletion (M. Ohala
1972, 1974) applied more often than not. Turkish subjects applied the MPR of
k-deletion to polysyllabic words rather than to monosyllabic ones (Zimmer & Abbott 1978). Hebrew speakers applied AMRs of vocalic ablaut and stop spirantization (e.g., *p* → *f*) the better the input fitted the morphological system of Hebrew (cf. morphological integration of loanwords, 5.13.2.8): E.g., E. *panel*
looks like a perfect Hebrew triliteral/triradical verb stem /pnl/, whereas E.
patent does not. Thus it cannot surprise that in Bolocky's (1978:16ff) productivity tests, 30% of his subjects produced *hifnil* as a *hi-f'il* form of *panel*,

but none produced *hi-ftint or similar from *patent* (cf. Farrar 1977). One relevant conclusion that can be drawn from Bybee & Pardo's (1981) interesting Spanish tests is, that under the same test conditions, native speakers applied (and
abstained from applying) Spanish diphthongization more often 'correctly' (p.
942f) than velar insertion (p. 954ff).[176] Now diphthongization of unstressed *e*
to stressed *ie* (e.g., *comenzár* 'to begin', 1.sg. *comiénzo*) is phonologically
more natural than velar insertion (e.g., *sal-ír* 'to leave', 1.sg. *sál-g-o*). And
this --in addition to Bybee & Pardo's (1981) conclusions on productivity-- may
explain why subjects manipulated no verbs such as inf. *megár*, 3.sg. *miéga* (3.sg.
pret. *megó* to be elicited) better than inf. *ronér*, 1.sg. *róngo* (2.sg.pres. *rónes*
to be elicited). Second, the alternation *e/ie*, as in *comenzár/comiénzo* was consistently better manipulated than *o/ue*, since the first can be matched with one
process of diphthongization (5.2.1, 4.4.3), the second only with two processes
(with additional polarization *uo → ue*, 5.22, 5.2.6).

5.13.4.4. At least we can conclude that in psycholinguistic experiments as
well, productivity is a matter of degree. In order to test the correlation between productivity and other gradual criteria of phonological naturalness, very
similar rules or even subrules should be compared in order to restrict the effect of test conditions on test results as much as possible to differences in
naturalness (cf. 6.1.5.4). Obviously allophonic PRs are always applied and, in
general, PRs more often than MPRs or AMRs.

5.13.5. Much less work has been done in testing productivity of more vs. less
natural rules in foreign language learning, i.e., when a native speaker of L_1
learns a foreign language L_2. It is claimed that MPRs do not transfer.[177] Obviously we must exclude naturalistic learning, i.e., in natural settings without formal teaching and before the (mythical) critical age of 12± years (cf.
Wode 1977, 1978). And we exclude the complications of several languages being
involved (cf. Mioni 1971b).

5.13.5.1. Does naturalness play a role in the transfer of L_1 rules to L_2? PRs
clearly transfer, thus producing the well known effect of a 'foreign accent',[179]
e.g., Germans, Poles, and Russians are known for devoicing final obstruents when
learning English or French.[180] But not all PRs do (Linell loc.cit.). Thus this
criterion is not very good for differentiating PRs and MPRs. AMRs such as G.

umlaut or E. Great Vowel Shift are clearly not transferred because AMRs are not even easy to loan (5.13.6.1.1). Rubach (1980) claims that only 'postcyclic rules [cf. 5.2.7.1.5] which are automatic and context-sensitive may cause phonological interference,' i.e., fairly natural and concrete PRs (including neutralizing, not just allophonic ones). If the transfer of PRs is restricted to those PRs that are identical to universal natural processes, then we may say that it is the universal availability of these process types that renders transfer possible.

5.13.5.2. Since we consider MPRs not simply as denaturalized PRs but as rules depending on both phonology and morphology, we may expect MPRs to be transferred only if they both fit universal process types of phonology and if morphological conditions in L₁ and L₂ are similar. E.g., the Polish MPR or rather the AMR of alveolar formation (see 7.4) which changes *k* to *c* [ts] before certain endings (mostly front vowels) is never applied to English by Poles when learning English (Rubach 1980). Rubach (1980) cites words like *hockey* and *keep*. But apparently they do not transfer the AMR of alveolar formation even in cases like E. *electric, electricity*, i.e., instead of E. velar softening. Thus the identical condition of a morpheme boundary (i.e., similar domain of application) and similar phonological properties of the first phoneme of th suffix do not suffice, nor does partial overlap of the structural description of the respective rules.

5.13.5.3. The situation is different when Poles learn Russian, since both languages have similar 'palatalization' rules which apply in similar morphological categories. Rubach (1980) leaves the question open. My informants R. Laskowski (Cracow) and F. Grucza (Warsaw) deny transfer, whereas Mr. and Mrs. S. Dyła (Łódz) have provided me with examples of the transfer of the Polish (still very MPR-like) AMR *k → c* into Russian in the first two years of Polish L₂ acquisition of Russian:

	meaning	Polish	Russian cognate	Russian form used in L₂ acquisition
nom. sg. fem.	'hand'	ręka	ruká	ruka
dat.		ręce	ruk'é	ruce
nom.	'flour'	mąka	muká	muka
dat.		mące	muk'é	muce
nom.	'pain'	męka	múka	muka
dat.		męce	múk'e	muce

I.e., the Polish learners of Russian identified the dative endings *-e* of both languages and replaced the Russian surface palatalization (phonemic) PR *k → k'* with the Polish AMR *k → c* before this dative ending. Notice that Russian has no AMR or MPR *k → c*. Similar problems are reported for Czechs starting to learn Russian.

5.13.6. Loaning of rules

5.13.6.1.0. A counterpart of transfer in foreign language learning from L₁ to L₂ can be found in loaning of rules from L₂ to L₁. This process illuminates the different nature of MRs, MPRs, and PRs.

5.13.6.1.1. Inflectional or derivational morphemes and MRs are loaned very rarely.[181] However when a considerable number of words are loaned where a given MR of L₂ is applied and if L₂ is fairly well known to the group of L₁ borrowers, then this MR can be taken over together with the words. E.g., when Albania was dominated by the Turks, Albanian did not only borrow Turkish *paşa* 'pasha', *beg* = *bey* 'master', etc., as *pasha, beg,* etc., but also the plurals *paşa-lar, beg-ler* as *pasha-llarë, beg-lerë*. (Since Albanian independence in 1912 these plurals have been becoming obsolete and are dying out.)

5.13.6.1.2. In the same way, MPRs (or AMRs as subparts of MRs) may be borrowed in the appropriate loanword stratum with its respective inflectional/derivational MRs (see the first systematic investigation in Baudouin de Courtenay 1895). In this way English velar softening has been borrowed and reconstituted within the Latinate vocabulary of English (Donegan 1978:6f). The same holds for the German parallel in G. *Elektrik-er* 'electrician', *Elektriz-ität* 'electricity', *Fabrik* 'factory', *fabriz-ieren* 'to manufacture' with the substitution of the monophonemic affricate [ts̯] for /k/. Most of these derivations have no direct French/Italian or Latin model but are productive within the Latinate vocabulary of German (cf. 5.10.3).

5.13.6.1.3. If the morphological structures of L₁ and L₂ (being in close contact) are very similar to each other, then MPRs (or AMRs as subparts of MRs) can be borrowed without lexical borrowing, but restricted to the respective paradigms. This has been shown for the East Cushitic languages Boni and Galla

(Orma dialect) by Sasse (1979): Boni has borrowed rules such as postvocalic
loss of glottal stop and *h* before inflectional endings (presumably a MPR), and
substitution of *m* for stem-final *s* before suffix-initial nasal (an AMR as part
of the inflectional MRs, telescoped (5.2.7.1) from s → š → f → b → m). All
All these rules are morphologically restricted and are not of a kind that they
could be mistaken for PRs. But notice that the rules were borrowed in a position before identical or near-identical suffixes. This shows that what counts
in a MPR are the exact morphological conditions, a concept of 'morphologized
rules' that Kiparsky (1982b) emphatically attacks (cf. 5.17.1.6.3).

5.13.6.2. On the other hand, history is full of examples of PRs being loaned,
both allophonic and phonemic neutralizing ones such as diphthongization (e.g.,
from German into Friulian) or final devoicing.[182] Such PRs may be taken over as
PRs or MPRs.

5.13.6.3.1. More interesting are cases which highlight the graduality of depho-
nologization/morphologization of PRs. One case is the diffusion of Northern
Greek deletion of high unstressed vowels through pre-Turkish northern Asia Minor
to Cappadocia in southeastern Asia Minor (Adams 1977:146f). At the time of diffusion, these dialects must have been lexically and morphologically very similar
and at the center of diffusion in Constantinople (and northeastern Greece), deletion of unstressed *i*, *u* was a natural PR.

5.13.6.3.2. At the other end of the diffusion area, in the (Southern Greek)
Cappadocian dialect of Pharasa,[183] its impact is smallest: First it applied only to *i*. In most lexical items deletion was not applied, in the others its application resulted in restructuring (and loss of the rule in these items), e.g.,
/aráp/ (< /arápis/) 'negro', pl. /aráp#i/ (Andriotis 1948:23, 36-8), /kór,
kórtsa/ 'girl' (< /kóri, kóris:a/), or in suppletion /rotá#o/ 'I ask', aorist
['rotsa] < /róti+s#a/. But it is a non-general MPR in verbal inflection, e.g.,
/θeríz#o/ 'I harvest', 3.pl.aor. ['θertsan] < /θériz#s#an/ (Andriotis 1948:23,
44) and a general MPR before clitics, as in ['θiri] 'door', [to##'θir##tsu] 'his
door', cf. gen. [θi'ru].[184] In other Cappadocian dialects the rule is less restricted, but never a PR.

5.13.6.3.3. In an intermediate dialect of the diffusion process, in Trebizond

Pontic,[185] deletion applied to *i* and *u* and to the greater part of the lexicon
(now restructured). It remains as a MPR in certain inflectional categories,
e.g., the genitive of /aðɛlfós/ 'brother' is [aðɛl'fu], but of /ánθropos/ the
genitive is [anθróp] (papadoupoulos 1955:46-48). The comparison with nouns like
[aðɛl'fu] (belonging to the same declensional paradigm) and the stress shift
which occurs only before certain inflectional endings allow the synchronic reconstruction of genitive /anθrópu/.

5.13.6.3.4. Modern high vowel deletion has been most 'denaturalized' (from the
phonological point of view) in the latest area of diffusion (3.2), less so in an
intermediate area (3.3). Thus it is plausible to assume a successive, gradual
denaturalization in the borrowing process of diffusion. While in northern Greek
dialects vowel deletion of unstressed /i, u/ has applied to the whole lexicon
(including loanwords) and is still active (cf., e.g., Kretschmer 1905:73-94),
this is much less so in Trebizond Pontic dialects. Cappadocian diachronic vowel
loss in many lexical items shows that vowel deletion must have been more general
and less morphologized earlier on in Cappadocia.[186]

5.13.6.4. In conclusion, we may state that MPRs and AMRs may be loaned only under the appropriate lexical and morphological conditions, i.e., this fits with
treating them as subregularities of the lexical and morphological structure.
PRs can be loaned as such or in a 'denaturalized' form as phonologically less
natural PRs or MPRs. However there seems to exist no example of a MPR of L_2 being loaned as a PR of L_1 or of an AMR of L_2 being loaned as a MPR of L_1.

5.13.7. As we have seen, productivity is not a homogeneous[187] criterion. Moreover, in principle, MPRs may be either productive or unproductive similarly to
PRs and AMRs, but on the whole, MPRs are less likely to be productive than PRs.

5.14. Speech errors

5.14.0. Productive rules (5.13) should apply in speech errors, where new inputs
are created for rule application, whereas unproductive rules should not.

5.14.1. The rich literature on slips of the tongue[188] contains statements that
PRs (or equivalents) are relevant to slips, in contrast to MPRs and allomorphic

MRs.[189] E.g., it is often said[190] that slips of the tongue always respect surface phonotactic constraints. This claim is falsified by forms such as [štn]u-
diert nicht instead of studiert nicht 'does not study', Bro[tsr]u.. instead of
Blutzulauf vergrößert 'blood supply increases', and [vl]ucie instead of the name
Lucie, [dl]eissig for dreissig 'thirty' (Meringer 1908:903), since *[#štn] and
*[tsr] are prohibited sequences in German. Cf. E. [æskə'bæθkənz] ← Athabaskans,
with *[θk] (Fromkin 1973:268 AA6), possibly [s]range and other instances in
Garnham et al. (1981:808ff), but certainly [sliːpš] (ibid. 809, 5.1.14), Fr.
dilemne ← dilemme 'dilemma' with Fr. *[mn#] (Frei 1929:52). Thus the hypotheses
that (1) obligatory PRs coincide with surface phonotactic constraints and (2)
such PRs cannot be violated (5.6) even in speech errors, cannot both be true.
Obviously AMRs are violated more often in slips of the tongue (Fromkin 1973:28f,
257ff).

5.14.2. Obligatory allophonic PRs always apply to speech errors; but also neutralizing PRs always seem to apply. This seems to be true of German final devoicing, e.g., Badehaus 'bathhouse' ['baːdəhaos] metathesized to Hausebat
['haozəbaːt], where underlying /d, z/ of /baːd, haoz/ are devoiced in the appropriate environment (W. U. Wurzel, personal communication). In the same way, un-
voicing of plural and Saxon genitive /z/ is always applied in case of transposition, e.g., in oxen's yoke → oxen yokes [z] is changed into [s],[191] while the
MPR of voicing fricatives, as in houses (/s/ → [z]) may be suppressed in speech
errors (cf. 5.14.4). And in wage hikes [hajks] → hike wages [wejdʒɨz] (Fromkin
1973:259 S 20), it is not [s] which is transposed, but the underlying /z/.

5.14.3. Some authors[193] explicitly claim that this last type of error may occur
only with PRs, i.e., the putative inputs of MPRs (and AMRs?) may never surface,
such as the /k/ underlying velar softening in electricity. But at least two
such cases can be found in Fromkin's corpus (1973:258 R 15, R 40): explanations
→ explanatings (cf. Fromkin 1975:57) and introduction → introducting, where the
abstract /t/ surfaces which is changed by a MPR to [š] in -tion.[193] No counterexamples such as *introdu[kš]ing seem to be attested. And speech errors such
as ['haõsɨz] have been observed (Wojcik 1979, cf. 5.14.2) where the input of a
MPR surfaces. Whereas this is a concrete input (identical to the sg. house),
introduct-, explanat- are not.

5.14.4. Obviously MRs can be misapplied (e.g., in Fromkin 1973:28f, 162, 199f). Interestingly, suppletion between *a* and *an* is correctly applied most of the time as in *a system* → *an istem,* vs. *a occurrence.*[194] As for AMRs, Meara & Ellis (1981) have found Welsh speech errors where consonants moved before allomorpjoc mutation MRs applied, i.e., concrete inputs of allomorphic MRs surfaced.

5.14.5. As we have seen with productivity (5.14), equally well evidence from slips of the tongue does not distinguish shaply between PRs and MPRs (nor APRs). As far as the data goes, there seems to be an important quantitative difference of degree between PRs and MPRs as to their application to slips.

5.14.6. Slips of the ear, which have been recorded[195] much less than slips of the tongue, do not show any evidence for the psychological reality of MPRs.[196] But they do not for MRs either, and if MPRs are the result of an interaction of MRs and PRs (the thesis of this book), why should slips of the ear evidence MPRs?

5.14.7. For slips of the pen (orthographic errors of normal adults),[197] I have not found any relevant data.[198] For acquisition of writing skills, see below 5.15.

5.14.8. Speech errors supply first rate evidence on processes of ongoing speech performance. And therefore they are even more important for the delimitation of mohphonology because it is often claimed[199] that PRs (or their counterparts in other theories) correspond to processes in on-going speech performance, whereas MPRs do not.[200]

5.14.8.1. Phonemes play an important role in perception[201] and therefore allophonic PRs must have some correspondence in processes of speech perception which reduce allophones to phonemes. Manaster-Ramer (1984) convincingly showa that analogy in diachronic change operates on phonemes only, never on allophones. All PRs of speech variation (cf. 5.11)[202] must be 'psychologically real'[203] in the same sense because, e.g., not too radical PRs of casual speech remain unnoticed, i.e., forms such as ['sɛ̃ʔə̃s] are usually perceived as /'sɛntɛns/ *sentence.* Such evidence for neutralizing MPRs AND PRs is much less clear, as is the case in slips of the ear (5.14.6).

5.14.8.2. In addition to PRs of speech variation, allophonic and neutralizing PRs are clearly shown by slips of the tongue (5.14.1f) to correspond to processes of speech production, including less low level rules such as those transducing /ng/ to [ŋ].[204] And then there is some (although much less) evidence for the 'psychological reality' of MPRs (5.14.3).

5.14.8.3. We may draw two conclusions from the discussion above: (1) Speech errors seem also to point to an asymmetry of speech production and speech perception. The term quasi-phoneme[205] can be aptly used for segments which contrast perceptually at least sometimes, but are clearly derived and are not input segments in terms of a description with rules. (2) The difference between PRs and MPRs in speech production is not so clear-cut as many theories would let us believe, but only one of degree, although of a quantitatively very important nature. (3) Distinctiveness as expressed by (basically structuralist) phonemes and distinctive as opposed to redundant features is important in perception and phonological behavior based on perception such as rhyming and assonance (5.16), the abductive mechanisms of analogy. However, in the competence (and performance) of production, many PRs apply identically to both phonemes and allophones irrespective of the distinction between distinctive and redundant features.[206]

And I must add that the few MPRs for which we have found evidence in slips of the tongue (5.14.3) are of a rather concrete form. Therefore this claim of 'psychological reality' may not be extended easily to abstract rules of classical generative phonology, although they often correspond directly or indirectly to MPRs.

5.14.9. Aphasic evidence will shortly be treated in 7.6.12 and 10.8.4.3. More in Dressler & J. Stark (in prep.)(cf. Dressler 1977a:43ff).

5.15. Acquisition of writing. The acquisition of writing by a competent speaker of his mother tongue is a prima facie source of evidence about his intuitions and thus about the 'psychological reality' of PRs vs. MPRs.[207]

5.15.1. In teaching native speakers of Southern Paiute, Sarsee, and Nootka to write, Sapir (1963/1933) observed them writing graphemes corresponding to input forms of MPRs, e.g., Nootka <ḥi> for /ḥi/ = [ḥɛ] (cf. Kenstowicz & Kisseberth

1979:157f). Similar experiments[208] have supplied similar positive evidence for MPRs. However, Mithun (1979) reports on unsuccessful attempts to eliminate non-automatic and automatic (!) alternations from orthographies taught to speakers of Mohawk. At first sight these findings would seem to speak against recoverability of both MPRs and neutralizing PRs.

5.15.2. More difficult to interpret are spelling strategies of children, such as those reported by Read (1971): Do spellings such as <DA> for *day*, <TIGR> for *tiger*, but the use of different vowel symbols for the second *i* in *divine* vs. *divinity* tell anything about the psychological reality of putative MPRs of the English Great Vowel Shift?[209] Unfortunately, children learn such MPRs very late, and spelling rules intermesh in complicated ways with the effects of MPRs and neutralizing PRs.[210]

5.15.3. Still, 5.15.1 supplies us with evidence for the psychological reality of (admittedly not very abstract) MPRs.

5.16. Poetic devices

5.16.1. There has been a considerable debate[211] whether poetic techniques may vouch for the 'psychological reality' of abstract underlying representations and thus also of certain MPRs if they correspond to higher level generative rules. A positive answer to this question may invoke, as bridge-theory between poetics and linguistics, the old and always more elaborated concept of poetic language being the only full and complete usage of the means of language, so that 'normal' everyday language represents a deviation from poetic language rather than the reverse.[212]

5.16.2. It is generally believed that differences among allophones of the same phoneme are irrelevant for poetic techniques. In rhyming, syllabic nucleus and offset are pertinant (called rhyme in Metrical Phonology, 3.2.2): Thus only different syllabic onsets might considerably differentiate the nucleus, so that one may conceive of vocalic allophones which would not rhyme with one another. I have not been able to find any such constellation. In alliterations, however, where only syllable onsets count, critical cases are easier to find: Kenstowicz & Kisseberth (1979:162f) cite Chao's (1957/1934) case of the Beijing dialect of

Chinese where [č] is an allophone of /k/ and where [či] and [ku] etc. alliterate. Thus it seems differences among phonemes (in the sense of perceptual contrasts) are relevant for poetry. However in Old French the difference between
between intrinsic and extrinsic allophones seems to be important for assonance:
According to Rheinfelder (1968:71ff) pre-nasal vowels (/ᵛN/) were slightly nasalized in open syllables ([ṽ$N]), strongly, but still allophonically in closed
ones ([ṽN$]). Now assonance between [v$_i$] and [ṽ$_i$] is quite general, whereas as-
sonance between [v] and [ṽ] is often avoided. Thus, in contrast to the Chinese
example, extrinsic allophones seem to have been felt as non-identical.

5.16.3. In Old Irish alliteration,[220] syllable initial stops[221] (e.g., *t* and *d*)
alliterate with their lenited counterparts (e.g., *t* with θ, *d* with δ) and with
their nasalized counterparts (e.g., *t* with *d*, *d* with *n*), but only those output
consonants alliterate with each other that are derived from the same input stop,
i.e., [d] lenited from /t/ alliterates with [t] and [θ], but not with perceptually (phonematically) identical [d] from underlying /d/. Initial mutations were
already MPRs and/or AMRs, but alliteration, with all probability, originated in
prehistoric times when they were still PRs. 'Errors' in alliteration support
the idea that these alliteration devices were 'anachronistic' in historic times
when the texts were written down (see Manaster-Ramer 1984).

5.16.4. The same 'conservation hypothesis' has been advanced for Icelandic,
Scaldic internal rhymes (cf. Sommerstein 1977:218ff, Linell 1979b:93), glide-
vowel alternation in Rigvedic metrics (Kiparsky 1972), and similar instances
(cf. Kenstowicz & Kisseberth 1979:159ff) where metrical structure makes reference to inputs of MPRs (not necessarily to an abstract morphophonemic representation). At least some of these MPRs are certainly 'psychologically real', such
as those all-pervasive Irish initial mutations which have persisted as AMRs of
sentence phonology up to modern Irish dialects. But the traditional character
of poetic devices which may carry on anachronistic phenomena (evidence in Manaster-Ramer 1984) weakens their validity for our purposes.

5.16.5. Moreover, poetic evidence is weakened not only by the danger of anach-
ronism (conservation), but also by the phenomenon of 'poetic licence',[222] which
may go far beyond any reasonable 'psychological reality' of a normal or idealized native speaker. E.g., the isolated jocular comparative G. *rökököer* of *ro-*

koko 'rococo' (a nonce-form and hapax legonemon of the 19th century Austrian
playwright J. Nestroy) does not prove anything for the vitality of the G. umlaut
AMRs, because a triple umlaut has no parallel whatsoever in umlaut rules of any
language (not to speak of German), but it does show that G. umlaut AMRs can be
consciously manipulated.

5.16.6.   What is at stake here is, first of all, the relative degree of consciousness of segments.[223]   I.e., the more easily the effects of a rule can be
elevated to consciousness, the easier it should be to manipulate this rule.
Since contrasts between phonemes have been proven to be of paramount importance
in perception (5.14.8.1) and evaluation (cf. Jaeger 1980), AMRs, MPRs, and PRs
which transform one phoneme into another (i.e., autonomous, taxonomic) phoneme
should be easier to manipulate than allophonic PRs (cf. speech error evidence,
5.14.2).   Second, MPRs and AMRs have more complex conditioning than do neutralizing PRs, so that there, effects have more chance to be consciously manipulated, such as in jocular formations (5.16.5);   and in rigorous poetic traditions (5.16.3f), conventions can be consciously continued.

Now we come to more theory-specific criteria:

5.17.   Rule order

5.17.0.   Problems of rule ordering have always attracted utmost attention within
Generative Phonology.[224]   Rules are formulated 'as operating in a particular order, such that the "later" process can be applied to the output of the "earlier"
but not conversely.'[225]

It is impossible to review the enormous literature here;[226]   instead, I
want to treat succinctly only two problem areas relevant for the differentiation
of AMRs, MPRs, and PRs (or corresponding classes of rules or alternations):
(a) inter-level rule ordering (5.17.1): Are all MPRs ordered after all AMRs and
    before all PRs, i.e., is there a segmental ordering of levels or blocks of
    rules?
(b) intra-level rule ordering: Are the types of rule order (including no order)
    within one block (or level) of rules (e.g., morphonology) different from
    those within another one (e.g., phonology)?
(c) The question of ordering in case of multiple application of the same rule
    (see earlier, 1.3.2) can be omitted, since AMRs, MPRs, PRs, and prosodic

rules seem to behave in similar ways.

5.17.1.1. If in any model of grammar
(a) there are distinct components/levels of morphology and phonology, and if
(b) there is either a distinct component or subcomponent of morphonology, and if
(c) there is a linear arrangement of components/levels,
then morphonology comes between morphology and phonology, or if it is a subcomponent of morphology, then morphonology is 'next to' phonology, or if it is a subcomponent of phonology, then it is 'next to' morphology.

Thus in American structuralism, the level of morphology is followed by the level of morphophonemics (roughly corresponding to our AMRs, all MPRs, and the neutralizing, phonemic PRs) and then by the level of phonology (corresponding to our allophonic PRs) if one proceeds from larger to smaller levels, as in all descendent models, including stratificational and generative grammar.

5.17.1.2. Going back to this structuralist distinction, Koutsoudas[229] has established the morphophonemic-allophonic principle: A morphophonemic rule application (i.e., of a neutralizing AMR, MPR, or PR) has precedence over an allophonic rule application (i.e., of an allophonic PR). But the division between neutralizing (some PRs, all MPRs and AMRs) and allophonic rules (allophonic PRs) is less important than the division between MPRs and PRs; and that between MPRs and MRs: Thus it is of little help for the delimitation of morphonology. Moreover, this principle has not stood the test in several instances.[230]

In one interpretation of Natural Phonology, all rules (= AMRs, MPRs) apply before all processes (= PRs).[231] Similarly, Lightner (1972:430),[232] Drachman (1973:166), Wilbur (1973:686, 1974:393, 1975), Lapointe & Feinstein (1982:81ff), Cearly (1974), Mayerthaler (1977), Derwing & Baker (1977:92f),[233] and Coates (1982:170) have claimed that all rules which correspond to our AMRs and MPRs precede all PRs. Odden's (1981:247) thesis 'Any rule containing a rule exception feature must be ordered before any rule containing a phonological feature in its structural change' goes too far, because it would order those casual speech PRs which do not apply to certain lexical categories (e.g., [+foreign]) before obligatory PRs.

5.17.1.3. A threeway distinction is made within the model of Derivational Phonology,[228] namely in (1) allomorphy rules (our AMRs), (2) derivational rules (our MPRs), (3) phonetic rules (our PRs), and these blocks are postulated to be ordered successively in rule application. For similar views, see Linell (1979b: 190), Booij (1981b:384f), Dressler (1977g). If true, rule ordering would be another criterion for the delimitation of morphonology. Unfortunately, many counterexamples have been found (although reanalyses circumventing the ordering paradoxes may be possible in some instances).

5.17.1.4.1. Examples of MRs applying after PRs are given by Noske et al. (1982: 404), who cite Javanese reduplication ordered after allophonic laxing of high vowels in closed syllables, i.e., counterexamples to both 5.17.1.2 and 5.17.1.3. More in Plank (1982). English *a* is in allomorphic suppletion with *an:* Skousen[234] cites a casual speech PR of deleting *h* before unstressed syllables which has to be ordered before morphological suppletion in order to derive examples such as *an (h)istorical rule, an (H)awaiian vacation.*

5.17.1.4.2. Examples of MRs applying after MPRs are the Javanese MR of elative formation (Dudas 1974), MRs of reduplication ordered after MPRs in Javanese (Noske et al. 1982:401f) and Tagalog (Churma 1981:82f). More in 5.19.3.

5.17.1.4.3. Examples of MPRs applying after PRs are Western Scottish English fronting of ʌi → ae (a PR) ordered before the MPR of voicing (f → v) in [wʌivz] 'wives' (Noske et al. 1982:394ff), optional devoicing (PR) applying before vowel harmony (if a MPR) in the Chachvila dialect of Yokuts (Kenstowicz & Kisseberth 1977:167f). Early Latin allophonic velarization of syllable final *l* (in most positions) and morphophonemic change of *i, e* → *u* before velarized *l* resulted in contrasts such as *faci$lis* 'easy' vs. *facul$tas* 'easiness',[235] *vult* 'he wants' vs. subj. *ve$lit.*

5.17.1.4.4. Other instances of ordering paradoxes have been discussed by S. Anderson (1975), Darden (1982). Clearly all these paradoxes represent exceptions to the normal arrangement, i.e., the default case of inter-level rule ordering, and must be specially marked.

5.17.1.4.5. A typical and genuine class of diachronic change (cf. 5.17.2.6) involves then interlevel rule reordering. E.g., the morphologization of German umlaut[236] caused its application prior to all vocalic PRs.[237] Thus interlevel rule reordering is not an autonomous mechanism of diachronic change, but a consequence of rule morphologization. However, this does not account for the origin of the ordering paradoxes cited above (5.17.1.4.1-4) and below (5.17.2.3-5).

Rule morphologization corresponds to rules climbing up in Derivational Phonology (5.17.3: from phonetic to derivational to allomorphy rules) and in Cyclical/Lexical Phonology (5.17.5f: from post-cyclic/post-lexical to cyclic/lexical rules and then from later cycles/lexical levels to earlier ones).

5.17.1.5.1. In Cyclic Phonology,[238] ordering of blocks of rules is achieved by having all cyclic rules apply before all postcyclic rules; moreover, the principle of strict cyclicity guarantees a clear division of what is done on each phonological cycle. In general, cyclic rules correspond to our MPRs and AMRs, postcyclic rules to our PRs. However, Rubach (1981:151ff, 171f) considers English velar softening and Great Vowel Shift to be postcyclic, which makes difficult a comparison of our framework with his. Thus we had better turn to a discussion of Lexical Phonology (5.17.1.6), which is an offspring of Cyclic Phonology.

5.17.1.5.2. But first, those who are not familiar with cyclic segmental rules may like to have an illustration of how Cyclic Phonology works. The following example (Rubach 1981:170) displays the derivation of *perceptual* and *perpetuity* from the root //perpet// (cycle 1); in cycle 2 the suffix or root extension //u// is added; in cycle 3 the suffixes *-al* and *-ity*. Only two cyclic rules are crucial in this example, Spirantization and j-Insertion, which apply in each cycle (i.e., whenever new morphological matter is added), and always in the same order.

Underlying representation:	(perpe) t+u+æl	t+u+iti	
Cycle 2	t+u	t+u	
	---	---	Spirantization
	t+ju	t+ju	j-Insertion
Cycle 3	t+ju+æl	t+ju+iti	
	BLOCKED		Spirantization
	---	---	j-Insertion
Postcyclic	t+jū+æl	t+jū+iti	Prevocalic tensing
	t+ju+əl	---	Vowel reduction
	t+ju+əl	---	Laxing
	---	t+iū+iti	Vocalization
	č+ju+əl	---	Palatalization
	č+u+əl	---	j-Deletion

5.17.1.6.1. The recent generative theory of Lexical Phonology[239] represents the most advanced theory of interlevel rule ordering so far, both for phonology and morphology: The rules of inflectional morphology and of word formation are 'organized in a series of levels.... Each level is associated with a sort of phonological rules for which it defines the domain of application.'[240] These 'phonological rules' are cyclic lexical rules (and correspond roughly to our AMRs and MPRs).[241] They are sensitive to morphological categories and may have idiosyncratic lexical (and also morphological) exceptions. The input of the first level of lexical rules is the underlying representation, which may be very abstract.[242] The output of the last level of lexical rules is the lexical representation, which matches rather closely the phonemic level of Stampean Natural Phonology, less so the phonemic level of structural (or taxonomic) phonemics. Afterwards, the non-cyclic (or post-cyclic) postlexical PRs apply, which correspond both to PRs of Natural Phonology and to all sorts of rules of sentence phonology (see 2.4.1), i.e., they comprise (a) all allophonic rules, (b) all exceptionless (automatic phonemic) neutralization PRs,[243] and (c) all casual/fast speech rules,[244] and moreover (d) all rules of sentence phonology/morphonology/morphology, apparently regardless whether they are PRs, MPRs, or AMRs.[245] However, PRs of lexical diffusion (5.10.5) are lexical rules (according to Kiparsky 1982d).

5.17.1.6.2. One may regard the program of Lexical Phonology and of this book as substantial and formal and related research as largely complementary. Here substantive and formal criteria are discussed which supplement the list of contrasts between lexical and post-lexical rules in Lexical Phonology, which --at least in its present state-- seems to be most interested in working out precisely in which domains and in which order rules are applied. Moreover, Lexical Phonology tries to remove most exceptions and irregularities by assigning lexical rules to specific levels (cf. Rubach 1981:179). It remains to be seen whether this will be possible with the details elaborated in this chapter which show that the division of PRs and MPRs is far less neat than described or adumbrated in most treatments.

However, there are mismatches between the two models:

5.17.1.6.2.1. Probably a biunique correspondence of post-lexical rules of present Lexical Phonology and PRs of this book is impossible, and I believe that I have more arguments for retaining my category of PRs than Lexical Phonology presents counterarguments.

5.17.1.6.2.2. My distinction of MPRs and AMRs corresponds much better to the distinction of phonological rules and rules of allomorphy in derivational phonology[246] than to anything in Lexical Phonology. Particularly the highest level(s) of Lexical Phonology mean(s) more abstractness than more MR-like behavior of rules.

5.17.1.6.2.3. The original concept of Lexical Phonology[247] seems to have been that one and the same rule may apply cyclically as a lexical rule in levels of lexical morphology and phonology and also postcyclically as a postlexical rule, whereas in Stampean Natural Phonology a process (i.e., PR) may not be a rule (i.e., MPR or AMR) at the same time. This chapter has shown that the distinction of PRs and MPRs is not that neat, which seems to diminish the difference between Lexical Phonology and Natural Phonology. However, Kiparsky (1982d) suggests that 'the versions of a rule appearing at different levels possess some degree of independence ... each level has its own phonology.' This concept would allow MPR-like applications of a PR to be singled out and transformed into a separate lexical rule of a specific level. How much then can rules be split up?

5.17.1.6.3. Kiparsky (1982c:150ff = 1982b:59ff) has criticized three concepts of 'morphologized rules.' His third version, 'morphophonemic processes are integral parts of morphological operations ... the most unfortunate treatment of all', is not ours, but Linell's.[248] His second version, the complete omission of phonological conditions on MPRs, has not been followed in this book at all. His first version, which consists in adding a list of conditioning formatives (i.e., morphological conditions) to the phonological environment, is partially unavoidable even in Lexical Phonology in the case of lexical and morphological idiosyncracies.[249] In other instances (as with Kiparsky's case of trisyllabic shortening), all suffixes in question (here *-ous*, *-ate*, *-ar*, *-al*, etc., as in *ŏmin-ous* vs. *ōmen*) could be unified into one category as here 'Latinate' (cf. 5. 10.3).

5.17.1.6.4. Ideally the properties of rules in this chapter should fall out from their formal properties in Lexical Phonology -- and vice versa, if both

approaches were completely compatible and if also the details of the formal organization of language specific rule application were treated in this book. Finally, there is an additional difference (which will come out more clearly in
chapter 10): I am trying to find, in a rather schematic way, semiotic and functional explanations, which apparently lie outside the interests and scope of
Lexical Phonology: It accounts for the essential observation that MPRs are
triggered by MRs/morphological categories, and indeed, if a modified version of
(Lexical Morphology and) Lexical Phonology should work, it would express just
that (structural description). In my model (Dressler 1977a, 1981b; 10) MPRs are
co-signs of MRs/morphological categories, and for this functional reason they
are subordinated to specific MRs/morphological categories, which can be struc-
turally described in terms of rule ordering.

5.17.2.1. Nearly all the literature on rule ordering (5.17.0, 5.17.12) is relevant for the problems of intra-level rule ordering, i.e., ordered application of
rules within blocks of rules. Nevertheless I must assign to this topic still
much less space than to inter-level ordering for the following reasons: (a)
Whereas for inter-level ordering it is easy to deduce from the general arrangement of a grammar the expectation that the block of MPRs should be applied between the block of MRs and that of PRs, no such transparent deductions are possible for intra-level rule ordering. (b) Any adequate discussion of the literature would go beyond the framework of this book. (c) Little has been written,
and with little result, under the specific angle of characterizing morphonology
in contrast to morphology and phonology.[250]

5.17.2.2. Classical generative phonology basically assumes extrinsic ordering,
and so do Cyclic and Lexical Phonology (5.17.1.5f) for rule application within
each level/cycle and within postcyclic/postlexical rules, i.e., rules are specifically ordered, once and for all, for each language/dialect in such a way
that all correct outputs and no incorrect one, are derived from the inputs (Extrinsic ordering). Other basic options are: (a) No ordering, i.e., rules apply
whenever their structural description is met so that several rules may apply simultaneously to the same inputs.[251] (b) Ordering of rules according to general
structural properties of the rules involved, of the strings they may apply to,
or of relations among rules (extrinsic ordering).[252] Here one may add conditions such as the 'elsewhere condition' (which Kiparsky 1982b, 1982c uses in
Lexical Phonology). (c) Ordering according to functional properties[253] of rules

or of rules preserving underlying contrast (impeding neutralization),[254] 'fortition before lenition.'[255]

5.17.2.3. AMRs can be formulated with explicit statements of conditions on application so that no ordering is necessary. However, description becomes more
economical if no conditions have to be stated for the basic allomorph, a common
practice in structural morphology,[256] continued by the Elsewhere Condition.[257]
In fact this is just another instance of the more general default principle, cf.
5.17.1.4.4, 5.20.8.2.1. E.g., in English plural formation *ox, child, brother*
(of a brotherhood) would be specified for attachment of the allomorph *-en; foot,
goose, mouse, louse,* etc., for being subject to umlaut (an AMR which has wrongly
been considered a PR); to all the other words (*sheep, fish,* etc., excluded) /z/
would be attached without any further specification.

However, extrinsic ordering is still called for in cases such as the sup-
letion of the Welsh article *yr* vs. *y* (Coates 1983): *yr* is used before vowels
(e.g., *yr afal* 'the apple'), *y* before consonants (e.g., *y gwaith* 'the work');
however if the article is followed by a feminine singular noun starting with *g-,*
initial mutation (lenition) to zero applies: thus *gardd* 'garden', *geneth*
'girl', but *yr ardd, yr eneth:* Here morphological suppletion follows an AMR of
mutation. For extreme ordering of AMRs in Polish and Russian declension, cf.
Pohl (1983:123ff).

5.17.2.4. MPRs are considered by so many phonologists as 'crazy rules' (Bach &
Harms 1972), 'unnatural PRs', etc., that complex ordering statements (especially
extrinsic ordering) necessary for their correct application may not surprise.[258]

5.17.2.5. PRs would be really quite different entities if no ordering statement
were necessary for them: This idea is captured by the 'No-Ordering Condition'
of Natural Generative Phonology (Hooper 1976:18ff, 116f). Others believe in simultaneous application of PRs,[259] others in general principles of intrinsic ordering (cf. note 252).

However, ordering problems remain with many PRs which have neutralizing
('morphophonemic') effects (merger of phonemes, deletion, or epenthesis
rules).[260] One case is Danish (neutralizing) nasal assimilation ordered after
allophonic, context-sensitive *a*-coloring (backing before /ŋ/) which gives
[saŋkrabə] 'sand crab' (*sand+krabbe*) vs. [saŋkrɛʔs] *sang + kreds* 'song cycle'.[261]

In the first form [a] is not backed before [ŋ], and this can be described with
the device of ordering lowel vowel backing before phonemic assimilation. This
case is also problematic for Cyclic and Lexical Phonology, since allophonic PRs
should be postcyclic or postlexical and thus apply after interphonemic assimilations.

5.17.2.6. Reordering of PRs in diachronic change has been seen as a major mechanism of change in generative phonology.[262] Closer inspection of the examples
given usually shows that these are either instances of inter-level reordering
(5.17.1.4.5) or that the structural descriptions of the rules may have changed
(restructuring) so that the concept of reordering is a superfluous device.[263]

A case of gross misuse of reordering is Sommerstein's (1977:242f, 245) example of Ancient Greek fricative weakening (s → h) and nasal deletion (before
/s/): Prehistoric s → h / $\begin{Bmatrix} \# \\ v \end{Bmatrix}$__v did not apply to such forms as [paːsa] 'each
all' (fem.sg.) ← /pansa/ ← /pant+ja/, except in a few dialects of the 1st mil-
lenium B.C. such as Laconian (e.g., dat.pl. *pahín* 'to all' ← /pansin/). However, Laconian (etc.) fricative weakening is only intervocalic, whereas prehistoric fricative weakening has been telescoped with *h*-deletion to s → ∅ / v__v.
Furthermore this *s*-deletion was quickly morphologized to an AMR which was restricted to a few morphological alternations such as *nós-to-s* vs. *né-o-mai* (<
nés-o-mai) 'I return', *akú-ō* (< *akús-ō*) 'I hear', passive aorist *ēkús-thē-n*,
passive perfect *ékus-mai*, verbal adj. *akus-tó-s* (derivative: *akus-tikós*); but
in these categories *s* expanded so that (by rule inversion, 5.2.7.3) we have
rather an expanding AMR (cf. 5.12.7) of *s*-insertion. Also word-initial fricative weakening had morphologized already in prehistoric times, so that we are
left with an AMR (or sometimes even suppletion) in a few alternations such as
the root *stē/sta*, as in 1.sg. aorist *é-stē-n* vs. reduplicated present *hi-stē-mi*
'I cause to stand', reduplicated perfect *hé-stē-ka*.[264] Under these circumstances how could the PR of prehistoric fricative weakening have survived many
centuries until it would have been reordered? Clearly the Laconian (etc.) PR is
a partial recapitulation of the older prehistoric PR of fricative weakening -- a
view unanimously held by pre- and non-generative Greek linguistics and philology.[265]

Few examples of diachronic intra-level reordering may remain, such as in
German /ng/ (Kohrt 1980). In Natural Phonology, the concept of reordering is

used, if at all, for very early stages of first language acquisition (Stampe 1969).

5.18. Iconicity

5.18.0. Iconicity is used here as a descriptive cover term for similarity relations between the inputs and the putputs of PRs, MPRs, and MRs. Later on it will be explained within a theoretical semiotic framework (10.4.5.3, 10.7.10). First, inputs have to be characterized (5.16.1), then outputs (5.18.2), and finally their relations (5.18.3f).

5.18.0. Iconicity is used here as a descriptive cover term for similarity relations between the inputs and the outputs of PRs, MPRs, and MRs. Later on it will be explained within a theoretical semiotic framework (10.4.5.3, 10.7.10). First inputs have to be characterized (5.16.1), then outputs (5.18.2), and finally their relations (5.18.3f).

5.18.1. Any rule whose input is an allophone should be a PR. This holds, rather trivially for the lowest level rules, which describe minimal details of phonetic production, if phonologists were to write them. More important cases are PRs which refer to extrinsic allophones, such as Austrian German [ɐ], as in ['leːdɐ] 'leather', which must be derived either from underlying /'leːdr/ via via intermediate ['leːdɐr] or, alternatively, from underlying /'leːdɐr/ via intermediate ['leːdər] (and possibly ['leːdɐɾ] or ['leːdɐr]).[266] Since neither [ə] nor [ɐ] are phonemes, any PR which weakens or deletes /r/ or [ɾ] after [ə, ɐ] or fuses [ər] to [ɐ] or lowers [ə] to [ɐ] before /r/ must refer to at least one of the allophones [ə], [ɐ], [ɾ]. This situation is frequent in casual speech (5.11) and would be quite general if those phonologists were right who regard 'normal style' outputs (which are allophonic by definition) as inputs of casual/fast speech PRs (5.11.2).

However if in rule ordering a MPR or AMR applies after an allophonic PR (5. 17.1.4), then the input of the respective MPR or AMR may be an allophone. PRs may have and MPRs and MRs do have phonemic inputs. For the crucial question of non-phonological input elements, see 5.7-10. Let us give score 1 to rules which have allophonic input, score 2 to those which have phonemic inputs.

5.18.2.1. Rules which introduce new segments, i.e., allophones, must be PRs.[267]
If one makes a distinction between intrinsic and extrinsic allophones,[268] then
PRs introducing intrinsic allophones (e.g., slight nasalization of [ɑ] Ruhlen
1978:231f, Ohala 175:299), and of all vowels before nasals (Ruhlen 1978)) are
phonologically more natural than those introducing extrinsic allophones (e.g.,
strong vowel nasalization before tautosyllabic nasals (cf. Clumeck 1975, Bhat
1975:33)). I.e., an intrinsic allophone, as an automatic and totally context-
determined variant whose deviation from the input target is hardly perceptible,
is maximally similar to its input. An extrinsic allophone, as a language-specific (conventional) and more easily perceivable deviation, is less similar to
its input (cf. 10.7.10). Let us give score 1 to rules producing intrinsic allophones, score 2 to those producing extrinsic allophones.

5.18.2.2. Still more conventional (language-specific) are quasi-phonemes[269]
(score 3), i.e., segments which (1) are in perceptual contrast with other segments (phonemes or quasi-phonemes) but (2) can always be derived from a different underlying phoneme and (3) behave, in other respects, partially like extrinsic allophones, partially like phonemes. E.g., this holds of [ŋ] in many languages where it is in perceptual contrast with /n, m/ but can be derived from
underlying /n/ (Dressler 1981). Other instances of quasi-phonemes are prenasalized stops when derived from underlying *nC*-sequences (Herbert 1977b), marginally
German [ç] vs. [x] (Dressler 1977a:52), cf. 5.18.3.4. (4) A quasi-phoneme must
always be derived from an underlying phoneme by a PR. But such a PR is to be
considered less iconic than one which introduces an extrinsic allophone.

A PR, MPR, of AMR which is phonemic by merging two input phonemes results
in an output which is still less similar to its input (score 4).

5.18.3.1. If we put together the criteria of 5.18.1f, we can either add input
and output scores in a mechanical way, with an unrevealing result (points 2-6):
e.g., PRs or MPRs which have an allophonic input and PRs which have a phonemic
input would both have score 4 -- this is like counting together apples and
pears. A more insightful scale of the respective phonological iconicity of
rules concentrates on the degree of structural change: Score 1: phonetic detail rules (including all PRs producing intrinsic allophones); Score 2: phonostylistic PRs of speech variation (5.18.1); Score 3: PRs changing phonemes into extrinsic allophones; Score 4: PRs changing them into quasi-phonemes;

Score 5: PRs, MPRs, AMRs changing them into other phonemes. Here degree of iconicity equals degree of automaticity and of similarity.

5.18.3.2. Degree of similarity between input and output of a rule can be operationalized by using the distinctive feature framework (2.3). One can count the number of features changed and test this classification in perceptual experiments. But as we have seen (5.3), the operation of process matching is more important if we want to differentiate synchronically MPRs from PRs and from AMRs.

However, we may profit from feature counting for diachrony. We can argue that barely perceptible deviations of outputs from inputs cannot express morphological differences and thus expect that the greater the perceptual deviation is, the more easily the respective PR can be morphologized, i.e., the less its stability as a PR. Since perceptual experiments are impossible for by-gone epochs, feature counting is a viable substitute if the distinctive features used are perceptually validated. E.g., we may expect a PR leniting /s/ → [z] to be more stable than a PR weakening /s/ → [h] (5.2.7.1, 5.3.1).

5.18.3.3. Following Generative Phonology, we can consider discrete PRs, MPRs, and AMRs less iconic than phonetic detail rules since they operate with binary features (e.g., /s/ → [z] = [-voiced] → [+voiced]) whereas phonetic detail rules operate with n-ary (multivalued) features, i.e., they are gradual instead of being discrete (e.g., in specifying the exact degree of aspiration of stops, cf. Linell 1979b:188f, Roberge 1980:notes 47, 57). However, this criterion may differentiate only among PRs (e.g., as to the diachronic stability, cf. 5.18.3.2) and it loses its reliability in a model where all distinctive features are n-ary, as in Stampean Natural Phonology. In contemporary structural phonemics, invariant and variant features of a phoneme are often distinguished, and a phoneme is defined by its invariant features (cf. Stankiewicz 1979:18). The diachronic change of a phoneme to morphophoneme may then be characterized as the introduction of changes in invariant features.

5.18.3.4. Allophonic PRs may again be differentiated into the more iconic subset of those which leave all input feature values intact but add new features, e.g., aspiration of English stops, and into the subset of those which change input feature values: e.g., the French PR which devoices word final sonorants after voiceless obstruents (as in *peuple*, *prêtre*), or the German PR ç → x =

[-back] → [+back]. All (quasi-)phonemic PRs (5.16.2.2) belong here, as well as
all MPRs and AMRs (5.18.3.5). Iconicity is disturbed in case of phonemic overlap, i.e., if under certain conditions the phonetic deviation from the phonemic
input is such that the resulting allophone is phonetically more similar to a
different phoneme, e.g., Danish word-final [d] reflects underlying /t/, but not
/d/, cf. 5.20.2.2.

5.18.4. Another possibility is to compare the relation between strings of segments in the input and in the output in order to differentiate PRs as to their
respective iconicity and putative diachronic stability. Let us symbolize an input strong consisting of three phonemes with XYZ (more in 10.7.10.8):

5.18.4.1. A relatively high degree of iconicity (similarity) can be attributed
to the relation between the input string /X Y Z/ and the output string [x y z]
if the number of segments remains identical and if each phoneme is represented
by a relatively similar allophone,[270] i.e., /X/ → [x], /Y/ → [y], /Z/ → [z], and
if the linear order (sequence) of corresponding phonemes and allophones is identical, as in E. /tedi/ → [tʰeɾɪ] (cf. Hooper 1977).

5.18.4.2. There is less similarity if the linear order is changed via metathesis (4.4.1.2, cf. Moravcsik 1977b): /X Y Z/ → [y x z] and worse /X Y Z/ → [z y
x], and the worse the more distant the metathesized segments are from one another, e.g., Hixkaryana sh → hs, xh → hx (Derbyshire 1979:187f), Ivrit metathesis
of coronal stop and fricative/affricate, as in reflexive prefix *hit* + pret.
sader 'arranged' → *histader* 'arranged one's affairs'.[271]

5.18.4.3. Linear order is less disturbed by an insertion (epenthesis) process
(4.4.1.4) /X Y Z/ → [x y a z], e.g., *kiss* + pl. /z/ → [kisəz], because the linear order is preserved, only adjacency is diminished.

5.18.4.4. Whereas insertion processes preserve the input phonemes, deletion
processes (4.5.2.1) destroy at least one of them /X Y Z/ → [x z] or [x y] or
[y z] as in consonant cluster reduction, e.g., *fast+en* → ['faːsn, 'fæsn]. Since
the similarity relation is disturbed by loss of input information, we may expect
that such PRs of deletion are diachronically less stable than insertion PRs, unless they are restricted to casual/fast speech where loss of information is less

disturbing.[272]

Deletion PRs are better if they leave a trace (partial preservation of information), e.g., in many German dialects (cf. Mansell 1973) vowels are nasalized by a following nasal unless an in-between segment has been deleted, e.g.,

rein	*Reihe-n*	*Lehm*	*leb-en*	
'pure'	'row-s'	'loam'	'to live'	
/raen/	/raeɛ+n/	/leːm/	/leːb+n/	
---	raeən	---	---	Vowel weakening
---	---	---	leːbm̩	Nasal assimilation
[raẽn]	---	[lẽːm]	---'	Vowel nasalization
	[raen]		[leːm]	Deletion

5.18.4.5. PRs of fusion (coalescence, 4.4.4) and of polarization (4.4.3) diminish similarity as well: /x y z/ → [x y͜z] with reduction of segment number, as in *can't* /kæn#t/ → [kæ̃t] (Hooper 1977); /x y z/ → [x y_1 y_2 z] with an increase of segment number, as in diphthongization [oː] → [ŭo, oŭ].

5.18.5. As we have seen, iconicity in the descriptive sense of this section is more interesting for diachronic than for synchronic morphonology. When we take it in its full semiotic sense (10.7.10, 10.8.3.4) its explanatory power will increase considerably.

5.18.6. Following Kruszewski (cf. Klausenburger 1979:12ff), Baudouin de Courtenay (1895:31ff) gave the first systematic description of the diachronic change from embrionic (G. 'keimende') but still invisible 'microscope of divergents' (= intrinsic allophonic PRs, 5.18.1, 5.18.2.1) via unconscious but visible and noticeable 'macroscopic divergents' (= extrinsic allophonic PRs or maybe even quasi-phonemic or phonemic PRs) to 'correlations' = 'psychophonetic alternations' (≈ MPRs) and 'traditional paleophonic alternations' (= MPRs and AMRs). A well known reformulation in our times is Hyman's (1977) concept of phonologization and subsequent dephonologization (more frequently called morphologization).[273] For all structuralist and many other[274] phonologists, the decisive turning point is the change from allophonic to phonemic outputs, whereas it is the thesis of this book that this change is a necessary, but not a sufficient precondition for PRs becoming MPRs. Walker (1979) claims the possibility 'to move directly from allophonic variation to morphophonemic alternation without ever affecting the phonemic inventory of a language,' exemplifying this claim with the diachronic

change of vowel nasalization in Old French, as in *don* 'gift' ∿ *doner* 'to give' >
O.Fr. [dõn ∿ duner]. But his 'morphophonemic alternation' covers both the PR/
MPR of vowel raising and the still allophonic vowel nasalization, i.e., he does
not prove that vowel nasalization changed directly from an allophonic PR to a
MPR.

5.18.7. Bjarkman (1975:68), Hooper (1976:84ff), and Dressler[275] have claimed
that this type of change (phonologization and then, possibly, morphologization)
is unidirectional. This claim seems to be immediately contradicted by Kuryłowicz's (1968:80) remark that 'the change of morphemes into morphonemes is also
easily illustrated.' But all his examples illustrate the rise or the desemanti-
cization of MRs, and never the change from AMRs to MPRs.

5.18.7.1. A more serious threat to my claim seems to be constituted by Malkiel's[276] findings on the morphological origin of sound laws. E.g., in addition
to the synchronic Spanish alternation *e* ∿ *ie*, *o* ∿ *ue* (with the inverted MPRs *ie*
→ *e*, *ue* → *o*),[277] there was a change *ié* > *i*, *ué* > *e* in Old Spanish, which partially originated in the conflict of two heterodialectal inflectional patterns.
Thus *afruenta* 'offense' changed to *afrenta*, and thus a synchronic alternation
with 1.sg.pres. *afruento*, inf. *afrontar* 'to insult, confront' might have resulted (Malkiel 1976). But would such an alternation represent a MPR? The inverted
MPR *ue* → *o* (*afruento*, *afrontar*) can be classified as a MPR because monophthongization in unstressed position is still a remnant of phonologicalness. On the
other hand, a putative rule *ué* → *é* (or *é* → *ue* or *é* → *o* or *o* → *é*) would not have
any phonological motivation but would be entirely conditioned by morphological
category and be thoroughly lexicalized; thus it would be a lexicalized, allomorphic MR. Moreover Malkiel (1976:771) himself states that the 'complication[278]
was avoided through split of the original verb into (a) *afrentar* 'to affront,
insult', flanked by the noun *afrenta*, and (b) *afrontar* 'to confront, bring to
fact', neither of them radical-changing.' Also the morphology-induced change
sieglo > *siglo* 'century' alongside with *segral* 'secular' (Malkiel 1976:769) does
not give birth to a MPR or even any rule at all, since both the (merely diachronic) metathesis (*l* – *r* > *r* – *l*) and the meaning difference preclude a rule-
governed alternation.[279] Similarly Hudson's (1976) example from Hadiya does not
constitute a synchronic alternation *rr* ∿ *ll*.[280]

   To regard such examples as proof for phonologization of MRs (e.g., Bailey

1982:84f) pertains to the common fallacy of regarding all sound changes (including restructuring) and even mere sound correspondences between language states distant in time as synchronic PRs.

Malkiel's[280a] work on dialect mixture and 'weak phonetic change' contains other examples of such morphology-induced change.

5.18.8. The scenario of 5.18.6 does not imply that all new PRs must be allophonic PRs, e.g., new vowel harmony rules can be phonemic and may even have morphological exceptions.[281] Nor do we maintain that all AMRs come from earlier PRs via MPRs (see 5.18.7).[282] But I claim that all MPRs come from earlier PRs (or possibly also from effects of earlier PRs, cf. Darden 1982). Both the development formulated as PR > MPR > AMR and the introduction of new AMRs from other (morphological, lexical, syntactic) sources can be subsumed under the heading of de-iconization.

5.18.9. The claim of 5.18.7 must not be confused with the similar-sounding claim that 'neither new phonemes nor new combinations of phonemes can ever come into existence by the agency of morphological analogy' (Trnka et al. 1958), which Stankiewicz (1979:57) correctly criticized. Stankiewicz goes on acknowledging 'that morphological alternations have their origin in phonetically conditioned alternants,' which is equivalent to our claim of 5.18.7; however he also points to 'the opposite phenomenon, i.e., the de-morphologization of alternations.' But 'de-morphologization' is a very ambiguous term, and in fact his two examples do not falsify our claim (5.18.7): the first one is demorphologization of the Slavic accentual shift, which corresponds to rule-loss (i.e., loss of a prosodic AMR) in our model; his second class of cases is 'a similar process ... when an alternation becomes an inherent feature of a grammatical form.' This corresponds to lexicalization in our model, e.g., stress placements becomes lexical for a given morpheme.

This discussion may exemplify our basic conviction that item-and-process techniques allow more precise models than item-and-arrangement techniques.

5.19. Indexicality

5.19.0. Similar to iconicity (5.18.0), indexicality will be dealt with within its full semantic range only later on (10.4.5.2, 10.7f), in a unified and syste-

matic review of topics already studied earlier on, e.g., process matching (5.2),
phonological vs. morphological lexical conditions and domains (5.7-10), speech
variation (5.11), generality (5.12). Here we need to examine a few questions
of context sensitivity left over there.

5.19.1. With 'the possible exception of very low level phonetic detail rules
which add new redundant phonetic features[283] and of pure preservation PRs of the
type /a/ → [a] (4.4.1), all PRs are context-sensitive (cf. Dressler 1977a:26).
Either they must refer to a segmental or to a prosodic phonological context (3f,
5.7f, 10.7.11.1). In the case of phonologically context-free phonostylistic
PRs, they refer to a sociolinguistic context (5.12). And we must be able to
match them to a universal phonological process type (5.2).

E.g., English or German context-free umlaut in plural formation, e.g., *foot*
→ *feet*, G. *Bruder* 'brother' → pl. *Brüder*, cannot be a PR. Moreover, it must be
an AMR because it has score 4 on the scale of phonological matching (5.2.4).

If we find a rule in grammar such as in Chimalapa Zoque (Knudson 1975:41f)
ŋ → w / __v, which has only a phonological context (no morphological or lexical
one), but does not correspond to any process type so far established, then either this description is incomplete or we must elaborate a new universal phonological process type (5.2).

5.19.2. Reference to morphological or lexical ,context itself is no obstacle for
a rule to be classified as a PR (5.9f), although most such rules are MPRs or
even AMRs. But there are specific formal classes of rules (used in generative
phonologies) which can be no PRs: e.g., Rubach's (1981:90) observation that
very complicated rules must be MPRs (or AMRs) may reflect the intuition of many
phonologists.[284]

Such complications arise from various morphological and lexical factors (5.
9f).

But one class of rules can be singled out: exchange rules. We can confidently say that all exchange rules which have no relevant phonological context
(see 5.2.4) must be AMRs,[285] cf. Anderson's (1974:92f, cf. Anderson & Browne
1973:495f) rule for plural formation in Dinka $\begin{bmatrix} +syll \\ \alpha long \end{bmatrix}$ → [-αlong] / $\underset{\text{PLURAL}}{\underline{\qquad}}$, e.g.,
sg. *čiin* 'hand', pl. *čin*, sg. *nin* 'sleep', pl. *niin*. Here exchange of vowel
quantity has no phonological context.

For plural formation in Luo, Anderson & Browne (1973:468f) consider the ex-amples *got* 'mountain', pl. *gode*, *kitabu* 'book', pl. *kitepe*, etc. The MR $\begin{bmatrix} +\text{obstr} \\ \alpha\text{voiced} \end{bmatrix} \rightarrow [-\alpha\text{voiced}] / \underline{\quad} + \begin{smallmatrix} e \\ [\text{PLURAL}] \end{smallmatrix}$ has an irrelevant phonological context because it cannot be matched to any universal process type: Why should the val-ue of [±voiced] be changed before /e/ and only before /e/?

5.19.3. Adjacency is a property of indexicality: The structural change of a rule indicates its condition the better the nearer they are to each other. But this can be formulated more precisely in terms of process matching. In a pro-cess of contact assimilation (4.5.3) the conditioning phoneme must be immediate-ly adjacent to the assimilated segment. If not, the respective rule cannot be a PR.

The Sanskrit MPR of retroflexion changes $s \rightarrow \underset{.}{s}$ after r, u, k, i, not only in *abhi-ṣiñc-* 'anoint' vs. *siñc-* 'sprinkle', but also in the (3.sg.) imperfect /abhi+a+sinc+a+t/ *abhyaṣiñcat* (Kiparsky 1982b:122, 131f), where the a (exponent of past tense indicative) intervenes. One may order the inflectional MR of a-prefixation (and other MRs as well) after the MPR of retroflexion. But still surface adjacency is reduced, and this type of rule order suggests in itself the morphologization of the retroflexion rule.

In Harari and in related languages (Kenstowicz 1981:438f, Hetzron 1977:48; for labialization, see Hetzron 1971) an AMR of palatalization /k, t → č, s → š/, etc., applies before non-adjacent /i/ in the 2.sg.fem. form.

Thus Jensen's (1974:685) 'strict adjacency condition' which 'disallows any intervening material between determinant and focus in processes' must be re-stricted to PRs.

Similarly a vowel harmony process can be a PR only if the vowel quality of, e.g., a suffix vowel depends on the next vowel to its left as in Turkish *İstan-bul-u*, *Gaziantep-i*, *Afyonkarahisar-ı*, acc. of *İstanbul*, *Gaziantep*, *Afyonkarahi-sar*. If they were *İstanbul-ı*, *Gaziantep-ı*, *Afyonkarahisar-i*, so that the second next vowel would be decisive, Turkish vowel harmony would now by this criterion be a MPR or an AMR (cf. Jensen & Strong-Jensen 1979:129ff and the re-ply by Odden 1980).

5.19.4. Basically the afore-mentioned criteria of indexicality can be handled

within the operation of process matching (5.2). But indexicality will reappear
as an important semiotic principle (10.7.11).

5.20. (Bi-)/(non-)uniqueness

5.20.0. The literature on morphonology, process phonologies, etc., is full of
overlapping concepts such as neutralization,[286] transparency/opacity,[287] direc-
tionality/predictability,[288] recoverability.[289] Discussion of these concepts
can hardly be separated from each other. Moreover, semiotic terms such as the
one-meaning-one-form principle[290] = relational invariance = biuniqueness in contrast to uniqueness and non-uniqueness have been used much more than in any other area discussed so far in this book.

So we can afford to use the schema of a scale biuniqueness-uniqueness-non-
uniqueness as the guiding principle of our discussion. This scale also expresses the unidirectional change PR > MPR > AMR (cf. 5.18.6-8).

5.20.1. Score 1 on the uniqueness scale is biuniqueness in its strict, set theoretical interpretation: Two sets, e.g., a set of input phonemes and a set of
output (allo-)phones, are equivalent if each element of one set corresponds biuniquely to one element of the other set, i.e., if one phoneme is mapped into
just one (allo)phone and vice versa; of course divergent intrinsic allophones
of the same phoneme are not counted. A notation would be /A/. Such a situation

$$\begin{array}{c} /A/ \\ \downarrow\uparrow \\ [a] \end{array}$$

of perfect biuniqueness is often true for single phonemes, but rarely for whole
natural classes of phonemes, e.g., for most vowel phonemes of Standard German
which have just one (extrinsic) allophone each --but much less so in casual
speech styles. Of course such rules of transduction/preservation, e.g., G. /iː/
→ [iː], /i/ → [ɪ] (with the exception of foreign words), etc., are PRs. They
express bidirectional relations[291] since all instances of /iː/ are realized (can
be predicted to be pronounced) as [iː], and an /iː/ has to be retrieved/inferred
/recovered from every instance of [iː], and there is optimal transparency of a
phoneme in its phonetic realization.

5.20.2. In phonology biuniqueness is used in a broader sense.

5.20.2.1. According to American structuralism,[291a] biuniqueness is preserved

even if a phoneme has more than one allophone, provided bidirectional inference
is unambiguous, e.g., the allophones [t] and [tʰ] of English /t/ are in predictable complementary distribution, but always unambiguously correspond to the
same phoneme /t/. Similarly in Austrian German (cf. 5.20.1) all non-low long
vowels are lowered before [ʀ] as in [vɪːʀ] *wir* 'we' vs. [viː] *wie* 'how'. Although inferability/recoverability is not diminished, additional processing is
demanded from the hearer to retrieve/recover the one underlying phoneme from two
different extrinsic allophones. Therefore I assign score 2 to this type of biuniqueness which occurs only with allophonic PRs. In set theory this is uniqueness, symbolized /A/.

$$/A/$$
$$[a]\quad[b]$$

In American structuralism, biuniqueness was postulated as an absolute constraint on relations between a phoneme and its allophones. This is an example
of a typical research strategy, found often in modern phonology, which consists
in elevating the optimal/most natural/most efficient, etc., state of affairs to
being the only state of affairs allowed by the given theory or model.

5.20.2.2. A still weaker type of biuniqueness can be found in cases of phonemic
overlap,[292] as in Danish where in syllable final position tense stops become lax
(e.g., t → d / __$), lax stops becoming fricatives (e.g., d → ð / __$). Underlying phonemes can still be unambiguously derived. But the conditions of the
PRs must be precisely observed in production, perception, and evaluation in order to avoid confusion (for decrease in iconicity, cf. 5.18.3.5). A notation
may be   /A/   /B/.

[a]/X   [b]/Y   [c]/Y
        [b]/X

Another example is [ŋ] in advanced French (Walker 1982): Underlying /ŋ/
occurs in LWs (e.g., *slang*) but never before nasals, where allophonic [ŋ] is due
to assimilation of /g/ in casual speech, e.g., *vaguement* [vaŋmã] 'vaguely',
whereas in Canadian French the source of [ŋ] is ambiguous.

All these rules are still PRs and can be assigned score 3. We predict that
score 1 PRs are the most stable in diachrony, score 3 PRs the least.

5.20.2.3. All rule types (= PRs) treated so far are transparent according to
the definition of Kiparsky[293] because they capture surface generalizations in

such a way that neither do there exist contradictions to the respective PR nor
is there any obstacle (in perception or evaluation or language learning) to
reading the rule off the surface forms.

5.20.3.   Score 4 can be assigned to uniqueness or unidirectional mapping, i.e.,
a unique mapping is predictable in one direction only.[294]

5.20.3.1.   A first subtype is represented by 'free variation', e.g., in many
German lects /r/ can be realized as [r, ʀ] in all positions and, moreover, as
[ɾ] in syllable-final position. When for some speakers [ɾ] is derived by a phonostylistic PR of casual speech, then there is a supplementary sociolinguistic
condition. Such unique rules are always PRs and are difficult to morphologize.

5.20.3.2.   Very rarely a special allophone occurs only under grammatical conditions: E.g., some speakers of Austrian German use the variant [æ:] of /ɛ:/ only
in the second subjunctive such as *gäbe* ['gæ:bə] 'would give' as opposed to the
first subjunctive *gebe* ['ge:bə]. This is a hypercorrect pronunciation intended
to avoid merger of these rarely used standard forms. Thus the rule is artificial.   In formal speech of some Breton dialects (Dressler 1972) /ɛ/ is weakened to its allophone [ə] only in two unstressed endings, but this is of course
still a PR.

5.20.3.3.   The other instances of uniqueness are various types of neutralization[295] where the derivation is always predictable but where inference in analysis (e.g., in perception) is not. First of all a rule may effect neutralization in part of its applications only. These are PRs with mixed allophonic and
phonemic changes, such as assimilation of /n/ to the place of articulation of a
following obstruent, e.g., German n → ŋ in *Tank* [taŋk] 'tank' (with the quasi-
phoneme [ŋ], 5.18.2.2) and the normal pronunciation of *fünf* [fʏɱf] 'five' (allophone [ɱ]), *an+park+en* ['ampakŋ̩] 'to seize' (with merger of the phonemes /n/ and
/m/).[296]   Or Maltese obstruents are voiced before sonorants so that the phonemes
/f/ and /v/, /t/ and /d/, etc., merge, whereas [ž] is an allophone of /š/ (Krier
1975).   Similarly Russian word-final voice assimilation is both 'morphophonemic'
and allophonic.[297] Martinet (1965:18, 27) attributes instances of such combinatorial conditions still to phonology.

5.20.3.4. A PR may always and only neutralize two underlying phonemes, e.g., phonemic final devoicing in varieties of German, Russian, Breton, Albanian, Ladakhi, etc., or sr → hr in Capanahua (Loos 1969:184) or p → k / __$ in Tetelcingo Nahuatl (Tuggy 1979). This is called automatic neutralization by L. Bloomfield (cf. Kilbury 1976:47). Trubetzkoy's (1939.V) distinction between context-determined and structure-determined neutralizations is of no relevance for out proposes because both dependency on surrounding phonemes (A → B / C__D) and dependency on prosodic features (syllable, word, stress, etc.) exclude biuniqueness in the same way.

5.20.3.5. One class of allophonic PRs is neutralizing,[298] e.g., ə-formation in English;[299] therefore the adjective of a name like *Newton* ['njuwtən] can be formed correctly with [ow] (*Newton+ian*) only if one knows the orthography: When Michaels (1980:391) presented subjects with the name ['ziŋkən], they could not decide on the derivations *Zinken+ian, Zinkan+ian, Zinkon+ian* without knowing the orthography of the second vowel.[300]

The PR of ə-insertion in plurals (*kiss-es*) adds another source for [ə] (in those dialects where they are homophonous). Such an output segment is still unambiguously derived from its inputs, but these various inputs cannot be inferred/recovered unambiguously from their identical output. The extension of this class of PRs is unclear since all conceivable cases can be classified as phonemic neutralizations (5.20.3.4).

However in a processual phonology, a PR v → ə / _____ does not mention
                                                    [-stress]
any specific underlying segment, whereas in a PR of final devoicing, a /d/ is considered to be neutralized with and to merge into a specific input segment, viz. /t/. Thus E. v → ə / _____ is an allophonic PR (although neutraliz-
                                       [-stress]
ing), G. [+obstr] → [+tense] / __$ is a phonemic PR. Another case of allophonic neutralization is optional merger of poststressed /i/ and /e/ into [ɪ] and of prestressed /u/ and /o/ into [ʊ] in Nawdm (Nicole 1979:47ff).[301] On flapping of E. /d, t/, cf. 5.20.6 note 310.

5.20.3.6. All PRs of 5.20.3.3f are non-transparent or opaque[302] according to Kiparsky (1973b) because the output tokens of a rule A → B / C__D do not comprise all the tokens of B, i.e., there are B's which have some other source, e.g., one part is rule-derived, the other part underlying, as in German, Polish, Russian [t] which may represent underlying /t/ or be derived from underlying /d/ in word-final position. However, English allophonic ə-formation (5.20.3.5) is not opaque in itself, because one and the same PR applies to several vowels and can be read off the surface, but only because of ə-insertion in pl. *kiss-es*, etc., where [ə] is also always unstressed. Thus [ə] has the two sources: v or zero. In other words, there is a two-way ambiguity.

According to our analysis, E. [ə] is many-ways ambiguous since the hearer or learner cannot infer which of the many English vowels may underly. Whereas it is the inference of the rule which matters in Kiparsky's conception, the inference of the respective underlying phoneme from a surface segment is relevant in our uniqueness conception. Accordingly, scaling of uniqueness would result in counting possible inputs (but cf. for default 5.20.8).

5.20.3.7. A special case of uniqueness is effected by deletion rules (PRs if general, etc.) such as deletion of /t/ in E. *hast-en, soft-en* (cf. 4.5.2.1, 5. 18.4.4). A zero output, i.e., nothing, may either be due to deletion (and there may be more than one deletable segment, cf. 5.20.3.6) or simply mean lack of semiosis. Therefore the ambiguity does not lie in the choice between two or more different input phonemes, but in the uncertainty whether any rule has applied at all.[303] This is a worse kind of ambiguity. Thus we may assume that deletion PRs may fare worse in diachrony than other PRs involving uniqueness.[304] E.g., the PRs of final ə-deletion and consonant-deletion in French /plat/ → [pla] 'plain' (masc.) and fem. /plat+ə/ → ['platə, plat] were replaced by the AMR of consonant addition in feminine formation (rule inversion): masc. /pla/ → [pla], fem. /pla/ → /plat/, and a stylistic MPR of ə-addition in songs and theater: /plat/ → ['plat(ə)].[305]

5.20.4. Rules typically involved in non-uniqueness are (score 5 on the uniqueness scale)[306] non-general neutralizing rules, classified as opaque rules, type (i) by Kiparsky (1973b),[307] i.e., rules of the form A → B / C__D which do not apply to all underlying tokens of A, e.g., umlaut in Germanic languages such as in E. *goose*, pl. *geese* as opposed to *moose(s)*. Non-uniqueness can be schematized as 　/A/　/B/, e.g.,　/uː/　/iː/

　　　　　[a]　[b]　　　　[uŭ]　[iĭ]
　　　　　　　　　　　　mooses　geese

Viz. neither does /uː/ have a unique derivation nor [iǐ] a unique inference.
Still worse is indeterminacy (non-uniqueness) effected by Palauan vowel deletion and weakening rules (Wilson 1972).

All such opaque rules are MPRs or AMRs, with the exception of neutralizing
fast speech PRs and neutralizing PRs of lexical diffusion.

Since Kiparsky (1973b) assigns morphological conditions as well to the environment / C__D, he can differentiate only between general (= visibly transparent) and non-general (= opaque) rules, but not between phonologically and morphologically general rules, a differentiation which usually entails a distinction between PRs and MPRs or AMRs.

5.20.5. The main thrust of Kiparsky's (1973b) opacity concept is rule interactions which make a rule A → B / C__D opaque: This is the case if another rule
introduces new strings CAD (type i, cf. 5.20.4) or changes CBD to either CED or
to EBD or CBE (Kiparsky's type iia). E.g., at a certain period of Republican
Latin, rhotacism s → r / V__V, as in *hōnos* 'honor', gen. *hōnōr-is*, was made (i)-
opaque by degemination ss → s / V__V; lexical exceptions (partially loanwords)
such as *asinus* 'donkey' increased (i)-opacity. Analogy in the new nom. *hōnor*
'honor' added (iia)-opacity because / V__# equals CBE in the above formula.
Mayerthaler (1977) has identified such 'opacity accumulation' as a major type of
diachronic change. This goes well with Kiparsky's (1982a:77f) observation that
opaque rules (i.e., MPRs) fade away and get lost eventually. On the other hand,
his claim (Kiparsky 1982a:75, cf. 1973:75ff) that 'rules tend to be ordered so
as to become maximally transparent' is of dubious importance insofar as all
cases of rule reordering do not represent primary change, and seem to be results
of morphological/lexical reorganizations (particularly of analogy).[308]

However also PRs may be opaque, e.g., Madurese tensing which is optionally
made opaque by a fast speech PR (Stevens 1980:641); such interactions of fast
speech PRs are typical (Linell 1979b:184). Another case is obligatory nasal assimilation in Austrian German[309] which changes /geːb+n, leːg+n/ 'to give', 'to
lay' into ['geːbm̩, 'leːgŋ̩]; this PR is followed by a fast speech PR of voiced
stop deletion before tautosyllabic, homorganic nasal, which results in [geːm,
leːm], with deletion of the very environment that caused assimilation (cf.
Skousen 1981:66f).

5.20.6. To conclude on opacity vs. transparency, we may confidently state that all phonologically transparent rules must be PRs, and all MPRs and AMRs must be opaque, since they necessarily change one phoneme into another. This goes well with Rubach's (1981:181) observation that all cyclic rules are opaque, and with Mohanan's (1982:8, 29ff, 136ff) that all lexical rules are opaque. However, a neat separation of phonology and morphonology is prevented by the set of opaque PRs, which are either PRs made opaque by fast speech and by lexically diffusing PRs (i.e., 'optional' rules) or (unique) neutralizing PRs. The first subset can be juggled away within the usual, idealized models which banish 'optional' PRs into the wastebasket of performance (or 'parole') or do not take them seriously.

The other subset could be eliminated if Dinnsen's (1983) claim[310] were correct that no phonological neutralization is truly neutralizing in production. E.g., in the case of German final devoicing the vowel in [vt#] ← /vd#/ would be about 10% longer than the vowel in [vt#] ← /vt#/, and this distinction was identified by 70% of the subjects in a perception experiment. Taken at its face value,[311] final devoicing may still be neutralizing, but due to a preceding PR of vowel lengthening before underlying voiced obstruents, underlying voiced obstruents are still recoverable/inferable. I.e., there is uniqueness if we look at the final obstruent only, but biuniqueness if we look at the sequence /vc#/, e.g., /aːd#/ → [aːˑt#] vs. /aːt#/ → [aːt#]. Moreover, Dinnsen (1983) allows for a set of PRs (e.g., /r/ → [w] in American children)[312] which do not neutralize in production, but do so in perception (even of their producers); these would have to be counted as unique in regard to recoverability/inferability.

If Dinnsen's (1983) further suggestion, that there are no neutralizing rules in phonetic production,[313] should prove correct, then we might have a clear criterion distinguishing PRs and MPRs, i.e., if we suppose that MPRs do neutralize both in production and in perception. However if there are PRs that neutralize in perception, as is commonly supposed, then there is still uniqueness in phonology. It must be noted that very similar sounds (even if they have different phonemic sources) are difficult to differentiate both in production and in perception. This renders experiments more difficult and also explains how gradual allophonic change may suddenly shift into phonemic neutralization (10.7.12.5).

5.20.7.0. In cases of uniqueness and non-uniqueness, the question arises whether and how underlying phonological structures can be recovered or inferred, and if there are degrees of recoverability/inferability. Eliasson (1977, 1978, 1981) points to 'transparent rule-blocks' which guarantee non-ambiguous recoverability, as in the case of Dinnsen's (1983) analysis of German devoicing (5. 20.6). One may add various traces of deleted segments[314] such as non-assimilation beyond a deleted segment, as with vowel-nasalization (5.18.4.4) in Bavarian and Austrian dialects.[315] These traces would belong to Eliasson's (1981) various anti-homonymy constraints which block too much surface neutralization. Finally he elevates the awkward situation of global ambiguity to an absolute constraint against abstract solutions in generative phonology, insofar as global ambiguity involved in abstract underlying forms should be disallowed. Here I find four flaws:

5.20.7.1. An exaggeration similar to American structuralism in regard to biuniqueness (5.20.2.1): A rather unnatural situation which seems to occur rather seldom and which is liable to be avoided in diachronic change is elevated to an absolute constraint.[316] In my view there is again a gradual continuum from natural and therefore very frequent phenomena (biuniqueness) to less natural and therefore rarer phenomena (types of uniqueness where inferability is possible under certain conditions) to very unnatural phenomena (non-uniqueness) which may become so disturbing for communication that no native speakers accept it in their phonologies. In this view, the task for the linguist is therefore reversed: Instead of speculating deductively about absolute constraints, he should set up (again deductively) naturalness scales and find inductively how much unnaturalness occurs in natural languages and under which conditions. An absolute constraint may then be found at the end of this search.

5.20.7.2. In Eliasson's studies there is no consideration whether the putative rules involved are MPRs or PRs.

5.20.7.3. Some neutralization must be allowed, but there is no proviso for how much is allowed. Thus this approach may run into the same difficulties as the phonematic concept of functional load (cf. the critique by King 1967).

5.20.7.4. A constraint on competence is derived from considerations of performance without investigating performance itself; see below 5.20.8, cf. 5.20.6.

5.20.7.5. Similar comments can be made on Kaye's[317] use of the concept 'recoverability'. As for diachrony, he correctly describes how new PRs may render old
PRs (and hence MPRs) less recoverable and that, as a result, rule changes such
as rule loss or rule inversion (cf. 5.20.3.7) again increase recoverability.

5.20.8.1. Semiotic considerations on biuniqueness, uniqueness, non-uniqueness
are metalinguistic contributions to language universals based on problems of
performance (see 10.3ff), i.e., degrees of difficulty how to derive outputs
from inputs and how to retrieve/infer/recover inputs from outputs. Thus a discussion of inferability or recoverability must not be restricted to inspections
of rules, rule schemata, and representations of phonological competence (5.20.
7.4). We must remember that also early generative syntax occupied itself much
with output ambiguity in syntactic surface structure, as in the famous sentence
Flying planes can be dangerous = *Planes that are flying can be dangerous* or *It
can be dangerous to fly planes;* but discussion has been limited on modeling
syntactic competence, whereas it is clear that most seemingly ambiguous sentences are disambiguated by prosodic means[318] or by context, i.e., by text linguistic means (cf. Beaugrande & Dressler 1981:V.1, V.9.7, X.6) or they are
avoided or one of the readings is avoided. Thus an investigation of ambiguity
(uniqueness or non-uniqueness) in syntactic competence only is incomplete. One
answer is perceptual identification experiments as shown in Dinnsen (1983), cf.
5.20.6.

5.20.8.2.1. Another way out is the application of a notion not yet used in phonology, morphology, or morphonology, the frame-theoretical concept 'default value'. Within a frame (cf. Metzing 1980) where one slot can be filled by more
than one filler (uniqueness or non-uniqueness), a default value is 'a value
which is taken to be the slot filler in the absence of explicit information to
the contrary.' E.g., in the derivation of English phonological outputs, [k] may
be said to be the default output of /k/ unless a suffix such as *-ity* follows
Latinate stems, where the output is [s] as in *electric-ity*. In retrieval/infer-
ence the default input of [s] is /s/, whereas the input /k/ is lexically, morphologically, and phonologically restricted (= 'explicit information to the contrary'), the input /z/ phonologically (e.g., plur. *cat-s*). In these cases the
preservation processes /k/ → [k] and /s/ → [s] may be called the 'default
rules'.

5.20.8.2.2. Several previously debated concepts come close to aspects of this
notion of default rules: major rules as opposed to minor rules (5.9.5, 5.17.1.
2), the elsewhere condition (5.17.2.3), Raible's (1980) concept of the regularity of exceptions, Ohlander's (1976:166ff) notion of typicalness. But what is
the most 'typical' rule, the default assumption 'in reference to the whole state
of knowledge' (Hayes 1980:55)?

5.20.8.2.3. Token frequency may seem the most obvious criterion. But notice,
e.g., that Mayerthaler (1977) has shown for plural formation of French nouns in
-*al* that plurals in -*aux* ([o]) are the most frequent ones, whereas only plurals
in -*als* are productive. And surely we want to capture this latter plural formation as the default rule.

5.20.8.2.4. Next we may be tempted to use all the criteria of naturalness that
we have discussed so far. But since criteria for the linguist may not be criteria for the native speaker, I want to mention those that I think to be at any
rate psychologically real for the native speaker/hearer in order to attribute
default status to a rule. Of course, this will have to be confirmed by appropriate experiments, but first, as is usual in such artificial intelligence inspired studies, one has to generate concepts and hypotheses:

5.20.8.3.1. As already illustrated in 5.20.8.2.1, the degree of phonological
iconicity (5.18) must be an important factor in default assignment. E.g., both
in German and in Breton (Dressler 1972), various vowels can be and have been
weakened to [ə][319] in casual speech. However, in the most formal stypes only
unstressed /ɛ/ may be backgrounded to [ə]. Why has just this one weakening process expanded from casual to formal speech? One answer is that /ɛ/ → [ə] is
phonologically more iconic than /a/ → [ə] or /i/ → [ə], etc., because [ə] is in
both languages a (lower) lax mid vowel and rather more front than back. Note
that in both languages --much more so in German-- many other vowels have been
reanalyzed as /ɛ/, e.g., OHG *sing-an* 'to sing' became MHG *sing-en*, with the following reanalysis of the unstressed vowel: /a/ → [ə] > /ɛ/ → [ə]. Thus [ə] has
and has had for a long time in both languages /ɛ/ as its primary synchronic
source, i.e., as its default input. Similarly in languages with phonemic final
devoicing, the voiceless obstruent is the default input, and diachronic restructurings have always or predominantly gone in this direction, such as the well-

known examples G. *weg* /vɛk/ = Yidd. *(a)vek* 'away' with /g/ > /k/ vs. G. *Weg* (with [k]), gen. *Weg-es* ['veːgəs] 'way'.

5.20.8.3.2. At least the child in language acquisition should use process matching (5.1f). A candidate for default assignment must be either a PR which can be matched with a universal phonological process type, or if none of the competing rules can, then the one which is most similar to such a process type should be chosen.

5.20.8.3.3. Productivity (5.13) must play a role in default assignment (cf. 5. 20.8.2.3), both phonological and morphological productivity. Among competing rules, the most productive one should be assigned the default status. Both phonological and morphological productivity have been proven to be accessible to native speakers in psycholinguistic experiments.[320] This criterion is also in line with the earlier concepts 'major rule', 'elsewhere condition', 'typical- ness' (5.20.8.2.2).

5.20.8.3.4. Do these criteria come into conflict? The second one (process matching, 5.20.8.3.2) may be superseded in the adult native speaker in the way that universal properties may be superseded by phenomena of language specific system adequacy in general,[321] but it may reappear in second language acquisi- tion (5.13.5).

   If a PR is totally productive, then either there is no conflict with a pu- tative, but non-existing more iconic rule, i.e., with biunique PRs such as Rus- sian palatalization, Spanish lenition of stops in intervocalic position, etc. (5.20.1), so there is certainty about input-output relations and no default as- signment is needed; or in case of competition between rules, or parts of rules for the same output (in retrieval/inference), the more iconic one is always the default rule. E.g., in case of Latin rhotacism s → r / V__V, the preservation rule /r/ → [r] is the default rule in inference, and not rhotacism even when it was totally productive. The same holds for final devoicing (4.20.8.3.1), where two parts of rules compete, e.g., /d/ → [t] and /t/ → [t].

5.20.8.3.5. A default rule is a rule which is to be chosen in either derivation or inference 'in the absence of explicit information to the contrary' (5.20.8.2. 1); let us call the inverse an exception rule. This information may concern

The larger phonological context. E.g., in those German dialects that Dinnsen (1982) refers to (5.20.6), [raːt] goes back to *Rat* 'advice', [raːˑt] to *Rad* 'wheel'. Thus the default inference /t/ → [t] is superseded by the explicit condition: 'In case of an extra-long vowel before final fortis, the input is the corresponding lenis.' And similarly in all instances of traces or transparent rule interaction (5.20.7.0). All such rules are PRs. In German dialects where *Rat* (masculine) and *Rad* (neuter) have the same phonetic representation [raːt], the default inference *Rat* may be superseded by morphological, syntactic, or semantic information coming from the context.

5.20.8.3.6. Phonological and morphological information is involved in other cases. Let us take the inferential analysis of [ə] in E. *kiss-es* ['kisəz], *ash-es*, *breez-es*, etc. This [ə] could go back to many vowels, such as the [ə] in ['njuwtən] (5.20.3.5). By historic accident there exist Latinate words and names such as *bonus*, *census*, *Jesus*, *Horace* with final [əs], but apparently none with final [səz, zəz, šəz, žəz, čəz, ǰəz]. Here the phonological information establishes the default. Thus it is a fairly safe default inference to recover ə-insertion in *kisses*. If there existed words of foreign origin in [səz], etc., then the morphological information 'plural; Saxon genitive; 3.sg. present' would be needed in addition. But ə-insertion would still be a PR as long as *[sz#, zz#, šz#, žz#, čz#, ǰz#] remain unpronounceable.

5.20.8.3.7. Other unique PRs with morphological conditioning previously discussed are G. /ɛː/ → [æː] and Breton /ɛ/ → [ə] (5.20.3.2). If we compare them with Latin rhotacism (5.20.8.3.4, 5.20.5), then we see that the former two rules represent very clearly defined morphological exceptions to the more iconic default preservation rule /ɛ/ → [ɛ], whereas rhotacism originally did not: The phonological condition / v_v in *honōs*, gen. *honōr-is* 'honor', *herī* 'yesterday' (adj. *hes-ternus*), the first -*r*- in *soror* 'sister' held also for the preservation rule /r/ → [r] in *soror*, gen. *sorōr-is*. Therefore *herī* and *soror* were restructured by default as /herī, sorōr/, and synchronic rhotacism was restricted to well-defined morphological categories such as neuters (*genus*, gen. *gener-is* 'gender') and monosyllables (*flōs*, gen. *flōr-is* 'flower'), cf. 5.2.7.3. Then the general preservation rule /s/ → [s] became again the default rule in derivation also in the phonological context / v_v.

For the various roles of morphological factors, see 5.9.

5.20.8.3.8. Other 'explicit information to the contrary' may be lexical exceptions (5.10). E.g., to the morphological default conditions of Latin (cf. 5.20.
8.3.7): 'Use in derivation rhotacism in the declension of monosyllables in *-s*'
there are lexical exceptions such as *bōs*, gen. *bōv-is* 'cattle', *sūs*, gen. *su-is*
'pig', and *vās*, gen. *vās-is* 'vase', where /s/ is preserved. These lexical exceptions had to be learned by rote,[322] like the few original lexical exceptions
(e.g., *asinus* 'donkey'), before rhotacism was restricted to certain morphological categories. The inverted AMR r → s / __+{s, t} (perfect; derived adjectives), as in *gerō* 'I lead', perfect *ges-s-ī*, perfect participle *ges-tu-s* is a
lexicalized exception rule itself and can be assigned non-lexical default value
only if more morphological and phonological information is added: (1) the trace
of a deletion rule blocks it as in *torqueō*, *tor-s-ī*, *tor-tu-s* 'I turn', (2) the
participle is in *-s-tus* only if the active perfect has no *-r-* (as in *aperiō*,
aperuī, *apertus* 'open'). But the formulation of such default assumptions would
be less economical than lexical learning by rote.[323]

5.20.8.3.9. If general lexical conditions can be stated such as in loanwords
(cf. 5.3.2), default assumptions can be formulated, e.g., for Russian: 'No palatalization in non-integrated foreign words' (but see Holden 1976 on the gradual
application of palatalization), or for English: 'Velar softening of /k, g/ in
Latinate words before Latinate suffixes starting with /i/.'

5.20.8.4.0. To recapitulate our discussion of 'default', we can suppose that
default assumptions play a role in all MPRs and at lease in some AMRs, but also
in some PRs. Thus they too are not a clear criterion for neatly differentiating
MPRs from PRs and AMRs. Nevertheless we can establish the following (phonological default) scale: Biunique PRs (uniqueness scale 1-3), where no default assumptions are necessary, must have score 1. First order default rules have
score 2 and are PRs. Second order default rules may be the term for those rules
which formulate exceptions to first order rules but themselves have no exceptions. They may be PRs, but all MPRs and AMRs fall into this class.[324]

Moreover, default assumptions seem to be useful for diachronic changes,
provided that we always look at both derivation (production) and inference (reception).

5.20.8.4.1. Biunique PRs,[325] where no default assumptions are necessary (score

1), are the most stable rules (with gradual differentiations as mentioned in 5.
20.1f). They are symmetric in derivation and inference. They can develop to
MPRs only if other rules (including preservation rules as in loanwords) come to
interfere with them so that they become unique. Symmetric relationships are
more stable than asymmetric ones. Conversely, the other case of symmetry, non-
uniqueness, is stable in the sense that no non-unique AMR or MPR may become
unique (or even a biunique PR) by itself, but only by loss of a rule or sub-
rule. Unique PRs may remain PRs either if in inference (retrieval in perception) they do not have any competitor (i.e., if no ambiguity is created, 5.20.
3.1f) or if in case of ambiguous inference (5.20.3.3f) they are default rules
of reception, where the default assumption can be stated in phonological terms
(score 2), e.g., in reference to phonological iconicity (5.20.8.3.1), to a
larger structure, or to traces. (This holds also for deletion PRs, 5.20.3.7).
Clearly rules must be more stable if they are default rules in both ways (derivation and inference) than if they are default rules in one way and exceptions
in the other way.

5.20.8.4.2. In addition, totally or partially allophonic PRs cannot be morphologized (5.20.3.1, 5.20.3.3, 5.20.3.5) even if they do not fulfill the above mentioned conditions (5.20.8.4.1). However, if a PR becomes phonemic and must be
formulated as an exception rule in inference (reception) but can still be formulated as a default rule in derivation (production), it is a PR liable to be easily morphologized, e.g., Latin rhotacism (default: s → r / v__v vs. default: [r]
← /r/, exception: [r] ← /s/, even in intervocalic position). In contrast, a
partially allophonic PR such as the Italian assimilation of /n/[326] in articulatory place to the following obstruent (cf. 5.20.3.3) (e.g., in *cinque* 'five',
trionfo 'triumph') cannot be an exception rule where the allophones [ɲ, ŋ] are
concerned, because all instances of [ɲ, ŋ] come from /n/, as opposed to [m],
which has /m/ as its default source.

Now I hypothesize that exception rules (even if only exceptional from the
inferential point of view) tend to fade away, i.e., to become more exceptional,
unless one of two conditions is fulfilled (5.20.8.4.3 and 5.20.8.4.5):

5.20.8.4.3. If the exception holds for a large set of items that is formulated
in a general way (phonologically, morphologically, or lexically) or if it holds
only for a few lexical items, easily learned by rote (e.g., Latin *r* → *s*, 5.20.

8.3.8). Thus it expresses an exceptionless subregularity or it is a default rule by itself (for this subset of items); here a general or default condition usually can be formulated neither phonologically nor lexically (unless there are clearly differentiated lexical strata) but only morphologically. E.g., when Latin rhatacism acquired too many disparate exceptions (cf. lexical ones like *asinus* 'donkey', phonological ones (dissimilatory) such as *rosa* 'rose'), no phonological or lexical generalization could be formulated for the default assumption either in derivation or in inference. As for morphology, no single, but only several morphological generalizations were possible (5.20.8.3.6); thus the application of rhotacism became more and more restricted.

5.20.8.4.4. If we compare German and English umlaut, then the MPR (and later AMR) of umlaut in German could be formulated as a default for derivation in morphological subcategories such as the plural *Kämm-e* 'comb-s' from masc. *Kamm*, and in this very category umlaut has expanded, i.e., lexical exceptions have diminished in time, cf. 5.12.7.

Due to the loss of morphological subcategories (inflectional paradigms) in English, no default could be formulated for English umlaut plurals. Thus they remained lexical exceptions, i.e., they gradually faded away, e.g., *cow*, pl. *cy* > *cyne* (like *brethr-en*) > *cow-s*. As the result of elimination of a MPR or PR, biuniqueness can be restored (Eliasson 1977:104, 107).

5.20.8.4.5. The status and fate of sociolinguistically variable exception rules is quite different. Whereas fading MPRs or AMRs are obligatory for most items and optional just for a few items simultaneously (i.e., for those for which the application of the rule is about to be withdrawn), variable PRs of speech styles are largely optional. For these --despite much sociolinguistic work done in many schools of thought-- application cannot be precisely predicted, i.e., no general conditions are available, but only either sociolinguistic defaults or preferences.[327] Diachronically the application of such PRs frequently expands, e.g., by lexical diffusion (Wang 1977) or by sociolinguistic change from below or above (Labov 1972) or by loans from casual speech into more formal speech styles (Dressler 1973, 1975b). In contrast to the afore-mentioned rules and rule changes, these diffusion processes are predominantly determined by social/ sociopsychological factors which play no role in those other changes.

5.20.8.4.6. Proponents of lexical diffusion (e.g., Wang 1977, Bailey 1973) and others have shown that in all cases they have investigated, the degree of application of a rule changes like an S-curve. I.e., a rule applies for a long time to a small number of items it could apply to, and for a long time to 80% or more of these items (before it reaches total generality), but for a very short period to 40%, 50%, or 60%.

This follows automatically from the assumption that of two or more rules (including preservation rules) competing for the same items, one must be the default rule, the other(s) the exception rule(s). Thus the S-curve displays the sudden switch of a rule from the status of an exception rule to that of the default rule in diffusion, and the reverse in fading.

5.20.8.5. Default concepts may prove helpful for synchronic phonological analysis as well:[328]

5.20.8.5.1. A central debate of generative phonology has been over abstractness of underlying segments and over rules changing them into quite different surface segments.[329] First, Postal's (1968:53ff) naturalness condition eliminated phonologically non-interpretable underlying segments used by some phonematicians.[330] Then Kiparsky (1973b [1968], 1982a:127ff) proposed the 'alternation condition' and later[331] the 'revised alternation condition', which prevent the linguist (and, as it is believed, the native speaker as well) from reconstructing abstract underlying segments in the total absence of alternation; e.g., in the case of German final devoicing a final /g/ for non-alternating [k] in [vɛk] (cf. 5.20.8.3.1). Kaye used recoverability and Eliasson inferability for the same purpose (cf. 5.20.7). And proponents of Natural Generative Phonology proposed even more stringent constraints.[332] Now such proposals can be elevated from phonology to a higher level of discussion by using the concept of default: If we take the example [vɛk], then /vɛk/ is the default inference (1) because /k/ → [k] or [kʰ] is more iconic than /g/ → [k], (2) because underlying voiced stops, with very few exceptions, nearly never occur after short vowels in German.

5.20.8.5.2. Trubetzkoy (1939) and other phonematicians have worked with archiphonemes in cases of neutralizations, e.g., /T/ (unspecified for [±voice]) for /t/ and /d/ in final devoicing. Others too[333] have argued for partially specified archisegments. Stampe[334] excludes such assumptions in his analysis because he considers an underlying segment to represent the phonological intention of the speaker; if this intention happens to be unpronounceable for the speaker in a given environment, then he adapts it by using a PR. Clearly the speaker must intend a specified segment.[336] In this way unspecified segments are banned from the derivational (production) direction of phonological mapping.

If we use the concept of default, we must criticize archisegments from the inferential direction as well: If the listener or learner makes an inferential default assumption about the possible input, he cannot have the choice open between various segments by inferring /T/ for /t/ or /d/ (see above) or an unspecified nasal archiphoneme /N/ for /n, m, ɲ/ in Italian nasal assimilation (5.20.3.3, 5.20.8.4.2); he must decide, by default, on one definite alternative.

5.20.9. Most adherents of structural phonematics make a great distinction between allophonic distribution and phonemic alternation or neutralization.[337] Some (post-SPE) generative phonologists have followed suit by sharply contrasting allomorphic and morphophonemic rules.[338] This distinction cannot coincide (as Trubetzkoy thought) with the distinction between phonology and morphonology because the class of neutralizing phonemic PRs (5.20.3.4) which express automatic neutralizations is general, fully productive, etc., and thus clearly belongs to phonology.[339]

This disturbing set of PRs would be reduced or even collapsed with allophonic PRs if Dinnsen's (1982) suspicion were correct that such rules do not effect complete phonetic neutralization in production (5.20.6). However, it is doubtful whether this radical extension of Dinnsen's (1982) and others' observation is true; and there would still remain Dinnsen's (1982) class of perceptually neutralizing rules.

Therefore we may maintain our results that also in respect to uniqueness, neutralization, recoverability, etc., there is a gradual continuum between phonology and morphonology and thus return to Baudouin de Courtenay's (1985) old position (1) on the synchronic typology of gradual differences within and between phonology and morphology, (2) on the gradual diachronic change from phonological to morphonological and morphological phenomena.

5.21. Conclusion

5.21.0. A process model such as ours puts emphasis on rules (1). Therefore morphonology can be characterized by characterizing MPRs. At the end of this descriptive chapter devoted to the distinction of PRs, MPRs, and AMRs, we may then sum up the properties of MPRs. But anyone who expects a catalogue of exceptionless definitions and tight distinctions will be disappointed, for MPRs --like many other categories--[340] have fuzzy boundaries. Nevertheless many properties cluster, often only by default.

Let us first recapitulate properties any MPR must have (5.21.1) or has by default (5.21.2), then enumerate those properties of a rule that tell us that this rule either must be a MPR (5.21.3) or is a MPR by default (5.21.4) or that this rule must be either a MPR or an AMR (5.21.5) or that this rule must be either a MPR or a PR (5.21.5). Then diachronic/developmental properties of MPRs are enumerated (5.21.7).

5.21.1. All MPRs (of the word domain) have the following properties:

5.21.1.1. They attain score 5 on the scale of phonological domains (5.8.6f), i.e., they have both phonological and morphological domains -- but this is true for certain subclasses of PRs and AMRs as well.

5.21.1.2. No MPR is a phonostylistic rule sensitive to the parameters of either speed of pronunciation or of formality/casualness of the speech situation (in the sense of 5.11) -- but this is true for all obligatory PRs and, apparently, for all AMRs as well.

5.21.1.3. MPRs seem to be extrinsically ordered among themselves if an elsewhere condition is included under this heading (5.17.2f) -- but this holds for AMRs and, apparently, some PRs as well.

5.21.1.4. The outputs of all MPRs are phonemes (5.18.2.1) and thus they attain score 4 on the phonological iconicity scale (5.18.3.1) -- the same for all AMRs and certain PRs.

5.21.1.5. In their structural change MPRs change at least one (phonological distinctive) feature value (5.18.3.4) -- item all AMRs, all (quasi-)phonemic PRs (including phonostylistic PRs), some allophonic PRs.

5.21.1.6. All MPRs are (phonologically) opaque (5.20.6) -- item all AMRs and some PRs.

5.21.1.7. Their output is neutralizing (5.20.3.3-7) and thus they attain score 5 on the phonological uniqueness scale (5.20.4) -- item all AMRs and certain subclasses of PRs.

5.21.1.8. If we combine properties, we can state that MPRs are non-general (or non-automatic) neutralizing rules (5.20.4) -- item many AMRs and some PRs (notably certain phonostylistic and lexically diffusing PRs).

5.21.1.9. This enumeration is not impressive, neither in quantity (compared with the numerous criteria proposed in the literature) nor in quality (no property excludes all AMRs and PRs, all properties hold even for many AMRs and some PRs).

5.21.2. MPRs have even fewer properties by default.

5.21.2.1. Generally MPRs attain score 3 on the scale of aid to pronunciation (5.6.3-5) -- item some AMRs; most AMRs and some MPRs attain score 4.

5.21.2.2. Generally MPRs are ordered between AMRs and PRs (5.17.1).

5.21.2.3. Thus, generally, their inputs are phonemes (5.18.1) -- item AMRs and neutralizing PRs.

5.21.3. Let us turn around now and scrutinize which properties assign a rule under investigation unambiguously to the class of MPRs. The result of our scrutiny is: ZERO. There is no single property which belongs to MPRs only. The same result has been obtained in the much less ample scrutiny of Dressler (1977g, 1977a:9).

5.21.4. The following two properties refer to MPRs by default:

5.21.4.1. If a rule is blocked by a morphological boundary, it is usually a MPR (5.9.1), rarely a PR, never an AMR. Notice that only the smaller part of MPRs fulfill this criterion.

5.21.4.2.   If a rule attains score 3 on the scale of aid to pronounceability it is usually a MPR (5.6.3-5) -- rules of score 1 and 2 must be PRs, rules of score 4 are AMRs by default, but there are MPRs of score 4 and AMRs of score 3.

5.21.5.   The following two properties never pertain to AMRs, but only to PRs and to MPRs:

5.21.5.1.   if a rule applies productively to the outputs of word games (5.13.3),

5.21.5.2.   if there is evidence for psychological reality in the acquisition of writing (5.15).

5.21.6.   Interestingly, many more properties never pertain to PRs, but only to MPRs and to AMRs:

5.21.6.1.   if a rule attains score 2-4 on the scale of process matching (5.2.6);

5.21.6.2.   if a rule attains score 3-4 on the scale of aid to pronounceability (5.6.3.5);

5.21.6.3.   if the application of a rule is restricted to morphological categories (5.9.5), unless it is a PR of casual speech or, maybe, a lexically diffusing PR;

5.21.6.4.   if the application of a rule is lexically restricted (5.10.6f), unless it is a PR of casual speech or a lexically diffusing PR;

5.21.6.5.   if a rule is not always applied in morphological neologisms (5.13.1.6);

5.21.6.6.   if a rule is never applied in psycholinguistic experiments (5.13.4);

5.21.6.7.   if a rule is never applied in foreign language learning (5.13.5) in transfer from L_1 to L_2, unless L_1 and L_2 are very similar in morphology and phonology;

5.21.6.8. if a rule is not always applied in speech errors (5.14);

5.21.6.9. if a rule is not generally applied in rhyming and alliteration (5. 16);

5.21.6.10. if the phonological condition is non-adjacent (5.19.3).

5.21.6.11. By default, the application of a PR is not limited to a single morphological category, whereas an AMR must be, and a MPR often is (5.9.5.1).

5.21.6.12. The fact that many more properties refer to both MPRs and AMRs than to both MPRs and PRs (5.21.5) may have induced so many scholars to consider morphonology as part of morphology and to lump MPRs and AMRs together as morphophonemic rules or alternations.

5.21.7. Diachronic/developmental properties of MPRs are:

5.21.7.1. MPRs originate as PRs and may develop further to AMRs (5.2.7, 5.4.7, 5.6.6, 5.8.5, 5.10.8) by acquiring morphological and reducing phonological domains (5.8.7, 5.9.7). This development is unidirectional (5.18.6-8) and can be understood as (unidirectional) de-iconization (5.18.8), removal from biuniqueness (5.20.0), accumulation of opacity (5.20.5).

5.21.7.2. MPRs may be subject to lexical fading (5.12.5, 5.20.8.4.2ff), also many AMRs.

5.21.7.3. MPRs and AMRs may be lost (5.12.6, PRs only under very specific conditions) so that biuniqueness can be restored (5.20.8.4.5).

5.21.7.4. MPRs --in contradistinction to both PRs and AMRs-- may not expand/ generalize in diachronic change (5.12.7).

5.21.7.5. MPRs may be loaned under very restricted conditions (less so for AMRs, much less so for PRs, 5.13.6).

5.21.8. Many properties used in the literature have been reduced to other criteria that fit better into our descriptive (and explanatory) system; other
properties seem to have, unfortunately, too little discriminatory power for the
moment: regularity (5.4), exclusion from specific morphological categories (5.
9.4), generality/automaticity (5.12.4), productivity in loanword integration (5.
13.2).

5.21.9. The enumeration of these properties (5.21.1-8) confirms the view that
there is no distinct level or component of morphonology. Nevertheless, it has
become clear that most PRs and most AMRs are quite different from MPRs and that
the PRs or AMRs which resemble MPRs are relatively few. In other words, there
are prototypical PRs and AMRs and, to a lesser degree, prototypical MPRs which
properties of PRs and AMRs, and there are in-between rules.

5.21.10. I do not attempt a hierarchy of properties here because this fits better the explanatory part (10). Some of the examples given in this chapter may
be observationally inadequate, I may have misinterpreted relevant data, and I am
sure to have overlooked relevant data available in books and journals. At least
I hope that I have provided a framework within which such defects can be easily
discussed and improved. But I believe that these improvements will not easily
change the global picture.

I add two detailed descriptive case-studies on Italian and Polish rules.

Notes

1. Cf. 1, 10.7.1.

2. For the latest appraisal, see Manaster-Ramer 1984, cf. 5.

3. Baudouin de Courtenay 1895, Kilbury 1976, Haslev 1972:115ff, Kuryłowicz 1968, Hooper 1976:84ff, Kiparsky 1982a:54ff, 199ff, Klausenburger 1979, Roberge 1980, Dressler 1977g.

4. Most radically criticized in 'developmental linguistics' (Bailey 1973, 1982, cf. W. Mayerthaler 1981, E. Mayerthaler 1982).

5. I.e., of a morphological, lexical, sociolinguistic, psycholinguistic, etc. nature.

6. Zwicky 1975b, Derwing 1979, Singh 1981; cf. 4.4.1.4, 5.6.2.3, 5.9.4.

7. Dobó 1980, Rédei 1978:47f, 1975:104, 112; cf. 5.10.2.

8. Darden 1977, Kenstowicz & Kisseberth 1977:56.

9. Skousen 1975:56ff, 106ff, Holman 1975, Comrie 1979, Hellberg 1983.

10. E.g., I have not come across any (uniquely) plausible synchronic matching with four processes so far.

11. Dressler 1977g:325, 1980c:106ff, Vennemann 1972e.

12. This mutual exclusion of perceptual backgrounding and foregrounding must be strictly separated from the ideal combination of perceptual foregrounding and greater ease of articulation; see 4.3.3.2, 4.6.

13. Hyman 1975:173ff, Wang 1969, Mayerthaler 1976:117ff, Hooper 1976:90, Dressler 1977a:26f, Hogg 1979:80, Roberge 1980, Kenstowicz 1981:434ff.

14. If one starts with an input /au/, then process matching is not possible any more.

14a. Wang 1969, Vennemann 1972e, Plank 1975, Magnus 1973, Baxter 1974:II, Schindler 1976, Hyman 1975:176ff, 183ff, 1977:410ff, Dressler 1977a:27, 1977g: 319f, Klausenberger 1979 (cf. E. Mayerthaler 1981:137). Earlier, Kuryłowicz often dealt with the interchange of 'terme de fondation' (A in A → B) and 'terme fondé' (B in A → B).

15. Dressler 1977a:21, 52, 27f, 1977g: §3.2, 3.4.2.4.

16. Cf. Dressler 1977a:29f, Ralph 1977:173.

17. Dressler 1977a:59f. In the case of rule inversion there is an interaction with MRs (cf. 10.8.3.5.2) or PRs. Wurzel (1981a:424ff) gives an excellent classification of interactions among PRs which result in dephonologication of one of the PRs concerned, but he underrates the simultaneous morphological factor; cf. 10.8.6.9f.

18. Bjarkman 1975:68, Knudson 1975:39, Dressler 1977g:317ff, 1977a:26f, 32, 51, 60, Cena 1978, Hooper 1979c:108f, Comrie 1979, Roberge 1980. For earlier work, see Kilbury 1976:21ff, Baudouin de Courtenay 1895:31ff, 61, 86, 93; cf. 5.18.6.

19. For (ir)regularity of alternations in Bloomfieldian morphophonemics, cf. Kilbury 1976:47.

20. For critical discussion, cf. Istre 1981, Lass 1976:168ff, Hyman 1975:139ff, 147ff.

21. If a language has /l/ and /ł/, then velarization applies to /ł/ vacuously, whereas in Mangarayi (Merlan 1982:180) both the alveolar and the retroflex laterals velarize.

22. This solves part of the hierarchy problem; cf. 4.2.2, Rennison 1979. Note that very abstract solutions may posit spurious regularities at an underlying level; cf. the critique by Elson 1975.

23. There may be problems with allophonic fast speech PRs, but nobody would mistake such PRs for MPRs or AMRs anyway.

24. See Anderson & Browne (1973) for this and similar examples; cf. Darden 1979:87f, Kenstowicz & Kisseberth (1977:87) on a Yuma exchange rule.

25. Cf. Hyman 1977. This belongs to what Vennemann (1972:184ff), following H. Schuchardt, calls 'phonetic analogy'; cf. Ralph 1977:173.

26. See Mel'čuk 1976, 1982:110ff.

27. Cf. Schwarze 1970, Werner 1977, Mayerthaler 1977:138f, Plank 1981:29ff, Roberge 1980, Rudes 1980; cf. 1.10.

28. Bach & Harms 1972, Zwicky 1975b:159ff, Hooper 1976:132f, Walker 1975:191f, Dressler 1977a:10, 32, 45ff (critically p. 37), Donegan & Stampe 1979b, Hogg 1979:80, Roberge 1980; for a critique, see Dinnsen 1978.

29. Hooper 1976:176 (if one presses her use of 'phonetically motivated'), Dressler 1977g:317ff; only AMRs: Wurzel 1981a, Benhallam 1977.

29a. Hooper 1976:89, Dressler 1977a:29, Comrie 1979:59, Roberge 1980, Hellberg 1980:4f, Wurzel 1980c:450.

30. /k', g'/ are written q, gj.

31. Stampe 1980, Donegan & Stampe 1979b:144, Hooper 1979c, Bjarkman 1975:68ff, Ford & Singh 1983a, 1983b; on perceptibility, see Ułaszyn 1931, Manaster-Ramer 1984.

32. Donegan & Stampe 1979:144, Donegan 1978:5; earlier noted by M. Kruszewski, cf. Kilbury 1976:26f.

33. Dressler 1972:56ff, Rubach 1976b: This renders the concept of 'surface phonetic constraints' or well-formedness conditions (Ford & Singh 1983) highly dubious; cf. 9.1.9.

34. In contrast to disyllabic sibilants in *dis$service, grass$snake, mis$shapen, goose$step, fish$slice, church$service*, etc. In *dis#satisfaction* /s#s/ is degeminated in syllable-initial position. I.e., in syllable-initial position two sibilants are assimilated and degeminated, whereas in syllable-final position vowel insertion applies (which aids perceptibility as well).

35. According to all adherents of Natural Phonology; see 5.6.22; cf. Kalnyn' 1981:207.

36. Cf. Linell 1979b:180ff, Roberge 1980, Kubrjakova & Pankrac 1983, Rischel 1984:354ff.

37. Cf. Karlsson 1974:32, Hooper 1976; critical: Kalnyn' 1981:206.

38. Cf. Dressler 1977a:50f, Linell 1979b:181f; cf. 5.11.5f.

39. E.g., Kubrjakova & Kankrac 1983:18, Ford & Singh 1983:65f.

40. Or: c___D where x contains supplementary information about A, e.g., pro-
    X   sodic, morphological, syntactic, lexical specifications.

41. Particularly in some dialects (e.g., Dressler & Hufgard 1980) allophonic
    [β] is derived from /b/ in casual speech.

42. For the history of exception devices in generative phonology, see Zonnefeld
    1978.

43. Cf. the critiques in Roberge 1980, Nyman 1980; cf. 10.3.

44. Cf. 5.5.2, Linell 1979b:181, Kenstowicz 1981; cf. 10.5.

45. Syntactic factors refer either to sentence (mor)phonology (2.4.1f) or to
    rule ordering (cf. 5.17.1.5f).

46. E.g., Vennemann 1974b, 1981, Skousen 1975:99, Hooper 1976:14f, Hyman 1978:
    22; more differentiated: Linell 1979b:180ff, 193.

47. Also the pause domain belongs here, i.e., the criterion whether rules can
    be blocked by intervening pauses: only PRs seem to be, according to work
    done so far; see Mohanan 1982:78ff, Ford & Singh 1983:12.

48. Cf. 1.3.4, and for Polish, Kenstowicz & Kisseberth 1979:418ff.

49. Wurzel 1970:209ff, Herok & Tonelli 1977, Dressler 1981a.

50. Selkirk 1980a, de Ceseris 1981; cf. Kenstowicz & Kisseberth 1979:411ff.

50a. Outside the scope of this book; cf. 2.4, 3.1.4.1, 3.3.2; cf. Selkirk
    1980a:114ff, Mascaró 1978:19 (Catalan fricative voicing).

51. Dressler 1977g:315, 320, 323 (where possible ambisyllabicity was neglect-
    ed).

52. Such as in speech errors (slips); cf. Fromkin 1973:18f, 125.

53. Selkirk 1980a:119ff, Schindler 1976:622.

54. A counterexample might be constituted by Hock 1979.

56. However, alternative formulations of this umlaut rule can avoid this prob-
    lem; notice *Bischof* 'bishop', adj. *bischöf-lich*, *Mittag* 'mid-day', adj.
    mittäg-lich, and the possibility of deriving *-er* in *Bauer* from underlying
    /r/, i.e., /baor/, so that *bäuer-lich* may be bisyllabic in the input repre-
    sentation (see Wurzel 1970:170ff, 106ff, Rennison 1981). Yet umlaut in
    -isch-formation is still productive, but not long-distance formations with
    -lich.

57. Clearly the claim (tentatively in Donegan & Stampe 1979a) that only PRs,
    but not MPRs or AMRs may refer to prosodic domains such as to the position
    of accent/stress is wrong (cf. Dressler 1977a:10 point 33).

58. Cf. Kenstowicz & Kisseberth 1977:63ff.

59. Cf. Kenstowicz & Kisseberth 1977:83ff (where morphological and phonological
    word boundaries are not distinguished, nor in Stanley 1973:187ff); cri-
    tique in Ohlander 1976:141ff; cf. Rubach 1981:175, Angenot & Dillinger
    1981:70ff.

60. These cases refute Rubach's (1977:159) implicit view that the application
    of phonostylistic processes would not be delimited by morpheme boundaries.

61. Stanley 1973:189ff, Langdon 1975:223ff.

62. In Imbabura Quechua (Cole 1982:200, 211f) /p, t, k/ are voiced when they
     follow a nasal, but the affricate /č/ changes to [ž] only when it follows a
     nasal and a boundary; note that /č/ → [ž] involves a greater structural
     change than /p/ → [b], etc., and must be matched to two universal process
     types rather than to a single lenition process.

63. For the most detailed description, see Ternes 1970:141ff, 331f, 341f; cf.
     Allen 1975.

64. Other examples in Hyman 1978, Booij 1977:81ff (cf. van Marle 1978).

65. Thus Angenot & Dillinger (1981:68ff) and Gaspar de Oliveira (1981:127) are
     not justified in putting morpheme boundaries at a par with boundaries of
     prosodic phonology.

66. Or in the stronger form: 'non-automatic neutralization processes.' Cf. on
     generality 5.12.1. For critical appraisals, cf. Kenstowicz & Kisseberth
     1977:210ff, Manaster-Ramer 1984, Orešnik 1979 (who further restricts Kipar-
     sky's constraint by eliminating the factor of morpheme boundaries), . An-
     derson 1980:76ff, Selkirk 1980:122ff; cf. Kiparsky 1982b.

67. Hock 1979, who revises previous simplified treatments.

68. As in Orešnik's (1979) Icelandic rule v → b / V__l{v, #}.

69. Another candidate for PR status is context-sensitive Basque palatalization,
     restricted to derived environments, cf. Iverson & Oñederra 1983.

70. These rules are termed major rules (with exceptions) in Generative Phonol-
     ogy, and exceptions may be subdivided into cases where an input fails to
     undergo a rule, and others where an environment fails to trigger a rule,
     cf. Kenstowicz & Kisseberth 1977:124f, Zonneveld 1978:143ff.

71. For counter-arguments against such rules in Finnish see Skousen 1975:59ff.
     But note the examples in Picard 1977, 1981, Darden 1982.

72. Labov 1970:53ff, 1975:49ff; cf. Kiparsky 1982:89f, 104, 115.

73. Zonneveld 1978:132ff, Darden 1981; cf. 5.9.4 note 70. But minor rules are
     usually defined by positive rule features in the lexicon (on words as lexi-
     cal entries, cf. 5.10), whereas purely morphological information is often
     neglected. Therefore our class has been better identified in structural
     morphonology; see Kilbury 1976:20.

74. Barkai 1975, Farrar 1977; cf. 5.10.

75. E.g., cf. Ternes 1970:141ff, 331f, 341f (in idiomatic morphosyntactic cate-
     gories within the phrase as well). For other examples, see Kenstowicz &
     Kisseberth 1977:71ff, 79ff, 1979:401ff; Capanahua deletion of present
     tense a (Loos 1969:145f); Greenlandic consonant deletion and spirantiza-
     tion (Rischel 1974:154, 156, 209ff, 242ff); Roberge 1980; Dell 1978; the
     inverted AMR of Latin rhotacism, 5.2.5; Bulg. k, g → c, z before pl. -i,
     especially in certain derivational suffixes (Bjørnflaten 1981); many con-
     sonant assimilations in Maung prefixes vs. suffixes vs. particles (Capell &
     Hinch 1970:35ff).

76. If the vowel of is is deleted in fast/casual speech after sibilants, then
     [ə, ɨ, ɪ] (different qualities according to the respective dialects) is in-
     serted (Zwicky 1975b).

77. More examples in Dressler 1972:51, 53, 55, 1973:133, 135f, 1975b:224, 1977a:50, Wodak & Dressler 1978:42, Linell 1979b:181f; cf. 5.11.6.

78. A state of affairs which many phonologists seem to regard as an absolute constraint on phonologicalness, e.g., adherents of Natural Generative Phonology: Vennemann 1972c, 1974b, 1978, 1981, Hooper 1976, 1979b.

79. Dressler 1977g:324ff, 1977a:20, 28f; cf. Klausenburger 1979:37ff, Roberge 1980; cf. 10.7f.

80. Dressler 1977g:324ff.

81. See Dressler 1977a:28f; cf. Vennemann 1974a, Mayerthaler 1977:153ff; cf. Kiparsky 1982a:64f, 99ff, Klausenburger 1979:37ff, Roberge 1980, Janda 1982.

82. Wurzel 1980c:448ff, 1981:425; cf. Russ 1975:57ff, Janda 1983. Robinson (1976) includes this in his notion 'scattered rule'. For research in Icelandic umlaut, see the survey by Benediktsson 1982.

83. Therefore I cannot follow Morin's (1983) suppletion analysis.

84. Benhallam (1979), by defining MPRs as 'phonologically plausible and applying in a lexical environment,' overestimates lexical factors greatly.

85. Cf. Zonneveld 1978:128ff, 150f, 193ff, Kenstowicz & Kisseberth 1977:113ff, 1979:393ff, Odden 1981. On a hierarchy of 'costliness' of lexical exceptions, see Kiparsky 1982b. Cf. Derwing & Baker 1977:91. Lexical items, not morphemes are marked, cf. Bochner 1981.

86. Saciuk 1969, 1974, Walker 1975; and earlier: Mathesius 1934, Fries & Pike 1949, Benton 1971.

87. For lexical diffusion, cf. Lass 1969:141, Dressler 1978c:152.

88. Jensen 1959:20ff, Meillet 1936:20f, 63, 168, 170, 191.

89. I have to thank Ralph P. Ritter (Berlin) for the following examples from FB = P'awstos Biwzandaçi and MX = Movsēs Xorenaçi.

90. If lost, a [ə] would be inserted between the two /s/'s: *[ĭisə'seː]; cf. Dressler 1980c.

91. Baudouin de Courtenay 1895:72ff, 62ff, 24, 30, Kilbury 1976:27, Pilch 1965, Kučera 1958; critically Waight 1980, Chomsky & Halle 1968:174, Saciuk 1969, 1974, Dressler 1977g:328f, Roberge 1980, Plank 1981:129ff, Zonneveld 1978:131f. Of course the degree of synchronic foreignness does not equal the historical depth of borrowing.

92. But even then with a few lexical exceptions such as *stich-ic*; more in Rubach 1981:152. For Portuguese velar softening, cf. Araujó 1981:108ff.

93. Other cases in Walker 1975 (French), Dell & Selkirk 1975 (French), M. Ohala 197 (Hindi), van Marle 1978 (Dutch), Lass 1980 (Yiddish), Rubach 1981 (Polish), Mohanan 1982:121ff, 141 (Malayalam); most of the English rules in Chomsky & Halle (1968), such as the synchronic Great Vowel Shift, trisyllabic laxing, etc.

94. Cf. Kiparsky 1982a, Kenstowicz & Kisseberth 1977:69ff; cf. 5.9.4, 10.8.3. 4.3.

95. In fact the notion 'derivational paradigm' plays a role mostly in Russian word formation theories (cf. Zemskaja 1978) only.

96. Bjørnflaten 1981; cf. Kenstowicz 1981:443; more in Elson 1975.

97. For other examples, cf. monophthongization of Spanish diphthongs (Harris 1977, Schwartz & Saunders 1977), Sanskrit *ruki*-rule and retroflexion (Hock 1979), Hebrew spirantization (Barkai 1975), Breton lenitions (Ternes 1970), etc. In fact most of the rules when being restricted to certain morpho- logical categories (5.9.5.1) have also lexical exceptions, e.g., English trisyllabic shortening is both restricted to the Latinate vocabulary and barred from certain lexical items such as the root *-note-* in *de-nŏt-ative* (Kiparsky 1982b).

98. Wang 1977 (with references), Dressler 1977g:328f, 1977a:49, 1978:151f, Krishnamurti 1978, Linell 1979b:182, Janson 1979:55ff, 124, Wurzel 1981a: 415, Labov 1981; cf. 5.20.8.4.6.

99. Labov (1981) claims that lexically diffusing sound change is always phone- mic. But notice non-phonemic ə-insertion which applies to different lexi- cal items in different Breton dialects (Jackson 1967:404f, Sommerfelt 1921:27f) so that we must suspect processes of lexical diffusion.

100. Zimmer 1975:561, Comrie 1979:58, Kenstowicz 1981:434f, Sezer 1981:375ff.

101. Holmer 1947:33ff.

102. Cf. Horn 1921, Dworkin 1975, 1977; cf. 10.8.5.3.

103. Rules with lexical exceptions are likely to be lexical/cyclic rules in the models of Lexical/Cyclic Phonology, cf. 5.17.1.5f.

104. This is Skousen's (1972:573f) criterion of PRs eliminating surface viola- tions such as lexical exceptions.

105. Cf. Mayerthaler (1977:158ff) for the French AMR of plural formation *-al* → *-aux* as in *cheval,* pl. *chevaux* 'horse(s)', Skousen (1975:68ff) for Finnish *k*-deletion and (pp. 107ff) for Finnish gradation rules creating exceptions to themselves.

106. Cf. Karlsson 1974:43f, Miller 1975, Dressler 1977a:20, 30, 34, 38f, 56ff.

107. Cf. Walter 1983; Waight (1980:80) calls this word-variation.

108. 'Optional application' is therefore a criterion (Linell 1979b:177f, Hooper 1976:104ff, Hock 1979, Campbell 1981:166f); Walter 1984 does not distin- guish these different classes of phenomena.

109. A first stage of this methodology, represented by Dressler 1972a, 1973, 1975b, 1976a, is similar to that of Zwicky 1972; a second stage repre- sented, e.g., by Dressler 1977a:48f, 1979a, 1980b, Vanacek & Dressler 1977, and especially by Wodak & Dressler 1978, Dressler & Hufgard 1980, Dressler & Wodak 1982, emphasizes phonological and/or sociopsychological theory and thus differs from the pioneering work of Labov (1972 and else- where).

110. Vanecek & Dressler 1977, summarized in Dressler & Wodak 1982 §5; Hasega- wa's (1979) distinction is untenable.

111. On the difficulty of perceiving fast speech, cf. Kasevič & Šabel'nikova 1983.

112. Cf. 4.3.3.3.2f. Moreover there are purely psychological factors which in- crease/decrease attention paid to speech and thus trigger/inhibit fore- grounding or backgrounding processes; cf. Vanecek & Dressler 1977, Dress-

ler & Wodak 1982:352ff.

113. Cf. Zwicky 1972, Dressler locc.citt., Barinova 1971a, 1971b, Lee & Howard
      1974, Rubach 1977, Herok & Tonelli 1977, Donegan & Stampe 1979b:131, 139f,
      Lyche 1979, Dell 1981, Abaurre Gnerre 1981, Gaspar de Oliveira 1981. Mo-
      rin's (1978:218) putative counterexample is a MPR which does not share the
      properties of variable PRs as mentioned here (cf. also optional Finnish
      gradation in Campbell 1981:167).

114. Obviously such hyperarticulate styles cannot be taken as the most direct
      reflection of the input, as Gaspar de Oliveira (1981) wrongly thinks.

115. This is the default style, so to say. Identical preferences of a social
      group may then be identified as a sociolect.

116. Linell 1979b, Lee & Howard 1974, Rudes 1976, Gaspar de Oliveira 1981; cf.
      the critique by Lyche 1979 and several examples in Dressler 1972, 1973,
      1975b.

117. Freeman 1970, Seidler 1978, Dressler 1981c, 1983a.

118. Dressler locc.citt., Rubach 1977, Kenstowicz & Kisseberth 1977:84, Bailey
      1978.

119. Morin 1981, Herok & Tonelli 1977, Rudes 1977:94f, Wodak & Dressler 1978:
      39f, Dressler & Wodak 1982. I cannot agree with Wurzel (1981a:421f) when
      he calls German velar assimilation of /n/ in /tank/ → [taŋk] a MPR and
      separates it from casual speech assimilations of /n/ to following labials,
      labiodentals, and velars across boundaries. I assume rather one single
      process of /n/-assimilation which applies in three places: (1) as a MSR
      which outlaws underlying intramorphemic */nb, np, nm/, (2) as an obliga-
      tory PR which changes intramorphemic /ng, nk/ to [ŋg, ŋk], (3) as a phono-
      stylistic PR of casual speech.

120. Malmberg 1962:135, Dressler 1973:137f, Fidelholtz 1975, Hooper 1976:104,
      Dressler & Wodak 1982.

121. Dressler 1973:137f, 1978c:151; cf. 5.13.2.1.

122. Personal communication by G. Nathan (Carbondale).

123. See Trudgill 1974:140ff, 146ff, Dressler 1975b:222f, Mioni & Trumper 1977:
      330f, Wodak & Dressler 1978:38f, 42, Dressler & Wodak 1982. Of course,
      the selection of a specific backgrounding process as snobistic index of a
      high social stratum does not render this sociolect 'casual', cf. French
      /r/-deletion as an index of the aristocratic *Inc(r)oyables* (Scherfer 1983:
      24).

124. See Linell 1979b:176f, 182f, Roberge 1980; on productivity, see 5.13.

125. Kilbury 1976, Linell 1979b:183 (both with references), Sommerstein 1977:
      42f, Kalyn' 1981, Ford & Singh 1983b:66f.

126. Cf. Linell 1979b:183, Iverson & Ringen 1978, Zonnefeld 1978.

127. For criticisms of this principle, see Gussmann 1978a chapter I, Goyvaerts
      1978:125f, van der Hulst 1979, Darden 1979 (answered by Hudson 1982), Od-
      den 1979, Lyche 1979, Stevens 1980, Kristofferson 1980, Hoel 1981.

128. Cf. Stankiewicz 1972:23.

129. Dressler 1972b, Linell 1979b:209f, Vachek 1981:100ff, Hock 1979, Angenot &
      Dillinger 1981:73, 76f, Araujó 1981, van Coetsem & McCormick 1982.

130. Kiparsky 1982a:18f, 31f, 137, 221, Campbell 1973, King 1976, Lass 1980b.

131. Miranda 1972, Vennemann 1972b:161, Schindler 1974:5ff, Skousen 1975:94ff, King 1976:19f, Dressler 1977a:30, Sommerstein 1977:240, Kiparsky & Menn 1977:73, Hogg 1979:79ff, Linell 1979b:208ff, Klausenburger 1979:119.

132. Campbell (1973) calls this 'rule obliteration'; cf. Miller 1973:698, Kiparsky 1982a:66, 72ff, 102ff, 136f on bleeding.

133. Russ 1975:66ff, Wurzel 1980a:110, 1984, Roberge 1980. Continued productivity of umlaut in diminutive formation (Singh & Ford 1983b:63) must be distinguished from spread, i.e., increase of productivity.

134. Williams 1962:120ff, Lipsky 1973:80, Klausenburger 1979:98. Another example is 5.17.2.6.

135. Often called regularity and confused with productivity, cf. Kilbury 1976: 53.

136. Aronoff 1982, Schindler 1972, Neuhaus 1973, Plank 1981, Motsch 1981, Ölander 1976, Anshen & Aronoff 1981, Górska 1982, Romaine 1983.

136a. E.g., Hellberg 1983, Hooper 1979b, Ford & Singh 1983b.

137. Dressler 1977g:320ff, 1977a:34ff, Linell 1979b:194ff; cf. Kiparsky 1982: 165ff.

138. Cf. Baudouin de Courtenay 1895:62, Dressler 1977a:34f, Linell 1979b:195.

139. Cf. Waugh 1979:315. It must be stressed that, generally, devices of forming abbreviations and acronyms cannot be included into the WFRs of the respective language, in contrast to neologisms (5.13.1.1); one consequence is that German and Russian final devoicing always applies to neologisms, but not to abbreviations. Still abbreviations are usually new native words.

140. Reformatskij 1979b:50f; confirmed by my Russian informants.

141. Cf. Baudouin de Courtenay 1895:62, Martinet 1965:22f.

142. Cf. for Hindi M. Ohala 1974.

143. Cf. for English Michaels 1980.

144. Cf. Darden 1977:123 for the non-application of Lithuanian n-deletion to neologisms; cf. Kiparsky 1982:167.

145. Kiparsky 1982:169f.

146. Abundant material in Filipović 1982; cf. Dressler 1977a:35ff, Linell 1979b:195ff, Waight 1980, Roberge 1980, Angenot & Dillinger 1981:68ff, Picard & Nicol 1982, Holden 1982, Manaster-Ramer 1984.

147. E.g., Skousen 1975, Linell 1979a, Kaye & Nykiel 1981, Rubach 1981; Holden (1976) prefers a weaker claim: fully productive rules apply more than less productive ones. For studies in terms of Natural Phonology, see Lovins 1973, Donegan 1978:138ff, Darden 1979:88, Smith 1980 chapter 5, Bjarkman 1982.

148. Cf. Flier to appear §1.1.

149. /ae/ → /oa/ ([ɔæ]) is a dialect input switch rule, cf. 5.11.8. Other examples in Lovins 1973:48f, Poldauf 1982.

150. Holden 1976; cf. Linell 1979b:196, Waight 1980, Flier to appear.

151. In such styles only truly integrated LWs are commonly used, since non-integrated LWs hardly match the intimacy of the speech-situation necessary for the choice of very casual style, cf. 5.11.7.

152. E.g., Baudouin de Courtenay 1895, Gusmani 1973:25ff (with ample references), Scott 1975.

153. Personal communication (J. Molnár, Budapest).

154. Kenstowicz 1981:434f, Zimmer 1975, cf. 3.10.6. The exclusion from Arabic and Persian LWs is another instance of lexical stratification, cf. Zimmer & Abbott 1978, 5.13.2.4.

155. Dressler 1977a:36, Zemskaja 1973:83, Linell 1979b:136 n.18, 196.

156. Kiparsky 1973b:93ff, 1982:166f, Skousen 1975:64ff, B. Orešnik 1982.

157. If it is not a native neologism, then it is not loaned from English but from either F. *ministère,* It. *ministero,* or G. *Ministerium,* i.e., with a stressed *e* in the source.

158. Dressler 1977g:325f, 1977a:37.

159. Mathesius 1964, Linell 1979b:196, Poldauf 1982:60.

160. Linell 1979b:196f, Holden 1982, passim in Filipović 1982.

161. Dressler 1977a:36; cf. Rubach 1981:26ff.

162. For the pronunciation variants, cf. Kučera 1958:9, Waight 1980:81, 87.

163. Dodi 1968:282f, Dressler 1977a:28f; cf. 5.13.2.3.

164. Cf. Farrar 1977, Barkai 1975, Werner 1981.

165. Kiparsky 1973b:103ff; cf. Lovins 1973:50f, Thomason & Kaufman 1976, Field 1981, Gerritsen 1982.

166. <gm> would be pronounced as [ŋm]; apparently the name was connected by popular etymology with *ek-baín-ein* 'to go out', verbal adj. *ékbatos.*

167. Dressler 1977a:39, Fields 1981.

168. Trubetzkoy 1939, VI.4 (on phonotactics), Kučera 1958, Pilch 1965, Bluhme 1965; cf. 8.3.3f, 8.4.2.

169. See Linell 1979b:20, Campbell 1979:75f, 1981a, 1981b, Donegan 1978:5f, Mohanan 1982:87ff, Kenstowicz & Kisseberth 1979:162ff, Ohala forthc. II E, Manaster-Ramer 1984. Four word games in Sango are discussed by Coupez 1981.

170. E.g., the Pig Latin form of *electricity* is derived from /s/, not from /k/ (Donegan 1978:5f); however the inputs for word games may be intermediate levels of representation. Nothing can be inferred from [oːkjeː] (not *[oːsjeː, oːšjeː]), the Pig Latin form of E. *yoke* (Linell 1979b:20), because velar softening applies only to Latinate vocabulary before Latinate suffixes starting with /i/: neither condition is met by [oːkjeː].

171. See earlier Sherzer 1970:346ff, 1976:33, criticized by Manaster-Ramer 1984.

172. Cf. also J. Ohala (forthc. II E) on conventionality. Manaster-Ramer (1984) thinks that anachronistic traditions may be as important in secret languages/language games as in poetic devices (5.16), but the latter carry much more prestige than the former.

173. Surveys in Linell 1979:201f, Dressler 1977a:34f, Jaeger 1979, 1980a,
      1980b, J. Ohala forthc. II F, III. Cf. Krohn & Steinberg 1973, Steinberg
      & Krohn 1975, Fromkin 1975, Mugdan 1977, Cena 1978, McCawley 1979, Derwing
      & Baker 1977, Derwing 1979:126ff, Baker & Derwing 1982 (vouching for /z/
      as basic form of the English plural), Bybee & Pardo 1981.

174. Kiparsky & Menn 1977; cf. Kiparsky 1975:196f, Jaeger, Linell, Dressler
      locc.citt.; see 5.13.4.2.

174a. Cf. Myerson 1973, Jaeger 1973, Michaels 1980; cf. Derwing 1979:128, Kase-
      vič 1979 for Russian.

175. See Kiparsky 1975:196f. J. Ohala (forthc. II F) strongly defends psycho-
      linguistic experiments in general, but he does not discuss these --mostly
      avoidable-- defects.

176. Or monophthongization *ie → e*, if one assumes rule inversion; see 5.18.7.

177. Linell 1979b:197ff, Rubach 1980, Ford & Singh 1983b:67. As for transfer
      in general, cf. Eliasson 1982.

178. Cf. Linell 1979b:197ff.

179. Cf. Donegan 1978:5, Thráinsson 1978:12f, Eliasson 1978, Wode 1978, Rubach
      1981:145, 173, Hurch 1983.

180. For an interpretation in terms of markedness within Generative Phonology,
      cf. Eckman 1977.

181. Weinreich 1967:35, Gusmani 1981:12ff, 129ff, Sasse 1979:93f.

182. See Ralph 1981 for the latest theoretical treatment, where the number of
      spontaneous, independent instances of final devoicing is reduced; this
      does not diminish its character as universal phonological process type (4.
      5.3.1), because many instances of non-borrowed devoicing are left over,
      even within Europe (e.g., Maltese, Albanian dialects).

183. Andriotis 1948, simplified by Adams 1977:147; cf. Dressler & Acson forthc.

184. Andriotis 1975:23, 33, 36f. Notice that the unstressed /i/ in phrase-fi-
      nal ['θiri] is not deleted.

185. Papadopoulos 1955:17ff, Oeconomides 1955:79ff, 85f (unfortunately without
      dialect differentiation).

186. Degeneralization of the input from the natural class of high vowels to /i/
      only (Adams 1977:146f) follows a phonological hierarchy, but this concept
      does not exclude the possibility of inputs being generalized.

187. Cf. Baudouin de Courtenay 1895, Kubrjakova & Pankrac 1983:30.

188. Starting with Meringer & Mayer 1895, Meringer 1908; cf. Fromkin 1973,
      1975:50ff, 1980, Linguistics 19.7/8 (ed. Cutler 1981), Söderpalm 1979,
      Foldvik 1979, Kettemann 1981, Stemberger 1982, Cutler 1982, Manaster-Ramer
      1984, J. Ohala forthc. II D.

189. Linell 1979b:110ff, 202, Donegan 1978:5f.

190. See Fromkin 1973:24, 86, 126, 229, Linell 1979b:138, 202, Foldvik 1979:
      119, Keller 1980:35, Crompton 1981:686, Cutler 1981:565, Stemberger 1982:
      251, J. Ohala forthc. II D.

191. Fromkin 1973:26, 258f, 162, Linell 1979b:110, Nöth 1979:71, Keller 1980:
      34, Meara & Ellis 1981:797f.

192. E.g., Linell 1979:202, Crompton 1981:678, 689f, Mohanan 1982:93f.

193. Rubach (1981:147ff) divides this rule into a cyclical rule of spirantiza-
      tion (t → s) and a postcyclic rule of palatalization (s → š).

194. Fromkin 1973:27f, Linell 1979b:110f, Keller 1980:37.

195. See Celce-Murcia 1980, Garnes & Bond 1980, Cutler 1981:566ff, Linell 1983
      (all with references).

196. Cf. Garnes & Bond 1975:221, Linell 1979b:203.

197. See Fromkin 1980:11, 22f, 99.

198. For the complicating strategies of transduction between phonology and or-
      thography, see references in Linell 1979b:197 n.41.

199. Cf. Linell 1979b:179, Stampe 1980, Mohanan 1982:92ff, 96.

200. More cautiously Donegan 1978:6.

201. Robinson et al. 1977, Tillmann & Mansell 1980, Jaeger 1980b, Manaster-Ra-
      mer 1984.

202. Cf. recently Mohanan 1982:87.

203. On 'psychological reality', see references and discussion in the second
      symposium of PICPhS 9,2 (1979) 63-128.

204. For English, see Fromkin 1973:223, often cited in later literature. For
      German, cf. the anticipation of /n/ in the slip *Bündinger*, obviously
      ['bʏndɪŋe], for the name *Büdinger* ['byːdɪŋe] (Meringer 1908). For a dif-
      ferent analysis with archiphonemes, cf. Kettemann 1981.

205. Korhonen 1969, Dressler 1977a, 1980b, 1981a; cf. Dressler's (1972) 'sec-
      ondary phonemes'. Hačatrjan (1979) suggests a similar analysis for Modern
      Armenian [ə].

206. Dressler 1971:344; Stampe has always held this view; cf. Jakobson.

207. We leave aside the much debated question to what extent historical writing
      systems are phonemic rather than allophonic or morphophonemic; cf. Penzl
      1957, 1973, King 1969:202ff, Swiggers 1983:380f; cf. 6.2.1.

208. Gudschinsky 1958, Gudschinsky et al. 1970, Payne 1981:161ff; but cf. Ken-
      stowicz & Kisseberth 1979:158f. Twadell's (1935:11f) criticism against
      Sapir's experiments is too general and inconclusive.

209. Negative: Myerson 1973:249.

210. Such orthographic evidence for MPRs or for abstract rules of Generative
      Phonology has been criticized by Sampson 1970:621f, Steinberg 1973, Stein-
      berg & Krohn 1975:256, Linell 1974, Fischer-Jørgensen 1975:294, Manaster-
      Ramer 1984. On spelling in general, cf. Frith 1980. Still one more level
      of problems is involved in spelling pronunciations; therefore I cannot
      share S. Anderson's (1981:532ff) optimism about inferences to be drawn
      from such data; his only relevant example, English vowel neutralization,
      is wrong as it stands; see 5.20.3.5.

211. Kiparsky 1973c, Sommerstein 1977:218ff, Kenstowicz & Kisseberth 1979:
      159ff, Linell 1979b:92ff, J. Ohala forthc. II C, Manaster-Ramer 1984. For
      early generative contributions in general, cf. Freeman 1970.

212. Coseriu 1971, Kristeva 1969, Seidler 1978, only marginally represented in

Freeman 1970:13ff. More in Dressler 1981c, 1983a. Many poets and writers have taken this view, very explicitly G. Hamann, A. W. Schlagel, P. Valéry, C. Morgenstern, H. Heißenbüttel, etc.

220.   Murphy 1961:6f, 36ff, Campanile 1968:6ff, Bergin 1921, Marstrander 1942: 185f, 196ff, 204ff, Manaster-Ramer 1984.

221.   In the sense of the only onset or part of the onset: thus *l*- alliterates with *fl*-, etc.; similar in Old Germanic alliteration.

222.   Cf. Miller 1977, Dressler 1981c: in general, poets are more prone to reflect on language and do (meta)linguistic analyses than 'normal speakers' do; cf. 5.16.1 note 212.

223.   Cf. Dressler 1977a:58f, Linell 1979b:204f.

224.   E.g., Csik & Papa (1979:115ff, under the headings: cycle, global rules, rule ordering (= historical change), rule order) enumerate more than 220 (out of 915 generative or related) contributions which have rule ordering as a primary subject matter.

225.   Sommerstein 1977:159. Note that rule ordering is basically a descriptive problem: Rules and rule interactions are formulated in order to generate the correct phonetic representation (output of the rule apparatus) from a hypothetical phonological representation (input to the rule apparatus). In Generative Phonology it is not claimed that the brain applies the rules in the particular order of the rule apparatus (this holds especially for 5.17.2). Only a few adherents of Generative Phonology, at times, have argued --in addition, but unsuccessfully-- for some psychological reality of rule order (i.e., that something in the brain may correspond systematically to certain properties of descriptive mechanisms of rule order), notably in arguments for reordering and medial rule insertion in diachronic change and language acquisition (cf. Kiparsky 1982a s.v. rule reordering). Notice that rule order is a non-problem in Natural Generative Phonology and other concrete process phonologies which have reverted to basic assumptions of structural phonematics. In Natural Phonology the role of rule order is very reduced, but with claims of psychological reality. Morphology needs rule order or equivalent distributional statements as in structural morphematics.

226.   Cf. note 224, Koutsoudas 1976, 1980, Koutsoudas & Sanders 1979, Kenstowicz & Kisseberth 1977:155ff, Iverson & Sanders 1978, Goyvaerts 1978:51ff, Pelletier 1980, Rubach 1982:138ff, Noske et al. 1982, Manaster-Ramer 1984.

227.   Cf. Kilbury 1976, Akhmanova 1971.

228.   Michaels & Lasnik 1978, Michaels 1981, Allen 1978.

229.   Koutsoudas 1977, 1980, Pullum 1983.

230.   See Noske et al. 1982; cf. 5.17.4f.

231.   Stampe 1980 (written 1972); cf. Linell 1979b:190; cf. 10.7.9.1.

232.   All minor rules 'always apply before all major rules.'

233.   More precisely they claim that phonotactic rules come last.

234.   Skousen 1975:122ff, Kiparsky 1982a:73.

235.   Cf. Matthews 1972:386f, Sommerstein 1977:122f, 206.

236. Cf. Russ 1975, Wurzel 1980a:110.

237. For an example from Athapaskan Hare, see Rice 1980.

238. Cf. Mascaró 1978, Rubach 1981, 1982, 1984, Booij 1981. For earlier work
      on cyclicity, see Zwicky 1976; cf. Chung 1983.

239. Kiparsky 1982b, 1982c, 1982d, Mohanan 1982, Strauss 1982. Criticized by
      Ford & Singh 1983a, 1983b:70f, Aronoff & Sridhar 1983.

240. Kiparsky 1982c:131, 1982b:1. Mohanan (1982) calls these levels 'strata'.

241. Also to MSRs, see 8.

242. Nearly as much as in Chomsky & Halle 1968; cf. Rubach 1981:96ff, 178, Ki-
      parsky 1982b:46ff = 1982c:143ff.

243. Mohanan 1982:94ff. Notice that these rules correspond to segmental pro-
      cesses of Stampean Natural Phonology (casual speech processes included).

244. Apparently even if sensitive to morphological categories (cf. 5.11), which
      Kiparsky's (1982b, 1982c) model does not allow.

245. As far as I know, the role, application, and properties of rules type (b),
      (c) have not yet been worked out in detail within Lexical Phonology;
      probably these details will present many problems to such simple and
      streamlined models of Lexical Phonology as cited in note 239.

246. Cf. 5.17.1.3 note 228.

247. See, e.g., Mohanan 1982:97.

248. Linell 1979b; cf. Hooper 1976, Stankiewicz 1979:19.

249. Cf. Kiparsky 1982b:39ff.

250. See Linell 1979b:190ff.

251. Cf. Kenstowicz & Kisseberth 1977:318ff, Vincent 1977, Coates 1982, Goy-
      vaerts 1978:63, 121.

252. Koutsoudas 1982 with references.

253. Although they may overlap with structural properties.

254. Cf. Iverson & Sanders 1978, Muraki 1982.

255. Stampe 1980; i.e., foregrounding processes should apply before back-
      grounding processes, cf. 10.7.9.2ff. This claim, which holds for PRs
      only, has the main effect of ordering MSRs (prelexical PRs) before (post-
      lexical) PRs of transduction, which correspond to backgrounding processes
      most of the time.

256. E.g., in the works of R. Jakobson and J. Kuryłowicz, cf. Matthews 1972:
      193ff; cf. for phonology Greenberg 1966:22, Reider 1981, Clements 1982.

257. Kiparsky 1983a, 1982b, 1982c:159ff, Goyvaerts 1978:66ff, Iverson 1983b.

258. Linell 1979b:190ff.

259. E.g., Coates 1982.

260. Cf. Noske et al. 1982, Linell 1979b:192f, Sommerstein 1977:206f, Kohrt
      1980, Rubach 1982:146ff, Herbert 1977c.

261. Noske et al. 1982:406f (after H. Basbøll and S. Anderson).

262. Sommerstein 1977:242ff.

263. Hogg 1976, Iverson 1981 against Kiparsky 1982a:37ff, 70ff, Moses 1982.

264. Note that new instances of word-initial [s] appear beginning with the earliest documents.

265. For such recapitulations (often called 'drift'), cf. Lass's (1974, 1975) concepts of orthogenesis and family universals.

266. Cf. Rennison 1981, Wodak & Dressler 1978:36ff.

267. Linell 1979b:186.

268. References in Fischer-Jørgensen 1975:216, Pilch 1964:4, 81, Hyman 1977, Roux 1981.

269. This term was introduced by Korhonen (1969:334f) and used by Dressler (1977a:52ff, 1981a) who previously (Dressler 1972) had used the term 'secondary phoneme'.

270. Where similarity is measured according to principles of 5.18.3.

271. Personal communication by Alexis Manaster-Ramer.

272. Sociolinguistic compensation by the social context of routine communication and/or intimacy between the speech partners.

273. For references, see 5.3; for phonologization, Dressler 1971, S. Anderson 1981:512ff, Roux 1981, etc.; for morphologization, also Hooper 1976: 102ff, Linell 1979b:208ff, Morin 1980, Wurzel 1980c, 1981a, 1982, Hellberg 1978, 1983, Klausenburger 1979, S. Anderson 1981:512ff.

274. E.g., Skousen 1975:108, Houlihan & Iverson 1977, Bjarkman 1975, Klausenburger 1979, Flier 1983.

275. Dressler 1977g:330, 1977a, 1980a, 1980b, 1981b: for semiotic reasons; cf. Roberge 1980, Hellberg 1983; cf. 10.7f.

276. Malkiel 1964/1968, 1968, 1969a, 1969b, 1976.

277. See Schwartz & Sanders 1977 for this particular rule inversion.

278. I.e., of an alternation *e* ∿ *o* in *afrenta/afrontar*, 'an unproductive scheme' that 'loomed on the horizon' (Malkiel).

279. This relation must not be confused with the (metaphonical) AMR *e* → *i*, *o* → *u* in the verbal paradigms of *herir* 'to wound', *dormir* 'to sleep', etc., with 1.pl.pres. subjunctive *hiramos*, *durmamos* (cf. Hooper 1976:156ff).

280. See Hudson's (1976:217, 227) own formulations. Neither did Sihler's (1977) Old English 'morphologically conditioned sound change' create a synchronic PR.

281. Cf. Picards 1977, 1981, Walker 1980:84, Darden 1982 against Hooper 1976: 102ff; cf. 5.9.4, 5.10.5, 5.10.8.

282. Both views rejected here are held by Hooper (1976:84ff) and Klausenburger (1979:20, 29ff), who is inconsistent insofar as he seems to argue (p. 49) with the view that the Indo-European MR of nasal infixation has no phonetic origin; this contradicts his view that all morphological alternations originate in PRs.

283. Linell 1979b:179f, if they are really context-free.

284. I omit the discussion of non-rules, e.g., of too-abstract generative rules
      which start with Proto-Germanic, Proto-Slavic, or even PIE inputs for con-
      temporary English, German, Russian, etc. (as often proposed by T. Light-
      ner), cf. Foley's (1965) fancy rules for the paradigm of Latin *sum, es,
      est* (cf. Dressler & Drachman 1977:293ff). The question which criteria
      justify the assumption of a PR/MPR has been very well argued in Zwicky
      (1975a) and most systematic treatments of the various schools of process
      (mor)phonologies.

285. S. Anderson 1974:95ff, Anderson & Browne 1973:461, Dressler 1977a:10 (af-
      ter 1977g:323), Linell 1979b:207f. Zonneveld's (1976) putative counter-
      example is only partially an exchange rule (/u:/ → [o], /o:/ → [u]) and
      not a PR.

286. Trubetzkoy 1939, Kilbury 1976:34ff, 57ff, Davidsen-Nielsen 1978, J. Ander-
      son & Ewen 1981.

287. Kiparsky 1982a(1971):75ff, 1973b, 1975.

288. Kaye 1974a, 1981, Kaye & Morin 1978, Gussmann 1976, 1978a, Linell 1979b:
      185f, Hale 1979; cf. 'upside-down-phonology' as in Leben & Robinson 1977.

289. Eliasson 1975, 1977, 1978, 1981, Rischel 1974:357; cf. Skousen's (1979)
      'inducibility'.

290. Anttila 1972:100ff, 278, Vennemann 1972b, Klausenburger 1979:123, Waugh
      1976:46ff, Ohlander 1976:47ff, Hudson 1980:115.

291. Eliasson 1975, 1977, 1981.

291a. Bloch 1941, Fischer-Jørgensen 1975:89f, 112f, 282ff; cf. Hyman 1975:67ff,
      Eliasson 1981:486ff.

292. See note 291, 5.20.2.1.

293. Kiparsky 1982a(1971):75ff; a more differentiated version in Kiparsky
      1973b:56ff, cf. 1975:195, Eliasson 1977:109.

294. 'Translucency' in Eliasson's (1977:109) terminology. This type of one-way
      predictibility was first described by Baudouin de Courtenay 1895:20f.

295. See 5.20.0 note 286 and Rubach 1978 on the non-uniqueness debate.

296. Cf. Herok & Tonelli 1977; for Italian, see also Matthews 1974:20ff; cf.
      Clayton 1981:576, Wojcik 1981, Manaster-Ramer 1984. For Arči phonemic-
      allophonic voicing assimilation, see Kodzasov 1976:26, 49.

297. Halle 1959:21ff, Bondarko 1979:68f, Wojcik 1981, Manaster-Ramer 1984, who
      cites Ułaszyn (1931) for a similar PR of Polish.

298. This class is disallowed by Houlihan & Iverson 1979, although Jakobson
      (1931) had dealt with it.

299. Krohn 1975:399ff, Fidelholtz 1979, Griggs 1982. It is assumed that there
      is no underlying /ə/ in English.

300. Thus S. Anderson's (1981:532f) speculations about the correctness of de-
      riving *Fult*[ow]*nian* from *Fulton* are inconclusive.

301. This issue bears also on Houlihan & Iverson's (1977) claims about the
      close link between neutralization and phonemization.

302. I.e., iib-opaque, following Kiparsky's (1973b) enumeration.

303. Note that we assumed preservation rules (4.4.1) so that 5.20.3.6 presents
      the choice between the rule A → B / C__D and the preservation rule B → B.
      Here there is the choice between the deletion rule A → ∅ / C__D and no
      rule at all.

304. Cf. Eliasson 1977:107, Kaye 1981:472, Dressler & Acson forthc.

305. Kaye & Morin 1978, Klausenburger 1979:55ff, which replace Schane's (1968)
      truncation analysis.

306. We might assign scores 6, 7, 8, ... n according to the degree of non-
      uniqueness, i.e., according to the number of ambiguous outputs and inputs,
      but this mechanical counting did not prove fruitful when I tried it.

307. Cf. Barkai 1975, Hellberg 1980:9; for Greenlandic lenition rules, cf.
      Rischel 1974:242ff.

308. Hogg 1979.

309. Dressler & Wodak 1982:343.

310. Cf. Cressey (1978) for the phonetic distinction between underlying and de-
      rived glides; Fox & Terbeek (1977) for differential vowel lengthening be-
      fore flaps derived from E. /d/ vs. /t/.

311. But note regional and sociolinguistic differentiation of the results of
      final devoicing/tensing within the German-speaking area.

312. Cf. Janson & Schulman (1983) for neutralization of Swedish /e/ and /ε/ in
      perception only, and for further references to similar examples.

313. But cf. Robinson et al. 1977.

314. E.g., Rubach 1982:161. But in Albanian dialects the MPR i → u / {k, g, h}
      +__ is maintained after the application of the PR of h-deletion (Desnicka-
      ja 1979).

315. Mansell 1973. Often this is treated under the heading of global rules
      such as for Sea Dayak vowel nasalization in Hyman (1975:123): /naŋga/
      'to set a ladder' is derived to [nãŋa] (not *[nãŋã]) because of g-deletion
      (leaving a trace); this is often described in terms of vowel nasalization
      being a global rule which refers to the underlying representation where
      /ŋ/ is not adjacent to the second /a/.

316. For a discussion of this strategy of argumentation within generative gram-
      mar, cf. Zwicky 1973.

317. Kaye 1974a,1981, etc.; cf. Kaye & Morin 1978, Gussmann 1976, 1978a:157ff,
      Hale 1979. It must be noted that these authors are less rigorous than
      Eliasson in matters of abstractness and more interested in questions of
      rule order, cf. Kaye's (1981:472) constraint 'deletion rules may not in-
      volve classes of segments with more than three or four members,' which
      contains the quantitative ambiguity limit '3 or 4' which is not deduced
      from any higher-order concept.

318. Cf. Lehiste 1973, 1983, Lehiste, Olive & Streeter 1978, Kooij 1971.

319. Which is a phoneme in neither language.

320. See 5.13.4; for word formation, cf. Aronoff 1983.

321. Cf. 10.10.

322. For the moment I neglect the differences in declension classes (paradigms).

323. Note that there was no analogical leveling between passive (deponent) *quer-or* 'I lament', perfect participle *ques-tus* and *or-ior* 'I arise', *or-tus, ex-per-ior* 'I ascertain', *ex-per-tus*, because deponents have no active perfect, and that *Xs-tus* may have other sources as well, as in *pās-tus* from *pāsc-or* 'I graze'. And yet this does not account for adjective formation as in *hes-ternus*, adj. of *herī* 'yesterday'.

324. Further subdivisions into unidirectional vs. bidirectional default assumptions, the postulation of third-order default rules, etc., does not seem to lead to better characterizations of MPRs.

325. Similarly, biunique and thus totally productive MRs of inflection and word formation are typical for agglutinating languages (cf. 10.9.2).

326. The sources /m, ɲ/ of [n] in the past participles *assun-to, spen-to* (Herok & Tonelli 1977:49) are obviously exceptions in inference, where /n/ is the default source.

327. For the concept of preference in artificial intelligence and work inspired by it, see Wilks (1979), Beaugrande & Dressler (1981: III.18, VII. 12). Of course neither 'default' nor 'preference' is used in these sociolinguistic studies, but notions such as variable rules/probabilities (e.g., in Labov 1972), implications (e.g., in Bailey 1973), style switching (Wodak & Dressler 1978, Dressler & Wodak 1982).

328. Since morphonology is concerned only indirectly, I must be brief.

329. Nearly 100 references in Csik & Papa (1979:115); cf. Hyman 1975:82ff, Sommerstein 1977:211ff, Kenstowicz & Kisseberth 1979:179ff, Gussmann 1978.

330. E.g., by Heger 1968, Issatschenko 1974.

331. Cf. Kiparsky 1982a:59ff, 1982b:56f, 63; cf. 5.9.3.

332. Vennemann 1972c, 1974b, Hooper 1976:116f, Klausenburger 1979.

333. Davidsen-Nielsen 1978, Hudson 1974, Hooper 1975, 1976:119ff; criticized by Rubach 1978; cf. Skousen 1979:126, Ohala forthc. 29ff.

334. At least since 1968, when he gave his unpublished paper 'Yes Virginia...' which defended the phoneme; cf. Lovins 1973:30.

335. Following Baudouin de Courtenay's (1895) 'Lautabsicht' ('sound intention', cf. Hermann 1932:118).

336. For arguments from assimilations, see Malecot & Metz 1972:205f, Scherfer 1983:22.

337. Trubetzkoy 1939, Martinet 1949, Hockett 1955, Pilch 1974, Davidsen-Nielsen 1978.

338. Schane 1971, Koutsoudas 1977, Houlihan & Iverson 1977, 1979, Dinnsen & Eckman 1978; cf. Linell 1979b.

339. In Cyclic and Lexical Phonologies (5.17.5f) they are postcyclic/postlexical rules such as allophonic PRs.

340. Bos 1967, Bolinger 1981, Sadock 1983, Dressler, Mayerthaler, Panagl & Wurzel, to appear.

6. THE ITALIAN PALATALS

6.0. Standard Italian has two velar phonemes /k, g/ and two palatal ones /č, ǯ/; the sibilant phonemes are /s/ (with the allophone [z]) and /š/; some varieties also have /ž/ (< /ǯ/). The orthography for the velars and palatals with following vowels and non-vowels (only after velars; consonants after velars are exemplified by /r/) is:

/k/: *ca, che, chi, co, cu, cr;* with glide plus vowel /ŭv, ĭv/: *qua, que,* etc., *chia, chie,* etc.

/g/: *ga, ghe, ghi, go, gu, gr; gua, gue,* etc., *ghia, ghie,* etc.

/č/: *cia, ce (cie), ci, cio, ciu.*

/ǯ/: *gia, ge, gi, gio, giu.* (The [ŭ] in *giuoco* 'play' is part of the diphthong /uo/ which alternates with /o/, cf. *giocare* 'to play'.)

The alternations between /k/ and /č/, /g/ and /ǯ/ are restricted to stem-final consonants before suffixes, which fall into three categories: plurals of nouns and adjectives (6.1-2), verbal inflection (6.3), derivational morphology (6.4).

6.1.1. Italian noun declension consists of the alternation between one singular and one plural form (there are no cases). The classes are (according to gender: m. = masc., f. = fem.):

	I m.	II m.	III f.	IV m./f.	V.	VI.
sg.	-o	-a	-a	-e	m. -o	no
pl.	-i	-i	-e	-i	f. -a	change
e.g.	romano	papa	donna	classe	frutto	film
	romani	papi	donne	classi	frutta	film
	'Roman'	'pope'	'woman'	'class'	'fruit'	'film'

Since the direction of the morphological alternation is unequivocally sg. → pl., we may safely speak of MRs of plural formation. These MRs add the vowel *i* to masculine nouns (I, II, IV) but the vowel *e* to the feminine nouns (III); but in class IV -*e* is replaced by -*i*; V is the special class of collectives. The stem-final vowels -*o/a/e* are then deleted.[1] Only in the possessives *tuo* 'your', *suo* 'his, her' is there no truncation: pl. *tuoi, suoi.* Truncation can be classified as an AMR.

The alternation of velars (sg.) and palatals (pl.) follows the same direction: This is the rule of palatal formation (PF) which applies to the plural as does the morphological spell-out rule of plural formation.

6.1.2. PF occurs only before plural *i* (there are no other declensional *i*-suffixes; for the elative *-issimo*, see 6.4.1.2). Of these classes of plural formation (6.1.1), class II includes only one example of PF: noun, adj. *belga*, pl. *belgi* 'Belgian'. Otherwise class II[2] retains the velars, e.g., *duca - duchi* 'duke', *collega - colleghi* 'colleague'.

Class IV or rather VI has a few words ending in *-che*, *-ghe* in the sg.: Compounds like *attaccabrighe* 'wrangler' do not change in the pl. (thus class VI). Informants avoided forming a pl. (in *-i*?) of the feminines *sineddoche* 'synecdoche' and (the rare plant name) *orobanche*.

Class III words ending in *-ca*, *-ga* retain the velar, e.g., *amica - amiche* 'girl friend'.

6.1.3. Within the first class the following sub-classes are relevant for PF:[3]

6.1.3.1. Among the words with penultimate stress, only a few nouns have PF: *amico* 'boy friend', pl. *amici*, *nemico* 'enemy', *greco* 'Greek' (also adj.), *porco* 'pig', but *per quattro porchi soldi* 'for four piggish dimes' (maybe influenced by adj. *sporco* 'dirty', pl. *sporchi*). All the other nouns, and all the adjectives retain the velar, e.g., *parco* 'park', pl. *parchi*, *bosco* 'wood', pl. *boschi*, *franco* 'frank', pl. *franchi*, *bergamasco* (adj.) 'of Bergamo', pl. *bergamaschi*. Note also *scorcio* 'shortening', pl. *scorci* with palatal in both sg. and pl.; but most plurals in *-ci* come from singulars in *-ce* (class IV), e.g., *complice* 'accomplice', pl. *complici*.

/g/ → /ǯ/ is to be found only in the idiomatic plurale tantum *i (re) magi* 'the three Magi'; the normal pl. of *mago* 'magus, sorcerer' is *maghi*, cf. *lago* 'lake', pl. *laghi*. PF is optional with *chirurgo* 'surgeon', pl. *chirurg(h)i*.

6.1.3.2.1. All adjectives in *-co* (mostly suffixes in *-ico*) with antepenultimate stress undergo PF, e.g., *comico* 'comical', pl. *comici*, *classico* 'classical', *maniaco* 'maniacal', *linguistico* 'linguistic', *magnifico* 'magnificent'. The only exceptions are *carico* 'loaded' (from *carico* 'load', pl. *carichi*, also *scarico* 'unloaded', both following the basic noun), a few words with penultimate vowels other than *i* fluctuate: *reciproco* 'reciprocal', pl. *reciproc(h)i*, *in/estrinseco* 'in/extrinsic'.

6.1.3.2.2. Most nouns in *-co* with antepenultimate stress undergo PF, e.g., *medico* 'doctor', *sindaco* 'mayor', *monaco* 'monk', *clerico* (*chierico*) 'clergyman', *distico* 'distich', *dittico* 'diptych', *lessico* 'lexicon', *mosaico* 'mosaic', *narcotico* 'narcotic', *portico* 'p.', *villico* 'peasant', *zodiaco* 'zodiac', all nouns in *-atico* (Dardano 1978:91f), e.g., *viatico* 'viaticum'.

The following nouns do not undergo PF: *pizzico* 'pinch', *carico* 'load, task' (with the derivatives *incarico, scarico*), *risico* 'risk', and the rare words *abbaco* 'abacus', *rammarico* 'lamentation', *valico* 'mountain pass, ford'.

PF is optional in the pl. of: *manico* 'handle', *farmaco* 'medicament', *parroco* 'parson', *indaco* 'indigo', *panico* 'panic', *stomaco* 'stomach', *fondaco* 'draper's hall', *traffico* 'commerce, traffic', *intonaco/-ico* 'plaster'.

6.1.3.3. Nouns and adjectives in *-go* with antepenultimate stress usually do not undergo PF, e.g., *dialogo* 'dialogue', *catalogo* 'catalogue', *analogo* 'analogous', *prodigo* 'prodigal', all with pl. *-ghi* only. Exceptions (with PF) are *asparago* 'asparagus' and certain nouns in *-logo* (signifying specialists) such as *glottologo* 'linguist'. PF is optional with *astrologo* 'astrologer' (but unlearned *strologo* has only a *-ghi* pl.), *filologo* 'philologist', *ginecologo* 'gynaecologist', *sarcofago* 'sarcophagus', *antropofago* 'cannibal', etc.

6.1.3.4. Long velars are never subject to PF, e.g., *sacco* 'sack', pl. *sacchi*.

6.1.4.1. Saltarelli (1970:77f) restricts PF to isolated words and to *k*-suffixes. This accounts for adjectives in *-ico* (6.1.3.2.1), *-ifico* (ibid.), and for nouns in *-atico* (6.1.3.2.2), but he also has to structure *am=ic+o, mon=ac+o, med=ic+o*. Maybe some Italians sense a relationship between *amico* 'friend' and *am+are* 'to love', *am+ore* 'love', but in all other cases no basis can be found for *k*-derivations derived from them.

Words which have a consonant immediately before *-co* never have antepenultimate stress, e.g., the suffix *-asco:* The penultimate syllable is heavy and attracts the stress.

6.1.4.2. The rule of PF must be split into several subrules:

$$
\begin{bmatrix} +obstr. \\ +back \\ \langle -voice \rangle \\ -long \end{bmatrix} \rightarrow \begin{bmatrix} -back \\ +delayed \\ release \end{bmatrix} \Big/ \begin{array}{c} V \\ \langle -stress \rangle \\ \begin{bmatrix} +high \\ -back \end{bmatrix}! \end{array} \underline{\hspace{1cm}}_{\langle +adj! \rangle} + \begin{bmatrix} i \\ pl. \\ I \ declens. \end{bmatrix}
$$

Interpretation:

(1) If one of the first two angled brackets (⟨-voice⟩, ⟨-stress⟩) is missing,
     then PF is a minor rule (6.1.3.1, 6.1.3.3): Certain morphemes (words or
     e.g. *-logo*) have a positive rule feature.

(2) With both angled brackets PF is a major rule (6.1.3.2): Certain nouns and
     a very few adjectives have a negative rule feature.

(3) Adj! = especially/most with adjectives in the major rule.

(4) For certain words the (positive or negative) rule feature exists in the
     lexicon of only some of the speakers. For some words even the same speaker
     wavers.

(5) $\begin{bmatrix} +high \\ -back \end{bmatrix}!$ = especially/most after the vowel /i/.

6.1.5. The evaluation of synchronic PF in Italian plurals gives the following
results if we apply our criteria of 5:

6.1.5.1. PF must be matched with two universal process types at the same time
(see 4.5.3.2, 4.6.2): (1) palatalization, (2) palatal affrication. Thus PF can
be no PR; input /k, g/ and output /č, ǯ/ are natural classes. But beyond this
phonological regularity (5.4.1), PF is morphologically conditioned (on generality, see 6.1.5.3), which is phonologically unnatural. It is phonetically plausible that long velars (e.g., *stucco* 's.') resist palatalization better than
short ones. Subsequent and preceding /i/ is the best environment among vowels,
however there is no PF before (or after) the still more plausible environment
[ĭ]; of course there are no such suffixes. Therefore the phonetic plausibility
of PF before plurals in *i*, but not before those in *e, a* is good. On the other
hand, the distance (5.3) between input and output is too great for a truly natural process (still more so in those variants of Italian with /č, ǯ/ → /š, ž/,
e.g., in *ami*[k]*o* 'friend', pl. *ami*[š]*i*). In the universal hierarchies of palatalization and of palatal affrication stress plays no role: there is no reason

for the process to apply after unstressed rather than after stressed vowels. Therefore the productivity in words with antepenultimate stress like *linguistico, filologo* is a property of the morphological elements *-ico* and *-logo*. Thus according to the criterion of phonological process matching, we can establish medium naturalness, typical for a MPR.

6.1.5.2. PF is neither a constraint on, nor a help for pronounceability and perceptibility (5.6). This is phonologically most unnatural. PF co-signals the MR of plural formation. As a MPR it is applied after the respective MRs, necessarily after the spell-out rule of plural formation.

PF is totally opaque, non-uniqueness/inferential ambiguity is high, recoverability low (5.20): (a) *fico* 'fig', pl. *fichi* does not undergo PF. (b) An irregular extension of PF derives *belga → belgi*. (c) There are input palatals, e.g., in *luce* 'light', pl. *luci, scorcio*, pl. *scorci*.

Obligatoriness (5.12) is a question of morphological category (e.g., adjectives in *-ico*) or of lexical marking. Optionality does not depend on phonological style (and it cannot, since palatal affrication as part of PF is not a backgrounding process, cf. 5.11), e.g., *chirurgi* is not more casual than *chirurghi*. This is again phonologically unnatural.

PF is not general (5.12). Exceptions do not follow a phonologically plausible pattern: (a) There is more PF after unstressed syllables than after stressed ones (6.1.5.1). (b) /k/ undergoes PF more readily than /g/. Domains are morphological, not phonological (5.8): again phonologically unnatural, and typical for MPRs and AMRs.

6.1.5.3. There is no biuniqueness because of neutralization and opacity (6.1.5. 2): PF merges phonemes, iconicity is low (features are changed and added, cf. 5.18). Therefore recoverability is low. But PF is the default rule in plural formation if /k/ is both preceded and followed by /i/ (cf. 5.20.8.4).

Productivity (cf. 5.13): When PF is a minor rule, productivity is low; only if new words with *-logo* (neologisms) or borrowed (loanwords) does PF have a chance to apply; e.g., a specialist in error analysis might be called a *lapsologo*, and all of my informants applied PF in the plural. When PF is a major rule, it is productive, completely so with adjectives in *-ico*, e.g., *lapsologico* 'pertaining to error analysis' (G. *Lapsologie* 'lapsology' was coined by G.

Nickel), with pl. always *-gici* [-ǯiči].

6.1.5.4. I ran a production test with nonsense words (cf. 5.13.4) at the University of Padua. The 88 subjects were all students of a foreign language and proficient speakers of Standard Italian.[5] I translate from the instructions: 'A medical doctor has invented the following terms (noun and adjective) for new diseases. Please form the respective plurals. In order to facilitate the task, I have added stress signs.' The first test pair 'il tràbo nefritóso' seemed quite medical because of the adjective derived from *nefriti* by the productive suffix *-oso* (the normal derivation is *nefritico*). All the subsequent nonsense noun-adjective pairs ended in *-co* or *-ca*.

The results were: (I) Only one subject applied PF to a fem. class III test item in *-ca* (and only once), perfectly in line with the non-existence of PF in this class.

(II) For test items in *-co*, the distribution of produced *-ci* and *-chi* forms was highly significant in the following respects:

(1) PF was applied in 85% (nouns) or 95% (adjectives) on nonsense words with antepenultimate stress, but only in 55% (57%) of nonsense words with penultimate stress.

(2) Immediate precedence of the vowel /i/ favored PF only in penultimate stress test items, both in nouns and adjectives. Notice that in existing antepenultimate stress words morphological categories are more relevant than in penultimate stress words. However, the morphological difference of nouns and adjectives (more general and productive) did not show up in the production test.

Thus our experiment seems to confirm the relevance of certain morphological and phonological factors.

6.1.6. From the point of view of morphology, the distance between input and output of PF is sufficient for a MPR or AMR since it is phonemic and thus guarantees easy perception of the morphological sign vehicle (5.3.1, 5.20.6). PF applies to the output of the MR of plural formation, i.e., it follows its direction (cf. 5.2.7.3). It is lexicalized, which is both phonologically and morphologically unnatural (cf. 5.10). It is general (cf. 5.12) only in small morphological subclasses (6.13.2.1, 6.1.3.3).

As we have already seen and as we will see still more clearly, PF has been split into several rules according to the MRs and morphological categories involved (cf. 5.9.8).

6.1.7. According to the criteria of 5.21.1.1f, 5.21.1.4-9, 5.21.2.2f, 5.21.6.1, 5.21.6.3, 5.21.6.5, 5.21.6.7, 5.21.6.8, 5.21.6.11, PF is or maybe is a MPR; according to many of these criteria it cannot be a PR; none of these criteria exclude the possibility of its being an AMR, although the relevance of preceding and following /i/ points to the class of MPRs. So we still must inspect diachronic criteria in order to see whether the adjacency of /i/ is accidental or not (see 6.2.5).

6.2.1. The diachrony of PF (especially in plurals) can be followed back for more than two millenia. For /k/ Old Latin inscriptions use Q before /o, u/, C before /e, i/, K before /a/ and all consonants. This is an (allophonic!) orthography for extrinsic allophonic labialization and palatalization before labiovelar and palatal vowels respectively.

At the end of antiquity the rule of PF was presumably:

$$\begin{bmatrix} k \\ g \end{bmatrix} \rightarrow \begin{bmatrix} k' \\ g' \end{bmatrix} \ / \ \underline{\quad} \begin{Bmatrix} \breve{\imath} \\ i \\ e \\ \varepsilon \end{Bmatrix}$$

Or the output was already [t', d'], where d' merged with Latin /ĭ/ > j > d', e.g., in Lat. *iam* 'already' (> It. *già*). After /kw, gw/ changed to [k, g] before palatal vowels, t', d' became contrastive (Tekavčić 1977.I:151ff): Thus t' presumably became a quasi-phoneme (only derived = never input, but contrastive), which made the process of palatalization a less natural PR. /d'/ was a phoneme since it was an input segment in all instances of earlier Latin /ĭ/ before nonpalatal vowels. /ĭ/, the most plausible phonetic environment of the palatalization process, was lost from the environment because of the development $g'\breve{\imath}$ > $d'd'$ (or [d':]).

6.2.2. Now the quasi-phoneme t' and the phoneme d' became subject to (presumably context-free) palatal affrication (in the antecedents of Standard Italian): Since context-free phonological processes are not stable synchronic PRs, palatalization and palatal affrication were telescoped (cf. 5.2.7.1):

$$\left.\begin{array}{c}\begin{bmatrix}k\\g\end{bmatrix} \rightarrow \begin{bmatrix}t'\\d'\end{bmatrix} / \underline{\quad} \begin{array}{c}V\\{[+pal]}\end{array}\\[2ex]\begin{bmatrix}t'\\d'\end{bmatrix} \rightarrow \begin{bmatrix}\check{c}\\\check{3}\end{bmatrix}\end{array}\right\} > \begin{bmatrix}k\\g\end{bmatrix} \rightarrow \begin{bmatrix}\check{c}\\\check{3}\end{bmatrix} / \underline{\quad} \begin{array}{c}V\\{[+pal]}\end{array}$$

Because of the greater distance of phonological change (i.e., non-match-ability with a universal phonological process type) and because of their con-trastiveness, č, ž were presumably restructured as the input phonemes in all cases where there was no alternation. And this in turn made alternations more likely to be exposed to analogical pressures of leveling.

6.2.3.   In this process, /ž/ was analogically leveled more than /č/, both in de-clension (number) and in conjugation, since its phonemic status had been better and longer established; so [-ži] plurals (plural being the marked form) were leveled to [-gi] in accordance with the (unmarked) singulars in [-go]. But /ž/ resisted in *i re magi* (6.1.3.1) since this was a plurale tantum, similarly in *asparagi* (6.1.3.3) since asparagus is primarily conceived of as a collective (also *belgi?*, 6.1.2), therefore the sg. was leveled to *(a)sparagio* with /ž/ in the Tuscan vernacular (Goidánich 1940:160). Moreover /ž/ remained (at least op-tionally) in learned words where the pronunciation of Latin ⟨gi⟩ as [ži] was of some influence (Goidánich 1940), and where pl. /ži/ was supported by derivations in /žía/ as in *filologi* 'philologists' and *fililogia* 'philology', *chirurg(h)i* 'surgeons' and *chirurgia* 'surgery' (6.1.3.3, 6.4.1.2).

6.2.4.   When early Romance /fíco/ (from Lat. *fīcūs*, thus a *u*-stem), the pl. of *fico* 'fig', was displaced into class I and got the suffix *-i*, PF was not applied (thus It. pl. *fichi*). This means that PF was no longer a totally productive PR, at least in cases of words with penultimate stress. This (and only this) sub-class also included many Germanic loanwords such as *franco* 'frank', *albergo* 'hostel' (cf. Goidánich 1940:160ff), which did not undergo PF. Therefore in this subclass, PF became lexicalized and a minor rule (6.1.4.2).

On the contrary, nouns and adjectives with antepenultimate stress did not include either morphologically reclassified words such as /fíko/ > /fíki/ or Germanic loanwords. But they included many learned words (some of Greek origin) where the palatal pronunciation of the identically written Latin words (with nearly identically pronounced singulars) helped. (All learning was done in Lat-in and the pronunciation of Latin ⟨ci, cae, ce, gi, gae, ge⟩ was invariably palatal.) Thus in this subclass PF remained a major rule.

6.2.5. However old Italian texts show much fluctuation between ⟨c⟩ and ⟨ch⟩,
less between ⟨g⟩ and ⟨gh⟩ before palatal vowels.[6] Examples of deviations from
today's norms are: *antici* 'old' (Jacopone), *bianci* 'white' (Dante; a Germanic
loanword), *grammatichi* 'grammarians', *filosofichi* 'philosophic' (Bocaccio), and
also in class III *pubblice* 'public' (Alberti), *biece* 'oblique' (Dante).

Later on, in emerging Standard Italian, PF was standardized according to
usage as explained in 6.2.3f and restricted to the position before *i*, the most
palatal vowel, which is the most plausible agent of palatalization. And even
preceding /i/ must have played a role (cf. 6.1.4.2, 6.1.5.4, 6.1.6).[7] This is
a strong argument for (at least vestigial) phonologicalness of pl. PF in early
Modern Italian (and this, even if grammarians may have played an important role
in standardization -- and why should grammarians be immune to phonological naturalness?). If Goidánich (1940, criticized by Tekavčić 1972.II:72f) is correct
in his emphasis on the artificiality of older Italian orthographical evidence,
then the restriction of pl. PF to the position before *i* must have occurred earlier.

6.3.1. The situation is much clearer with PF in verbal inflection. It is restricted to the old (= Latin) III and IV conjugations;[8] there is no PF in the
old I conjugation, and there are no velars in the old II conjugation (e.g.,
piaccio < Latin *placeo* 'I please'). Contrast *legg+ere* 'to read' (Latin III
conjugation = Ital. II conjugation) with *pag+are* 'to pay' (Latin I conjugation
= Ital. I conjugation):

```
Lat. III = It. II:  prs. 1. leggo          2. leggi           3. legge
Lat. I   = It. I :       pago                paghi              paga

          1.pl.(also sub- leggiamo [ǯːa]  2. leggete  (subj. leggiate)
                junctive) paghiamo [gǐa]     pagate   (subj. paghiate)

              impf. leggevo           fut. leggerò
                    pagavo                 pagherò
```

In dialects there has been the leveling *leggo > leggio*.

6.3.2. In my opinion, this PF is an AMR or part of the respective MRs. In addition to phonologically unnatural features parallel to those discussed for pl.
PF in 6.1f, we have the following criteria vouching for the morphological nature

of PF in conjugation: There is no restriction to the position before the phonologically most plausible vowel (cf. 6.2.5, 6.1.5.1). Rigorous leveling has occurred, according to purely morphological categories, so that PF is a totally
reliable cosignal of the respective morphological class. Length of the velar
as in *leggo* ['leg:o] is no barrier to PF (cf. 6.1.3.4, 6.1.5.1).

There has been more telescoping, and thus there is a greater distance of
structural change (and a worse score of phonological process matching) in the
conjugation of *cresco* [sko], 2.sg. *cresci* [š:i] 'I, you grow' or *finisco, fini-
sci* 'I, you finish' (dialectal leveling to *feni*[š:]*o* in Lazio).

PF is completely general with *-sc-* verbs as with the other verbal forms
shown; but it is not unique because *leggere* may be the infinitive both of 1.sg.
prs. *leggo* (standard) and *leggio* (dialectal).

6.4. In derivational morphology (Dardano 1978), PF is morphologically governed
and partially lexicalized.

6.4.1.1. Suffixes (i.e., the respective MRs) which always cause PF are: the
archaic verbal suffix *-icare*, e.g., *bianc+iare* 'to pass into white' from *bianco*,
pl. *bianchi, teolog+icare* 'to theologize'; the nominal suffix *-izia*, e.g.,
sporc+izia 'dirtiness' from *sporco*, pl. *sporchi, amic+izia* 'friendship' from
amico, pl. *amici;* the productive adjectival suffix *-istico*, e.g., *classic+isti-
co* 'classicist', presumably from *classicismo* rather than *classico* 'classical'.

6.1.4.2. Productive suffixes which almost always cause PF are: the nominal
suffixes *-ia*, e.g., *pedagogia* from *pedagogo*, pl. *pedagoghi;* *-ità*, e.g.,
opac+ità 'opacity' from *opaco*, pl. *opachi* 'opaque'; *-ismo*, e.g., *grec+ismo,
classic+ismo; ista*, e.g., *music+ista* 'musician' from *musica* 'music', *grec+ista,
classic+ista, pedagog+ista;* the adjectival suffix *-ico*, e.g., *pedagog+ico, chi-
rurg+ico;* the elative *-issimo*, e.g., *amic+issimo* 'very friendly', *cattolic+is-
simo* 'very Catholic', from *cattolico*, pl. *cattolici*, but *sporch+issimo* 'very
dirty'; the verbal suffix *-izzare*, e.g., *grec+izzare* 'to hellenize' from *greco*,
pl. *greci*,[9] but exceptions are *turch+izzare* 'to make Turkish' from *turco*, pl.
turchi, cech+izzare 'to make Czech' from *ceco*, pl. *cechi;* and as with other
derivational suffixes, /k/ after /s/ or long /k:/ is not subject to PF, e.g.,
slovacch+izzare 'to make Slovak' from *slovacco*, *tedesch+izzare* 'to Germanize'
from *tedesco*.

6.4.2.1. Productive suffixes which are never cosignalled by PF are: the verbal suffix *-eggiare*, e.g., *grech+eggiare* 'to use Greek expressions'; the verbal diminutives *-ettare*, *-erellare*; the nominal suffixes *-eria*, e.g., *medich+eria* 'doctor's surgery' from *medico*, pl. *medici*; *-ezza*, e.g., *sproch+ezza* 'dirtiness', *bianch+ezza* 'whiteness'; fem. *-essa*, e.g., *musich+essa* 'fem. musician', *duch+essa* 'duchess' < Late Latin *ducissa* to masc. *duca*; *-iere* (diphthongal variant of *-ere*), e.g., *musich+iere* 'musician'; *-iero* (diphthongal variant of *-ero*), e.g., *albergh+iero* 'inn-keeper' from *albergo* 'inn'; the diminutives *-ino*, *-etto*, *-iccio*, e.g., *musich+ina* = *musich+etta* from *musica*, *cattolich+etto*, etc.; the adjectival suffixes *-evole*, e.g., *domestich+evole* 'domesticable' from *domesticare* 'to domesticate', *domestico* 'domestic', pl. *domestici*, *amich+evole* 'friendly' from *amico*; *-ereccio*, e.g., *porch+ereccio* 'piggish' from *porco* 'pig', pl. *porci*; *-esco*, e.g., *grech+esco* 'in the Greek way'; *-ese*, e.g., *pragh+ese* 'Praguian' from *Praga* 'Prague'.

6.4.3.1. A first class of lexical exceptions is explainable with some general principle: *-eto* never triggers PF with the exception of *asparag+eto* 'asparagus field': Since asparagus is conceived of collectively (see 6.2.3), the plural *asparagi* seems to have been decisive. The nominal deadjectival suffix *-ismo* causes PF, but *pressappoch+ismo* 'lack of precision' is exceptionally derived from an adverb, *pressappoco* 'nearly', not from an adjective.[10] *-ico* causes PF, but not if the derivate comes from a Greek word in *-k^hikós*, e.g., *monarch+ico* 'monarchic'; the same holds for *-ia*, e.g., *monarch+ia* 'monarchy' and *-ismo*, e.g., *monarch+ismo* 'monarchism'; cf. all the derivations of *monaco* 'monk' (< Gk. *monak^hós*), pl. *monaci* (!), e.g., *monach+ismo*, archaic adj. *monach+ile* (but *porc+ile*, *bar+ile*). *Porc+ello* 'piglet' seems to contradict the prohibition of PF in diminutives (cf. 6.4.4.1.2), but the whole word is inherited from Latin *porc+ellus* and it is supported by the augmented diminutive suffix *-cello* (as in *monti+cello* from *monte* 'mountain').

6.4.3.2. Certain stems never undergo PF: Class I nouns such as *repubblica* 'republic' → *repubblich+ista* 'republican' (but *pubblico* 'public' → *pubblic+ista* 'publicist'), *droga* 'drug' → *drogh+ista* 'druggist'; foreign names, e.g., *Franco* with *franch+ismo*, *franch+ista* (a follower of the Spanish dictator); *antico* 'old' (with /k/ < Latin /kw/), pl. *antichi* with *antich+ità* 'antiquity' and elative *antich+issimo*; *fuoco* 'fire', pl. *fuochi* with *fuoch+ista* 'fireman', but similar exceptions occur with other *-ista* agent nouns as well.

6.4.3.3. There are fluctuations in *dialog(h)+izzare* 'to converse' (cf. *dialog+i-co*, *dialog+ista*, *dialog+ismo*), *grammatic(h)+ista* 'grammarian' (archaic), *cec+ità* 'blindness' from *c(i)eco* 'blind', pl. *cechi*, older *c(i)ech+ità* (Tekavčić 1972. III:127).

Earlier variants with /k/ such as *pratich+ista* 'practitioner', *cattolich+i-smo* were no longer accepted by my informants.

6.4.4.1.1. All suffixes that cause PF either obligatorily or nearly so, start with *i* (6.4.1). Suffixes starting with another vowel (even *e*) never cause PF.

6.4.4.1.2. *-i-* suffixes which shun PF are partially only apparent counter-examples (cf. 6.4.2): *-iere*, *-iero* (both of French origin) are diphthongal variants of *-ere*, *-ero*; verbal *-ire* is unproductive. Synchronic diminutives never allow PF whether they start with *i* or another vowel,[11] although in other languages (e.g., Basque dialects, cf. Iverson & Oñederra 1983) phonological palatalization is an iconic signal of diminutives.[12]

6.4.4.1.3. Fluctuations between velars and palatals occur only before *i* (6.4.3. 3).

6.4.4.2. Examples such as *antich+ista* (6.4.3.2) might make us think of a very early date for the restriction of PF to the position before *i*. However the fluctuations (6.4.4.1.3) and even a certain increase of PF in fluctuations (6.4. 3.3) suggest that *i* still functions as a phonologically plausible environment. Of course there may be an influence of the role of *i* in plural formation (6.1). Progressive lexical fading of PF seems to have stopped long ago, similarly of PF in plural formation.

6.4.5. PF in plural formation and in derivational morphology behave similarly in the other evaluative criteria as well: Also in derivational morphology PF is no constraint on/help for pronounceability; it has multiple opacity (one sure case of irregular extension of PF is *asparageto* (6.4.3.1)); non-phonostylistic optionality; morphological domains.

But in derivation there is more (lexical) generality if we assume rule split into subrules according to the various commanding MRs. PF equally has in word formation low phonological recoverability, similar productivity (or more), the same input-output distance.

6.5. Our approach allows us to differentiate PF in plurals and derivational morphology on the one hand and in conjugation on the other, according to the descriptive criteria of 5 (see 6.1.7, 6.2.5, 6.3.2, 6.4.5). Although all (sub)-rules of PF are heavily morphologized, the first two PF rules (6.1, 6.3) still seem to be MPRs; PF in conjugation is not, but rather an AMR (or part of the respective MRs). In any event, there has been rule split of Proto-Italian PF, which is predicted by our model just in those cases where a MPR becomes subser-viant to and linked to several highly different MRs (see 5.9.8).

Notes

1. The alternative claim that the MRs change the sg. vowels into the pl. vowels would not account for the popular *i film+i* 'the films', sg. *il film* (in literary Italian words such as *film, golf* belong to class VI: *i film*).

2. Class II comprises few underived words, but the productive suffix *–ista*. Since it applies also to loanwords and neologisms, it is still a productive MR.

3. Costabile 1973:120ff, Wanner 1972, Salterelli 1970:77f, Lepschy & Lepschy 1981:99.

4. *Dimentico,* pl. *dimentichi* 'forgetful' is derived from *dimenticare* 'to forget' which never shows PF, and thus has no *–co* suffix.

5. The Venetan dialects in and around Padua have a slightly different rule of PF: its outputs are the affricates /c, ʒ/ ([ts, dz]) instead of Standard /č, ž/. Otherwise the rules are very similar, but I could not control the possible impact of diverging lexical exceptions. Therefore I picked nonsense words which (1) did not evoke specific, very similar existing words, (2) which belonged to a lexical area which excludes the use of dialect words.

6. Tekavčić 1972.II:71, Migliorini 1960:156, 159, 224ff, 288f, 388f, 469.

7. A similar role was played by /i/ in the evolution of palatalization/palatal formation PRs in Albanian (5.9.5.1, Dressler 1977a:18), Serbo-Croatian (Thomason 1976:374), and Swedish (Ralph 1981:345).

8. As in *leggere* 'to read', *mugire* 'to low', cf. Rohlfs 1968.II:96ff, Tekavčić 1972.II:73, 348ff, Salterelli 1970:78.

9. The putative counter-example *catechizzare* comes from *catechismo,* which has no independently existing basis.

10. Cf. *menefreghismo* without PF, derived from *me ne frega* 'I don't mind'.

11. *Baccillo* 'bacillus' is not a synchronic diminutive of *bacco* 'warm', nor *baccello* 'husk' of *bacca* 'berry'.

12. Has Italian simply de-iconicized diminutives such as in the sound changes of diminutive suffixes *–illus, –ittus* > *–ello, –etto*?

7. PALATALIZATION OF VELARS IN POLISH

7.0. While in Italian (6) there is but one rule of palatal formation, which affects only two velar phonemes, in Polish --since Proto-Slavic-- many palatalizations have affected many consonants. This allows us to study the processes of the palatalization of velars which have been phonologically denaturalized to various degrees in the same language.

First (7.1) I characterize the relevant segments of the Polish phonemic/allophonic inventory, before summarizing the diachronic changes involved (7.2). Then (7.3-5) I study the synchronic classes of three palatalization processes, while concentrating on their application to velars. I use Polish orthography and a broad transcription. 7.6f is devoted to the evaluation of the rules studied.[1]

7.1.1. The Polish vowel phonemes and their graphic representations are:[2]

	/ i	e	ɨ	a	o	u	ẽ	õ /
orthography	i	e	y	a	o	u,ó	ę	ą
palatal	+	+	-	-	-	-	+	-
labial	-	-	-	-	+	+	-	+
high	+	--	+	-	-	+	-	-
low	-	-	-	+	-	-	-	-
nasal	-	-	-	-	-	-	+	+

Y represents a strongly centralized high, palatal vowel, which is of course less palatal than i, e. If /ẽ, õ/ (or diphthongs [ew̃, ow̃]) are only quasi-phonemes, to be derived from underlying /VN/-sequences, then this derivation has to be ordered before the palatalization processes which interest us here (Laskowski 1975:103, 127, Gussmann 1978a:101ff, 155), so that we can treat them safely as underlying vowels. /ɨ/ can be derived from /i/ after non-palatalized consonants and/or vice-versa.[3] Laskowski (1975:20), Gussmann (1978a), Rubach (1981:16ff) posit an abstract (underlying) tense-lax distinction (cf. 3.3.2). If we assume n-ary features, then we have the following scale of decreasing palatality: i - e - ẽ - ɨ - a - õ - o - u.

7.1.2. The relevant consonants are:[4]

/ ć 3̌ ś ź c 3 s z t d č 3̌ š ž x' x γ k' k g' g ł l r j /

orthography	ć	dź	ś	ź	c	dz	s	z	t	d	cz	dż	sz	ż	chi	ch	h	ki	k	gi	g	ł	l	r	i
	ci	dzi	si	zi										rz	hi	h		k		g	[ɥ]				j
anterior	−	−	−	−	+	+	+	+	+	+	−	−	−	−	−	−	−	−	−	−	−	−	+	+	−
palatal	+	+	+	+	−	−	−	−	−	−	−	−	−	−	+	−	−	+	−	+	−	−	−	−	+
high	+	+	+	+	−	−	−	−	−	−	+	+	+	+	+	+	+	+	+	+	+	+	−	−	+
distributed [palatalized]	+	+	+	+	−	−	−	−	+	+	−	−	−	−	+	−	−	+	−	+	−	−	−	−	+
continuant	−	−	+	+	−	−	+	+	−	−	−	−	+	+	+	+	+	−	−	−	−	+	+	+	+
delayed release	+	+	−	−	+	+	−	−	−	−	+	+	−	−	−	−	−	−	−	−	−	−	−	−	−
voice	−	+	−	+	−	+	−	+	−	+	−	+	−	+	−	−	+	−	−	+	+	+	+	+	+

prepalatal · alveolar · post-alveolar · velar

Nearly all of these consonants are phonemes or at least quasi-phonemes (i.e., derivable, but they occur in minimal pairs, e.g., [k'e] vs. [ke]).[5]

7.2.0. The diachronic background of the changes of velars, alveolars, and other consonants to prepalatal, postalveolar, and palatalized (distributed) consonants is, in a simplified form (for more details, see Stieber 1973, cf. 7.9):

7.2.1. 1st Slavic palatalization: $k > k' > t' > č$ / __ $\begin{bmatrix} +voc \\ +pal \end{bmatrix}$; similarly $g > \check{3}$ > ž (originally intervocalically), $x > š$.

The synchronic reflexes --which I will call postalveolar formation (PF)-- will be dealt with specifically in 7.3.

7.2.2. 2nd Slavic palatalization: $k > k' > t' > c$ / __ $\begin{bmatrix} +voc \\ +pal \end{bmatrix}$, i.e., before i, e originating from older diphthongs); similarly $g > 3$, $x > š$ (but $x > \acute{s}$ / __i).

The synchronic reflexes --which I will call alveolar formation (AF)-- will be dealt with in 7.4.

7.2.3. 3rd Slavic palatalization: $k > ... > c$ / $\begin{bmatrix} +voc \\ +pal \end{bmatrix}$ __ (under specific conditions only). In certain abstract analyses, words like *owca* [ofca] 'sheep' are derived from underlying /ovĭk-ā/ or /ovek-a/ with this rule.[6]

7.2.4. Before palatal vowels, consonants palatalized again (e.g., k, s, t, r > k', s', t', r') and merged with consonant + /j/ combinations (such mergers also occurred with PF). Later t', d', s', z' became /ć, 3́, ś, ź/, and r' > ř > ž. The pair /l' - l/ changed to /l - ł/ and finally to /l - u̯/.

Synchronic reflexes of these palatalizations --which I call surface palatalization (SP)-- will be dealt with specifically in 7.5.

7.3.1. The oldest process is postalveolar formation (PF), which is very similar to Italian palatal formation (see 7.6). Its usual name is 1st Slavic/velar palatalization. If we try a concrete formulation, we can write the rules

$$(P\ 1)\ \begin{bmatrix} -pal \\ +cont \\ (+high) \end{bmatrix} \rightarrow \begin{bmatrix} +pal \\ +del.release \\ -high \end{bmatrix} /\ \_\_\ +\ [suffix_{PF}]$$

which results in $k \rightarrow cz$ [č], $g \rightarrow d\check{z}$ [ǯ] (the output remains [-anterior]) and

$$(P\ 2)\quad \begin{vmatrix} +pal \\ -ant \\ -cont \\ +voice \end{vmatrix} \rightarrow [+cont]\ /\ [-obstr]\ \_\_ + segment$$

for $d\dot{z} \rightarrow \dot{z}$ [ž].[7]

Notice the diminutives in $-ek$ and $-ka$ with [ž] vs. [č] and [ǯ]:

rok	pastuch	bóg	mózg	drobiazg	waga	warga	rózga
'year'	'shepherd'	'god'	'brain'	'trifle'	'balance'	'lip'	'whip'
rocz-ek	pastusz-ek	boż-ek	móżdż-ek	dobriażdż-ek	waż-ka	warz-ka	różdż-ka
[č]	[š]	[ž]	[mužǯek]	[ǯ]	[ž]→[š]	[ž]→[š]	[ǯ]→[č]

Cf. also the alternations *drżeć - drgnąć* 'to tremble' (see 7.3.2.2.3), but *miazga* 'mash' → *miażdżyć* 'to mash' (cf. 7.8.4.3) and the loanword *alonż* < Fr. *allonge* without a change of *nż* to [nǯ]. *Patuszek* exemplifies *ch* [x] → *sz* [š]:

$$(P\ 3)\quad \begin{vmatrix} -pal \\ +cont \\ +high \end{vmatrix} \rightarrow \begin{vmatrix} +pal \\ -high \end{vmatrix}\ /\ \_\_ + [suffix_{PF}].$$

(P 3), which can be collapsed with (P 1), if desired,[8] changes /x/ to *sz* [š] and (abstract) /γ/ to $\dot{z}$ [ž] in a few words such as *wataha* [-xa] 'Cossack band', dim. *watażka* /vataška/, gen.pl. *watażek* [vatažek].

7.3.2. Suffixes which trigger postalveolar formation (PF) are:

7.3.2.1. In declension, there are only a few isolated forms:

7.3.2.1.1. The only (masculine) vocatives in $-e$ are:

Bóg [ɓuk]	kozak	człek	≈	człowiek [ču̯ov′ek]
'God'	'Cossack'	'man'		
Boże [bože]	kozacze	człecze	≈	człowiecze [ču̯ov′eče]

The normal vocative ending after velars is $-u$, e.g., *Polak* 'Pole', voc. *Polaku;* also *kozaku, człeku, człowieku* are the usual forms (Brooks 1975:69ff, Gussmann 1978c:33), the $-e$ variants are stylistically marked (Laskowski 1975:92 note 16). Non-velars undergo surface palatalization (SP), e.g., *pan* 'Mr.', voc. *panie* [pańe].

7.3.2.1.2. The neuter plurals (< duals) in *-y* (/ɨ/): *ocz-y* 'eyes', *usz-y* 'ears' (Brooks 1975:80, Laskowski 1979:50) from sg. *oko, ucho*. However the pl. of *oko* in the secondary sense 'blob of fat, point of a dice/playing card, look-out' is *ok-a*, and of *ucho* 'handle, sling, loop' generally *uch-a*, which confirms the morphological irregularity (lexicalization) of this neuter ending. In other paradigms the ending [ɨ] triggers either AF, the variant [i] SP, or there is no change at all (for details, see 7.4.2.3).

7.3.2.1.3. The locative plural of *Włoch-y* [vu̯oxɨ] 'Italy' (pl. like E. *The Netherlands*) is *Włosz-ech* [vu̯ošex], with the recessive ending *-ech* (instead of *-ach*), which occurs in a few other geographical names and triggers SP (P 7) with non-velars.[9]

7.3.2.2.1. A few adjectives with stem-final *g* undergo PF before the comparative suffix *-szy*,[10] e.g., *tęg-i* 'thick', comp. *tęż-szy;* but *such-y* 'dry', comp. *such-szy*.

7.3.2.2.2. Adverbs regularly undergo PF of velars, but irregularly SP of non-velars before the comparative suffix *-ej* (Brooks 1975:284, Laskowski 1979:168), e.g., *dzik-o* 'wildly', comp. *dzicz-ej* [ʒ́ičej]. However the comparatives of *szybk-o* 'quickly', *miękk-o* 'softly' are *szybci-ej, miękci-ej* with [ćej] or *miękc-ej*, against our rule.

7.3.2.3. In conjugation, PF plays a much more important role:

7.3.2.3.1. A subclass of the 'suffixless' group of the small, unproductive, and recessive class of verbs with infinitives in *-c*,[11] e.g., *piec* 'to bake', has the conjugation of the present: *piek-ę, piecz-esz, piecz-e,* pl. *piecz-emy, piecz-ecie, piek-ą*. The preterit is (3.sg.) *piek-ł*, impersonal pret. *piecz-ono*, pres. gerund *piek-ąc*, past gerund *piek-ł-szy*, past passive participle *piecz-ony*, 2.sg. imperative *piecz;* in a parallel way *g* is replaced by *ż*. Thus the relevant suffixes start with oral vowels. In other verb classes, non-velars undergo SP before the same suffixes, e.g., *niosę* 'I carry', PPP *niesiony* [ńeśonɨ]. The same holds for imperatives, so that the hypothesis of an underlying /i/ or /j/ (such as after vowels in *drży-j* 'tremble!' from inf. *drże-ć* and 2.sg. *drży-sz*) seems to be an attractive alternative[12] to the concrete hypothesis that postalveolar formation is the only signal of the imperative (cf. 7.5.2.4, 7.11.1.1. SP applies to non-velars, 7.5.4.3).

7.3.2.3.2. Velar-final verbs with infinitive in *-ać* have PF (of *k*, *g*) in the entire present, e.g., *płak-ać* [pu̯akać] 'to weep', 1.sg. *płacz-ę*, 2. *płacz-esz*, etc., pres. gerund *płacz-ąc*, impv. *płacz*, but preterit *płak-ał*, PPP *(o)płak-any*. Non-velar verbs have SP (Laskowski 1979:131, Gussmann 1978b:101f). The condition is clearly morphological.

7.3.2.3.3. Imperfective verbs in stem-final *-cz*, *-ż* alternate with perfective verbs in *-k-ną-*, *-g-ną-* (Laskowski 1979:157f), e.g., *krzycz-eć* [kšičeć] and *krzyk-ną-ć* 'to cry', *drż-eć* and *drg-ną-ć* 'to tremble'; the base stems recur in *krzyk* 'a cry' and *drg-awka* 'a trembling'. This is rather a case of (productive) derivational stem formation[13] of verbs with the infinitives *-eć* and *-yć* (underlying /ić/, see 7.5.4.1 note 35) which triggers SP with non-velars, e.g., *znak* 'sign' → *znacz-yć* 'to signify', *patałach* 'blunderer' → *patałasz-yć* 'to blunder', *skrzyp* 'creak' → *skrzypi-eć* 'to creak', *gon* 'chase' → *gon-ić* [gońić] 'to hunt' (cf. 7.3.2.4.1).

7.3.2.4. General and productive PF, parallel to SP with non-velar stem-final consonants, is triggered by the following suffixes (which all start with oral vowels, i.e., /e, i, a/, or /j/, cf. 7.3.2.3.1):

7.3.2.4.1. Verbs in *-eć*, *-yć* (see 7.3.2.3.3) with their verbal nouns in *-enie*, e.g., *krzycz-enie*, *znacz-enie*. Non-velar stems take *-ić* with SP.

7.3.2.4.2. Denominal adjectives in *-asty* or rather *-/j/asty*, e.g., *mącz-asty* from *mąka* 'flour' (Gussmann 1978b:75-77, 1978c:33), cf. *krow-iasty* [krov'astɨ] from *krowa* 'cow' (Rubach 1981:75).

7.3.2.4.3. Denominal adjectives in *-ysty* (Gussmann 1978c:33), e.g., *śnież-ysty* [śńežɨstɨ] 'snowy' from *śnieg* 'snow', *miażdż-ysty* from *miazga* 'mash'. SP is triggered by the variant *-isty*.

7.3.2.4.4. Denominal adjectives in *-any* or rather *-/j/any* (≠ participles in *-any*),[14] e.g., *ziemniacz-any*, *blasz-any* from *ziemniak* 'potato', *blacha* 'sheet metal' (< G. *Blech*).

7.3.2.4.5. Expressive derivations in *-yna* (*-ina*), *-yca* (*-ica*) (see Gussmann 1978b:50, 63, 1978c:32), e.g., *śnież-yca* 'blizzard' from *śnieg* 'snow', *druż-yna* 'team' from *druh* /druɣ/ 'boy scout' (Gussmann 1977:56). There is one exception to (P 7) with *-y/ica*: Russian-loaned *car-yca* 'empress' from *car* 'emperor' (not *[caẑɨca]).

7.3.2.4.6. The relatively infrequent result nouns in *-eń* (Gussmann 1978c:33), e.g., *tłucz-eń* 'fallen stone' from *tłuk-ę* 'I hit' (inf. *tłuc*). There is one, at least possible, exception (to P 10): *dur-eń* 'idiot' ← *dur-nieć* 'to get stupid' ← *dur-ny* 'stupid'.

7.3.2.4.7. The fem. suffix *-anka*, e.g., *panna Różdż-anka* 'Miss Rózga' (Brooks 1975:275), *koleż-anka* from *kolega* 'colleague', *Sapież-anka* from the noble name *Sapieha*, *blasz-anka* 'box of sheet metal' from *blacha*, *ziemniacz-anka* 'potato (*ziemniak*) soup'.

7.3.2.5. The following parallel set is not general, i.e., PF has exceptions before the following suffixes (which start with vowels AND consonants):

7.3.2.5.1. Agent nouns[15] in *-nik*, fem. *-nica* (Gussmann 1978a, 1978b:53, 65f), e.g., *orzesz-nik* 'hickory' from *orzech* 'nut', *dłuż-nik* 'debtor' from *dług* 'debt', *rocz-nica* 'anniversary' from *rok* 'year', but *ciąg-nik* 'tractor' from *ciągn-ąć* 'to tug' rather than from *ciąg* 'train'; deverbal also *wy-krzyk-nik* 'exclamation point' to *wykrzyk-nąć/wykrzycz-eć* (7.3.2.3.3) 'to exclaim'. For other final consonants (triggering SP), cf. (for P 7) *wietrz-nik* [vʹetšńik] 'air hole' from *wiatr* 'wind', but *piekar-nik* 'oven' to *piekarz* 'baker' (Gussmann 1978a:33), *kwartal-nik* 'quarterly' from *kwartał* 'quarter' (SP is regular only with *ł* → *l*, cf. 7.3.2.5.3).

7.3.2.5.2. Agent nouns in *-arz*, fem. *-arka* (Gussmann 1978b:75, 1978c:33), e.g., *tabacz-arz* [tabačaš] 'tobacco sniffer' from *tabaka* 'tobacco'; but *druk-arz* 'printer' from *druk* 'print' (< G. *Druck*), *księg-arz* 'book seller' from *księga* 'book', and all modern loanwords such as *kajak-arz* 'kayak sportsman', *pudling-arz* 'puddlinger'. Cf. the variation[15a] in *bajcz-arz* = *bajk-arz* 'fable teller' from *bajka* 'fable, fairy tale', *fajcz-arz* = *fajk-arz* 'pipe producer' from *fajka* 'pipe', *sklepik-arz* = dial. *sklepicz-arz* 'shopkeeper' from *sklepik* 'small shop'. Also SP is recessive with non-velar stems. Of teh derived local suffix *-arnia*: *królik-arnia* and *królicz-arnia* 'rabbit warren' from *królik* 'rabbit', *ampułk-arnia* and *ampułcz-arnia* from *ampułka* 'ampoule' (cf. Górska 1982:155).

7.3.2.5.3. Denominal adjectives in *-ny*,[16] e.g., *rocz-ny* 'yearly' from *rok* 'year', *strasz-ny* 'terrible' from *strach* 'fear'. But there are a few exceptions with *ch* [x]: *zmierzch-y* from *zmierzch* [zm'ešx] 'dawn', deadverbal (or depronominal) *po-wszech-ny* 'general' and expressive compound suffixes *-uchny*, *-achny*, e.g., *mil-uchny* = *mil-utki* = *mil-usieńki* 'very dear' from *mił-y* 'dear', *cich-uchny* = *cich-usieńki* 'completely silent',[16a] *dług-achny* 'very long', *grub-achny* 'very gross' from *cich-y*, *dług-i*, *grub-y*. SP is general only with *ł* → *l* and occurs in a few cases with *r*, e.g., *wiatro* 'wind' → *wietrz-ny* 'windy' (cf. 7.3.2.5.1).

7.3.2.5.4. Nominal suffix *-ak* (laskowski 1975:105), e.g., *strasz-ak* 'dummy pistol' from *strach* 'fear', but *drug-ak* 'pupil of the second class' from *drugi/a* 'second'.

7.3.2.5.5. There is a series of still less general suffixing MRs, for which I simply refer to Laskowski (1975:42, 104), Gussmann (1978a:70f, 1978b:59, 77, 1978c:33, 36), and Rubach (1982:74ff) (cf. 7.4.5).

7.3.2.6.1. The diminutive formation with m. *-ek*, f. *-ka*, n. *-ko* (underlying /ek, eka, eko/, cf. Gussmann 1978a:73, 1978b:34f, 47-50, 1978c:32, 35) is totally general and productive with velars, e.g., *człowiek* 'man', dim. *człowiecz-ek*; *flacha* 'bottle' (with diachronic back formation), dim. *flasz-ka* (cf. G. *Flasche* ['flašə]), *druh* /druɣ/ 'boy scout', fem. *druż-ka*, gen.pl. *drużek* (Gussmann 1977: 56, cf. 7.11.5.4.2). However, there is no SP before *-ek*, etc., with non-velars, e.g., *dom* 'house', dim. *dom-ek*, double dim. *dom-ecz-ek*. This is strikingly different from the completely general SP of non-velars before the suffix *-ik* (see 7.5.5.1).

7.3.2.6.2. PF before the adjectival suffix *-liwy* is not general and has no parallel SP of non-velars, e.g., *moż-liwy* 'possible' from *mog-ę* 'I can' (inf. *móc*), *płacz-liwy* 'tearful, whining' from *płak-ać* 'to weep', but *zapobieg-liwy* 'precautious' from *zapobieg-ać* 'to be precautious', cf. the variation in *strach-liwy* = *strasz-liwy* 'terrible' from *strach* 'fear'.

7.3.3. Now it is time to discuss alternative, more abstract formulations of PF:

7.3.3.1. The main option is to split up PF (P 1) into two successively applying PRs: The first could be identical with SP (7.5, P 7) and change /k/ to /k'/, the second PR would then change /k'/ into [č] in the appropriate conditions. This would give PF a free ride (Zwicky 1975:158 Q) and make the PR generating *cz* a more natural one since its input would be /k'/, which is closer to [č] than the more remote /k/, at least in diachrony.

Synchronically, /k'/ and [č] are [+pal], whereas /k/ is [-pal], but /k'/ is palatalized (distributed), which is the case with neither [č] nor /k/. Therefore we would have a Duke of York gambit (Pullum 1976) in changing [-distr] /k/ first to [+distr] /k'/ and then back to [-distr] [č]. This is fine in diachrony but less so in synchrony.

7.3.3.2. This split-up alternative would seem to work well with verbs in *-ać* (7.3.2.3.2), *-eć*, *-yć* (7.3.2.3.3, 7.3.2.4.1) and all other suffix derivations which trigger both general PF of velars and general SP of non-velars (7.3.2.4). For the suffix derivations with lexical exceptions (7.3.2.5), we have to assume negative rule features anyway.

7.3.3.3. However, SP would have to be blocked only for non-velars with diminutives in *-ek* (7.3.2.6.1) and the suffix *-liwy* (7.3.2.6.2), which would mean an ad hoc complication. In comparative formation (7.3.2.2) there is no strict parallelism between the treatment of velars (PF) and non-velars (SP). If we put the vocatives (7.3.2.1.1), the plurals (7.3.2.1.2), and the verbal paradigm (7.3.2.1.1) of velars and non-velars on the same foot by applying SP to velars as well (and only then PF), then we miss the important distinction that SP of non-velars is a regular and general cosignal of major morphological classes, whereas PF occurs only in minor morphological and morpholexical classes and is thus much less general, i.e., a general morphological class is cosignaled by general SP, a non-general morphological class is cosignaled by non-general PF.

7.3.3.4. If we use the free ride (7.3.3.1), then we have to cope with the further complication that SP of velars and/or non-velars occurs in many other conditions than PF of velars (7.5), particularly always before /i/, i.e., in reality there is not so much parallelism between the two types of alternation. In
addition, the phonological nature of th initial segments of suffixes before
which SP, AF, and PF of velars take place, is different, and we will find general SP of non-velars before all morpheme-internal and postprefixal /i/ (and of
/k, g/ even before /e/).

7.3.3.5. SP unmistakeably appears to be more of a low level rule than PF.
Therefore /k → k'/ would be expected to be ordered later than /k → č/ or /k' → č/
(see Linell 1979:190ff). In Stampean terms (Donegan & Stampe 1969:142ff, Donegan 1968:131ff), SP would be a lenition process, PF a fortition process, and
lenition processes should be ordered after fortition processes (5.17.2.2);
moreover, PF would be rather a rule (MPR or AMR), SP a process (PR), and rules
should apply before processes (5.17.1).

7.3.3.6. Abstract alternatives such as the masterpieces of abstract analysis in
Laskowski (1975), Gussmann (1978a, 1978b), Rubach (1981, 1982, 1984 using Cyclic
Phonology, cf. 5.17.1.5) are based on split-up analysis. In addition they introduce abstract palatal vowels which cause anticipatory palatalization; thus,
e.g., Gussmann's (1978a:22, 155) PR /16/ (or /5/) for PF becomes as simple as
[-syl] → [-back] / __ [-back]. Moreover they introduce an abstract underlying
distinction between tense and lax vowels. E.g., the suffix -n(-y) as in rocz-ny
(7.3.2.5.3) gets an underlying form /ĭn/, but /ĭ/ never surfaces as such and
there is rarely a surface vowel corresponding to the /ĭ/ of the suffix /ĭn/.[17]

7.3.3.7. I do not want to give the impression of ruling out abstract solutions
for their abstractness. But any further discussion of advantages and disadvantages of the abstract solutions cited in 7.3.3.6 is overshadowed by the following obstacle:

    /š, ž, č, ǯ, c, ʒ/ themselves undergo SP before /i/, including the outputs
of PF (/š, ž, č, ǯ/) and of AF (/c, ʒ/).

    Thus whoever splits up PF and AF into SP and PF' (and AF' respectively) has
to have SP reapply, i.e., has to assume the derivation /k/ → /k'/ → /č/ → /č̣/,
with SP applying both to /k/ and to /č/ (see 7.5.1.3).

7.3.4.1. For reasons presented in 7.3.3, it seems better to remain with PRs (P 1-3) and to mark suffixes for being subject to PF and/or AF and/or SP.[18] If PF acts as a major rule (within a morphological class, i.e., linked to MRs), then there are either no lexical exceptions (7.3.2.3.2, 7.3.2.4, 7.3.2.6.1 for PF) or the relatively few lexical exceptions are marked with a negative rule feature in the respective lexical entries (7.3.2.2.2, 7.3.2.5.1, 7.3.2.5.3, 7.3.2.5.4); if it acts as a minor rule, lexical items undergoing it are marked with a positive rule feature (7.3.2.1-2, 7.3.2.2.2 for SP only, 7.3.2.5.2, many subrules of 7.3. 2.5.5). In 7.3.2.3.1, PF cosignals a minor MR.

7.3.4.2. One might think of splitting PF into several PRs or considering some/ most/all of them as being part of the respective MRs.

7.4.1. The historical 2nd velar palatalization or synchronic alveolar formation (AF) can be formulated in two (three) synchronic PRs:

$$(P\ 4)\quad \begin{bmatrix} +high \\ -pal \\ -cont \end{bmatrix} \rightarrow \begin{bmatrix} -high \\ +pal \\ +del.rel \end{bmatrix} / \underline{\quad} + \begin{matrix} V \\ [-nas] \\ [Suffix_{AF}] \end{matrix}$$

which results in $k \rightarrow c$, $g \rightarrow dz$ [ʒ].

$$(P\ 5)\quad \begin{bmatrix} -pal \\ +cont \end{bmatrix} \rightarrow [+pal] / \underline{\quad} + \begin{matrix} V \\ [-nas] \\ [Suffix_{AF}] \end{matrix}$$

which results in ch [x] $\rightarrow sz$ [š], h [ɣ] $\rightarrow \dot{z}$ [ž], as with (P 3).

Before i-endings (among suffixes$_{AF}$), sz /š/ (also underlying /š/, see Brooks 1975:264, Rubach 1981:93ff) is changed to [ś] (prepalatalization) (cf. 7. 5.1.4).

$$(P\ 6)\quad \begin{bmatrix} +pal \\ -ant \\ +cont \end{bmatrix} \rightarrow [+high] / \underline{\quad} + \begin{matrix} V \\ [+high] \\ [Suffix_{AF}] \end{matrix}$$

7.4.2. AF is predominantly anchored in declension, i.e., before the following suffixes (cf. Rubach 1981:86ff).

7.4.2.1. Dative-locative sg. in $-e$ of (mostly fem.) substantives whose nom.sg. is $-a$ (after non-palatalized consonants) or of masc. nouns with nom. $-o$,[19] e.g., *ręka* 'hand', dat. *ręc-e*, names *Kościusko*, dat. *Kościuszcz-e*, *Sapieha*, dat. *Sa-*

pieha, dat. *Sapież-e, noga* 'leg', dat. *nodž-e, monarcha* 'monarch', dat. *monarsz-e.* Non-velars undergo SP.

7.4.2.2. Nom. pl. allomorph *-e* only in *ręc-e* 'hands' (former dual) from a velar. With non-velars (other than dentals), this *-e* triggers SP. Therefore the isolatedness of this form is due to morphology rather than to morphonology.

7.4.2.3. Personal nominal plurals in *-y* (Brooks 1975:82, 93ff, Gussmann 1978b: 73f, 1978c:33f), e.g., *kierownik* 'leader' → *kierownic-y* [k'erovńici], *zbieg* 'fugitive' → *zbiedz-y* [zb'eʒi]. Underlying this [i] must be an /i/: First, it palatalizes (AF) *k, g, ch* → *c, dz, sz* /š/. Then there applies a rule of *i*-retraction i → i (cf. Gussmann 1978:22f) after *c* (also if underlying), *dz* /ʒ/, since sequences *[ci, ʒi] are not permitted, e.g., *sportowiec* 'sportsman' → pl. *sportowc-y.*[20]

The pl. of *mnich* 'monk' /mnix+i/ gives /mniši/ with (P 5), and with prepalatalization (P 6) *mnisi* [mńiśi].[21] *-i* also remains after labials, dentals, and the lateral and causes SP, e.g., *agronom-i* [m'i] 'agronomists', *Arab-i* 'Arabs', *markiz-i* [źi] 'marquises', *studenc-i* [ći] from *student* 's.' (with SP and prepalatalization /t/ → [ć], /d/ → [ʒ́], /s/ → [ś], /z/ → [ź], /n/ → [ń]), *diabl-i,* pl. of *diabeł* [eu̯] 'devil'.

Whereas the ending of the personal plural is /i/, the non-personal pl. ending is /i/ (which is non-palatalizing), e.g., *arab-y* 'Arabian horses', *informator-y* [ri] 'guide books', *diabł-y* [d'jabu̯i] 'demons, hellhounds' (contrast above personal *Arab-i* 'Arabs', *informatorz-y* [ži] 'informants', *diabl-i* 'devils'), *ocz-y* 'eyes', *usz-y* 'ears' (7.3.2.1.2), *duch-y* 'ghosts', *watah-y* 'Cossack bands' (sg. *wataha*). For exceptional non-personal *-i*-plurals, see Stankiewicz (1955: 565). Non-personal *-y*-plurals can be used for personal nouns with a derogative connotation (Stankiewicz 1955:570f).

However, sequences [ki, gi] are not permitted in Polish.[22] Therefore *i*-fronting is applied after velar plosives (Gussmann 1978b:59f) with following SP: /ki, gi/ → /ki, gi/ → [k'i, g'i]; notice non-pers. pl. *kierownik-i* [k'erovńik'i] 'steering handles (on a bicycle)', *zbieg-i* 'circumstances' (contrast above pers. pl. *kierownic-y* 'leaders', *zbiedz-y* 'fugitives'). The same *i*-fronting applies after surface-palatalized consonants, e.g., in the plural of nouns ending in *-ość.*

Thus the antagonistic PRs of *i*-retraction and *i̇*-fronting help to distinguish (1) personal and non-personal nom.pl., (2) underlying /k, c/ vs. /t/, /g,
ʒ/ vs. /d/.

7.4.2.4. In the plural of adjectives (Brooks 1975:266ff, Gussmann 1978b:73f)
the distinction between personal and non-personal nominative plurals is already
guaranteed by the use of the non-pers. (usually non-palatalizing) ending *-e*.
The pers.pl. ending /i/ causes the same changes as with personal nouns (7.4.2.
3), e.g., *wielki* [v'elk'i] 'great' = /v'elk+i/ vs. pl. *wielc-y* [v'elcɨ] = /v'elk+i/
where one sees clearly the difference between sg. masc. /i/[22a] and nom.pl. /i/,
wszystek 'the whole' → pl. *wszysc-y*, *nag-i* 'naked' → pl. *nadz-y*, *dobr-y* 'good' →
pl. *dobrz-y* [dobʒi], *mał-y* [mau̯ɨ] 'small' → pl. *mal-i*, *młod-y* [mu̯odɨ] 'young' →
młodz-i [mu̯oʒi], *piesz-y* 'pedestrian' → *pies-i* [p'eśi], *głuch-y* 'deaf' →
głus-i[22b] (cf. 7.4.5).

7.4.2.5. The deadjectival adverbial ending *-e* triggers AF with velars, SP with
non-velars (Brooks 1975:283f, Gussmann 1978b:13, 1978c:33f), e.g., *wielk-i*
'great' → *wielc-e*, etc.; the only case of *g* → *dz* seems to be *srog-i* 'severe' →
srodz-e. This ending does not seem ever to be suffixed to stems in *-ch* /x/.

7.4.3. Whereas PF applies much more in conjugation than in declension, AF is
much better represented in declension than PF, but never does apply in conjugation.

7.4.4. In striking contrast with PF, AF has little application in derivational
morphology. Beyond the structural description of (P 4), the suffix *-stwo* triggers the change *k* → *c* and SP of non-velars (Gussmann 1977:46), e.g., *ptak* 'bird'
→ *ptacwo* 'poultry', *heretyk* 'heretic' → *heretyctwo* 'heresy', *górnik* 'miner' →
górnictwo 'mining', cf. *pan* 'lord' → *państwo* 'lordship'.

The same occurs before adjectivizing *-ski* (Gussmann 1978b:103f, 114), e.g.,
heretycki 'heretical'. Before these suffixes *g* and *ch* are deleted; e.g.,
Brzeski from *Brzeg* '(placename; G. *Brieg*)'; morpheme-initial *s* is fused with
preceding *c*, thus /k+stvo/ → /c+stvo/ → [ctvo] (cf. Laskowski 1981:9ff). There
is the alternative hypothesis that a special rule (AF') applies before these
suffixes.

Certain items must be marked for *k*-deletion (similar to *g/ch*-deletion, e.g., *Suwałki*, adj. *suwalski*, and all placenames in *-bork* (Laskowski 1981:9, 32)).

7.4.5. Having discussed the alternations between *-i* and *-y* in 7.4.2.4f, we are ready to make up for a lacuna in 7.3.2.5.5 and discuss the denominal adjective formation with the suffix *-y/-i* which triggers PF with velars, SP with non-velars. We find *-y* in: *kierownicz-y* 'leading' (≠ pl. *kierownic-y* 'leaders' ≠ pl. *kierownik-i* 'steering handles', 7.4.2.3) from *kierownik* 'leader', *boż-y* 'godly' from *bóg* 'god', *monarsz-y* [ršɨ] 'monarchal' from *monarcha* 'monarch'. However, *-szy* [šɨ] and *-ży* [žɨ] may be replaced with *-si* [śi] and *-zi* [źi] respectively, e.g., *mnisz-y* = (preferred) *mnis-i* from *mnich* 'monk' (pl. *mnis-i*), *pastusz-y* (preferred) = *pastus-i* from *pastuch* 'shepherd' (Laskowski 1975:113), *papuż-y* = *papuz-i* from *papuga* 'parrot', *mys-i* = *mysz-y* (?) from *mysz* 'mouse'.[23]

Elsewhere this rare suffix seems to be *-i* (causing SP), e.g., *małp-i* [mau̯p'i] from *małpa* 'ape', *wdow-i* from *wdowa* 'widow', *liliput-i* [ći] from *liliput* 'dwarf', *bez-nog-i* 'legless' from *noga* 'leg' (cf. Gussmann 1978b:59f). Recessive PF and subsequent SP applying also to velars seems to have resulted (or to have begun to result) in a split of adjective formation into suffixation with parallel /+i/ and /+ɨ/.

7.5.1. Surface palatalization (SP) can be formulated in the following PRs:

7.5.1.1. First, palatalization before certain suffixes, most of them starting with /e/.

$$
\text{(P 7)} \quad
\begin{bmatrix} +\text{cons} \\ -\text{pal} \\ -\text{cont} \end{bmatrix}
\rightarrow
\begin{bmatrix} +\text{pal} \\ +\text{distr} \end{bmatrix}
\Big/ \underline{\hspace{2cm}} \underset{\sim \begin{bmatrix} -\text{pal} \\ +\text{cont} \end{bmatrix}}{} +!
\begin{bmatrix} -\text{cons} \\ -\text{high} \\ +\text{pal} \\ -\text{nasal} \end{bmatrix}
[\text{suffix}_{\text{SP}}]
$$

This rule never applies to /x/ (or /ɣ/) and for /k, g/ is triggered by a few suffixes only (for details, see 7.5.3f).

7.5.1.2. Then we have palatalization of all non-palatalized[24] consonants including /x/ (and abstract /ɣ/) before /i/.

$$
\text{(P 8)} \quad
\begin{bmatrix} +\text{cons} \\ -\text{distr} \end{bmatrix}
\rightarrow
\begin{bmatrix} +\text{pal} \\ +\text{distr} \end{bmatrix}
\Big/ \underline{\hspace{1cm}}
\begin{bmatrix} -\text{cons} \\ +\text{pal} \\ +\text{high} \end{bmatrix}
$$

(P 8) turns /k, g, x, p, b, m, f, v, t, d, s, z, n, ł, r̂/
into   [k', g', x', p', b', m', f', v'] /t', d', s', z', n', ł', r̂'/.[25] (P 8) also
applies to /š, ž, č, ǯ, c, ʒ/, i.e., conceivable outputs of PF (P 1-3) and AF (P
4-5), e.g., in connected speech *już ide* 'I'm going already' and *noc i dzień*
'night and day' are pronounced with [ž'i, c'i] respectively.[26] For loanwords,
cf. e.g., *Djibuti* [ǯ'ibut'i] 'Djibouti'.

7.5.1.3. In connected speech (P 8) applies also to imperatives where (P 1) has
applied, e.g., to *skocz i* 'jump and' or *piecz i* 'bake and', *pomóz i* 'help and'
(cf. 7.3.2.3.1ff).

In 7.3.3.7 we noted that this allophonic application of SP undermines the
hypothesis of replacing PF (P 1) with the following rule sequence: (1) a common
core palatalization, identical with SP, changes also /k/ (subject to PF and AF)
first into /k'/; (2) this /k'/ is affricated by PF to /č/ or by AF to /c/. For
(3) this /č/ would undergo SP again and become /ć/ before /i/ as exemplified
above. I.e., an AMR or MPR of imperative formation would reapply as a casual
speech PR, which would run counter to everything we know about casual speech
PRs (see 5 passim).

On the other hand, the casual speech PR is identical with (P 8) except that
its domain is generalized from the word to the phrase (cf. 7.6.8.2). One who
wants to separate these two PRs nevertheless is faced with still another problem, i.e., where to assign both instances of SP in foreign words such as *Djibuti*
(see above).

Of course most instances of PF are triggered by suffixes which are at least
partially present at the surface. But in addition to imperatives we can mention
non-general word formations (7.3.2.5.5) such as the deverbal and deadjectival
nouns *płacz, straż, dzicz* derived from *płak-ać* 'to weep', *strzeg-ę* 'I guard',
dzik-i 'savage' respectively (Gussmann 1978b:77).

There are no such cases with AF, but non-general derived instances of /c/,
as in *móc* 'to be able', undergo casual speech SP before /i/ as well.

7.5.1.4. (P 9) 'Monophthongization' of /ł'/ → [l]. The secondary feature of
palatalization (which is strongest during the final portion of the segment) becomes a primary feature of palatality (extended to the total duration of the
lateral), which implies that [+back, +anterior] is changed to [-back, -anterior].

(P 10)   /r'/ → /ř/ → [ž]   (cf. 7.4.2.3 note 18)

7.5.1.5. (P 11) Prepalatalization of /t', d', s', z', n', c', z'/
                          to [ć, ʒ́, ś, ź, ń, ć, ź]. This PR can be
collapsed with the prepalatalization of prealveolars (P 6 in 7.4.1). Note that
neither (P 6) nor (P 11) apply in new borrowings or words sensed to be foreign
such as *sinus* [s'inus], *Djibuti* [ʒ'ibut'i], nor across word boundaries in casual
speech, as *kosz jabłek* 'a basket of apples' with [š'j] (Wierzchowska 1980:156ff,
Gotteri 1981:45ff).

In our presentation, the more concrete PR of SP (P 8) would precede the
less 'concrete' PRs of prepalatalization (P 11, 6) which apply only across suffix boundaries (7.5.2.6). An alternative is to posit a combined PR (or MPR?) of
(P 6, P 11) which would change /s, z, c, ʒ, n, š, ž, č, ʒ/ directly to [ś, ź, ć,
ʒ́, ń], similarly (P 11) which turns /r/ directly into [ž], (P 9') which turns
/ł/ (or /w/?) directly to [l]. The slightly non-general combined rule (P 11 &
P 6) would be followed by the general PR (P 8). The discussion of such options
lies outside the scope of this chapter.

What is important for us is that the nasals of *pan i pan+i* 'Mr. and Mrs.'
are different in casual speech ([n'] vs. [ń]), similarly *płacz i płacz* 'weep and
weep!' ([pu̯ač' i pu̯ač]), while the velars in *druk i druk+i* 'print and prints' are
not ([druk' i druk'i]),[27] nor are the prepalatals of *płać i płać* 'pay and pay!'
([pu̯ać i pu̯ać]). In other words, (1) casual speech palatalization of velars is
identical with their formal speech palatalization in morphological alternations,
(2) both processes are different for alveolars and postalveolars (7.5.2.6), (3)
prepalatals do not undergo further palatalization in casual speech.

7.5.2.1. Morpheme-internal distribution of palatalized ('soft') vs. non-palatalized ('hard') velars:[28] *[ki, gi, xi] are impermissible sequences (as are
*[pi, ti, ni, zi], etc.) (cf. Gussmann 1978a:10f), also *[k'ɨ, g'ɨ, x'ɨ] (simi-
larly *[p'ɨ, ć'ɨ, ń'ɨ, ź'ɨ], etc.). There are nearly no [kɨ, gɨ] (see 7.4.2.3),
whereas [xɨ] is freely permitted. [k'i, g'i] are frequent, *chi* [x'i] occurs only
in loanwords and in the onomatopoetic stem *chichot* 'tittering'. At least word-
initially, *kie, gie* [k'e, g'e] or their variants [k'je, g'je] are much more frequent than *ke, ge*, which occur only in loanwords.[29] [xe] occurs, but neither
*[x'e] nor *[x'ẽ], cf. *kuchnia* [kuxńa] 'kitchen', gen.pl. *kuchen* [kuxen] (cf. 7.
5.1, 7.6.5). *gię, chę* occur freely; word-initially, *kię* does not exist, *kę* is

rare, e.g., *kędy* 'whither', *kępa* 'bushel'. Before other vowels, [k′, g′, x′] occur only in a few loanwords and in *giąć* [g′onć] 'to bend' (see Gussmann 1978: 129f).

7.5.2.2. Minimal pairs with velars never occur morpheme-internally, e.g., acc. sg. *Polskę* [polske] 'Poland' vs. nom./acc.pl. *polski-e* [polsk′e] 'Polish', acc. sg. *drog-ę* 'way' vs. neuter nom.sg. *drog-ie* 'dear'. There are many more minimal pairs between velars and with the results of PF and AF, e.g., [č] and [c], than with [k′].[30]

7.5.2.3. There are morpheme-internal minimal pairs among non-velars (Brooks 1975:7ff), e.g., *bies* [b′es] 'devil' vs. *bez* [bes] 'without', *pasek* 'belt' vs. *piasek* 'sand'. For both types of cases (before /e/ and before other vowels), one could propose an underlying distinction /b, p/ vs. /bj, pj/, etc. A PR converting /Cjv/ into [C′v] is needed anyway for derived adjectives, e.g., nom. masc. *ryb-i* [rɨb′i], fem. *ryb-i-a* [rɨb′a], non-pers.pl. *ryb-i-e* [rɨb′e] from *ryb-a* [rɨba] 'fish'.[31] Thus we can restrict SP (P 7) before [e] to velars.[32]

7.5.2.4. This implies the assumption of an underlying /j/ (or even /i/) and postconsonantal *j*-deletion (cf. Gussmann 1978a:60) in those many alternations such as *panna* 'Miss, girl', gen.pl. *panien* /pańen/, adj. *panieński* (see Laskowski 1975:28ff). But *geolog-ia* [geolog′ja] 'geology' from *geolog* 'geologist', *astronom-ia* [m′ja] 'astronomy' from *astronom* 'astronomer' (Gussmann 1978a:67f) must then contain either a /j/ which is not deleted, or an underlying sequence /ija/ or /jia/ which gives a different result than underlying /i+a/ as in *rybia* (7.5.2.3).

7.5.2.5. The *j*-hypotheses of 7.5.2.3f are complicated and abstract, although still much more abstract solutions have been advanced by Lakowski (1975) and Gussmann (1978a, 1978b). A simpler analysis is the concrete analysis, namely that there exist underlying palatalized non-velars, but no underlying palatalized velars. Instead of *j*-deletion (7.5.2.4), we have to suppose more applications for independently necessary depalatalization PRs.[33] Of course all consonants palatalize before /j/, as in *geolog-ia, astronom-ia* (7.5.2.4).

Even under this analysis (P 8) must be upheld, since there are no non-palatalized consonants before [i, j] and generally palatalizing suffixes. Thus [p'i] may be either underlying /p'i/ or /pi/ (the latter presumably only in the competence for loanwords of those speakers who are able to suppress palatalization, which is very difficult).

7.5.2.6. However, underlying prepalatals (/ći, śi/, etc.) can be distinguished from /ti, di, si, zi/ (cf. 7.5.1.5) which give the outputs [t'i, d'i, s'i, z'i] in (1') loanwords, such as *tinta* 'tint', *dinosaur* 'd.', *silos* 'silo'; (2) onomatopoetic words such as *tikać* 'to tick'; (3) over prefix boundaries (after indigenous prefixes), such as *z+iritować* 'to irritate', *z+iszczać* 'to make true', *od+izolować* 'to isolate', *roz+igrać sie* 'to get exuberant', *bez+imienny* 'nameless', *pod+inspektor* 'subinspector', *przed+istnenie* 'preexistence'. As a consequence, the prepalatalization rules (P 6, 11) are restricted only to the position before palatalizing suffixes.

7.5.3. Suffixes which cause SP of velars are:

7.5.3.1. In declension, the masc., neuter instrumental *-em* palatalizes only /k, g/,[34] i.e., triggers (P 7), e.g., in *Polak* 'Pole', instr. *Polakiem* [k'(j)em]. It does not palatalize *ch* /x/ or any other consonant.

7.5.3.2. For nom.pl. /i/ triggering (P 8), see 7.4.2.3f.

7.5.3.3. Genitive *-i* (fem. declension) of stems in /k, g/ or surface palatalized consonants (Brooks 1975:50ff), e.g., *kolega*, gen. *koleg-i* [g'i]. All other consonants take non-palatalizing *-y* [ɨ] as genitive ending. Similarly to 7.4.2.3, we can apply *ɨ*-fronting to underlying /ɨ/.

7.5.3.4. All *-i/-e* endings in the adjective (only velars are affected), e.g., fem *wielk-a* 'great', gen., dat., loc. *wielki-ej* [v'elk'ej], pl. nom., acc., voc. *wielki-e*, gen., loc. *wielk-ich*, dat. *wielk-im*, instr. *wielk-imi*, masc. dat.sg. *wielki-emu*, gen.sg. *wielki-ego* (cf. Rubach 1981:124f).

7.5.3.5. In nominal derivation we have nouns in /ja/, see 7.5.2.4.

7.5.3.6. In verbal derivation, imperfectives in (infinitive) *-iwać* palatalize all velars, and we find *-iwać* also after surface-palatalized consonants, but

-ywać after all other consonants (Gussmann 1978a:14f), e.g., *wymyśl-eć* 'to con-
trive' → *wymyśl-iwać*, *koch-ać* 'to love' → *podkoch-iwać* [x'ivać]. If we start
with underlying /iv-ać/, then we can apply *i̯*-fronting (7.4.2.3), but this time
also after /x/. Notice also the alternation with PF in, e.g., *pobecz-eć* 'to
beat a bit' vs. SP in *pobek-iwać* (Laskowski 1975:160).

7.5.4. Most morphological categories (or MRs) which trigger PF or AF with velars, trigger SP (P 7) with non-velars (cf. 7.3.3.6):

7.5.4.1. General SP and PF apply before vocative *-e* (7.3.2.1), partially before
comparative *-szy* (7.3.2.2.1), in the present stem of verbs in inf. *-ać* (7.3.2.3.
2), in verbs in inf. *-eć* (7.3.2.3.3, 7.3.2.4.1) and *-yć/-ić* (ibidem).[35] Nouns
in *-yna/-ina*, *-yca/-ica* (7.3.2.4.5), *-ysty* (7.3.2.4.3), *-/j/asty* (7.3.2.4.2),
-/j/any (7.3.2.4.4), *-eń* (7.3.2.4.6), *-anka* (7.3.2.4.7), all starting with oral
vowels or /j/.

7.5.4.2. Non-general SP and PF apply in agent nouns in *-arz* (7.3.2.4.5) and
nouns in *-ak* (7.3.2.5.4).

7.5.4.3. Only PF applies before the diminutive suffix *-ek* (7.3.2.5.1, but cf.
-ik) and the adjectival suffix *-liwy* (7.3.2.6.2). PF before agent suffix *-nik*
(7.3.2.5.1) and adj. suffix *-ny* (7.3.2.5.3) corresponds to SP of *ł* → *l* (and a
few instances of *r* → *rz* [ž]) only. The minor verbal class in *-ec* (7.3.2.3.1)
with PF has a correspondence with the surface palatalizing class in inf. *-eść*,
e.g., *wiodę* 'I lead', 2.sg. *wiedzi-esz* [v'eźeš], inf. *wieść* (Gussmann 1978b:99).

7.5.4.4. SP and AF are general before dat.-loc. and nom.pl. in *-e* of nouns (7.
4.2.1f, not of adjectives 7.4.2.4), nom.pl. in *-i/-y* (7.4.2.3f, PF: 7.3.2.1.2),
adverb suffix *-e* (7.4.1.5), nouns in *-stwo*, adjectives in *-ski* (7.4.4).

7.5.5. Two suffixes triggering SP simply do not occur after velars, which is a
question of morphology:

7.5.5.1. The diminutive suffix *-ik/-yk* (Gussmann 1977:46, 49, 1978b:30, 37).
After velars, *-ek*, which triggers PF, is used instead (7.3.2.6.1).

7.5.5.2. The frequent nominal suffix -*ec* (Gussmann 1977:46) is productive after non-velars. For velar stems I found hardly any examples, e.g., *głusz-ec* 'a deaf man' (a word which not all informants accepted) from *głuch-y* 'deaf' and derivations from *róg* 'horn', such as *jedno-roż-ec* 'unicorn'.

7.5.5.3. The suffixes of 7.5.3 cause SP of velars only and therefore neither PF nor AF.

7.5.6. In accordance with 7.3.3, I propose that MRs of relevant suffixes (i.e., the suffixes within these MRs) should be marked positively and disjunctively for PF, AF, and SP.[36] So if PF has applied (non-vacuously), SP can no longer apply to the same item, etc.

7.6. The comparative evaluation of Polish synchronic PF, AF, and SP gives the following results:

7.6.1. Most of these PRs must be matched with more than one universal process type (see 5.2), which is phonologically the more unnatural the more processes one PR must be matched with.

7.6.1.1. PF (P 1, 3) and (P 5) must be matched with at least (1) palatalization, (2) palatal (af)frication of the shibilant type (7.4.5.3.2, 7.4.6.2). *dż* → *ż* (P 2) is a context-sensitive spirantization process of affricates (between vowels/sonorants) which reflects a natural hierarchy (cf. 7.4.5.2).

7.6.1.2. Similarly, AF (P 4) must be matched with (1) palatalization, (2) palatal affrication of the sibilant/alveolar type (7.4.5.3.2, 7.4.6.2).

7.6.1.3. In addition to (P 2), only SP (P 7) and (P 8) can be matched with a single universal process type, i.e., palatalization and fronting in palatal environment (7.4.5.3.2) respectively. Thus SP (score 1) is phonologically more natural than PF and AF (score 2 or 4 if without phonologically relevant context).

7.6.3. The distance between input and output is small in (P 7, 8, 2), but relatively great in (P 1, 3, 4, 5). This is a consequence of 7.6.1.

7.6.3.1. (P 1, 3, 4) are symmetric and thus regular (5.4.1) PRs as far as the input is concerned; (P 7) shows a hierarchical asymmetry: /x/ is palatalized before /j, i/, not before /e/ (as are /k, g/), e.g., Standard *chemia* [xemʹja] 'chemistry'. This seems to be particularly true in eastern Poland (e.g., Lublin), whereas in Warsaw colloquial speech the pronunciation is [xʹemʹja] and the instrumental of *groch* 'pea' is [groxʹem] instead of Standard [groxem], so that (P 8) also applies before /e/ as well. There is a phonetic explanation for the non-application of (P 7) to /x/ before /e/ in eastern Poland, where /x/ is more back than /k, g/, therefore palatalization is more difficult (an instance of the rich-get-richer principle).

The inputs and outputs are natural classes if more than one phoneme is involved. Thus all rules which interest us have score 1.

7.6.3.2. In their various applications, (P 1, 3, 7) behave quite differently to the point of being candidates for being split up into different PRs according to different types of conditions; (P 4, 5) are to be split up only into two rules (7.6.3.2). In SP, there is completely general (P 8), but not so (P 7). In most morphological types of application, (P 1) does not apply to the whole input set /k, g, x/.

7.6.4. (P 1, 3, 4, 5) are neither constraints[37] on, nor helps for pronounceability or perceptibility (5.6). As for (P 2), [žǯ] is easier to pronounce than [zž],[38] [vžv] easier than [vǯv], but [ž] after vowels and sonorants is easily pronounceable. SP (P 7) presents an aid to, (P 8) a constraint on pronounceability and perceptibility, as I have noticed with informants.

7.6.5. Conditioning is morphological and phonological, but to varying degrees (cf. 5.7, 5.9). Let us give score 1 to mere phonological, score 2 to mainly phonological, score 3 to mainly morphological, score 4 to mere morphological conditioning.

7.6.5.1. The conditioning of (P 1, 3) is morphological. The suffixes involved start with /j, i, e, ɨ, a, o, š, n, ł/ (and *ǫ* /õ/ in 7.3.2.3.2). The imperative *piecz* (7.3.2.3.1) has a zero-suffix (or no suffix), unless one assumes an underlying /j/-suffix and then *j*-deletion or *j*-fusion. In 7.3.2.3.2, PF is the signal of present formation, irrespective of the following suffix-initial phoneme.

The conditioning of (P 2) is phonological, but also morphological insofar as it applies only to derived /ž/ (derived from /g/) and only before suffix boundary.

7.6.5.2. The conditioning of (P 4, 5) is morphological. However --with the exception of the derivational suffixes *-ski*, *-stwo* (7.4.4)-- all (= declensional) suffixes start with oral palatal vowels, which is a phonologically natural environment,[38a] so that one can think of a rule split of AF into rules (a) in declension before /i, e/, (b) in derivational morphology.

7.6.5.3. SP (P 7, 8) can be assigned to two types of applications: (a) before suffixes identical or similar to those triggering PF, AF (7.6.5.1f); (b) before following /(+) j, i, (e)/, the natural hierarchy of palatalization (P 8 applies only before /i, j/). Notice that all suffixes which trigger only SP, but not PF, AF, start with /j, i, e/. Thus we have a clear scale of phonological naturalness: SP > (P 8) > (P 7) > AF > PF.

7.6.6.1. The domians involved are phonological (5.8) in the following cases: (P 8) always applies syllable-internally, but in more casual speech certain regions of Poland have it even cross-sylabically but phrase-internally, as in [vruk'irka] (7.5.1.2f). The other palatalization rules apply within and across the syllable, but only within the morphological word.

7.6.6.2. (P 1, 3, 4, 5, 7) apply only beyond morpheme-boundary; for historical reasons the application is mostly syllable-internal. (P 2) never has the occasion to apply within a morpheme.

7.6.7. Lexical factors (5.10) play a role in PF (P 1, 3) insofar as within certain categories it has many lexical exceptions (7.3.2.5) or even applies only to a few lexical items (7.3.2.1, 7.3.2.5.5). This holds also for the corresponding applications of (P 7) of SP, but not to (P 7) as applied to velars.

7.6.8.1. SP (P 8) is obligatory before /j, i/; (P 2) is phonologically obligatory as well. For (P 1, 3, 4, 5, 7), obligatoriness is a factor of morphology and lexical exceptions/marking.

7.6.8.2. Similarly, hierarchic phonostylistic optionality (5.11) is a characteristic only of (P 8): Gussmann (1978a:12) cites optional palatalization of velar stops (only before [i], not before [e], which again follows a phonologically natural hierarchy) in sandhi (= less formal speech), e.g., in *jak idziesz* 'how are you going?' → [jak'iǯeš]. My informants have confirmed this for *ch* /x/ as well and agree that *wróg Edward-a* 'E.'s enemy' is [vruk$edvarda] in careful speech, [vru$gedvarda] or [vruk$edvarda] without palatalization of /g/ in less careful speech, but *wróg Ireneusz-a/Irk-a* 'I.'s enemy' becomes [vru$g'i] or [vruk'$i] in casual speech.[39] For other consonants subject to (P 8), see 7.5.1.3, 7.5.1.5. There is no phonostylistic variability (characteristic of very natural PRs) with other PRs.

7.6.9. As for generality (5.12), (P 8) is completely general, without morphological or lexical exceptions, as far as velars are concerned. Morphologically restricted, but without lexical exceptions are (P 4-6) and the corresponding parts of (P 7). (P 1, 3) and the corresponding parts of (P 7) are partly general, partly major rules with few lexical exceptions, partly minor rules. Thus, following the distinction of Kenstowicz & Kisseberth (1977), they are not only minor environment rules (Kenstowicz & Kisseberth 1977:124f), i.e., morphemes are marked for triggering these PRs (when there is no such positive rule feature on a morpheme, then these PRs do not apply); there are also minor input rules among them, i.e., the lexical inputs have to be marked for triggering these PRs (7.3.2.1.1f, 7.3.2.5.2, 7.3.2.5.5, 7.4.5). (P 2) is general, if phonological and morphological conditions are taken together. Thus for generality we again have the scale: SP > AF > PF. Let us assign score 1 to phonological generality, score 2 to morphological generality, score 3 to lack of both.

PF has to be split into several rules in order to separate major and minor rules, or minor environment and minor input rules.

7.6.10. One meaning of productivity (5.13) refers to the integration of loanwords (5.13.2). On Polish, see particularly Rubach (1980).

7.6.10.1. (P 7, 8) are completely productive, and the hierarchy /j, i/ vs. /j, i, e/ of (P 7, 8) is respected. /j, i, e/-suffixes always trigger SP (at least for velars), e.g., instr. *Planki-em, banki-em, tangi-em* of *(Maks) Plank,*[40] *bank, tango* (Gussmann 1978a:13, Rubach 1981:131).

Morpheme internally all /k, g, x/ are palatalized before [j, i], e.g., in *chinina* 'quinine', *historia* [x'i], *geologia* [g'ja], *kiks* 'a kick', *gips* 'gypsum' (G. *Gips*), *girlanda* 'garland' (It. *ghirlanda*), cf. *whisky*, *groggy* (7.4.2.3 note 22) and Rubach (1981:78f).

Before [e], all /k, g/ used to be palatalized, and this palatalization has been preserved in earlier loanwords, e.g., *kielich* [k'elix] 'chalice' (G. *Kelch*), *kiermasz* 'kermis', *gielda* 'purse' (G. *Geld* 'money'), cf. Gussmann (1978b:61). Later loanwords were still palatalized, but this SP was dropped a few decades ago, e.g., *gieografia* [g'eograf'ja], *gieolog, gieometria* > *geografia, geolog, geometria* 'geography, geologist, geometry'. Other palatalized velars are heard only from the older generation, e.g., *kielner* 'waiter' (G. *Kellner*) instead of present-day *kelner*. Modern loanwords do not palatalize, e.g., *bakelit, kemping* 'camping'.[41]

Interestingly, SP seems to be more productive in (unstressed) final sylla- bles, where there is some partial fluctuation, e.g., *lag(i)er* 'concentration camp' (G. *Lager*); older loans are *szlagier* [šlag'er] 'hit' (G. *Schlager*), *krytykier* 'niggling critic' (G. *Kritiker*), *blagier* 'hoaxer' (F. *blagueur*).

Or [k'e, g'e] are replaced by [k'je, g'je] (Rubach 1981:122f). All this shows clearly that SP of velars has been lost before morpheme-internal /e/.

7.6.10.2. Also AF is productive in loanwords, e.g., the dative of *koka* 'Coke' is *koc-e* (Gussmann 1978b:29, 44f), cf. learned words such as *fonetyka* 'phonet- ics', *replika* → dat. *fonetyc-e, replic-e*, or nom.pl. *pedagodz-y* from *pedagog* 'pedagogue', foreign placename *Saratoga*, dat. *Saratodz-e* (Rubach 1981:87).

7.6.10.3. At lease certain subrules of PF are productive in loanword integra- tion. E.g., the diminutive (7.3.2.6.1) of *koka* 'Coke' is *kocz-ka* (cf. Gussmann 1978b:29), of *befsztyk* 'beefsteak', *befsztycz-ek* (Rubach 1981:77); the adjec- tive of *fonetyka* is *fonetycz-ny* 'phonetic', etc.[42] The same holds for infini- tives in *-yć* (7.3.2.4.1), e.g., *Prusak* 'Prussian' → *prusacz-yć* 'to Prussianize'; for *kajak* 'kayak', one can easily form the acceptable denominal verb *kajacz-yć* 'to paddle a kayak'. But this type of productivity holds even for non-general parts of (P 1), e.g., *buldoż-y*, adj. of *buldog* 'bulldog' (7.4.5). But Russian *carica* was borrowed as *caryca* (7.3.2.4.5) and not transformed to **carz-yca* *[cažica]. (P 2) does not apply to the Albanian personal name *Hodža* (Alb. *Hodxa*) (cf. 7.3.2.5.2) because there is neither a boundary before the /a/ nor an underlying /g/.

On the other hand, no MPRs or AMRs seem to be applied to loanwords from French in the Polish language used by Poles living in northern France. But since these Poles never inflect these French words (Gogolewski & Kopec 1980) and since no Polish derivations from French words are recorded, how could MPRs and AMRs be applied? Foreign words which are not integrated into native morphology are not subject to native MPRs and AMRs (cf. 5.13.2.8).

7.6.10.4. We see again that productivity in loanword integration does not properly differentiate between phonologically more or less natural rules. Morphological integration is a necessary but insufficient condition for the application of MPRs, but often also for PRs.

7.6.10.5. Another meaning of productivity refers to indigenous neologisms and abbreviations (5.13.1). Here my material is scanty. As for SP, Gussmann (1978a:13) reports the instr. *branki-em* formed from the nonsense word *brank* (confirmed by my informants).

If abbreviations are inflected at all, they follow at least SP (P 7), e.g., *Fablok* = *Fabryka Lokomotyw* and *Pafawag* = *Państwowa Fabryka Wagonów* have the instrumentals *Fablokiem*, *Pafawagiem* and the nom.pl. *Fabloki* [kʹi], *Pafawagi* [gʹi]. The pronunciation of *EKG* (= *elektrokardiogram*) as [ekagʹe] is a consequence of the pronunciation of the letter *G* as [gʹe].

7.6.10.6. As for experiments (5.13.4), there are some data for (P 2) (7.3.1). First I induced informants to form non-existing diminutives from *targ* 'market', *chirurg* 'surgeon', *Belg* 'Belgian', *pudding* [nk] (underlying /ng#/) 'p.', *kemping* 'camping'. They agreed on *Belžek*, preferred *taržek*, *chiruržek* over *tardžek*, *chirurdžek*, but *puddindžek*, *kempindžek* over *puddinžek*, *kempinžek*, i.e., there is no constraint on pronounceability. Cf. also *folga* 'alleviation' → dim. *foldžka*. Rubach (1981:77, 84f) arrived at similar results. This fluctuation corroborates the distinction between (P 1) and (P 2), i.e., /g/ does not change to /ž/ at once.

7.6.10.7. As for transfer of rules in second language acquisition (5.13.5), the PR of SP (P 8) clearly is applied to English by Polish learners, e.g., in *to hear* being pronounced as [xʹijer] (Rubach 1980); cf. the wrong Russian object case *sobak-i* 'dogs' with (P 8) in Wewiór (1978:161). But as we have seen in

5.13.5.3, Polish AF (P 4) can be applied in the learning of Russian under the appropriate morphological conditions.

7.6.11. I have no reliable data on slips of the tongue (5.14). Słoński (1947: 55) cites erroneous *Gewont* for the name *Giewont*, which might confirm the loss of SP (P 7, 8) before morpheme-internal /e/ (cf. 7.7.10.1). This is presumably a foreign name, and Słoński, as usually, does not fulfill the minimal 'philological' requirements for data gathering in this field.

7.6.12. Interesting aphasic data have been elicited by Halina Mierzejewska and Stanisław Grotecki (Polish Academy of Sciences, Warsaw) in a test elaborated at my suggestion (in view of this chapter). Their (yet unpublished but available) results seem to agree with my prediction that the degree of morphotactic transparency (relatable to phonological naturalness) correlates with the degree of both retention and the direction of substitution of morphological operations used by aphasics.

In a plural production test, patients had to form plurals from singulars such as I *kot* 'cat', II *kajak* 'kayak', III *pilot* 'p.', IV *Polak* 'Poke'. The respective plurals are:

I   *kot-y* [ko$^\$$tɨ]: Here only entirely productive and transparent PRs of resyllabification and hardly observable intrinsic allophony interfere.

II   *kajak-i* [ka$^\$$ja$^\$$k′i]: In addition to resyllabification the PR of SP (P 8) applies.

III   *piloc-i* [pi$^\$$lo$^\$$ći]: Here we have in addition the PR of prepalatalization (P 11), which effects a larger distance between /t/ and /ć/ than between /k/ and /k′/. Moreover this is a neutralizing PR with all its consequences.

IV   *Polac-y* [po$^\$$la$^\$$cɨ]: In addition to resyllabification we have the MPR (P 4) of AF.

As predicted, the number of errors rose from categories I through IV. Moreover, class III plurals were more often replaced by erroneous class I plurals than the other way around. And the same happened with class II and IV plurals.

7.6.13. All PRs and MPRs discussed are ordered after all MRs involved. But there are problems with subrules of SP (see 7.5.1.5). For a cyclic treatment, see Rubach (1981).

However, there is a morphology-conditioned selection of suffixes for triggering PF, AF, and SP (P 7). In ordering PF and AF before SP (P 7, 8) one can describe some of these conditions phonologically instead. This would be an ordering of phonologically less natural PRs before more natural ones (cf. also 7. 5.1.5).

7.6.14. Phonological iconicity (5.18) is good in (P 7, 8) since in addition to fronting of velars, only a secondary feature is added. One can write (P 5) so that they involve only one feature specification change, but the phonetic difference between input and output is at least as great as with [k] → [k̍]. There is only one feature specification change in (P 2), but more in (P 1, 4). On the scale of 5.18.3.1, (P 8) obtains score 2, (P 8) score 4, all the others score 5.

7.6.15. As for phonological indexicality (5.19), so-called 'semi-palatalization' of /ci, ti/ to /ći, t'i/, etc., looks more like a case of coarticulation in performance than other instances of (P 8) such as /ki/ to /k'i/ and more like it than any other rule.

(P 8) is more phonologically indexical than (P 1, 2, 3, 4, 7), which involve morphological indexicality as well. Imperative formation (7.3.2.3.1) is not indexical insofar as it cannot refer to an element present on the surface, but it leaves a trace. MPRs and AMRs refer indexically to morphological categories.

7.6.16. Nearly all rules discussed are phonologically one-way or more-ways opaque (5.20):

7.6.16.1. Morphological and lexical exceptions are found to (P 1, 3, 7). (P 4-6, 2) have no lexical exceptions. (P 8) is transparent in this respect.

7.6.16.2. /č, š, ž, c, ʒ/ generated by (P 1-5) neutralize with identical underlying segments, e.g., waž-nik 'weighing inspector' ← wag-a 'balance' vs. kabotaž-nik 'coastal vessel' ← kabotaž 'coastal shipping', fem. kolež-anka (7.3. 2.4.7) and Paryž-anka 'Parisian' ← Paryž 'Paris' (cf. Gussmann 1976:299f, 1978b: 78). Palatalized consonants may either be derived by (P 7) or (P 8) or be underlying, although the probability of ambiguous forms is small in pre-suffixal position.

[x′, k′, g′] are only derived and are thus totally transparent like [s′, z′, t′, d′, ć, ʒ′], etc.

7.6.16.3. Many output segments can be derived from several input segments (not identical with their respective output segments) or by more than one rule (similar to overkill, Rubach 1976), e.g., *sz* [š] may come from /x/ by (P 3, 5) or from /š/, [ž] may come from /g/ by (P 1 + 2) or from /r/ by (P 7 + 10) (cf. Gussmann 1978a:33) or from /ž/, *cz* [č] may come either from /k/ by (P 1) (e.g., *rocz-nik ← rok* 'year') or from /c/ by a similar rule (e.g., *ulicz-nik* 'urchin' ← *ulic-a* 'street') or from /č/. *dż* [ǯ] is derived from /g/ by (P 1), whereas in fast speech [ǯ] can be derived from /dž/ as in *Andrzej* 'Andrew', *wiedrze,* dat. of *wiadro* 'bucket' (i.e., [ǯ] ← ← /dr/), and in Cracow *idź* /#/ *że* [iǯže] 'come now!' can become [iǯ:e]; and there is underlying /ǯ/.

7.6.16.4. Only (P 4) is a possible candidate for a PR applying beyond its structural description.

7.6.16.5. Transparency is not achieved if extrinsic ordering or an equivalent device is imposed. In various ways (7.3.3) we have tried to avoid extrinsic ordering of PRs. However the ordered morphological and lexical features [±PF, AF, SP] in the lexical entry of words and morphemes is an equivalent. In whatever way we describe it, SP (P 7, 8) before /j, i, (e)/ are the most transparent among the rules compared here. For the ordering of Polish rules in a more abstract framework, see especially Gussmann (1978b:74, 77f, 80ff, 1978c:39).

7.6.16.6. Thus as for biuniqueness between phonological input and output (5.20) of velars, we find it only in (P 7, 8), and only for the never underlying [k′, g′, x′] (score 2). All other rules are non-unique (score 3); there are no unique rules among them like Polish final devoicing (score 2). Of course the phonemic status of palatalized consonants is still shaky (1) since their functional load is small and (2) since experimental perceptual studies by W. Jassem (cited by Paulsson 1969:218) show that the relevant contrast between [ć′i] and [ćɨ] is not the palatalization contrast, but the contrast between /i/ and /ɨ/.

7.6.16.7. Recoverability (5.20)[43] of velar inputs is excellent with (P 7, 8), bad in (P 1, 2, 3, 4, 5) since there are always several sources conceivable.

7.6.17. Important diachronic characteristics of phonologicity vs. morphologicity are:

7.6.17.1. There has been rule telescoping in PF and AF (P 1, 3, 4, 5) producing better morphological signals but phonologically less natural rules. (P 2, 7, 8) are not telescoped.

7.6.17.2. We must assume that several rule splits have occurred within (P 1, 3, 4, 5, 7), which is phonologically unnatural, but morphologically natural.

7.6.17.3. Parts of (P 1, 7) have become subject to lexical fading (7.3.2, 7.4. 5), which is morphologically bad, but phonologically worse.

7.6.17.4. Application and morphological domain of (P 1, 3-5) have undergone analogy, which is not to be expected from phonologically very natural PRs, e.g., colloquial 1.sg. *pieczę* instead of *piekę* (7.3.2.3.1, cf. Stankiewicz 1960:198).

7.6.17.5. In some Polish dialects (Stieber 1973:136) /k', g'/ have changed to /c, ʒ/, which shows that AF is a recurring phenomenon in Polish and could be used as an argument for the language specific phonological naturalness of AF in Polish, i.e., as a base of articulation based on a 'family universal' (Lass 1975) or Sapirean drift or as a phenomenon which fits the phonological system (system adequacy in the sense of Wurzel 1979).

7.6.17.6. PF has been eliminated in several Slavic languages and dialects (cf. Stankiewicz 1966:512). By cautious interpretation of this comparative evidence, we may consider this as a symptom of PF producing the most unstable alternations. 'The less phonologically natural a rule is, the easier it is lost.'

7.6.18. For first language acquisition, the relevant data at my disposal are scanty: According to Zarębina (1965:98), children start to palatalize /p, k/ before /i/ very early and have much optional SP, whereas they seem to learn PF and AF much later. The rich material of Smoczyński's (1955) children Anka and

Pawełek shows very early (age 1;0) non-application and then nearly exception-less[44] application of velar surface palatalization before [i] (P 8): The adult input /ki, gi/ is always represented by the children's output [k'i, g'i] and there is no output *[ki, gi], as with adults. But there is never such general application of (P 7) or velar palatalization in general before /e/; only single correct forms are attested, e.g., the correct instrumental [kóńik'em] 'with the horselet' (Pawełek 2;2) from *konik*.

On the other hand, many outputs [si, zi, ci, ʒi, ti, di, ni, pi, bi, mi, vi] are attested, i.e., (P 8) is not totally general and productive with conso-nants other than velars, which goes well with the universal hierarchy of pala-talization (4.5.3.2). As for transparency/opacity of (P 8) with these conso-nants, the majority of these outputs [ci] come from underlying /cɨ/ (both chil-dren were generally neutralizing /ɨ/ with /i/ as [i]); in fact nearly all in-stances of underlying /cɨ/ were realized as [ci], e.g., Pawełek had at age 2;1 [zampńij] = *zamknij* [zamk'ńij] 'shut!', [ʒ́emi] = *będziemy* [benʒ́emɨ] 'we'll', [pauk'i] = *zapałki* [zapauk'i] 'matches'; [dv'i, dźi] = *drzwi* [džv'i] 'door' (age 2;0); [mikaj] = *zamykaj* [zamɨkaj] 'shut!' (age 2;2); [im'i] = *zdejmij* [zdejm'ij] 'let's take off!' (age 2;3), [m'i] and rarer [mi] = *mi* [m'i] 'to me'. Thus non-palatalization seems to have been partially functionally constrained.

According to Smoczyński's (1955) material, his children had not acquired PF and AF and the respective MRs triggering them by the age of 2;5.

7.7.1. On the following table the most important facts are displayed. The ver-tical columns show (I) PF of stops (P 1) in conjugation, except imperative for-mation (II), (III) PF (P 1) in derivational morphology if general, (IV) if not general, (V) PF of fricatives (P 3) in derivational morphology when general, (V) PF of fricatives (P 3) in derivational morphology when general, (VI) AF of stops (P 4) in declension, (VII) in derivational morphology, (VIII) AF of fricatives (P 5) in declension, (IX) PF of affricate spirantization (P 2), (X) SP of velars before /+e/ (P 7), (XI) SP of velars before /i, j/ (P 8).

The horizontal represents outstanding criteria or bundles of criteria. In the cells the numbers refer to the scores in 7.6 and 5; + means presence, - means absence of a criterion, blank means lack of data. Alternative assignments are in parentheses.

Rules	I	II	III	IV	V	VI	VII	VIII	IX	X	XI
	PF	PF	PF	PF	PF	AF	AF	AF	PF	SP	SP
	P 1	P 1	P 1	P 1	P 3	P 4	P 4	P 5	P 2	P 7	P 8
	conj.	impv.	der. gen.	der. nong.	der. gen.	decl.	der.	decl.			
7.6.1. process matching	2(4)	2(4)	4(2)	4	4(2)	2	4	2	1	1	1
7.6.3. regularity	2	2	1	1	1	1	1	1	1	1	1
7.6.4. constraint/aid pron.	4	4	4	4	4	4	4	4	3(4)	3	1
7.6.5. phonolog. conditions	4	4	4	4	4	4(3)	4	4	2(3)	3(2)	1
7.6.6. phonolog. domains	5	5(6)	5	5	5	5	5	5	5	5	1
7.6.7. no lexical factors	-	-	+	-	+	+	+	+	+	+	+
7.6.8. phonostylistic var.	-	-	-	-	-	-	-	-	-	-	+
7.6.9. generality	3	3	2	3	2	2	2	2	2	2	1
7.6.10.1-4 loanword integr.			+	+		+	+		+	+	+
7.6.10.5. neologisms			+						(+)	+	+
7.6.14. phonolog. iconicity	5	5	5	5	5	5	5	5	5	4	2
7.6.15. indexicality	+	-	+	+	+	+	+	+	+	+	+
7.6.16. phonolog. (bi)unique	3	3	3	3	3	3	3	3	3	1	1
7.6.17.1. no telescoping	-	-	-	-	-	-	-	-	+	+	+
7.6.17.2. no rule split	-	-	-	-	+	+	+	-	+	-?	+
7.6.17.3. no lexical fading	-	-	-	-	-	+	+	+	+	+	+
7.6.18. early child acquis.	-	-	-	-	-	-	-	-	-	-	+
7.6.12. retention in aphasia						4					2(3 in nonvel.)
global sum	34/36	35/38	33	35	32	30	32	30	24/26	22	9

7.7.2. Let us start with a global count, where plus is counted as 0, minus as 1. Blanks are signaled with +. If we leave out degree of retention in aphasia (7.6.12), then we arrive at the following groups:

(1) XI (P 8) with a score of 9.

(2) X (P 7) and IX (P 2) with scores of 22 and 24(26) respectively.

(3) AF (VI-VIII) ranging from 30+(+) to 32+ ((P 4) in derivational morphology).

(4) PF (I-V) ranging from 32++ ((P 3) = fricatives) to 35+ ((P 1) in non-general derivational morphology) or 34(37)++ (imperative formation).

This clustering gives a first indication that SP (P 8) before /i, j/ is a PR, that SP before /+e/ (P 7) and (P 2) may be either MPRs or PRs, that PF and AF may be either MPRs or MRs. But this global count --which, so to say, adds pears to apples-- does not allow any finer differentiation.

7.7.3. If we apply the qualitative weighting of criteria in 5.21, then the following are particularly interesting.

MPRs generally attain score 3, sometimes score 4 on the scale of aid-to-pronunciation (5.6.3ff, 5.21.2.1, 5.21.4.2). Thus SP (P 7) before /+/ and affricate spirantization (P 2) are likely to be MPRs. Moreover, SP (P 7) can be no PR because it applies only in certain morphological categories (5.9.5, 5.21. 6.3).

Prepalatalization of dentals (P 11), 7.5.15, seems to be on the way to becoming a MPR,[45] whereas SP (P 8) before /i, j/ is definitely a PR.

7.7.4. Our table shows important diachronic differences between affricate spirantization (P 2) and PF and AF rules. Both PF and AF rules have undergone rule telescoping and have been split into several rules, whereas (P 2) fails both criteria (cf. 7.6.10.6). Thus PF and AF rules are firmly connected with MRs, a property characteristic of AMRs. Another typical distinction between AMRs and MPRs lies in the weighting of conditions: PF and AF rules are clearly morphologically conditioned, (P 2) is both morphologically and phonologically conditioned.

Also according to the amount of structural change, (P 2) and (P 7) clearly contrast with PF and AF. All the other criteria are consistent with the classification of PF and AF as AMRs and (P 2) and (P 7) as MPRs.

According to several criteria, PF rules are rather prototypical AMRs, whereas AF rules have retained more resemblance to MPRs.

7.8.1. The Polish data analyzed here support the conclusions of 5.21. MPRs have many properties in common with PRs and MRs. There are transitions between MPRs and AMRs, and between MPRs and PRs both in synchrony and in diachrony.

If we take morphonology in its large interpretation of the interaction between phonology and morphology, then most of the phenomena discussed fall into this area. In its narrow interpretation as the system of MPRs, morphonology can claim only a small part of what we have discussed, i.e., what pertains to affricate spirantization (P 2) and to SP (P 7) before /+/. Both MPRs are fine examples of morphological and phonological factors combined. E.g., the MPR (P 2) is triggered by the AMR of PF (P 1) only, but within a plausible phonological environment which recalls a PR in all its respects.

7.8.2. Our analysis of Polish morphonology is very fragmentary since we have concentrated on velars only. If we compare it with the brilliant generative analyses by R. Laskowski, E. Gussmann, and J. Rubach, then it lacks their sweeping generalizations and looks rather clumsy. But it has respected more the role of morphological factors and it has not lumped together as PRs rules that behave quite differently in several respects. Although Rubach (1981, 1984) represents considerable progress because he classifies (P 8) as a postcyclic rule and the others as cyclic rules, there is still an enormous difference between the MPRs (P 2, P 7) and some odd rules of PF.

The morphology (and therefore also the morphonology) of a highly inflecting language such as Polish does not lend itself to sweeping generalizations in descriptive analysis, whereas the PRs such as (P 8) or final devoicing allow sweeping generalizations. However on the explanatory level, as has been found both in generative models of morphology and in Natural Morphology, all this complexity of descriptive morphology is regulated by rather few principles of sweeping generality, as will be seen.

7.8.3. If we compare our analysis with investigations within the framework of structural grammar (e.g., Schlenker 1964, Stankiewicz 1955, 1960, 1967, or ear-

lier, Baudouin de Courtenay 1895, or Trubetzkoy's (1934) systematic treatment of
Russian morphophonemics, all brilliant pieces of work as well), then it lacks
their sweeping reduction of morphonology to morphology. It unites certain types
of morphophonemic alternation under the same MPRs or AMRs and tries to correlate
the rules with facts, particularly of external evidence which structuralists are
usually not interested in.[46]

Their insights in morphological semiotics will be developed in 10, but the
same semiotic principles will be used for both phonological and morphological
explanation. The Polish material analyzed in this chapter will be one of the
main data sources for illustrating these principles.

Notes

1. For the compilation of data (beyond available descriptions), which proved to be necessary in nearly all sections, I used the 'Wielki Słownik Polsko-Niemiecki', W. Doroszewski's 'Indeks a tergo', and informants.

2. Cf. in general Paulsson 1969, Koźbiał 1980, Laskowski 1975, Rubach 1982: 95ff; for phonetics, cf. Wierzchowska 1980.

3. Paulsson 1969, Stieber 1973:126, Gussmann 1978b:33f, 59f, 1978a:16f, 22, Mikós 1979b, Rubach 1981:75, 100ff; cf. 7.4.2.3f, 7.4.4.

4. For the whole inventory, see Laskowski 1975:16ff, cf. Gussmann 1978a:21, Rubach 1981, 1982:98ff, 1984; for phonetics, cf. Wierchowska 1980; for fricatives and affricates, also Gotteri 1981.

   Only the distinctive features which are relevant for our chapter are given here. The phoneme /γ/ is only dialectally preserved on the surface (Stieber 1973:70, 12§); in the standard, it has merged with /x/, at least on the surface (see Gussmann 1977:54ff).

5. Speakers who replace [k'e, g'e] with [k'je, g'je] have only allophonic [k', g'], like always allophonic [x'].

6. Laskowski (1975:107), cf. Gussmann (1978b:140, 63ff), criticized by Rubach (1984).

7. Notice the formal speech differentiation between [č] in *czy* 'that' and [tš] in *trzy* 'three', between [ž] in *drożdża* 'yeast' and [dž] in *dżdży* [džžɨ] 'it rains', *dżdżowy* 'rain' (adj.), and other derivations from *deszcz* [dešč] 'rain', gen. *dżdżu* [džžu], with final devoicing in the nominative singular.

8. I keep (P 1) and (P 3) apart for easier reference.

9. Brooks 1975:92, 105, 114, Laskowski 1979:49, Stankiewicz 1966:198.

10. Whereas stem-final /ł, n, r, t/ undergo SP; see Brooks 1975:278f, Laskowski 1979:84.

11. Brooks 1975:190f, Laskowski 1979:128, 136, Gussmann 1978b:99, Tokarski 1978:229.

12. Gussmann 1978a:62, 1981, Rubach 1984.

13. Gussmann 1978b:89f, 97, 1978c:32, Rubach 1981:74f.

14. See Gussmann 1978b:75f, 1978c:33, 35f, Rubach 1981:75.

15. Including instrument nouns, etc.; cf. Dressler 1980a.

15a. With connotational and slight denotational differences.

16. Gussmann 1976:283f, 1978a:33, 1978b:74, 109f, 1978c:33, 36f.

16a. Cf. Gussmann 1978b:83f, and p. 85 for depalatalization.

17. The gen. plural of words like *pewny* 'sure' is *pewien* [pev'en], where a palatalizing /e/ surfaces. In the abstract analysis, the putative /ɨ/ is lowered to palatalizing /e/ in just this one form but deleted in all other environments.

18. Gussmann (1978c:35) discards morphological conditioning of these PRs with

argumentation.

19. Brooks 1975:50, 53, 101, 272, Laskowski 1979:22, 30, Gussmann 1978b:72f, 94.

20. *i*-retraction also takes place after *rz* [ž], but not after *ż* [ž], e.g., *informator* 'informer', pl. *informatorz-y*. Thus /r+i/ gives [žɨ], whereas /š+i, ž+i/ give [śi, źi] according to (P 6). This distinction can be captured by assuming that *i*-retraction applies to /r'/, or rather /ř/, the intermediate step between /r/ and [ž]. For a different type of *i*-backing, see 7.5.4.1.

21. The pl. of *druh* is *druh-owie*, with a different ending. For /ž/ → [ž] / __ i, cf. *groż-ę* 'I threaten', inf. *groz-ić* [groźić].

22. Gussmann (1978a:10) cites as exceptions two personal names (pronounced with [k'] in unguarded speech) and *kynolog* 'cynologist'; cf. also the foreign word *gymkhana* [gɨ] 'g.'. *Whisky* and *groggy* are pronounced with final [k'i, g'] respectively, i.e, they are nativized.

22a. Cf. Rubach 1981:87 note 4.

22b. This plural formation has expanded in diachrony. Rubach (1981:90) apparently takes this as an instance of a phonologization of a MR (cf. 5.18. 6ff), whereas it is simply an instance of a generalization of a MR.

23. *ptasz-y* = *ptas-i* from *ptak* 'bird', instead of expected *ptacz-y, is exceptional and a diachronic accident: *ptak* comes from earlier *ptach* with an isolated change x > k / __# (cf. Stieber 1973:70, Rubach 1981:92 note 6).

24. I.e., it does not apply to underlying /ć, ʒ́, ś, ź, ń/, cf. 7.5.1.5.

25. I assume (with most authors) that /ł/ underlies [u̯] (cf. 7.4.4.6.1).

26. Wierzchowska 1980:156ff, Sawicka 1974:34f, Gotteri 1981:45ff, Rubach 1981: 137.

27. The same holds for *chłop i chłop+i* 'farmer and farmers' with two identical [p'i] sequences, cf. Rubach 1981:114f.

28. Cf. Paulsson 1969, Gussmann 1978a:10f, 24, 1979b:59f, Rubach 1981:110ff.

29. When *ę* /ẽ/ is denasalized, new sequences [ge, ke] arise from /gẽ, kẽ/ word-finally; see Gussmann 1978a:24.

30. Paulsson 1969:230ff, Gussmann 1978a:20f, 1978c:37ff.

31. See Gussmann 1978a:70f, 1978b:31f.

32. Gussmann (1978b:42f) favors an additional abstract solution: He derives non-palatalizing [e] from an abstract non-palatal vowel.

33. Schenker 1964:34f, Gussmann 1976:285, 290f, Laskowski 1979:16.

34. Brooks 1975:71, Gussmann 1978b:43, 60, Mikoš 1979a:42f, Rubach 1981:111f, 120.

35. If we start with underlying /ić/, then we get the derivation /znak+ić/ → /značić/ (PF) → [značić] (*i*-backing after /č, ǯ, š/ and /ž/ (both *ż* and *rz*, cf. 7.14.2.3). After all other finals, surface palatalizing –*ić* is maintained. Of course all /k, g, x/ are subject to PF (see 7.3.2.3.3), so that there are no infinitives in *[k'ić, g'ić, x'ić] (cf. 7.4.5).

36. Unless the suffix triggering general SP (P 8) starts with /i, j/ (or /e/ if

(P 7) palatalizes only /k, g/);   see 7.5.3.1-3.

37.   See earlier Baudouin de Courtenay (1895:19).

38.   A similar assimilation to [žž] would blur the underlying distinction between /z/ and /g/.

38a. *y* /ɨ/, *ę* /ẽ/ are already more central, i.e., less palatal.

39.   Final devoicing is limited to the domain of the phonological word in Polish
and is applied, in some regions, even in casual speech of external sandhi.

40.   But also *Maks-em Plank* is used, which is an avoidance strategy, which implies that speakers are not completely at ease in applying SP productively
to foreign names.

41.   Paulsson 1969:223, Gussmann 1978b:60 note 9, Rubach 1981:78, 121ff.

42.   Gussmann 1976:284, Rubach 1981:77, 7.3.2.5.3.

43.   Gussmann (1976) is too optimistic about recoverability of morphologized and
lexicalized Polish PRs, e.g., an agent in *-cz-nik* (7.3.2.5.1) may come from
a stem with final *cz, c, k.*

44.   Two clear exceptions pp. 164, 171, one doubtful p. 163;   p. 164 Pawełek realized *kotkę* /kotke/ as [kaki], see below.

45.   Notice that the collection of maternal baby talk by Sussex (1976:98f) contains examples of overuse of prepalatalization before /e/ (i.e., mothers
can manipulate such substitutions consciously), but none of palatalization
of velars. On the other hand, all maternal substitutions recorded can be
matched with universal process types. Thus the lack of overused PF and AF
in these data is no surprise.

46.   Nor generativists: Notice the lacunae in our coverage of 'external evidence' due to the typical lack of interest in such matters. And it should
be rather Poles whom we would expect to elaborate monographs about various
types of external evidence for problems of Polish (mor)phonology.

8. PRELEXICAL RULES AND MSRs (MORPHEME STRUCTURE RULES)

8.1.1. According to Trubetzkoy (1931), the first part of morphonology is 'the study of the phonological structure of morphemes.' However, he did not take up this study himself later on, in contrast to some of his followers.[1] Following Trubetzkoy, Jakobson (1962.I:108f. [1949]) underlined that 'the different grammatical classes of formal units can be characterized by a different utilization of phonemes,' adding 'and even of distinctive features.'

8.1.2. In American structuralism and generative phonology, the term morphophonemics has been limited to the area of phonemic alternations. But within generative phonology, morpheme structure rules and then morpheme structure constraints (MSRs, see 2.2) have been developed in order to characterize the notion 'possible morpheme'; i.e., they predict of what underlying segments and in which order, a morpheme may be made up.

Without going into technical details and problems, I want to stress two of their properties: They hold for underlying representations, not for surface phonetics (phonetic representations), and for the morpheme, not for the lexical or morphological or phonological word, e.g., in Latin for the morphemes *nō-* 'we', *vō-* 'you', not for the lexical words *nōs*, *vōs*[2] nor for the morphological words (or inflectional word forms) *nō-bis*, *vō-bis* (dative and ablative) nor for the phonological words *nō-bis-cum*, *vō-bis-cum* 'with us, with you'.[3]

Finally it must be mentioned that there has been much debate about the duplication problem,[4] e.g., in Russian there is both a MSR of voicing agreement, as in *vostok* 'east' and *zdes'* 'here', and a PR of voicing agreement, as in *vozdvigat'* 'to erect' vs. *do vos-trebovanija* 'poste restante', where both a MSR and a PR express the fact that /st, zd/ and [st, zd] are permitted sequences in Russian, */zt, sd/ and *[zt, sd] are not.

8.1.3. MSRs have come under serious attack: The duplication of information on phonological constraints is uneconomical and may miss valid generalizations.[5] If correct constraints are formulated that hold only for the phonetic representation, not for the underlying one, i.e., surface structure/phonetic constraints (SPCs),[6] then duplication can be more easily avoided. Finally the relevant units for phonotactic constraints are the syllable and the word, but not the morpheme.[7]

8.1.4. In defense of MSRs, good countercases have been discussed, where phonotactic constraints/rules hold for morphemes only and at the underlying level --
or at least at a remote level if one follows the underlying level -- or at least
at a remote level if one follows a model where MSRs and MPRs and PRs are inter-
mingled in derivation.[8]

8.1.4.1. My first example (already in Dressler 1977a:54f) comes from the East
Caucasian language Hinalug,[9] which has vowel harmony restricted to roots: palatal /i, y, e, ø, æ/ vs. velar /u, ɯ, o, ɑ/. Thus its domain is the morpheme,
not the word. MPRs do not violate it (Kibrik 1972:56), but PRs do, such as the
casual speech PR which changes and merges (neutralizes) unstressed /i, ɯ/ into
their common allophone /ə/. This counterexample may not impress all those phonologists who do not take phonostylistic PRs as seriously as other PRs.[10] But
there is also a relevant obligatory PR (Kibrik 1972:28): ɑ → e / __ j, e.g., in
[p,ej'rɑm] 'shirt'.[11] Thus vowel harmony does not hold in the phonetic representation, but only in the underlying phonological representation (or at some
other remote level a model may postulate between the input and output levels),
i.e., for /pɑjrɑm/. Now a critic of MSRs may suspect that purported Hinalug
vowel harmony represents a spurious generalization. However, it holds for all
roots without exception, even for recent loanwords from Russian, i.e., it is
productive; cf. R. *stol* 'table' > H. *ustul* with a harmonic prothetic vowel, R.
stakan 'glass' > H. *isteken* where the prothetic vowel has influenced the harmonic quality of the following vowels (velar ɑ → palatal e), R. *tramvaj* 'tram' > H.
durumbe,[12] where the /u/ of the first and second syllable harmonize with underlying /ɑ/ of the third syllable before the application of the PR ɑ → e / __ j.

   In Hindi, nasal-stop sequences must be homorganic only in underlying morphemes, but not necessarily beyond a morpheme boundary or within the morpheme
beyond (the trace of) a syncopated vowel.[13]

   Kekchi speakers apparently differentiate borrowed (Spanish) intramorphemic
clusters from identical, but intramorphemic indigenous clusters (Campbell 1979:
76).

8.1.4.2. Another Hinalug example (Kibrik 1972:29) is voicing agreement between
adjacent consonants, which holds only within a morpheme and thus pertains to the

domain issue only. The same is true for agreement in voicing and glottalization of Circassian consonants.[14]

8.1.4.3. In Desano, nasal harmony holds for the domain of the morpheme, not of the word (Kaye 1976b, Kenstowicz & Kisseberth 1977:147f). Within the same morpheme all vowels are either nasal or oral and in agreement with them *m*, *n*, *ŋ*, *ñ*, *w̃* alternate with *b*, *d*, *g*, *y*, *w*, e.g., in *keo+ri+mĩhĩ* 'a ruler'. In Desano, morpheme boundaries always coincide with syllable boundaries, which is not the case in Hinalug and Circassian.

8.1.5. Examples of underlying constraints which are not true of the phonetic representation have been given by Kaye (1974a). Kaye (1981:472ff) cites the Northern Algonquian dialect of Lac Simon, where a word-initial constraint voices all word-initial obstruents, only to be contradicted by a PR of transduction which devoices initial and final obstruents.[15]

　　As Benveniste (1939:29) observed, Latin word-initial (and morpheme-initial!) *spr-* occurs only in perf. *sprēv-ī*, participle *sprē-tus*, agent noun *sprē-tor* from *spern-ō* 'I scorn'. It has to be added that word-internally, *-spr-* occurs only in the respective compound forms of *spern-ō*. Thus one may posit a constraint against initial *spr-* which holds for morphemes, syllables, and words, but only for the underlying level before the application of the MRs which derive the perfect, the participle, and the --productive and verb-like-- agent nouns.[16] If a model does not allow such MRs to apply after the definition of word or syllable constraints, then the constraint against initial *spr-* must hold for underlying morphemes. However, who guarantees that the lack of other initial *spr-* clusters is not fortuitous, considering the existence of *spl-*, *str-*, *scr-* (but not of **scl-* and **stl-*) in Classical Latin?

8.1.6. So far we have seen some internal evidence for MSRs separate from SPCs. If we claim psychological reality for MSRs, then 'external' evidence is even more important. Ohala's (forthc. III A) report on psycholinguistic experiments is rather inconclusive, whereas Wright's (1975) report vouches for the productivity and psychological reality of morphemic domains in (surface) phonotactics of English homorganic nasal-stop sequences as in necessarily homorganic *lend*, **lemd* vs. *scream-ed* with /m+d/, cf. 8.2.6.

8.1.7. Livia Tonelli[17] has found a new type of external evidence from an Italian strategy of avoiding stigmatized words. This strategy consists in pro-
nouncing the first syllable of the obscene word or malediction or curse and then
--after a short pause-- switching to an innocuous word which starts with the
same syllable. E.g., instead of *ca$zzo* 'penis' they say *ca$volo* 'cabbage', or
for a curse with *Ma$donna* they substitute *ma$ttino* 'morning'. An example relevant for our discussion is *stron$zo* 'shit', which is changed to *stron$boli*, or
without a pause, *Stromboli* (name of a volcanic island). The sequence **stronboli*
is prohibited by a MSR (duplicated by neutralizing PRs and casual speech PRs of
nasal assimilation, cf. Herok & Tonelli 1977, cf. 5.20.3.3). Now the /n/ in
stronzo and the /m/ in *Stromboli* are the same only if either (1) *Stromboli* is
derived from underlying /stronboli/ by the same PR we need anyway (see above),
an abstract solution (using the free ride principle) which most contemporary
schools of phonology rule out; or (2) if we assume an archisegment /N/ in
stro/N/*zo* and *Stro*/N/*boli* --but we have ruled out archisegments for other reasons (5.20.8.5.2); or (3) if we assume a MSR (as foreseen in the theories of
Natural Phonology (8.2.1)[19] and of Cyclic and Lexical Phonology) which relates
underlying /m/ in *Stromboli* to /n/.

A similar analysis is possible for the metathesis *rubber baby bubby bunkers*
of the tongue twister *r. b. buggy bumpers* (Schourup 1973) and paraphasias such
as G. *Bambus* 'bamboo' → *pandus* (Stark 1974:24).

8.1.8. Further evidence comes from loanword phonology (cf. the Hinalug example,
8.1.4). E.g., Spanish loanwords in Desano such as *María* > *baria, ventana* 'win-
dow' > *wetanã* confirm the reality of the Desano morpheme constraint on nasal
harmony (Kaye 1974b:58f).

Kaye & Nykiel (1981) cite loanwords in Lac Simon Algonquian (p. 26ff, cf.
8.1.5) and in cognate Odawa (p. 29ff) which seem to obey underlying word structure constraints.[20]

8.1.9. SPCs as the putatively exclusive phonotactic constraints still suffer
from other deficiencies.

8.1.9.1. They can be violated in word games (5.13.3.1), cf. Manaster-Ramer
1984.

8.1.9.2. They can be violated in slips of the tongue (5.14.1).

8.1.9.3. Often they do not hold for casual speech. Rubach (1976b, 1977:38ff) cites, e.g., Shibatani's (1973:91) prohibition of English word-initial stop-nasal clusters which is violated by casual pronunciations of *complete, concern, contain,* e.g., as [km$^\$$p.., kn$^\$$s.., kn$^\$$t..].

But this has been noted earlier for other languages:[21] In the Breton dialect of Buhulien (Dressler 1972), all underlying /Vns/ sequences are pronounced as /Vːs/, but in rapid speech (presto) /patronːeːz/ is not pronounced like lento [paˈtronːes] but as [paˈtrons] (Dressler 1972:54, 58), which violates the putative SPC against *[Vns] sequences, but not the underlying MSRs. Many Russian examples can be found in Barinova (1971a, 1971b) and Thelin (1971:123ff, 134ff), e.g., [ˈpžalsta] (cf. Reformatskij 1979:245) for [paˈžalujsta] 'please' violates both (1) a constraint against a sequence of labial and shibilant, (2) obstruent voicing assimilation (cf. 8.1.2).

SPCs can also be violated in emphatic speech (Manaster-Ramer 1984).

Now many phonologists discard, implicitly or explicitly, casual speech and speech variation in general. Linell (1979b:126) states explicitly that 'conditions pertain to careful pronunciations at the surface level.' This is unsatisfactory for several reasons:[22] (1) Careful pronunciations (in Linell's sense) comprise a very small part of actually pronounced utterances, maybe not more than 1%. (2) According to Linell (1979b:120), they have an elevated status among all types of pronunciations (from the most emphatic to the sloppiest): Their psychological reality is, so to say, increased. This seems to me rather the idealization of linguists and a tradition going back to earlier linguistic field work relying on dictation style. Now can such an analysis claim to be concrete as opposed to the 'abstract' MSR analyses? In my opinion there is only a difference of degree in abstractness. (3) Finally this view misses the fact that there are constraints which hold for the outputs of all styles and others which hold only for certain styles such as careful pronunciations. E.g., as I have noted in Dressler (1972:58, cf. 1975b:224), an unstressed sequence # stop-vowel-stop cannot be reduced to # stop-stop in Breton (e.g., *[ptrons]) nor in Welsh (Zwicky 1972 §3.3) nor in most local dialects and regional variants of German, e.g., the perfect participle *getan* may become [taːn] and similar forms, but never *[ktaːn], in contrast to [kseːn] from *ge-seh-en* 'seen' (cf. Wodak &

Dressler 1978:36f), cf. 10.10.1.3.

8.1.10. This does not mean at all that I refute the validity of phonotactic
generalizations for the domains of syllables, words, or phrases[23] and for phonetic outputs (both for careful and sloppy pronunciations!). Rischel (1974),
who notes 'the mismatch between underlying representations and surface representations' (p. 384) in West Greenlandic, especially for consonant clusters (p.
387ff), judiciously observes that 'statements about structure should not just
refer to one level. The phonological structure of single formatives should be
specified with reference to the level of underlying representations. ... Underlying structure ... provides the reason why rules are needed to accomplish the
goal defined by surface structure,' and he considers MSRs rather as an inheri-
tance from the past (p. 391f).

   With these statements Rischel (1974) remarkably prefigures the treatment of
MSRs in Cyclic and Lexical Phonologies (cf. 5.17.1.5f) where there are cyclic/
lexical rules that apply to the earliest cycle/level (as redundancy rules) and
where there is a diachronic change from postcyclic/postlexical rules, which may
be said to express surface phonetic constraints, to gradually higher and higher
level cyclic/lexical rules of smaller domains up to the morpheme level. According to Kiparsky (1982c:167ff), the duplication problem has ceased to be problematic because reapplication of any lexical rule at later levels/cycles is demanded by the model. Instead of morphemes, different lexical categories (e.g.,
N, V) are the domains of rules -- however this does not work for rules defining
grammatical morphemes only (8.2.6, 8.3.7, 8.2, 8.4.4.3) or clitics (8.3.6) which
may belong to different lexical categories (pronouns, conjunctions, adverbs).
If 'predictable feature specifications are left unspecified in lexical entries'
(Kiparsky 1982c:167), then they do not represent strings of intended phonemes
(5.20, 8.5.2).

   A theory of MSRs has to account for the fact that there are constraints
which hold for syllables, morphemes, words,[24] phrases, and for the underlying
(input) and all output levels in the same way, and that there are others which
hold only for some (or only one) of these domains and levels, and how these constraints change in diachrony. In the following, I will sketch such a theory
(much more explicit than in Dressler 1977a:54ff), however a full treatment would
demand a monograph of its own.[25] Unlike the above treatment of PRs, MPRs, and
MRs, here I will include more elements of Natural Morphology and its semiotic

metatheory.

8.2.1.   In Natural Phonology,[26] phonological processes have two main functions
(cf. 2.1). On the one hand they transduce the phonological input (phonological
representation in phonemes) into the phonetic output (phonetic representations
of various speech styles). These I have simply called PRs. On the other hand
they govern the phonological input, insofar as they merge all possible sounds of
human language into the phonemes of the respective language (segment-structure
rules, 2.2.1) and restrict their possible concatenations (sequential-structure
rules, 2.2.2).[27] These I have called prelexical rules. Now the same PR may
serve as a prelexical PR and as a (postlexical) PR of transduction (in practice
only if it is context-sensitive, a sequential-structure rule in its prelexical
function), i.e., it may apply at the input level and reapply later on in transduction (both as obligatory and/or optional PRs of hyperformal and casual
speech)[28] so that no duplication problem exists.[29]

8.2.2.   For PRs of transduction, I have given examples for their various phonological domains (5.8). They may hold for syllables, feet, phonological words,
and phrases or only for syllables or only for phrases (PRs of sentence phonology), etc. If we take the double function of PRs seriously, then the syllable,
the foot, and the word must be the relevant domains for a prelexical PR, either
all or one or two of them.[30] Then (in 5), for synchrony and diachrony, I discussed the gradual morphologization and lexicalization of PRs via MPRs to AMRs.
If I want my theory to be consistent, I am obliged to claim also that prelexical
PRs may gradually be morphologized to prelexical MPRs and MRs. My respective
remarks in Dressler (1977a:56)[31] must now be extended.

8.2.3.   How does the domain of the morpheme, which I could not list among the
phonological domains of 8.2.2, come in? This depends on the language type that
a language or a part of a language is approaching.[32] For the sake of optimal
perception and processing (cf. 10.8.5.3), the optimal morpheme boundary coincides with the syllable boundary. Thus optimal morphemes should have, seen from
the aspect of this principle, the shape of just the syllable (i.e., morphemes
should be mono-, di-, trisyllabic, etc.). This is typical for both the agglutinating and the isolating language types.

       If the identification of morpheme and syllable is extended to the word,[33] then we obtain the isolating language type, as approached by South East Asian languages with typically monosyllabic words.[34] In these languages there is relatively little distinction between lexical and grammatical morphemes.

If a language distinguishes systematically between grammatical and lexical morphemes, then the principle of optimal size (cf. 10.7.3, 10.8.5.3) tends to have longer lexical than grammatical morphemes. Thus an optimal solution is to have monosyllabic grammatical and disyllabic lexical morphemes. Agglutinating languages (cf. Ladakhi, and, to a lesser extent, Turkish) approach this distribution. Of course the inherent advantages of these choices constitutive for these two language types are counterbalanced by disadvantages in other semiotic parameters.

Inflecting languages show a different mix of semiotic advantages and disadvantages (cf. 10.9.3). They do not price morpheme transparency highly. At least in inflection, morpheme boundaries typically do not coincide with syllable boundaries. Following the principle of optimal size, within a morphological word lexical morphemes are frequently larger than one or two syllables (i.e., they add syllable parts to one or two full syllables), whereas grammatical morphemes are often shorter than one syllable or even consist of two incomplete syllables if they are positioned between the root and a further affix, e.g., the Russian gen. /s+pa$t+ni$k+a/, a morphological word form which contains the derivational prefix /s/ 'together', the derivational suffix /nik/ (agent), and the inflectional suffix /a/.

Introflecting languages have additional prelexical characteristics (cf. 8.3.8).

8.2.4. As we have seen in 8.2.3, in inflecting (and introflecting) languages, within morphological words morpheme shapes do not (or only rarely do) coincide with syllable shapes. Thus prelexical PRs (sequential-structure rules) of the syllable domain cannot hold for morphemes. Since prelexical PRs have psychological reality, many phonologists seem to have concluded that sequential-structure rules that hold only for morphemes do not. This is a logically fallacious conclusion of the most elementary kind:[35]

first premise:	$p \rightarrow q$	= Syllable constraints (p) are psychologically real.
second premise:	$\neg p$	= Some MSRs are not syllable constraints.
false conclusion:	$\neg q$	= Therefore these MSRs are not psychologically real.

Moreover such a conclusion seems to mask an astonishing lack of insight into the nature of morphology: Should a native speaker/hearer be supposed to have internalized many generalizations about his phonology and syntax, but none or very few about his morphology, not even the most elementary ones about the shapes of morphemes?[36] Should he rather be supposed to learn an odd list of idiosyncratic morphemes like learning a catalogue of monomorphemic proper names? Or should he even be supposed not to be able to analyze morphological word forms into their constitutive morphemes? Anyone who negates the last two questions will be induced to negate the first question as well. At least an adherent of Natural Morphology must do so. On the psychological reality of morpheme shapes (before the application of PRs), cf. 8.1.4, 8.1.6 and Sapir's (1963 [1933]) famous paper on the psychological reality of phonemes, which concerns inputs to PRs and thus vouches, indirectly, for the psychological reality of morpheme shapes prior to the operation of PRs.

8.2.5. Now a critic of MSRs who grants our argumentation so far may recede to the position that generalizations about the shapes of morphemes and those of syllables may have nothing to do with each other. However the native speaker/hearer should know whether there is a default (5.20.8.2.1) coincidence or non-coincidence between morpheme and syllable shapes.

Next there are diachronic relations: If a language changes from an agglutinating type to an inflecting type, many generalizations about syllable shapes are due to remain valid for morpheme shapes as well, at least for some time and as default assumptions. Then many inflecting languages have a rather agglutinating type word formation component.[37] Thus there is another reason why there cannot be such a neat separation of generalizations.

Finally, when a child is learning an inflecting language, it learns generalizations about morphology later than generalizations about phonology, and thus is likely to cling to phonological default assumptions even in morphological parsing.

8.2.6. In this process the language learner must become aware of the fact that certain phonotactic sequences, particularly complex consonant clusters, occur only if there is a morpheme boundary within the sequence,[38] e.g., in the German sequences /nkst, lkst, rkst, rmst, lmst/, etc., i.e., /CCst/ or even /CCCC$/, there is (as a default) a morpheme boundary before the /s/, as in *du sink-st*

'thou sinkest', *welk-st* 'witherest', *wärm-st* 'warmest', *film-st* 'takest shots',
stärk-st 'strengthenest' and *wärm-st-er* 'warm-est', *stärk-st-er* 'strong-est',
and there are more sequences of the form /CCst/ in casual speech which are for-
bidden in 'careful pronunciation'. Therefore such sequences give the hearer a
clue for morpheme processing. The exceptions are very few: *ernst* 'earnest',
Herbst 'autumn'.

The same holds, at least in the form of defaults,[39] for the other Germanic
languages, cf. E. dimorphemic *the/he ship-s, warm-th, wid-th* (8.1.6, Selkirk
1982:349f) and is typical for all languages which show at least some degree of
fusion, cf. Mangarayi (Merlan 1982:193f), Zyrian (Rédei 1975:104), Somali (Cardona & Agostini 1981:18), Latin (Benveniste 1939:29f).

To reject the morpheme as a relevant unit for phonotactic constraints must
be justified not only by criticizing and discussing generative work, but also by
doing so with, e.g., the common practice of European phonematics, cf. Trubetzkoy
(1939.VI:3), who explicitly stated that simpler and more general phonotactic
constraints can be formulated for the morpheme than for the word, i.e., he used
the argumentation for valid generalizations the other way around.

However, it is clear that we are already in the presence of prelexical MPRs
and MRs if different constraints hold for morphemes and syllables.

8.2.7. Considerations of space forbid a (necessarily detailed) discussion of
the various proposals at which levels and how syllabification takes place.[40]

So I briefly state my views: I have assumed that there are prelexical prosodic PRs (8.2.2 note 30), i.e., that words and morphemes enter phonological
derivation with assigned stress and/or pitch. Consistency forces me to assume
that they are already syllabified, i.e., that there are prelexical syllabification rules (see 8.3.1). Therefore the prosodic counterparts of segmental PRs of
transduction are PRs of resyllabification (e.g., if morphemes are combined), of
stress shift, etc. I have also assumed that there are prelexical sequential-
structure PRs. Since one of the domains is the syllable, consistency forces me
again to assume prelexical syllabification rules.

8.3.1. If we start with sequential-structure rules, then we should first exemplify the rule formats of PRs. Let us take the example of an open syllable
language which allows only two syllable shapes: CV, V. There is just one pre-

lexical syllabification PR, namely for the structure

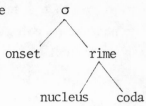

there is the prelexical syllabification PR 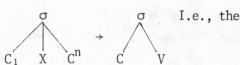 I.e., the

onsets c, cc, ccc, etc., are replaced by c. The nuclei v and c are replaced by
v. And the codas ∅, c, cc, ccc, etc., are replaced by ∅. The structure

 remains unchanged.[42]

Such a language may have the following prelexical sequential-structure PRs:
$$c_{[-nas]} \rightarrow \emptyset / \_\_^{\$} \text{ and } v\, c_{[+nas]} \rightarrow \tilde{v} / \_\_^{\$}$$ if both oral and nasal vowels occur
in the underlying phonemic inventory.

In a language like Maori there would be the more generalized prelexical PR
$c_1 \rightarrow \emptyset / \_\_^{\$}$. This PR was earlier a PR of transduction as Hale (1973) has
noted: Earlier the surface forms [hopu, aru] 'to catch, to follow' were derived
by this PR of syllable-final consonant deletion from the underlying forms
/hopuk, arum/, as seen in the passives *hopuk-ia, arum-ia*. When this PR changed
its role from a rule of transduction to a prelexical one (cf. Krupa 1968:38ff),
the underlying forms became /hopu, aru/ and the passives were analyzed as
hopu-kia, aru-mia.

At the same time the passive morphemes fell in line with the general default shape of morphemes (8.3.10) insofar as they start with a cv syllable,
which makes morphological processing easier (morpheme boundary = syllable boundary, see 8.2.3), a common type of suffix change (cf. Stein 1970).

8.3.2. A sequential-structure rule is an optimal prelexical PR if it holds for
all domains and for underlying and phonetic representations as well, i.e., if it
effects a real SPC (8.1.3). This is still another case where the best state of
affairs has been elevated to an absolute constraint on possible states of affairs in sectors of modern phonology (cf. 5.20.7.1).

Let us assume that a sequential-structure rule that holds only for morphemes, but not for phonological domains such as syllables or phonological
words, is a prelexical MPR.

8.3.3. Dephonologization of a prelexical PR may start with loanwords to which
it is not applied. Trubetzkoy (1939.VI:4) implicitly distinguished prelexical
PRs and MPRs when he stated (with German examples) that loanwords disobeying
MSRs can be more easily tolerated if the same sequence is permitted intermorphemically, i.e., if they do not correspond to a prelexical PR, but only to a
prelexical MPR.

Let us briefly survey vowel harmony in Turkish: We may assume that Turkish
originally[42] had a completely productive PR of back[43] vowel harmony, both prelexically and in transduction.

Massive borrowing of Arabic and Persian words created a mass of exceptions[44] for both prelexical vowel harmony and suffix harmony (transduction), so
that today one can clearly distinguish prelexical 'root harmony' and 'suffix
harmony' (transduction).[45]

The terms 'root' and 'suffix' harmony are misnomers: Rather prelexical
back vowel harmony holds morpheme-internally both in roots and in suffixes,
i.e., there are suffixes such as *-siniz, -seniz,* etc., but not like **-sinuz.*
Prelexical harmony has no exceptions within inflectional suffixes because no
disharmonic suffixes have been borrowed.[46] What is commonly called 'suffix harmony is a MPR of transduction which harmonizes suffixes with roots.[47] Exceptions to the prelexical MPR of back harmony occur even in older Greek borrowings
such as the placename *İstanbul < is tan pol(in)* 'into the city', where the first
front vowel is in disharmony with the two following back vowels, or in the partially identical placename *Boli*. Also old foreign words retain disharmonic
vowels, e.g., *birader* 'brother'. A recent borrowing may be exemplified by
/šɨ/*vester* 'hospital nurse' from G. *(Kranken)/šv/ester,*[47a] where disharmonic /ɨ/
has been inserted instead of harmonic /i/, which seems to confirm the character
of 'root harmony' as a prelexical MPR. Yavas (1980) claims that in loans such
as g[ɨ]*rip* (< Fr. *grippe* 'influenza'), the disharmonic [ɨ] is due to a PR of velar conditioning; under the analysis vowel harmony would hold for the underlying form /girip/, i.e., it would be abstract.[48]

What is really remarkable about the Turkish prelexical MPR of back vowel

harmony is its liveliness. Zimmer's (1969) experiments[49] showed that his Turkish subjects often applied back harmony to monomorphemic nonsence words.

Children do not seem to have problems with learning vowel harmony, but with
learning exceptions to it. Vowel harmony is not disturbed in aphasia, neither
in Turkish (Peuser & Fittschen 1977) nor in Finnish nor in Hungarian (according
to complete agreement among several aphasiologists of both countries) -- but
note that prosodic phonology can be severely disturbed in these languages, which
does not confirm prosodic analyses of vowel harmony, but fits with what happens
with phonologically natural rules in aphasia (cf. 7.6.12).

Still more remarkable: It has been observed that Turks starting to learn
Spanish,[50] German,[51] and Norwegian[52] apply back (root) harmony to Spanish, German, and Norwegian words respectively in their first stage of learning.[53] This
is unheard of any MPR of transduction in second language acquisition (unless L_1
and L_2 are closely related, 5.13.5.3).

And such transfer has not been observed with other prelexical MPRs, e.g.,
Swedish palatalization: $\begin{bmatrix}k\\g\end{bmatrix} \rightarrow \begin{bmatrix}\varsigma\\j\end{bmatrix}$ / __ $\underset{[+palatal]}{v}$ This was originally a PR of
transduction (cf. Eliasson 1973, Linell 1979b:102f). Then it split into a pre-
lexical PR and a MPR of transduction. Then increasing loans such as *gips* 'gypsum' with [g] from G. *Gips* transformed the prelexical PR into a prelexical MPR
(Wurzel 1981:428f): This rule seems never to be applied to foreign languages
learnt.

An explanation for this difference between Swedish and Turkish will be proposed in 10.9.2.5.

If a language has different lexical strata, different MSRs may hold for
them.[54] In Hungarian, old loanwords were adapted to native syllable structure
which prohibits (or rather, prohibited) syllable-initial consonant clusters;
later loanwords retain such initial clusters (cf. Siptár 1980). Languages may
vary even synchronically in (non)application of MSRs under sociolinguistic conditions like those that Rodríguez González (1982) has found for Spanish abbreviations.

8.3.4. Another type of partial or total dephonologization can be characterized
by separate prelexical sequential-rules for special classes of morphemes. This
is not the case with Turkish prelexical back vowel harmony (8.3.3), which holds

both for roots and suffixes intramorphemically, or the Desano prelexical nasal harmony (8.1.4). This is still a PR because (1) its domain is defined both phonologically (syllable domain) and morphologically (morpheme domain) and (2) it is exceptionless, whereas Turkish back harmony has the morpheme as its only domain and has many exceptions (loanwords).

In Circassian, the prelexical rules of voicing agreement (8.1.4) cannot apply in affixes because they are too short and do not contain relevant clusters.[55] Thus we do not know whether they would apply to affixes as well. Prelexical sequential-structure MRs constrain the length of these affixes (see below 8.3.7, 8.3.8.2).

8.3.5. Since (and even before) Trubetzkoy (1939.VI:4, Introd. 2) it has been well known that MSRs may have exceptions in interjections, onomatopoetic, and expressive words (cf. Benveniste 1939:30). E.g., German has the interjections *pst* [pst] 'hush!' and *hm* [hm̥, m̥m̥] 'uh'. Both violate constraints against syllabic consonants. A Russian name such as *Mstislav* can be pronounced neither with the Russian syllabification [msti$slaf] nor as *[ms$tis$laf] similar to [pst], nor as *[m̥$stis$laf] or *[mstislaf] after the model of *hm*, but is pronounced by admirers of *Mstislav Rostropovič* as [məstislaf], or with vowel harmony [mistislaf], whereas nobody pronounces *pst* as *[pəst]. Note also the onomatopoetic designation of a waltz rhythm ['(h)m̥tata], but not *['(h)mə ta ta] (??['(h)əmtata]). Notice also the non-formal/casual (in effect quite normal) pronunciations ['reːdn̥, 'haːbm̥] for *reden, haben* (/reːd+ɛn, haːb+ɛn/), formal ['reːdən, 'haːbən] 'to talk, to have'.

Thus the phonotactic constraint against syllabic consonants is still truly phonological (despite the exclusion of interjections, etc.) and holds prelexically (for underlying syllables) and on the surface for stressed syllables and for unstressed syllables in the case of obstruents (for post-stress sonorants only in (very) careful speech). It is effected by a prelexical syllabic (i.e., prosodic) PR (cf. 8.2.2) and by PRs of vowel insertion.

8.3.6. Special word classes that may be characterized by MSRs of their own may be ideophones (Derbyshire 1979:182) and clitics,[56] e.g., the Italian clitic *gli* [lʼi] is the only Italian word with initial /lʼ/.

8.3.7. It is commonly assumed that there exist special MSRs[57] for roots vs. af-

fixes, an important division among morphemes. However, often they apply to affixes in a very radical form if these are very short; e.g., Circassian inflectional affixes are limited to the shapes v, c, cv, vc by default rules because
other shapes (suffixes CC, CVC) are extremely rare (Kumahov 1971). In inflecting languages, affixes are typically shorter than lexical morphemes (8.2.3, 8.3.
4): This is governed by prelexical (prosodic and segmental) MPRs: E.g., English and German inflectional suffixes are restricted single syllable codas or
rimes (E. *-s*, *-(e)d*, *-en*, *-ing*, *-er*, *-est*); this is the default in Latin declension (exceptions *-rum*, *-bus*).

The English and German codas have the forms C or CC; if c_1c_2, then c_1 is a
nasal or /s/, and c_2 is a stop. Latin declensional suffixes can end only in one
consonant, the conjugational ones also in nasal plus stop.[58] German derivational suffixes can easily be divided into foreign and native[59] ones. For the native ones, the following generalizations hold: They are at most monosyllabic,
otherwise rimes or codas, and by default they are unstressed (except stressed
-ei in *Fischer-ei* 'fisher-y'); accordingly, the suffixes *-heit*, *-haft*, *-schaft*,
-tum, *-mal*, which earlier were compound final words, have become partially de-
stressed, *-lich* completely.

For Spanish, cf. Hooper (1976:187); for Polish, Schenker (1964:30f); for
Slavic languages in general, Stankiewicz (1960:189f); for Mataca, Viñas Urquiza
(1970.I:39).

If we compare the MSR characteristics of 8.3.5 and 8.3.6f, then we see that
typically interjections, etc., are exempted from general prelexical PRs, i.e.,
they are 'negative exceptions', whereas grammatical suffixes (and the classes of
8.3.6) can be characterized by prelexical MRs of their own, i.e., by 'positive
exceptions'. These special prelexical rules, I claim, have the semiotic function of cosignaling that the respective morpheme belongs to a specific grammatical class, at least in inflecting and introflecting languages or language components. At the same time their relatively bad perceptual saliency (rimes, codas)
which renders morphemic processing more difficult, is a typical disadvantage of
the inflecting language type (see 8.2.3, 8.3.8.2). However, these suffixes that
consist of a syllable coda only, often contribute to forming word-final clusters
which are excluded from monomorphemic words, which is an aid for morphemic processing (8.2.6).

8.3.8. On the other hand, there are MSRs which apply to lexical morphemes only, e.g., the canonical form of Igbo lexical morphemes /C(y)V/ (Hyman 1975:112).

8.3.8.1. The most famous prelexical MRs of this sort are the Semitic restrictions of lexical roots to a three-consonant skeleton, e.g., for Classical Arabic we may assume the two related default rules:[60]

MR(1) nominal monomorphemic stem → CVC(V)C, i.e., *qatl*, *qitl*, *qutl*, *qatal*,
   qatil, *qatul*, etc.

MR(2) verbal stem → CaCVC, i.e., *qatal-*, *qatil-*, *qatul-*

These are default rules (1) because they hold only for given word classes,[61] (2) because there are some two- and four-consonant stems (although the two middle consonants of the four are never separated in verb forms so that they function like a complex phoneme).[62] Still such MRs are productive in loanword integration, cf. Modern Hebrew *le-flartet* 'to flirt' with the radicals /fl-r-t/ extracted from E. *flirt*, cf. /t-lf-n/ or /t-lp-n/ extracted from *telephone*, and in more artificial neologisms such as *me-fustar* 'pasteurized' with /p-st-r/ extracted from *Pasteur*.[63]

8.3.8.2. Another well known example is represented by Benveniste's (1935) theory of the early Proto-Indo-European root and word structure, for which we can formulate the following three prelexical MRs:

MR(1) root → /CeC/

e.g., /sed/ 'to sit', /əₗed/[64] 'to eat', /peə₃/[64] 'to drink', cp. Lat. *pō-culum* 'drinking vessel', /pel/ 'to fill'. This rule defines all verbal, nominal, adjectival, and (at least some) numeral roots, but does not refer to clitics or pronouns.

MR(2) suffix → /eC/

e.g., /eg/ in /i̯u-n-ég/ 'to join' (> Lat. *jung-ere*), /eə₁/ in /pl-n-éə₁/ 'to fill'.

MR(3) élargissement[65] → /C/

e.g., /u̯/ in /péə₂-u̯-r/ 'fire' (with /-r/ of the neuter nominative-accusative), /n/ infix in /i̯u-n-ég, pl-n-éə₁/. The same shape may occur with inflectional endings, prefixes, etc. Together with other MRs and with PRs (e.g., of vowel deletion and syllabification in /pel/ vs. /pl̥-n-éə₁/), this is a coherent reconstruction.

8.3.9.   Still more specific prelexical MRs may characterize special morpheme
classes: Trubetzkoy (1931) cites Caucasian verbs and pronouns (with only one
consonant) as opposed to nouns, Slavic pronouns (with one consonant only), etc.
Capanahua nouns may end in no other stop than /p/ (Loos 1969:124). In Alawa the
root pattern /CVC/ is restricted to verbs (Sharp 1972:4) with only the exception
of the conjunction *mal* 'because'; but this prelexical MR is being made opaque
by English loanwords. For default MRs of German gender, cf. Altmann & Raettig
(1973).

Even within one morpheme class subclasses may be defined by exclusive or
default MRs, e.g., the different ablaut classes of Germanic strong verbs;[66]
e.g., MRs for the Gothic strong verb classes can easily be formulated:[67]

$\text{root} \to {}^{\$}c_0^3 \text{ v } c_1^2{}^{\$} \text{ / Verb}$[68]

$c_0^3 \text{ v } c_1^2 \to c_1 \text{i:C}$ / strong V_I e.g., *beit-an* /biːt+an/ 'to bite'

$c_0^3 \text{ v } c_1^2 \to c_1 \text{iuC}$ / strong V_{II} e.g., *kius-an* 'to choose'

$c_0^3 \text{ v } c_1^2 \to c_1 \text{iRC}$ / strong V_{III} e.g., *bind-an* 'to bind'

Due to the PR $\begin{array}{c} \text{v} \\ \text{[+high]} \end{array} \to [\text{mid}] \text{ / \_\_ r}$ this MR is clearly restricted to the underlying phonological representation and is invalid on the surface, as in
wairp-an /werp/ 'to throw'.

$c_0^3 \text{ v } c_1^2 \to c_1 \text{iR}$ / strong V_{IV} e.g., *qim-an* /k^{w}im+an/ 'to come'

And the same PR operates, e.g., in *bair-an* /ber/ 'to carry'.

$c_0^3 \text{ v } c_1^2 \to c_1 \text{iC}$ / strong V_V e.g., *gib-an* 'to give'

$c_0^3 \text{ v } c_1^2 \to c_0 \text{aC}$ / strong V_{VI} e.g., *swar-an* 'to swear'

The differentiation of most of these prelexical MRs is due to the sound laws,
i.e., PRs of transductions were morphologized or led to restructurings of inputs.

The relevance of such prelexical MRs has appeared even in psycholinguistic
tests with nonsense words, e.g., Spanish verbs of the class *miento* 'I lie', inf.
mentir whose roots end in *r*, *rt*, or *nt* (Harris 1969:113f) have displayed a definite productivity of their own in vowel alternation.[69]

8.3.10. A short clarification on default rules:[70] Prelexical default MRs[71] are of two kinds. The first class has well-defined exceptions, either of a general character amenable to rule formulation or a small number of lexical exceptions easily learned by rote (cf. MacWhinney 1978, 8.3.9). The other class is of a more dubious nature since the defaults are based only on statistical significance of frequency distributions. E.g., the Bratislava group led by Gabriel Altmann and Viktor Krupa and later the school of West German Quantitative Phonology led by G. Altmann[72] have established statistical profiles for morpheme shapes in many languages.[73]

These prelexical default MRs can be diachronically rather stable, e.g., the prelexical MR of the Gothic strong verb class III still has its correspondences in default MRs in modern German and, less so, in contemporary English, e.g., *to bind, find, grind* and *ring, sing, drink, shrink, sink, stink* (cf. Bybee & Slobin 1982:269, 277ff, 288). Now this might be considered a mere historical residue of an earlier historical stage which it would be anachronistic to capture in a synchronic grammar. However, such generalizations show some psychological reality in first language acquisition, cf. the common children's ablaut forms *bring, brang, brung*.[74] Or the German default MR that nouns in *-e* are feminine[75] operates in morphological loanword integration, i.e., foreign words in *-e* tend to become feminine in gender irrespective of their original gender, e.g., F. *l'étage* (m) 'floor' became G. *die Etage* (f), F. *le garage*, G. *die Garage*.[76]

8.4. Prelexical 'paradigmatic'/'context-free' PRs, MPRs, and MRs (segment structure rules) will even more briefly, in view of wide-spread parallels to 8.3.

8.4.1. Prelexical segment-structure PRs (2.2.1, 8.2.1) as representatives of universal process types (foregrounding processes) reduce the possible sounds of the human language faculty to the phonemic inventory of a specific language. At this prelexical level, verbal process types also express Jakobson's implicational laws of phonemic inventories and generative markedness rules.[77]

These PRs can be prosodically restricted: Structural descriptions of phonemic inventories often juxtapose different (particularly vocalic) phoneme inventories for the stressed vs. the prestressed and poststressed syllables[78] or the first vs. the second syllables, etc.[79] For consonants, see Trubetzkoy (1932).

If there are alternations between a specific vowel in one prosodic position and another specific vowel in another prosodic condition, no PRs of transduction can be established. But prelexical PRs can be. E.g., the short vowel system of the Lule Lappic dialect (Wickman 1975) of the first syllable /u, o, a, i/ is determined by the following prelexical PRs:[80]

$$\underset{\text{[insufficient coloring]}}{V} \rightarrow \text{[+low]}$$

Thus the short monophthongal correspondents of the diphthong /oa/ and the long vowels /ä, á/ and similar conceivable sounds are replaced by low /o/ and /a/ respectively.

$$\underset{\text{[sufficient coloring]}}{V} \rightarrow \text{[+high]}$$

Thus the short monophthongal correspondents of the diphthongs /uo/ and /ie/ and similar conceivable labial and palatal vowels are replaced by high /u/ and /i/ respectively.[81] Central vowels are excluded by the prelexical coloring PRs

$$\underset{\text{[-labial]}}{V} \rightarrow \text{[+palatal]} \quad \text{and} \quad \underset{\text{[-palatal]}}{V} \rightarrow \text{[+labial]}.$$

In the second syllable only the phonemes /u, a, i/ occur. Here the prelexical PR of lowering is generalized:

$$\begin{bmatrix} V \\ \text{insufficient coloring} \\ \text{weak prosodic position} \end{bmatrix} \rightarrow a$$

Conceivably /o/ of the first syllable might be replaced by /u/ in the second syllable. But the change from low to high would be a more drastic change than the shift of one low vowel with little labiality to another low vowel with no labiality.

Second, we see the close connection between /a/ and /o/ in the monophthongization PR:

oa → oː / [weak prosodic position]

Third, there is a vowel harmonic PR which shifts (short and long) /a/ of the second syllable to /o/ and /oː/ respectively if they follow an /a/ of the first syllable.

8.4.2. Similarly to 8.3.3, phonemes may be restricted to (or absent from) loanword strata. E.g., context-free nasalized vowels in standard British English

and German are foreign (particularly French). Thus the prelexical PR
v → [-nasal] (cf. 2.2.1) has the exception / [-foreign]. And among non-integrated or only partially integrated loanwords, nasal vowel phonemes have the default connotation 'French'.[82]

  The German affricate phoneme /pf/ never occurs in non-integrated loanwords,
which is rather accidental because there is no other language with /pf/ whose
contacts with German have been close enough.

8.4.3. Similarly to 8.3.4, prelexical segment-structure PRs may be violated in
interjections, onomatopoetic and expressive words. E.g., dental clicks occur in
German only as an expression of surprise and indignation, the bilabial vibrant
for cold temperature and as a sign for horses.

  Wojcik (1981) cites English clicks, syllabic /m/, nasalized /ə/, and the
bilabial fricative in [ɸiu̯]. Or Bengali [ɦ] occurs only 'in interjections implying suffering or disgust' (Nigam 1975:22).

8.4.4.0. Similarly to 8.3.7, the class of grammatical affixes may be characterized by the presence or absence of specific phonemes. If this were a pure accident, then one would expect a normal statistical distribution of the following
situations: (1) all phonemes do occur, (2) only one does not, (3) only a few
do.[83] Moreover, if, e.g., only six phonemes were absent or present, accidental
sets like /b, n, s, k, a, y/ should occur more frequently than natural classes
like all stops /b, p, d, t, g, k/ of the respective language.

  But, as we expect from working with the notion default (3.10), only three
situations are frequent:

8.4.4.1. All phonemes occur both in roots/stems and in grammatical affixes.
We would expect this situation to prevail in agglutinating languages, where both
classes are not well-distinguished in general (8.2.3). This expectation is confirmed in, e.g., Turkish, where 15 of 21 consonants occur in inflection (19 in
derivation), Hungarian (16[84]/20 of 25 consonants), Finnish (10/12 of 13 consonants), Vogul (12/17 of 17 consonants). The missing consonants of Turkish are
v, f, g, ǧ (spirant), h, j (spirant [ž]); of Hungarian, the fricatives f, v,
zs, the affricates c, dz, cs, dzs, ty, gy, the nasal ny; of Finnish g, r, j
(glide; r, j both occur as rule-derived from /d, i/); of Vogul, the stops p,

t', the fricatives x, s', the sonorants r, n', l'. These sets do not have complete natural classes of consonants.

8.4.4.2. Only a set of a few phonemes is excluded from grammatical affixes and this set is not fortuitous.[85] /ɛ, ɔ/ are absent in Lomongo, /u, o/ in Yawelmani (Kenstowicz & Kisseberth 1977:148), /e, o/ in Mangarayi (Merlan 1982:181). In Latin inflectional suffixes, the phonemes /l, g, k, p, ae,[86] ao/ do not occur, i.e., the diphthongs, /l/, and half of the stops. All vowels but /u/ occur in Polish verbal suffixes, but all in declension.

8.4.4.3. A marginal phoneme may occur only in grammatical, but not in lexical morphemes. Job (1977:65) assumes a Circassian (Adyge) labialized labial nasal phoneme /m̩/, which seems to be restricted to grammatical morphemes.

8.4.4.4. Phonemes occurring in grammatical affixes are restricted to a few, and these seem to form more natural sets than in 8.4.4.2. In view of their semiotic function to cosignal grammatical morphemes, this is to be expected from positive signals (8.4.4.3) as opposed to negative ones (8.4.4.2). Jakobson[87] observed that of 23 Czech consonants, only three occur in nominal endings, only six in verbal endings, and that only /m/ occurs in both classes; that only /z, d, n, ŋ/[88] occur in English inflectional suffixes. The only vowel present in German inflectional suffixes is /ɛ/, the only consonants are the nasals /n, m/, the dental stops /d, t/, the vibrant /r/, and the fricative /s/, i.e., mostly den-tals.[89] In Polish declensional suffixes, /v, f, g, x, j, m/ are the only conso-nants. Floyd (1981) notes that Ancient Greek (Attic) inflectional endings com-prise no consonants other than /t, tʰ, s, n, m/, i.e., the voiceless dentals and the nasals.

All these restrictions can be expressed by prelexical segment-structure MRs, e.g., for Attic Greek:

$$\begin{matrix} \text{C} \\ \text{[+obstr.]} \end{matrix} \rightarrow \begin{bmatrix} +\text{coronal} \\ -\text{voice} \end{bmatrix} \quad / \quad \text{inflectional endings}$$

$$\begin{matrix} \text{C} \\ \text{[-obstr.]} \end{matrix} \rightarrow [+\text{nasal}] \quad / \quad \text{inflectional endings}$$

All these restrictions are the results of sound laws[90] AND the failure to restructure suffixes in such a way that a random distribution of phonemes would be restored. This failure of random restructuring[91] is, I submit, connected with the semiotic function of default assumptions in language types such as the inflecting type. Turkish, Hungarian, Finnish, Vogul (8.4.4.1), which are predominantly agglutinating but have minor inflecting ingredients, do not have a truly random distribution, insofar as certain consonants are excluded from inflectional suffixes, whereas others are greatly favored. The assumption then is that a language passing from a predominantly agglutinating to a predominantly inflecting type would restrict the phonemes used largely to those favored in its earlier agglutinating stage.

Notes

1. Cf. Isačenko 1963, Horecky 1981, Skalička 1935:29, 36f, 41, 47f, 54f, 58. But even in Trubetzkoy's times, constraints were formulated for the word domain, e.g., by Benveniste 1939. For later phonematics, cf. Scholes 1966, Ševoroškin 1969, Lupaş 1972.

2. If one says that the nominative as unmarked case represents the unit 'lexical word' of Latin nouns. Incidentally, *vōs* (and *nōs*) is also the accusative and vocative. Moreover, such as in most nouns, the relation between these cases in *-s* and *-bis* is identical with those in the *e*-stems and the input forms of other nominal paradigms.

3. Of course *nōbis* in, e.g., *Dōna nōbis pācem!* 'Give us peace!' is also a phonological word.

4. See Kenstowicz & Kisseberth 1977:136ff, 1979:427ff. For the latest discussion showing the inevitability of duplication and its place in phonological theory, see Manaster-Ramer 1984.

5. See above, note 4.

6. Hudson 1974, Hooper 1975, 1976:179ff, Clayton 1976, Brink 1977 following Shibatani 1973 and Sommerstein 1974; cf. Goyvaerts 1978:101ff, Linell 1979b:117ff, Kahn 1976:39 note 2, Crothers & Shibatani 1981:73ff.

7. Hooper 1976:179ff, Linell 1979b (on page 126 he allows surface structure constraints to apply to various domains, including morphs, which the other critics disallow).

8. Linell (1979b:126) accuses countercritics (Kaye 1974b, Morin 1975, Dressler 1977a) of confusing the issue of domains (whether there are phonotactic constraints which hold for morphemes only) with the issue of the level of application (underlying or surface/phonetic representation or both). It is up to the reader to judge the following counterexamples accordingly.

9. After Kibrik et al. 1972. Dešeriev's (1950) description is less detailed and used a different transcription system. Note also that Kibrik et al. (1972) simplify their transcription system starting with p. 47.

10. Incl. Linell 1979b, whose surface structure constraints hold only for careful pronunciations, cf. 8.1.9.

11. The derived palatal vowel /e/ is responsible for the palatalization of the /p/ before it.

12. These are examples from Dešeriev (1950:18), who writes *e* for *ej* of Kibrik (1972), who has no relevant examples.

13. Narang & Becker 1971, Bhatia & Kenstowicz 1972, Kenstowicz & Kisseberth 1977:148.

14. Paris (1974:132); cf. Klimov & Alekseev 1980:43f.

15. But this solution is criticized by Iverson 1983a and Picard & Nicol 1982.

16. Cf. Panagl 1975, Matthews 1972:170ff.

17. Seminar paper, MS.

18. Note the existence of *stronzato* 'uptailed' and other words starting with *stron-*, so that *Stromboli* could have been avoided.

19. A PR of nasal assimilation which is used here in its prelexical function and reapplies as a PR of transduction obligatorily (5.20.3.3) and then again in casual speech, e.g., *hanno ballato* 'they have danced' → casual *han ballato* → more casual [amba'lːato].

20. Criticized by Picard & Nicol 1982, Iverson 1983a.

21. For Burushaski, see Morin 1975a, 1976; for Chukchee, Ševoroškin 1969:69f.

22. Cf. also 5.11.2.

23. Morin (1975b) gives a French example of even sentence-final position being phonotactically relevant.

24. Cf. Payne 1981:74.

25. Therefore the graduality of distinctions between prelexical PRs, MPRs, and MRs cannot be explored in such detail as I have tried to do with PRs, MPRs, and MRs of transduction (cf. 5). Also I cannot discuss other approaches and views.

26. Stampe 1969, 1973, 1980, Rhodes 1972, Donegan & Stampe 1979b, Donegan 1978.

27. I.e., all phonotactic constraints are the results of rules!

28. Here also context-free PRs of foregrounding reapply after their prelexical function as segment-structure rules.

29. Cf. 8.1.2f, 8.1.7 note 19, 5.17.1.6f, 8.1.10.

30. By definition the phrase domain is ruled out for segmental PRs (except for idiomatized, i.e., lexicalized, syntactic phrases), but not for prosodic PRs where PRs of transduction can be contrasted with prelexical functions for all possible domains. But this is completely outside the scope of this book.

31. Cf. Wurzel 1981a:428.

32. Cf. 10.9, Skalička 1935, 1979.

33. As also in early language acquisition, cf. 9.

34. Cf. 10.9.1, Skalička 1979:187f, Trubetzkoy 1939:264.

35. Cf. also Geis & Zwicky's (1981) notion 'invited inference'.

36. E.g., their integrity in morpheme combinations, i.e., their degree of morphotactic transparency plays a role in perception (MacKay 1978). Of course morphotactic segmentation in human processing is not identical with morphological parsing in a computer program (cf. Janson 1979:62ff).

37. Cf. Skalička 1979, 10.9.3.3, Dressler 1982a:80f.

38. In phonology first mentioned by Trnka (1931), cf. Trubetzkoy 1939.VI:2-4, Greenberg 1965:6, 9, 11f, 17f, Seiler 1965:137, Campbell 1979:76, Kahn 1976:39f note 2. In order to avoid this acknowledgement of the interference of morphology, Lupaş (1972:116ff, 124ff, 159) introduces a zero phoneme!

39. Cf. Greenberg 1965:11f; for details, see 5.20.8.

40. Pulgram 1970, Vennemann 1972d, Kahn 1976, Bailey 1978, Donegan & Stampe 1979a, Lowenstamm 1979, Selkirk 1982, Poser 1982.

41. Any replacement of ccv by cvcv or of vc by vcv must be handled by resyllab-

ification PRs.

42. Hovdaugen 1971:167ff, Krámský 1956:121ff, Hazai 1973:364ff.

43. There is multiple evidence that the front vowels are basic, e.g., Turks themselves call the case forms *i hâlı*, *e hâlı*, *de hâlı*, *den hâlı*, and not **ı/a/da/dan hâlı*. They are generalized in the Vindin dialect (Németh 1965: 44ff). Labial harmony exists only for high vowels: *-ü*, *-u*, *-i*, *-ı*.

44. Cf. Zimmer 1969:310f, Yavas 1982:127.

45. Here I neglect the long-debated issue of whether one should write a single rule or two different rules for 'root' and 'suffix' harmony (cf. Ringen 1981, Crothers & Shibatani 1981): first, because there is no problem of a PR or MPR functioning both prelexically and in transduction; second, because both functions should be clearly distinguished; third, because in case of less than total generality, vowel harmony (as in Turkish, Finnish, Hungarian, etc.) does not behave identically in all details intramorphemically and intermorphemically and because such differences of detail should not be ignored. For a detailed differentiation, cf. Vértes (1977) on Ostyak vowel harmony. For autosegmental treatments of Turkish (and other) vowel harmony, see Clements & Sezer 1982, Kaye 1982, Poser 1982, and critique in S. Anderson 1982:10, Ringen 1983.

46. Except disharmonic derivational suffixes such as locative *-istan* (Clements & Sezer 1982:231f), which were originally compounded.

47. Forms like *geliyor* 'he is coming', from *gel-mek* 'to come', are not counterexamples since the underlying suffix is *-yor* /ĭor/, as in *koru-yor* 'he is protecting' from inf. *koru-mak*: After the root-final consonant a high vowel is inserted which harmonizes with the root, as in *geli-yor*, *bulu-yor* 'he is finding', from *bul-mak*, etc. The *-yor* suffix is one of those suffixes which do not harmonize with the root but cause harmony in the following suffix, e.g., *geli-yor-um* 'I'm coming'.

47a. Other examples in Yavas 1982:125f, 1980:129f. But harmonic epenthesis is more frequent, cf. Clements & Sezer 1982:246ff.

48. More on disharmony in Clements & Sezer 1982, who also (p. 224ff) refute the putative rule of labial attraction.

49. Cf. Campbell 1981a, 1981b for an external piece of evidence for the productivity of Finnish vowel harmony. Generalization of vowel harmony in casual/fast speech has been observed in languages other than Finnish (cf. Skousen 1975:53) as well.

50. Personal communication by Zülâl Balpınar.

51. Meyer-Ingwersen 1975, Yakut 1981:104, 109, Neumann & Reich 1977:85, 96f, 100ff, 114, 395ff.

52. Personal communication by E. Hovdhaugen, Oslo.

53. Cf. Dobozy 1978a on stem vowel harmony in American-Hungarian.

54. Cf. Saciuk 1969; cf. Payne 1981:54, 74ff, Fries & Pike 1949, Benton 1971: 66, Wilson 1972:30; cf. Plank 1981:234ff, Benveniste 1939:27f, 30.

55. With the exception of Adyge *-ɣ't* (Kumahov 1971:269, 271f).

56. Zwicky 1977:34f, Morin 1979. Of course there are more PRs, MPRs, and MRs of the sentence/phrase domain that characterize them; cf. 2.4.2 and Dress-

ler 1977a:54 §28.

57.   Trubetzkoy 1931, 1939.VI:4, Hyman 1975:111f.

58.   This entails the segmentation of the 2.sg. perf. *leg-is-tī* 'you have read'
      (cf. Matthews 1972:77ff). On the rarity of consonant clusters in Latin,
      see Janson 1979:68ff.

59.   According to morphological criteria, the (originally borrowed) suffixes
      -ei (stressed), *-lei* (both of French origin), agent *-er* (of Latin origin)
      have to be considered as: native or [-foreign].

60.   Justified in Kilani-Schoch & Dressler, to appear, cf. Kuryłowicz 1972.
      Other views, e.g., in Bar-Lev 1978, cf. 10.9.4.

61.   Pronouns, conjunctions, numerals, particles, etc., are grammatical words
      for which MRs of lexical roots do not apply.

62.   Cf. Žuravlev's (1967) concept 'gruppofonem'; cf. Ewen 1980, 1982, Selkirk
      1982:346ff.

63.   Cf. Werner 1983:47, 64f and Werner 1982.

64.   With the reconstructed laryngeals $/ə_1, ə_2, ə_3/$, which in syllable-final po-
      sition later lengthen the immediately preceding vowel and behave like a $/ə/$
      in syllabic position.

65.   'Amplificatory element', of which only one may be combined with a suffix in
      verbs.

66.   Cf. van Coetsem 1980, Barbour 1982, Prokosch 1939:147ff.

67.   Krause 1963:216ff.

68. c_1 means 'at least one consonant', c^3 means 'three consonants at most', $^\$x\$$
      means that the root must be a possible syllable.

69.   Bybee & Pardo 1981:944ff, cf. in general Bybee & Slobin 1982.

70.   Cf. 5.20.9, 8.3.3, 8.3.7f, 8.4.4.0; cf. the statistical ideas of Trubetz-
      koy 1932.

71.   After elaboration of this chapter Bybee & Moder (1983) appeared. They use
      prototype theory and Wittgenstein's family resemblances in a way which is
      partially intertranslatable with the default concept. Their conception
      works best if there is a fuzzy class which displays gradually diverging
      distances from a prototype. This, it seems, is not the case in the exam-
      ples investigated here. Anyway, the results of their psycholinguistic ex-
      periments prove the psychological reality of some sort of morpheme shapes,
      whatever model may prove best in describing these phenomena.

72.   Cf. Altmann & Lehfeldt 1980 and the series Quantitative Linguistics edited
      by G. Altmann & R. Grotjahn.

73.   E.g., Krupa 1967, Altmann 1968, 1971, cf. note 72.

74.   Cf. Bybee & Slobin 1982:270, 280, Bybee & Moder 1983.

75.   Altmann & Raettig 1973; for other gender default rules of German, see Zu-
      bin & Koepcke 1981.

76.   Also in dialects, cf. Kirchmeier 1973:79f; for gender adaptation and simi-
      lar morphological integration phenomena ('transmorphemizations') in general,
      see the contributions in Filipović 1982.

77.   Stampe 1969, 1972, 1973, 1980, Donegan 1978, Donegan & Stampe 1979b; cf. 2.1f, 4.1.

78.   Cf., e.g., Saporta 1963, Valentin 1978, Itkonen 1975:35f, 39, 45, 49f, Gulya 1975:123f, Sauer 1975:131f, 134f, 145. Unstressed and non-first syllable position are both weak prosodic positions within the foot.

79.   E.g., Korhonen 1975:11ff, 17ff, Wickman 1975:1f, Hovdhaugen 1971:168ff, Skalička 1979:239f.

80.   Cf. Donegan 1978 for these process types.

81.   The question of where Lule Lappic establishes the boundary between sufficient coloring for the second PR and insufficient coloring for the first PR must be investigated by studying language acquisition, loanword integration, etc.

82.   For other cases, see Saciuk 1969, Fries & Pike 1949, Lovins 1973 ch. IV, Wilson 1972, Benton 1971.

83.   The presence of only one phoneme in grammatical affixes is excluded by the distinctivity principle; the total absence (i.e., only ∅-morphemes) is logically impossible.

84.   Of the nine consonants which do not occur in inflectional affixes, five are very rare throughout the whole language.

85.   The absence of /o, ɔ, ø, œ, y, r, j, v, pf, p/ from native German derivational suffixes seems to be, at least partially, accidental. This list shrinks if one adds prefixes.

86.   Provided that one analyzes gen./dat. *rosae* as /rosa+ī/.

87.   1962 (1949).I:108; cf. Stankiewicz 1961:189a, Shapiro 1969:8, Plank 1979: 142ff.

88.   Not exact, see 8.3.7.

89.   Earlier R. Jakobson in Trubetzkoy 1939.VI:3 note. The only prefix is /gɛ/.

90.   Cf. now Bybee & Moder 1983:266.

91.   On the Latin diachronic conspiracy that resulted in prelexical default rules, cf. Janson 1979:69ff.

9. LANGUAGE ACQUISITION

9.1. Recent studies in first language acquisition in morphophonology[1] have concentrated rather on the acquisition of those types of inflectional allomorphy or morphological paradigms which show no phonological conditioning, e.g., of verbal paradigms in Portuguese and Russian, of the forms of the German article, etc. So what we think can be called morphonology has played a rather marginal role in these studies. Also, studies in the acquisition of phonology have rather neglected morphonology.[2] However, in view of the enormous role that language acquisition plays within generative and 'naturalist' models as well as in psycholinguistics, a book with heavy emphasis on substantive evidence (cf. 10) cannot bypass language acquisition. Since I have not made longitudinal or cross-sectional empirical studies of my own, I can only give a very fragmentary picture of the acquisition of language.

9.2. There is no integrated bridge-theory in the framework of which I can discuss all the concepts of my approach. A certain number of these concepts, however, can be discussed within the psycholinguistic model of MacWhinney (1978, cf. Berman 1981b) which can easily be fitted to a revised model of Stampe's (1969) Natural Phonology. In this way 9 is a prelude to 10.

9.2.1. The three basic terms of MacWhinney's (1978:5ff) model are application, correction, and acquisition. In production (= 'expressive application') the child starts with his intention ('a set of things he wants to say') which he has to map onto surface forms. In this task the lexicon and morphological operations (if already acquired) have semiotic priority over phonological operations because intention must be packaged first into words and morphemes before it can receive its phonological and phonetic shape (cf. 10.4.4.4).[3] Reception (= 'receptive application') is the inverse of productive application. However in normal maturation, the child masters difficulties in phonological perception earlier than in phonological production, although the extreme view that perception is completely mastered before the acquisition of phonological production starts cannot be upheld anymore.[4]

9.2.2. 'Correction serves to monitor the accuracy of expressions and receptions

in terms of both internal and external data' (MacWhinney 1978:7). E.g., when
English child has acquired the MR of plural formation still in a simplified form
by always utilizing the morph /s/ (MacWhinney 1978:7f), he forms the plural of
[waɪfs] (the 'thesis' in MacWhinney's terms); but he may have stored the plural
[waɪvz] learnt by rote (the 'antithesis'). If the antithesis is strengthened in
reception, then it will eventually correct the thesis and lead to a restructuring (cf. MacWhinney 1978:12, 82) of his morphological and phonological system,
e.g., by taking the later learnt /z/ as base form of the plural from which the
[s]-form has to be derived (cf. Zwicky 1975b). This is one way of the acquisition of items and processes (rules).[5]

9.2.3. MacWhinney (1978:17-19, 30, 40-44, 51, 83) found clear evidence for phonological predispositions, interpretable in the sense of Stampe's (1969) universal natural processes (cf. 4, 10.7). However he does not firmly integrate them
into his model nor include them in the computational simulation of acquisition
(1978:85ff), and he does not consider morphological or other predispositions.
In my view, all linguistic and semiotic predispositions can be integrated as a
special class of internal data (2.2) following the acquisitional model of H. Andersen (first published in Anttila 1972:197): The child establishes and cor-
rects his grammar (i.e., grammatical hypotheses) by inferring it from universals
and from the perceived adult outputs by abduction. His output is deduced from
universals and grammar (lexicon and phonological system included).

9.2.4. According to Chomsky's (still 1980) strong innateness hypothesis, linguistic universals are inherited predispositions and not reduceable to inherited
physiological or cognitive properties of the human species. For Stampe's universal natural processes that the child has to suppress (unlearn) or limit according to the adult model, Stampe (1969 and later) does not decide explicitly
whether they are all strictly innate or may also be due to general principles of
maturation. On my functionalist approach, see 10.

9.2.5. In MacWhinney's model (1978:1ff, 6), three principles of acquisition are
at work: rote, analogy, and combination.

9.2.5.1. Rote memorization is learning of unanalyzed forms, including amalgams
which may be analyzed later on (such as *wives*, 9.2.2). Forms learned by rote

are used and reproduced easily, but neologisms cannot be formed nor can nonce forms be handled (e.g., in metalinguistic tests). Strong suppletion, e.g., *go* ∿ *went* can only be learned by rote.

9.2.5.2. According to MacWhinney (1978:2, 6), learning by analogy is quite complicated; evidence is, e.g., 'When the child produces real forms and nonce forms of very different shapes ... The use of priming should serve to increase the use of analogy.' Learning by analogy is assumed by adherents of the concept of weak suppletion in morphonology, e.g., the plural *leaves* of *leaf* is learned/ formed in analogy to the model *wives*, plural of *wife* (or vice versa). Analogy means surface analogy in the sense of one form being shaped after another surface form without any rule-governed analysis.

9.2.5.3. Combination means learning according to an item-and-arrangement or an item-and-process model; evidence for combination is, e.g., when the child produces erroneous real forms and regularized nonce forms: Thus, learning of regularity by combination is strong evidence against suppletion analysis of this regularity.

9.3. Findings about the acquisition of morphology relevant to morphonology are:

9.3.1. MPRs can be learned only if the appropriate MRs which trigger these MPRs have been learned (single output forms learned by rote are only an apparent exception since they do not involve learning of a MPR). E.g., English MPRs of the Great Vowel Shift (whatever form they may have) in, e.g., *divine – divin+ity* cannot be learned before the appropriate derivational MRs of suffix formation with *-ity* have been learned (see the evidence, e.g., in Read 1971:12, Ingram 1976b:8; more in 9.5.4). Cf. for Portuguese, Scliar-Cabral (1979) and Hooper (1979a:31ff), for Russian, Sorokin et al. (1979), for Dutch *d*-insertion, Snow et al. (1980), for Hebrew spirantization, Berman (1981a:279f).

When MPRs triggered by MRs are learned at the same time as the respective MRs (e.g., Czech 1st palatalization k → č in derivational morphology, see Dressler (1977a:40 note 83)), then this may be seen as an argument that this putative MPR is rather an integral part of the MR (as Linell (1979b:200, 211) claims for all MPRs).

These facts fit with the principle of morphology having priority over phonology (cf. 9.2.1, 9.4.1, 10.4).

9.3.2.   In accordance with claims of Natural Morphology (10.8), good signs,
e.g., perceptually salient and unambiguous (especially biunique) morphemes, regular and productive rules, are acquired before less good signs.[6]

9.3.3.   In our model, lexical storage of complex morphological forms is a filter
which checks rule-generated forms (10.8.3). This can be seen as an ontogenetic
continuation and result of the acquisition procedure described by MacWhinney
(1978:8, 13f; see 9.2.2).

9.3.4.   Children learn more frequent forms earlier and better than less frequent
corresponding forms (MacWhinney 1978:9f, 12, 16f). Although frequency of use is
a consequence of more essential factors (pragmatic and functional importance,
appropriateness to speech situations, structural basicness, naturalness and semiotic excellence, productivity, etc.), this may not be as important to the
child, so that the frequency of exposure to a form is of relevance for itself.

9.4.   Findings about the interaction of morphology and phonology are:

9.4.1.   Semiotic priority of morphology over phonology (9.2.1, 9.3.1) does not
necessarily mean acquisitional priority. If a child does not unlearn, suppress,
or limit radical phonological processes of early childhood, he would obscure or
even eliminate (e.g., inflectional) morphemes, and thus could not express his
intentions; i.e., what would be the sense of acquiring the production of morphemes that would be ununderstandable? This conforms with D. Slobin's acquisition principle of 'overt and clear marking of underlying relations' (cf. Hooper
1979a:25f, Linell 1979b:211).

Consider the case of Amahl Smith (Smith 1973): First all English plural
morphemes would have been obliterated by final consonant deletion. In a later
stage he preserved final /z/ as [ḍ], but first only in plural morphemes: i.e.,
he produced *these, those, horses* as [ḍiːḍ, ḍoːḍ, ɔːḍiḍ] but *cheese, always* as
[ḍiː, ɔːlweː], cf. also preservation of the final consonant in *bees, cars,
scales, owls,* but not in *backwards* or in *trousers,* which has no singular so that
-*s* is not a useful sign of plurality; see Smith (1973:68, 212ff). So Amdahl

unlearned final consonant deletion first in plural morphemes,[7] which again shows
the semiotic priority of morphology over phonology. Of course, morpheme identification and decomposition in polymorphemic word forms is impeded by the other
early phonological processes as well.

9.4.2. In striking contrast to this natural sequence of acquisition, children
with deviant, pathological acquisition of phonology have not unlearned all early
radical processes when they have started to learn morphology (see Ingram 1976a:
115ff, Dressler 1977a:42, Klein 1978:3 (with references), Eisenwort-Schelz 1979,
all with literature).

9.4.3. There is an inherent conflict between the tendencies towards morphotactic transparency (cp. 9.4.1, 9.5.1.4f, 10.8.1) and phonological productivity.
In the process of unlearning easy phonological substitutions and acquiring morphology, children get involved into this conflict.

     According to Stampe's (1969) model of phonological acquisition, children
should progressively limit or suppress early substitutions in the direction of
the adult system, i.e., when they reach a stage where they limit a natural process in the same way adults do, they should maintain this acquisition stage.

     However, this simple model is not confirmed by the way that Greek children
are reported to acquire Greek plurals (Theophanopoulou-Kontou 1973); e.g., the
adult plurals of ['poδi, lu'luδi, te'traδi̯o/te'traδ'o, tra'pezi] 'foot, flower,
textbook, table' are ['poδi̯a, lu'luδi̯a, te'traδi̯a, tra'pezi̯a] or ['poδ'a], etc.,
with a totally productive process of prevocalic gliding of unstressed /i/. All
children first say ['poi̯a, lu'lui̯a, te'tai̯a, 'pei̯a], i.e., they glide stem-final
/i/ prevocalically before the neuter plural morpheme /a/ and simplify the resulting clusters /δi̯, zi̯/. Some children then seem to switch immediately to the
adult form. However others have an intermediate stage with forms such as
['poδia, lu'luδia, tra'pezia], etc., i.e., they suppress the natural process of
i-gliding of their previous and their later phonologies temporarily in neuter
plurals (and only there, according to Theophanopoulou-Kontou's (1973) data).
The explanation I can think of for this strategy is that they prefer morphotactic transparency to phonological naturalness before they conform to the adult
model.[8] For other instances in Modern Greek, see Dressler (1977a:41).

     The tendency towards morphotactic transparency is also fulfilled as a con-

sequence of using more regular morphological patterns without MPRs than irregular ones with MPRs (9.3.2) such as in acquisition of Russian morphology as summarized and interpreted by Andersen (1979:§3, after Gvozdev (1949.[9]   Children
form present tense 1st persons such as [p'i'saju, i'skaju] 'I write, look for'
to infinitives [p'i'sat', i'skat'] instead of normal [p'i'šu, i'ščú] (with the MPR
of palatal formation),[10] cf. the respective imperatives [p'i'saj, poi'skaj] instead of [p'i'ši, poi'šči], cf. 5.1.2.

9.4.4. MacWhinney (1978:6f, 72) established the acquisition principle of 'affix
checking':[11] 'children will have trouble learning to add suffixes to roots that
appear to already contain the affix,' e.g., plural /s/ (9.2.2). This, I suggest, is the acquisitional precedence of the 'weaker dissimilation constraint'
defended by Dressler (1977b): This constraint prohibits the addition of morpheme-initial $v_i c_j$-sequences to roots ending in $v_i c_j$, e.g., in *fish-ish,
*linen-en. I.e., the avoidance of forms where a suffix looks like a copy of the
preceding stem termination may start with the strategy of 'affix checking' (cf.
Stemberger 1981, Menn & MacWhinney 1984).

9.5. Degrees of phonological naturalness (4f) play a role in the acquisition of
morphonology as well:

9.5.1. MacWhinney (1978:8, 16, 18, 30f, 40ff, 51, 83) has found that phonological predispositions result in phonologically plausible and general rules (cf.
typical PRs) being learned earlier and better than other rules (typical MPRs)[12]
and he claims that this influence corresponds to the relative degree of phonological naturalness. This fits with our approach of degrees of naturalness (5),
but not with the dichotomies between natural PRs and unnatural rules (MPRs,
AMRs) or alternations (or similar) as espoused by Stampe (1969), Hooper (1976),
Linell (1979) and many others.

Additional evidence can be found in the following instances:

9.5.1.1. Kergoat (1972:25) has observed that Breton children acquire the (phonologically now very unnatural) Breton mutations with the exception of the least
general mutation of k → <c'h> (realized as [x, ç, h] according to the dialect)
after the definite article *ar* in masculine singular nouns, e.g., [a kɔ'kɔk] 'the
cock' instead of *ar c'hilhog* from *kilhog* 'cock'.

9.5.1.2. Vowel deletion is acquired later than *j*-insertion by Russian children (Andersen 1979a:§3.2, §4.2), both MPRs having the function of eliminating the hiatus. Now vowel deletion is still less productive and general than *j*-insertion in Russian. However the tendency towards morphotactic transparency and morphological regularization may be more important (see 9.4.3): verbal stem *pisa-* 'write', normal adult 1.sg. [p'i'šu], child form [p'i'saju]; *j*-insertion serves morphological transparency better than vowel deletion (on the semiotic badness of synchronic deletion rules, see 10.7).

9.5.1.3. The PR (P 8) of surface palatalization (a very natural, but neutralizing PR) is learned earlier and better than the other Polish palatalization rules (but see 9.5.1.5) and in the correct position before /i/ (cf. 7.5), and the related MPR of surface palatalization (P 7) is used early as well.[13]

This case becomes problematic for Stampe's (1969) model of phonology acquisition: Surface palatalization (PR P 8) is a natural process (7.5), thus it should be a remnant of the innate universal process of palatalization (4.5.3.2). Now when Anka produces [gi-gi] instead of *[g'i-g'i] at age 1;0;27 (Smoczyński 1955:61) or when Pawełek pronounces [kuki][14] at age 1;11;10 (p. 161), this can be interpreted (e.g., in a generative model) as non-acquisition of surface palatalization (PR P 8) or --within Stampe's model-- in the following way: First there is an unordered application of natural palatalization, transforming the phonological intention /gi/ into [g'i] and of (the antagonistic) natural context-free depalatalization, inverting it into [gi]. Optional ordering would explain the variation between palatalized and non-palatalized forms. Then context-sensitive palatalization would be ordered after context-free depalatalization, according to one or both of the following principles: (1) fortition first - lenition last (5.17.2.2, 10.7.9.2), (2) context-free processes are relegated to the status of prelexical processes.

However, according to this model palatalization should be first applied in its most general form, i.e., in all palatalizing environments, before it is limited to the hierarchically most natural and adult position before /i/. But there is not a single instance of palatalization of /k, g/ before [e, ɨ] in the abundant data of Smoczyński's (1955) children Anka and Pawełek (the data start at age 0;10). Furthermore, according to Stampe (1969), palatalization should first be applied more generally than later. However Anka and Pawełek first applied it only to velars systematically, and only later and gradually acquired palatalization of the other consonants which are palatalized before /i/ in Polish. Thus they show a successive generalization of a natural phonological process during acquisition of phonology. Cf. Locke's (1983:21ff) report on the Afrikaans boy who did not apply Afrikaans final devoicing to final stops.

9.5.1.4. Russian has a surface palatalization similar to Polish, i.e., a very natural, but still neutralizing PR with exceptions (cf. Holden 1976). Its acquisition by Ženja Gvozdev is amply documented in Gvozdev (1949.I): Before age 2, all consonants are palatalized in the position before [i, e], even if the adult form has another vowel, e.g., ['t'i ku'p'ila 'n'is'ka] at age 1;11 = adult *ty* [tɨ] *kupila knižku* 'did you buy a book?' (Gvozdev 1949.I:38). The first depalatalized forms (age 2;0) are ['kon'cil'i] 'they ended' = *končili*, [ma'tet'] 'to look' = *smotret'*, [l'u'bit'] 'to chop' = *rubit'*, [a'ni] 'they' = *oni*, ['budit] 'becomes' = *budet*. Before age 2 we find cases of excessive, i.e., 'unmotivated' palatalization, e.g., [s'a'baka] 'dog' = *sobaka*, [d'om] 'house' = *dom*.[15] After age 2 such excessive palatalization is vanishing. Unlearning of excessive palatalization seems to result in cases of incorrect depalatalization. According to Stampe's model, Ženja first would apply the natural process of palatalization in its most natural environment, and then he would make errors while trying to limit it. However, all the instances of non-palatalized consonants before *i, e* uttered during ages 2 and 3 are deviant (in relation to adult speech); none correspond to cases in the position before non-palatalizing adult /e/ or adult /ɨ/ which Ženja merged with /i/ for a long time. Nor can Stampe's model explain cases of excessive palatalization before age 2.

Although Russian surface palatalization is not a completely natural PR and thus somewhat diminished (cf. 10.2.1.2.1) morphotactic transparency, Ženja applied it without exception in morphological alternations, e.g., at age 1.10: [ma'ka] = *bašmak+a* 'shoe' (gen.sg.) and [ma'k'i] = *bašmak+i* (nom.pl.). This case is not in contradiction with the situation of 9.4.1 where Amahl, for the sake of morphological transparency, did not apply final consonant deletion, a process which does not exist in adult English; but in the Greek case of 9.4.3, morphotactic transparency outweighed application of a natural PR of both adult and child language during an intermediate stage of language acquisition.

9.5.1.5. Let us compare the acquisition of phonologically much less natural

'palatalizations' in Polish and Russian: Since Smoczyński (1955) has no inflectional data and no derivations other than diminutives, whereas Gvozdev (1949)
has, I restrict my discussion to Russian, and there to the rules transforming
/k, g, x/ (<k, g, h>) into č, ž, š (similar to Polish postalveolar formation, 7.
3).[16] In diminutives (as Anka and Pawełek did), Ženja always applied them correctly (Gvozdev 1949.II:93ff, 103): e.g., at age 1;9: ['n′iga, 'n′is′ka, 'maka,
ma'c′ka] = *knig+a* 'book', dim. *knižka, bašmak+a* 'shoe', dim. *bašmačka*, also in
neologisms. At age 4;6, Ženja started to produce popular etymologies, including
back formations (Gvozdev 1949.I:227, 232) where he reconstructed velars, e.g.,
the accusative *log-u* (age 4;9, Gvozdev 1949.II:103) from *ložka* 'spoon', which
looks like a diminutive.[17] Certain regularities in verbal inflection have been
mentioned in 9.4.3.

   Palatal formation (k → č, g → ž) in comparatives of adjectives is not acquired separately from comparative formation itself (Gvozdev 1949.II:170); only
the morphophonemically correct comparative *čišče* of *čistyj* 'tidy' is produced at
age 6;11, whereas a regularized comparative (i.e., without morphophonemic alternation) [č′i's′t′ej] is produced at age 6;6. Notice that the structural change
between *st* and *šč* is greater than that between *k* and *č* or *g* and *ž* (e.g.,
[da'rožь] 'dearer', age 3;9, to *dorogoj* 'dear').

   In derivational morphology, data of adjectival derivation are richer than
of nominal derivation: E.g., the possessive and relational suffix *-in-* is first
used without change of *k* → *č*, etc., e.g., age 2;8 ['tang′inɑ], adj. to the dog's
name *Tango*; age 3;9 [suda'k′inьj], adj. to *sudak* 'pike perch'; later velars
are changed first in [bambu'č′inьjь] (age 6;4), adj. of *bambuk* 'bamboo' (Gvozdev
1949.II:161), i.e., morphological suffixation is acquired before separately
learned palatal formation. Ženja formed many neologistic verbs with the verbal
stem-forming suffix *-i-* which triggers palatal formation (Gvozdev 1949.II:119,
137f): In all instances he applied palatal formation, starting at age 2;1:
[mьla'toč′it′] 'to hammer' from *molotok* 'hammer' (Gvozdev 1949.I:81), cf. deverbal [talč′ilьs′] (age 4;3) fem. preterit = correct adult /tolk=a+la#s′/ from
tolkat-sja 'to rove about'. However as for position before the analogous *-e-*
suffix, Ženja did not apply palatal formation in [zьpla'h′ejьt] 'he becomes bad'
from *plohoj* 'bad' (Gvozdev 1949.II:139). Verbal stem formation with *-e-* is less
frequent than with *-i-* in Ženja's speech and produces many fewer neologisms. So
we may conclude that the degree of generality of palatal formation depended, in
Ženja's speech, at least partially on how productively he used the respective

MRs (diminutives and −*i*− suffixation most).[18]

Sorokin et al. (1979) conclude that phonology is learned before phonology.

9.5.2. Relative productivity of adult grammar is reflected by relative productivity of rules in child language. There, MacWhinney (1978:31) claims to have found two convenient cut-off points. He defines full productivity as application 'of at least 90% of the time to nonce roots', whereas at least 50% is the threshold for moderate productivity. In cases where no experimental data are at our disposal (e.g., for Polish, 9.5.1.3, and Russian, 9.5.1.4), productivity in child language can only be inferred from natural data, especially from the degree of application of a (M)PR in neologisms.

9.5.3. It has been known for a long time[19] that very unnatural PRs or MPRs can also be generalized during language acquisition. However MacWhinney (1978:12ff, 54, 81; cp. 9.2.2) has found that it does not happen in the form of analogies after a model form, but as a generalization of patterns (i.e., combination or rule learning, 9.2.5.3). Hellberg's (1978) conclusion that phonetic naturalness has nothing to do with learnability is unwarranted because (quite apart from the evidence of 9.5.1) he does not consider (1) that the stages of learning unnatural MPRs are later (se 9.5.1), (2) that his main counterexample (lowering of Swedish /ε/ before retroflexes) involves sociolinguistic problems of diffusion.

9.5.4. Linell's (1979:200ff, 215ff) discussion of language acquisition contains harsh critiques of the generative model. Since neither he nor any published work reports the morphonological findings of Myerson's (1976) unpublished thesis, we must briefly recall her respective results:

(1) Like previous investigations (e.g., Moskovitz 1973) but in a more cogent way, Myerson (1976:41f, 219, cf. 28) found that knowledge and manipulation of some AMRs of English Vowel Shift (which are all fairly unnatural MPRs) depends on previous acquisition of reading and correlates significantly with reading capability: This means an important difference from PRs, although I do not deny the psychological reality of orthographical representations (cf. 5.15, 5.20.3.5).

(2) Linell's thesis (e.g., 1979:96, 200-202) that morphophonemic rules (MPRs or AMRs) are not entities separable from the respective MRs faces the

problem that in Myerson's test results (1976:114ff), recall of (derivational) MRs was different from recall of their respective MPRs and AMRs: The morphological error type of suffix substitution (i.e., use of different MRs) decreased from the first recall (one day after teaching the derived nonce words) over the second one (after one week) to the third recall (after six weeks). On the contrary, the morphophonemic error type of keeping the base vowel (instead of changing, e.g., [ei] of the nonce word *skane* to [æ] or *[ɛ] in the nonce derivation *skanity*) increased from the first over the second to the third recall.

Notice also Myerson's (1976:145) report about an 8-year-old boy answering the question how he remembered the nonce words: 'On *trævity* the "A" changes when you take away the "E" on *trave* and add the "I".' I.e., the boy mentioned an orthographic or phonological trigger, which means that not only morphological triggering is psychologically real.

9.6.   The findings discussed so far may allow the following, at least tentative, conclusions:

9.6.1.   Some of the evidence adduced (9.4.3, 9.5.1, 9.5.1.3f, 9.6.5) poses problems for the Stampean model of the acquisition of phonology and morphonology,[20] but not for our model. Our approach would be vitiated if it could be shown that the degrees of morphological and phonological naturalness (10) have no positive correlation either with early age or degree of excellence of acquisition.[21] The universality of phonological processes (4, 10.7) does not necessarily mean that they are innate as such, but that they are and/or become universally available in maturation. An important factor is the child's environment.[22]

Notice also that the multiple strategy approach of a functionalist model (10.3.5.3) fits with rich variation in language acquisition data,[23] whereas other models rather predict parallel ways of acquisition for all children. For a functionalist model always allows various strategies to overcome a difficulty; children have to acquire the routine and norm of their native language, which of competing PRs are to be applied to a given input.

9.6.2.   A basic claim of our model of morphonology would be vitiated if the suppletion analysis of morphonology as practiced in Natural Generative Phonology (NGP) (Hooper 1976, 1979a, 1979b, Hudson 1980, 1982) were to be correct. Although to my knowledge no detailed investigations of the acquisition of weak

suppletions have been made within this framework, it seems to presuppose learning by analogy, and not by combination, for adherents of NGP reject both taxonomic item-and-arrangement grammars and item-and-process models of morphonology,
and moreover impute great importance to analogy.[24] Now, MacWhinney (1978:6, 8f,
14, 54f) has found that 'children will only apply analogy when rote and combination fail' (p. 6), that 'if the child has exhausted all possible ways of controlling allomorphic selection through phonological principles and still encoun-
ters disequilibrated pairs[25] he must finally resort to lexical principles to determine the choice of allomorphs' (p. 14), i.e., restriction by a lexical filter
is late, whereas NGP presupposes that forms like *brung* are learned one after another by analogy (or even by rote?) and are connected by a via-rule (or redundancy rule in other models) only as a secondary generalization.

MacWhinney's (1978) findings seem to refute both current overestimation of
analogy and its underestimation by classical standard Generative Phonology, cf.
9.4.3, 9.5.1.

Now Bybee & Slobin (1982:278) have published their investigation on past
tenses like *brung* in language acquisition which are supposed to support their
concept of a 'schema'; this concept corresponds much more to formats of complicated (but not abstract!) MPRs or AMRs rather than to surface analogy or surface
suppletion (cf. Peters 1983:92, 100).

9.6.3. Many recent studies in generative phonology amply acknowledge the importance of at least certain notions of naturalness. So far, my argumentation for
the importance of naturalness holds for their approach too. However, one distinction made in many generative (and all structural) studies does not seem to
receive any support from language acquisition, i.e., the strict distinction between allophonic and neutralizing, phonemic PRs. Both types of PRs abound in
early child language, and those neutralizing PRs of children that correspond to
several adult neutralizing PRs seem to be as well preserved throughout all
stages of language acquisition as are allophonic PRs. Note the general application of final devoicing in German (e.g., Mugdan 1977:139; on surface palatalization in Russian, see 9.5.1.4).

Therefore language acquisition as well does not support the amalgamation of
phonemic PRs and MPRs (and AMRs) into a unified class of morphophonemic rules.
Again morphonology is not identical with traditional morphophonemics.

Notes

1. See MacWhinney 1978, Hooper 1979a, Andersen 1979b, Berman 1981a, 1981b.

2. E.g., Yeni-Komshian et al. 1980, Edwards & Shriberg 1983, Locke 1983.

3. Cf. Peters 1983. On the mutual temporal order relations in the acquisition of different components of language, see Klein 1978:8.

4. See the symposium no. 3 in PICPhS 9 (1979):131-182, Klein 1978, Yeni-Komshian et al. 1980.II.

5. MacWhinney (1978) distinguishes five different cycles of acquisition.

6. Šahnarovič 1973, Hooper 1979a:25ff, Andersen 1979b:§3, MacWhinney 1978:11f.

7. Cf. Fey & Gandour (1982) on children's strategies for preserving underlying contrasts.

8. The data do not give evidence whether the plurals of the first stage were learned by rote. If yes, one could say that children preferred to preserve morphotactic transparency when they switched from rote learning to combination learning (9.2.5) of plurals.

9. Andersen's reports about Gvozdev's data must be supplemented: (1) Andersen does not list the earliest forms used by Gvozdev's son Ženja. (2) Often the deviant, regularized forms, highlighted by Andersen, are used later and less frequently than the irregular but correct adult forms. (3) Regularizations sometimes go in different directions, so at least some of them show learning by analogy, not by rule (or 'combination' in MacWhinney's terms, see 9.2.5).

10. But there is also the other direction of levelling: [i's'it] = *iščit'* (age 1;10) instead of the adult inf. *iskat'*, modeled after 1.sg. *iščju*, etc.

11. 'Affix checking' is another instance of the comparison between internal and external data.

12. Cf. MacWhinney (1978:40ff, 50ff) on Hungarian and Finnish.

13. Notice that Pawełek formed the instrumental [kon'ik'em] of *konik* 'horselet' with correct surface palatalization (MPR P 7) before the instrumental suffix *-em* already at age 2;2 (Smoczyński 1955:163), whereas no case forms with the less natural palatalizations (AMRs!) can be found in Smoczyński's data.

14. As an undefinable case form of *kółko* [kuwko] 'small wheel'. The important fact is non-palatalization of /k/ before [i].

15. In addition, (1) adult /l/ ([ł]) and /r/ are generally rendered as [l] (or [l'], not distinguished by Gvozdev), i.e., we may assume a context-free process of replacing all liquids with *l*, with an optional velarization before non-palatal sounds; (2) all shibilants are obligatorily replaced by palatalized sibilants, i.e., š, ž → s', č → c'; (3) many cases of distant assimilation can be found, e.g., ['s'as'a] = *Saša* 'Alexander' with anticipation of [s'] corresponding to adult š.

16. According to current terminology these are clearly morphophonemic rules (since they neutralize phonemes). As we will see, Gvozdev's Russian data are in striking contrast to Ingram's (1976b:10, 17f) inference from English data when he claims that morphophonemic rules are acquired between 7 and 12

years. The reason for this discrepancy may be that English AMRs of Great Vowel Shift are non-general rules of the Latinate vocabulary of English, whereas certain Russian palatal formation rules are highly general or even exceptionless, and phonologically much more natural, thus to be classified as MPRs; and secondly, complex morphology (and hence MPRs) is learned earlier in languages with rich morphology (e.g., Russian and German) than in English on which Ingram (1976b) relies; for the difference between the strongly and the weakly inflecting language types, cf. 10.9.3.2.

17. For similar back formations in adult language, see Uluhanov 1975:102.

18. It can be inferred from the exceptionless use of palatal formation in neologisms that here palatal formation has been learned by rule, not by analogy or rote, cf. 9.2.5.

19. Cf. Mugdan 1977:139, 162f for German umlaut, Linell 1979:200, Hooper 1979a: 28f.

20. For other critiques, see especially Linell 1979b:220 note 13, Drachmann 1978, Greenlee & Ohala 1980 with references. Clearly no model of phonology acquisition can exclude strategies such as those described in Fey & Gandour 1982.

21. Cf. Jakobson's (1941) views on markedness and acquisition and the claim of generative syntacticians that marked structures are acquired later than less marked/unmarked structures (Pustejovsky & Burke 1981), cf. Bates & Rankin 1979.

22. Cf. Wells & Robinson (1982) with their destructive criticism against the Chomskyan myth of vastly incomplete, inadequate, and degenerate stimuli presented to the child during language acquisition, cf. Snow & Ferguson (1977), Malshen (1980, with further references on motherese), Locke (1983: 195ff) on the importance of the child's linguistic environment.

23. On variation, see Klein 1978 and Leonard et al. 1980; cf. the problem-solving approach in the case study by Fey & Gandour (1979).

24. Thus the argumentation here holds also for other schools of thought which replace process models with analogical ones.

25. I.e., a conflict between, e.g., rule-generated past and participle *brung* and lexically stored *brought*.

10. TOWARDS AN EXPLANATORY MODEL OF MORPHONOLOGY: ON THE INTERACTION OF
NATURAL PHONOLOGY AND NATURAL MORPHOLOGY WITHIN A SEMIOTIC FRAMEWORK

CAUSARUM INVESTIGATIO[1]

10.1. Introduction

10.1.1. This chapter has been written with great hesitation because it may dissatisfy many readers: So far the content of this book has been largely descriptive; I have tried to account for all the sorts of morphonological phenomena I could think of, and to show how the concepts used in this book can cover them. 'Covering' and 'accounting for' facts is taken by many linguists as sufficiently explanatory, so that to them this chapter may seem superfluous. But any method of description presupposes an explanatory foundation, be it explicit of implicit, ambiguous or unambiguous. I prefer to make these presuppositions explicit and to dissolve the theoretical ambiguities deliberately upheld so far in order to offer a useful platform of discussion to as many readers as possible.

Treating the topics of this chapter adequately would have resulted in a lengthy monograph of its own. On the other hand many of the topics discussed in this chapter will be dealt with at greater length in the forthcoming volume by Dressler, Mayerthaler, Panagl & Wurzel and in Dressler (in prep.), as far as Natural Morphology is concerned. And as for Natural Phonology, I may refer the reader to Stampe (1980), Donegan (1978), Donegan & Stampe (1979b), Dressler (1980b/1983, 1984b). This may excuse the often sketchy character of this chapter.

10.1.2. The structure of this chapter is as follows: After dealing with generalities of explanation (10.2), I will present what I mean with a functional explanation of morphonology (10.3), show the usefulness of semiotics as a metatheory (10.4), delineate how Natural Phonology and Natural Morphology refer to their extralinguistic foundations (10.5), and how the model is structured (10.6); then phonology (10.7) and morphology (10.8) will be treated in their relations with morphonology: This will conclude the discussion of universals. In 10.9 morphonology will be inserted into language typology, in 10.10 into system adequacy.

10.2. On explanation

10.2.1. An explanatory model must strive towards predictiveness or --with a different time perspective[2]-- towards explanation. Since no total or complete explanations are possible, at most only partial explanations can be offered, i.e., the hypothetical explanams can explain only certain aspects of the explanandum. And even partial explanations given are usually no effective explanations, but only claims of explanability[3] in the form of explanatory sketches. This is all I can try to achieve here (on problems of multicausality, see 10.3. 5.3). Of course explanation does not equal diachronic derivation (cf. Stankiewicz 1979:43), although this so-called 'genetic explanation' is a necessary element in system adequacy (cf. 10.3.18.6).[4]

Most of this chapter will also lack formalization.[5] For partial formalizations of Natural Morphology and Natural Phonology, see Mayerthaler (1981, 1982), cf. also van den Boom (1983).

10.2.2. The properties of a theoretical model depend on the orientation and research interests of the model builder(s);[6] e.g., someone who is interested only in synchronic phonological or morphological classification of corpus data may easily lose sight of morphonology (e.g., Buyssens 1980). But whoever is interested in diachronic change in phonology or morphology, in the connection of phonology with morphology, etc., inevitably has to account for morphonological phenomena.

10.2.3. And whoever is interested in 'external/substantive' evidence[7] may come to question the wisdom of reducing linguistic theory to a theory of grammar (as in Chomsky 1975, 1980, Newmeyer 1980, 1983) because so much else is involved in substantive evidence besides Chomsky-type grammatical competence. Should the linguist try to account for some of these facts within a broader theory of language, or should he always restrict himself to a theory of grammar which would then always have to interact with other, non-linguistic theories in order to account for facts of language change, acquisition, impairment, variation, etc.?[9] E.g., when an adherent of a strict theory of grammar deals with language change, he is stepping outside his self-imposed boundaries unless he uses, in addition, a general theory of diachronic system change, which no grammar theoretician has done so far.

Since I consider grammar (including morphonology) a tool for communication and for supporting cognition involving the use of many linguistic devices beyond what is traditionally called 'grammar', I follow those[10] who want to construct language theories. This does not mean that a linguistic theory conceived along these lines can explain the above-cited types of substantive evidence on its own. It still needs bridge-theories[11] to psychological, sociological, and other theories. As has become evident in many sections of 5, such bridge-theories are most of the time still rather embryonic, irrespective of whether they are attached to grammar theories or language theories. However, proponents of language theories apparently try harder to bridge the gap than the average adherent of a grammar theory.[12]

10.2.4. If language serves communication and cognition, and if this is regarded as an essential property of language that a linguist must take into consideration, then this approach leads inexorably to functionalist positions (10.3) and possibly to the inclusion of semiotic considerations (10.4). However even if this is granted, 'form follows function, but not very far,' as Zwicky & Zwicky (1980:83f) have put it nicely, because 'the shape of a language cannot be predicted in full or in detail from the functions the language is called upon to serve.' But, in addition to functions, physiological, psychological, and social factors (10.5) directly or indirectly constrain the variability of linguistic form.

Clearly such a research program is too ambitious to have come very far in its implementation. Therefore I must rally to what adherents of generative grammar have not tired of repeating: Such a model cannot be falsified by the enumeration of putative counterfacts,[13] but only by the establishment of a counter-model which explains the same facts better -- and there will be quite a few explanations of facts in this chapter which have been explained either not at all so far or only within the framework of Natural Phonology/Morphology. Evidently a model of the kind we have in mind cannot be as simple (cf. Popper 1959: 137ff, Grassl 1979) as others whose scope is much more limited.

10.3. Functionalism

10.3.0. In justifying functionalism in linguistic theory I will first sketch its actual use in linguistics (10.3.1-5), then criticize critics of functional-

ism (10.3.6, cf. 10.3.13, 10.3.15) and outline a proper functional explanation
of morphonology (10.3.7ff, especially 10.3.17ff).

10.3.1. Classical functionalist models can be exemplified by Prague School
functionalism with its means-ends model,[14] further developed by Martinet (e.g.,
1949, 1965), Jespersen (1949), and more recently by Sgall et al. (1969), Dik
(1978, 1980) or Givón (1979 with much more specific claims of explanability) and
Halliday's (e.g., 1984) Systemic Grammar; for morphonology and phonology, cf.
Phonologica 1980 and Maslov (1979).

Some of these models exhibit a rather restricted functionalist format[15] because (1) they are limited to the communicative function (and functions derived
from it) and do not separate it clearly from communicative intent (as in 'the
function of a plural suffix is to signal plurality'); (2) they contain, in addition to function, only one conceptually different unit, i.e., structure (thus
'functional structuralism'); (3) their connections between explanatory functions and the structural explananda are often too short, simple, and vague;
(4) attempts to test functional explanations empirically are too infrequent.

Some of the contributors to Grossmann et al. (1975) are aware of these
shortcomings, but none of them deal with morphonology.

10.3.2. However, there is a functionalist model which is much more similar to
the approach proposed here (cf. Dressler 1979b): The UNITYP (= universals & typology) model elaborated by H. Seiler and his group in Cologne,[16] which unfortunately includes neither morphonology nor phonology. This model explicitly and
correctly distinguished (a) functions, operations serving them, and dimensions
where functions are served by operations, (b) the levels of universals, typology, and language-specific systems. Moreover, the cooperation of philosophers
(Holenstein 1978, cf. 1976, van den Boom 1983) improves the explanatory basis,
and substantive empirical evidence is adduced from diachrony, psycholinguistics,
language acquisition, aphasia, etc.

A transposition of concepts (a)-(b) to morphonology could be exemplified
with different types of palatalization PRs, MPRs, and AMRs (cf. 4.5.3.2, 4.6.2,
6, 7) serving, as operations, with varying degrees of success, the functions of
pronounceability and perceptibility (which are functions subordinated to the
communicative function of language). The dimensions where these operations

serve are phonological features, phonemes/allophones, allomorphs. The level of universals where they serve has been discussed descriptively in 5 (for functional explanation, see 10.3-8); for the level of typology, see 10.9; for the level of language-specific systems, see particularly 6 (Italian), 7 (Polish), and 10.10 on system adequacy.

10.3.3. Functionalism is called for if a language theory is supposed to cover communicative aspects of language because communication is goal-oriented and purposeful. This is true both of discourse theory or text linguistics[17] and of phonetic strategies.[18] Thus those antifunctionalists are quite consistent who sharply separate phonetics from phonology (e.g., some phonematicians or Foley 1977) and discourse from grammar (as in orthodox Generative Grammar). On the contrary, adherents of Natural Phonology take phonetics as an explanatory background of phonology (Bailey 1982 even demands an integrated phonetology), and adherents of Natural Morphology are interested in the function of morphology in discourse structure (cf. Dressler, Mayerthaler, Panagl & Wurzel, forthc.).

10.3.4. If language is understood as a social institution,[19] then too functional explanations are called for, as in functional systems theory.[20] Cybernetic models of language and language change[21] may be regarded as (technocratic) variants of communication theoretical models.[22]

10.3.5.1. Language change is a classical touchstone for functionalist explanation.[23] Simple explanations such as with A. Martinet's 'functional load/yield' of phonemes have lacked persuasiveness[24] because intervening variables were not systematically considered. Such explanations fall within the realm of the concept 'efficiency in linguistic change'.[25] If individuals use an operation (including MPRs) for communicative (and other) functions, then they, and the speech community as a whole, have an interest in making this tool more efficient for serving these functions. If therefore they improve the tool, language change results. As a corollary, one assumes that a speech community does not willingly make a language tool less efficient, i.e., change towards less efficiency is imposed by other factors (cf., e.g., 10.3.18.4, 10.3.18.6). Evidently there are 'non-adaptive' changes (Lindblom 1984) which are not connected with efficiency (or are so only very marginally).

10.3.5.2. Of course this is a grossly simplified picture of efficiency in language change. Taken literally it would mean that languages, as wholes, always
get more efficient and that, in a not very distant past, would have been very
inefficient. Such an absurd conclusion could be reached only by someone unaware
of an essential property of functional explanation: goal conflict.[26] As the
reader will have inferred from 5, PRs are more natural than MPRs on several accounts (cf. 10.7.1, 10.7.8, 10.7.10, 10.7.12, etc.), but as we will see (particularly in 10.7.11, 10.8), PRs are less natural than MPRs for other reasons. If
'more natural' corresponds to 'more efficient', then the change of a PR into a
MPR would make this rule (as an operation) less efficient on certain counts but
more efficient on others because after the change certain functions are served
better, others worse, i.e., optimalization is local, not global.[27]

In order to become explanatory, a functional model must be testable, and
therefore it must offer principled solutions to goal conflicts, show which goals
are more important, or at least restrict the conceivable number of solutions to
a goal conflict (cf. 10.3.18.4). This will be done here for the levels of universals (10.3-8), language types (10.9), and language-specific system adequacy
(10.10). Of course goal conflict prevents functional explanation from being
very short and straightforward.

10.3.5.3. Another problem for functional explanation is the fact (a) that one
function can be served by several operations (multiple strategies), (b) that one
operation may serve several functions simultaneously (multifunctionality).[28]
Here the typical phenomenon of multicausality[29] comes in. Therefore one and the
same MPR may serve several subfunctions, and one and the same subfunction may be
served by several MPRs. The establishment of a functional connection between a
MPR and a subfunction does not hinge on the achievement of the enumeration of
all other subfunctions the same MPR serves and of all the rules that serve the
same subfunction. Only if we want to evaluate the relative importance of a subfunction being served by a MPR, or the efficiency with which a MPR serves a subfunction, must we compare various subfunctions of a MPR and various rules serving the same subfunction (cf., e.g., the concept 'conspiracy' in Kenstowicz &
Kisseberth 1977:143ff, Lapointe & Feinstein 1982:91f).

10.3.6. In the theory of science, functional explanations --starting with the
Aristotelian causa finalis-- are intimately connected with teleology.[30] Teleol-

ogy has been attacked since Francis Bacon[31] as obscurantist and unempirical, and with such success that it has been renamed 'teleonomy' or simply 'functionalism'. In addition to criticism cited in 10.3.1, I should mention two objections often leveled against the functional enterprise of Natural Phonology/Morphology:

10.3.6.1. Putative 'natural tendencies' are considered as phoney,[32] i.e., circular: If, e.g., final devoicing occurs in many languages, it must be natural → final devoicing is a natural process, therefore it tends to occur in many languages. This is 'atheoretical naturalism', only faintly resemblant of a theory of Natural Phonology which inserts a process type such as final devoicing (4.5. 3.1) into a well-defined slot within a consistent model and adduces substantive evidence (10.2.3) in order to overcome circularity.

10.3.6.2. Functionalist theories are criticized for their proliferation of functions and asked to provide, once and for all, an exhaustive list of functions (cf. Woodfield 1976:118). This is tantamount to asking for a complete explanation (cf. 10.2.1). A realistic goal is to provide all main and many secondary/subordinate functions.[33]

10.3.6.3. More detailed criticisms against functionalism in phonology and morphonology have been leveled by Drachman (1981a) and Lass (1980a, 1981) and, at least partially, have been answered by Campbell & Ringen (1981) and Dressler (1981b).[34] At this point it may suffice to comment on the consequences of these critiques, which --albeit on an unusually sophisticated level-- represent two trends in the field (10.3.6.4f).

10.3.6.4. Drachman (1981:109) ends up in allowing only 'afterthought teleologies' of function (in addition to teleologies of goals, cf. 10.7). Thus the inquiry --typical for all social sciences-- into functions as covering the contributions of elements (or an ordered system) towards the preservation of the system containing these elements (cf. Emmet 1958:46) is branded as unscientific in linguistics and relegated to the status of speculative afterthoughts; explicit search is abandoned in favor of implicit intuitions. If linguistics belongs --at least partially-- to the social sciences, why should its research taboos resemble less those of other social sciences than those of physics[35] or biology (Lass 1981:257 note 2)? Note that functional explanations have been rehabilitated even in biology.

10.3.6.5. Lass[36] is even more radical: True to his motto 'What isn't predicted isn't explained,' he accepts only deductive-nomological or covering-law explanations and condemns functional ones. But then he ends up admitting that deductive-nomological explanations are impossible in language change. This conclusion comes as no surprise to those who have always held that 'language, like other human institutions, cannot be investigated according to ... a genuine model of a predictive science.'[37]

A consequence of Lass's argumentation is that we should resign from trying to explain language change. This is another instance (cf. 5.20, 10.7) of the dire consequences when linguists equate the 'best way/method/state of affairs' with the only one to be allowed.

10.3.7. One type of teleological explanation holds for goal-intended behavior in purposive, conscious actions,[38] as in speech performance and in certain phenomena of diachronic change. Here also MPRs can be involved, e.g., Campbell & Ringen (1981:59) cite the replacement of Finnish [ð] (due to consonant gradation of plain stops in closed syllables) by '[d] in Standard Finnish due to spelling pronunciation based on a Swedish reading model.' This is a sociolinguistic change which made the Finnish gradation MPR more irregular. Similar sociolinguistic purposes of imitating prestige registers may change a phonostylistic PR into an obligatory PR and thus initiate the irreversable change of phonologization (and, possibly, morphologization, cf. 5.18.6ff, 10.7.11.4, 10.7.12.4f, 10.8.6.9f). Notice that not only individuals, but also a whole speech-community may act on purpose (Woodfield 1976:207). Finally I want to mention that terminologists following international norms (cf. Wüster 1979) should coin morphologically complex terms which are morphotactically transparent and thus exclude the operation of MPRs, which would disturb the morphotactic transparency (cf. 10.8.1, 10.8.4.1).

10.3.8. Another type of explanation holds for teleology of function, where no conscious, purposive actions can be assumed.[39] Accordingly a MPR X can be attributed a function F within a system S[40] if X does an activity A (or has a property A) which 'characteristically and normally contributes to F' and if 'F is good for S (in normal circumstances), either intrinsically or because it characteristically contributes to some further good' (Woodfield 1976:208).

In 5 we have defined MPRs (in contrast to PRs and AMRs) and a large number of perperties of A, be they constant or only typical and accidental; evidently the constant and typical (default) properties are important for functional explanation. The systems S involved are the inflectional and derivational morphologies, i.e., the paradigms, classes, categories, and MRs. In anticipation of 10.7.11 and 10.8.6, we may say that MPRs have more indexical function within a morphological system than do PRs. E.g., the MPR of Turkish 'suffix harmony' (8.3.3) in *tut-acak* 'he will hold' (with the property/operation $e \to a$) has the indexical function of signaling that /ecek/ is a suffix connected with the root *tut* 'hold', whereas the sequence [tu$^\$$te$^\$$ʒek] may be the beginning of *tut ecektör* 'hold an ejector!'.[41] The vocalic changes of vowel harmony indeed 'characteristically and normally[42] contribute' to signaling that a suffix is connected with a specific preceding root or suffix. This subfunction 'F is good' for morphologically complex words/word-forms because 'it characteristically contributes to some further good', viz. receptive processing. In receptive recognition, morphological word-forms are important units of processing, so that helps for recognizing word(-form) boundaries or the extent of word-forms are good for communication, less for cognition.

10.3.9. This identification of the function of a MPR is not enough. For the question arises whether this indexical function of vowel harmony is important or irrelevant. Clearly a Turkish hearer can distinguish *tut-/ecek/ tör(pü)* 'he/she will hold a wood file' from *tut ecektör* 'hold an ejector!' by pragmatic, semantic, syntactic means and by sentence intonation without recourse to vowel harmony;[43] but in a syllable-timed language such as Turkish, the hearer lacks the prosodic clues for word(-form) boundary identification that exist in stress-timed languages.

In other words, a MPR (in contrast to many AMRs) is redundant.[44] Now communication theories and cybernetics (cf. Klaus 1968) distinguish useful redundancy and dead redundancy: Elements of a piece of information are usefully redundant if they can be left out without diminishing the informational content but if they can be used to preserve or restore the set of information communicated if other parts are left out in production or reception. Dead redundancy cannot help to supplement, preserve, or restore information. Since all communication systems are unreliable (Ungeheuer 1972:204, Beckhausen 1978:14), useful redundancy is needed.

Evidently the difference between useful and dead redundancy is gradual. This immediately leads to the question: How useful is the redundancy[45] of, e.g., the MPR of Turkish vowel harmony? Results of a first experiment where subjects had to guess the location of word boundaries in continuously written Turkish sentences seem to validate the assumption that vowel harmony is useful in recognition of word boundaries.

In general it can be decided (following Sanders 1977:163) (1) whether a property of an operation (e.g., MPR) is only compatible with the function of the operation, or (2) whether it is justified by its function, in that the operation --due to this property-- serves its function better, more simply, faster, in a less error-prone or energy-consuming way, or (3) whether the property is deter- mined by the function of the operation because otherwise the operation would be incapable of serving the function, cf. diachronic examples in Campbell & Ringen (1981). Properties of MPRs can only be compatible (1) or justified (2) but not determined (3) by the functions of the respective MPRs.

Again, the usefulness of a MPR depends also on the other properties of the linguistic type (10.9) and of the language-specific system (10.10).

Redundancy and multifunctionality (10.3.5.3) are preconditions for language acquisition, innovation, and thus language change (Holenstein 1982:103).

10.3.10. In diachronic change a function may become vestigial (Wright 1976:89), e.g., useful redundancy may gradually become useless (dead). This, I claim (cf. 10.7.11), happens to phonological functions of PRs if these PRs turn into MPRs. The same is bound to occur in first language acquisition, e.g., to the function of aiding/constraining pronounceability (10.7.1), if Turkish vowel harmony first has the status of a PR and then changes, during acquisition, to the status of pre- and postlexical MPRs. In the format of a functional explanation it is as- sumed that this change occurs because Turkish children notice that vowel harmony serves morphology rather than pronounceability (cf. 10.7.11.4).

10.3.11. On the other hand, a fortuitous accident can be used for establishing a functional connection.[46] This seems to happen in phonologization and subse- quent morphologization (10.7.11.4f): The morphological indexicality of a PR, i.e., the fact that it often (redundantly) signals a morphological category, is first an accident of the phonologization of intrinsic allophones[48] and of its frequency of use in morphological alternations. Then the phonological indexicality of a PR may be downgraded in favor of its morphological indexicality, and thus the PR may be reinterpreted[49] as a MPR.

10.3.12. Of course having a function does not equal achieving its goal (Wright 1976:73ff), e.g., in articulatory undershoot the articulators move towards an articulatory goal without reaching it, but this does not eliminate the function of an articulatory movement or of the PR which determines this movement. However, typical non-achievement may lead to diachronic change: If a lenition PR of intervocalic spirantization is performed more and more with articulatory undershoot in the course of generalizing casual speech properties, the hearer may reinterpret this lenition PR as a deletion PR, cf. the history and prehistory of Celtic and French lenitions and of Finnic gradations (5.2.2, 5.2.4).

The spread of a linguistic change may be explainable as goal-intended, purposive behavior (cf. 10.7.3): Since the speaker has internalized which linguistic rules or units are appropriate to a given (more or less formal) speech situation, he can be assumed to know unconsciously (to 'cognize' in Chomsky's (1980) terms) which tools are adequate for formal vs. informal situations. Now if a speaker generalizes some formal or informal speech behavior, he can be assumed to know (cognize) which PRs (or other rules or units) to generalize or degeneralize. It would seem absurd to me --and in discrepancy with sociolinguistic findings on sociophonological stereotypes and indicators-- if the speaker did not know the function of these PRs (e.g., backgrounding for informal situations, foregrounding for formal ones), i.e., if he did not know what the respective linguistic operation is good for. In this way teleology of purpose (10.3.7) and teleology of function (10.3.8) are connected in diachronic change.

10.3.13. Therefore we can answer the following objections to linguistic functionalism (10.3.13.1-3):

10.3.13.1. Language variation does not at all 'drive the final coffin-nails into functionalism' (Lass 1980a:93f, 1981:268) (i) because variation is normal in functional systems (cf., e.g., Sanders 1977:162, van Parijs 1981), (ii) because linguistic variation is controlled by social and psychological factors, i.e., it is functional itself (cf. 10.3.12, 5.11), and (iii) because in other domains

also change occurs via variation and selection/survival of the more efficient
alternatives.[50]

10.3.13.2. Lass (1980a: chapter 3, 1981:268ff) and Romaine (1981:104ff) attack
'methodological individualism' in models of language change: 'It is not the individual speakers who change grammar, but grammar changes itself.' But if
speakers are aware of the relative efficiency ('goodness') of the operations
they use[51] and thus either increase or decrease their use, and if spread is an
important part of grammar change, then the speakers' involvement in grammar
change can be subjected to functional explanation in regard to efficiency (cf.
10.3.5.1f, 10.3.7, 10.3.11f).

This does not entail the assumption of either a spurious group-mind or of
historic knowledge of what one's ancestors have done. E.g., the long history of
the inefficient AMRs of umlaut in Germanic languages (cf. 5.2.4, 5.8.6) displays
a slow decrease of umlaut forms, although new umlaut forms are occasionally attested, i.e., there has been fluctuation, but the great majority of speakers
must have been quite aware of the inefficiency of recessive umlaut AMRs, and
thus reduction or mere conservation of lexicalized umlaut forms has prevailed.
The slowness of decrease is due both to lexicalization and to strong social control in language acquisition.

The anthropomorphic metaphors that we find in many functional accounts of
language change are thus less a danger than an abbreviatory shortcut which
covers the mechanisms of functional explanation with a smoke screen (cf. Campbell & Ringen 1981:63f).

10.3.13.3. While attacking functionalists for treating grammars like individuals acting on purpose,[52] supporters of the view that 'grammar changes itself'
are subject to the core to the same attack, i.e., against treating grammars like
active entities. Or, one who speaks of simplification in grammar change[53] presupposes purposive behavior again, viz. purposive behavior of children, but usually does not bother to supply the necessary functional explanation which would
vouch for explanatory adequacy.

10.3.14. This remark leads us to a functional account of first language acquisition (9). According to Stampe (9) 'rules' (i.e., MPRs, AMRs) have to be
learned, 'processes' (PRs) unlearned. In the case of PRs, Wright's (1976:127)

(1976:127) account holds that we (i.e., learners) 'discovered that we naturally behaved in that way [e.g., by using a universal process type identifiable with a PR of the given language -- WUD] and nurtured the disposition against attenuation'; as for MPRs and AMRs, 'we trained ourselves to behave in that way.' As for MRs, their conventional part is learned by 'training' alone, whereas their universal, natural properties (cf. 10.8) are 'discovered' in learning and are less subject to 'attenuation'. In this way language acquisition falls within the scope of a functional account of human action. One who believes in the innateness of phonological processes --an assumption compatible with, but not necessary for our position-- will find a functional account in Woodfield (1976: 154ff).

10.3.15. Lass (1980a:86ff, 1981:265, 272) doubts the explanatory power of functional explanation since it does not define dysfunctions (but cf. Pateman 1982: 171f). However, in addition to pidgins (Lass 1981:272), one can mention early, still 'dysfunctional' stages of language acquisition, and language decay and language death: When a minority language becomes dysfunctional in respect to its communicative and cognitive function, speakers tend to use it less and thus accelerate its decay and dysfunctionality.[54] Also there are language disturbances (cf. 5.14.9).

If there were no dysfunctionalities, why would various endeavors of language planning or language engineering try to correct them? Finally, certain poetic 'deviations' would be dysfunctional in 'normal' speech, e.g., the two contradictory radical strategies employed by the Viennese poet Konrad Bayer: (1) In his text 'Karl ein Karl' he replaces all nouns with the one name *Karl*. (2) The hero of his short text 'mutationen 2' gets a different name in each sentence so that conceptual coreference is contradicted by lexical non-reoccurrence.

So if there are dysfunctions in language, and if innovations can lead to dysfunctionalities, how can we explain the fact that no or few dysfunctionalities arise in 'normal' language change? If grammar change were only structural without regard to functional relations, how can an explanation of grammar change exclude dysfunctional change, i.e., explain why it does not occur or occur only very rarely? The answer is: Explanation of language change MUST include functional explanation! And this answer is complementary to Lass's conclusion (10. 3.6.5) that explanation of language change is impossible, which can now be seen as following from his rejection of functional explanation.

10.3.16.   Whereas in language change certain aspects of grammar, at the expense of others, may become more efficient in serving certain functions (cf. 10.3.5.2, 10.7.11.4, 10.8.2), there are only two cases where a language system as a whole may become more efficient:

10.3.16.1.   When a jargon develops via a stabilized pidgin into an expanded pidgin or a creole language, the specific language system develops from a reduced ('dysfunctional') language into a fully developed language which has the same overall efficiency for communication and cognition as other natural languages.[55]

Early pidgins do not have MPRs, (1) because they have little morphology and (2) because they have no antecedent history of PRs being morphologized. This lack of morphonology fits with the overall observation that early pidgins have little redundancy.[56] Evolution to expanded pidgins or creoles results in the elaboration of morphology (cf. Mühlhäusler 1979, 1981, 1983). This creates the necessary precondition for the development of MPRs (cf. Mühlhäusler 1981), although they are still rather rare in creole languages, e.g., in Haitian Creole (Hall 1953:22, 28, 34f, Valdman 1977b), Jamaican Creole (Akers 1981), Sri Lanka Creole Portuguese (Smith 1978, who in comparing Portuguese Indian Creoles found a correlation between morphological complexity and the number of morphophonemic alternations, as expected); cf. Tinelli's (1981) enumeration of MPRs, which are more numerous within the sentence domain than within the word domain (MPRs in the strict sense of this book).

Thus we may reach two general conclusions in regard to MPRs and functionalism:

(1) The occurrence of MPRs presupposes a language system which is as 'efficient' as and serves the functions of communication and congnition as well as a fully developed natural language.

(2) It presupposes the cooccurrence of a fairly elaborated morphology.[57] MPRs again seem to serve morphological ends.

These conclusions are confirmed by the following facts:

(1) In language decay --which represents, to a certain degree, a mirror-image of the expansion from jargon phases of pidgins to creoles-- MRs and MPRs are heavily reduced (cf. 10.3.15), PRs much less so.

(2) The reduced 'languages' of technical terminology have very few MPRs, if

any at all (Wüster 1979), but morphotactically very transparent morphologies (cf. 10.8.2.4).

(3) In first language acquisition MPRs are learned rather late (9), when grammar has expanded to near-adult completeness, and notably after most of morphology has been acquired.

(4) In aphasia (cf. 5.14.9, 7.6.12) MPRs are more disturbed than the PRs of the given language, and these disturbances seem to correlate with disturbances in morphology.

10.3.16.2. The other case where language as a whole became less 'dysfunctional' or more efficient must have been the phylogenetic evolution of the human language faculty;[58] during its evolution it must have served better and better the communicative and cognitive functions that natural languages have.[59] And if we may --in the vein of Bickerton (1981)-- extrapolate from the conclusions of 10. 3.16.1, then we may assume that the appearance of morphonology comes late in phylogenetic evolution.

10.3.16.3. As for the areas of this (10.3.16), we cannot decide how far 'form follows function' and how far structural poverty limits efficiency (e.g., in language decay both conditions favor each other), but we have established the relevance of functionalism for the study of morphonology.

10.3.17.0. To a certain extent the teleological connection between form and function from an explanation of 'form follows function' to predictions of 'function predicts form.'[60] Because of the existence of multiple strategies, multi-functionality (10.3.5.3), and redundancy (10.3.9), predictiveness is of a weaker form than in deductive-nomological explanation, so that we can achieve only probabilistic predictions --but even deductive-nomological explanations of empirical facts must be reduced to probabilistic ones.[61] In this sense our approach is weakly deductive. In order to underline the limited nature of our predictions, I will express predictions in the form of expectations whose fulfillment is to be checked in empirical research (cf. Lass 1980c:98f).

10.3.17.1. As far as morphonology is concerned, we must refer to the formula of the teleology of function (10.3.8): An entity X has the property A which serves the function F within a system S. S is language, which has the functions of communication and support for cognition. If we assume that form follows function to some extent, and if efficiency in serving a function is a preferred stage, then we can construct premises and draw conclusions like:

I.   In order to serve a function F, an entity X must have at least one property A_i which can serve F efficiently.

II.   If an entity X and an entity Y serve the same function(s) F_i, then X and Y are likely to have some property/properties A_n in common.

III.   If X and Y have no common function, then no common property can be predicted (or excluded).

IV.   If X and Y serve more common functions than X and Z, then X and Y are expected to have more properties A_n in common than X and Z.

       Now let us replace X, Y, Z with MPRs, PRs, and AMRs:

V.   MPRs have more phonological (sub)functions in common with PRs than with AMRs.

VI.   MPRs have more morphological (sub)functions in common with AMRs than with PRs.

VII.   Therefore it is expected that MPRs share more phonological properties with PRs, more morphological properties with AMRs

This expectation is fulfilled (see 5.21.10.7f).

10.3.17.2. A continuation of this argumentation is:

VIII. If X and Z have different, distinct functions F_i, F_k and F_a, F_b respectively, they are expected to have distinct properties A_i, A_k and A_a, A_b respectively (this does not exclude shared properties).

IX.   If Y has no function which is not included in the sets of functions of either X or Z, then Y is not expected to have a property A_y which is distinct from all the properties of X and Z, i.e., its properties are expected to consist of properties of the set A_i, A_k ... and A_a, A_b ... or of composite properties composed from these properties (e.g., A_{i+a}, A_{k+c}, A_{l+b} ...).

X.   Let us assume (cf. 10.3.9ff, 10.7ff) that morphonology has no distinct function of its own.

_____

XI. Then it follows that morphonology is not expected to have properties of its
     own, but only properties it shares with phonology and/or morphology.

And indeed in 5 we have seen that MPRs have only properties which recur
among the properties of PRs and/or AMRs. This explanandum will receive a probable functional explanation if we can confirm that assumption X is probably
true.

10.3.17.3. Despite all claims of isomorphy (and thus similarities) among components of language (or grammar), it has been assumed (at least tacitly) that each
component of language has its distinct properties, e.g., phonology, morphology,
syntax, etc. In combining assumptions I and VIII we can assume XII:

XII. Each distinct component X of the system S has its distinct properties A
      which serve functions F.

XIII. The set of MPRs has no distinct properties of its own (10.3.7.2).

_____

XIV. Therefore the set of MPRs of a language does not represent a distinct com-
      ponent of a language (in all possible senses of language, cf. 10.5).

If we add the basic assumption (2) of our item-and-process model that a
component consists of its rules with their inputs, outputs, and restructions
(all to be subsumed as properties of these rules), then our basic hypothesis is
functionally explained: 'There is no distinct component of morphonology.' And
MPRs share all their properties with PRs and/or AMRs, we can infer the second
part of our hypothesis: 'Morphonology is the intersection of phonology and morphology.'

But we need to account for this intersection --or in our dynamic model:
interaction-- between phonology and morphology. Therefore I propose that the
theory of interaction between phonology and morphology be the proper domain of
theoretical morphonological studies. And in this sense we may speak of a theory
of morphonology.

10.3.18.0. It is of course much easier to give functional explanations for
properties and subfunctions of a distinct component (with distinct functions)
such as phonology and morphology than for a secondary field of dubious status

like morphonology. Nevertheless I take up this challenge. Our functional account proceeds according to the following research strategy:[62]

10.3.18.1. First, both in phonology and morphology, secondary functions must be subordinated to main functions, and properties must be assigned to functions they serve. This will be done within a semiotic framework of naturalness (10.4, 10.6ff).

10.3.18.2. Then probabilistic predictions (cf. 10.3.17.0) are made on the basis of frequency distributions of morphonological phenomena and properties (and of similar phonological/morphological properties) in the languages of the world. These predictions are derived from assumptions on parameters of Natural Phonology, Natural Morphology, and their interactions, assumptions which are themselves derived from a small set of higher-order principles. The (phonologically or morphologically) most natural phenomena are expected to be most frequent[63] since they are supposed to contain the most efficient operations (on the respective parameter) and because efficiency should be preferred; the most unnatural phenomena should be extremely rare or not occur at all. The functional explanation would account for these frequency distributions best if a correlation between relative degree of naturalness and overall frequency could be established. I stress the qualification 'OVERALL frequency' because many marginal variables may intervene. These deductive predictions and their inductive scrutiny, i.e., attempts at (dis)confirmation, belong to the level of universals (cf. 10.6.1f).

10.3.18.3. Based on the same framework, negative predictions can be made, i.e., conceivable phenomena can be defined which are either phonologically or morphologically too unnatural to occur in any language, item conceivable morphonological phenomena with contradictory phonological and morphological properties so that they cannot occur (cf., e.g., 10.7.1.1, 10.7.3, 10.7.10.8, 10.8.2.2f). These exclusions --which would correspond to universal (not language-specific) asterisks in generative grammar-- must be predictable, whereas the boundary between very unnatural phenomena which are rare (cf. 10.3.18.2) and those which do not occur can often be found only by induction. This research pertains to the level of universals as well.

10.3.18.4. In comparing the separate predictions for each parameter of phonological and morphological naturalness we are bound to find numerous conflicts among parameters, i.e., phenomena which are relatively natural on one parameter, but rather unnatural on another. It is our task to limit possible outcomes of such conflicts to a minimum and to construct conditions for preferences in solving such conflicts. In other words, we must predict both solutions which may occur and solutions which may not. To that effect we need subtheories of language typology (10.9) and of system adequacy (10.10).

10.3.18.5. In this connection 'substantive' (external) evidence (cf. 10.2.3) is of paramount importance. For in various domains of substantive evidence the relevant intervening variables of each domain are different and therefore we can often predict how the same conflict should be solved differently in different constellations of factors, e.g., in normal language acquisition as opposed to language acquisition by children with Down's syndrome or in one aphasic syndrome as opposed to other aphasic syndromes. Hence, in contrast to psycholinguistic experiments, substantive evidence provides us with 'natural experiments'.

10.3.18.6. Finally there is the 'devil's case'. Just as within theology the assumed existence of the devil flies in the face of any decent theodicy, so too do highly unnatural phenomena within theories of Natural Phonology and Natural Morphology. If we want to convince our colleagues of the virtues of these theories, then we must demonstrate why and how highly unnatural phenomena can occur at all. In this way a devil's case represents a sort of crucial experiment.[64]

In dealing with a devil's case, one must first run through the five steps enumerated above (10.3.18.1-5). In addition, 'genetic' or historical explanation is necessary,[65] i.e., one has to account diachronically for the genesis of the highly unnatural phenomenon. Most of the time historical accidents are involved which have resulted in rampant language contact (cf. Campbell 1980) or other peculiar historical constellations.

In this respect Lehmann (1952:23) is partially correct when he states: 'The only explanation for a linguistic form is an older linguistic form.' In fact genetic explanation is a contributive kind of explanation and the last step within an attempt towards a full explanation. The impossibility of a complete explanation (cf. 10.2.1, 10.3.6.2) follows now from the involvement of teleology of purpose in explanation: Human purposive action always contains elements of human freedom (cf. Stegmüller 1979:126ff).

10.3.19. What I have argued for in this section (10.3) is the admissibility and feasibility of functional explanation (at least in connection with a 'natural-ist' approach) and its relevance for a theory of morphonology, but I have not argued for the necessity of functionally explaining morphonology.

Anyone who wants to limit his endeavors to strictly synchronic questions of grammatical form and structure occurring in a corpus or in his informants' dic-tation styles[66] can largely dispense with functionalism. But he is often left with bizarre morphonological phenomena which cannot be explained deductively or which can be explained only with the help of homologically bizarre explanations.

Functional explanation by concepts of naturalness, I hope to have been able to show already by now, is neither haphazard nor a matter of intuition, but de-mands a serious methodological enterprise comparable to other carefully devised research programs in linguistics and beyond. If I plead for mutual tolerance among linguistic theories throughout this book, I do not plead 'against method' (Feyerabend 1975).

10.4. On a semiotic metatheory of naturalness theory

10.4.1. Why semiotics?

10.4.1.1. The influence of semiotics on linguistics started with F. de Saus-sure's (1916/1968) 'semiology', where we find a very contracted conception of semiotics which is virtually reduced to the arbitrary connections between signi-ficants (F. 'signifiants') and significates (F. 'signifiés') in certain classes of conventional symbols.[67] The semiotic theory of Peirce (1965) found its way into linguistics mainly through the works by Jakobson[68] and his pupils such as H. Andersen, T. Sebeok, M. Shapiro (see Shapiro 1983). R. Anttila and U. Slagle even founded a semiotic model of 'Gastaltlinguistik' whose predicaments are in-teresting for morphonology, but without sufficient explanatory power.[69] Later on the enormous expansion of semiotics outside linguistics[70] has led to an im-pact in linguistics as well. Particularly the notion of iconicity or iconism (cf. 10.4.5.3ff) has become very fashionable.

But this is not the reason why I have proposed a semiotic framework (cf. Dressler 1980b, 1981b, 1981d, 1982a, 1982c), but my main motives have been two:

10.4.1.2. 'Natural' is often used in a very vague, intuitive sense, and this has been correctly criticized. If an adequate metatheory can be found, this metatheory would constrain the many possibilities of constructing naturalness theories. Semiotics is a good candidate because it deals with the polarity 'natural - conventional' (cf. 10.4.5, 10.7f) and is largely functionalist.[71]

10.4.1.3. The axioms on which linguistic models are built are often entirely ad hoc, based on intuitive insights of fashionable views. This situation is not bad in itself (cf. Popper 1959), but again it allows an extremely wide array of possible starting points for theories. If we find a larger superposed theory to which a linguistic theory might reasonably be subordinated as a special subtheory, then the choice of promising starting-points can be rigorously delimited. Semiotics as the theory of signs in general, which has been applied to many fields, is a good candidate for playing the role of a metatheory for a theory of language if languages are systems of verbal signs.

10.4.1.4. Additional motives for choosing Peircean semiotics are: (1) It suggests a processual model (cf. 10.4.4.2, 10.4.4.4), which fits well with our processual approach. (b) It has many concepts which closely correspond to well-established linguistic concepts (cf., e.g., 10.4.3, 10.4.4.4). (c) Chains of signs (10.4.3) lead gradually from the referent via levels of language structure to phonetic substance and back and thus bridge the gap between form and substance.

10.4.2. We define language as a system of verbal signs with the two main functions (following many linguists, psychologists, neurologists, etc.):

(1) of enabling man to communicate better than with non-verbal signs (communicative function);

(2) of supporting and guiding cognition better than with non-verbal signs (cognitive function.[72]

   If we want to understand what language --and morphonology, phonology, and morphology within language-- accomplishes for the language user, we have to concentrate on the achievement of man's verbal means of communicating and aiding cognition; therefore we must have a way to compare his verbal and non-verbal means.

A discipline apt for serving as the basic framework for our approach is semiotics, the theoretical and practical study of signs in general. An adequately elaborated theory of semiotics[73] is the most promising candidate for supplying a metatheory to Natural Morphology, Natural Phonology, etc., because its object is the more general category (genus proximum) of signs, of which language signs are a specific subclass. But which semiotic theory (cf. Harvey 1982, Eco 1984) should we choose? In my view, the precise system of the first large semiotic theory is still the safest choice, viz. the semiotics of Charles Sanders Peirce.[74]

10.4.3. According to Perice, a sign consists of 'something [= signans, WUD] which stands to somebody [= interpreter] for something [= signatum] in some respect or capacity [= interpretant]' (Buchler 1955:99). Thus we have four aspects of a sign:[74]

(1)   The interpreter is the user of the sign when inventing or producing or perceiving or processing or evaluating or storing or retrieving etc. a sign. The adequacy of the same sign for these different tasks may be different. 'Nothing is a sign unless it is interpreted as a sign' (Peirce 1965.II:170, cf. VII:216).

(2)   The signatum is what is expressed in the sign.

(3)   The signans (sign vehicle) is what expresses the signatum.

(4)   The interpretant is described as the 'idea to which [a sign] gives rise' (Buchler 1955:99, Peirce 1965.I:275), its 'proper effect', e.g., as a specific habit-change in the interpreter (Buchler 1955:276f, cf. Peirce 1965. VIII:179, 226). The sign 'creates in the mind [of the interpreter] an equivalent sign, or perhaps a more developed sign. That sign which it creates I call the interpretant of the first sign' (Buchler 1955:99).[75]

This results in a chain of signs: Signs stand for signs for signs for signs.[76] This might pose the problem of infinite regression because due to these chains of signs, in the end, everything might be indirectly connected to anything else. But this danger does not exist in linguistics because within language the number of sign types is very limited. However the chain of signs that relate linguistic signs to cognitive concepts and their referents (cf. McNeill's notion of semiotic extension) has no definite boundary within concepts and referents, as can easily be seen in literary criticism: The linguistic units (or signs) inter-

preted are finite, the comments by literary critics are not.   In general, chains
of signs mediate between substance and form.

10.4.4. Let us start with the chain of signs in phonology and then continue
with morphology:

10.4.4.1. In phonology, phonemes, quasi-phonemes,[77] extrinsic and intrinsic
allophones are sign vehicles (signantia) without any meaning than otherness (G.
Andersheit, F. *altérité*), as Jakobson (1962.I:280ff, II:707) has argued for
phonemes: They distinguish the sign vehicles of morphemes, as signs on signs,
i.e., their purpose is otherness.[78]

10.4.4.2. But a phoneme, in turn, is the signatum of a signans (in the semiotic
formula: *aliquid stat pro aliquo*), especially of allophones (cf. Jakobson 1962.
I:296f, 656), i.e., the input phonemes intended by speakers (Donegan & Stampe
1979b, Donegan 1978) are replaced by other segments (cf. 10.4.4.4).   The possible relations between a signatum and its signans are according to the types of
segments involved:

(1)   A phoneme as a signatum is signaled by the signans of an allophone or
      quasi-phoneme as in E. /t/ → [tʰ] in *ten*, /n/ → [ŋ] (/ __g → ∅) in *long*.

(2)   A phoneme is signaled by the signans of another phoneme in neutralizing
      PRs, MPRs, AMRs, as in /k/ → /s/ in *electric-ity*.

(3)   A phoneme is signaled by an intermediate segment which occurs in a deriva-
      tion as a false step, as in Polish /g/ → /ǯ/, if this /ǯ/ is obligatorily
      changed to /ž/ by spirantization (7.3.1). This is not allowed in all pho-
      nological models (cf. 10.7.10.4).

(4)   A phoneme is replaced by a zero signans, as in deletion PRs (e.g., *let us
      go* → *'s go*), MPRs, and AMRs.

      As we will see in 10.7, these four types of signatum-signans relations are
not equally efficient from the semiotic point of view, cf. Peirce's insistence
on the fitness/efficiency of sign classes for representation (e.g., Peirce 1965.
V:86ff on 'goodness') and Morris's (1971:173, cf. 359, 367) dictum: 'Signs adequate for some purposes may be inadequate for others.'

10.4.4.3. When we hear a complex word-form, e.g., E. *(he/she) rewrites*, the al-

lophones [ɹiɹai̯ts] are signantia of the phonemes /riraitz/ as their signata.
The signs composed of phonemes and their respective allophones are signs on the
signs of morphemes whose signantia are the formatives (morphs, exponents), e.g.,
re, write, z, and whose signata are the derivational meaning 'REPETITION', root
meaning 'WRITE', inflectional meaning '3rd SG. PRES.'. Morphemes are again
signs on the signs of words (*rewrite*) or word-forms (*rewrites*), whose signatum
is in our case the meaning of *to rewrite* and of *(he/she) rewrites* respectively.
The interpretant of a word are the concepts, connotations evoked, its perlocu-
tionary force, which can also be expressed as sign relations.

Since morphemes and MRs are signs on signs (= words), words are primary
signs, morphemes and MRs secondary signs, phonemes and PRs tertiary signs (namely, as signs on the signs of morphemes). Therefore the lexicon (or, a fortiori,
the syntax) has a general (semiotic and epistemological) priority over morphology and so does morphology over phonology.

10.4.4.4. Peirce differentiates several triads of signs, one being the triad
qualisign, sinsign, legisign.[79] Of these, the legisign is most relevant for our
study of Natural Phonology and Natural Morphology. 'A legisign is a law that is
a sign' (Buchler 1955:102), i.e., a conventional rule[80] connects signans and
signatum in order to 'render insufficient relations efficient' (Peirce 1965.
VIII:227) and to guarantee the interpretant for the interpreter.

Therefore we can conceive of PRs, MPRs, and MRs as signs whose signatum is
the input of the respective rule, and whose signans is its output; or more generally: 'rules are signs of mediation which relate the 'underlying' structure
to that of actual speech' (Shapiro 1983:81). Sinsigns are replicas of the respective legisigns, i.e., actualizations in performance of legisigns (which belong to the level of competence or Saussurean 'langue').

10.4.4.5. Prelexical processes merge conceivable phonological inputs into the
phonemes of a given language (8). Their teleology is quite different from that
of postlexical processes (cf. 10.7.1, 10.7.1.1). Paradigmatic prelexical PRs,
which establish the phonemic inventory of a given language, can hardly be understood as signs because no language can have an established sign relation between
conceivable sounds and their subset, the phonemes of the respective language;
for these conceivable sounds cannot be intended[80] and thus cannot be signata.
Syntagmatic prelexical PRs (which govern phonotactics) have phonemes of the giv-

en language as both inputs and outputs. They can be understood as signs on signs, i.e., on morphemes or words, specifying their shapes, i.e., they can be understood as indices (10.4.5.2).

10.4.5. Another[81] Peircean triad is totally relevant for us: Signs can be classified as having more or fewer properties of symbols, icons, and indices:[82]

10.4.5.1. A symbol is characterized by a conventional or habitual connection between signans and signatum; thus all language signs are symbolic, at least to a small extent (cf. Shapiro 1980:54, Eschbach 1978). However it is not true that almost all language signs are purely symbolic as F. de Saussure and many of his followers tended to believe. Moreover conventionality is reduced by the decisive role of the interpreter (10.4.5).

10.4.5.2. An index is a sign which focusses the attention of the interpreter on the object intended without describing it and which is common to the experience of speaker and listener: Pronouns and all grammatical morphemes (inflectional and derivational)[83] are indexical (and, of course, symbolic at the same time). An index (at least ideally) stands unequivocally for the object it refers to (Peirce 1965.V:414).

10.4.5.3. An icon exhibits a similarity[84] or analogy between signatum and signans. Icons are the most natural signs.

10.4.5.4. 'Symbols grow. They come into being by development out of other signs, particularly from icons' (Peirce 1965.II:169). The change from more iconic to less iconic symbols can be classified as deiconization (Plank 1979) as it has occurred in the evolution of writing systems (Diringer 1949, Gelb 1963, Ivanov 1982, cf. 10.7.11.4f). Thus symbols are the highest achievement of human language, whereas animal communication functions much more by iconic and indexical means (cf. Nöth 1976). Also sign language is more iconic than verbal language (cf. Klima & Bellugi 1979:79ff), but the constitution of symbols[85] is based on icons (and also on indices), as illustrated by the process of language acquisition (ontogeny)[86] and storage in memory. 'The only way of directly[87] communicating an idea is by means of an icon; and every indirect method of communicating an idea must depend for its establishment upon the use of an icon'

(Peirce 1965.II:158), i.e., in icons there is an intrinsic connection between signans and signatum.

10.4.5.5. The most natural icons are images which 'partake of simple qualities' (Peirce 1965.II:157) shared by signans and signatum, e.g., onomatopoetic words.[88] The least 'iconic icons' are metaphors, which exhibit some mere parallelism or partial similarity between signans and signatum.[89]

10.4.5.6. Most important for Natural Morphology are diagrams, whose degree of iconicity lies between that of images and metaphors (Peirce 1965.III:211). Diagrams are icons 'which represent the relations, mainly dyadic, or so regarded, of the parts of one thing by analogous relations in their own parts' (Peirce 1965.II:157). For example, when we regard a technical diagram of a car in a drivers' handbook, we know (by convention) that up and down on the paper (signans) means verticality in the signatum (the car), that right and left mean front and back, that uninterrupted lines refer to visible, dotted lines to invisible parts of the car, etc.

The important role of diagrammaticity in grammar has become clearer and clearer,[90] and it is a dominant theme in Natural Morphology.[91] For phonology all three types of icons have been used.[92]

10.4.6. Let me clarify the semiotic terminology of this chapter: If I speak of 'icons, iconic, iconicity' without further specification, I mean signs or sign relations which are not only symbolic (or maybe also indexical), but also iconic to a non-negligible degree; more precisely, they are the Peircean 'iconic rhematic sinsigns' in the context of performance (or Saussurean *parole*); in all other contexts (competence, universals, typology), they are the Peircean 'iconic rhematic legisigns', and similarly with indices. And I will speak of symbols only in the sense of 'symbolic rhematic sin/legisigns' if their iconic/indexical components are non-existent/negligible or neglected for the sake of argumentation (which will be duly stressed). For other principles of semiotics, especially various semiotic parameters of efficient signing which help to evaluate the relative efficiency of a linguistic sign, see 10.7.2-7, 10.8.

10.4.7. Of course hypotheses must be derived from semiotic theorems and empirically tested either via substantive evidence (cf. 10.2.3, 10.4.5.4f, for aphasia,

cf. Nöth 1976, Plank 1978) or via specific psycholinguistic experiments (e.g.,
Tarte & O'Boyle 1982, Luftig 1983, Seifert, to appear). This leads us to 10.5
on the extra-linguistic foundations of Natural Phonology and Natural Morphology.

10.4.8. But before this next step I want to point to important differences between my model and the full-blown semiotic model of grammar by Shapiro (1983),
particularly since Shapiro's book concentrates on phonology, morphology, and
morphophonemics (which covers the domains of our AMRs, MPRs, and most neutralizing, phonemic PRs). Shapiro's approach is neo-structuralist (his own term)
insofar as he insists on items and their distribution and alternations within a
(sub)system and greatly reduces the role of rules (much more than in H. Andersen's work, to which he is much indebted, cf. Shapiro 1983:98f); contrast our
chapter 1. Shapiro stresses the distinction between form and substance --al-
though chains of signs relate them (10.4.3.4).[93] It is thus consistent with his
approach that he undervalues both substance and substantive bases of linguistic
structure (e.g., p. 108ff in regard to the 'naturalness fallacy'[94]). His approach is functional, but in the narrow sense of 10.3.1. He overextends, with
insufficient justification, the Peircean notion of interpretant (cf. 10.4.3.4)
and elevates it to the basis of markedness in a rather cryptic way. Markedness
is not founded in universal substantive principles,[95] so that the assignment of
markedness values is often ad hoc;[96] moreover the expedient concept of markedness reversal may serve as a protective device against falsification.

However, I can fully agree with some statements such as Shapiro's (1983:97)
contention that 'rules cease to be viewed as divorced from the sign relations
they implement', and with his warning (p. 156) that 'morphophonemic rules must
not be viewed merely as a 'junk' pile of old phonological rules which have fall-
en into desuetude.'

10.5.   On the extralinguistic bases of Natural Phonology and Natural Morphology

10.5.1. When criticizing Natural Phonology for its reliance on phonetics, S.
Anderson (1981) hit at an essential property of Natural Morphology as well: The
quest for extralinguistic foundations (as *causa materialis*, cf. Pateman 1982:
165f) in the sense of extralinguistic factors which either determine/prohibit or
(dis)favor conceivable properties of linguistic structure. Thus questions arise
such as 'In which cases is physiology resistable, and resisted by human agents?'

(Pateman 1982:165). This section (10.5) will deal rather briefly with generalities because there are no extralinguistic bases of morphonology itself, but only of phonology and morphology, and because these factors are better treated together with the specific parameters of naturalness they are connected with (10. 7f).

10.5.2. The means that are available to language for serving its communicative and cognitive functions are limited (Oller 1971), and unreliable in actual performance (Ungeheuer 1972:204, Backhausen 1978:14), or to put it more positively, there are finite choices open how to serve these functions (and subfunctions), some of them being more, some less efficient. These extralinguistic factors are physiological, neurological, psychological, and social.

10.5.2.1. Physiological limits of perceptual space and of articulation restrict the number of possible sounds, of distinctive features and their combinations. Among the articulatory options available there are best points, and the problem is to find the 'optimum position'[97] which has the best perceptual effect while 'entailing minimum physiological energy', i.e., 'minimum displacements of lips and tongue from their natural positions' (Lindblom 1972:79) so that they achieve maximal perceptual contrast with least effort. In other words, those means are most efficient which follow the minimax principle, which Carroll & Tannenhaus[98] cite in the following form (which is more adequate for grammar than for phonetics): 'The speaker always tries to optimally minimize the surface complexity of his utterance while maximizing the amount of information ... he effectively communicates to the listener.'

These are not concerns only of the individual speaker in performance or when acquiring language, but should also have played a role in the phylogeny of language. In this way Lindblom, MacNeilage & Studdert-Kennedy (forthc.) derive formal phonological universals from self-organizing processes of substance.

10.5.2.2. Psychological limitations on perception and receptive processing go far beyond phonetics,[99] e.g., the principle of ground and figure favors processing of stimuli which clearly contrast with their background.[100] Memory problems, restrictions on storage, retrieval, selective attention, etc., come in, cf. for the ease of learning signs, Luftig (1983).

10.5.2.3.   In many accounts of language either as a 'mental organ' or as conditioned by physiological/neurological/psychological factors, social factors are
treated only as secondary, disturbing variables.[101] However communications systems are purposive, interactive, and adaptive.[102] Therefore if language has a
communicative function, and if we allow that form follows function to some extent (10.3), then social factors are constitutive for language. E.g., the
above-mentioned trade-off relation between optimal perceptual contrast and least
articulatory effort (10.5.2.1) presupposes the speaker's empathy[103] with the
hearer's receptive role.

Or the morphosemantic tendency towards an unmarked status of the first person, of proximal distance, and of the present tense derives from the social attitude of the prototypical speaker centered on 'ego, hic et nunc'.[104]

10.5.3.   Thus extralinguistic factors underdetermine linguistic structure, but
they limit the choice of linguistic operations open to languages and favor/dis-
favor alternative operations. The need to overcome or to avoid extralinguisti-
cally determined difficulties can be considered as subordinate functions of operations (subordinate to the main functions of language or of its respective
components) because certain devices become very costly (the inverse of the minimax principle, cf. 10.5.2.1).

The speaker (and the child in language acquisition) has the tasks of a
problem solver who has to attain goals (e.g., functions of language) and to
overcome difficulties in attaining them, and who has a collection of methods
available (i.e., universal linguistic operations as conditioned by extralinguistic factors).[105] Again, solving problems of communication and cognition requires goal-intended actions, but the operations used by the problem solver have
their own teleologies of function (10.3.7f).

Seiler (1978c, 1978) has introduced the concept of problem solving into his
UNITYP model (cf. 10.3.2) so that universal linguistic operations can be regarded as devices for solving problems in serving functions of language. Elements
of a language-specific grammar, e.g., MPRs, are thus problem solving devices
themselves, albeit in an indirect way, insofar as individual grammars are connected with universals (10.6ff).

10.5.4.   It is in connection with functional principles of problem solving that

we must evaluate devices for economizing effort such as the minimax principle
(10.5.2.1). Similarly Martinet's (1949, 1955) principles of economy or Zipf's
principles of least effort[106] can be used within a functionalist framework. In
my view, these principles do not reflect separate, independent functions of language, but only functions which must be subordinated to the main functions of
language and language components; their relative importance can be evaluated
only within a hierarchical model of the various (sub)functions and operations
involved.

10.5.5. After having delineated the role of extralinguistic factors within a
functional, semiotic model of Natural Phonology and Natural Morphology we can
answer another set of objections[107] against 'strong naturalism' as pioneered by
models of Natural Phonology.

10.5.5.1. Deductive-nomological explanations demanded by Lass (1980a, 1981),
Drachman (1981), and other contributors to Phonologica 1980 (cf. also S. Anderson 1981) have been devised for (relatively) closed systems.[108] Only under lab-
oratory conditions may a relatively closed system of controlled variables be obtained (cf. Pateman 1982). This is the reason why we devised experiments for
testing our sociopsycholinguistic model of phonological variation (Vanecek &
Dressler 1977, cf. Dressler & Wodak 1982). But this is much more difficule for
morphonology because several theories are involved (cf. 10.6); still quite a
few predictions have been and will be derived.

10.5.5.2. Lass (1981:264) assails functionalists for falling victim to 'the
fallacy of affirming the consequent' as in the argumentation imputed by him to
functionalists:

  'a. Here is a function F.
   b. Implementation of F would cause X.[109]
   c. X occurs.
   d. ∴ X implements F.'

Unfortunately Lass does not cite any author who follows this line of argumentation even to some extent. In any case it cannot be imputed to all functionalists. At least my line of argumentation consists of the following stages:

(A) Identification (simplified):

    I.   There is a hierarchical system of universal functions[110] F_1, F_2, F_3, F_4, ...

    II.   The properties P_1, P_2, ... make an operation fit to implement the functions F_1, F_2, ... respectively.

    III.   There is a set of universal operations (e.g., universal phonological process types, chapter 4) O_1, O_2, O_3, O_4, ...

    IV. O_1 has the properties P_1, P_2; O_2 has the properties P_1, P_3, ...

    V.   Because of its properties P_1, P_2, O_1 implements the functions F_1, F_2, ...

    IV.   Rule X of language L_i has the properties P_1, P_2, ...

_____

    VII.   Rule X of language L_i represents O_1.

    VIII.   Rule X of language L_i implements the functions F_1, F_2, ... (cf. the identification of universal process types with language-specific PRs via the method of process matching (5.2)).

(B)   <u>Evaluation</u> of the relative efficiency with which function F_i is implemented by operation O_i. Here criteria of chapter 5 are used. In chapter 4 we saw already that generalization/maximalization of a backgrounding process according to its hierarchy serves ease of articulation better (cf. 10.7).

(C)   <u>Predictions</u> are made according to the strategies delineated in 10.3.18 (cf. 10.3.17) and exemplified in 10.6ff.

Lass (1980c) is pessimistic about the results of such an enterprise, but this is of course another matter than imputing a fallacy to it.

10.5.5.3. Drachman (1981:104) objects (1) that 'no rule-block dichotomies consistently and coherently correlate with subsets of ... functions' -- but how could he expect anything else from functions? (cf. 10.3.5.3, 10.5.2.1, 10.5.5.2; but still there are not chaotic connections, e.g., between phonological processes and the two main functions of segmental phonology, see 4, 10.7); (2) that 'the major Peircean trichotomy ..., into icon, index and symbol, already faced such serious demarcation problems' -- this second remark on demarcation displays a profound misunderstanding of Peircean semiotics and is an inconsistent reproach against Dressler (1980b) because there (Dressler 1980b:50, 8.4.3) the non-exis-

tence of pure icons and pure indices and the mixed character of signs is explicitly mentioned.[111]   The problem is one of comparisons, e.g., of evaluating
which one of two signs is more iconic, whether indexicality of a sign is more
of a phonological or morphological nature, etc. (cf. 10.7ff).

10.5.5.4.   S. Anderson (1981:531) proclaims that 'constraints on the linguistic
system per se are in principle independent of such "functional" explanations
from other domains,' such as language acquisition.   This remark begs the question whether (universal/general) properties of synchronic systems are the results of (universal/general) properties of language acquisition and language
change or vice versa.[112]   But even granted the epistemological priority of synchronic systems, this remark presupposes a highly theory-specific separation and
evaluation of 'internal' evidence as important and of 'external' evidence as unimportant (cf. 10.2.3, 10.5.5.5).[113]

      There are fewer absolute external constraints than relative ones, which
render many conceivable operations/structures highly marked;   e.g., Anderson's
(1981:531ff) identification of Kiparsky's 'alternation condition' (cf. 5.20, 10.
7.11.1) as an extralinguistic one is relevant only for models which place absolute constraints on 'crazy' phenomena, whereas we claim only that unnatural phenomena are highly marked and therefore very rare (cf. 5.20.7.1, 10.3.18.2f, 10.
7f).

10.5.5.5.   S. Anderson's (1981:535f, cf. 495f, 509) credo that formal constraints do not directly mirror the properties of other, not specifically linguistic cognitive systems has also been shared by any serious adherent of Natural Phonology (and Natural Morphology) from its very beginnings and is the gist
of 10.5.   Extralinguistic facts underdetermine linguistic structure, but this
does not mean that they do not constrain structure at all (in terms of both absolute and relative constraints).   Due to such assumptions Natural Phonology/
Morphology does not fall into the trap of reductionism.

      Therefore Anderson (cf. 10.5.5.4f) is attacking a strawman.[114]   The basic
differences lie elsewhere: His model strictly separates (1) grammar[115] from
other domains of language, (2) competence from performance.   In both respects my
model is different (10.6).

10.6. The structure of the model

10.6.1. The model of morphonology I propose is a processual model of interaction between (processual) phonology and morphology (cf. 2). Processes modeled
by rules are more than a generative device which transduces one structure into
another on the level of describing language-specific competence;[116] they are
also operations serving functions (cf. 10.3.2, 10.3.5ff, 10.5), and this on each
level of the quintuple: (I) universals/human language faculty (10.6.2), (II)
type (10.6.3), (III) language-specific competence (10.6.4), (IV) norm (10.6.5),
(V) performance (10.6.6). This quintuple, established by L. Hjelmslev and E.
Coseriu (cf. 1968, 1980), replaces the Chomskyan triple (I), (III), (V) and the
Saussurean quadruple (I), (III), (IV), (V).

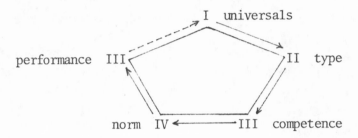

10.6.2. The level of universals (of the human language faculty, (I) on the diagram) comprises functions (10.3, 10.5), operations, and principles which can be
assigned to parameters of naturalness. These parameters[117] usually can be given
the form of implicational scales from most to least natural; one type of examples is phonological process types (4). For scales of morphological naturalness, see 10.8; cf. Mayerthaler (1981), Dressler (1982a, 1982c, in prep.),
Dressler, Mayerthaler, Panagl & Wurzel (forthc.); for scales in the UNITYP
framework (10.3.2), cf. UNITYP-Forschergruppe (1983).

    The main functions of language and of phonology, syntax, text, lexicon must
be implemented by any language as well as some of the functions subordinated to
them. Still 'lower' functions depend on the operations used. A small number of
operations and principles seem to be strictly universal in the sense that no
language is 'able to resist' their inclusion into its system.[118] Others are
parametric in the sense of an implicational choice of operations from these
parameters.[119] Similarly certain principles (e.g., the minimax principle, 10.5.
2.1) are followed to a greater or smaller extent and in different manners within
individual languages. Finally, certain operations are universally available,

but avoidable within individual languages, notably (suppressible) phonological
processes and all the operation types of morphology and morphonology, such as
the principles of affixing, reduplication, etc.[120]

In order to avoid the often misused word 'natural', W. Mayerthaler[121] has
been using the term '(universal) markedness' instead of 'naturalness'.

10.6.3.   Universal properties are the basis of typological properties ((II) on
the diagram in 10.6.1), i.e., they are restricted or filtered by the system of
choices (and the ensuing compensations) of a linguistic type, in the sense of an
ideal construct of a language type (Skalička 1979).[122]   Individual languages use
more or fewer natural operations on each parameter of naturalness in the sense
of implicative parametric choices;   cf. for phonological hierarchies 4.5.3.2,
10.7.1.4.   An example from the morphological naturalness scale of diagrammaticity would be: If a language uses an operation of modification such as ablaut (E.
sing → sang/song) or umlaut (E. *foot → feet*), then it also uses the more natural
operation of affixation (e.g., E. *work-ed, root-s*) but not vice versa.

A language type cannot always 'choose' the best procedure or operation of
each naturalness scale because of the dialectic conflicts within language (10.6.
7.2f).   A language type is constituted by the specific choices from the naturalness scales;   a language type 'sacrifices', as it were, the naturalness in some
parameters for the sake of greater naturalness in other parameters (cf. Mayerthaler 1982:234ff on markedness compensation and local optimization, Skalička
1979:267f on equilibrium in change).

Due to its richness in morphonology, the language type whose properties are
studied most extensively here is the inflecting type (cf. 10.9.3);   but also
discussed are properties of the agglutinating type (10.9.2), the introflecting
(10.9.4), polysynthetic (10.9.5), and isolating (10.9.1) types.

10.6.4.   Universal and typological properties are both restricted/filtered and
further specified by the system of an individual language (competence, *la
langue*, (III) on the diagram of 10.6.1).   Within any given language, a language
type is realized according to the system-defining properties of the specific
language subsystem.   Compliance with these properties equals system adequacy in
the narrow sense.   A morphological phenomenon (inflectional class, paradigm, a
morphological form, marker, or rule) or a phonological phenomenon (e.g., sylla-

ble constraints, MSRs, postlexical PRs) may be rather unnatural in terms of universal markedness theory (10.6.2), but at the same time it may be very 'normal'
within the language-specific grammar in terms of system adequacy.

A theory of morphological system adequacy has been elaborated by Wurzel
(1982, 1984, in Dressler, Mayerthaler, Panagl & Wurzel, forthc.) for inflectional morphology. For phonological system adequacy, cf. the concept 'language-
specific basis of articulation' and, within Generative Phonology, work on conspiracies or on cycles (cf. 10.10).

On the language-specific level, 'genetic' (i.e., diachronic) explanation
(10.2.1, 10.3.18.6) becomes mandatory; e.g., only by taking the emergence of
the Latinate part of English vocabulary and word formation into account can one
evaluate the peculiar language-specific properties of English morphonology (cf.
10.10).

10.6.5. The options permitted by the system of a language are further filtered
by the norms ((IV) on the diagram of 10.6.1) of a language as a social institution (cf. Coseriu 1958, 1968, 1971). Here no proper theory has been aimed at by
proponents of Natural Phonology/Morphology, but cf. the sociopsycholinguistic
bridge-theory to Natural Phonology in Dressler & Wodak (1982).

10.6.6. The norms of a language are realized in individual performance (*la parole*), the proper domain of psycholinguistics (cf. 5.13.4, 5.14, 9, (V) on the
diagram of 10.6.1). Thus performance is based on norms, norms are based on language-specific competence, competence is based on type, and types are based on
universals. But what are universals based on? Our model flatly states that
they are based on (general properties of) performance, or more precisely, on the
needs of linguistic performance serving functions of language and having to meet
extralinguistic conditions.[123]

10.6.7. The interactions among parameters of naturalness are based on goal conflicts of performance as displayed in universal markedness theory and partially
constrained in theories of type and of language-specific system adequacy. The
problem of how conflicts among parameters are resolved is crucial for a model of
morphonology (and of Natural Phonology/Morphology). If resolutions of conflicts
could not be predicted at all, then no disconfirmable and thus testable hypotheses could be constructed. On the other hand, total predictability is excluded

by interlinguistic and intralinguistic language variation (cf. 10.3.18.2, 10.3.
18.4, 10.5.5.5).

10.6.7.1. Since 1977 (Dressler 1977a, 1977e, 1978b, 1980b, 1980d), when I proposed a 'polycentric' model, I have tried to deal with specific interactions;
cf. similar and larger enterprises in the UNITYP-group (10.3.2). Trade-off relations between 'efficiency in one area' and 'non-efficiency in another area'
have been repeatedly noted by R. Jakobson (Waugh 1976) and many others (recently
Haiman 1983:812ff).

10.6.7.2. Wurzel (1980d, 1981b) has elaborated on the dialectic character of
what I had called a polycentric approach (10.6.7.1) and dealt with it in terms
of Marxist dialectical materialism, which allows the modeling of the conflict
between tendencies towards optimization of phonology and morphology (cf. 10.7f).
This entails a dynamic relation or structural contradiction between phonology
and morphology and results in the diachronic change of PRs to MPRs and AMRs.[125]
Note that Marxist dialectics involves functional explanation (discussed in van
Parijs 1981:174ff).

An important element of historical change, according to Marxist dialectics,
is 'the shift of quantitative into qualitative change' ('Gesetz des Umschlagens
quantitativer in qualitative Veränderungen': Wurzel 1980d:172). This would refer to morphonology insofar as certain criteria of a PR may change without affecting its phonological character; e.g., Russian final devoicing can still be
classified as a PR although it is phonemic/neutralizing (5.18.3, 5.20.3.4) and
may be suspended in prepausal truncated vocatives and abbreviations (5.13.1.2f).
But if a certain quantum of criteria is changed, such a PR may suddenly be reanalyzed as (i.e., turn into) a MPR, a qualitative shift. And as Wurzel (1980d:
172f) underlines, a property of qualitative shift can also be identified in morphologization: dominance reversal (G. 'Dominanzumkehr'). Whereas in the conflictual interaction of phonology and morphology PRs are clearly dominated by
phonological factors, MPRs are dominated by morphological factors. Therefore
such a model of morphologization differs drastically from those models (cf. 5.
18.6) which predict a simultaneous change of all relevant criteria when a PR
turns into a MPR. However, dialectics in itself does not provide predictions
for the outcomes of conflicts, i.e., which one of several conceivable results
will occur or probably occur or never occur. For this purpose semiotic princi-

ples can be used (cf. 10.7f).

Moreover Marxist dialectics is open to more general objections: Hegel laid down the dialectical principle of the three-stage evolution of ideas via THESIS, ANTITHESIS (contradicting the THESIS), and SYNTHESIS, which suspends[126] and retains[126] in itself THESIS and ANTITHESIS. Marx and Engels transferred this dialectical principle to the evolution of activities, events, structures, etc., of the real world (G. 'Realdialektik', cf. Hörz & Wessel 1983) and this transfer has been resented by many Hegelians and other philosophers (cf. Stegmüller 1979: 141ff). The relevance of this controversy for an application of dialectics to morphonology is further complicated by the controversy over the status of rules: Are they ideas or 'things'? (cf. 10.6.1 note 116).

Finally it must be noted that alternative explanatory approaches may replace Marxist dialectics (Stegmüller 1979:141ff).

10.6.7.3. In recent years modularity has become a catch-word in Generative Grammar.[127] The essence of modularity is the interaction of autonomous modules.[128] Internal modularity refers to interactions among modules of grammar such as between phonology and morphology (or parts of them), external modularity to interactions between grammar and non-grammatical modules such as discourse, pragmatics, belief systems, etc. Clearly our model of morphonology engulfs both internal and external modularity/interactionism.

Surprisingly the notion of modularity/interactionism has not been highlighted in generative work for the interactions of phonology and morphology in morphonology or morphophonemics (cf., e.g., Hulsty & Smith 1982.I, II): The inherent potentialities of the modular/interactionist framework have not been put to profit; rather the interactive/modular relations between Lexical Phonology and Lexical Morphology have been reduced to interdigitated rule applications (rule order relations, cf. 5.17.1.6).

10.6.7.4. Our interactive approach has important consequences for the demarcation problem of morphonology (cf. 1, 11): Although there are gradual (synchronic and diachronic) transitions between PRs and MPRs, MPRs and AMRs, the modules of phonology and morphology are mutually discrete and clearly demarcated. However the interactions between them (and with the lexicon) may produce results that differ only gradually; presumably all overlapping or borderline categories[129] have a similar origin.

10.7. Phonological universals and morphonology

10.7.1.0. Natural Phonology can be supplied with and based on a functional semiotic theory (cf. Dressler 1980b, 1979). It has always been held by D. Stampe
and the other Natural Phonologists that the two main functions of segmental phonology are to make language pronounceable and perceptible. For that purpose
words and morphemes are segmented into phonemes (understood as sound intentions
as in Baudouin de Courtenay 1895) and postlexical phonological processes apply
in order to adapt these phonemes to articulatory and perceptual needs and to
overcome difficulties of articulation and perception. Many properties of processes can be deduced from, or connected with these two main functions (10.7.8).

The definition of phonemes as sound intentions implies that they are fully
specified because they could not be intended otherwise. As a consequence (and
not for reasons of constraining phonological descriptions) there can be no archiphonemes (as in Natural Generative Phonology), cf. 5.20.8.5.2.

Three predictions concern the distribution of foregrounding (fortition,
dissimilatory) and backgrounding (lenition, assimilatory) processes. Notice
(1) that the distinction between foreground and background corresponds to the
semiotic distinction between figure and ground,[130] a distinction which sharpens
the contours of what is to be perceived; (2) that the two classes of process
types are antagonistic because they serve the often conflicting needs of hearer
and speaker respectively.[131]

10.7.1.1. If phonemes are defined as phonological intentions, and if phonology
serves communication, and if the most important goal in communication is to be
understood, then phonemes must serve primarily optimal perception rather than
ease of articulation, i.e., the function that foregrounding (dissimilatory) processes have as well.[132] Since prelexical PRs (2.2, 8), which constrain the number and combination of phonemes, govern the phonological intentions themselves,
we can predict that they will predominantly consist of foregrounding (dissimilatory) processes. All the prelexical processes defining the phoneme inventory of
a language (segment structure processes) are foregrounding processes. With prelexical phonotactic (sequential structure) processes the semiotic principle of
sign combinability (10.7.5) comes in, which takes both perception and production

into account, so that there are also backgrounding processes to be expected.

On the other hand, the main function of backgrounding (assimilatory) processes is to adapt phonemes to the needs and difficulties of the speech tract.
Since this is also a function of postlexical PRs, we can predict that both sets
of processes will coincide largely within the phonology of any language. This
does not hold for MPRs and AMRs if they can be matched with universal processes
at all (5.2).

All these synchronic predictions are borne out spectacularly, as any phonological description in terms of Natural Phonology shows (cf. Donegan 1978, Knudson 1975 for Zoque, Lovins 1973 for Japanese, Dressler & Hufgard 1980 for Breton, Dobö 1980 for Zyrian, Tonelli 1981 for German and Italian, Scherfer 1983
for French, etc.).

If postlexical foregrounding processes are rare (except according to 10.7.
12), then we can exclude the sequence of two postlexical foregrounding PRs in
the same derivation.

10.7.1.2. A second set of equally synchronic predictions concerns speech variation. According to the sociopsycholinguistic theory of socio-phonological
speech variation (Dressler & Wodak 1982), formal speech situations can be characterized as those where the speaker subordinates his speech strategies to the
exigencies of the hearer(s): He monitors speech so as to render perception
easiest. Casual speech situations can be characterized as those where the
speaker is less concerned about understandability of his production either because he has less respect for the hearer (etc.) or because the communication
situation itself carries more/enough clues for understanding the message (pragmatic redundancy). Therefore we can predict that foregrounding (dissimilatory)
processes are preferred in formal speech situations, backgrounding (assimilatory) processes in casual ones. And indeed this has been found by all investi-
gators (see 5.11).

10.7.1.3. Having explained why postlexical processes in normal (i.e., more or
less casual speech) almost exclusively consist of backgrounding processes, we
may ask why diachronic change often involves foregrounding processes such as
diphthongization in the English Great Vowel Shift.

If language change is connected with language learning, then one main pur-

pose of acquiring phonology is to acquire the phonemes, the phonological intentions. This goal is helped by adults using 'baby talk', which employs more
foregrounding and fewer backgrounding processes than other forms of adult language. Both the goal and th strategy mentioned explain why foregrounding
processes are bound to crop up in diachronic change.

However, the conclusions of 10.7.1.1 which disfavor postlexical foregrounding processes predict that they not survive as well as backgrounding processes
among postlexical processes. Also this prediction is fulfilled insofar as some
diachronic foregrounding changes simply restructure the phoneme input and never
become synchronic postlexical processes, such as many chain shifts or /x/ > /f/
in E. *laugh* (cf. J. Ohala 1974a, Javkin 1979). Restructuring entails semiotic
recoding of the input-output relations (cf. Jakobson 1962.I:651).

Other foregrounding processes are soon morphologized into rules (or lost),
such as the diphthongizations of the English Great Vowel Shift, and thus removed
from the set of postlexical phonological processes for which out predictions
hold.

Finally, a typical scenario of diachronic change consists in the generalization of backgrounding processes which are first limited to casual speech into
always more formal speech situations until they become obligatory processes
(Dressler 1973, 1975b, etc., cf. 10.7.12.3). All this easily explains why 'lenition processes are rarely compensated ... by ... fortitions' (Drachman 1981a:
107), not to speak of clear cases of compensation as in Back (1979, 1981), Thomas (1979); mostly they are compensated by morphological change, as demonstrated
since the Neogrammarians.

10.7.1.4. Universal process types have inherent hierarchies (Donegan & Stampe
1977, 1979b:138ff, formalized in W. Mayerthaler 1982:208ff, 230ff). They are
sometimes (i.e., only rarely!) violated in language-specific hierarchies, similar to grammatical hierarchies.[133]

Now it is totally unjustified to demand from an adherent of Natural Phonology --as Lass (1980 §2.7, 1981:206ff, cf. S. Anderson 1981:507) does-- that he
should be able to predict which language picks which threshold on the hierarchies of each process type. Let us take Lass's (1981) example of nasal assimilation and reduce the hierarchy to three thresholds: (1) total suppression of
the process type, no assimilation at all; (2) assimilation of /n/ to following

stops in place of articulation;   (3) assimilation of all nasal consonants to all
adjacent obstruents, the most general form of this backgrounding process type.
What Natural Phonology can predict is that in casual speech threshold *k* of formal speech may be generalized to threshold *k + 1* but not vice versa;   that --if
a language allows only threshold *k*-- Wernicke aphasics may relax this inhibition
because they cannot monitor speech production sufficiently.   Both predictions
have been confirmed: e.g., in German, nasal assimilation is restricted to
threshold (1) in formal speech, but generalized to threshold (2) in casual
speech;   and Austrian Wernicke aphasic have produced threshold (3) forms such as
[nɪnt, gŋɒːlt] for *nimmt* 'takes' and *g(e)malt* 'painted' (cf. Dressler 1979a,
1982).

10.7.2.   Among semiotic principles, let us mention first the principle that the
signantia of a sign should be distinguishable.[134]   This is the basis for the
distinctive function of phonemes and features (also of allophones!), for the
well known notions of maximum differentiation and phonological space, but also
for the minimization of fusion (e.g., contraction) and deletion process types in
formal speech.   Only in casual speech where the verbal message may be reduced
for sociopsychological reasons do fusion and deletion processes become more common (cf. 10.7.10.4).

     Prelexical processes (PRs and MSRs) may not merge too many phonemes, but
prelexical MPRs may merge more phonemes, e.g., restrict the number and sequence
of phonemes used in specific morphological categories because there a much
smaller number of morphemes has to be distinguished than the ten thousand words
of general vocabulary.   Of course there are many trade-offs, e.g., between number of phonemes and phonotactic constraints, number both of types of phonological mergers and of length of morphemes/words, or productivity of MRs, etc. (cf.
Ronneberger-Sibold 1980).   On the other hand, reasons of economy favor a limitation of the number of phonemes (cf. Goodman 1968:154).

     The property of efficient signantia to be distinctive and perceivable makes
intermediate false steps in phonological derivations costly, e.g., when we assumed for Polish (7.3.1f) that [ž] in voc. *boż-e* 'o God' is derived first via
AMR (P 1) from /g/ to intermediate (non-perceivable) /ž̧/ and second via MPR
(P 2) from /ž̧/ to perceivable [ž] rather than directly (/g/ → [ž]), we chose
this semiotically costly derivation only for several reasons (7.3.1, 7.6.10.6);
but we rejected splitting up (P 1) /k/ → [č] into the two rules /k/ → /k'/, /k'/

→ [č] because the justification seemed to be insufficient (7.3.3). Therefore the relative concerteness of analyses in terms of Natural Phonology represents neither an ad hoc assumption nor a research strategy designed to restrict the number of possible, competing analyses of the same data (as in Natural Generative Phonology), but follows from a higher-order principle.

10.7.3. Another aspect of the same semiotic principle refers to the efficient size of a signans,[135] i.e., it must be neither too big nor too small, for otherwise the sign might not easily be produced or perceived. This principle allows the predictions that (1) ultrashort sounds will be rare and easily lost (e.g., Old Slavic ĭ and ŭ) (cf. 10.7.10.3, 10.7.10.8b); that (2) vowels will be more frequent than diphthongs or triphthong, that stops and fricatives will be more frequent than affricates (cf. Luschützky, to appear). The existence of 'tetraphthongs can be excluded (cf. 10.3.18.3) because their input would be either triphthongs, which do not occur on the phonemic level, or diphthongs with two synchronic foregrounding PRs, which is excluded (10.7.1); either they would apply in a feeding relation or only one could apply in a prosodically strong position, the other would have to apply in an adjacent weak position, but there the application of foregrounding processes is very unlikely (4.3.3.3.1).

10.7.4. Signs are either only (conventional) symbols or, at the same time, also icons and/or indices (10.4.5). Icons are the most natural, symbols the least natural, which allows several predictions (10.7.10f).

10.7.5. Signs should be easily combinable, especially in production (articulation).[136]

10.7.6. Signantia of signs should be reliable (Goodman 1968:156, Morris 1971: 198, 365, 368). This preference favors a biunique relationship between signans and signatum, which optimized semiotic transparency (Koj 1979) of directness of semiosis, the optimum for respective processing.[137] Notice that iconicity favors the choice of biuniqueness (cf. W. Mayerthaler 1981). On predictions, see 10.7.12.

10.7.7. Words are primary signs, morphemes and MRs secondary signs (i.e., signs on words, analyzable within the word), phonemes and phonological processes tertiary signs (i.e., signs analyzable within the morpheme). In communication and cognition words have precedence over morphemes (and MRs), these over phonemes and PRs (cf. 10.4.4.3, 10.7.11.4).

10.7.8.   In making predictions first we derive predictions from the two main functions of segmental phonology (10.7.1, 10.7.8.1):

10.7.8.1.   If phonology has the function of making language pronounceable and perceivable (10.7.1), then processes should aid pronunciation (backgrounding processes) or perception (foregrounding processes). Based on a theory of back-grounding process types (Donegan 1978, Dressler forthc. §4) and of ease of ar-ticulation (Lindner 1975), we can identify Polish PRs and MPRs (SP P 7, 8) and (SPIR P 2) as backgrounding. Backgrounding processes aid ease of articulation most when they are genrealized in casual speech (5.11). Now only (SP P 8) --the only Polish process discussed-- is generalized in casual speech insofar as it applies across word boundaries, as in *wróg Ireneusz-a* 'I.'s enemy' pronounced with [g′] (7.6.8.2).

10.7.8.2.   As for the word domain itself, any obligatory PR must represent a constraint on production and perception, whereas a MPR does not. This defining criterion can be derived from the two primary functions of segmental phonology, which do not hold for MPRs because inputs to MPRs can be pronounced and percep-tually identified/discriminated in the given language, provided that PRs apply (5.6, 5.11f);   however the non-application of PRs in the obligatory word domain results in unpronounceability and inaccurate perception of the segment. Only (SP P 8) fulfills this criterion: *[gi] (as input to SP (P 8)) is not pro-nounceable, whereas [ge] (as input to SP (P 7)) is.

  If a PR represents a constraint on pronounceability and perceptibility, several predictions can be made:

10.7.8.3.   A process must be general, i.e., exceptionless (cf. 5.12), MPRs need not be but may be. Of our Polish examples only (SP P 8) is general, the MPRs (SP P 7, SPIR P 2) are not as far as phonological conditions are concerned. As for morphological conditions on MPRs, (SP P 7) is general, (SPIR P 2) not neces-sarily (10.7.8.4).

10.7.8.4. A process should apply productively to loanwords, neologisms, and abbreviations (5.13): (SP P 8) does, but even MPRs and AMRs, such as (SP P 7) and
(AF P 3, 4), if both phonological and morphological conditions are met. There
is fluctuation with (SPIR P 2) (cf. 7.6.10.3, 7.6.10.6).

10.7.8.4. PRs should apply in speech errors, MPRs may or may not -- which is
true (cf. 5.14).

10.7.8.5. PRs must be phonologically conditioned because the constraint is phonological. Among the Polish rules of 7, (SP P 8) is clearly phonologically conditioned, but applies also in alternations which present conditions that are
both phonologically and morphologically appropriate, i.e., the phonological condition is always present, the morphological condition only sometimes. For MPRs,
the morphological conditions must always be present and there rules may apply
without exceptions, which is not true for their phonological conditions.

    Therefore distribution is a more important criterion than alternation for
processes (PRs), the reverse for rules (MPRs, AMRs). In this respect Natural
Phonology resembles structural phonematics more than it does Generative Phonology (cf. Zwicky 1975:155f).

10.7.8.6. Phonological domains such as syllable, foot, phonological word/phrase
can be seen as another aspect of phonological conditions.

10.7.9. As for rule ordering, the following predictions can be made:

10.7.9.1. 'Rules before processes!' In 10.4.4.3 we derived the semiotic priority of morphology over phonology. AMRs are MRs themselves, MPRs are strictly
bound to morphology. Thus we expect the applicational precedence of 'rules'
(AMRs, MPRs) over processes (PRs) postulated by Donegan & Stampe (1979b:156).

10.7.9.2. 'Fortitions first, lenitions last!' Fortitions (foregrounding processes) refer to the perception of the phonological intentions, backgrounding
processes to their adaptation to the speech tract. Since this adaptation presupposes the formation of intentions, we expect backgrounding processes to presuppose foregrounding processes. This is trivially true of (1) backgrounding
prelexical sequential structure processes following foregrounding prelexical

segment structure processes, and (2) backgrounding postlexical processes following foregrounding prelexical processes (though the precedence of backgrounding
prelexical over backgrounding postlexical processes follows only from the makeup
of the model itself). More important is the consequence that among postlexical
processes the few 'fortitions' come 'first', the many 'lenitions last' (Donegan
& Stampe 1979b:153ff) and that, after all AMRs, MPRs, and fortitions, lenition
PRs apply whenever their structural description is met, i.e., simultaneously or
in feeding order. In other words, we do not expect any extrinsic order statements for PRs (but do not exclude them for MPRs and AMRs, for which they were
devised in Generative Phonology).

10.7.9.3. This derivation of expectations on ordered application presupposes an
analog between 'logical' ordering of operations in the model and 'temporal' ordering in speech planning and production. Such an analog may seem strange in a
theory which strictly separates performance from competence, but not in a model
where competence is understood as competence of performance (cf. Donegan &
Stampe 1979b:135f, Kodzasov & Krivnova 1981:153f, the UNITYP model 10.3.2); and
this is not an ad hoc assumption but follows from the same relation between legisigns and sinsigns in Peircean semiotics (10.4.4.4).

10.7.9.4. On the other hand, 10.7.9.1f represents only the most natural order
to be expected, and --as often in naturalness/markedness theories-- our deduction of predictions does not exclude the possibility of exceptions under special
conditions, i.e., the occurrence of marked order (Stampe 1969, cf. 5.17.1.4, 5.
17.2.5f), cf. S. Anderson's (1974:147ff) notion of 'local order'.

10.7.9.5. Still many cases of marked order given in the literature are no counterexamples to 10.7.9.1f; e.g., both alleged counterexamples that Drachman
(1981a:103) throws against ordering principles of Natural Phonology: (1) The
paradoxical relation between the American English process of flapping and AUX-
contraction must be seen in light of the distinction between word and sentence
phonology (and morphonology): Flapping belongs to word phonology, AUX-contrac-
tion to the larger domain of sentence morphonology, and Lexical Phonology is
quite right in giving the word domain applicational precedence before the sentence domain (cf. 2.4.1, 5.17.1.5f). (2) Drachman (1981:103) wants to disprove
the principle of ordering fortitions before lenitions by the example of Northern

Modern Greek consonant insertion (fortition) being ordered after unstressed high
vowel deletion (lenition) as in ['kintsi] from /'kinise/ 'moved'. However Northern M.Gk. unstressed high vowel deletion is undoubtedly a 'rule' (MPR)[138] because it has many surface exceptions (such as final unstressed [i] from underlying /e/ in ['kintsi] itself) and is also morphologically conditioned.[139] Thus
we have a confirmation of the principle that 'rules' are ordered before processes! And even more, our theory explains why historically later insertion was not
preserved as a synchronically later process after deletion (see 10.7.1.3, etc.).

10.7.10. Other predictions can be derived from the principle of iconic naturalness.[140] If (1) a sign is more natural the more iconicity it has, and if (2) a
process or rule is a sign whose input is the signatum and whose output is the
signans, and if (3) the input-output relations are more iconic in PRs than in
MPRs or AMRs (see 10.7.10.2), and if (4) more naturalness results in higher frequency (10.3.18, cf. Mayerthaler 1982:218), then we predict:

10.7.10.1. Processes (PRs) must be much more common in the languages of the
world than MPRs (and AMRs), which is true. There are two deficiencies in S. Anderson's (1981:496) critical and rhetorical questions: 'Should the set of rules
admitted in the grammars ... be limited to ... "natural rules" [i.e., PRs, WUD]?
Or might grammars contain as a central part rules that are not grounded (synchronically, at least) in such phonetic explanations [i.e., MPRs, WUD]?' Our
system does not exclude MPRs, but assigns to them, deductively and correctly, a
marginal rather than a central role.

There are no MPRs in isolating languages, but many pre- and postlexical
PRs, cf. Donegan & Stampe (1979b:135). There are few pre- and postlexical MPRs
in agglutinating languages and even in inflecting/fusional languages there are
more PRs than MPRs and AMRs.

10.7.10.2. The degree of iconicity correlates with resemblance between signatum
and signans (e.g., as counted in distinctive features).[141] Therefore intrinsic
allophonic processes are most iconic, extrinsic allophonic processes less, phonemic neutralization processes and MPRs still less. And as predicted by 10.7.
10.1, among postlexical processes, the number of intrinsic allophonic processes
is so high in any language that no phonologist has bothered to count them,
whereas the number of the other classes of PRs, MPRs, AMRs decreases according

to their relative degree of iconicity. One consequence is that processes appear much more to be 'universal' (5.1) in cross-language distribution than MPRs.

10.7.10.3. Signs which have no perceptible signans are very uniconic. Thus we can predict again (cf. 10.7.3.1, 10.7.3.3, 10.7.10.8, 10.7.11.1, 10.7.12.1, cf. Dressler & Acson, forthc.) that deletion and fusion processes are rare. This is true with the exception of (optional) casual speech processes because they do not always apply, so that an overt signans can be perceived and learned at least in formal speech. E.g., the nasal fusion PR which derives [kæ̃t] from intermediate /kæ̃nt/ (from underlying /kænt/) is an optional, casual speech process in most varieties of English.

Obligatory deletion or fusion PRs are diachronically unstable and liable to be lost or to be transformed into MPRs (cf. 5.18.4.4f, 10.7.1), e.g., Slavic and French vowel and consonant deletion processes or Maori final consonant deletion (Hale 1973) are no longer PRs.

10.7.10.4. But even within MPRs deletion and fusion rules are unstable, for the same reason as PRs. Thus French final ə- and consonant truncation has been largely inverted (5.2.7.3) to ə- and consonant insertion.[143] Only in abstract analyses of Slavic phonologies such as Lightner's (1972) for Russian or Gussmann's (1978a, 1978b) and Rubach's (1981, 1982, 1984) for Polish are abstract high vowels assumed as phonemic inputs which are then deleted. Notice that both abstract input phonemes and ∅-outputs are semiotically inefficient in view of the distinctiveness principle (10.7.2). For indexicality, see below 10.7.11.1. Although the assumption of such rules is by no means excluded in our model, the burden of proof is heavy.

10.7.10.5. Another version of the prediction (cf. 10.7.10.3) is that phonological processes preferably involve a small change/distance between input and output (5.3), as in Polish (SP P 8) as opposed to all AMRs and MPRs discussed (except (SP P 7)). The distinctiveness principle (10.7.2) has a controlling effect so that only languages with few vocalic phonemes have rather distant vocalic allophones, e.g., [i, ε, y, u] for /i/ in Circassian (Paris 1974, Jakovlev 1948). I.e., distinctivity favors larger distance, whereas iconicity favors smaller distance.[144] Similarly, only languages with few phonemic consonants have distant allophones, e.g., Rotokas (Firchow & Firchow 1969) has [b, β, m] for /β/, [d, ɾ, l, n] for /d/, cf. Kuki (1979) on Tuamotu.

10.7.10.6. If iconicity of input-output relations is counted in features, then regularity (5.4) is preferred in processes, i.e., natural classes defined by features should be affected by the more iconic processes. Since the prototypical domain of phonological features is PRs (processes), our prediction is not expected to have much importance for MPRs and AMRs anyway. True enough, among our Polish examples, the PR (SP P 8) holds for the whole natural class of velar phonemes /k, g, x/, the MPR (SP P 7) only for the subset /k, g/, the MPR (SPIR P 2) only for /g/. The AMRs (AF P 3, 4) and particularly (PF P 1) have exceptions which are irregularly distributed for /k/ vs. /g/ vs. /x/ or they often apply to only one or two of these phonemes in morphological subcategories.[145]

Typically PRs are better written in terms of distinctive features, AMRs and often MPRs in terms of single phonemes.[146] Also, among prelexical MSRs of sequential structure, PRs typically refer to natural classes defined by distinctive features such as fricatives, sibilants, nasals, MPRs to a lesser extent (8.3.7ff).

10.7.10.7. It is assumed in Natural Phonology that, ceteris paribus, more natural phenomena are simpler than less natural phenomena. In any neurolinguistic theory it is assumed that simpler structures/rules of a given parameter are less disturbed in aphasia than less simple ones of the same parameter. Therefore we may predict that among comparable processes/rules the degree of iconicity should co-vary with the degree of non-impairment in aphasia.

This prediction is borne out by the Polish data elicited by H. Mierzejewska and S. Grotecki (7.6.12).

10.7.10.8. A diagram is an icon where the relations in the signatum and the signans are analogous. The types of phonetic realizations of phonemic sequences can be connected with diagrammaticity. Let us notate input phonemes with capital letters, their outputs with small letters, and connect the respective input and output with an association line (examples in 5.18.4).

(a) The following relations are diagrammatic:

```
/W   X/      /W   X/      /W   X/      /W   X/ etc.
 |   |        |   |        |   |        |   |
[w] [x]     [w'][x']     [w] [y]      [z] [y]
```

(b, c)   The following relations are non-diagrammatic:

(b)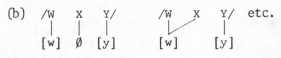

(c)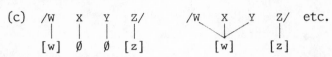

(d)   The following relations are anti-diagrammatic:

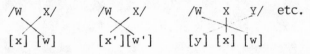

The relations (a) exhibit complete analogy/diagrammaticity, irrespective of the decreasing iconicity between /W/ → [w], /W/ → [w'], /W/ → [z]; the relations (b) are incompletely analogous;   (c) relations are still worse;   and (d) relations are flatly anti-diagrammatic, i.e., the output relation between [x] and [w] in the first case contradicts the input relation between /W/ and /X/.

Now if degree of naturalness predicts relative frequency (cf. 10.5, 10.7.1, 10.7.3, 10.7.9.4, 10.7.10.1f), we can predict again that synchronic deletion and fusion processes should be rare (b, cf. 10.7.3.1, etc.), particularly if two or more phonemes in a row are deleted[147] or fused with another phoneme -- and in fact such processes are still rarer.   But the rarest should be synchronic processes of metathesis (5.18.4.2).   Hooper's (1976) 'linearity condition' is an absolute constraint against metatheses (even against such MPRs and MRs, which are not that rare);   we are against exaggerating unnatural situations to prohibited ones (cf. 10.7.3.2, 10.11.1f, 10.12).

Notice that in metatheses association lines cross.   Crossing of association lines (although between two tiers) are prohibited in Autosegmental Phonology.[148] This is another instance of the tendency in linguistic theories to transform semiotically inefficient and thus rare phenomena into prohibited phenomena (via an absolute constraint).

10.7.11.   An index (cf. 10.4.5.2) is a sign which exhibits a direct connection between signans and signatum, such as an anaphoric pronoun indicating a coreferential noun.   Now indexicality (cf. 5.19) can be used in its full semiotic sense: i.e., a MPR such as Pol. (SPIR P 2) /ž/ → [ž] / [-obstr] __ + segment is a moderately iconic sign which relates the signatum /ž/ to its signans [ž] under specified conditions; on the other hand the signans [ž] points indexical-ly to the phonological environment as its phonological indexical signatum and to the following suffix as its morphological indexical signatum. Four classes of predictions can be made: (1) as to the presence or absence of indexicality, (2) as to the efficiency of the signatum, (3) of the signans, (4) of the relation between signans and signatum.

10.7.11.1. Indexical signs are more natural than symbolic signs lacking indexi-cality. Context-sensitive PRs are indexical insofar as they indicate their pho-nological context (cf. Anttila 1975, 1980, Dressler 1977a:24, 48); context-free PRs are phonologically non-indexical. Thus we can predict, due to our natural-ness and frequency connection, that context-free PRs should be rare.

We have to exclude prelexical segment structure processes because they are not signs (10.4.4.5); but postlexical context-free PRs are extremely rare --un-less we believe proponents of abstract context-free neutralizations (cf. 5.10.8.5, 10.7.10.4).

Interestingly the discussion of constraints on context-free neutralizations has peaked in several proposals which allow only those neutralizations that leave traces (5.20.7.0, cf. S. Anderson 1981:530ff), i.e., are indexical. E.g., if Gussmann (1977:54ff) assumes that the *h* [x] in the Polish name *Sapieha* is an underlying abstract /γ/, then he assumes a context-free rule which devoices /γ/ to [x], whereas the voicedness of underlying /γ/ appears in the output of PF (P 1) [ž] as in the feminine derivation *Sapież-anka*, as opposed to voiceless [š] in *blasz-anka* 'box of sheet metal' from *blacha* [blaxa] 'sheet metal' (< G. *Blech*). Thus the phonetic voicedness of [ž] is an iconic trace of underlying /γ/. Now if the context-free devoicing rule /γ/ → [x] is restricted to those morphemes whose /γ/ leaves a trace in alternants in [ž], then such constraints represent a limitation of context-free rules to indexical rule applications. Moreover such rules are only unique (10.7.12, 10.7.12.5 note 155) and thus un-natural for two reasons.

Abstract context-free deletion rules are even more unnatural because they are also non-iconic insofar as their output is zero (cf. 10.7.10.3f, 10.7.10.8b). E.g., Gussmann (1978a, 1978b) and Rubach (1981, 1982, 1984) derive Polish *rocz-ny* [ročnɨ] 'yearly' from underlying /rok+ĭn+ɨ/. After PF (P 1), which turns /kĭ/ to /čĭ/ and thus leaves a trace of supposedly underlying /ĭ/, this abstract vowel undergoes a context-free deletion rule.

In contrast to other concrete phonologies,[149] abstract neutralizations are not prohibited but designated as very unnatural and thus very costly (cf. 10.7.3.2, 10.7.10.6, 10.7.11.2), so that natural languages will barely permit them.

Or they must be assigned to the set of MPRs or AMRs because these rules indicate morphological categories, i.e., they are (morphologically) indexical, e.g., PF (P 1) in the Polish imperative *piecz* [p'eč] 'bake' from the stem /p'ek/ indicates this specific morphological form, even if additional phonological indexicality is assumed when assuming an underlying imperative ending /j/ (thus /p'ek+j/) which is deleted after triggering PF.[150] Note that deletion rules are more unnatural if they are context-free than if they are context-sensitive.

10.7.11.2.   As has been corroborated by psycholinguistic studies in syntax,[151] indexical sign relations are more efficient the nearer the signans is to its signatum, i.e., in case of adjacency.   Again, non-adjacency is only marked but should not be excluded by phonological theory (cf. S. Anderson 1982:8f, 11, cf. 5.19.2.3).

Nevertheless it is remarkable that postlexical vowel harmony rules (governing so-called affix harmony) --which refer to non-adjacent vowels in the linear string of phonemes-- nearly always seem to be MPRs and not PRs, e.g., they do not represent absolute constraints on pronounceability and usually have many exceptions.

10.7.11.3.   An index is the better the better its signans (i.e., the output of a process/rule) can be perceived.   Clearly processes which effect a great distance of change (cf. 10.7.10.4) are best, processes involving intrinsic allophones worst.   If we predict frequency, then these predictions are exactly opposite to those based on phonological iconicity (10.7.10.2, 10.7.10.4), so that we have a conflict between the parameters of iconicity and indexicality.   E.g., Polish PF, AF, SPIR are better indices than SP (P 7, 8), but SP (P 7, 8) are more iconic than these other rules.

This conflict is solved in the following ways: Icons are more natural signs than indices (10.7.4), therefore the parameter of iconicity is more important than the parameter of indexicality so that our predictions of 10.7.10.1ff about allophonic PRs being more frequent than phonemic ones are still justified

(cf. on biuniqueness 10.7.12.1). But these predictions hold only for phonological iconicity, and such a phonological parameter is only fully applicable to PRs
but not to MPRs and AMRs, whereas indexicality fully applies to MPRs and AMRs as
well. This leads us to the next conflict:

10.7.11.4. In phonological indexicality the signata are phonological entities
(phonemes, allophones, cf. Jakobson 1962.I:296f), in morphological indexicality
morphological entities or categories (cf. 10.7.8.6). Due to the principle of
semiotic precedence of morphology over phonology (10.7.7), morphological indexicality is higher valued than phonological indexicality.

A further premise is the principle of local efficiency of linguistic
change, i.e., the tendency of linguistic subsystems to become more efficient,
even at the expense of other subsystems (cf. 10.3.5.1f, 10.6.7).

From these two premises (hierarchy of indexicality and efficiency of
change) we can predict that PRs diachronically tend to become MPRs and AMRs, but
not vice versa.

(a) When a PR becomes a MPR, there is first a preponderant phonological
signatum and sometimes a morphological one (cf. 10.7.8.5), and the child when
learning morphology will tend to prefer morphological indexicality over phonological indexicality in the case of morphophonemic alternations. Due to this
abductive change (Andersen 1973), morphological indexicality becomes preponderant; e.g., in Pol. *Plank-iem* (derived by SP (P 7)) the morphological indexical
signatum 'sg. instrumental' is more important than the phonological signatum
'/e/' of the ending *-em*.

(b) When a MPR becomes an AMR, the phonological indexical signatum becomes
irrelevant (clearly in Polish PF), i.e., the phonological properties become vestigial if they subsist at all (cf. 10.3.10).

(c) An AMR may not change diachronically to a MPR nor a MPR to a PR. Alleged counterexamples to this unilateral change are due to misinterpretations
(cf. 5.18.6ff).

(d) Thus we find a diachronic improvement of indexicality corresponding to
progressive diachronic de-iconization (which we also find in onomatopoetic words
and diminutives, due to sound change). The precedence of morphology over phonology (10.4.4) explains the 'disconcerting' (S. Anderson 1981:512, cf. Drachman

1981:105) diachronic tendency of PRs to become MPRs. It is even less 'disconcerting' insofar as only a very small percentage of the PRs within any language
ever become MPRs.

10.7.11.5. What remains to be clarified is how allophonic PRs change into phonemic ones. As long as they are allophonic, their signans is indexically inefficient but iconically efficient. When they are phonemic, they are indexically
more efficient and are --only then-- capable of indexing morphological categories, but their phonological iconicity has been decreased so that it is no obstacle any more for morphologization of PRs to MPRs, which equals further de-iconization (10.4.5.4, 10.7.12.5).

10.7.11.6. A side effect of de-iconization and improvement of indexicality is
the phenomenon that phonemic or morphophonemic differences are better manipulated for purposes of orthography (5.15) and for poetic devices (5.16).

10.7.11.7. The indexicality of an obligatory process/rule is more reliable than
that of an optional casual speech PR. The output of such a backgrounding process may or may not indicate a phoneme it assimilates to. This will be impor-
tnat for the relative position of processes on the biuniqueness scale (10.7.12.
4).

10.7.12. Phonological biuniqueness (cf. 5.20, 10.8.2) must not be seen as an
absolute constraint on input-output relations in phonology, as was assumed by
many structuralist phonematicians (cf. 5.20.2.1). In his critique of semiotically based Natural Phonology, Drachman (1981:105) seems to have succumbed to
the same fallacy of confusing preference for, with restriction to biuniqueness
(which 'condemns phonology to a degree of concreteness ...'). But biuniqueness
is better than uniqueness, and non-uniqueness (particularly multiple ambiguity)
is worst.

      The effects of the (bi)uniqueness parameter (5.20) are similar to those of
the iconicity parameter (10.7.10.2) as far as phonological (bi)uniqueness is
concerned. MPRs and AMRs are non-unique, allophonic PRs biunique most of the
time, phonemic PRs are in between (5.20.1f).

10.7.12.1. Therefore the same predictions can be made as from iconicity in re-

gard to frequency of PRs vs. MPRs and AMRs, frequency of intrinsic/extrinsic allophones vs. phonemic PRs (10.7.10.2), rarity of deletion and fusion rules (10.
7.10.3) because there is no unique signans (i.e., output of such rules). The
convergence of iconicity and (bi)uniqueness predictions comes as no surprise
because iconicity favors biuniqueness (cf. Mayerthaler 1981).

10.7.12.2. The more ambiguous outputs or inputs are the more (phonologically)
unnatural the respective rules are. E.g., in Polish (7) [ž] may go back to the
input /ž/ or to /r/ (as does [r]) or to /g/ (via PF (P 1) and SPIR (P 2)), but
/g/ may be represented by [g] or [g'] or [ʒ] or [ž] (via PF (P 1)), or [ž] may
go back to /ɣ/ (via PF (P 1)).

Now I claim that non-unique relations must involve MPRs or AMRs, and that
in multiple ambiguity AMRs are predominant (cf. 5.20.4ff). Phonological (bi)u-
niqueness is relatively unimportant for MPRs and AMRs as is phonological iconicity (10.7.11.4).

10.7.12.3. A phonologically biunique relation or a phonologically unique relation

$$
\begin{array}{ccc}
/X/ \quad /Y/ & \text{or} & /X/ \quad /Y/ \\
\mid \qquad \mid & & \diagdown \quad \diagup \\
[x] \quad [y] & & [x]
\end{array}
$$

is by definition general and productive. This is a property of obligatory PRs
as opposed to MPRs and AMRs (cf. 10.7.8.3f), which follows from their respective
positions on the (bi)uniqueness scale.

10.7.12.4. Optional casual speech PRs are worse on the (bi)uniqueness scale
than respective obligatory PRs. Thus the diachronic change of such optional to
obligatory PRs (10.7.1.3) can be explained as a change towards biuniqueness[152]
and to better indexicality, provided that we accept the principle of efficiency
in linguistic change. An obligatory PR may become optional again only if it has
been changed to a MPR/AMR which fades away (5.12.5).

10.7.12.5. Since only obligatory PRs can morphologize, we must assume that the
position on the (bi)uniqueness scale is of importance. But this is also a question of indexicality (10.7.11.7).

Now if we come back to the problem (10.7.11.4f) of what happens when allo-

phonic PRs turn into phonemic PRs (phonemization), before turning into MPRs, we
have to distinguish type and token biuniqueness:

(a) Token (bi)uniqueness refers to the relation between the tokens of a
phoneme and its output tokens. Obligatory PRs are biunique, whereas phonostylistic PRs of casual speech are not because the same input phoneme token within
a given word has one or another output (according to sociopsycholinguistic factors). Now the following scenario of diachronic change becomes perfectly under-
standable: Casual speech abounds with processes of deletion, fusion (10.7.3,
10.7.10.3), and mergers (phonemic neutralization) and thus goes strongly against
the principles of iconicity and biuniqueness so that it becomes much less com-
prehensible per se. But as we have seen (10.7.1.2), this is not harmful; serving the function of ease of articulation (backgrounding) is more important.[153]
I.e., the consequences of this main function of segmental phonology override the
consequences of biuniqueness and iconicity.[154]

Therefore, as a first step, in casual speech allophonic PRs may easily
change into phonemic (neutralizing) PRs, even if they remain allophonic PRs in
formal speech. As a second step, phonemic PRs of casual speech are generalized
to more formal speech styles (as are other phonostylistic PRs) due to sociopsycholinguistic pressures (cf. Labov's 1972 change from below). The final change
to an obligatory (phonemic) PR raises token biuniqueness (cf. the argumentation
on default, 5.20.8.3.5ff). In a fourth step, this obligatory phonemic PR is
available for morphologization (10.7.11.4).

(b) Type (bi)uniqueness primarily refers to the relation between phonemes
and their allophones in obligatory PRs and in competence. In this respect an
extrinsic allophonic PR is more efficient than a phonemic PR on both the (bi)u-
niqueness and the iconicity scales. Phonological indexicality is by definition
less important. So why should an obligatory PR ever change from an extrinsic
allophonic PR to a phonemic PR if we assume a tendency towards efficiency of
change? We cannot invoke an interaction with morphology, because this conflict
explains only the change of obligatory phonemic PRs into MPRs.

Let us take the example of German final devoicing: There are dialects
where this PR is extrinsically allophonic, i.e., the devoiced output of final
/d/ does not neutralize with the output of final /t/. In other dialects it
does, i.e., the PR is phonemic,[155] which is a diachronically later stage. How
can we imagine that extrinsic devoicing changed to phonemic devoicing in some

dialects? Two explanations come to mind:

(1) It is perceptually difficult to discriminate the devoiced output of /d/ from the output of /t/. Hence hearers may be induced to merge them, according to the line of argumentation in J. Ohala (1974a, etc.) and Javkin (1979). The elimination of a difficult perceptual distinction which is easily confused may be seen as serving perception. This scenario fits into Andersen's (1973) model of abductive change.

(2) A more generalized version of a phonological process is more natural. If final devoicing of /d/ is an assimilatory backgrounding process (4.5.3.1), then it is more natural to devoice it completely, so that it merges with the output of /t/.[156]

But where are backgrounding processes most likely to be generalized? In casual speech. And where is perceptual confusion most likely to occur? In casual speech as well. Thus scenario (b) may have to be reduced to scenario (a). The resulting importance of casual speech for phonemicization will not strike us as exeggerated when we realize that presumably 99% of what we speak and hear is casual speech.

Phonemization is the prerequisite for the change of PRs to MPRs,[157] and this change (morphologization), which is much more important fro morphonology, has already been explained in 10.7.11.4, 10.7.1.3.

10.8. Functionally and semiotically based morphological universals and morphonology

10.8.0. My account of Natural Morphology will be strictly limited to aspects relevant to morphonology. Systematic treatments of large fragments of the model can be found elsewhere.[158]

10.8.1.1. One of the functions of both inflectional morphology and of word formation (comprising derivational morphology and compound formation, cf. 1) is to motivate existing complex words and word forms. First of all we must distinguish semantic and morphotactic motivation, second, more or less efficient motivation. E.g., the inflectional word form *long-er* is motivated morphotactically from the basic form [lɔŋ] via the MR (spell-out rule) of comparative formation, and 'simpler' in those dialects where the comparative is pronounced ['lɔŋəʴ]

than in those where it is pronouced ['lɔŋgəˑ], i.e., the complex word form
['lɔŋəˑ] is morphotactically more transparent than ['lɔŋgəˑ]. Semantically
long-er is motivated from the meaning of *long* via the morphosemantic rule of
comparative formation; the semantic transparency of *long-er* seems to be excellent. For word formation (WF), let us cite the two derived nouns *long-ing* and
long-itude: both are motivated morphotactically and semantically from the base
form *long* (verb or adjective respectively) via the respective MRs (WFRs), but
long-ing is clearly both semantically and morphotactically more transparent than
long-itude ['lɑnǰitĭuːd]. These linguistic intuitions must be expressed by the
theory of Natural Morphology in a descriptively and explanatorily adequate way.

Since morphonology (or at least morphophonemics) is directly involved in
the degree of morphotactic transparency of forms like ['lɔŋgəˑ, 'lɑnǰitĭuːd],
this type of transparency will be our first topic:

10.8.1.2. The parameter of morphotactic transparency can be stated in the form
of a scale of morphotactic transparency. Morphotactic transparency is more natural than its opposite, morphotactic opacity. This follows from the semiotic
principle of semiotic transparency (cf. 10.7.6) and has found empirical support
in psycholinguistic experiments (cf. MacKay 1978): The more transparent the
base and the derivational operation is, the better perceptible and identifiable
they are, i.e., clear morpheme boundaries[159] facilitate morpheme discrimination
and identification.

On the following seven-point scale of morphotactic transparency, I is most
natural, VII least natural. Of course this scale can be further subdivided,
like a thermometer.

I	II	III	IV	V
intrinsic	extrinsic	neutralizing	MPRs	MPRs
allophonic	allophonic	PRs intervene	(no fusion)	with fusion
PRs intervene	PRs, resyllab-ification	e.g., flapping	e.g., velar softening	
excite$+ment	*exis$t+ence*	*rid+er$*	*electri$c+ity*	*conclusion*
excite	*exist*	*ride*	*electric*	*conclude*

VI	VI	VII		
AMRs	weak --	strong		
e.g., E. Great Vowel Shift	suppletion	(no rules!)		
decision	*childr+en*	*Glaswegian*	*am, are, is, was, were, be*	
decide	*child*	*Glasgow*		

10.8.1.2.1. On this scale, morphotactic transparency decreases from threshold I through threshold VII. This corresponds to differences in the rules involved: From I through VI (and in *children, Glaswegian*) we find spell-out MRs. In addition we find in I (E. *excite-ment*) intrinsic allophonic PRs which differentiate word- and syllable-final /t/ very slightly; or take It. *sacch-i* ['sa$^{\$}$kːˈi] with slight palatalization, as pl. of *sacco* ['sa$^{\$}$kːo] 'sack'; Polish SP (P 8, 7.5.1. 2) is more extrinsic and thus diminishes morphotactic transparency more.

In II (*exist-ence*) a PR of resyllabification also intervenes. In III (*rider*), in some English dialects, a neutralizing PR of flapping intervenes in addition.

In IV, MPRs intervene, e.g., velar softening in *electric-ity* or Italian palatal formation in *amic-i* 'friend-s' (6) or Polish MPRs of spirantization (P 2, 7.3.1) and SP (P 7, 7.5.1.1), with or without resyllabification. In V (*conclusion*) an MPR fuses the final /d/ of *conclude* with the suffix-initial glide.

In VI, AMRs intervene such as the English Great Vowel Shift, which relates *dec*[i]*sion* to *dec*[ai]*de*, in addition to the MPRs and PRs referred to above. Polish PF (P 1, 7.3) and AF (P 4, 7.4) are AMRs, but since they are the only rules interfering --besides resyllabification-- their effect on transparency still refers to stage IV (although a MPR is less opaque); imperative formation with PF in *piecz* [pʹeč] 'bake!' from /pʹek+j/ (7.3.2.3.1) refers to stage V (more opaque than a MRP, lack of an overt suffix, df. 10.7.11.1).

In VII the relation between *ch*[ai]*ld* and *ch*[i]*ld*[r]*-en* exemplifies weak suppletion (alternation of single segments), the realtions in *am - are - is - was - were - be* strong suppletion (alternations of whole stems), cf. 1.9, 5.4.8.

10.8.1.2.2. Parts of this scale of morphotactic transparency closely correspond to the scale of phonological iconicity (10.7.10) which establishes the gradation

intrinsic allophonic PRs (cf. transparency threshold I) - extrinsic allophonic
PRs (cf. II) - phonemic PRs (cf. III) - MPRs (cf. IV, V). We have also seen in
10.7.10.3f that fusion and deletion PRs/MPRs are worse than other rules, which
corresponds to less transparency in V than in IV.

Therefore the phonological parameter of phonological biuniqueness and the
morphological parameter of morphotactic transparency do not contradict each other, but converge, i.e., their effects should add up. This convergence is not
surprising because both parameters are divided from the principle of semiotic
transparency. In this respect, the consistency of our model is confirmed.

10.8.1.3. The consistency of our model is confirmed in yet another respect:
The same predictions (mutatis mutandis) can be derived from the scale of morphotactic transparency equally as from the scale of phonological biuniqueness (10.
7.10), and they are correct as well. Another --true-- prediction can be added:
On the average, morphotactically more transparent rules will be more productive
than less transparent rules within a given language. But there are two problems:

10.8.1.3.1. In many languages more MRs seem to involve resyllabification
(transparency II) than not (transparency I); notice the very productive English
WFRs of agent formation in -er and of deverbal -able adjectives. Now resyllabification and allophonic PRs are so little noticed by the hearer that they do not
disturb morpheme perception (identification of morphemes and morpheme boundaries) very much, as has always been the position of structural phonematics. A
preponderance of threshold I techniques is constitutive for agglutinating languages only (10.9.2) at least as far as lack of resyllabification is concerned.
Of course the frequent constellation of vowel-final stem and consonant-initial
suffix favors resyllabification.

10.8.1.3.2. Inflecting languages sometimes may have a preponderance of threshold III and IV derived words and word forms over threshold I and II derived ones.
This is type-specific (cf. 10.9.3).

10.8.1.3.3. One way of avoiding fusion in inflecting languages is to apply epenthetic PRs or to insert interfixes (semantically empty morphs), such as in
Russian the interfix -ov- in *bank-ov-skij*, adj. derived from *bank* 'bank' vs. an-

other derived adj. *banč-nyj* (with the AMR $k \rightarrow č$);[160] of course insertions weaken biuniqueness (10.8.2).

10.8.1.4. Three other predictions are:

10.8.1.4.1. Morphotactically more transparent sign combinations are easier to process and to separate into their constitutive elements. Therefore we can predict for slips of the tongue that production errors should be sensitive to relative ease of processing/separability, i.e., the more easily two elements are separated the more likely replacements are in slips of the tongue. Now all examples of anticipated/persevered/metathesized WF morphemes recorded are morphotactically very transparent (threshold II), e.g., prefix metathesis in G. *Verbrecher-ge-hirne* 'brains of criminals' → *Ge-brecher-ver-hirne* or metathesis in the compound *Laut-wert* 'sound value' → *Wert-laut* (Fromkin 1973:196, MacKay 1979 with references). In contrast to these transpositions, MPRs and AMRs may sometimes be involved in substitutions, e.g., in the replacement of *introduction* by *introducing*, etc. (Fromkin 1973:257f R 40, 7, 15f), where the substitution occurred before the application of the MPR, another proof for the psychological reality of WFRs (and thus processing, see MacKay 1979) and of the MPRs connected with them.

10.8.1.4.2. As MacWhinney (1978) has shown for the process of the acquisition of morphology, children use regular patterns (semantically and morphotactically transparent MPRs of affixation) with far fewer errors than opaque patterns, and opaque MPRs are more often replaced by transparent MPRs than vice versa.[162]

10.8.2.1. The next relevant parameter is implemented in the scale of biuniqueness - uniqueness - non-uniqueness/ambiguity. Biuniqueness means relational invariance between signatum and signans. If we notate signata (morphosemantic entities in morphology) with capital letters A, B, ... and signantia (the shapes of, e.g., stems and suffixes) with small letters a, b, ..., then morphological biuniqueness equals $A \equiv a$, $B \equiv b$: A is uniquely represented by a and vice versa, B by b, etc. Let us notate a biunique stem with $A \equiv a$, a biunique suffix with $B \equiv b$, as in Turkish *Türk-ler* 'Turks', where A = 'Turk' $\equiv a$ = *Türk*, B = PLURAL $\equiv b$ = *-ler*.

In morphonology, either uniqueness means (1) allomorphy, i.e., B (e.g., English PLURAL) is represented non-uniquely by either b = /z/ (*garden-s*) or c = -*en* (*ox-en*), whereas c = -*en* represents B uniquely (in the case of -*en* only within the noun, where it only means PLURAL).

Or uniqueness means (2) multifunctionality, i.e., one affix has two morpho-semantic meanings, e.g., in nouns 'past' can be expressed only (= uniquely) by the prefix *ex*- (as in *ex-president*), whereas *ex*- has yet a second meaning, viz. 'out', as in *ex-clude, ex-halation*.

Non-uniqueness (with varying degrees of ambiguity) can be exemplified within English verbs with the suffix -*en* which can function in deadjectival verb formation (*to whit-en*) or in past participles (*writt-en*), and there are other means for expressing deadjectival verb formation and past participles.

Relational invariance enhances the reliability of a sign in its communicative and cognitive functions. A biunique sign is most reliable in production because there is no (allomorphic) competition, i.e., no alternative in planning. Perception and processing by the receiver of a signans which uniquely represents a signatum (uniqueness or biuniqueness) is easiest, for it does not impede semiotic transparency at all (Koj 1979, cf. Hervey 1982:84ff).

Even in the case of unique allomorphs, allomorphy entails additional effort in processing (cf. MacKay 1978). Biuniqueness has often been called an optimal goal (difficult to obtain).[164]

10.8.2.2. Now, PRs, MPRs, and AMRs create allomorphy, but as we have seen in 10.8.1.3.1, PRs create many fewer problems for semiotic transparency than do MPRs and AMRs. Therefore we can make the same predictions for morphology as those based on the scale of morphotactic transparency. And this convergence of the two parameters is again to be expected because both derive from the principle of semiotic transparency.

Since both parameters derive from the same principle, we can also predict the non-existence of operations that are very natural on one parameter but very unnatural on the other (cf. 10.3.18.3), such as conceivable rules which are simultaneously most transparent (morphotactically) and very ambiguous.

10.8.2.3. If we compare the phonological (10.7.10.1) and the morphological scales of (bi)uniqueness and their respective predictions, then again the two parameters converge, as far as MPRs are concerned. The more phonologically am-

biguous a MPR is, the greater is the likeliness of ambiguity in the morphological signatum-signans relations because MPRs contribute directly to morphological
ambiguity in terms of both type and token uniqueness/ambiguity.

And we can predict (cf. 10.3.18.3, 10.8.2.2) the non-existence of rules
which are phonologically ambiguous but which cosignal biunique morphological
relations.

10.8.2.4.   From the cognitive point of view (i.e., implementing the cognitive
function of language), biunique signs are most precise. Thus they are preferred
goals in the planning of technical terminology (cf. Wüster 1979:79, 82f), where
precision is a very important goal: Terms which are biunique are the most reliable labels. However, the more a language attains biuniqueness, the more storage is needed, which is unproblematic only in artificial languages and technical
terminology. On morphological productivity, cf. 10.8.4. Due to the convergence
of parameters discussed in 10.8.2.2f, we can predict that in planned technical
terminology there will be fewer MPRs than in natural languages at large.

10.8.2.5.   Again we are faced with the paradox: Four parameters (morphological
and phonological biuniqueness, morphotactic transparency and phonological iconicity, cf. 10.8.1.2) converge in assigning highly marked (unnatural) values to
MPRs and AMRs in contrast to less marked (more natural/efficient) PRs; and
still PRs unidirectionally change to MPRs, which seems to fly in the face of any
belief in the efficiency of language change (10.3.5.1f). We have already given
several answers to this challenge (10.7.11.4), some of which will be elaborated
on in a larger explanatory context (10.8.2.6, 10.8.3.4, 10.8.6.2ff); more are
to come (10.8.3.4f, 10.9.3) in the sense of multicausality (cf. 10.3.5.3).

Of course greater efficiency is restored in all four parameters if a MPR/
AMR is eliminated (dies out), i.e., the convergent scales predict correctly (in
conjunction with the premise of local change towards more efficiency) that rules
(MPRs, AMRs) are much more likely to die out than processes (PRs); in fact PRs
die out only if they are collapsed with or obliterated by another PR.

10.8.2.6.   The paradox is slightly mitigated by the principle of default (5.20.
8.2). We can say that a morphological or phonological input-output relation is
biunique by default if normally a morphosemantic meaning A and a phoneme B are
expressed by the affix a and the allophone b respectively 'in the absence of ex-

plicit information to the contrary'. Let us enlarge on the example of 5.20.8.2.
1: Nominalization of English adjectives (A) is normally expressed by the suffix
-*ness* (a) unless it is a Latinate stem where we have the option of -*ity*. /k/ is
normally realized as [k, kʰ] unless a Latinate *i*-initial suffix is added to
stem-final /k/ so that the MPR of velar softening applies. Thus **electric-ness*
would be the default derivation of *electric* if there were not the above cited
'explicit information to the contrary' in the form of positive exception/rule
features.

The principle of default permits a number of predictions which we have already discussed in 5.20.8.

10.8.2.7. In connection with the concept of default we must discuss lexical exceptions or lexical factors in MPRs (cf. 5.10). How can we explain that rules
become more ambiguous by admitting lexical exceptions? For this purpose we must
discuss semantic transparency (10.8.3).

10.8.3.1. The function of semantic motivation of complex words (derivations or
compounds) and (inflectional) word forms (10.8.1.1) favors semantic transparency. In addition, semantic transparency follows from th principle of (bi)u-
niqueness:[165] If a complex word (form) is morphologically biunique, then the
same signans should always be represented by the same signatum so that it should
have a constant meaning. This is also known as Frege's principle of compositionality: 'The meaning of a complex expression is a function of the meanings
of the constituent parts.' Semantic transparency has been brought into the format of a scale, the scale of descriptiveness in Seiler's UNITYP model.[166]

10.8.3.2. The principle of compositionality (full semantic transparency) nearly
always holds in inflection, whereas it plays a rather marginal role in derivation. As a result, words derived via WFRs show significantly greater tendency
towards idiomaticity (lexicalization) than inflectional word forms.

10.8.3.3. The reason for this difference between inflection and word formation
lies in a conflict between morphological and lexical biuniqueness. The formula
for morphological biuniqueness (e.g., in *rid-er*) is $(A \equiv a) + (B \equiv b)$, i.e., the
lexical signatum A (e.g., RIDE) should always be expressed by the root/stem a
(e.g., *ride*), the derivational signatum B (e.g., AGENT) by the suffix b (e.g.,

-er).

However there is an antagonistic trend towards lexical (or holistic) biu-
niqueness/invariance (Dressler 1977a:19f, 48f, 1977e:16) represented by the formula $(A + B) \equiv (a + b)$, i.e., the meaning of the whole derived word should be in
an invariant relation with the whole form of the word irrespective of semantic
and morphotactic compositionality.

As we have stated in 10.4.4.3, words are primary signs but morphemes are
only secondary signs, which establishes semiotic priority of lexicon over word
formation: Lexical invariance is more important than morphological biuniqueness
for all words that are stored, and this is the case for nearly all derived forms
with the exception of occasionalisms (neologisms not yet accepted or nonce
forms). Therefore most derived words are more or less lexicalized (semantically
opaque): The MR governing the morphosemantic relation between base and derica-
tion is lexically affected in that its effect must be supplemented by lexical
information.

However inflectional word forms have precedence over morphemes composing
them only in perception,[167] but only extremely frequent tokens of inflectional
word forms can be assumed to be stored as such. Therefore, whereas WFRs are
semiotically clearly subordinated to existing lexical items (which they motivate, i.e., word formation serves the lexicon), inflectional word forms refer to
lexical items only indexically insofar as th base forms motivate them.

In this way we have explained why inflection is in general much more semantically transparent than word formation (10.8.3.2).

10.8.3.4. Postlexical MPRs are signs on signs, i.e., on complex words/word
forms, and they are thus connected with the morphotactic MRs deriving complex
words/word forms. Now we may ask (cf. 10.8.2.7) whether there are any conditions on lexical exceptions/factors of these spell-out MRs.

Here the principle of diagrammaticity (10.4.5.6, 10.7.10.8) based on diagrammatic[168] relations between morphosemantic and morphotactic relations comes
in. There is diagrammaticity if the morphotactic relations between the signantia *a* and *b* are in some way analogous to the morphosemantic relations between
the respective signata *A* and *B*.

10.8.3.4.1. There is diagrammaticity in the following two cases: (a) if seman-

tic transparency of the signatum $A + B$ (e.g., verb meaning LONG + PROGRESSIVE)
is reflected by morphotactic transparency of the signans $a + b$ (e.g., *long+ing*);
(b) if semantic opacity of the signatum $A + B$ (e.g., adj. meaning LONG + SUB-
STANTIVATION $\neq$ meaning of *long+itude*) is reflected by morphotactic opacity of
the complex signans $a + b$ (e.g., /lɔng/ + /ity:d/[168a] → ['lɑnǰitĭud]).

On the other hand, *leng-th* is a less diagrammatically derived word because
a rather high degree of semantic transparency is contradicted by a high degree
of morphotactic opacity because an AMR of umlaut intervenes, as also in
streng-th.

10.8.3.4.2.   Therefore we can predict that MPRs (because they produce morphotactic opacity (10.8.1.2ff) should occur more often with semantically opaque than
with semantically transparent complex words. This prediction has not yet been
sufficiently tested (but cf. on productivity, 10.8.4), however there are telling
contrasts within English *-land* compounds (see 5.9.1, 5.10.8) between semantically and morphotactically transparent *pet-l*[æ]*nd, waste-l*[æ]*nd* and semantically
and morphotactically opaque *main-l*[ə]*nd* (cf. 5.9.1, Karpf 1976).

10.8.3.4.3.   Next we can predict that --ceteris paribus-- MPRs should occur more
often in word formation than in inflectional morphology because inflections are
much more transparent semantically (10.8.3.2, cf. Plank 1981:72; for an exception, cf. 5.10.4).

This has been observed under the heading of paradigm conditions or paradigmatic coherence/constancy/uniformity/regularity/constraint.[169] A paradigm is
based on diagrammatic relations in a set of parallel words or word forms. This
parallelism is based on semantic transparency. Inflectional paradigms are nearly always semantically transparent, e.g., the meaning of a 3rd person sg. active
indicative pluperfect is usually compositional. As we have seen in 10.8.3.2,
derivational morphology is usually semantically more opaque. Therefore word
formation paradigms (cf. Zemskaja 1978, Guilbert 1975) must be marginal in contrast to inflectional paradigms, as they are. For MPRs, see 10.9.6.3.

If diagrammatic reflection of semantic transparency by morphotactic transparency is semiotically efficient, then morphotactic transparency, then morphotactic transparency can be preserved at the expense of generality of MPRs (not
of PRs, because they represent an absolute constraint on pronounceability and

disturb transparency much less);   e.g., Roberge (1980) cites the suppression of
ə-deletion (better: of the MPR deleting underlying /ɛ/) in the Standard German
verbal paradigm 3.sg.pres. *rett-et* 'saves' because the application of this MPR
would result in a fused form *[rɛt].[170] This may also be called a case of preservation of 'functional' distinctions, which is an instance of diagrammaticity
between the relations of meaning and form.

10.8.3.4.4.   In speaking of paradigms we must touch on analogy as well.   Forms
of an inflectional paradigm are in general much more subject to analogical leveling than derivationally related words, cf. the leveling of Latin nom.sg. (reconstructed) /oleiom/ 'oil', gen. /oleiw-ī/, etc., derived noun /oleiw-ā/ to
oleum, oleī, etc., with leveling of the oblique cases, but *olīva* without leveling (Schindler 1974:3, cf. in general, 10.8.3.3).

We cannot go into the enormous literature on analogy,[171] which goes back to
the Neogrammarian concept of a conflict between sound law and analogy, as proto-
types of phonology vs. morphology.   I only want to mention that analogy of morphemes presupposes semantic transparency and that its semiotic function is to
enhance corresponding morphotactic transparency, thus increasing diagrammaticity.

Frequent forms are more resistant to analogical leveling than infrequent
forms since they are better stored in memory.   Therefore it is more economic to
retrieve very frequent forms directly from storage than to compute them from
their bases via the respective MRs (cf. Mayerthaler 1977:139ff).   Therefore also
MPRs which occur in frequent forms are more stable than those which apply in
less frequent forms;   note, e.g., among verbal auxiliaries, modal verbs, and the
frequently used strong verbs.

10.8.3.4.5.   Another prediction based on diagrammaticity refers to lexical factors in morphonology (5.10, 10.8.2.7): MPRs should refer to lexical factors if
the respective words/word forms are lexicalized (semantically opaque, cf. 10.8.
3.4.1).   This prediction does not carry us very far[172] because most existing
words are lexicalized, whereas most inflectional forms are not.   Still, Plank
(1981:33f) has verified that MPRs have fewer exceptions in inflection than in
word formation, and we have seen the same distribution in Italian (6) and Polish
(7) palatalizations.   On an intervening typological variable, see 10.9.3.3.

10.8.3.4.6. There is another principle which governs lexical factors in morphonology: the default principle (5.20.8.2, 10.8.2.6). There is less ambiguity in
case of default (bi)uniqueness, as we have seen in 10.8.2.6.[173] If there are
very few lexical exceptions to a MPR, then these can be learned by rote and represent 'explicit information to the contrary'. Therefore --with the help of the
default principle-- we can predict that MPRs which are not general (exceptionless) should fall into two classes: (a) major rules which have few, easily
learnable exceptions (with negative/minus-rule features for the respective lexical items); (b) minor rules which apply to only a very few lexical items (with
positive rule features for the respective items to which the rule applies, and
which can easily be learned). This division is clear in Italian PF MPRs in plural formation (6.1, cf. 5.10.4).

10.8.3.4.7. And as for diachronic change, we can predict that MPRs (and AMRs)
should rapidly change from the status of major rules to minor rules or vice versa, i.e., according to diagram (a) or (b):

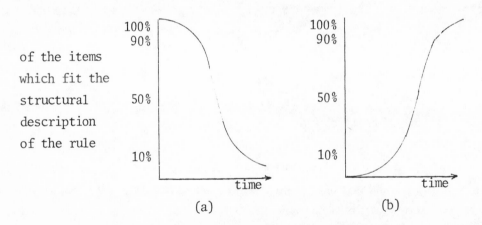

We have already claimed that MPRs can follow only scenario (a) with lexical fading before final rule loss (5.20.8.4, cf. 5.12.5f), whereas AMRs can follow both
scenarios (5.12.7, 5.20.8.4.4, 5.20.8.4.6). One reason is the respective role
of morphological indexicality, which has not to compete with recessive phonological indexicality in AMRs (5.7.11.4, 10.8.6).

PRs can only follow scenario (b) lexical diffusion, 5.10.5, 5.20.8.4.6),
and this because of phonological biuniqueness being implementable in PRs but not
in MPRs (10.7.12.4). If they start to have lexical exceptions (beginning of
scenario (a)), morphologization to MPRs has already begun.

10.8.3.5.1. Diagrammaticity (10.4.5.6, 10.7.10.8, 10.8.3.4) allows still another prediction exemplified with Latin paradigms such as *ger-ō* 'I lead', *ges-s-ī*, perf.pass.participle *ges-tus*. On the morphosemantic level the present is basic or unmarked, the perfect is derived or marked. In a diagrammatic way, normally, inflectional spell-out MRs derive perfect and perfect pass.part. forms by adding suffixes to the present stem and/or AMRs change the present stem into the perfect stem.[175] Similarly the Italian MPR of PF (6) is diagrammatic because it applies only in derived forms (e.g., sg. *ami*[k]*o*, pl. *ami*[č]*i*), and in Polish word formation all rules discussed in chapter 7 apply to derived forms, similarly in inflection before plural suffixes vs. suffixless singular, etc.

However, in Lat. *ger-ō*, perf. *ges-s-ī* it is the unmarked present stem which is derived from the basic stem form /ges/ via the (earlier) PR or (later) MPR of rhotacism (5.2.3, 5.9.5.1). This is antidiagrammatic, because the direction of derivation of the MPR contradicts the directions of the MRs involved.

Now we can classify antidiagrammaticity as marked/unnatural and thus predict that the directions of MPRs and MRs cosignaled by them will be parallel more often than the reverse.[176] And via the second premise of local efficiency in language change we can predict (probabilistically as always) that antidiagrammatic relations, such as in Lat. *ger-ō*, perf. *ges-s-ī*, are likely to be changed.

10.8.3.5.2. One type of change is rule inversion (5.2.7.3, cf. Andersen 1980: 33). E.g., the Latin MPR of rhotacism changed its direction in perfect formation from $s \rightarrow r$ to $r \rightarrow s$ / __ {s, t} (in certain suffixes). Since this inverted rule violates several criteria of MPRs (referring to phonological naturalness), it must be an AMR.

When the directions of MRs and MPRs are antagonistic, and if this is antidiagrammatic, and if therefore rule inversion is likely to occur, then, a priori, we cannot exclude an alternative format of rule inversion, i.e., the diachronic scenario of the given MPR retaining its direction and of the respective MR inverting its direction. However systematicity renders this conceivable alternative highly unlikely because MRs have both semiotic and applicational precedence over MPRs. Therefore MPRs are expected to adapt their direction according to MRs and not vice versa.

Notice that our prediction of rule inversion does not hold for PRs whose

directions of structural change often contradict the directions of the respective MRs they interfere with. PRs are more iconic and less indexical than MPRs
and disturb morphotactic transparency much less (10.8.1.3). Therefore antidiagrammaticity provoked by PRs is less cumbersome in processing than MPR-provoked
antidiagrammaticity. Even phonemic PRs do not change direction easily, as the
many final devoicing PRs show which apply only to base forms (typically endingless nom.sg.) but not to morphologically derived forms, e.g., in G. *Hun*[t]
'dog', gen. *Hun*[d]-*es*.

I do not claim that all antidiagrammatic relations are immediately changed,
but only that they are highly marked and thus more likely to be changed than
diagrammatic relations. Nor do I claim that all cases of rule inversion have
this source (cf. 5.2.7.3).

10.8.3.5.3. Another type of change is modification of the rule or lexical fading (5.12.5), so that 'antidiagrammatic' MPRs or AMRs die out. An example for
both changes is what happened to the AMR of nasal infixation in Latin (a) pres.
ta-n-g-ō 'I touch', perf. *te-tig-ī*, part. *tac-tus* (cf. 10.8.3.5.1 note 175);
(b) *ru-m-p-ō*, *rūp-ī*, *rup-tus* 'break'; (c) *vi-n-c-ō*, *vīc-ī*, *vic-tus* 'win', etc.,
and to its Italian correspondents (a) ∅; (b) *rompo*, *ruppi* (2.sg. *romp-esti*,
etc.), *rotto*; (c) *vinco*, *vinsi*, *vinto*. Either the respective Latin verbs were
lost[177] as in subclass (a); or the /n/ was analogically carried through the
whole paradigm as in (c); only in a very few words (b) has the *n*-less perfect
been kept (and only in the 1/3.sg., 3.pl., cf. Lepschy & Lepschy 1981:139ff):

I.   *prendo*, *presi* (and derivates);   *accendo*, *accessi*;   *tendo*, *tesi* (and deri-
     vates);   *dif-/of-fendo*, *-fesi*;   *rendo*, *resi*;   *(so)spendo*, *(so)spesi*;   *scen-
     do*, *scesi*.

II. *fondo*, *fusi* (and derivates);   *dispongo*, *disposi*;   *rispondo*, *risposi*;   *rom-
     po*, *ruppi* (and derivates).

Group II is suppletive because no rule can be established which holds for
most of these forms (no two verbs are exactly parallel). The same holds for
isolated *n*-less participles such as *stretto* from *stringo*, *strinsi*. The small
and homogeneous group I does not display an inverted AMR of *n*-deletion, as Klausenburger (1979:49ff) claims --a change from a less marked insertion rule to a
more marked deletion rule would be astonishing anyway (10.7.2, 10.7.10.3f, 10.7.
10.8)-- but a new, very minor rule (AMR) of *nd*-replacement in perfect formation:

$nd \rightarrow s \ / \ e \ __ + $ perfect suffix.

10.8.3.5.4. A weaker form of diagrammaticity is achieved if MPRs (and AMRs) apply to morphosemantically more marked forms but not to corresponding less marked
forms (cf. 10.10.2.5). Let us inspect our Polish rules (7) in this regard: AF
(7.4) marks dat.-loc.sg. vs. acc.sg. (7.4.2.1), and indeed DATIVE-LOCATIVE is
morphosemantically more marked than ACCUSATIVE (cf. Jakobson 1962.II:45f, 65ff,
Kuryłowicz 1964:84ff, 321, Schenker 1964:13f). AF cosignals marked masculine
vs. unmarked common gender nom.pl. (where the PR of SP (P 8) applies, 7.4.2.3).
This analysis is supported by the fact that in the gen.pl., masculine variants
take the suffix *-ów* [uf] while common variants are endingless, i.e., also less
marked on the expression level (Schenker 1964:67).

However the contrast between AF applying in human/personal pl. *Polac-y*
'Pole-s' and the PR of SP (P 8) applying in pejorative/metaphorically deperson-
alized *Pola*[k']-*i* is hardly diagrammatic. Similarly in conjugation, present is
morphosemantically less marked than past (Kuryłowicz 1964:25, 95, Mayerthaler
1981); but in the verbal class of 7.3.2.3, present is cosignaled by PF. The
principles of Natural Morphology would predict that this contradiction to morphological diagrammaticity should result in a diachronic instability of this
class -- and it is a recessive class.

10.8.4.1. So far we have discussed only one main function of word formation:
semantic and morphotactic motivation. The other main function is lexical enrichment (F. *enrichissement verbal*) by creating new words as signantia for already existing concepts in view of new interpreters and/or new interpretants
(e.g., fashion). Desirable qualities of new words are (a) precision, if the
cognitive function of language is the goal of the interpreter as in terminology;
(b) reliability of signs, in view of the communicative function. The most precise and reliable signs are biunique and the best WFRs to serve this goal are
biunique, unique ones next best, etc. (cf. the uniqueness scale in 10.8.2).

If a WFR is biunique, then by deduction it is fully productive[178] because
the same morphosemantic signatum is always expressed by the same signans, e.g.,
by a suffix such as E. *-able*, to cite the most productive English WFR. Since
there is a gradual degree of efficiency between biuniqueness and many-way ambiguity on the uniqueness scale, productivity should also be a matter of degree,
and the more productive WFRs should serve lexical enrichment more efficiently

than the less productive ones.

Our model is consistent in correctly predicting the obvious, namely that the more productive a WFR is, the more it will be used for lexical enrichment, provided that the interpreter makes the rational choice of using the most efficient means for his cognitive and communicative goals. Of course poets, advertisers, and others who envisage the poetic function of language may choose otherwise.[179]

10.8.4.2. The less ambiguous a MR is --including inflectional MRs-- the more semantic transparency it has. And the more semantically transparent a complex sign is, the more likely it is --due to the preference for diagrammaticity-- to be morphotactically transparent as well (10.8.3.4.1). If we tie in productivity, then we have all the premises for predicting what has often been observed:[180] The more productive a MR is, the more likely it is to generate morphotactically transparent complex words/word forms, or in other words, the less likely it is that a MPR interferes. In case of inflectional MRs, a typological intervening variable interferes in the inflecting type (10.9.3.6.2).

10.8.4.3. Our model predicts this correlation between the productivity of MRs and the absence of MPRs for other domains also, e.g., language acquisition. And indeed children's WFRs seem to be most productive when AMRs and MPRs have not been fully acquired.[181]

10.8.4.4. Clearly our model does not predict that non-application of MPRs to the outputs of MRs implies that these MRs are productive (but only the other way around). Such a claim would be absurd with rather isolating languages which have few MRs and no MPRs (10.9.1), and it would be incorrect for decaying and dying languages: There[182] productivity of MRs fades away, though morphotactic transparency of existing complex words and word forms often increases. The reason is easy to find: Complex words and word forms of the recessive language are worse stored and less often processed and computed than those of the dominant language, therefore morphotactic motivation is very important for memory and productive/receptive performance. As a consequence, morphotactic transparency and thus absence of MPRs is even more preferred than in non-decaying languages.

10.8.5. Semiotic principles referring to the shape of a signans (10.7.2) have some relevance for MRs and MPRs as well:

10.8.5.1. The principle of syntagmatic contrastiveness of signs following each
other in the speech chain is connected with the figure-ground relation of sharp-
ening the contours (cf. 10.7.1) of roots/stems/lexical bases vs. derivational
and inflectional morpheme shapes. This principle favors morphotactic transparency and thus disfavors postlexical MPRs (because MPR-induced opacity is more
opaque than PR-induced reduction of transparency, 10.8.1).

Sharpness of contours is increased by reserving specific MSRs (prelexical
MPRs and MRs) to specific derivational and inflectional categories (cf. 8), or
by concentrating consonants in roots and vowels in morphological operations as
in Semitic languages (cf. 8.3.8.1, 10.9.4). All this involves indexicality as
well (10.8.6.1).

This reflection of morphosemantic divisions (viz. morphological categories)
by morphonological distinctions is diagrammatic.[183] Also due to diagrammaticity, semantically simpler morphemes tend to be phonologically simpler as well.[184]

10.8.5.2. Syllable onset consonants are more salient than vowels (3.2.1.1, 4.3.
3.3.1) and more distinguishable consonants can be articulated and perceived than
vowels, so that almost all languages have more phonemic consonants than vowels.
Since there are many more lexical than grammatical morphemes, it is both economical and diagrammatic to concentrate lexical meaning in consonants, grammatical
meaning in vowels, as in Semitic languages[185] and in Proto-Indo-European. Notice that umlaut and ablaut phenomena are much more frequent than comparable,
equally systematic consonant modifications (cf. Yokuts, Athabascan languages).

Even in languages without productive ablaut or umlaut, in redundancy tests,
vowels can be omitted more easily than consonants (provided that there is little
morphology involved), such as in an advertisement in the New York subway (I indicate the deleted material in parentheses): *if (yo)u c(an) r(ea)d th(is)*
m(e)s(sa)g(e) (yo)u c(an) b(e)c(o)m(e) a st(e)n(ographer) & g(e)t hi(gh) pa(y).

10.8.5.3. The syllable is an important perceptual unit (cf. 3, 5.8); morphotactic transparency (10.8.1) is enhanced if syllable boundaries coincide with
morphological boundaries (10.8.1.2.1, Plank 1981:67ff).

It has been noticed in studies of diachronic chnage (Stein 1970, Plank

1981:69ff, 139) that a common type of suffix change consists in a vowel-initial suffix acquiring a consonantal syllable onset. The conceivable inverse change, loss of morpheme- and simultaneously syllable-initial consonant has not been observed. For a further diachronic prediction, cf. 10.8.5.4.

10.8.5.4. The optimal length of signantia (Oller 1971:27) is difficult to ascertain. According to the respective language type, optimal word form length seems to vary between one and three syllables (cf. 5.10.7). Due to principles highlighted by Zipf (1949, cf. 10.5.4), affixes can be shorter than roots/stems (cf. 8.2.3, 8.3.4, 8.3.7, 10.9.3.1). The optimal length of derivational affixes seems to fluctuate (according to my own counts) around one syllable, whereas inflectional suffixes are often shorter. While phonology tends to reduce the length of morphemes in diachrony, morphology tends to compensate by making them longer, cf. Skalička (1979:242, 282ff).

If the affix is very short, a MPR cosignaling this affix facilitates its identification (cf. 10.8.6.6). Since MPRs are diachronic remnants of PRs, and PRs apply more easily within a syllable than across a syllable boundary (cf. 5.8.4.1), MPRs are more likely to occur before those very suffixes which are more difficult to identify because morpheme and syllable boundaries do not coincide (10.8.5.3); cf. the palatalizations in 6, 7 which outweigh heterosyllabic MPRs.

Now we can make two diachronic predictions: (a) Since tautosyllabic MPRs (and AMRs) are more usefully redundant (cf. 10.8.6.6) than heterosyllabic MPRs (AMRs), they should have more diachronic stability, and (b) among them those MPRs (AMRs) which apply before shorter suffixes rather than before longer ones. The Polish AMR of PF (7.3) confirms the first hypothesis because all general PF applications are tautosyllabic and all heterosyllabic applications are non-general (recessive: 7.3.2.5).[186]

10.8.6.1. We have already discussed the indexicality of all MPRs and of all context-sensitive PRs and AMRs (10.7). Indexicality is often in a wider sense, such that all morphology is indexical.[187] Then, of course, pre- and postlexical MPRs are much more indexical than PRs because the morphological factor is much more important for MPRs than for PRs. Here we use indexicality in a narrower sense, as the relation of a morpheme, phoneme, or rule to a co-present signatum (which may again be a phoneme, morpheme, word, or rule).

10.8.6.2.   In 10.7.11.3 we already duduced that that phonemes are better indexical signantia than allophones, and thus also that AMRs, MPRs, and phonemic PRs are indexically better than allophonic PRs.   And in 10.7.11.4, 10.7.11.7 we have deduced that morphemes are better indexical signantia than phonemes, and that in this respect the transformation of a phonemic PR into a MPR represents an improvement of indexicality.   Add the semiotic precedence of morphology over phonology (10.7.11.3, 10.7.11.4f, 10.7.11.7, 10.7.12.5).   The greater importance of morphological than phonological indexicality also shows in rule split (5.9.8), e.g., Italian PF (6) has split into several MPRs and AMRs according to the morphological categories indexically co-signaled.   If phonological indexicality were as important as morphological indexicality, we would expect that rule split according to different phonological contexts would occur as easily as morphology-induced rule split;   this is clearly not the case.   The history of Italian PF (6) shows that the phonological context (importance of /i/ following the velar) may play a contributive role in the modification of MPRs.   Polish palatalization rules (7) have split phonologically insofar as different rule formats hold for the input phonemes /k, g/, and /x/, but the extent of morphological rule split has been much greater.

10.8.6.3.   Now we must elaborate on the question why shift from phonological to morphological indexicality is so great a semiotic improvement that it can override deterioration in three semiotic parameters (10.8.2.5), a deterioration only partially diminished or counterbalanced by diagrammaticity between morphosemantic and morphotactic opacity (10.8.3.4.1), frequency (10.8.3.4.4) and the concept of default (bi)uniqueness (10.8.3.4.6).   Of course we cannot quantify the relevance of each scale/parameter and of their various thresholds.   Presumably this undecidability is not just a shortcoming of descriptive or explanatory adequacy, because different choices/solutions of our conflect are constitutive for language types (10.9, 10.8.6.8).

10.8.6.4.   Morphological indexicality is higher valued than phonological indexicality[188] not only for semiotic precedence of morphology over phonology (10.4.4.4), but also because morphemes have meaning, phonemes do not, i.e., phonology implements sense discrimination, morphology and morphonology sense determination (Jakobson & Waugh 1979:53f).   Therefore diachronic morphologization of a PR entails semanticization (Maslov 1979:196ff).

The end point of semanticization is reached when an AMR is the only signans of a morphosemantic signatum such as plural umlaut in E. *feet, geese* and G. *Mütter* ['mʏtər], pl. of *Mutter* 'mother'. The Polish imperative *piecz* [p'eč] (7.3. 2.3.1) has PF as its only overt signans; if we assume that speakers still derive [č] in this form from underlying /k+j/, then final semanticization has not yet been reached, although the difference in performance may be small, because here the PF must be planned as much as any MR.

10.8.6.5. Peirce (1965.VIII:137) mentions the usefulness of concomitants[189] of signantia. PRs and MPRs are concomitants of morphemes or MRs (cf. Roberge 1980: 201ff) or cosignals, as I have called them (Dressler 1977a, cf. Maslov 1979:139). Only the cosignaling signantia established by PRs are less efficient than those established by MPRs (10.7.11). In the process of morphologization their cosignaling function becomes successively more important, or as Roberge (1980) puts it, concomitants are on their way to becoming exponents, i.e., their morphological redundancy becomes ever more useful (cf. 10.3.9).

10.8.6.6. Morris (1971:85, 365) insists on a specific subtype of (usefully redundant) indices, the 'preparatory stimulus = a stimulus that influences a response to some other stimulus.' E.g., the umlaut of *u → ü* [ʏ] in G. *Hünd-chen* 'dogg-ie', *Hünd-in* 'bitch', adj. *hünd-isch* can be seen as a preparatory stimulus for a small set of umlauting suffixes; or palatal formation in It. *ami*[č]-*i* 'friend-s', *ami*[č]-*izia* 'friend-ship' as a preparatory stimulus for just two suffixes (6.1.3.1, 6.4.1). These are typical examples of a MPR which applies to the stem and prepares the hearer for a suffix to come. MacWhinney & Pléh (forthc.) have found psycholinguistic evidence for their importance for suffix identification.

10.8.6.7. At the same time such MPRs increase the cohesion of the word (form)[190] and thus enhance indexicality. Another cohesive technique, vowel harmony (10.3.8f, 10.9.2.5) hardly furnishes prepatory stimuli (10.8.6.5).

10.8.6.8. MPRs and AMRs do not simply cosignal a chaotic set of morphemes and MRs, as a casual reader of 5-7 may infer, but often they cosignal (sometimes by default) large morphological classes or categories:

10.8.6.8.1. E.g., Stankiewicz (1960, 1961, 1979:26, 42ff) and Laskowski (1979b, 1981) have insisted on the restriction to, or concentration on word and inflectional classes of given alternations in Slavic languages. Van Coetsem & McOrmick (1982) have pointed to the different development of Germanic umlaut in verbs and nouns, which has a parallel with Italian PF in declension vs. conjugation (6). But sometimes these indexed categories are quite small, such as sg. present other than 1st sg. present of a subclass of verbs in German, e.g., 2nd sg. *hält-st*, 3rd sg. *hält* vs. 1st sg. *halt-e*, pl. *halt-en/et* 'hold';[191] or PF in Italian plural formation (6.1) signals only masculine *o*-stems.

10.8.6.8.2. This holds also for Polish redundant AMRs such as PF (7.3) and AF (7.4): PF cosignals conjugational and word formation categories and very few declensional ones; AF cosignals declensional categories and only two WFRs. Thus these two AMRs are rather complementarily distributed in Polish morphology.

E.g., the declensional categories cosignaled by major rules are nom.pl. vs. dat.-loc. vs. accusative sg., where minimal pairs are established by AF, e.g., *drodz-e* 'way' vs. acc. *drog-ę* [droge] (with merger of word-final /ẽ/ with /e/); adverb vs. adjective, comparative vs. positive. Among plurals, AF cosignals (in addition to the nom.pl. -*y*) either human/personal, whereas -*i* (triggering surface palatalization (P 8)) signals non-human/non-personal (with the secondary meaning of pejorative, as in *Polac-y* 'Pole-s' vs. *Polak-i* 'lousy Poles') or male vs. common gender plurals, e.g., *włóczędz-y* 'male vagabond-s' vs. *włóczęg-i* 'vagabond-s'.

10.8.6.9. What is then the driving force behind the unidirectional change: PRs > MPRs > AMRs? There are basically two accounts: (1) the dephonologization model,[192] (2) the morphologization/grammaticalization model.[193] Of course there exist varying mixtures of both (e.g., Roberge 1980), but generally one of the two accounts plays a very minor role.

According to the dephonologization model, technical mishaps such as interactions of PRs[194] render PRs more and more phonologically unnatural (or crazy or whatever other label). These are rather 'unfortunate accidents' without any unifying generalization such as simplification or whatever, not to speak of any higher-level explanation. Even assignment of function to accidents (10.3.11) occurs before a PR turns into a MPR.

The morphologization model as I have defended it, starts with the unifying principle of semiotic precedence of morphology over phonology (and, less directly, of meaning over form, 10.8.6.4) and with the hypothesis of local change towards efficiency (optimalization, 10.3.5).

This is not an ad hoc assumption. For if we survey the semiotic parameters discussed in 10.3, 10.7, 10.8, then iconicity and (bi)uniqueness favor the loss of MPRs but disfavor the genesis of MPRs from PRs (10.8.6.3); also the principle of successivity/combinability of signantia (10.7.5, 10.7.12.5) is disfavorable.

Diagrammaticity between semantic and morphotactic opacity is only a contributing and regulating principle because it contributes only to (dis)allowing MPRs to occur and because it cannot account for MPRs in semantically transparent inflection (10.8.3.4, 10.8.6.3). Similarly, token frequency can explain only why certain items are more resistent to analogy (which levels MPRs), cf. 10.8.3.4.4, 10.8.6.3.

The principle of distinctive signantia (10.7.2) is ambiguous in regard to our conflict of parameters: Although phonemes (produced by MPRs) are better distinguished than allophones (produced by the great majority of PRs), MPRs neutralize underlying distinctions. The concept of default (bi)uniqueness (10.8.3.4.6, 10.8.6.3) can only mitigate the effect of rising ambiguity when a PR changes into a MPR.

When an obligatory phonemic PR is no longer obligatorily applied, i.e., when it ceases to represent a constraint on pronounceability/perceptibility, then this drastic deterioration of phonologicity can be understood in our model only as a 'sacrifice' in favor of other, more important parameters:

10.8.6.10. The main driving force we may look for is increase in morphological indexicality and replacement of phonological by morphological indexicality (10.7.11.3f, 10.8.6.2ff), which has no semiotic explanation other than precedence of morphology over phonology.

Also the principle of efficient size/shape (or ground-figure contrast, 10.7.3) points in the same direction because what is better signaled are morphological, not phonological categories when a PR changes into a MPR; e.g., if an ultrashort vowel inserted by a PR (as in Koromfe and other West African languages, cf. Rennison 1984) is changed into a full vowel inserted by a MPR.

Or there is a decrease of unnaturalness when an overall deletion PR (8.7.2, 8.7.10.3f, 10.7.10.8) is changed and restricted to a MPR or AMR of subtraction which occurs only in a very limited and morphologically fully predicted environ- ment and usually accompanied by secondary motivations from other semiotic param- eters (cf. Dressler 1984b, Dressler & Acson, forthc.), e.g., when the Northern Greek PR deleting all unstressed high vowels was replaced by a MPR deleting un- stressed /u/ in the gen.sg. and unstressed /i/ in the nom.pl. of masculine *o*- stems, as in nom.sg. *ắθropos* 'man', gen.sg. = nom.pl. *aθróp* (underlying /aθróp-u, aθróp-i/).

Beyond morphology we have the lexicon, words being semiotically primary signs, morphemes secondary signs (cf. 10.8.3.3). PRs may have exceptions with non-integrated loanwords. If these elements are accepted as a separate stratum of a language, and if these rules still do not apply, then they become MPRs (cf. 5.10, 5.13.2, 10.8.2.7, 10.8.3.4.5f).

The morphologization model has been established on a very small semiotic basis. Now, our enlarged semiotic basis and the hypotheses of local change to- wards efficiency have limited explanation of the genesis of MPRs in terms of ef- ficiency to morphological factors.

10.8.6.11. What we have tried to explain within our semiotic model up to this point is how, due to the additional premise of local efficiency (optimization) of linguistic change, PRs may change to MPRs and AMRs but never in the opposite direction. Now we have to discuss which general principles, not yet inserted into our explanatory chain, may control/regulate/check the unidirectional change PRs > MPRs > AMRs, i.e., the genesis and survival of MPRs. First we discuss the more general typological principles (10.9), then the more specific principles of system adequacy (10.10).

10.9. Morphonology in language typology

10.9.0.1. If Natural Phonology and Natural Morphology consisted only of univer- sal markedness theories (10.7f), then only probable tendencies, probable con- flicts of tendencies, and possible solutions of tendencies could be predicted. If we want to specify which possible solutions of conflicts are probable within a given language, and how the solution of one conflict influences the solutions of other conflicts, then we need a theory which accounts systematically for co-occurrent conflict solutions, and this is a theory of language types,[195] in the sense of 10.6.3.

10.9.0.2. A typological parameter most important for morphonology is the amount of agglutination vs. fusion (Sapir 1921, 1922:52ff): The more fusional a language is, the more PRs, MPRs, and AMRs are needed to implement morphological fusion (cf. Skalička 1979:335ff). This is an instance of parameters/tendencies of different language components 'not precluding one another' (Seiler 1979:7): Here phonological parameters are subordinated to morphological ones according to typological adequacy.

10.9.1. The isolating language type has little (ideally: no) morphology (with functional/semiotic advantages and disadvantages) as in Semai, Vietnamese, many Sino-Tibetan and Polynesian languages.[196] Lack of morphology results in lack of postlexical MPRs, AMRs, phonemic PRs, but not of segmental allophonic PRs. This may sound trivial, but it is less trivial that prelexical MPRs seem to be lacking as well. I.e., lack of (prelexical and postlexical) morphology results in lack of MPRs of any sort. Again, there are many prelexical PRs which restrict the phonemic inventory and phoneme sequences of, e.g., Vietnamese. A prelexical rule (probably to be considered a MPR) typical for isolating languages restricts morphemes to monosyllabic shapes (Skalička 1979:27, Kasevič 1983:118ff); lack or poverty of morphology (particularly affixation) results in lack of resyllabification PRs so that morphemes are monosyllabic on the phonetic surface as well.

        In our model, prelexical and postlexical MPRs (or PRs, mutatis mutandis) are the same entities, only they operate at two different levels. Therefore if the notion 'language type' is consistent, we should expect that the class of MPRs (whether pre- or postlexical ones) should be treated in a uniform way. This expectation has been confirmed in the isolating language type.

10.9.2.1. The agglutinating language type (as rather well represented by Turkish)[197] can be briefly outlined in the following way:[198] Advantages of this type are: Morphological (bi)uniqueness (10.8.2) is highly favored, and thus there is much semantic and morphotactic transparency (10.8.1, 10.8.3), diagrammaticity (as related to transparency, 10.8.3.4) and great productivity of MRs (10.8.4), little allomorphy. MRs introduce only affixes, neither ablaut nor umlaut, and these affixes are only continuous and either prefixes or suffixes (no in-, inter-, circum-, transfixes). There is a tendency towards monosyllabic morphemes (cf. 10.8.5) and these are fairly autonomous, morphotactically because morpheme and syllable boundaries tend to coincide, semantically because many affixes may occur as independent lexical items as well.

Disadvantages are: Lack of multifunctionality (10.8.2.1), which is a burden for memory storage; this lack and the relative length of affixes (at least one syllable) result in long word forms, which may pose problems for processing. Because of little non-uniqueness, there is little indexicality in the form of syntactic redundancy, therefore compensation (for slips of the tongue and of the ear) is difficult in perceptual processing, hence also phonological reductions in casual speech are difficult. There is little indexicality due to lack of closeness between signans and signatum (cf. 10.7.11.2) in long word forms insofar as the most peripheral affix can be fairly distant from the root/stem (cf. 10.9.2.2). There are no clear word classes (including inflectional morpheme classes), no specific properties of affixes as opposed to roots. Since morphological (bi)uniqueness is favored, the unity of the word (form) is less revealed so that the MPR of vowel harmony is typically used as a binding device (10.9.2. 5).

10.9.2.2. As an example let us contrast a Turkish word form with its Latin equivalent:

ada   - *lar*   - *ım* - *ız* - *dan*   = *insul*   (-)*is*   *nostr*(-)*is*
'island' - PL(URAL) - '1' - PL - ABL(ATIVE)   'island' (-)ABL 'our' (-)ABL
                        'our'   PL   PL
'from our islands'

-*lar* is biuniquely connected with plurality (on vowel harmony see 10.9.2.5) because it is the only signans of nominal plurality (as contrasted with -*ız*, the signans of possessor plurality) and does not express anything other than plurality -- Latin -*is* expresses plurality and dative or ablative (multifunctionality), and plurality is expressed by all its other plural case-forms; there is another DAT/ABL.PL allomorph -*bus* (in other declensional paradigms). Whereas in Latin there is redundant congruence of grammatical number between subject and predicate, noun and modifier; there is none in Turkish: Plural is expressed only once (biuniqueness) in the subject/noun; even after a numeral there is the singular, as in *bir/iki/bin ada* 'one/two/thousand island(s)'. Similarly -*dan* is biuniquely connected with ABLATIVE -- in Latin ABLATIVE is expressed in various singular allomorphic case endings ($-\bar{a}$, $-\bar{o}$, $-\bar{\iota}$, $-\bar{u}$, $-e$, $-\bar{e}$) in addition to pl. $-\underset{.}{i}s$, $-bus$. Latin has syntactic redundancy in the congruence of *nostris* with *insulis* -- Turkish has none: If the hearer mishears the ending in *insulis* he can still compensate with the ending of *nostris*. The Turkish ablative suffix $-dan$ is far away from the root it refers to indexically, Latin $-is$ is adjacent.

The underlying and surface shapes of roots and affixes are similar in Turkish (but not in Latin), typically one syllable or more. The Turkish morphemes are morphotactically very transparent (except for resyllabification of *lar+ım+ız* → *la\$rı\$mız* -- if /im+iz/ and not /mi+z/ is the underlying form); if we compare Latin abl.pl. *insulis* with nom.sg. *insula*, then we may assume either truncation of the feminine stem vowel $-a$ or fusion with it -- both operations are rare in Turkish; and so on.

But we do have vowel harmony (10.9.2.5), cf. *ev-ler-im-iz-den* 'from our houses'.

10.9.2.3. Let us summarize the role of MPRs in a very agglutinating language such as Turkish: There are very few prelexical MPRs (cf. 8.3.3, 8.4.4.1); in the ideal construct of the language type there are none. There are no inflectional paradigms to cosignal via prelexical MPRs (cf. 10.9.2.1, 10.9.3.6.2).

10.9.2.4. Postlexical MPRs (and AMRs) --and we have seen many of them in ininflecting languages such as Russian, Polish (7), Italian (6)-- are very rare[199] and are not assumed at all in the ideal construct. These are the very MPRs which arise due to a conflictual interaction between phonology and morphology and are remnants of earlier PRs which have been morphologized.

10.9.2.5.1. But there is one type of MPR which is notably absent in inflecting languages but typical for agglutinating languages: vowel harmony. Note that Estonian when changing from an agglutinating to an inflecting language has lost vowel harmony (typical for Finno-Ugric languages) but has acquired many pre- and postlexical MPRs of the type of 10.9.2.4.

Our system can explain, I think, the difference between the other MPRs and vowel harmony --which is also a MPR-- because it does not represent a constraint on pronounceability and typically has numerous lexical exceptions.

10.9.2.5.2.   In inflecting languages, postlexical MPRs serve fusion of morphemes to words and word forms and thus morphological indexicality in terms of adjacency;   they are in many ways phonologically unnatural and they reduce naturalness on morphological parameters other than indexicality (10.7.8, 10.7.10, 10.7.1.2, 10.8.1f).

Vowel harmony too is an index of the extension of the word (form) domain. But it does not disturb morphotactic transparency (10.8.1).

Vowel harmony-induced allomorphy (e.g., Turkish pl. *-ler/-lar*, abl. *-den/ -dan*, 1.pl.poss. *-im-iz/-ım-ız/-üm-üz/-um-uz*) poses fewer problems for processing[200] and storage because (e.g., in Turkish, both back and labial) vowel harmony can be matched with a single universal process type (4.5.3.3), whereas other MPRs cannot (5.2).   Allomorphy never refers to the many roots/stems but only to the relatively few affixes, whereas the opposite is true of the MPRs of umlaut. Vowel harmony, at least in languages such as Turkish, Hungarian, and Finnish, seems to be a (lexically and morphologically restricted) remnant of a PR of child language.   In other words, morphological biuniqueness is less affected by vowel harmony than by other MPRs.

Note also that vowel harmony does not affect consonants, which are more important for morpheme/word identification than vowels (10.8.5.2).

10.9.2.5.3.   What all this means is that with respect to vowel harmony, there is much less conflict between phonology and morphology than with respect to other MPRs and phonemic PRs;[201]   interaction between phonology and morphology is rather cooperative.   Since phonological and morphological naturalness contradict each other much less, vowel harmony can retain (and combine) much more phonological and morphological naturalness than other MPRs.

10.9.2.5.4.   This greater amount of phonological naturalness has telling consequences (cf. 8.3.3).   In L_1 and L_2 acquisition, in aphasia, in word games, in rule-loaning, vowel harmony differs greatly from other MPRs, and in loanword integration from many other MPRs.   There is a striking difference between vowel harmony and other MPRs even within the same language.

10.9.2.5.5.   Although the retention of so much phonological and morphological naturalness may sound ideal, we must not fall into the fallacy[202] of overlook-

ing the expence at which this high degree of transparency, biuniqueness, iconicity is bought (10.9.2.1).

10.9.2.6. The agglutinating language type embodies a consistent choice of a
great deal of naturalness on some parameters, little naturalness on others.
Again our expectation that pre- and postlexical MPRs are treated in the same way
(10.9.1) has been confirmed. There are few (ideally no) pre- or postlexical
MPRs, with the exception of vowel harmony, which typically occurs in both a pre-
and postlexical function.

10.9.3.1. After having discussed the agglutinating type (10.9.2) and having
contrasted Turkish, a decent representative of this type, with Latin, a decent
representative of the inflecting type, we can enumerate the constitutive features of the ideal construct of the inflecting (fusional) language type very
briefly.[203]

In many aspects the inflecting type is the reverse of the agglutinating
type: much indexicality in the form of redundancy due to congruence, easy re-
ducibility in casual speech, clear distinction of word/morpheme classes to be
signaled indexically by prelexical and postlexical MPRs and AMRs, therefore much
allomorphy; closeness of signans and signatum, shorter word forms due to much
less iconicity and morphological (bi)uniqueness; much multifunctionality; usually only one inflectional ending after the stem, more synonymy, less morphological productivity, less semantic and morphotactic transparency. More lexical
invariance, less diagrammaticity; infixes may occur.

10.9.3.2. These properties are well represented in strongly inflecting languages such as most ancient Indo-European languages and most modern Slavic languages;
Estonian, Baltic, some Bantu languages.

Characteristics of the inflecting language type are attenuated in weakly
inflecting languages such as modern Romance[204] and (many) modern Germanic languages, some Bantu languages. These languages have some ingredients of the isolating and some of the agglutinating language type. This is a frequent typological mix.

10.9.3.2. Another frequent typological mix must be mentioned: Many languages
with inflecting type inflectional morphology have rather agglutinating WF,[205]

but never the other way around, because syntactic redundancy refers to inflectional, not to derivational affixes, i.e., compensates for opacity of inflectional morphology only. This typological mix constrains predictions regarding
less transparency in word formation than in inflectional morphology (10.8.3.4.
3, 10.8.3.4.5).

10.9.3.4. Modern English displays a very weird typological mix in morphology.
In a nutshell, it combines weakly inflecting type inflectional morphology (including the tendency towards monosyllabic [Germanic] roots and lack of morphological gender and paradigm distinctions) with strongly inflecting (fusional)
type derivational morphology in its large Latinate lexical stratum, rather agglutinating Germanic derivational morphology, and polysynthetic aspects of com-
pounding.

It is a singular sight for contemporary linguists to see such a typologically atypical language serving as preferred testing ground for theories of morphology and morphonology (the proper domain of Generative Phonology). Typologically purer languages are less complicated to analyze, so that it might be a
better research strategy to first analyze decent representatives of each language type before tackling English. At least, hypotheses made on the basis of
English alone have often proved to be extremely short-lived.

10.9.3.5. This may sound like calling English a typologically inconsistent language and falling into the fallacy of the 'consistent language' that N. Smith
(1981) has denounced vividly and correctly. As a partial reply, I want briefly
to enumerate some differences between our typological approach and the one he
attacks.

10.9.3.5.1. Whereas word order typologies that N. Smith (1981) has in mind display a proliferation of types (e.g., Greenberg's 24 basic word order types), we
use Skalička's (1979) five ideal type constructs: isolating (10.9.1), agglutinating (10.9.2), inflecting (10.9.3), introflecting (10.9.4), polysynthetic (10.
9.5). It would be extremely difficult to devise ad hoc an additional type in
order to shield the theory against disconfirmation.

10.9.3.5.2. The properties of word order types are rather few and of a surface
syntactic nature, whereas Skalička's (1979) type properties are numerous and

pertain to all components/levels of language. And --as far as morphology and phonology are concerned-- I have tried to relate them to universal parameters of naturalness. This compares with the endeavors towards parametrization in recent generative work on universal grammar (e.g., Chomsky 1982).

10.9.3.5.3. Diachronic research in typology (unfortunately rather neglected by Skalička 1979) must guarantee a genetic explanation (cf. 10.3.18.6, 10.6.4, 10.3.10f) of typological mixes and limit conceivable typological mixes by establishing 'consistent changes' on many parameters (cf. also Sgall 1972, Korhonen 1980, Skalička 1979:263ff).

10.9.3.5.4. But also principles delimiting conceivable mixes from a purely synchronic viewpoint must be found, cf. 10.9.3.3.

10.9.3.6. A second methodological statement: Our discussion of morphonological typology can easily be transformed into the format of lengthy deductions (predictions) with ample discussions following. For lack of space, a few abridged deductions for morphonology with the inflecting language type (contrasted with the agglutinating type) must suffice:

10.9.3.6.1. Premise A: The higher a language type values the typological parameter x, the more rarely this type is allowed to choose bad/unnatural options on the respective naturalness scale of parameter x.

Premise B: The agglutinating type values the parameter of morphotactic transparency much more highly than does the inflecting type.

Premise C: MPRs reduce morphotactic transparency, ESPECIALLY fusional MPRs (cf. 10.8.1.2).

Conclusion: MPRs (especially fusional MPRs) occur much less in agglutinating languages than in inflecting languages.

Zero hypothesis: MPRs are randomly distributed in inflecting and agglutinating languages. But inspection of more than 50 inflecting and agglutinating languages has shown results which fit the conclusion, but not the zero hypothesis.

10.9.3.6.2. Premise D: Inflectional paradigm classes are type constitutive for

the inflecting language type but absent from the agglutinating type (cf. Skalička 1979, Wurzel 1984).

Premise E: Languages tend to mark input distinctions diagrammatically in
the output.

Premise F: Prelexical and postlexical MPRs represent input-output relations.

Premise G: Paradigm classes provide systematic subdivisions to the lexicon.

Conclusion: MPRs do mark paradigm classes.

Zero hypothesis: Prelexical and postlexical MPRs have the same relative
distribution in inflecting languages as in agglutinating languages, although
their absolute number is higher in inflecting languages.   The zero hypothesis
can be rejected: In agglutinating languages MPRs cannot mark paradigm classes
since there are none.   According to the zero hypothesis, the more numerous MPRs
of inflecting languages should mark existing paradigm classes either never or
only very rarely.   However Wurzel (1984) and Stankiewicz (1960, 1961, 1979) have
collected many examples of postlexical MPRs indexing paradigm classes, and Jakobson and his followers have identified many prelexical MPRs indexing paradigm
classes (8.3.7, 8.3.8.2, 8.3.9, 8.4.4).   As for the relation between productivity of MRs and MPRs cosignaling them (10.8.4.2), paradigms cosignaled by MPRs
restrict the productivity of inflectional MPRs to the respective class of words/
stems which belongs to the paradigm.   Therefore this typological variable may
modify but not eliminate the correlation between degree of productivity and
poverty/lack of MPRs.

10.9.3.6.3.   Similar predictions can be made for inflection vs. derivation since
paradigms are much more important for inflectional than for derivational morphology (10.8.3.4.3).   On the other hand we have predicted (10.8.3.4.4) that
analogy is easier in inflectional paradigms than in derivational morphology, and
similar predictions were made in 10.8.3.2f.   In order to overcome these contradictory predictions we must refine them contextually, e.g., analogy will level
MPR-induced irregularities within a paradigm whereas, e.g., prelexical MPRs
which index the whole paradigm are not subject to this system-internal sort of
analogy but only to leveling connected with typological change.   Further investigations demand principles of system adequacy (10.10).

10.9.3.7. Our deductive expectation of 10.9.1 (cf. 10.9.2.6) has been confirmed again: The inflecting type is the type which seems to have most MPRs both in pre- and postlexical function.

10.9.4.1. The interflecting language type (as in the Semitic languages)[296] is nearest to the inflecting type (10.9.3). It has disadvantages such as: partially discontinuous roots as bases of MRs; multiple derivational (and inflectional) ablaut AMRs as in the Classical Arabic inflectional forms *kātab-a*, *ʾa-ktab-a* from *katab-a* 'he wrote', and in its derived nouns *kitb-at, kitāb*, *kātib, ma-ktub, kutub-iyy-at*; little morphological (bi)uniqueness.

But the advantages are: short words/word forms; vowels are the only syllabic nuclei; great indexicality due to optimal closeness of signatum (root or stem) and signans (ablaut) and clear MSRs (consonants signal roots, vowels ablaut to a large extent); great motivation of WF due to great uniqueness of root relations, e.g., 'write, writer, book, desk, letter', etc. are formed from the same Arabic root /katab/, such that the signatum of the concept 'write' is expressed in a more unique way in Arabic than in English. Even textual semantic coherence can be signaled by means of roots much better than in other language types (Aphek & Tabin 1981).

10.9.4.2. We do not follow the transfix analysis[207] of Semitic languages, which postulates a three (or four) consonant discontinuous root, e.g., Arabic /k-t-b/ 'write', and discontinuous vocalic transfixes, e.g., Ar. /a-a, ā-a, ∅-a/, etc. for the verb or /i-∅, i-a, i-ā/, etc. for the noun because there are minimal pairs between roots/words with root-inherent vowels which cannot be predicted by the transfix analyses, as in Class.Ar. *jadd* 'grandfather' ≠ *jidd* 'diligence, effort', *ḥasab-* 'to count' ≠ *ḥasib-* 'to believe' ≠ *ḥasub-* 'to be considered'. If one starts with an ambiguous root /ḥ-s-b/, then the supposed transfixes /a-a, a-i, a-u/ would all have the same meaning 'base form' without predicting the appropriate lexical differences. But even if there were no minimal pairs, the specific vowel of the first syllable of a given noun and of the second syllable of a given verb cannot be predicted by any morphological or semantic rules.

10.9.4.3. Rather we postulate, e.g., for Classical Arabic, MSRs, i.e., prelexical MRs (cf. 8.3.8.1) which constrain the occurrence of the three vowel phonemes /a, i, u/ in nominal vs. verbal roots (Kilani-Schoch & Dressler 1984). These are prelexical default rules which hold for the great majority of roots and to which most loanwords are adapted; e.g.:

nominal monomorphemic root → $C_i a C_j (V) C_k$

which produces the noun types *qat(a)l, qit(a)l, qut(a)l,* etc., if we take the traditional illustrative consonants *q, t, l;* or:

verbal stem → $C_i a C_j V C_k$ or $C_i a C_j C_k a C_l$

This last rule correctly predicts that is a verb is formed from the loaned word *telephone* or *nickel* it must be *talfan-a, nakkal-a.* In our analysis, lexical meaning is still concentrated in consonants, grammatical meaning in vowels (cf. Anttila 1975a, 10.8.5.2), but to a lesser degree.

Then there are prelexical MPRs which restrain the cooccurrence of consonants within the same root (cf. Greenberg 1950). Of course there also exist postlexical MPRs such as vowel truncation or shortening, prefix *t*-metathesis, but they are rarer than AMRs of ablaut, reduplication, consonant lengthening, etc.

10.9.4.4. Our basic assumption of the unity of pre- and postlexical rules (of the same type respectively)(cf. 10.9.1, 10.9.2.6, 10.9.3.7) has again been confirmed. The introflecting type is the one which has most MRs governing root shapes and this both prelexically and postlexically, and there are fewer effects due to MPRs both prelexically and postlexically.

10.9.5. As for the polysynthetic type, I must resign from giving even a short consistent description as far as morphonology is concerned for the following reasons: (a) This type is not very well described by Skalička (1979:56ff, 340); (b) Sapir (1921:142f, 1922:52ff) insists that polysynthetic or incorporating languages may be either fusional/inflecting or agglutinating (and thus may not be of a single morphonological type), which is confirmed by descriptions such as those by Seiler (1965, 1977:37ff), Swanton (1911), Langacker (1977:133ff), L. Foley (1980). (c) My own attempts to generalize from West Greenlandic Eskimo and Classical Nahuatl --the only two polysynthetic languages I have studied-- have been severely --and justly-- criticized by the Amerindianists with whom I have discussed morphology.

Thus although this type can well be described in terms of morphology, this does not seem to be true for morponology. Either this type does not favor any particular sort of morphonology (a relation consistent with Skalička's theory of typology) or some more radical changes in typological theory are necessary; but since a multidimensional typology on the lines of Sapir (1921) would open up typological theory to the objections by N. Smith (1981) (cf. 10.9.3.5), I refrain from it.

10.10. Aspects of morphonological system adequacy

10.10.0. With the exception of inflectional morphology (Wurzel 1984), models of system adequacy are in an embryonic stage. Therefore this section 10.10 is rather fragmentary. Starting with phonological (10.10.1) and morphological (10. 10.2) system adequacy, we will go into various aspects of morphonological system adequacy.

10.10.1.1. A central place in phonological system adequacy appertains to the notion 'basis of articulation', which goes back to phoneticians and early phonologists such as H. Sweet, W. Vietor, O. Jespersen, E. Sievers, J. Baudouin de Courtenay, N. Trubetzkoy, etc.[208]

The basis of articulation is defined as the 'sum of the typical movements/ position of the vocal organs' and it affects whole sets of processes. Particularly Delattre's (1965, 1969 and earlier) work shows why certain universal phonological process types are totally suppressed in contemporary French (e.g., palatalization of dentals, cf. 10.7.1.3). The basis of articulation may account also for language-specific articulatory places of allophones (Ladefoged 1980a) and thus even for apparent exceptions to universal phonological hierarchies (cf. 10.7.1.3), e.g., that Seneca vowels are raised in unstressed position instead of being lowered and centralized (Dean-John et al. 1984:50).

10.10.1.2. Moreover the basis of articulation can be made responsible for the language-specific properties of distinctive features as posited for a given language: Martinet (1957) and others (cf. Dressler 1967:2ff) criticized Jakobsonian distinctive features sharply for their universality and for violating the structuralist principle of describing a language system autonomously. More recently Ladefoged (1980a) has stressed this cross-linguistic phonetic variability, and S. Anderson (1981:504ff) has used these facts as arguments against the

extra-linguistic basis of Natural Phonology (10.5). However this critique fails
to recognize (a) the dialectical interplay between universality and individuali-
ty necessary for theoretical linguistics (cf. our model in 10.6) and (b) the
fact that language-specific implementations of universal distinctive features
are not completely chaotic or idiosyncratic, but are subject to the unifying
principle of the language-specific basis of articulation.

10.10.1.3. At any rate, certain distinctive features may not be used or only
partially in a given language, e.g., Seneca has no labial or labialized consonants (Dean-John et al. 1984), Duwamish has no nasals, neither among consonants
nor vowels (Ranson 1945). This is clearly connected with the basis of articulation. I.e., this is another instance of a latent universal (viz. distinctive
feature) being suppressed in a language; this does not vitiate the universality
of, e.g., nasality or labiality.

    Other languages exclude certain combinations of distinctive feature combi-
nations. E.g., both German and Breton exclude the inter/addental non-strident
fricatives /θ, ð/ both from the phonemic inventory and from allophones; therefore lenition PRs may turn, in casual/rapid speech, /b/ into [β] and /g/ into
[γ, j], but not /d/ into *[ð] (cf. Dressler & Wodak 1982, Dressler 1972, 1975b,
Dressler & Hufgard 1980). These absolute phonetic constraints are connected
with the basis of articulation and therefore can never be violated in non-patho-
logical speech (cf. 8.1.9.2).

    Formally such exclusions are represented by prelexical paradigmatic PRs
(segment-structure rules, 8) which are not contradicted by antagonistic postlexical PRs (cf. 10.10.1.4).

10.10.1.4. A related aspect of phonological system adequacy are the notions of
phonemic and allophonic space (Moulton 1960, cf. Dressler 1977a:15ff, Tonelli
1981) definable in terms of Natural Phonology as clashes between prelexical PRs
(segment-structure rules) and antagonistic postlexical PRs (cf. 10.10.1).

    E.g., in German the phonemic space of vowels is restricted by prelexical
PRs to the peripheral vowel phonemes /i, iː, e, eː, (εː), a, aː, o, oː, u, uː,
y, yː, ø, øː/, but postlexical laxing and centralizing PRs produce less peripheral sounds such as [ɪ, ε, ɑ, ɔ, ʊ, ɣ, œ, ə, ɐ], i.e., the allophonic vowel
space is filled, e.g., with all conceivable transitions between [i, ɪ] and [ə],

but *[ɯ, ɤ] are excluded (in terms of 10.10.1.3). On the contrary, in West Caucasian languages, all vowel phonemes are central (e.g., /ə, a/), but more peripheral allophones exist than in German (including [ɯ, ɤ], cf. Job 1977, Paris
1974).

     Or Rotokas (Firchow & Firchow 1969), Wichita (Rood 1971), Hidatsa (Rood
1971:R 22 note 11), Puget Sound Salish (Ruhlen 1974:259), Snoqualmie (Swadesh
1952:238), Quileute (Andrade 1933:151, 156) have no nasal phonemes, but nasal
consonantal allophones. West Greenlandic Eskimo (Rischel 1974:23ff, 37) and
South Bigouden Breton (Dressler & Hufgard 1980, Dressler 1977a:15f) have only
one low vowel phoneme, West Greenlandic front /a/ (in addition to /i, u/) and
Breton back /ɑ/ (in addition to /i, e, ɛ, o, u/); Breton has more allophonic
space in front of its low vowel phoneme than 'behind' it, West Greenlandic the
other way around. Both languages have a postlexical PR of allophonic lowering
of vowels before uvular consonants. And according to allophonic space available, this PR backs West Greenlandic front /a/, but fronts South Bigouden /ɑ/.

10.10.1.5. Another aspect of phonological system adequacy are conspiracies.[209]
E.g., in Old Church Slavonic pre- and postlexical PRs conspire to achieve open
syllables and a preponderance of $c_i v$ syllables, e.g., vn → ṽ, monophthongization, metathesis *tort → trot*, consonant deletion in syllable coda, insertion of
the glides *j, v* before syllable-initial vowel (Shevelov 1969:203, 251, 427), cf.
the alternations[210] *mlě$ti* 'to grind', 1.sg.pres. *me$ljǫ; za$pę$ti* 'to set
snares', 1.sg.pres. *za$pǐ$no*, 1.sg.aor. *za$pę$sŭ; ljubiti* 'to love', 1.sg.
pres. *lju$bljǫ; be$zŭ* 'without', *be$z na$ro$da* 'without the people'. The grad-
ual diachronic breakdown of this conspiracy coincided both with new sound change
and with morphologization of some of the PRs involved.

10.10.1.6. The breakdown of the Old Church Slavonic syllable conspiracy corroborates an assumption that we must deduce from basic tenets of Natural Phonology:
Only PRs, but not MPRs, belong to phonology, therefore phonological system adequacy comprises only PRs but not MPRs. Conspiracies are a type of phonological
system adequacy. Therefore MPRs are not supposed to take part in conspiracies;
if they do, then their role is not effective, i.e., they do not express constraints on pronounceability (e.g., in Old Church Slavonic loanwords), but their
role is only vestigial (because MPRs originate from earlier PRs). In other
words, if a PR changes into a MPR, this is a symptom of the decay/elimination of

a conspiracy. An abstract phonology which does not differentiate PRs and MPRs (or corresponding entities) cannot express this generalization. In similar ways we can deduce that the basis of articulation does not constrain MPRs (10.10.1. 1ff); that a language-specific system of distinctive features (10.10.1.2f) does not have to take account of MPRs; that MPRs are not constrained by allophonic space (10.10.1.4) and by phonemic space only insofar as both their inputs and outputs are phonemes of the respective language and as their structural changes (distance between input and output) are usually not as great as of AMRs (5.2f, 5.21.5, 5.21.6.1).

10.10.1.7. Segmental phonology is typologically constrained by prosodic phonology (cf. 3.1, Donegan & Stampe 1983). If prosody-constrained PRs morphologize MPRs, then these MPRs indirectly show the effect of a contemporary or diachronically antecedent prosodic system.

10.10.1.8. Frequency distributions of phonemes (and at least of extrinsic allophones!) produce a 'normality' effect which appertains to system adequacy. Unfortunately the more advanced research in quantitative phonology[211] and in process phonology is done in mutual isolation (and disrespect, all too often). For MPRs, cf. 10.10.2.1ff.

10.10.2.0. As for morphological system adequacy, we may start with recalling that German morphologists of the 19th century created the notion of *Systemzwang* 'system coercion'; the translation *system pressure* correctly diminishes the connotation of necessity to that of probability. Neogrammarians used this notion for analogical 'pressures' within morphological paradigms.

The notion of *Systemangemessenheit* 'system adequacy, system congruity' or 'system-dependent naturalness' created by Wurzel (1984, cf. in Dressler, Mayerthaler, Panagl & Wurzel, forthc.) makes this and other more or less implicit traditional ideas explicit and fits them into a novel and coherent model of inflectional morphology. Due to the ample and precise description of the model in Wurzel (1984), I can recapitulate it very briefly and concentrate instead on the consequences for MPRs.

10.10.2.1. The inflectional morphology of a language can be characterized by a set of system-defining structural properties, some of which are clearly of a ty-

pological nature such as absence or presence of multifunctionality, of distinct
paradigm classes (cf. 10.9.2.1f, 10.9.3.1); others define the language-specific
selection and specification of universal morphological categories (number, case,
tense, aspect, mood, gender, etc.). System-defining structural are either exceptionless or defaults which tend to reduce the exceptions.

One system-defining property is highly relevant for morphonology, viz.
whether base form inflection (typical for agglutinating languages, 10.9.2, and
weakly inflecting languages, 10.9.3.2) or stem inflection (typical for strongly
inflecting languages, 10.9.3) is predominant. E.g., in Latin base form declension is rare, to be found only within the third declension class, e.g., *sōl*
'sun', acc. *sōl-em*, but even there we have subclasses such as nom.sg. *rēx*
(/rēg-s/) 'king', gen. *rēg-is*, cf. class I *rosa* 'rose', gen.,dat.sg, nom.pl.
rosae, abl.sg. *rosā*, dat.,abl.pl. *rosis*, class II *locus* 'place', gen.sg., nom.
pl. *locī*, dat., abl.sg. *locō*, class IV *lacus* 'lake', gen.sg., nom.,acc.pl. *lacūs*,
dat. *lacuī*, class V *spēs* 'hope', gen., dat. *speī*, abl. *spē*.

Stem inflection favors the application of phonemic PRs (e.g., in /rēg-s/ →
[rēks] 'king', /salut-s/ → [salus] 'health') and of MPRs (e.g., in dat.pl.
/rēg-bus/ → [rēgibus], /laku-bus/ → [lakibus]). And the AMRs in classes I, II,
IV, V produce still more opacity. Although stem inflection is more morphotactically opaque than word base inflection, it is system adequate and 'normal' (most
frequent in type and token) in Latin. In post-Classical Latin, word base declension paradigms were eliminated in favor of stem declension paradigms before
the whole declensional system changed to the Romance systems of the weakly inflecting type. But before this typological change Latin stem inflection and the
morphotactic opacity involved did not decrease, but rather it increased from the
time of reconstructed Proto-Indo-European onwards.

This is an instance of Wurzel's (1984) principle that system-defining
structural properties --such as preponderant stem inflection-- have a system-
stabilizing effect.

10.10.2.2. In 10.8.1, 10.8.6 we have seen that MPRs diminish morphotactic
transparency, but may increase morphological indexicality. This results in a
--synchronic and diachronic-- conflict between parameters of universal naturalness. This conflict may be resolved in favor of either of these two parameters.
From 10.9.2f we can deduce that typological adequacy favors more morphotactic

transparency in languages approaching the agglutinating type, but more indexicality in languages approaching the inflecting type. However this is still only
a general, probabilistic prediction that holds for sets of conflicts in sets of
languages. If we want to make still more precise predictions for a specific
conflict, we have to look at language-specific system adequacy, such as system-
defining structural properties (10.10.2.1).

Let us take the instance of Latin dat., abl.pl. *lacibus*. This case form is
less transparent than the archaic variant *lacu-bus* (e.g., in the archaizing Latin style of Varro); both variants are equally long (parameter of shape of
signs, 10.8.5) and indexical. Why then has *lacubus* not eliminated the variant
lacibus? Note that unstressed *-ub-* was perfectly pronounceable, e.g., in *incu-
bus* 'nightmare', *incubō* 'I inhabit'. In an inflecting language morphotactic
transparency is not a top priority (10.6.3, 10.8.3), therefore in stem inflection, surface shapes of morphemes may differ from underlying shapes and exert
analogical pressure (cf. 10.8.3.4.4). Now *lacus* may be perceived as either
lacu-s (i.e., *u*-stem plus nom. /s/) or *lac-us* (root plus surface ending); both
analyses are psychologically real, the second example in view of the fact that
in post-Classical Latin and Proto-Romance class IV nouns were gradually transferred to class II nouns (e.g., dat., abl.pl. *lac-is* like *loc-is;* Ital. *lag-o* <
Lat. *lac-us* like *luog-o* < *loc-us;* pl. *lagh-i*, *luogh-i,* cf. 6.2.4). The surface
ending of dat.pl. is clarely *-bus* in the small class V such as *rēbus* from *rēs*
'thing', but there is *-ibus* in the *i*-stems such as *navibus* from *navis* 'ship'
(underlying *navi-bus*) and in the frequent consonant-stem nouns such as *rēgibus*
(10.10.2.1). Therefore *-ibus* is the normal ending outside of the *u*-class, and
this supports the operation of the minor rule (MPR) of vowel change, which in
Classical Latin operates in a limited set of morphological categories:

   $$v \rightarrow i \; / \; \underline{\quad}\; ^\$$$

cf. *faciō* 'I make', compounds *af-ficiō, ef-ficiō; caput* 'head', gen. *capit-is;*
carmen 'song', gen. *carmin-is,* etc.

10.10.2.3. Stem inflection often comes together with another morphotactically
opaque device: modification, i.e., either in addition to or in place of affixation a MPR or an AMR of suppletion diminishes morphotactic transparency. Again
modification is highly disfavored in agglutinating languages but permitted in
strongly inflecting languages; weakly inflecting languages are in between (cf.
10.9.3).

		no modification		modification
	Hungarian		reconstructed Pre-Latin	Classical Latin
nom.sg.	idő	'time'	*tempos	tempus
acc.sg.	idő-t	--	"	"
dat.sg.	idő-nek	--	*tempos-ei	tempor-ī
nom.pl.	idő-k	'time-s'	*tempos-a	tempor-a
derived adj.	idő-szerű	'time-ly'	?	tempes-tivus[212] tempor-ālis

Or take Latin *iter* 'way' with suppletion, dat. *itiner-ī*, pl. *itiner-a* (Pre-Latin **itin-ei*, **iter-a*) but without modification: *iter-ī*, *iter-a*. In Latin (and reconstructed Pre-Latin), modification is normal in stem inflection and frequent even in word base inflection; in Hungarian and English, modification is rare, e.g., in English it occurs in strong verbs (suppletion in *go – went*, AMRs in *sing – sang – song*, etc., MPRs in *keep – kept*, etc.). In plural formation there are AMRs of umlaut and the recessive voicing MPR as in *roof – roove-s*, etc., whereas the PRs governing the [z] ∿ [s] ∿ [əz] alternation do not belong to modification because they are PRs.

If we enlarge Wurzel's model to word formation, we see that there too stem modification occurs in inflecting languages such as Latin (e.g., *tempestivus*, *temporālis*).

Inflectional morphology of the inflecting type is characterized by paradigms (10.9.3, 10.10.2.4). Various paradigms are signaled by modification since morphotactic transparency is not highly valued in the inflecting type. This implies the presence of MPRs and/or AMRs; in our Latin cases we have the MPR of rhotacism (5.2.5, 5.20.8.3.4, 5.20.8.3.6, 5.20.8.3.8, 5.20.8.4.2f) in *tempor-ī*, etc., various MPRs in vowel alternations *o* ∿ *e* ∿ *u*, add the declension classes I, II, IV, V (10.10.2.1). Thus modification is a system-defining structural property of Latin declension.

According to Wurzel (cf. 10.10.2.1), system-defining structural properties tend to be perpetuated in language change. E.g., Latin has lost most modification-signaled paradigms that can be reconstructed for Proto-Indo-European, e.g., the paradigm of the form *iter*, **itin-is*, **itin-i* was replaced by pure affixation *iter*, *iter-is*, *iter-ī*. But in addition to the small suppletive class of *iter*, *itiner-is* (with contamination of **itin-is* and *iter-is*) Latin introduced new in-

flectional paradigms with modification, such as *tempus, tempor-is,* where the PRs
of mid vowel raising before /s/, of high vowel lowering before /r/, and rhotacism have become MPRs and thus effected modification. Although affixation with
modification replacing pure affixation (**tempos, *tempos-is > tempus, tempor-is*)
implies a decrease of morphotactic transparency, i.e., a change towards less
naturalness on this parameter, such opaque paradigms proliferated and remained
productive as shown in loanword integration, e.g., AGk. *thúos* 'incense' was borrowed as *tūs* and integrated into the class of rhotacism (gen. *tūr-is,* etc.).
The relative diachronic stability of these MPRs is type consistent because Latin
remained a strongly inflecting language (10.9.3); also modification is system-
congruous and 'normal' (due to type and token frequency).

10.10.2.4. The preceding 10.10.2.3 also illustrates Wurzel's notion of paradigm
structure conditions which are constituted by implications: Syntactic and lexical categories (e.g., gender in Latin and most other Indo-European languages)
determine morphological paradigms which are indicated and diversified by morphonological and phonological properties, such as phonemes used in stem forms
(e.g., Latin *a-, o-, i-, u-, e-,* consonant-stems) and MPRs applied in these paradigms. If a paradigm is stable, then we may expect that the respective MPRs
will be stable as well and tend to be eliminated only together with the paradigms themselves. Latin rhotacism is a case in point: In declensions, the MPRs
of rhotacism were lost only where the respective morphological subclass would be
collapsed with an already existing *r*-stem class. E.g., *honōs* 'honor', acc.
honōr-em was replaced by *honor,* acc. *honōr-em,* because these words then inflected like *imperātor* 'commander, emperor', acc. *imperātōr-em.* On the other hand,
it was impossible to unite the subclass *flōs* 'flower', gen. *flōr-is, tūs* 'incense', gen. *tūr-is* with any existing *r*-class.

Similarly MPRs which cosignal many morphological categories and/or MRs are
more 'normal' than others which have a more limited distribution and therefore
they have more diachronic stability. E. Mayerthaler (1982) has shown this for
Surselvian vowel alternations (cf. 10.10.3.1f).

10.10.2.5. The interplay of universal, typological, and system-specific factors
can be easily illustrated with the shapes of inflectional endings of languages
of the inflecting language type: The connection between meaning and form, e.g.,
between a case meaning and a case form is symbolic (conventional) and thus lan-

guage-specific.

However the average length of case/number forms is subject to the typological principle that in the inflecting type grammatical morphemes should be considerably shorter than lexical morphemes (8.3.6, 10.8.5.4); this is a typological prelexical constraint on morpheme shapes. Then there is the universal diagrammatic preference for assigning longer shapes to morphosemantically more
marked categories (cf. 10.4.5.6 with references).

Andersen (1980:40) has shown this for Russian declension, W. Mayerthaler
(1981:65ff) for Romance declensions, Wurzel (1984) for German inflection. Let
us add for illustration a less diagrammatic instance, the declensional endings
of Lat. *rēx* [reːks] 'king':[213]

	nom.	acc.	gen.	dat.	abl.
sg.	/rēg-s/	rēg-em	rēg-is	rēg-i	rēg-e
pl.	rēg-es	rēg-es	rēg-um	rēg-(i)bus	rēg-(i)bus

Morphosemantically, SINGULAR is less marked than PLURAL, ACCUSATIVE and (mostly
adnominal) GENITIVE more marked than NOMINATIVE, DATIVE and ABLATIVE still more
marked than ACCUSATIVE (W. Mayerthaler 1981:51, 167f, 65ff, cf. 10.8.3.5.4).

These binary relations of morphosemantic markedness are diagrammatically
expressed in relative length of endings: (1) nom., dat., abl.pl. endings are
longer than the respective sg. endings; (2) acc., gen.sg. endings are longer
than the nom.sg. endings, (3) dat., abl.pl. endings are longer than the acc.pl.
endings: seven diagrammatic relations. Then we have three non-diagrammatic relations because no difference in length corresponds to difference in markedness:
(4) acc., gen.sg. = pl., (5) acc. = nom.pl. Finally we have two anti-diagrammatic relations because morphosemantic markedness corresponds to less length:
(6) dat., abl. vs. acc.sg.

As expected (10.3.18.2, 10.4.5.6, 10.8.3.5.4), diagrammaticity is most frequent, antidiagrammaticity least. These are prelexical constraints on MRs.

In *rēgibus*, a MPR of *i*-insertion applies to underlying /rēg+bus/ (10.10.2.
1f) and this is diagrammatic insofar as an MPR applies to a marked category (cf.
10.8.3.5.4); 'to the kings' is three-ways marked as PLURAL, NON-NOMINATIVE,
DATIVE/ABLATIVE. On the contrary, devoicing in /rēg-s/ → [reːks] is a PR and
thus irrelevant for this type of diagrammaticity (10.8.3.5.4).

Universal and language-specific principles mix in case syncretism (cf. Carstairs 1984). There is a universal probability that there is more syncretism in marked categories, e.g., in the plural as opposed to the singular, cf. nom. = acc. *rēg-es*, dat. = abl. *rēgi-bus*, but it is a specific Latin paradigm condition that nom. and acc., dat. and abl. undergo syncretism in many paradigms, both in sg. and pl. And the form of the endings themselves is language specific, partially constrained by language-specific MRs with regard to the phonemes and phoneme sequences used (8.3.7, 8.4.4).

10.10.3.1. So far we have seen that MPRs are excluded from phonological system adequacy (10.10.1), but are involved in morphological system adequacy (10.10.2). E. Mayerthaler (1982, especially p. 274) has tackled morphonological system adequacy itself, when she investigated vowel alternations in Surselvian Rhaeto-Romance, in synchrony and diachrony. System-adequate MPRs,[214] as predicted (5.18. 6ff, 10.7f), all go back to PRs of either unstressed vowel centralization as in [və'ñi:] 'to come' vs. ['veñ] 'comes', or unstressed vowel raising as in [num'na:] 'to name' vs. ['nʊm] 'name', or stressed vowel diphthongization as in [ɔrdi'na:] 'to order' vs. [ɔr'dəjnə] 'orders' or [kuš'ta:] 'to cost' vs. ['kuəštə] 'costs'.

10.10.3.2. According to E. Mayerthaler, phonological naturalness contributes to system adequacy of MPRs insofar as only those alternations have been preserved which change either non-labial to non-labial or labial to labial vowels. We may add that the number of MPRs is restricted and that the structural changes which occur in the same phonological condition do not contradict each other.

Moreover it can be observed that also in other languages the subset of MPRs that have been preserved and the subset of MPRs that have been lost (or changed to AMRs) among a larger set of MPRs (or PRs) seem to be differentiated by greater vs. lesser phonological homogeneity.

E.g., in Polish (7), only anticipatory palatalizations have been preserved, the perseverative, 'third Slavic' palatalization has not (7.2.3). Of the preserved palatalizations, only surface palatalization of velars ((P 7): k → k', etc.) and dental palatalization (e.g., t → ć, etc.) have remained MPRs; both effect very similar structural changes; AF k → c and PF k → č, with more diverging structural changes, have become AMRs.

Or in Germanic languages which had i-umlaut and a-umlaut, i-umlaut has out-lived a-umlaut. Also u-umlaut was lost early in Old English and split into various AMRs in Icelandic (Orešnik 1977).

10.10.3.3. Two (universal) criteria of phonological naturalness seem to be particularly relevant for making a MPR system adequate:

(a) Process matching (5.2): The fewer universal phonological process types a MPR is matched to, the less likely it is to become an AMR (as expected from 5.2). Phonological homogeneity of MPRs (10.10.3.2) can be expressed by the identity of processes that several MPRs are matched to, such as palatalization for Polish, MPRs of fronting for Germanic umlaut MPRs.

(b) Phonological uniqueness (5.20): If a language has both MPRs of i-umlaut and a-umlaut, then an i-umlaut MPR might front /a/ to /e/ and an a-umlaut MPR might back /e/ to /a/, and this might complicate the task of recognizing derived vowels. Of course it depends on the language-specific phonemic inventory and the inputs/outputs of MPRs how much ambiguity might be brought about. However antagonistic rules are not restricted to PRs (4.3.3, 10.7.1) but may also occur within MPRs and AMRs. Thus Polish has rules of palatalization and depalatalization, of vowel deletion and vowel insertion (cf. Laskowski 1975, Gussmann 1978a). So we must conclude that this particular aspect of morphonological system adequacy is still very unclear.

10.10.4. Language-specific systems are highly conventional or in semiotic terms, symbolic (10.4.4.1).[215] Whereas universal morphological and phonological naturalness (10.7f) rely to a great extent on substantive principles of iconicity and indexicality, system adequacy partakes much more of symbolicity.

According to Peirce (1965.VII:356, §593), 'the essence of a symbol is formal, not material.' Thus we may assume that it is the level of system adequacy where formal principles of morphonology should hold like those investigated in Generative Phonology and discussed in 5.9, 5.12, 5.17, 5.20. E.g., if we think of Lexical Phonology (5.17.1.6) and its concern with levels, then Kiparsky's contention that the number of levels may be highly language specific sounds very probable.

10.10.5. Principles of language-specific system adequacy hold only as long as

the system is not disturbed from outside. Wurzel (1984) has shown in detail how
at the end of the period of Old High German, sound change neutralized the phonological distinctions characteristic for different inflectional paradigms of Old
High German. Therefore, in Middle High German, new paradigms with new system-
defining structural properties and with new paradigm structure conditions replaced the old Old High German ones. The same is true for the transition from
Classical Latin to the Romance languages or from Classical to Byzantine Greek.

Such drastic changes of morphological systems obviously determine the fate
of morphonology as well: MPRs may be lost or changed into AMRs such as German
umlaut which then became a system-defining structural property of subclasses of
plural formation and has since expanded (cf. 5.20.8.4.4).

Another type of change from outside is massive impact from another language. E.g., the influx of numerous Arabic and Persian words has led to morphologization of Turkish vowel harmony (cf. 8.3.3). The genesis of the Latinate
part of English vocabulary has introduced many MPRs and AMRs into English derivational morphology where they are apparently system-adequate. Greek dialects
of Cappodocia have been influenced so much by Turkish (cf. 5.13.6.3.2, Dressler
& Acson, forthc.) that they not only changed their inflectional morphology in
the direction of the agglutinating type, but also took over 'suffix vowel harmony' in verb morphology and largely eliminated MPRs of high vowel deletion.

The basic claim about system adequacy of MPRs is then that only MPRs which
have become system-defining structural properties are preserved (or changed into
AMRs which may then expand) within the respective system. Other MPRs are liable
to fade away.

Notes

1. Motto on the fresco portraying the 'Philosophische Facultät' (Faculty of Letters and Sciences), painted by Gregorio Guglielmi (who followed a conceptual program by Pietro Metastasio, Mozart's favorite libretto poet) in 1754 for the former building of the University of Vienna (now Austrian Academy of Sciences).

2. Stegmüller 1969a:451 after Hempel 1965, Popper 1959, cf. Bunge 1963:39.

3. G. 'Erklärbarkeitsbehauptung'; see for these concepts Stegmüller 1969a: 449ff, 1969b:108ff.

4. Note that such genetic explanation pertains to historiography and thus demands hermeneutic or exegetic types of explanation.

5. Cf. the discussion of its values in Matthews 1981.

6. Cf. Wunderlich 1976:3f, Stegmüller 1979a:443ff, cf. the survey on explanations in linguistics by Enkvist 1979. For a marxist view, see Yartseva 1977.

7. Cf. Zwicky 1975, Skousen 1975, Bresnan 1978, Manaster-Ramer 1984, Rhodes forthc.

8. Cf. Linell 1979b, 1980, Halle et al. 1978, 'Psychological reality of phonological descriptions', Symposium 2, PICPhSc 9,2:63-128, 9,3:195-216, Dik 1980, Rhodes forthc. Critically, Chomsky 1980:106ff.

9. On the issue of modularity, see 10.6.7.3f.

10. Cf., e.g., Seiler 1978b, Bartsch & Vennemann 1982.

11. Botha 1979a, 1979b, cf. Dressler 1979a, 1980b, 1981a, 1984a, Dressler & Wodak 1982.

12. This impression has been very forceful in my personal experience.

13. Which show nothing other than present inadequacies of the model, but these are expected in any explanatory sketch.

14. Cf. Vachek 1968, Trubetzkoy 1939, Jakobson 1962 (especially 1962.II:383ff), Waugh 1976, Sgall et al. 1969, Horálek 1983.

15. Functionalism itself is the topic of Mulder & Hervey 1980, Hervey 1982: 155ff, Ronneberger-Sibold 1980:37ff. Notice that the vast majority of contemporary linguists follow a functionalist model of one or another persuasion.

16. Cf. Seiler 1978b, 1978c, 1977, and the contributions by E. Holenstein, H. van den Boom, W. Huber, F. Stachowiak, H. Seiler in Seiler 1978a, the series akup, Linguistic Workshop, the review-article by C. Lehmann (1981), etc.

17. Cf. Beaugrande & Dressler 1981.III (e.g., §17, 27f), V:15, Givón 1979.

18. Cf. Lindblom 1983, J. Ohala 1983 and often, albeit more implicitly.

19. At least in the sense of Hjelmslev's and Coseriu's *norme* (10.6.5).

20. See Luhmann 1973, Habermas & Luhmann 1971, Schweizer 1979.

21. E.g., Lüdtke 1970 and contributions to Lüdtke 1980, cf. Woodfield 1976:183ff

22. Ungeheuer 1972, Watzlawick et al. 1967, Backhausen 1978.

23. Cf. Coseriu 1958, van Parijs 1981:105ff, Campbell & Ringen 1981.

24. Cf. King 1967, Weinreich, Labov & Herzog 1968:133f, 137, van Parijs 1981: 113ff.

25. Jespersen 1949, Greenberg 1963, cf. Dressler 1980b, Ronneberger-Sibold 1980:110ff, critical Skalička 1979:264ff.

26. Woodfield 1976:141ff, 152f, van Parijs 1981:216, Greenberg 1963:84, Ronne- berger-Sibold 1980:34, 131, 177ff, 227ff, cf. 10.3.18.4.

27. W. Mayerthaler 1982:237, van Parijs 1981:61ff, Ronneberger-Sibold 1980: 228ff, cf. earlier Jespersen 1949 §4.3: 'No language is perfect in every respect.'

28. Woodfield 1978, van Parijs 1981:71f, Campbell & Ringen 1981:64, cf. Green- berg 1963:78, Sanders 1977:162, Voorhoeve 1981, Murray 1982.

29. Wright 1976:34, 129ff, E. Leinfellner 1980:36, Pateman 1982:163f, cf. Four- quet 1963:641f, Greenberg 1963:77, Malkiel 1967, 1976. S. Anderson (1981: 507f) criticizes the inability to decide among alternative hypotheses, which may occur in any model, but must not be confused with multicausality.

30. See Wright 1976, Woodfield 1976, van Parijs 1981, Emmet 1958, Holenstein 1976:117ff, von Wright 1974, Stegmüller 1969a:457ff, Leinfellner 1980:62f, Ringen & Campbell 1981, Pateman 1982:167ff.

31. De dignitate et augmentis scientiarum (1623): Causarum finalium inquisitio sterilis est et, tamquam virgo Dei consecrata, nihil parit (I owe this ref- erence to E. Holenstein). Cf. 5.7.4.

32. Or: Dispositions are non-explanatory, cf. Wright 1976:57ff.

33. Cf. Woodfield 1976:142, 251. Then, certain functions may be irrelevant or of marginal interest, as are Jakobson's (1962.II:703) conative, emotive, phatic, and poetic functions for the study of morphonology.

34. This chapter goes more into details.

35. Cf. the physicalism in Drachman 1981a:101 with note 1, Drachman 1981b, and of Lass 1980a, 1981:257 note 2.

36. Lass 1980a, 1981, cf. the refutations by Pateman 1982.

37. Coseriu 1958, Sommerfelt 1962:78f, Itkonen 1981, van Parijs 1981, Matthews 1982:23, cf. Stegmüller 1979:103ff.

38. Woodfield 1976, Wright 1976, van Parijs 1981:55, Campbell & Ringen 1981, Lass 1981, Drachman 1981, cf. 10.5.3.

39. Woodfield 1976, Wright 1976, Campbell & Ringen 1981:57ff, 61f, Sanders 1977, van Parijs 1981:113, cf. 10.5.3.

40. In terms of either a social practice/institution/system or a biological system. Therefore grammatical elements may have functions, irrespective of whether grammar is defined as a social institution or as a 'mental organ' (Chomsky 1980) or as both (depending on the aspects of grammar referred to).

41. This specific subtype of indexicality is called 'cumulative' function by Trubetzkoy 1939, cf. Jakobson & Waugh 1979:146ff. On its implementation in agglutinating languages, cf. Lehtonen & Koponen 1977.

42. This is the default case, non-harmonizing suffixes and roots which do not trigger vowel harmony being well-defined classes of exceptions.

43. Cf. other cases of homonymy in Campbell & Ringen 1981 and Lass 1981.

44. A long recognized fact, cf. Komárek 1964, Anttila 1974:47f, Haslev 1972: 31ff, Korhonen 1969:303ff, Dressler 1977a:24, 46, 48ff.

45. The problem of quantifying redundancy is another, very difficult problem, cf. the critical survey by McCalla 1984.

46. Wright 1976:114, Holenstein 1982:100, cf. Jespersen 1949 §7.1.

48. Or in Linell's (1979a §9) way of putting it: If a speaker becomes aware (conscious) of allophonic variation, he can use it on purpose and it may serve an indexical function.

49. This is a case of 'Umfunktionalisierung' (refunctionalization).

50. Van Parijs (1981:51f, 106); called 'selective variation control' by Lass 1981:265f.

51. Cf. Wright (1976:46) on observable goal-dependence: 'proprietary judgments vary with goals in a repeatable and intersubjective way'; cf. Campbell & Ringen 1981:63f, cf. 10.3.12.

52. This is commonly derided as 'Hypostasierung' (E. *hypostasis*) in German science theory.

53. King 1969, Kiparsky 1982a, cf. Sommerstein 1977:240ff.

54. Cf. references in Dorian 1981, Dressler & Wodak 1977, Dressler 1981d.

55. Cf. Bickerton 1981, Highfield & Valdman 1981, Markey 1981, Mühlhäusler 1979, 1983, Muysken 1981, Valdman 1977a.

56. Markey 1981, cf. Alleyne 1980, Manessy 1977:135f, Le Page 1977:224.

57. On language typology, see 10.9.

58. Cf. Wright 1976:105ff, Woodfield 1976:137f, Drachman 1981a:109, 1981b §4.2, Lass 1981:270, Lindblom 1984 for its connection with functionalism.

59. Cf. Riedl 1981:28f (and passim on the evolution of cognition), Hörz & Wessel 1983:188ff, Lindblom 1984.

60. Wright 1976:10, 29, 39ff, 100ff, Woodfield 1976:132, Campbell & Ringen 1981:63.

61. Cf. Stegmüller 1969a:453ff, 1969b, 1979:577ff, W. Leinfellner 1965:69ff, E. Leinfellner 1980, cf. Ronneberger-Sibold 1980:131, 224ff, Ringen & Campbell 1981.

62. This is of course not a discovery procedure, but a procedure for testing functional hypotheses empirically; cf. Ringen & Campbell on testability of functionalism. On indeterminism in semiotics, cf. Peirce 1965.VI:15.

63. I must warn explicitly against the frequency fallacy, i.e., of equating either type or token frequency with naturalness. High frequency is just a consequence of naturalness, unless more important factors intervene.

64. For skeptical attitudes to crucial experiments, cf. Lakatos & Musgrave 1964:173ff. 'Devil's cases' are discussed in Dressler, in prep.

65. Cf. Coseriu 1958, Stegmüller 1969b, Itkonen 1981:82, cf. 10.2.1, 10.10.

66. And in this respect generative grammar is truly structuralist, but more restricted than functional structuralism.

67. For the massive debate, cf. de Mauro 1967, Jakobson 1975:9ff, Gamkrelidze 1981. On (functional) semiology in general, see Hervey 1982:9ff, 155ff.

68. Jakobson 1962, Jakobson & Waugh 1979, Waugh 1976, Eco 1977.

69. Slagle 1974, Anttila 1977, 1980, Langhoff 1979.

70. Cf. Jakobson 1975 and Eco 1984 for its genesis; cf. Eco 1976, Hawkes 1977, Sebeok 1977, 1979, Hervey 1982, Norrick 1981. For the arts, see also Shapiro 1976, Goodman 1968, Eco 1979, Eschbach & Rader 1981. Many congresses (e.g., Rauch & Carr 1980), journals, and publication series are devoted to semiotics.

71. Cf. Greenlee 1973, Hervey 1982, Shapiro 1983, who insists on the teleological nature of semiosis, cf., e.g., Peirce's (1965.I:91) definition of natural class as 'a class the existence of whose members is due to a common and peculiar common cause'.

72. Whereas communication theory shares the first function, it does not deal with the second one. Thus semiotics, which shares both, is a better metatheory for linguistics.

73. With strictly defined semiotic concepts, in order to avoid the danger of reducing relatively well-defined linguistic entities to ill-defined entities of another field.

74. Here we rely particularly on Peirce 1965 and Buchler 1955. The theory of Morris 1938, 1971, 1981 (with a very useful critical introduction by K.-O. Apel) is too behavioristic; cf. also Eschbach 1981, Hervey 1982:38ff, Greenlee 1973, Shapiro 1983.

75. More precisely, a sign may produce several interpretants in the same act of semiosis, cf. Deledalle 1979. On the interpretant mediating between sign and object, cf. Hervey 1982:27f, Shapiro 1983:45ff; however I cannot follow Shapiro's (1983:73ff) identification of interpretant with the form of the content of a sign and even with markedness.

76. Peirce 1965.VII:217, Jakobson 1962, Eco 1976, Braun 1981, Shapiro 1980, 1983:47ff.

77. Korhonen 1969, Dressler 1977a:52ff.

78. Cf. Andersen 1979, Shapiro 1983:13, 76f. Thus I disagree with reducing phonemes, etc., to the status of merely being features of signs, cf. Eco 1984:20f. Jakobson (1962.I:297) has acknowledged indexicality as the only semiotic value of allophones, cf. 10.7.11.

79. Buchler 1955:101f, cf. Hervey 1982:29f, 33f, Shapiro 1983:33ff.

80. Unless the child tries to imitate an adult sound it cannot properly perceptually discriminate and identify; the same may happen with foreign languages.

81. Since for Natural Phonology/Morphology we are primarily interested in the sign formats of allophones, phonemes, morphemes, and words, but not in larger signs (clauses, sentences, utterances), we have to deal only with rhematic signs of still another Peircean triad: rhematic sign, argument, dicent (Buchler 1955:115ff, Peirce 1965.II:134ff, 146ff).

82. Buchler 1955:104ff, Peirce 1965.I:195f, II:143ff, 156ff, Shapiro 1983:39ff,
     Jakobson 1962.II:335, 349ff.

83. Anttila 1975; for the exact definition of indices, cf. Pape 1980, Pelc
     1981, Hervey 1982:169ff. For semantics, cf. Norrick 1981:46ff, Jakobson &
     Waugh 1979:44, Jakobson 1962.II:335.

84. The attack on resemblance theory by Thomason (1980:420) is only partially
     correct and can damage only very naive application of semiotic concepts to
     linguistics; see Goodman 1968, Gadamer 1972:391 (cf. 1975:374ff), Dressler
     1981d: note 49, Brekle 1981, Braun 1981:163, 166, Shapiro 1983:43. The
     same holds for similar critiques by Lyons 1977.I:102f, Eco 1976, etc.

85. Unless they are genetically inherited, i.e., 'innate ideas' (Chomsky 1975,
     1980).

86. Werner & Kaplan 1967, Nöth 1976, Fodor 1979:175, 184ff, McNeill 1979:236ff.
     This does not imply any claim about a purely (or preponderantly) iconic
     character of putative proto-languages of primitive mankind.

87. But not 'direct' in the sense that communication would dispense with the
     interpreter and the interpretant.

88. Wissemann 1954, Moravcsik 1980, Pesot 1980:13ff, Voronin 1983. Evidently
     they too are partially symbolic (conventional).

89. One instance is so-called 'sound symbolism', e.g., [i] or palatalization
     (e.g., in Basque: Iverson & Oñederra 1983) indicating smallness metaphor-
     ically: Fischer-Jørgensen 1978, W. Mayerthaler 1981:99ff. For other
     types, cf. Jakobson 1962.II:355ff, Jakobson & Waugh 1979:176ff, Kim-Renaud
     1976, Ultan 1978b, Plank 1979, Plank & Plank 1979, Tarte & O'Boyle 1982.

90. Jakobson 1962.II:349ff, 707, Waugh 1976:47ff, Gamkrelidze 1974, 1981:339,
     Moravcsik 1980, McNeill 1980, Haiman 1980, 1983; R. Posner, J. Pesot, W.
     Mayerthaler, J. Ross in: Zeitschrift für Semiotik 2,1 (1980), Enkvist
     1981. For semantics, cf. Norrick 1981:28ff.

91. Cf. Dressler 1977a, 1980b, 1980d, 1982a, 1982c, W. Mayerthaler 1980a, 1981,
     Wurzel 1980, 1982.

92. Cf. 10.4.5.5, Jakobson 1962.I:280-310, Moravcsik 1977a, Pesot 1980, Dressler
     1980b, Shapiro 1983.

93. This holds also for the relation between phonological and phonetic features
     (cf. S. Anderson 1981:503).

94. Within Generative Phonology the form-substance separation is less strict,
     even with critics of Natural Phonology such as S. Anderson 1981, Drachman
     1981a, Lass 1980a, 1980c, 1981. A better parallel to the structuralist
     separation would be Foley 1977.

95. Shapiro's (1983:18) qualification of the 'asymmetric character' of marked-
     ness as being 'clearly rooted in biological and neurophysiological isomor-
     phisms' is not followed up later in his book.

96. E.g., p. 146 that Japanese desinences 'beginning in a vowel are unmarked'
     (without any argument at all), although the universal preference for con-
     sonantal (i.e., syllable-initial) onsets has been known for a long time
     (cf. 10.8.5.3).

97. E.g., Lindblom (1972), who asks for substance-based theories of phonology
     and assails the concept of 'primacy of linguistic form'.

98. 1975:51; cf. Klaus (1968) on optimal strategies. Wurzel (1981b:1367 §4) criticizes correctly the assumption of an absolute optimum, which --due to the conflictual nature of language-- is impossible.

99. E.g. for syntax, cf. the massive work by Bever (e.g., 1970) or Givón 1979, McNeill 1979:119ff, 224ff, 293, Clark & Clark 1977; for morphology, W. Mayerthaler 1981.

100. Peipmann 1976:237, Holenstein 1976:93, W. Mayerthaler 1980a:31.

101. Cf., e.g., Tauli (1958:25ff, 44ff) on the social-cultural environment, or Dressler & Wodak (1982) and Romaine (1984) on correlational sociolinguistics.

102. Cf. Backhausen 1978:6ff, 34, Watzlawick et al. 1967 §4, cf. Romaine 1984 for the sociolinguistic perspective.

103. A concept of Symbolic Interactionism (Goffman 1974); for text production, cf. Beaugrande & Dressler 1981.VI §29.

104. Cf. Bühler 1933/1982, W. Mayerthaler 1980a:22ff, 1981:11ff.

105. See Newell 1969, Newell & Simon 1972, cf. Kleinmuntz 1966, Norman & Rumelhardt 1975, Beaugrande & Dressler 1981.III §17. In addition the language learner acquires (partially on inherited bases) a collection of evaluations and a memory of relevant information.

106. Zipf 1949, 1965, cf. Coseriu 1958:183ff, Birkhan 1979, Ronneberger-Sibold 1980:244f, and in a semiotic vein Moravcsik 1980 §4.1.1f, Haiman 1983: 801f, 807.

107. Cf. 10.3.6, 10.3.13. Here as elsewhere in this book we deal only with objections which bear --directly or indirectly-- on morphonology.

108. In fact the only closed system would be a complete theory of the world. In all smaller systems we have to acknowledge Kurt Gödel's incompleteness theorem about everything having yet another external cause.

109. Better: 'X, Y, or Z', cf. 10.3.5.3.

110. For simplification I omit the problems of typological variation, cf. 10.9.

111. Thus his reproach against putative 'pure iconism' must be directed against someone else's hypotheses. And all I have written about indexicality completely agrees with his remark 'Nothing compels us to confine "index" to Trubetzkoyan boundary signals, for allophones may even index deleted segments.'

112. S. Anderson's (1981:534f) speculations about understanding how a hearer understands different dialects seem to presuppose the empirically unsupported view (fashionable in the sixties) that different dialects have identical abstract underlying forms or that grammars are pandialectal (along the lines of Bailey 1982).

113. It is precisely this neglect of 'external' evidence that renders S. Anderson's (1981:532ff) discussion of English vowel neutralization beside the point (see 5.20.3.5, 5.15.2).

114. The strawman is still more rediculous in Newmeyer 1983:6ff. But S. Anderson's (1981:495) equation of 'natural' with 'entirely reducible to phenomena ... outside the system itself' is a stark exaggeration itself; cf. 5. 7.4.

115. The contents of his 'irreducible component' (p. 536) of (universal) grammar have far too often been reduced by critics with counterexamples and by
remodelers of his own persuasion than would have been expected for a theory that aspires to the status of physics. E.g., S. Anderson's (1981:516)
formal constraint on compensatory lengthening (it 'does not arise unless a
language already has distinctively long vowels and/or diphthongs') has
been falsified for Onondaga by Karin E. Michelson, Harvard U., pers.comm.

116. As in generative or stratificational grammars. For varying concepts of
rules, cf. Gumb 1972, E. Itkonen 1974 §3ff, Beaugrande & Dressler 1981 §3.

117. As far as description and cross-linguistic comparison is concerned, they
can be compared with parametrization (incl. parameter fixing) in recent
versions of generative grammar, cf. W. Mayerthaler 1982:206ff.

118. Such universals are also the goal of generative research in Universal
Grammar.

119. This is an old idea in Natural Phonology/Morphology, the UNITYP program,
etc., and recently also highlighted in Generative Grammar, e.g., Chomsky
1982.

120. At least Semai (Diffloth 1972) seems to be a language which has no mor-
ph(on)ology beyond reduplication.

121. Adopted in Dressler, Mayerthaler, Panagl & Wurzel, forthc.

122. Cf. Sgall 1971, 1972, Szabó 1970, and similar approaches in Sapir 1921:
ch. 6, Coseriu 1978, Ronneberger-Sibold 1980:45ff, 137ff.

123. See 10.3, 10.5, cf. McNeill 1979:284ff, Ronneberger-Sibold 1980:34, 131,
228ff.

124. The very title of Hermann 1931, cf. earlier Paul 1880.

125. For other contradictions as causes of diachronic change in a marxist
framework, see Serebrennikov 1970, Girke & Jachnow 1974:99ff, 235ff,
Böhme 1979.

126. The G. verb *aufhaben* means both 'to suspend' and 'to retain/preserve in
it'.

127. Chomsky 1978, 1982:135ff, S. Anderson 1981:494, Fodor 1982, highlighted in
Newmeyer 1983, but not yet in Newmeyer 1980.

128. Therefore the term 'interactionism' would be more appropriate, cf. Beaugrande & Dressler 1981.III:4, III:18, Newmeyer 1983:3 note 2. Interactive
models are common in Artificial Intelligence, Cognitive Science, and Text-
Linguistics where, e.g., the exigencies of hearer vs. speaker are considered as much as in Natural Phonology.

129. Cf. Bos 1967, Sadock 1983.

130. Holenstein 1976:44, 92f, Peipmann 1976:237, Gadamer 1972:145, 390, Clark &
Clark 1977. On perceptual salience, cf. Lindblom, MacNeilage & Studdart-
Kennedy, forthc.

131. Cf. Lindblom 1983, Donegan & Stampe 1979b, Wurzel 1981b:1366 §3.2, Janson
1979:126.

132. Let us exclude, for the moment, the small class of processes which serve
both functions (4.6).

133. Cf. Dressler 1979:266 §7 against the criticisms by Dinnsen 1978, Dinnsen 1977, 1978; the remarks there hold also against Drachman 1977, cf. 1981: 104f, Lass 1981:262.

134. Cf. 10.7.3, Peirce 1965.VII:216, Goodman 1968:156, Oller 1971:27, Watt 1979:32. This is a performance condition constituitive for phonological universals according to Lindblom, MacNeilage & Studdert-Kennedy, forthc.

135. Oller 1971:27, since a signans should be perceptible (Bühler 1933/1982).

136. Goodman 1968:156, Peirce 1965.V:171, Jakobson 1962.II:336, cf. 10.7.1.1, 10.7.12.5.

137. Cf. Peirce 1965.VII:216f, Morris 1971:198, 369, Hawkes 1977:141, cf. Moravcsik 1977b:24, Waugh 1978. The more the phonetic output as signans is different from the phonological input as signatum, the more attention is diverted towards the sign shape.

138. Other confusions of rules (MPRs, AMRs) and processes (PRs) in the literature can be exemplified with S. Anderson's (1981:509ff) Icelandic rule /k/ → /c/, his Fula alternations (p. 500ff), his Breton mid-vowel rules (p. 521ff), Helberg's (1980) Faroese rules (thus truly only 'apparently natural'): 'unnatural' properties of rules do not refute, but confirm the predictions of Natural Phonology!

139. Papademetre 1982, Dressler & Acson, forthc.; cf. the rich material in Georgios 1962 and Kretschmer 1905.

140. Cf. 5.18, Gadamer 1972:391, Norrick 1981:32ff, Braun 1981:136ff.

141. Cf. 5.18, 10.4.5 on the relativity of the resemblance model. On the iconic nature of phoneme-allophone relations, see earlier Andersen 1966 (inaccessible to me, but abundantly cited by Shapiro 1969:9ff), cf. Haiman 1983:816.

143. Cf. Kaye & Morin 1978, Klausenburger 1979:68ff, Tranel 1981.

144. Cf. Jakobson's (1931) and Martinet's (1955) equidistance principle, which counts for allophonic space as well (Dressler 1977a:15f), not only for phonological space (Moulton 1960).

146. The autosegmental approach of assigning features of segments to different tiers (e.g., consonant tier, vowel tier, nasal tier) is thus not expected to work as well with MPRs as with PRs, cf. S. Anderson 1982:5.

147. Therefore we can predict that --outside of extremely casual/rapid speech-- multiple application of mutually feeding deletion processes is excluded, cf. on Lardil, Kenstowicz & Kisseberth 1977:111ff, 300ff.

148. E.g., Goldsmith 1976, Clements 1982, S. Anderson 1982:1ff, and other papers in Hulst & Smith 1982.

149. E.g., Natural Generative Phonology: Hooper 1976, Vennemann 1972c.

150. Gussmann 1978a:62, 1981, Rubach 1984, cf. 7.3.2.3.

151. Beaugrande & Dressler 1981.III §26; as an unmarked option in Chomsky 1982:94f; semiotically interpreted by Moravcsik (1980 §4.3.1) and Hyman (1983:782ff).

152. Cf. H. Schuchardt's and Vennemann's (1972b) notion of phonetic analogy.

153. This also produces better sign combinations, cf. 10.7.5.

154. This picture is quite different from the one that proponents of abstract neutralization (10.7.11.1) portray.

155. A further complication is the possible trace in the quantity of the preceding vowel (5.20.6).

156. This corresponds to overshoot of a process resulting in merger (Drachman 1981a:106).

157. Another example can be found in the history of Breton mid vowels (S. Anderson 1981:521ff).

158. W. Mayerthaler 1981, Wurzel 1984 (cf. 1982), Dressler, Mayerthaler, Panagl & Wurzel, forthc., Dressler, in prep. For specifics of my own approach, see Dressler 1980d, 1982a, 1982c, Dressler & Acson, forthc., Kilani-Schoch & Dressler, to appear [1984].

159. Cf. Serebrennikov's (1970) internal mechanism.

160. Cf. Lopatin 1975, Shapiro 1967, Malkiel 1958 etc., Dressler, to appear.

162. Cf. Pačesová 1978:451f and the material in Panagl 1977.

163. Dressler 1977c:62, 67; cf. the neologisms in Cvetkova & Teplickaja 1975. Cf. the Polish data in 7.6.12, 5.14.9.

164. 5.20 note 290. See Vennemann 1972b:183ff, Anttila 1972:100ff, 1974/1977, Andersen 1980:36ff, Itkonen 1981:81, called uniform symbolization by W. Mayerthaler 1981. Cf. Quaderni di Semantica 2/80 (1980) 288f devoted to a discussion of the 'One-Form One-Meaning Hypothesis'. Naturally all languages have a certain vagueness (cf. Carnap's tolerance principle), which must not be confounded with ambiguity.

165. Cf. Dressler 1977a:19f, 48f, 1977e:16, Hooper 1979c:113ff.

166. Seiler 1975, Ultan 1976, Stachowwiak 1978, Stephany 1980 (with material from language acquisition).

167. On --rather rare-- impacts on morphological change, cf. Vincent 1980, Morpurgo-Davies 1976, 1978a, 1978b. What our model explains is that in analogy, changes of, e.g., stem-suffix combinations, are predominantly governed by the whole shape (beyond the morpheme boundary) in derivational morphology, but by the parts (separated by a morpheme boundary) in inflectional morphology.

168. Cf. Haiman 1980, 1983:783ff, W. Mayerthaler's (1980a,1981) central concept of constructional iconicity, called isomorphism by C. Lehmann 1974.

168a. Assuming that abstract /y:/ underlies [ĭu], as K. Hill (pers.comm.) suggests; cf. surface [y] in many, e.g., Scottish, Southern States, varieties of English.

169. Kiparsky 1982a, Hulst & Kooij 1981, Lass 1980b, Nyman 1980 §3.1.

170. Cf. Wurzel 1981a §2.1, Plank 1981:155ff. For transparency of (diagrammatic) reduplications barring the application of MPRs, see Wilbur 1973; cf. Moravcsik 1978.

171. See W. Mayerthaler 1980b, Anttila 1974/1977, Kiparsky 1982.

172. Note the Old Armenian counterexample (5.10.4) to the claim that MPRs are ALWAYS more general in inflectional than in derivational morphology.

173. A nice Russian example for restructuring of AMRs accoring to what I call
the default principle is given in Andersen 1980:41f: Alternations t → č
have been changed to ones in k → č, because among AMRs these represent the
default case.

175. Instances such as 1.sg.pres. *ta-n-g-ō* 'I touch', perf. *te-tig-ī* are exceptional, here an infix (more marked than suffixes, cf. Dressler 1982c) is
attached to the stem, then a minor MR of reduplication and a MPR of vowel
weakening (unstressed v → i) apply to the perfect, cf. 10.8.3.5.1.

176. Shapiro (1980b:90, 1983:164) expresses this in a different semiotic framework.

177. Maybe 'awkwardness' in the sense of Dworkin (1975, 1977) played a role.

178. Dressler 1977e, cf. 5.13 note.

179. Cf. Dressler 1981c, Jakobson 1962.IV, Panagl 1977b.

180. E.g., Stankiewicz 1979:26, Plank 1981:72.

181. Chmura-Klekotowa 1972, Panagl 1977b, Pačesová 1978, Dressler 1977e:20f
(with a critique of J. Berko-Gleason, etc.), cf. 10.8.1.4.2.

182. Dressler 1977d, 1981d.

183. Jakobson 1962.II:352, Andersen 1980:4, 6.

184. Moravcsik 1980 §4.1.1, Andersen 1980:36ff.

185. 8.3.2.1, Anttila 1975b:11, cf. 10.9, 10.8.5.1.

186. The second hypothesis is more difficult to test (in Polish as in other
languages) because paradigm constraints and the correlation of suffix
length with inflectional vs. derivational morphology intervene.

187. Anttila 1975b, Andersen 1980:34ff, 40ff.

188. Cf. Hooper 1977c:110ff, 1976:86ff.

189. Cf. Peipmann 1976:50 for the importance of secondary features for perception.

190. Anttila 1975b:6, 13, cf. Kenstowicz & Kisseberth 1977:104, cf. Peipmann
1976:165, Braun 1981:150.

191. Cf. the critique by Carstairs (1980:1155, 1982:488, cf. 491) against
Dressler (1977a) and Wurzel (1980c) respectively.

192. Bach & Harms 1972, Hyman 1977 and most generative literature (including
Lexical Phonology), W. Mayerthaler 1977, Wurzel 1980c, 1981a. In structural phonematics the crucial step is phonemization of allophones.

193. Dressler 1977a, 1980b, Dressler & Acson, forthc., Hooper 1977c (and Natural Generative Phonology in general), Maslov 1979.

194. Which of course occur but are rather rare; even the instance acknowledged
in Dressler (1977a:51f: German [ŋ]-formation) does not concern the genesis
of a MPR but the change from an allophonic into a quasi-phonemic PR; in
all the examples of dephonologization in Wurzel (1980c, 1981a) a morphological factor is also involved.

195. 10.6.3. Skalička (1979) has stressed that languages represent 'various
solutions of the same task' (cf. Sgall 1971:83), but he has never attempt-
ed to give a systematic account of universal tasks. The same holds for

Ronneberger-Sibold (1980:45ff, 137ff), who has not inspected Skalička's many relevant contributions (since 1934). A lacuna in these approaches (and in my own as well) is the neglect of prosodic typology. Donegan & Stampe (1983) concentrate on agglutinating vs. inflecting languages.

196. Skalička (1979:23ff, 339) exaggerates the isolating properties of English and French and misassigns Vietnamese and Chinese to the polysynthetic type.

197. Cf. the other Altaic, most of the Uralic and Caucasian languages, Basque, Tokharian, many Indonesian and West African languages.

198. Cf. Skalička 1979:36ff, 258ff, 334ff, Szabó 1970, Korhonen 1980, cf. Sapir 1922:53. Indonesian languages (Alieva 1970), though, have more ingredients of the inflecting type.

199. E.g., Turkish $k \rightarrow \check{g}$ or $k \rightarrow \emptyset$, or gradation in Finnish (which has important inflecting/fusional ingredients).

200. Note that in certain Turkic languages suffixes with $i/\imath/\ddot{u}/u$ rhyme with one another, whereas umlauted and non-umlauted vowels never rhyme with one another, which confirms the difference in ease of processing.

201. W. Lehmann (1978:217) ties certain MPRs to his syntactic typology: object-verb languages tend to have vowel harmony, verb-object languages umlaut. I cannot control his empirical basis, but I doubt that these typological connections can find an explanatory basis, unless prosodic typology is used as in Donegan & Stampe 1983.

202. This seems to be the reason why many morphologists and phonologists admire the agglutinating type and thus often construct synchronic, abstract underlying agglutinative forms for very non-agglutinative surface forms or reconstruct agglutinative proto-forms for later inflecting languages.

203. Cf. Skalička 1979:45ff, 198ff, 337ff, Sgall 1972, cf. Sapir 1922:53.

204. Cf. the typological characterization of Spanish by Geckeler 1983. Note that Romance languages are much richer in conjugation than in declension.

205. Skalička 1979:245, 250, Szabó 1971:84, Dressler 1982a, 1982c, Geckeler 1983.

206. See Kuryłowicz 1961, 1972, Kilani-Schoch & Dressler 1984, Kilani, forthc., cf. Cohen 1970, Cantineau 1950, Greenberg 1950, Werner 1982, 1983, Skalička 1979:54ff, 340f.

207. Cantineau 1950, Cohen 1970, Mel'čuk 1976:273, 282, still accepted in Dressler 1982a, 1982c.

208. For more recent studies (with references), see Delattre 1965, 1969, Drachman 1973b, James 1977, Lekomtseva 1983, Dean-John et al. 1984.

209. Kenstowicz & Kisseberth 1977:143ff, Kiparsky 1982a:106ff, Linell 1979a:121ff.

210. ⟨ě⟩ is a long front vowel, ⟨ę, ǫ⟩ are nasal vowels, ⟨ĭ, ŭ⟩ are ultra-short high vowels.

211. Altmann 1968, 1971, Altmann & Lehfeldt 1980, Krupa 1967, Job 1977.

212. Historically the chain of suffixation was *tempus* → *tempes-tas* → *tempes-(ta)t-ivus* (with haplology), but synchronically --for semantic and morphotactic reasons-- *tempes-tivus* refers directly to *tempus*.

213. The vocative has been omitted because there is additional but different

motivation for shortness, cf. W. Mayerthaler 1981:31ff, 97f, Dressler 1982c: §6.5.4.

214. Owing to the material at my disposal I cannot exclude the possibility of having mistaken some AMRs for MPRs.

215. Peirce 1965.II:167: A symbol is 'a conventional sign or one depending upon habit (acquired or inborn).'

11. CONCLUSIONS

> Bei Erweiterung des Wissens macht sich
> von Zeit zu Zeit eine Umordnung nötig,
> sie geschieht meistens nach neueren
> Maximen, bleibt aber immer provisorisch.
>
> Johann Wolfgang von Goethe[1]

11.1. Starting with the introduction (0) through chapter 10, we have often cited the two early protagonists of morphonology Jan Baudouin de Courtenay and Nikolaj S. Trubetzkoy. What progress has been made since then? And where can we locate this book?

External signs of progress --well documented for hard sciences in Rescher (1978)-- are the great increase in the number of linguists investigating morphonology, of pertinent publications (although here too the number of first-rate results has risen much more slowly than of results in general), and the increase in complexity of results.

11.2. A more important tentative in evaluating progress is to apply a grid of criteria that has been found useful in evaluating progress in some other science. One such grid is the matrix used by the physicist M. Moravcsik (1977):[2]

11.2.1. Moravcsik's (1977) first criterion of scientific progress is 'a close interaction between speculation and explanation on the one hand, and observation and measurement on the other.'

Whereas the various structuralist schools innovated in both respects between the thirties and fifties, it has been afterwards rather that generativists, 'post-generativists', and psycholinguists have excelled in theorizing about morphonology and in enriching its contents. Therefore discussions in this book necessarily reflect which schools have contributed most during the last twenty years.

A danger inherent in morphonological speculation is excessive abstractness in constructing inputs ('morphophonemes' in certain structural grammars, 'systematic phonemes' in Generative Phonology) of MPRs or morphonological alternations

Structural morphonology/morphophonemics had too few inbuilt mechanisms for inhibiting excessive abstractness (cf. 0.5.2). Generative Phonology had more, at least since Postal (1968), and developed even more constraints afterwards. Other and later process models are even more concrete, i.e., they allow only concrete operations (Laskowski 1981:19f), and in our model concreteness can be deduced from higher-order, metatheoretical principles (cf. 10.7.11.1f). In this respect Lexical Phonology represents a step backwards, because it again allows greater abstractness (cf. 5.17.1.6.1).

11.2.2. Moravcsik's (1977) second criterion is the cumulative nature of research in phases of great progress, in contrast to a 'field of science ... characterized by many different approaches, speculations, conjectures, models, and experimental directions, unrelated to each other.' Here several comments are in order:

11.2.2.1. Within the same research paradigm, research often has been cumulative, notice, e.g., the progress made in describing Russian morphonology in a structuralist format from Trubetzkoy (1934) to Čurganova (1973). Or if we transcend the limits of schools, we see that the criteria used for distinguishing PRs and MPRs have been greatly increased since Stampe (1969) and early generative work on natural vs. crazy rules (cf. 0.4.2, 5). Or if we go back to the very beginnings of morphonology, the description of diachronic change from PRs to MPRs has become much richer from Baudouin de Courtenay (1895) to Klausenburger (1979), Roberge (1980), Wurzel (1980c, 1981a), etc. Or notice the progress from Dressler (1977a) to this book. The cumulative nature of progress may be most evident in psycholinguistic investigations and in other studies of substantive evidence (5, 9); and progress is continuously going on.

11.2.2.2. But progress is hampered by a consequence of what Zwicky (1973) has called 'the analytic leap from "some Xs are Ys" to "all Xs are Ys"' and its consequences. E.g., having observed that there is usually a biunique relation between a phoneme and its allophones, some American structuralists exaggerated this observation to the claim that there must always be such a biunique relation (see 5.10.2.1). When irrefutable counterexamples were found, the principle of biuniqueness was thrown out completely by Generative Phonology. However biuniqueness (in its broader, linguistic conception, 5.20.2.1) still remains the most frequent and --more importantly-- the most natural relation between inputs and outputs of rules. Progress is achieved only if the thesis (e.g., the claim of biuniqueness) and the antithesis (counterexamples) are followed by the synthesis (e.g., the acknowledgement of biuniqueness as the most natural state of affairs and the explanation of exceptions by intervening factors). We have seen many instances of the above-cited fallacy (5.20.7.1) and have deduced why certain properties of MPRs or PRs or AMRs are both typical and not exceptionless.

11.2.2.3. Moravcsik's (1977) warning against 'different approaches' etc. 'unrelated to each other' may be addressed to many linguists working in either structural morphology or areas of Generative Phonology that correspond to morphonology in so far as they do not take notice of progress made in other schools of thought. This neglect of other approaches and of their findings (with all the consequences of duplication, blindness to problems raised by others, loss of scientific standards already reached by others) are much less frequent in 'postgenerative, post-structural' approaches including Natural Phonology/Morphology and in psycholinguistic investigations, and this is to their credit.

11.2.3. Moravcsik's (1977) third criterion stresses 'new conceptual idea[s]' and 'novel ways of looking at a problem'. This innovative spirit has been typical for approaches to morphonology, while they have been comparatively new, cf. 11.2.1.

11.2.4. Moravcsik's (1977) fourth criterion is the degree of mathematization. This laudable criterion is fulfilled only Quantitative Phonology when studying MSRs (cf. 8.3.10) and by some psycholinguistic investigations (e.g., MacWhinney 1978). Vennemann's (cf. 1981) recent endeavors towards strict formulation refer to a theory of phonology, not of morphology.

11.2.5. Moravcsik's (1977) fifth criterion connects progress with 'an increasingly broader unification of our view of nature.' Thus progress in morphonology is intimately connected with progress on the more basic levels of morphology and phonology. Trubetzkoy's morphonology was seriously encumbered by the lack of a proper theory of morphology. Also Generative Phonology has studied the area of morphonology for a long time without possessing a theory of morphology approximating the elaboration of its theory of phonology. Adherents of Natural Phonology and Natural Generative Phonology had no theory of morphology either, but most of them shied away from investigating morphonology.

The purpose of our chapter 10 was to combine theories of Natural Phonology and Natural Morphology both with one another and with a semiotic metatheory. Since this metatheory is claimed to hold for all acts of semiosis, far beyond linguistic, verbal semiosis, our approach is much more ambitious than the above cited ones in aiming at 'an increasingly broader unification of our view of [the] nature' of man. The dynamics of deriving morphonology from semiotic meta-theory and from theories of Natural Phonology and Natural Morphology makes mor-phonology a specimen of how a program of dynamic derivation may be worked out in linguistics.

11.3. Moravcsik's (1977) other criteria are hardly relevant for morphonology. Instead I want to add another criterion of progress: the judicious use of the theory of science.

11.3.1. Structural morphonology of the Prague School approach was hampered by the fact that its functional communication theory (of the Bühler 1933/1982 type) did not provide a function for morphonology because morphonological alternations are redundant and not relevant/pertinent from the structural-communicative point of view (cf. Komárek 1964, Kloster-Jensen 1975, cf. 10.3.9, 11.5.3), and the-ories of extra-linguistic communication used provided an excessively vague con-ception of redundancy (cf. McCalla 1984).

11.3.2. The emergence of Generative Grammar resulted in a deeper involvement of linguists in the theory of science and of philosophers in linguistics, often in a critical way, as in Botha (e.g., 1979a, 1979b). As for the choice of a theory of science, different approaches to morphonology or to its founding disciplines morphology and phonology were able to resort to different models of science the-ory, e.g., note the radical rejection of conventionalist theory (as taken for granted in Generative Grammar) by D. Stampe (see Donegan & Stampe 1979b:127f). And the application of different theories of science promoted hetergeneity of approaches. Notice, with regard to this book, the growing dissention between R. Lass and the present writer, which can be traced back, at least partially, to Lass's (1980a-c, 1981) increasingly rigorous adherence to hypothetic-nomological standards of explanation (cf. 10.3.6, 10.3.13, 10.3.15f, 10.7.1.4) and my grow-

ing involvement (Dressler 1977a, 1977e vs. 1980b, 1981d, 1982a, 1982c) in semiotics and functionalism (cf. 10.3f).

11.3.3.   Being aware of the frequent mistrust of functionalism and/or semiotics,
I have divided this book into a greater descriptive part devoid of functionalism
and semiotics as much as possible (1-9) and into a specific chapter (10) on a
functionally and semiotically based explanation of morphonology. Moreover, most
of the results in the descriptive part can stand without any semiotic of functional underpinnings, and their bases can be translated into other theories;
notice also our deductions in 10.3.17, 10.3.18.2f, 10.7.10, 10.9.3.6. On theoretical pluralism, cf. 11.6.

      Besides, as expressed in the subtitle 'the dynamics of derivation', the im-
plications of our explanatory approach in chapter 10 go far beyone morphonology.

11.4.1.   I can agree with Martinet's (1965) rejection of morphonology and its
inclusion into morphology to the extent that:

      (1) one should not assume a basic level/component of morphonology, on a par
with morphology, phonology, etc., and that:

      (2) phonology is less important for morphonology than is morphology.

However a Martinet-type approach cannot account for the gradual synchronic and
diachronic transition between PRs and MPRs.

11.4.2.   The conclusions of the descriptive chapter (5.21) have corroborated our
assumption about morphonology being an intersection of morphology and phonology.

      More specifically, our scrutiny of criteria (5) that define MPRs (morphono-
logical rules) and distinguish them from PRs (phonological rules) and AMRs (allomorphic morphological rules) has dramatically confirmed our assumption: There
is no single property that unambiguously defines a MPR and sets it apart from
both PRs and AMRs simultaneously --unless one constructs composite criteria that
contain several properties at a time. And even such combinations of properties
define prototypical MPRs only, whereas there exist at least a few fuzzy cases of
rules that are hard to classify --at least at the present level of empirical
studies and data available. Still our criteria should prevent misclassifica-
tions of, e.g., MPRs as PRs and vice versa as we have been able to identify in
publications even of experts such as S. Anderson (1981), Drachman (1981a:103),

Hellberg (1980), cf. 10.7.9.5.

11.4.3. The Italian and Polish case studies of chapters 6 and 7 have corroborated our findings of chapter 5 and demonstrated the advantages and disadvantages of our approach in contrast to other existing or conceivable accounts.
But I cannot conceal my conviction that it is the metatheoretical basis which
eventually will decide among rival accounts.

11.4.4. The next chapter (8) extended our differentiation of MPRs, PRs, and MRs
to MSRs (morpheme structure rules) as defining the underlying phonemic inventory
and phonotactics of morphemes. I hope this chapter has finally met Trubetzkoy's
(1931:161) engagement to study the phonological structure of morphemes by refin-
ing it according to our model into the study of morphonological structures of
morphemes.

     In our model, prelexical rules (as MSRs) and postlexical rules (as MPRs,
AMRs, PRs of transducing input phonemes into output phonemes/allophones) are
different only in distribution, degree, and function (prelexical vs. postlexical), but not in substance, i.e., they are either MPRs or PRs or MRs (in pre- or
postlexical function). This assumption has been corroborated by the observation
that both prelexical and postlexical MPRs behave in the same way in each different language type (see 10.9.1f, 10.9.2.3f, 10.9.2.6, 10.9.3.6.2, 10.9.4.4).

11.4.5. The chapter on child language acquisition (9) has illustrated out approach in a field of substantive evidence that has played a pivotal role in many
linguistic theories.

11.4.6. MPRs are morphologically AND phonologically conditioned at the same
time, morphological conditions being most important. Roberge (1980) tried to
differentiate the importance of conditions by contrasting the terms 'teleology'
and 'reference'; Flier (1979) distinguished 'condition' vs. 'constraint' vs.
'reference'. Since I found it difficult to operationalize these distinctions, I
preferred to evaluate the relative importance of morphological and phonological
conditions (10.7f).

11.4.7. Frequently we found connections between synchrony and diachrony. In
contradistinction to structural models,[3] our model allows synchronic and related

diachronic phenomena to be discussed together --without confusing synchronic and diachronic aspects.

11.5.1. Looking back to the explanatory chapter (10), we see morphonology as the interface of morphology and phonology or as the diachronic result of conflict (or cooperation) between principles of Natural Morphology and Natural Phonology. This dialectic relation of phonological and morphological principles has been found amenable to theoretic modeling with the help of a semiotic metatheory (10.4) and of functionalist science theory (10.3), which make all the difference from other (now often called 'modular') models. Hegelian and Marxian modeling of this dialectic relation is possible (Wurzel 1980d, 1981b), but not necessary (10.6.7). What is important to note (10.6.7.4) is that the components or 'modules' of phonology and morphology are discrete and mutually well-delimited, but the results of their interactions may differ gradually so that there are fuzzy boundaries between PRs and MPRs (and AMRs). On the other hand, the language learner can abductively shift quantitative into qualitative change (10.6.7.2) and thus shift a MPR-like PR into a prototypical MPR.

11.5.2. How are the conflicts between morphology and phonology resolved? A difficult questioned underlined by Fox (1980:318) in his review of Dressler (1977a). Since any determinism is out of the question, we must strive for probabilistic predictions. Our basic research strategy is to look first for the extra-linguistic bases (the 'natural' foundation so to say, cf. 10.5, 11.5.4) of an operation (MPR, PR, MR, etc.) and for the function(s) it is called to serve, then to look for semiotic categories which establish graded universal parameters, then reduce interactions and conceivable outcomes of conflicts and constraints on/preferences for outcomes (10.4, 10.7f). A theory of language types puts further constraints on/preferences for cooccurrence of MPRs with other grammatical elements (10.9), and principles of language adequacy (10.10) narrow down the language-specific choices available.

    This ambitious research program is hard to achieve all at once, therefore more specific research strategies (e.g., 10.3.18) are used for achieving immediate results, which so far have vouched for the feasibility and profitability of the whole program.

11.5.3. Whereas for all PRs (even phonemic PRs) phonological principles are

dominant, morphological principles are dominant for MPRs, and diachronic dominance shift (10.6.7.2) may happen only in the direction from PRs to MPRs, due to
semiotic priority of morphology over phonology (10.4.4.4, 10.7.11.4, 10.8.6.2).
This does not impeach the genesis of new PRs as intrinsic allophonic processes:
Since they are conditioned only by phonology and phonetics, and do not disturb
morphotactic transparency, no conflict arises between phonology and morphology.
Functionally accidental intrinsic allophonic PRs may receive specific phonological functions (cf. 10.3.11) and change into extrinsic allophonic PRs; these, in
turn, and especially phonemic PRs,[4] may receive morphological (non-dominant)
functions when they occur --accidentally-- in morphological alternations. After
dominance shift the non-dominant phonological function(s) of MPRs may become
vestigial (cf. 10.3.10), a change typically connected with the change from a MPR
into an AMR: Morphological conditioning becomes the default condition and tends
to be generalized to the exclusive condition (if we neglect lexical factors).
Another dominance shift applies to AMRs or turns MPRs into AMRs when instead of
(redundant) concomitants they become the exponents of a MR or morphological category (10.8.6.5).

MPRs are redundant (cf. 10.3.9, 11.3.1), and recent psycholinguistic experiments by MacWhinney & Pléh (forthc.) have proven the importance of these redundant cosignals of MRs and morphological categories for morpheme identification
and differentiation. But useful redundancy may become dead redundancy (cf. 10.
3.9): Reduction of morphological indexicality (cosignaling function) and ves-
tigiality of phonological function then contribute to rule loss.

In this vein we preferred to account for the genesis of MPRs from older PRs
in terms of morphologization rather than of dephonologization (cf. 10.8.6.9).
In Dressler (1977a:60, 1980b:71 §13) I reproduced a flow chart of morphologization: Although I still think these flow charts to be basically correct, the
number of factors found to be involved in morphologization has increased in the
meantime too much for an all-embracing flow chart to retain a diagrammatic value.

11.5.4. Natural Phonology has been criticized (cf. 10.5) for its reliance on
the presumed extra-linguistic bases of phonology. If consistent and justified,
this critique would have to be extended to Natural Morphology as well. The account of our research strategy in 11.5.2 and of the diachronic genesis of MPRs
in 11.5.3 has shown again the true dimension of the role that, in our approach,
the physiology of articulation and perception has as the extra-linguistic basis

of phonology, not to speak of morphonology.

Here two comments are in order:

(1) Natural Phonology/Morphology has not redimensioned the role of the extra-linguistic bases of rules except in the eyes of its critics who have misunderstood what has not been said with enough explicitness.

(2) The explicit enumeration of factors involved in 'naturalness' will hopefully result in replacing the often misunderstood word 'natural(ness)' with narrower and more precise terms and in relegating it to the status of a traditional, handy cover term.

11.6. Linguistics is a human science, but parts of it have close relations to biology and physics (morphonology very indirect ones only). Linguistics is also a social science, but at least partially also a formal science. This hetergeneity invites the use of diverse methodologies and theories of science, and a priori it is not clear where the usefulness of a given methodology or science theoretical model stops. Therefore methodological pluralism is more profitable in linguistics than in more homogeneous disciplines. This belief in methodological tolerance presupposes the consistent use of some methodology. I hope to have made explicit what mine is.

Notes

1. 'With the extension of knowledge, from time to time a rearrangement becomes necessary, it usually happens in accord with new maxims, but it always remains provisional.'

2. Being a physicist and a philosopher of physics, M. Moravcsik has used these criteria in several branches of both theoretical and applied physics. Moreover they have been accepted and successfully employed in policy decisions about foreign aid programs in physics for the Third World. Finally, being the brother of the philosopher Julius Moravcsik and of the linguist Edith Moravcsik (neither of whom could be accused of unwarrented 'physicalism'), he is convinced that at least some of his criteria can be profitably used in sciences radically different from physics (personal communication).

3. Cf. the radical critique in Bailey (1982), also against generative models.

4. On the change of extrinsic allophonic to phonemic PRs, cf. 10.7.11.5, 10.7.12.5.

BIBLIOGRAPHY

Periodicals, working papers, and monograph series are cited in this bibliography either by title or by abbreviation. The abbreviations are those found in the UNESCO supported *Bibliographie linguistique*.

Abaurre Gnerre, Maria B. M.
  1981   Processos fonológicos segmentais como índices de padrões prosódicos diversos nos estilos formal e casual do português do Brasil. Cadernos de Estudos Lingüísticos 3 (UniCamp).
Adams, Douglas R.
  1977   Inter-dialect rule borrowing: some cases from Greek. GL 17:141-51.
Akers, Glenn A.
  1981   Phonological variation in the Jamaican continuum. Ann Arbor: Karoma.
Akhmanova, Olga
  1971   Phonology, morphonology, morphology. The Hague: Mouton.
Alieva, N.
  1970   Indonesian sort of agglutinative morphological type. PICL 10,3:571-74.
Allen, Janice D., and Phyllis W. Hurd
  1972   Manambu phonemes. te reo 15:37-44.
Allen, Margaret R.
  1975   Vowel mutation and word stress in Welsh. Ling 6:181-200.
  1978   Morphological investigations. University of Connecticut dissertation.
  1980   Semantic and phonological consequences of boundaries: a morphological analysis of compounds. In Aronoff & Kean 1980:9-28.
Alleyne, Mervyn C.
  1980   Comparative Afro-American. Ann Arbor: Karoma.
Altenberg, Evelyn P., and Robert M. Vago
  1983   Theoretical implications of an error analysis of second language phonology production. Language Learning 33:427-47.
Altmann, Gabriel
  1968   Combinations of consonants in Indonesian morphemes of the CVCVC type. Mitteilungen des Instituts für Orientforschung 14:108-25.
  1971   Die morphologische Profilähnlichkeit. Ein Beitrag zur Typologie phonologischer Systeme der slawischen Sprachen. Phonetica 24:9-22.
Altmann, Gabriel, and Werner Lehfeldt
  1980   Einführung in die quantitative Phonologie. Bochum: Brockmeyer.
Altmann, Gabriel, and V. Raettig
  1973   Genus und Wortauslaut im Deutschen. Phonetica 26:297-303.
Andersen, Henning
  1966   Tenues and mediae in the Slavic languages. Harvard University dissertation (cited after Shapiro 1969).
  1969   A study in diachronic morphophonemics: Ukrainian prefixes. Lg 45:807-30.
  1972   Diphthongization. Lg 48:11-50.
  1973   Abductive and deductive change. Lg 49:567-95.
  1975   Variance and invariance in phonological typology. Phonologica 1972 (eds. W. Dressler & F. Mareš, Munich: Fink), 67-78.

1979a   Phonology as semiotic.   In A semiotic landscape (eds. S. Chatman et
         al., The Hague: Mouton), 377-81.
1979b   Russian conjugation: acquisition and evolutive change.   Paper presented
         at the 4th Int. Conf. Hist. Linguistics, Stanford.
1980   Morphological change: towards a typology.   In Fisiak 1980:1-50.
Anderson, John M.
1980   On the internal structure of phonological segments: evidence from
         English and its history.   FLH 1:185-212.
Anderson, John M., and Colin J. Ewen
1981   The representation of neutralization in universal phonology.   Phonolo-
         gica 1980:15-22.
Anderson, Stephen R.
1974   The organization of phonology.   New York: Academic Press.
1975   On the interaction of phonological rules of various types.   JL 11:39-62.
1976   Nasal consonants and the internal structure of segments.   Lg 52:326-44.
1981   Why phonology isn't 'natural'.   LInq 12:493-539.
1982a   Differences in rule types and their structural basis.   In Hulst & Smith
         1982.II:1-25.
1982b   Where's morphology?   LInq 13:571-612.
Anderson, Stephen R., and Wayles Browne
1973   On keeping exchange rules in Czech.   PIL 6:445-82.
Andrade, Manuel J.
1933   Quileute.   Handbook of American Indian languages III.   New York: Colum-
         bia Univ. Press:149-292.
Andriotis, N. P.
1948   To glōssikó idióma tōn Pharasōn.   Athens: Ikaros (Collections de l'In-
         stitut Français d'Athènes 8).
1974   La loi de prophylaxie dans le vocalisme néo-grec.   Salonika.
Angenot, Jean-Pierre
1981   Balanced ternarism in multinary phonology.   In Angenot et al. 1981:15-
         65.
Angenot, Jean-Pierre, and Mike Dillinger
1981   Against the binary classification of phonological rules.   In Angenot et
         al. 1981:66-81.
Angenot, Jean-Pierre, and Paulino Vandresen
1981   The Portuguese [r]'s revisited.   In Angenot et al. 1981:82-102.
Angenot, Jean-Pierre, et al., eds.
1981   Studies in pure Natural Phonology and related topics.   Universidade Fe-
         deral de Santa Catarina Working Papers in Linguistics 1. Florianópolis.
Anisfeld, Moshe
1969   Psychological evidence for an intermediate stage in a morphological
         derivation.   JVLVB 8:191-5.
Anshen, Frank, and Marc A. Aronoff
1981   Morphological productivity and phonological transparency. CJL 26:63-72.
Anttila, Raimo
1972   An introduction to historical and comparative linguistics.   New York:
         Macmillan.
1974/1977 Analogy.   University of Helsinki, Dress Rehersal 1. = The Hague:
         Mouton 1977.
1975a   Exception as regularity in phonology.   Phonologica 1972:91-9.
1975b   The indexical element in morphology.   Innsbrucker Beiträge zur Sprach-
         wissenschaft, Vorträge 12.
1977   Dynamic fields and linguistic structure -- a proposal for a gestalt
         linguistics.   Sprache 23:1-10.

1980   Language and the semiotics of perception.   In Rauch & Carr 1980.
Anwar, Mohamed S.
1974   Consonant devoicing at word boundary as assimilation.   Language Sci-
        ences 32:6-12.
Aphek, E., and Y. Tobin
1981   S. Y. Agnon: word systems and translation.   Text 1:269-77.
Araujó, Sumaia Sahade
1981   The velar softening rule.   In Angenot et al. 1981:107-12.
Aronoff, Marc A.
1976   Word formation in Generative Grammar.   Cambridge, MA: MIT Press.
1983   Potential words, actual words, productivity, and frequency.   PICL 13:
        163-71.
Aronoff, Marc A., and Mary-Louise Kean, eds.
1980   Juncture.   Saratoga: Anma Libri.
Aronoff, Marc A., and S. N. Sridhar
1983   Morphological levels in English and Kannaḍa or atarizing Reagan.
        Interplay 3-16.
Avanesov, R. I., et al., eds.
1979   Zvukovoj stroj jazyka.   Moscow: Nauka.
Bach, Emmon
1983   On the relationship between word-grammar and phrase-grammar.   Natural
        Language and Linguistic Theory 1.1:65-91.
Bach, Emmon, and Robert T. Harms
1972   How do languages get 'crazy rules'?   In Stockwell & Macauley 1972:1-21.
Back, Michael
1979   Sonorität und Lautwandel.   Festschrift for D. Szemerényi (ed. B. Bro-
        gyanyi, Amsterdam: Benjamins), 53-69.
Backhausen, Wilhelm J.
1978   Grundzüge eines Kommunikatormodells als ST-System.   Hamburg: Buske.
Bailey, Charles-Janes N.
1970   Towards specifying constraints on phonological metathesis. LInq 1:347-9.
1971   Vowel reduction and syllabic sonorants in English.   Hawaii WPL 3,2:35-
        104.
1973   Variation and linguistic theory.   Arlington, VA: Center for Applied
        Linguistics.
1978   Gradience in English syllabization and a revised concept of unmarked
        syllabization.   Bloomington: Indiana University Linguistics Club.
1982   On the ying and yang nature of language.   Ann Arbor: Karoma.
Baltaxe, Christiane
1978   Foundations of distinctive feature theory.   Baltimore: University Park
        Press.
Baker, William J., and Bruce L. Derwing
1982   Response coincidence analysis as evidence for language acquisition
        strategies.   Applied Psycholinguistics 3,3:193-222.
Barbour, J. S.
1982   Productive and non-productive morphology: the case of the German strong
        verbs.   JL 18:331-54.
Barinova, Galina A.
1971a   Redukcija glasnyh v razgovornoj reči.   In Raz vitie fonetiki sovremme-
        nogo russkogo jazyka.   Fonologičeskie podsistemy (eds. S. S. Vygotskij
        et al., Moscow: Nauka), 97-116.
1971b   Redukcija i vypadenie intervokal'nyh soglasnyh v razgovornoj reči.
        ibid.:117-27.

Barkai, Malachi
1975   On phonological representations, rules and opacity.   Lingua 37:363-76.
Bar-Lev, Zev
1978   The Hebrew morpheme.   Lingua 45:319-31.
Barnes, Mervin, and Helmut Esau
1973   Germanic strong verbs: a case of morphological rule extension?   Lingua
        31:1-34.
Bartsch, Renate, and Theo Vennemann
1983   Grundzüge der Sprachtheorie.   Tübingen: Niemeyer.
Basbøll, Hans
1972   Some conditioning factors for the pronunciation of short vowels in
        Danish.   ARIPUC 6:185-210.
1978   On the use of 'domains' in phonology.   PICL 12:763-6.
1979   Phonology.   PICPhS 9,1:103-32.
1981a   On the function of boundaries in phonological rules.   In Goyvaerts
        1981:245-69.
1981b   Metrical theory and the French foot.   Phonologica 1980:35-44.
1981c   Remarks on distinctive features and markedness in Generative Phonology.
        GLOW 1979:25-64.
1982   Nordic i-umlaut once more: a variational view.   FLH 2:59-85.
Bates, Elizabeth, and John Rankin
1979   Morphological development in Italian.   Journal of Child Language 6:29-
        52.
Batliner, Anton
1974   Überlegungen zur Assimilation im Altnordischen und dem Problem einer
        'Theorie der Natürlichen Regeln'.   Forschungsberichte, Inst.f.Phonetik
        und Komminikation, München 3:49-95.
Battle, J. H., and J. Schweitzer, eds.
1973   Mid-America Linguistics Conference Papers 7, 1972.   Stillwater: Oklaho-
        ma State University.
Baudouin de Courtenay, Jan
1895   Versuch einer Theorie phonetischer Alternationen. Ein Capitel aus der
        Psychophonetik.   Strasbourg: Trübner.   Cf. Stankiewicz 1972.
Baxter, Andrew R. W.
1974   Some aspects of naturalness in phonological theory with special refer-
        ence to Old English.   Lincoln College B. Litt. thesis.
Beaugrande, Robert Alain, and Wolfgang U. Dressler
1981   Introduction to text linguistics.   London: Longman = Einführung in die
        Textlinguistik.   Tübingen: Niemeyer.
Belgeri, Luigi
1929   Les affriquées en italien et dans les autres principales langues euro-
        péennes.   Université de Grenoble.
Bell, Alan, and Joan Hooper, eds.
1979   Syllables and segments.   Amsterdam: North Holland.
Benediktsson, Hreinn
1982   Nordic umlaut and breaking: thirty years of research.   Nordic Journal
        of Linguistics 5:1-60.
Benhallam, Abdu
1979   MIT phonology and Arabic.   PCLS 15:30-41.
Benton, R.
1971   Phonotactics of Pangasinan.   WPL (Hawaii) 3,9.
Benveniste, Emile
1935   Origines de la formation des noms en indo-européen.   Paris: Maisonneuve.
1939   Répartition des consonnes et phonologie du mot.   TCLP 8:27-35.

1946   Structure des relations de personne dans le verb.   BSL 43:1-12.
Bergin, Osborn
1921   The principles of alliteration.   Ériu 9:82-4.
Berman, Ruth A.
1981a   Regularity vs. anomaly: the acquisition of Hebrew inflectional morphol-
         ogy. Journal of Child Language 8:265-82.
1981b   Language development and language knowledge: evidence from the acqui-
         sition of Hebrew morphophonology.   ibid. 609-26.
Bertinetto, Pier Marco
1977   'Syllabic blood' ovvero l'italiano come lingua ad isocronismo sillabio.
         Studi di grammatica italiana 6:69-96.
1979   Aspetti prosodici della lingua italiana.   Padova: CLESP editrice.
Bethyn, Christina Y.
1978   Morphology in phonology: the case of syllable lengthening in Polish and
         Slovak. Glossa 13:251-62.
Bever, Thomas
1970   The cognitive basis for linguistic structures.   In Cognition and the
         development of language (ed. J. R. Hayes). New York: Wiley, 179-362.
Bhat, D. N. S.
1974   The phonology of liquid consonants.   WPLU 16:73-104.
1975   Two studies on nasalization.   Nasálfest 27-48.
1978   A general study of palatalization.   In Greenberg 1978.II:47-92.
Bhatia, Tej K.
1976   On the predictive role of the recent theories of aspiration.   Phonetica
         33:62-74.
Bhatia, Tej K., and Michael Kenstowicz
1972   Nasalization in Hindi: a reconsideration.   PIL 5:202-12.
Bickerton, Derek
1981   Roots of language.   Ann Arbor: Karoma.
Birkhan, Helmut
1979   Das 'Zipfsche Gesetz', das schwache Präteritum und die germanische
         Lautverschiebung. Vienna: Verlag der Österreichischen Akademie der
         Wissenschaften (Sitzungsberichte 348, phil-hist. Klasse).
Bjarkman, Peter
1975   Toward a proper conception of processes in Natural Phonology.   PCLS
         11:60-72.
1982   Process versus feature analysis and the notion of linguistic 'closest'
         sounds. PCLS 18:14-28.
Bjørnflaten, Jan I.
1981   Die zweite Palatalisierung im Bulgarischen.   Nordlyd 4:72-89.
Blache, Stephen
1978   The acquisition of distinctive features.   Baltimore: University Park
         Press.
Bloch, Bernard
1941   Phonemic overlapping.   American Speech 16:278-84.   (Reprinted in Makkai
         1972:66-70.)
Bloomfield, Leonard
1939   Menomini morphophonemics.   TLCP 8:105-15.
Bluhme, Hermann
1965   Zur phonologischen Behandlung von Fremdwörtern.   PICPhS 5:218-21.
Blumenthal, Peter
1972   Die Entwicklung der romanischen Labialkonsonanten.   Bonn: Romanisches
         Seminar der Universität.

1979   GAULLISTE - GAULLIEN - GISCARDIEN: zur Suffigierung von Politikernamen
        im Französischen. Beiträge zur Romanischen Philologie 18:257-65.
Blumstein, Sheila
1973   A phonological investigation of aphasic speech. The Hague: Mouton.
Blust, Robert
1980   More on the origins of glottalic consonants. Lingua 52:125-256.
Blochner, Harry
1981   The l → o rule in Serbo-Croatian. Harvard Studies in Phonology 2:17-49.
Böhme, U.
1979   Überlegungen zu einer funktionalen Betrachtung der Wortbildung. Lin-
        guistische Arbeitsberichte 22:36-43.
Bolinger, Dwight L.
1961   Generality, gradience, and the all-or-none. The Hague: Mouton.
Bolocky, Shmuel
1977   On the status of fast speech in natural generative phonology. NELS
        7:33-47.
1978   Word formation strategies in the Hebrew verb system: denominative verbs.
        Afroasiatic Linguistics 5,3:111-36.
Bondarko, L. V.
1979   On the phonological operations ensuring speech communication. PICPhS
        9.II:67-73.
Booij, Geert
1977   Dutch morphology. Lisse: P. de Ridder Press.
1981a   Rule ordering, rule application, and the organization of grammar.
        Phonologica 1980:45-56.
1981b   Review of Zonneveld et al. 1980. Lingua 55:369-88.
1984   French C/Ø-alternations, extrasyllabicity and Lexical Phonology. Vrije
        Universiteit WPL 7 (Amsterdam).
Boom, Holger van den
1983   Zum Verhältnis von Logik und Linguistik in Bezug auf UNITYP-Grundsätze.
        akup 52.
Bos, Gijsbertha F.
1967   Categories and border-line categories. Amsterdam: Hakkert.
Botha, Rudolf
1979a   External evidence in the validation of mentalistic theories: a Chomsky-
        an paradox. Stellenbosch Papers in Linguistics 2:1-38.
1979b   Methodological bases of a progressive mentalism. Stellenbosch Papers
        in Linguistics 3.
Brakel, C. Arthur
1974   Portuguese //r ≈ r̃//, Lusitanian and Brazilian allophones. Studies in
        Linguistics 24:1-15.
1979a   A gramática generativa e a pluralização em português. Boletim de Filo-
        logia 25.55-96.
1979b   Segmental strength, hierarchies, and phonological theory. The elements:
        a parasession on linguistic units and levels, Chicago Linguistic Socie-
        ty:43-51.
1981   Phonological markedness and distinctive features. MS. (Now: Blooming-
        ton: Indiana University Press, 1984.)
Brasington, R. W. P.
1976   On the functional diversity of phonological rules. JL 12:125-52.
Braun, Gerhard
1981   Präsentation versus Repräsentation. Zur Beziehung zwischen Zeichen und
        Objekt in der visuellen Kommunikation. Zeitschrift für Semiotik 3:143-
        70.

388 DRESSLER

Breen, J. G.
 1977 Andegurebenha vowel phonology. Phonetica 34:371-91.
Brekle, Herbert E.
 1981 'No U-Turn'. Zur Integration eines speziellen Typs ikonischer Elemente
    in schriftsprachlichen Wortbildungen. In Zeichenkonstitution, Akten
    des 2. Semiotischen Kolloquiums (ed. Lange-Seidl, Berlin-New York: de
    Gruyter):172-9.
Bresnan, Joan
 1978 A realistic transformational grammar. In Halle at al. 1978:1-58.
Brink, Daniel
 1977 On the role of the syllable in Natural Generative Phonology. JLASSO
    11:123-8.
Brooks, Maria Zagorska
 1975 Polish reference grammar. The Hague: Mouton.
Broselow, Ellen
 1982 On predicting the interaction of stress and epenthesis. Glossa 16.115-
    32.
Buchler, Justus, ed.
 1955 Philosophical writings of Peirce. New York: Dover.
Bühler, Karl
 1933/1982 Die Axiomatik der Sprachwissenschaft. Kantstudien 38:19-90. En-
    glish translation R. E. Innis in Semiotic foundations of language the-
    ory. New York: Plenum Press:91-164.
Bunge, M.
 1963 Causality: the place of the causal principle in modern science. Cleve-
    land/New York.
Buyssens, Eric
 1980 Epistémologie de la phonématique. Brussels: Université libre de Bru-
    xelles.
Bybee, Joan, and Elly Pardo
 1981 On lexical and morphological conditioning of alternations: a nonce-
    probe experiment with Spanish verbs. Linguistics 19:937-68.
Bybee, Joan, and Carol Modor
 1983 Morphological classes as natural categories. Lg 59:251-70.
Bybee, Joan, and Dan Slobin
 1982 Rules and schemas in the development and use of the English past tense.
    Lg 58:265-89.
Cagliari, Luiz C.
 1983 An experimental study of nasality with particular reference to Brazil-
    ian Portuguese. Florianópolis: Universidade Federal de Santa Catarina.
Cairns, Charles E., and Mark H. Feinstein
 1982 Markedness and the theory of syllable structure. LInq 13:193-225.
Campanile, Enrico
 1968 Metrica celtica antica e metrica germanica antica. Enciclopedia Clas-
    sica VI. Torino: Società Editrice Internazionale. Ch. II:56.
Campbell, Lyle
 1973 Rule loss and rule obliteration. In Battle & Schweitzer 1973:248-53.
 1974 Theoretical implications of Kekchi phonology. IJAL 40:269-78.
 1979 The quest for psychological reality: external evidence in phonology.
    PICPhS 9.II:74-8.
 1980 Explaining universals and their exceptions. Papers 4th Conference on
    Historical Linguistics (eds. E. C. Traugott et al., Amsterdam: Benja-
    mins):17-26.

1981a   Generative phonology vs. Finnish phonology: retrospect and prospect.
         In Goyvaerts 1981:147-82.
1981b   The psychological and sociological reality of Finnish vowel harmony.
         Vago 1981:245-70.
Campbell, Lyle, and Jon Ringen
1981   Teleology and the explanation of sound change.   Phonologica 1980:57-68.
Cantineau, Jean
1950   Racines et schèmes.   Mélanges W. Marçais.   Paris: Maisonneuve:119-24.
Capell, A., and E. E. Hinch
1970   Maung grammar.   The Hague: Mouton.
Cardona, Giorgio, and Francesco Agostini
1981   Studi somali I.   Rome: Il Bagatto.
Carroll, John R., and Michael K. Tanenhaus
1975   Prolegomena to a functional theory of word formation.   Papers from the
         parasession on functionalism (eds. R. Grossman et al., Chicago Linguis-
         tic Society):47-62.
Carstairs, Andrew
1980   Review of Dressler 1977a.   Linguistics 18:1153-7.
1982   Review of Fisiak 1980.   JL 18:486-92.
1984   Outlines of a constraint on syncretism.   FoL 18:73-95.
Catford, J. C.
1977   Fundamental problems in phonetics.   Bloomington: Indiana University
         Press.
Cearly, Alvin
1974   The only phonological rule ordering principle.   NatPhon 30-42.
Cedergren, Henrietta J., and David Sankoff
1975   Nasals: a sociolinguistic study of change in progress.   Nasålfest 67-80.
Celce-Murcia, Marianne
1980   On Meringer's corpus of 'slips of the ear'.   In Fromkin 1980:199-211.
Cena, R. M.
1978   When is a phonological generalization psychologically real?   Blooming-
         ton: Indiana University Linguistics Club.
Cerrón-Palomino, R.
1974   Morphologically conditioned changes in Winka-Quechua.   Studies in the
         Linguistic Sciences 4,2:40-75.
Chao, Y-R.
1957   The non-uniqueness of phonemic solutions of phonetic systems.   In Read-
         ings in linguistics I (ed. M. Joos, University of Chicago Press):38-54
         [originally 1934].
Chapin, Paul
1970   On affixation in English.   In Progress in Linguistics (eds. M. Bier-
         wisch & K. Heidolph).   The Hague: Mouton:51-63.
Chen, Matthew
1970   Vowel length variation as a function of the voicing of the consonant
         environment.   Phonetica 22:129-59.
1972   Predictive power in phonological description.   Lingua 32:173-91.
1974   Metarules and universal constraints in phonological theory.   PICL 11:
         909-24.
Chene, Brent de, and Stephen R. Anderson
1979   Compensatory lengthening.   Lg 55:505-35.
Chmura-Klekotowa, Marina
1972   Slovoobrazovatel'nye neologizmy v detsky reči na materialah pol'skego i
         russkogo jazyka.   Colloquium Paedolinguisticum (ed. K. Ohnesorg).   The
         Hague: Mouton:83-100.

Chomsky, Noam
  1951   Morphophonemics of Modern Hebrew. University of Pennsylvania MA thesis
  1957   Review of Jakobson & Halle 1956. IJAL 23:234-42.
  1975   Reflections on language. New York: Random House.
  1980   Rules and representations. New York: Columbia University Press.
  1982   Lectures on government and binding. The Pisa Lectures. Dordrecht:
         Foris.
Chomsky, Noam, and Morris Halle
  1968   The sound pattern of English. New York: Harper & Row.
Chung, Sandra
  1983   Transderivational relationships in Chamorro phonology. Lg 59:35-66.
Churma, Donald G.
  1981   Some further problems for upside-down phonology. WPL (Ohio State Uni-
         versity) 25:67-106.
Clark, Herbert H., and Eve V. Clark
  1977   Psychology and language. New York: Harcourt-Brace-Jovanovich.
Clayton, Mary L.
  1976   The redundance of underlying morpheme-structure conditions. Lg 52:295-
         313.
  1981   Word boundaries and sandhi rules in Natural Generative Phonology. Lg
         57:571-90.
Clements, George N.
  1976   Palatalization: linking or assimilation? PCLS 12:96-109.
  1977   The autosegmental treatment of vowel harmony. Phonologica 1976:111-9.
  1982   A remark on the elsewhere condition. LInq 13:682-4.
Clements, George N., and Samuel J. Keyser
  1983   CV phonology: a generative theory of the syllable. Cambridge, MA: MIT
         Press.
Clements, George N., and Engin Sezer
  1982   Vowel and consonant disharmony in Turkish. In Hulst & Smith 1982.II:
         213-55.
Clumeck, Harold
  1975   A cross-linguistic investigation of vowel nasalization: an instrumental
         study. Nasálfest 133-51.
Coates, Richard
  1980   The role of time in phonological representations. Journal of Phonetics
         8:1-20.
  1982   Why Hungarian isn't as extrinsic as Vago thinks. JL 18:167-72.
  1983   On a class of solutions to a phonological dilemma. Paper read at the
         LAGB spring meeting at Sheffield.
Coetsem, Frans van
  1980   Germanic verbal ablaut and its development. In Contributions to his-
         torical linguistics (eds. F. van Coetsem & L. R. Waugh). Leiden:
         Brill:281-339.
Coetsem, Frans van, and Susan McCormick
  1982   Old High German umlaut and the notion of optimal patterning. Amster-
         damer Beiträge zur Älteren Germanistik 17:23-7.
Cohen, David
  1970   Etudes de linguistique sémitique et arabe. The Hague: Mouton.
Cohen, David, and Jessica Wirth, eds.
  1975   Testing linguistic hypotheses. New York: Wiley.
Cole, Peter
  1982   Imbabura Quechua. (Lingua Descriptive Studies 5.) Amsterdam: North
         Holland.

Comrie, Bernard
  1979   Morphophonemic exceptions and phonetic distance. Linguistics 17:21-50.
  1980   The sun letters in Maltese: between morphophonemics and phonetics.
          Studies in the Linguistic Sciences 10,2:25-37.
Comrie, Bernard, and Gerald Stone
  1978   The Russian language since the Revolution. Oxford: Clarendon Press.
Coseriu, Eugenio
  1958   Sincronía, diacronía e historia: el problema del cambio lingüístico.
          Montevideo: Universidad de la República.
  1968   Sincronía, diacronía y tipología. Actas del 11. Congreso Internacional
          de lingüística y filología románicas. Madrid: C.S.I.C.:269-83. (Ger-
          man translation in E. Coseriu 1970: Sprache, Structur und Funktionen.
          Tübingen: Narr:235-66.)
  1971   Thesen zum Thema 'Sprache und Dichtung'. In Beiträge zur Textlinguis-
          tik (ed. W. Stempel). Munich: Fink:183-8.
  1980   Der Sinn der Sprachtypologie. TCLC 20:157-70.
Costabile, Norma
  1973   La flessione in italiano. Rome: Bulzoni.
Coupez, André
  1981   A linguistic lesson. In Angenot et al. 1981:113-21.
Cressey, William W.
  1978   Absolute neutralization of the phonemic glide-versus-vowel constraint
          in Spanish. In Contemporary studies in Romance linguistics (ed. M.
          Suñer). Washington: Georgetown University Press:90-105.
Crompton, Andrew
  1981   Syllables and segments in speech production. Linguistics 19:663-716.
Crothers, John, and Masayoshi Shibatani
  1981   Issues in the description of Turkish vowel harmony. Vago 1981:63-88.
Csik, Steven, and Eugene Papa
  1977 & 1979 Theoretical issues in Generative Phonology: an annotated bibli-
          ography. 2 vol. Bloomington: Indiana University Linguistics Club.
Čurganova, Valerija G.
  1973   Očerk russkoj morfonologii. Moscow: Nauka.
Cutler, Anne
  1981   Guest editorial: The reliability of speech error data. Linguistics 19,
          7/8:561-82.
  1982   Speech errors: a classified bibliography. Bloomington: Indiana Univer-
          sity Linguistics Club.
Cvetkova, L. S., and S. V. Teplickaja
  1975   Rol' slovoobrazovanija v formirovanii parafazij u bol'nyh s afaziej.
          In Materialy u vsesujuznogo simpoziuma po psiholingvistike i teorii
          kommunikacii ANSSR:179-83.
Daly, D. M., and L. M. Martin
  1972   Epenthetic processes. Papers in Linguistics 5:604-12.
Dardano, Maurizio
  1978   La formazione delle parole nell'italiano di oggi. Rome: Bulzoni.
Darden, Bill
  1971   Diachronic evidence for phonemics. PCLS 7:323-31.
  1977   A global rule in Lithuanian phonology. PCLS 13:116-24.
  1979   On the nature of morphophonemic rules. PCLS 15:79-89.
  1981   On arguments for abstract vowels in Greenlandic. PCLS 17:31-9.
  1982   Dissimilative glide insertion in West Greenlandic. PCLS 18.
Dauer, R. M.
  1983   Stress-timing and syllable-timing reanalyzed. Journal of Phonetics 11:
          51-62

Davidsen-Nielsen, Niels
    1978   Neutralization and archiphoneme. Copenhagen: Akademisk Forlag.
Dean-John, Hazel, Richard Demers, and Richard Oehrle
    1984   The articulatory base of Seneca. Discussion Papers, 47-51.
de Cesaris, Janet A.
    1981   'Functional' observations on some rules in Mallorcan Catalan. Phonolo-
            gica 1980:77-51.
Delattre, Pierre
    1965   Comparing the phonetic features of English, French, German and Spanish.
            London.
    1969   An acoustic and articulatory study of vowel reduction in four lan-
            guages. International Journal of Applied Linguistics 7:295-325.
Daledalle, Gérard
    1979   Pour une lecture sémiotique de la sémiotique de Pierce. Kodikas 1:5-8.
Dell, François
    1973   Les règles et les sons. Paris: Hermann.
    1978   Certains corrélats de la distinction entre morphologie dérivationelle
            et morphologie flexionelle dans la phonologie du français. Recherches
            Linguistiques à Montréal 10:1-10.
    1981   On the learnability of optional phonological rules. LInq 12:31-7.
Dell, François, and Elisabeth Selkirk
    1978   On a morphologically governed vowel alternation in French. In Recent
            transformational studies in European languages (ed. S. Keyser). Cam-
            bridge, MA: MIT Press, 1-51.
Derbyshire, Desmond C.
    1979   Hixkaryana. Amsterdam: North Holland.
Derwing, Bruce
    1979   Psycholinguistic evidence and linguistic theory. In Perspectives in
            experimental linguistics (ed. G. D. Prideaux). Amsterdam: Benjamins,
            113-38.
Derwing, Bruce, and William Baker
    1977   The psychological basis for morphological rules. In Macnamara 1977:
            85-110.
Dešeriev, Junus D.
    1950   Grammatika hinalugskogo jazyka. Moscow: Nauk.
Desnickaja, Agnija V.
    1967   Nekotorye voprosy morfonologii. Istoriko-Filologičwskije issledovani-
            ja. Festschrift Konrad. Moscow: Nauka, 86-91.
    1968   Albanskij jazykiiego dialecty. Leningrad: Nauka.
    1979   Morfonologičeskie processy v obrazovanii vtoričnoj fleksii v albanskom
            jazyke. Avanesov 1979:83-97.
Devine, A. M., and Laurence D. Stephens
    1977   Two studies in Latin phonology. Saratoga: Anma Libri.
    1980   On the phonological definition of boundaries. Aronoff & Kean 1980:57-
            78.
Diffloth, Gérard
    1972   Notes on expressive meaning. PCLS 8:440-7.
Dik, Simon C.
    1978   Functional grammar. Amsterdam: North Holland.
    1980   Funktionelle morfonologie. In Morfologie in Nederland (eds. T. Hoek-
            stra & H. van der Hulst). Glot Special, 73-100.
Dinnsen, Daniel A.
    1978   Phonological rules and phonetic explanation. Bloomington: Indiana Uni-
            versity Linguistics Club.

1979a (ed.) Current approaches to phonological theory. Bloomington: Indiana University Press.

1979b Atomic phonology. Dinnsen 1979a:31-49

1983 On the phonetics of phonological neutralization. PICL 13:1294.

Dinnsen, Daniel A., and Fred Eckman

1978 Some substantive universals in Atomic Phonology. Lingua 45:1-14.

Diringer, David

1949 The alphabet. London: Hutchinson.

Discussion Papers

1984 5th Intern. Phonology Meeting (eds. W. Dressler et al.). wlg, supplement 3.

Dipsey, Nicole

1967 Etude de l'acquisition de la morphologie française chez l'enfant. Université de Liège.

Dobó, Attila

1980 Zwei phonologische Prozesse in syrjänischen Dialekten. WlG 22-3, 25-30.

Dobozy, Maria

1978 Code-mixing and vowel harmony in American-Hungarian urban speech: evidence of regressive assimilation. MS. Applied English Center, University of Kansas, Lawrence.

Dodi, Anastas

1968 Fonetika e gjuhës së somte Shqipe. Tirana: University.

Dogil, Grzegorz

1980 Elementary accent systems. Wiener linguistische Gazette 24:3-22. (Abridged in Phonologica 1980:89-99.)

Donegan, Patricia Jane

1978 On the natural phonology of vowels. WPL (Ohio State University), 23.

Donegan, Patricia J., and David Stampe

1977 On the description of phonological hierarchies. CLS book of squibs (eds. S. E. Fox et al.). Chicago Linguistic Society, 35-8.

1979a The syllable in phonological and prosodic structure. Bell & Hooper 1979:25-34.

1979b The study of natural phonology. Dinnsen 1979a:126-73.

1983 Rhythm and the holistic nature of language. Interplay, 337-53.

Dorian, Nancy

1981 Language death. Philadelphia: University of Pennsylvania Press.

Drachman, Gaberell

1973a On the interpretation of phonological primes. WPL (Ohio State University) 15:161-73.

1973b Phonology and the basis of articulation. Sprache 19:1-19.

1977 On the notion 'phonological hierarchy'. Phonologica 1976:85-102.

1978 Child language and language change: a conjecture and some refutations. Fisiak 1978:123-44.

1981b On explaining 'all the explicanda of the previous theory': Popper and the growth of linguistics. Folia Linguistica 15:345-61.

Dresher, Bezalel E.

1981 Abstractness and explanation in phonology. In Explanation in linguistics (eds. N. Hornstein & D. Lightfoot). London: Langman, 76-115.

Dressler, Wolfgang U.

1965 Pamphylisch -d- zu -r-: ein weiterer Dubstrateinfluß? Archiv Orientální 33:183-9.

1967 Wege der Sprachtypologie. Sprache 13:1-19.

1971 Some constraints on phonological change. PCLS 7:340-9.

1972a Allegroregeln rechtfertigen Lentoregeln. Sekundäre Phoneme des Breto-
nischen. Innsbrucker Beiträge zur Sprachwissenschaft 9. (Abridged and
revised as: Essai sur la stylistique phonologique du breton: les dé-
bits rapids. Études Celtiques 14:99-120 (1974).)

1972b On the phonology of language death. PCLS 8:448-57.

1973 Pour une stylistique phonologique du latin. BSLP 68:129-45.

1975a Zentrifugale und zentripedale phonologische Prozesse. WlG 8:32-42.
(Revised WSLJb 23,1978:36-46.)

1975b Methodisches zu Allegroregln. Phonologica 1972:219-34.

1976 Können Morphemfugen die Domäne phonologischer Prozesse begrenzen?
Opuscula Slavica et Linguistica, FS. A. Isatschenko. Klagenfurt: Heyn,
123-37.

1977a Grundfragen der Morphonologie. Vienna: Verlag der Österreichischen
Akademie der Wissenschaften.

1977b Phono-morphological dissimilation. Phonologica 1976:41-8.

1977c Morphological disturbances in aphasia. WlG 14:3-11.

1977d Wortbildung bei Sprachverfall. In Perspektiven der Wortbildungsfor-
schung (eds. H. Brekle & D. Rastovsky). Bonn: Grundmann, 62-9.

1977e Elements of a polycentristic theory of word formation. WlG 15:13-32.

1977f Phonologische Prozeßtypologie. In Studies in linguistic typology (eds.
M. Romportl et al.). Prague: Acta Universitatis Carolinae. Philologi-
ca 5, 1974:135-46.

1977g Morphologization of phonological processes (Are there different morphonological processes?). Linguistic studies offered to J. Greenberg (ed.
A. Juilland). Saratoga: Anma Libri II:313-37.

1978a Phonologische Störungen bei der Aphasie. Badania lingwistyne nad
afazją (ed. H. Mierzejewska). Warsaw: Osselineum, 11-24.

1978b On a polycentristic theory of word formation (with special emphasis on
aphasiological evidence). PICL 12:426-9.

1978c How much does performance contribute to phonological change? Fisiak
1978:145-58.

1979a Arguments and non-arguments for naturalness in phonology: on the use of
external evidence. PICPhS 9,2:93-100.

1979b Remarks on the typology of segmental process types. Wiener linguistische Gazette 20:1-14. (Revised as: Reflections on phonological
typology. Acta Ling. Hung. 29, 1982:259-73.)

1980a Universalien von Agens-Wortbildungen. In Wege zur Universalienfor-
schung, Festschrift H. Seiler (eds. G. Bretschneider & C. Lehmann).
Tübingen: Narr, 110-4.

1980b A semiotic model of diachronic process phonology. WlG 22-3, 31-94.
Revised in Perspectives for historical linguistics (eds. W. Lehmann &
Y. Malkiel). Amsterdam: Benjamins, 93-131.

1980c Was erwarten Phonologietheorien von der Indogermanistik -- was kann die
Indogermanistik bieten? Lautgeschichte und Etymologie (eds. M. Mayrho-
fer et al.). Wiesbaden: Reichert, 102-19.

1980d Naturalness as a principle in genetic and typological linguistics.
TCLC 20:75-91.

1981a External evidence for an abstract analysis of the German velar nasal.
Goyvaerts 1981:445-67. Prepublished in: WlG 19 (1979) 3-28.

1981b Outlines of a model of morphonology. Phonologica 1980:113-22.

1981c General principles of poetic license in word formation. Logos Semantikos, Festschrift E. Coseriu 2 (ed. H. Weydt). Berlin-New York: de
Gruyter, 423-31.

1981d Language shift and language death: a Protean challenge for the
       linguist. FoL:5-28.
1982a Zur semiotischen Begründung einer Natürlischen Wortbildungslehre.
       Klagenfurter Beiträge zur Sprachwissenschaft 8:72-87.
1982b A classification of phonological paraphasias. WlG 26:3-13.
1982c On word formation in Natural Morphology. WlG 26:3-13. [Now in PICL
       13:172-82.]
1983   Konsequenzen einer polyzentristischen Sprachtheorie für die Stiltheorie
       der dichterischen Sprache. WlG 30:3-18. [Longer versions appear in
       Études Finno-Ougriennes 1983:119-31 and Glossologia 1 1982:17-25.]
1984a Conditions for the use of external evidence in phonology. In Rhodes,
       forthc.:35-48.
1984b Explaining Natural Phonology. Phonology Yearbook I:29-51.
1984c Subtraction in word formation and its place within a theory of Natural
       Morphology. Quaderni di Semantica 5:78-85.
to appear Zur Wertung der Interfixe in einer semiotischen Theorie der
       Natürlichen Morphonologie. Festschrift G. Hüttl-Folter. Vienna:
       Wiener slavistischer Almanach. [An enlarged English version in Dress-
       ler, in prep.]
in prep. Studies in Natural Morphology. Tübingen: Narr.
Dressler, Wolfgang U., and Vaneeta Acson
forthc. On the diachrony of subtractive operations: evidence for semiotically
       based models of Natural Phonology and Natural Morphology from Northern
       and Anatolian Greek dialects. In Proceedings of the 5th International
       Conference Hist. Linguistics (ed. J. Fisiak). Amsterdam: Benjamins.
Dressler, Wolfgang U., and Gaberell Drachman
1977   Externe Evidenz für eine Typologie der Vokalprozesse. Salzburger
       Beiträge zur Linguistik 3:285-97.
Dressler, Wolfgang U., and Alexander Grosu
1972   Generative Phonologie und indogermanische Lautgeschichte 77:19-72.
Dressler, Wolfgang U., and Josef Hufgard
1980   Études phonologiques sur le breton sud-bigouden. Vienna: Verlag des
       Österreichischen Akademie der Wissenschaften.
Dressler, Wolfgang U., Willi Mayerthaler, Oswald Panagl, and Wolfgang U. Wurzel
to appear Leitmotifs in Natural Morphology. Amsterdam: Benjamins.
Dressler, Wolfgang U., Heinz Stark, and Wilfried Grossmann
to appear Phonological strengthening processes in paraphasias. In Dressler
       & Stark, in prep.
Dressler, Wolfgang U., and Jacqueline Stark, eds.
in prep. Aphasic language: linguistic analyses. New York: Academic Press.
Dressler, Wolfgang U., and Ruth Wodak(-Leodolter)
1977   (eds.) Language death. International Journal of the Sociology of
       Language 12.
1982   Sociophonological methods in the study of sociolinguistic variation in
       Viennese German. Language in Society 11:339-70.
Droescher, W. O.
1974   PUHOI - Eine Egerländer Mundart in Neuseeland. Phonai 15, Monographien
       7:195-235.
Dudas, K.
1974   A case of functional phonological opacity: Javanese elative formation.
       Studies in the Linguistic Sciences 4,2:91-111.
Ďurovič, L'ubomír
1967   Das Problem der Morphonologie. In To honor Roman Jakobson I. The
       Hague: Mouton, 556-68.

Dvončova, Jana
  1972   Die Stellung der Intonation im Rahmen der Artikulationsbasis. Phoneti-
          ca Pragensia 3 (Symposium on Intonology, eds. M. Romportl & P. Janota),
          73-76.
Dworkin, Steven N.
  1975   Therapeutic reactions to excessive phonetic erosion. Romance Philology
          28:462-72.
  1977   Therapeutic reactions to phonotactic awkwardness: the descendants of
          alauda in Hispano-Romance. ZRomPhil 93:513-7.
Eckman, Fred R.
  1977   Markedness and the contrastive analysis hypothesis. Language Learning
          27:315-30.
Eco, Umberto
  1976   A theory of semiotics. Bloomington: Indiana University Press.
  1977   The influence of Roman Jakobson on the development of semiotics. In
          Roman Jakobson: echoes of his scholarship (eds. D. Armstrong & C. H.
          van Schooneveld). Lisse: de Ridder, 39-58.
  1979   The role of the reader: explorations in the semiotics of texts. Bloom-
          ington: Indiana University Press.
  1984   Semiotics and the philosophy of language. Bloomington: Indiana Univer-
          sity Press.
Eirikson, Eyvindur
  1982   English loanwords in Icelandic - aspects of morphology. Filipović
          1982:266-300.
Eisenwort-Schelz, Brigitte
  1979   Über den Phonologieerwerb geistig behinderter Kinder. WlG 21:17-26.
Eckblom, Richard
  1935   Die Palatalisierung von *k, g, ch* im Slawischen. Uppsala: Almqvist.
Eliasson, Stig
  1973   Generatif fonologie, morfofonemik och svenskans [š] och [ç]. Folkmåls-
          studier 23:195-213.
  1975   On the issue of directionality. In The Nordic languages and modern
          linguistics II (ed. K.-H. Dahlstedt). Stockholm: Almqvist-Wiksell,
          421-45.
  1977   Inferential aspects of phonological rules. Phonologica 1976:103-10.
  1978   Theoretical problems in Scandinavian contrastive phonology. In The
          Nordic languages and modern linguistics 3 (ed. J. Weinstock). Univer-
          sity of Texas at Austin, 217-43.
  1981   Analytic vs. synthetic aspects of phonological structure. Goyvaerts
          1981:483-524.
  1982   Transfer as evidence for phonological solutions. Studia Anglica Pos-
          naniensia 14:185-96.
Elson, Mark J.
  1975   Symmetry in phonology. Lg 51:293-302.
Emmet, Dorothy
  1958   Function, purpose and powers. London: Macmillan.
Enkvist, Nils E.
  1977   Stylistics and textlinguistics. In Current trends in textlinguistics
          (ed. W. U. Dressler). Berlin-New York: de Gruyter, 175-96.
  1979   'What' and 'Why': on causal explanation in linguistics. Folia Linguis-
          tica 13:1-21.
  1981   Experimental iconicism in text strategy. Text 1,1:97-111.
Ertel, Suitbert
  1969   Psychophonetik, Untersuchungen über Lautsymbolik und Motivation.
          Goettingen: Hogrefe.

Eschbach, Achim, ed.
  1981   Zeichen über Zeichen über Zeichen: 15 Studien über Charles W. Morris.
          Tübingen: Narr.   [Eight of these studies are in English.]
Eschbach, Achim, and Wendelin Rader, eds.
  1981   Literatursemiotik I, II.   Tübingen: Narr.
Escure, Geneviève
  1977   Hierarchies and phonological weakening.   Lingua 43:55-64.
Ettinger, Stefan
  1974   Form und Funktion in der Wortbildung.   Tübingen: Narr.
Ewen, Colin J.
  1977   Aitken's law and the phonatory gesture in dependency phonology.   Lingua
          41:307-29.
  1980   Segment or sequence?   Problems in the analysis of some consonantal
          phenomena.   Ludwigsburg Studies in Language and Linguistics 4:157-204.
  1982   The internal structure of complex segments.   Hulst & Smith 1982:27-67.
          [Revised version of Ewen 1980.]
Farrar, Christopher
  1977   Spirantization, stress shift and vowel reduction in Modern Hebrew.   WlG
          16:19-30.
Ferguson, Charles A.
  1978a   Phonological processes.   Greenberg 1978.II:403-42.
  1978b   Historical background of universals research.   Greenberg 1978.I:7-31.
  1980   Phonology as an individual access system: some data from language ac-
          quisition.   Fillmore et al., 189-201.
Fey, Marc, and Jack Gandour
  1979   Problem-solving in phonology acquisition.   Paper read at the 54th
          Annual Meeting of the Linguistic Society of America.
  1982   Rule discovery in phonological acquisition.   Journal of Child Language
          9:71-81.
Feyerabend, Paul
  1975   Against method.   Outline of an anarchistic theory of knowledge.   Lon-
          don: New Left Books.
Fidelholtz, James L.
  1975   Word frequency and vowel reduction in English.   PCLS 11:200-13.
  1979   Neutralization in English syllables and its relation to rhyme in poetry.
          Studia Anglica Posnaniensa 11:79-85.
Field, Thomas T.
  1981   Loanword phonology and phonological rule types.   Phonologica 1980:129-
          36.
Filipović, Rudolf, ed.
  1982   The English element in European languages.   Zagreb: Institute of Lin-
          guistics.
Firchow, Irwin, and Jacqueline Firchow
  1969   An abbreviated phoneme inventory.   Anthropological Linguistics 11:200-
          13.
Fischer-Jørgensen, Eli
  1967   Perceptual dimensions of vowels.   In To Honor Roman Jakobson.   The
          Hague: Mouton, 667-71.
  1972   Kinesthetic judgement of effort in the production of stop consonants.
          ARIPUC 6:59-73.
  1975   Trends in phonological theory.   Copenhagen: Akademisk Forlag.
  1978   On the universal character of phonetic symbolism with special reference
          to vowels.   ARIPUC 12:75-89.
  1980   Temporal relations in Danish CV sequences with stop consonants.   ARIPUC
          14:207-61.

Fisiak, Jacek, ed.
  1978   Recent developments in historical phonology. The Hague: Mouton.
  1980   Historical morphology. The Hague: Mouton.
Fleuriot, Léon
  1964   Le vieux breton. Paris: Klincksieck.
Flier, Michael S.
  1979   Review of Dressler 1977a. Lg 55:413-5.
  1982   Morphophonemic change as evidence of phonemic change: the status of the
          sharped velars in Russian. Slavic linguistics and poetics, Festschrift
          E. Stankiewicz (eds. K. Naylor et al.). Slavica = IJSLP 25/26:137-48.
  1983   The alternation $l \sim v$ in East Slavic. In American contributions to the
          9th International Congress of Slavists I (ed. M. S. Flier). Slavica,
          99-118.
Floyd, Edwin D.
  1981   Levels of phonological restriction in Greek affixes. In Bono homini
          donum: essays in historical linguistics in memory of J. A. Kerns (eds.
          Y. Arbeitmein & A. Bomhard). Amsterdam: Benjamins, 87-106.
Fodor, Jerry A.
  1979   The language of thought. Cambridge, MA: Harvard University Press.
  1982   The modularity of mind. Cambridge, MA: MIT Press.
Foldvik, Arne K.
  1979   Norwegian speech error data - a source of evidence for linguistic per-
          formance models. Nordic Journal of Linguistics 2:113-22.
Foley, James
  1965   Prothesis in the Latin verb sum. Lg 41:59-64.
  1978   Foundations of theoretical phonology. Cambridge University Press.
Foley, Lawrence
  1980   Phonological variation in Western Cherokee. New York: Garland.
Fontanella, María B.
  1962   Algunas observaciones sobre el diminutivo en Bogotá. Boletín del Ins-
          tituto Caro y Cuervo 17:556-73.
Ford, Alan, and Rajendra Singh
  1983a   Remarques sur la phonologie lexicale. Revue de l'association québéc-
          quoise de linguistique 3.
  1983b   On the status of morphophonology. Interplay, 63-78.
Fourquet, Jean
  1963   Pourquoi les lois phonétiques sont sans exception. PICL 9:638-44.
Fox, Anthony
  1980   Review of Dressler 1977a. JL 16:316-20.
Fox, R. A., and Dale Terbeek
  1977   Dental flaps, vowel duration and rule ordering in American English.
          Journal of Phonetics 3:27-34.
Freeman, Donald C., ed.
  1970   Linguistics and literary style. New York: Holt, Rinehart and Winston.
Frei, Henri
  1929   La grammaire des fautes. Paris: Geuthner.
Fries, Charles C., and Kenneth L. Pike
  1949   Coexistent phonemic systems. Lg 25:29-50.
Frith, Uta, ed.
  1980   Cognitive processes in spelling. New York: Academic Press.
Fromkin, Victoria A.
  1973   (ed.) Speech errors as linguistic evidence. The Hague: Mouton.
  1975   When does a test test a hypothesis, or, What counts as evidence? Cohen
          & Wirth 1975:43-64.

1980 (ed.) Errors in linguistic performance: slips of the tongue, ear, pen and hands. New York: Academic Press.

Fry, D. B.
1979 The physics of speech. Cambridge University Press.

Gadamer, Hans-Georg
1972 Wahrheit und Methode. Tübingen: Mahr. [English: Truth and method. New York: Seaburg Press, 1975.]

Gamkrelidze, Thomas V.
1974 The problem of l'arbitraire du signe. Lg 50:102-10.
1982 The 'principle of complementarity' and the problem of the arbitrary linguistic signs. Logos semantikos II, Festschrift E. Coseriu. Berlin-New York: de Gruyter, 335-42.

Gaprindašvili, Šota G.
1966 Fonetika darginskogo jazyka. Tbilisi: Mecniereba.

Garde, Paul
1980 L'accent. Paris: Presses Universitaires de France.

Garnes, Sara, and Zinny S. Bond
1975 Slips of the ear: errors in perception of casual speech. PCLS 11:214-25.
1980 A slip of the ear: a snip of the ear? a slip of the year. Fromkin 1980:231-9.

Garnham, Alan, et al.
1981 Slips of the tongue in the London-Lund corpus of spontaneous conversation. Linguistics 19:805-17.

Gaspar de Oliveira, Sidney
1981 Speeds and underlying representations - glides in Portuguese. Angenot et al. 1981:122-36.

Geckeler, Horst
1983 Description typologique de l'espagnol selon le modèle de V. Skalička. MS for the 17th International Congress of Romance Linguistics and Philology (Aix-en-Provence).

Geis, Michael, and Arnold M. Zwicky
1971 On invited inferences. WPL (Ohio State University) 8:150-5.

Gelb, Ignace J.
1963 A study of writing. University of Chicago Press.

Georgios, Christos
1962 To glossiko idioma Germa Kastorias. Salonica: Etairia Makedonikon Spoudon 23.

Gerlach, Peter
1978 'Panofsky: Perspective als symbolische Form' in semiotischer Sicht. In Die Einheit der semiotischen Dimensionen (ed. Arbeitsgruppe Semiotik). Tübingen: Narr, 319-36.

Gerritsen, Johan
1982 English influence on Dutch. Filipović 1982:154-79.

Girke, Wolfgang, and Helmut Jachnow
1974 Sowjetische Soziolinguistik. Kronberg: Scriptor.

Givón, Talmy
1979 On understanding grammar. New York: Academic Press.

GLOW
1979 Proceedings of the 1979 GLOW Conference: Theory of Markedness in Generative Grammar (eds. A. Belletti et al.). Scuola Normale Superiore di Pisa, 1981.

Glozman, Žanna M.
  1974a   Nejropsihologičeskij i nejrolingvističeskij analiz grammatičeskih naru-
          šenii reči pri raznyh formah afazii. Avtoreferat dissertacii. Izda-
          tel'stvo Moskovskogo Universiteta.
  1974b   K voprosy o narušenii morfologičeskoj struktury reči pri afazii. Vo-
          prosy Psihologii 1974,5:81-7.
Goffman, Erving
  1974   Frame analysis. New York: Harper & Row.
Gogolewski, Edmond, and Jerzy Kopec
  1980   Les emprunts lexicaux français dans la langue des émigrés polonais dans
          le nord de la France. Cahiers de l'institut de linguistique de Louvain
          6:143-52.
Goidánich, Pier Gabriele
  1940   La gutterale e la palatina nei plurali dei nomi toscani della prima e
          seconda declinazione. Saggi Linguistici. Modena: Società Tipografica
          Modenese, 154-96. [Improved version of the first edition of 1893.]
Goldsmith, John
  1976   Autosegmental phonology. Bloomington: Indiana University Linguistics
          Club.
  1980   Review of Fromkin, ed., Tone: a linguistic survey (New York: Academic
          Press, 1978). Lg 56:413-8.
Goman, Roderick D.
  1981   On the natural phonology of consonants. WPL (Ohio State University)
          25:107-73.
Górska, Elzbieta
  1982   Formal and functional restrictions on the productivity of Word Forma-
          tion Rules. FoL 16:149-62.
Goodman, Nelson
  1968   Languages of art: an approach to a theory of symbols. Indianapolis:
          Bobbs-Merrill.
Gotteri, Nigel
  1981   Getting the Polish grooved froctionals right. Journal of the Interna-
          tional Phonetic Association 11:44-50.
Goyvaerts, Didier L.
  1978   Aspects of Post-SPE Phonology. Ghent: Story-Scientia.
  1981   (ed.) Phonology in the 1980's. Ghent: Story-Scientia.
Goyvaerts, Didier L., and Geoffrey K. Pullum, eds.
  1975   Essays on the Sound Pattern of English. Ghent: Story-Scientia.
Grassl, Wolfgang
  1979   Einfachheit als Kriterium der Theorienwahl. Eine Studie zur Metatheo-
          rie der Linguistik. Dissertationen der Universität Graz 45.
Greenberg, Joseph H.
  1950   Patterning of root morphemes in Semitic. Word 6:162-81.
  1963   Structure and function. In J. H. G., essays in linguistics. Universi-
          ty of Chicago Press, 75-85.
  1965   Some generalizations concerning initial and final consonant sequences.
          Linguistics 18:5-34.
  1966   Language universals with special reference to feature hierarchies. The
          Hague: Mouton.
  1978   (ed.) Universals of human language. (IV volumes) Stanford University
          Press.
Greenlee, Douglas
  1973   Peirce's concept of sign. The Hague: Mouton.

Greenlee, Mel, and John J. Ohala
  1980   Phonetically motivated parallels between child phonology and historical
          sound change. Language Sciences 2:283-308.
Griggs, Silas
  1982   Atonic vowel neutralization in English. JLASSO 4:356-75.
Grossmann, R. E., L. San, and T. J. Vance, eds.
  1975   Papers from the parasession on functionalism. Chicago Linguistic So-
          ciety, University of Chicago.
Gudschinsky, Sarah C.
  1958   Native reaction to tones and words in Mazatec. Word 14:338-45.
Gudschinsky, Sarah C., and Harold & Frances Popovich
  1970   Native reaction and phonetic similarity in Maxakalí phonology. Lg 46:
          77-88.
Guerssel, Mohamed
  1978   A condition on assimilation rules. Linguistic Analysis 4:225-54.
Guilbert, Louis
  1975   La créativité lexicale. Paris: Larousse.
Guile, Timothy
  1972   A generalization about epenthesis and syncope. PCLS 8:463-9.
  1973   Glide-obstruentization and the syllable code hierarchy. PCLS 9:139-56.
Gulya, János
  1975   Phonologische Analyse des Wogulischen. Linguistische Studien 22:117-29.
Gumb, Raimond D.
  1972   Rule-governed linguistic behavior. The Hague: Mouton.
Gusmani, Roberto
  1973   Aspetti del prestito linguistico. Naples: Scientifica Editrice.
  1981   Saggi sull' interferenza linguistica. Florence: Casa Editrice le Let-
          tere.
Gussmann, Edmund
  1976   Recoverable derivations and phonological change. Lingua 40:281-303.
  1977   Variation and argumentation in phonology. Papers and Studies in Con-
          trastive Linguistics 6:43-62.
  1978a   Explorations in abstract phonology. Lublin: Uniwersytet Marii Curie
          Skłodowskiej.
  1978b   Contrastive Polish-English consonantal phonology. Warsaw: Państwowe
          Wydanctwo Naukowe.
  1978c   Is the Second Velar Palatalization a synchronic rule of Modern Polish?
          BPTJ 35:27-41.
  1981   The phonological structure of the Polish imperative. Studia gramatycz-
          ne 3:33-46.
Gvozdev, A. N.
  1949   Formirovanie u rebenka grammatičeskogo stroja russkogo jazyka, I-II.
          Moscow: Izdatel'stvo Akademii Pedagogičeskih Nauk RSFSR.
Hačatrjan, A. A.
  1979   O funkcijah glasnoj [ə] v sovremennom armjanskom jazyke. Avanesov
          1979:261-5.
Haiman, John
  1980   The iconicity of grammar. Lg 56:515-40.
  1983   Iconic and economic motivation. Lg 59:781-819.
Hale, Kenneth
  1973   Deep-surface canonical disparities in relation to analysis and change:
          an Australian example. Current Trends in Linguistics 11:401-58.
  1979   The problem of psychological reality in the phonology of Papago.
          PICPhS 9,II:108-13.

Hall, Robert A.
1953   Haitian Creole.   Philadelphia: American Folklore Society.
Hallap, Viktor
1965   Phonological problems of the Moksha-Mordvin language.   In Congressus
Secundus Internationalis Fenno-Ugristarum (Helsinki) I:161-7.
Halle, Morris
1959   The sound pattern of Russian.   The Hague: Mouton.
1983   On distinctive features and their articulatory implementation.   Natural
Language and Linguistic Theory 1:91-105.
Halle, Morris, Joan Bresnan, and George A. Miller, eds.
1978   Linguistic theory and psychological reality.   Cambridge, MA: MIT Press.
Halle, Morris, and Jean-Roger Vergnaud
1981   Harmony processes.   In Crossing the boundaries in linguistics (eds. W.
Klein & W. Levelt).   Dordrecht: Reidel, 1-22.
Halliday, M. A. K.
1984   An introduction to Functional Grammar.   London: Arnold.
Harris, James W.
1969   Spanish phonology.   Cambridge, MA: MIT Press.
1977   Remarks on diphthongization in Spanish.   Lingua 41:261-305.
1978   A rejoinder to 'Vocalic variations in Spanish verbs'.   Glossa 12:83-100
1983   Syllable structure and stress in Spanish: a nonlinear analysis.   Cambridge, MA: MIT Press.
Hartmann, Dietrich
1980   Über Verschmelzungen von Präposition und bestimmten Artikel.   ZDL 47:
160-83.
Hasegawa, Nobuko
1979   Casual speech vs. fast speech.   PCLS 15:126-37.
Haslev, Marianne
1972   Morfo-fonemikk.   Synkrone og diakrone aspekter.   Oslo: Universitetsforlaget.
Hawkes, Terence
1977   Structuralism and semiotics.   London: Methuen.
Hayes, Bruce
1981   A metrical theory of stress rules.   Bloomington: Indiana University
Linguistics Club.
Hayes, P. J.
1980   The logic of frames.   Metzing 1980:46-61.
Hazai, G.
1973   Das Osmanisch-Türkische im XVII. Jahrhundert.   The Hague: Mouton.
Heger, Klaus
1968   Die *liaison* als phonologisches Problem.   Festschrift W. von Wartburg
(ed. K. Baldinger).   Tübingen: Niemeyer, 467-84.
Heidolph, Karl Erich, et al.
1981   Grundzüge einer deutschen Grammatik.   Berlin: Akademie-Verlag.
Heine, Bernd, and Mechthild Reh
1982   Patterns of grammaticalization in African languages.   akup 47.
Hellberg, Steffan
1978   Unnatural phonology.   JL 14:157-78.
1980   Apparent naturalness in Faroese-Nordic.   Journal of Linguistics 3:1-24.
1983   'They never come back.'   On unproductive rules and allomorphs.   Färsk
Forsk (Institutionen för Nordiska Språk, Göteborgs Universitet) 3.
Hempel, Carl G.
1965   Aspects of scientific explanation.   New York: Free Press.

Hempel, Carl, and Paul Oppenheim
  1936   Der Typenbegriff im Lichte der neuen Logik.   Leiden.
Herbert, Robert
  1977a   Morphophonological palatalization in Southern Bantu: a reply to segmen-
          tal fusion.   Studies in African Linguistics 8:143-71.   [Also in WlG 14:
          12-40.]
  1977b   Phonetic analysis in phonological description: prenasalized consonants
          and Meinhof's Rule.   Lingua 43:339-73.
  1977c   Language universals, markedness theory, and natural phonetic processes:
          the interactions of nasal and oral consonants.   Ohio State University
          dissertation.
Hermann, Eduard
  1931   Lautgesetz und Analogie.   Abhandlungen der Gesellschaft der Wissen-
          schaften zu Göttingen, Phil.-Hist. Klasse, Neue Folge 23.3.
  1932   Phonologische Mehrgültigkeit eines Lautes.   Philologische Wochenschrift
          35/38:115-8.
Hervey, Sándor
  1982   Semiotic perspectives.   London: Allen-Unwin.
Hetzron, Robert
  1971   Internal labialization in the tt-group of outer South Ethiopic.   JAOS
          91:192-207.
  1977   The Gunnän-Gurage languages.   Naples: Istituto Orientale di Napoli.
  1980   Review of Greenberg 1978.   Lingua 50:249-94.
Highfield, A., and A. Valdman, eds.
  1981   Historicity and variation in Creole studies.   Ann Arbor: Karoma.
Hint, Mati
  1971   Osnovnye fonologičeskie i morfonologičeskie problemy akcentuacionnoj
          sistemy èstonskogo jazyka.   Aftoreferat dissertacii.   Tallin: Akademija
          Nauk Èstonskoj SSR.
Hjordt-Vetlesen, Ole
  1981   La tendance dissimilatrice dans la dérivation nominale en roumain.
          RIDS 92:39p.
Hock, Hans Herich
  1976   Final weakening and related phenomena.   1975 Mid-America Linguistics
          Conference Papers 10 (ed. F. Ingemann).   Lawrence: Department of Lin-
          guistics, University of Kansas, 219-59.
  1979   Retroflexion rules in Sanskrit.   South Asian Languages Analysis 1:47-61.
Hockett, Charles F.
  1955   A manual of phonology.   (IJAL Memoir 11) Baltimore: Waverly Press.
  1958   A course in modern linguistics.   New York: MacMillan.
Hoel, Thomas
  1981   Hooper's fonologi - naturlig eller 'over-naturlig'?   Nordlyd 4:1-71.
Hogg, Richard M.
  1976   The status of rule reordering.   JL 12:103-23.
  1979   Analogy and phonology.   JL 15:55-85.
Holden, Kyril T.
  1976   Assimilation rates of borrowings and phonological productivity.   Lg 52:
          131-47.
  1982   Borrowing and the perception of English vowels in Russian.   CJL 27:135-
          49.
Holenstein, Elmar
  1976   Linguistik, Semiotik, Hermaneutik: Plädoyers für eine strukturale Phä-
          nomenologie.   Frankfurt: Suhrkamp.

1978   Präliminarien zu einer Theorie der funktionalen Aspekte der Sprache. Seiler 1978a:32-52.
1982   Gehirn und Geist: Zur Renaissance von Bewußtseinstheorien. Philosophische Rundschau 29:90-106.
Holmann, Eugene
1975   Grade alternation in Baltic-Finnic. University of Helsinki, Department of General Linguistics, Dress Rehersal 3.
Holmer, Nils M.
1947   Critical and comparative grammar of the Cuna language. Göteborg, Etnografiska Museet.
Honikman, B.
1964   Articulatory settings. In Honour of Daniel Jones. London, 73-95.
Hooper, Joan Bybee
1975   The archisegment in Natural Generative Phonology. Lg 51:536-60.
1976   An introduction to Natural Generative Phonology. New York: Academic Press.
1977   Substantive evidence: vowel length and nasality in English. PCLS 13: 152-64.
1979a   Child morphology and morphophonemic change. Linguistics 17:21-50.
1979b   Formal and substantive approaches in phonology. PICPhS 9:143-52.
1979c   Substantive principles in Natural Generative Phonology. Dinnsen 1979a: 106-25.
Horálek, Karel, ed.
1983   Praguiana: some basic and less known aspects of the Prague Linguistic School. Prague: Academia.
Horecký, Jan
1975   Generatívny opis fonologického systému spisovny slovenčiny. Acta Facultatis Philosophiae Universitatis Šafarikanae. Jazykovedný zborník 4:5-41.
1981   Morfematičeskij aspekt morfonologii v slovackom literaturnom jazyka. Popova 1981:299-302.
Horn, Wilhelm
1921   Sprachkörper und Sprachfunktion. Berlin: Mayer & Müller.
Hörz, Herbert, and Karl-Friedrich Wessel
1983   Philosophische Entwicklungstheorie. Berlin: VEB Deutscher Verlag der Wissenschaften.
Hoskison, James T.
1975   Notes on the phonology of Gude. Columbus: Ohio State University MA thesis.
Houlihan, Kathleen
1977   On aspiration and deaspiration processes. In Current themes in linguistics (ed. F. Eckman). New York: Wiley, 215-39.
Houlihan, Kathleen, and Gregory K. Iverson
1977   Phonological markedness and neutralization rules. Minnesota Working Papers in Linguistics and Philosophy of Language 4:45-58.
1979   Functionally-constrained phonology. Dinnsen 1979a:50-73.
Hovdhaugen, Even
1971   Turkish words in Khotanese words: a linguistic analysis. NTS 24:163-78
Hudson, Grover
1974   The role of surface phonetic constraints in Natural Generative Phonology. NatPhon, 171-83.
1976   Paradigmatic initiation of a sound change in Hadiya. Studies in African Linguistics 7:211-29.
1980   Automatic alternations in non-transformational phonology. Lg 56:94-125

1982   Reply to Darden 1979. PCLS 18:202-8.
Hulst, Harry van der
1979   Recent developments in phonological theory. Review of Hooper 1976.
         Lingua 49:207-38.
Hulst, Harry van der, and Jan G. Kooij
1981   On the direction of assimilation rules. Phonologica 1980:209-214.
Hulst, Harry van der, and Norval Smith, eds.
1982   The structure of phonological representations I, II. Dordrecht: Foris.
Humboldt, Wilhelm von
1835   Über die Verschiedenheit des menschlichen Sprachbaus und ihren Einfluß
         auf die geistige Entwicklung des Menschengeschlichts. Gesammelte Werke
         7. Berlin.
Hurch, Bernhard
1982   Studi sull' /h/. Testi di laurea, Università degli Studi di Pasi.
1983   H. Eine Studie zur kontrastiven Phonetik und Phonologie. Parallela
         (eds. M. Dardano, W. U. Dressler & G. Held). Tübingen: Narr, 271-80.
Hurch, Bernhard, and Livia Tonelli
1982   /'matto/ oder /'mat:o/? Jedenfalls /'mat:o/! Zur Konsonantenlänge im
         Italienischen. WlG 29:17-38.
Hutcheson, James W.
1973   A natural history of complete consonantal assimilations. Ohio State
         University dissertation. (Cf. Remarks on the nature of complete con-
         sonantal assimilation. PCLS 9 (1973):215-22.)
Hyman, Larry M.
1977   Phonologization. In Linguistic studies Greenberg II. Saratoga: Anma
         Libri, 407-18.
1978   Word demarcation. Greenberg 1978. II:443-70.
Ingram, David
1976a   Phonological disability in children. London: Arnold.
1976b   Current issues in child phonology. In Normal and deficient child lan-
         guage (eds. D. & A. Morehead). Baltimore: University Park Press, 3-27.
Ingria, Robert
1980   Compensatory lengthening as a metrical phenomenon. LInq 11,3:465-96.
Interplay of phonology, morphology, and syntax, Papers from the parasession on
the
1983   (eds. J. F. Richardson et al.). Chicago Linguistic Society.
Isačenko/Issatschenko, Alexander V.
1965   Syllabe et morphème en allemand. Omagiu lui A. Rosetti. Bucharest:
         Editura Academiei, 413-5.
1974   Das 'Schwa mobile' und das 'Schwa constans' im Deutschen. Festschrift
         für H. Moser I (eds. U. Engel & P. Grebe). Düsseldorf: Schwann, 142-71.
Istre, Giles L.
1981   How natural are natural classes? The /l, n, r, s/ case in Portuguese.
         Angenot et al. 1981:173-85.
1983   Fonologia transformacional e natural. Uma introdução crítica. Floria-
         nópolis: Univerdidade Federal de Santa Catarina.
Itkonen, Esa
1974   Linguistics and metascience. Kokemäki: Studia Philosophica Turkuensia
         II.
1981   Rationality as an explanatory principle in linguistics. Logos semanti-
         kos II, Festschrift E. Coseriu (eds. H. Geckeler et al.). Berlin: de
         Gruyter, 77-87.
Itkonen, Terho
1975   Über die Phonemsysteme der finnischen Dialekte. Linguistishe Studien
         22:35-57.

Ivanov, Vjačeslav V.
   1982   Die Linguistik und die humanwissenschaftlichen Probleme der Semiotik:
           Zur Evolution vom darstellenden Zeichen zum syntaktischen Symbolzeich-
           en. Zeitschrift für Semiotik 4:41-54.
Iverson Gregory K.
   1978   Synchronic umlaut in Old Icelandic. Nordic Journal of Linguistics 1:
           121-39.
   1981a   On the directionality of paradigm regularization. Goyvaerts 1981:545-
           54.
   1981b   Rules, constraints and paradigm lacunae. Glossa 15:136-44.
   1983a   Voice alternations in Lac Simon Algonquin. JL 19:161-4.
   1983b   The elsewhere condition and h-aspiré. JL 19:369-76.
Iverson, Gregory K., and Miren L. Oñederra
   1983   On Basque palatalization. Paper read at the winter meeting of the
           Linguistic Society of America. [To appear in Folia Linguistica XIX,
           1985.]
Iverson, Gregory K., and Catherine O. Ringen
   1978   Exception devices in phonology. PICL 12:780-85.
Iverson, Gregory K., and Gerald A. Saunders
   1978   The functional determination of phonological rule interactions. Bloom-
           ington: Indiana University Linguistics Club. [= Studia Linguistica 34:
           168-96 (1980).]
Jackson, Kenneth
   1953   Language and history in early Britain. Edinburgh University Press.
   1967   A historical phonology of Breton. The Dublin Institute for Advanced
           Studies.
Jaeger, Jeri J.
   1979   Vowel shift rules vs. spelling rules: which is psychologically real?
           Paper read at the 54th Annual Meeting of the Linguistic Society of
           America (Loa Angeles).
   1980a   Testing the psychological reality of phonemes. Lg & Sp 23:233-53.
   1980b   Categorization in phonology: an experimental approach. University of
           California, Berkeley, dissertation.
Jakobson, Roman
   1931   Prinzipien der historischen Phonologie. Traveaux du Cercle Linguis-
           tique de Prague 4:247-67. [= Jakobson 1962.I:202-20. English version
           in A. R. Keiler, A reader in historical and comparative linguistics.
           New York: Holt, 1972, 121-38.]
   1941   Kindersprache, Aphasie und allgemeine Lautgesetze. Uppsala: Almqvist-
           Wiksell. [= 1968. Child language, aphasia, and phonological univer-
           sals. The Hague: Mouton.]
   1962   Selected writings I, II. The Hague: Mouton.
   1975   Coup d'oeil sur le développement de la sémiotique. Bloomington: Indi-
           ana University Press.
Jakobson, Roman, and Morris Halle
   1956   Fundamentals of language. The Hague: Mouton.
Jakobson, Roman, and Linda Waugh
   1979   The sound shape of language. Bloomington: Indiana University Press.
Jakovlev, N. F.
   1948   Grammatika literaturnogo kabardino-čerkesskogo jazyka. Moscow: Nauka.
James, Allen R.
   1977   On the phonological relevance of articulatory basis. ZPSK 30:280-96.
Janda, Richard D.
   1979   Double-cross in phonology: why word-boundary (often) acts like a con-
           sonant. BLS 5:397-412.

1982   On limiting the form of morphological rules: German *umlaut*, diacritic
        features, and the 'cluster-constraint'. NELS 12:140-52.
1983   Two umlaut-heresies and their claim to orthodoxy. Coyote Papers 4:59-
        71.
Janson, Tore
1979   Mechanism of language change in Latin. Stockholm: Almqvist & Wiksell.
Janson, Tore, and Richard Schulman
1983   Non-distinctive features and their use. JL 19:321-36.
Jarceva, Viktoria, ed.
1969   Edinicy raznyn urovnej grammatičeskogo stroja jazyka i ih vzaimodejstvie.
        Moscow: Nauka.
Javkin, Hector R.
1979   Phonetic universals and phonological change. Report of the Phonology
        Laboratory 4 (University of California, Berkeley).
Jensen, Hans
1959   Altarmenische Grammatik. Heidelberg: Winter.
Jensen, John T.
1974   A constraint on variables in phonology. Lg 50:675-86.
Jensen, John T., and Margaret Strong-Jensen
1979   The relevancy condition and variables in phonology. LAn 5:125-60.
Jespersen, Otto
1949   Efficiency in linguistic change. Historik-filologiske Meddelelser
        27,4.   Here cited after O. J., selected writings. [Tokyo: Senyo, 381-
        466.]
Job, Dieter M.
1977   Probleme eines typologischen Vergleichs iberokaukasischer und indoger-
        manischer Phonemsysteme im Kaukasus. Bern-Frankfurt: Lang.
Jonasson, Jan
1971   Perceptual similarity and articulatory reinterpretation as a source of
        phonological innovation. Papers of the Institute of Linguistics, Uni-
        versity of Stockholm 8:30-42.
Jones, Charles
1976   Some constraints on medial consonant clusters. Lg 52:121-30.
Kachru, Braj, et al., eds.
1973   Issues in linguistics, papers in honor of Henry and Renée Kahane.
        Urbana: University of Illinois Press.
Kahn, Daniel
1976   Syllable-based generalizations in English phonology. Bloomington: In-
        diana University Linguistics Club.
1980   Syllable-structure specifications in phonological rules. Aronoff &
        Kean 1980:91-105.
Kainz, Friedrich
1956   Psychologie der Sprache IV. Stuttgart: Enke.
Kaisse, Ellen M.
1983   The English auxiliaries as sentential clitics. Interplay 96-102.
Kalnyn', L. È.
1981   K voprosu o razdelenii zvukovyh čeredovanij na fonetičeskie i nefoneti-
        českie. Popova 1981:205-12.
Karlsson, Fred
1974   Phonology, morphology, and morphophonemics. Gothenburg Papers in
        Theoretical Linguistics 23.
1977   Morphotactic structure and word cohesion in Finnish. Jyväskylä Con-
        trastive Studies 4:59-74.
to appear Paradigms and word-forms in Natural Morphology. Studia Grammatycz-
        ne.

Karpf, Annemarie
  1976   Typologie idiomatischer Komposita und Nominalsyntagmen. University of
          Vienna dissertation.
Kasevič, Vadim B.
  1979   Interferencija fonologii, morfonologii, orfografii v rečevoj dejatel'-
          nosti. Avanesov 1979:137-43.
  1983   Fonologičeskie problemy obščego i vostočnogo jazykoznanija. Moscow:
          Nauka.
Kasevič, Vadim B., and E. M. Šabel'nikova
  1983   Temp, ritmiki i strategija vosprijatija reči. Fonetika 83:78-89 (cf.
          9f).
Katamba, Francis
  1979   How hierarchical and universal is consonant strength? Theoretical
          Linguistics 6:25-40.
Kaufman, Terrence
  1969   Teco - a new Mayan language. IJAL 35:154-74.
Kaye, Jonathan D.
  1974a   Opacity and recoverability in phonology. CJL 19:134-49.
  1974b   Morpheme structure constraints live! Recherches linguistiques à Mont-
          réal 3:55-62.
  1981   Recoverability, abstractness, and phonematic constraints. Goyvaerts
          1981:469-81.
  1982   Harmony processes in Vata. Hulst & Smith 1982.II:385-452.
Kaye, Jonathan D., and Yves-Charles Morin
  1978   Il n'ya pas de règles de troncation, voyons! PICL 12:788-92.
Kaye, Jonathan D., and Barbara Nykiel
  1981   Abstract phonotactic constraints. Studia Anglica Posnaniensia 13:21-42.
Kazazis, Kostas
  1969   Possible evidence for (near-)underlying forms in the speech of a child.
          PCLS 5:372-9.
Kean, Mary Louise
  1981   On a theory of markedness: some general considerations and a case in
          point. GLOW 1979:559-604.
Keating, Patricia A., and Wendy Linker
  1982   Physiological motivations for phonetic naturalness. WPP 54:57-64.
Keating, Patricia A., et al.
  1983   Patterns in allophone distribution for voiced and voiceless stops.
          Journal of Phonetics 11:277-90.
Keller, Eric
  1980   Manuel de psycholinguistique. Montréal, UQAM.
Kenstowicz, Michael
  1981   Functional explanations in generative phonology. Goyvaerts 1981:431-44.
Kenstowicz, Michael, and Charles Kisseberth
  1977   Topics in phonological theory. New York: Academic Press.
  1979   Generative phonology. New York: Academic Press.
Kergoat, Lukian
  1972   Yezh ar Vugale. Hor Yezh 79:7-29.
Kervella, Fanch
  1947   Yezhadur bras ar brezhoneg. La Baule: Skridoù Breizh.
Kettemann, Bernhard
  1981   Evidence for the reality of segmental and transsegmental features.
          Phonologica 1980:237-43.
Keyser, Samuel J., and Wayne O'Neil
  1980   The evolution of the English plural rule. Journal of Linguistic Re-
          search 1,2:17-35.

Kibrik, A. E., et al.
 1977 Opyt strukturnogo opisanija arčinskogo jazyka. Izdatel'stvo Moskovskogo Universiteta. IV volumes.
Kibrik, A. E., S. V. Kodzasov, and I. P. Olovjannikova
 1972 Fragmenty grammatiki hinalugskogo jazyka. Moscow: Izdatel'stvo
 Moskovskogo Universiteta.
Kilani-Schoch, Marianne
 1984 Base lexicale en arabe classique et en arabe tunisien. Bulletin de la
 section de linguistique de la faculté des lettres de Lausanne 6.
Kilani-Schoch, Marianne, and Wolfgang U. Dressler
 to appear Natural Morphology and Tunisian vs. Classical Arabic. Studia
 Grammatyczne (ed. R. Laskowski). [Also in WlG 33, 1984.]
Kilbury, James
 1976 The development of morphophonemic theory. Amsterdam: Benjamins.
Kilham, Christine
 1977 Thematic organization of Wik-Munkan discourse. Canberra: Pacific
 Linguistics B 52.
Kim, Chin-Wu
 1972 Directionality of voicing and aspiration in initial position. PICPhS
 7 (eds. A. Rigault & R. Charbonneau). The Hague: Mouton, 338-43.
 1973 Opposition and complement in phonology. Kachru 1973.
Kim, Kong-On
 1977 Sound symbolism in Korean. JL 13:67-76.
Kim-Renaud, Young-Key
 1975 Korean consonantal phonology. University of Hawaii dissertation.
 1976 Semantic features in phonology: evidence from vowel harmony in Korean.
 PCLS 12:397-412.
King, Robert D.
 1967 Functional load and sound change. Lg 43:831-52.
 1969 Historical linguistics and generative grammar. Englewood Cliffs, NJ:
 Prentice-Hall.
 1973 Rule insertion. Lg 49:551-78.
 1976 The history of final devoicing in Yiddish. Bloomington: Indiana
 University Linguistics Club.
Kiparsky, Paul
 1972 Metrics and morphophonemics in the Rigveda. In Contributions to
 generative phonology (ed. M. Brame). Austin: University of Texas
 Press, 171-200.
 1973a 'Elsewhere' in phonology. In A Festschrift for Morris Halle (eds. S.
 Anderson & P. Kiparsky). New York: Holt, 93-106.
 1973b Phonological representations. In Three dimensions of linguistic
 theory (ed. O. Fujimura). Tokyo: TEC, 1-136.
 1973c The role of linguistics in a theory of poetry. Daedalus = Proceedings
 of the American Academy of Arts and Sciences 102,3:231-44.
 1975 What are linguistic theories about? In Testing linguistic hypotheses
 (eds. D. Cohen & J. Wirth). New York: Wiley, 187-220.
 1979 Metrical structure assignment is cyclic. LInq 10:421-41.
 1981 Remarks on the metrical structure of the syllable. Phonologica 1980:
 245-56.
 1982a Explanation in phonology. Dordrecht: Foris. [A collection of
 republished articles.]
 1982b Lexical morphology and phonology. MS, MIT, 150p. (Cf. 1982c.)
 1982c From cyclic phonology to lexical phonology. Hulst & Smith 1982.I:131-
 75. [p. 131-43 = 1982b:1-20, p. 143-73 = 1982b:47-94.]

1982d   Lexical levels in analogical change: the case of Icelandic.   MS, MIT.
Kiparsky, Paul, and Lise Menn
1977   On the acquisition of phonology.   Macnamara 1977:47-78.
Kirchmeier, Monika
1973   Entlehnung und Lehnwortgebrauch.   Tübingen: Niemeyer.
Kirshenblatt-Gimblett, Barbara, ed.
1976   Speech play.   University of Pennsylvania Press.
Klaus, Georg
1968   Wörterbuch der Kybernetik.   Berlin: Dietz.
Klausenburger, Jürgen
1978   Mikołaj Kruszewski's theory of morphophonology: an appraisal.   His-
        toriographia Linguistica 5:109-20.
1979   Morphologization: studies in Latin and Romance morphonology.   Tübingen:
        Niemeyer.
Klavans, Judith L.
1983   The morphology of cliticization.   Interplay 103-121.
Klein, Harriet
1978   The relationship between perceptual strategies and productive strate-
        gies in learning the phonology of early lexical items.   Bloomington:
        Indiana University Linguistics Club.
Kleinmuntz, Benjamin, ed.
1966   Problem solving.   New York: Wiley.
Klima, Edward, and Ursula Bellugi
1979   The signs of language.   Cambridge, MA: Harvard University Press.
Klimov, Georgij A.
1978   Strukturnye obščnosti kavkazskih jazykov.   Moscow: Nauka.
Klimov, Georgij A., and M. E. Aleksev
1980   Tipologija kavkazskih jazykov.   Moscow: Nauka.
Kloster-Jensen, Martin
1975   Wohin gehört die Morphophonologie?   Festschrift Hugo Moser II.
        Düsseldorf: Schwann, 244-51.
Knudson, Lyle M.
1975   A natural phonology and morphophonemics of Chimalapa Zoque.   Work
        Papers SIL 19, University of North Dakota Session, Section II.
Kodzasov, Sandro V.
1976   Model' fonetičeskoj sistemy (na materiale arčinskogo jazyka).   Moscow:
        Institut Russkogo Jazyka ANSSR.
Kodzasov, Sandro V., and Ol'ga F. Krivnova
1981   Sovremennaja amerikanskaja fonologija.   Moscow: Izdatel'stvo Moskovsko-
        go Universiteta.
Kohrt, Manfred
1980   Rule ordering, rule extension, and the history and present status of
        /ng/ clusters in German.   Linguistics 18:777-802.
Koj, Leon
1979   The principle of transparency and semantic antinomies.   In Semiotics
        in Poland (ed. Jerzy Pelc).   Dordrecht: Reidel, 376-406.
Komárek, Miroslav
1964   Sur l'appréciation functionelle des alternances morphonologiques.
        Traveaux linguistiques de Prague 1:145-61.
Kooij, Jan G.
1971   Ambiguity in natural language.   Amsterdam: North Holland.
Korhonen, Mikko
1969   Die Entwicklung der morphologischen Methode im Lappischen.   FUF 37:
        203-62.

1975   Zur Phonologie des Skoltlappischen. Linguistische Studien A.
        Arbeitsbereichte 22 (Berlin), 11-34.
1980   Über die struktural-typologischen Strömungen (drifts) in den uralischen
        Sprachen. Congressus 5. Intern. Fenno-Ugristarum I (ed. O. Ikola).
        Turku: Suomen Kielen Seura, 28-42.
Koutsoudas, Andreas
1964   The handling of morphophonemic processes in transformational grammar.
        Papers Pappageotes (Word supplement 20), 28-42.
1976   (ed.) The application and ordering of grammatical rules. The Hague:
        Mouton.
1977   On the necessity of the morphophonemic-allophonic distinction.
        Phonologica 1976, 121-6.
1980   The question of rule ordering: some common fallacies. JL 16:19-35.
Koutsoudas, Andreas, and Gerald A. Sanders
1979   On the universality of rules and rule ordering constraints. Studia
        Linguistica 33:57-78.
Koźbiał, Jan
1980   Zur Geschichte der 'phonematischen Wertungen' im Bereich des polnischen
        Konsonantismus. Kwartalnik Neofilologiczny 27:335-45.
Krámský, Jiři
1956   Über den Ursprung und die Funktion der Vokalharmonie in den ural-
        altaischen Sprachen. Zeitschrift der Deutschen Morgenländischen
        Gesellschaft 106:117-34.
1981   Review of Dressler 1977a. JLASSO.
Krause, Wolfgang
1963   Handbuch des Gotischen. Munich: Beck.
Kretschmer, Paul
1905   Der heutige lebische Dialekt. Vienna: Hölder.
Krier, Fernande
1975   Analyse phonologique du maltais. Phonetica 32:103-29.
Krishnamurti, Bh.
1978   Areal and lexical diffusion of sound change: evidence from Dravidian.
        Lg 54:1-20.
Kristeva, Julia
1969   Séméoitikè. Recherches pour une sémanalyse. Paris.
Kristoffersen, Gjert
1980   Abstraksjonsproblemet i generativ fonologi, belyst ved data fra
        Arendalsdialekten. Nordlyd 3:7-61.
Krohn, Robert
1975   Underlying vowels in Modern English. Goyvaerts & Pullum 1975:395-412.
Krohn, Robert, and D. Steinberg
1979   The productivity of vowel alternations in English. WPL Hawaii 5,6:24-
        47.
Krupa, Viktor
1967   Dissociations of like consonants in morphemic forms. Asian and African
        Studies 3:37-44.
1968   The Maori language. Moscow: Nauka.
Kruszewski, Mikołaj
1881   Über die Lautabwechslung. Kazan: Universitätsbuchdruckerei.
Kubrjakova, Elena S., and Jurij G. Pankrac
1983   Morfonologija v opisanii jazykov. Moscow: Nauka.
Kučera, Henry
1958   Inquiry into coexistent phonemic systems in Slavic languages. American
        contributions to the 4th Int. Congress of Slavistics. s'-Gravenhage:
        Mouton, 1-21.

Kuki, Hiroshi
    1970   Tuamotuan phonology.   Canberra: Pacific Linguistics.
Kumahov, Muhadin A.
    1971   Slovoizmenenie adygskih jazykov.   Moscow: Nauka.
Kuryłowicz, Jerzy
    1949   La nature des procès dits 'analogiques'.   Acta Linguistica (Hafniensia)
            5:15-37.
    1961   L'apophonie en sémitique.   Wrocław: Wydawnictwo Polskieij Akademii
            Nauk.
    1964   The inflectional categories of Indo-European.   Heidelberg: Winter.
    1967   Phonologie und Morphonologie.   PhonGeg 158-72.
    1968   The notion of morpho(pho)neme.   Lehmann & Malkiel 1968:65-81.
    1972   Studies in Semitic grammar and metrics.   Wrocław: Wyd. Polsk. Akad.
            Nauk.
Labov, William
    1970   The study of language in its social context.   Studium Generale 23:30-67.
    1972   The internal evolution of linguistic rules.   In Linguistic change and
            generative theory (eds. R. Stockwell & W. Macauley).   Bloomington:
            Indiana University Press, 101-71.
    1975   Il continuo e il discreto nel linguaggio.   Bologna: Il Mulino.
    1981   Resolving the neogrammarian controversy.   Lg 57:267-308.
Ladefoged, Peter
    1971   Preliminaries to linguistic phonetics.   University of Chicago Press.
    1980a   What are linguistic sounds made of?   Lg 56:485-502.
    1980b   Cross-linguistic studies of speech production.   WPP 51 (UCLA), 94-104.
Laferriere, Martha
    1974   Some theoretical properties of rule addition and rule loss.   NELS 5:
            192-9.
Lakatos, Imre, and Alan Musgrave, eds.
    1974   Criticism and the growth of knowledge.   Cambridge University Press.
Langacker, Ronald W.
    1977   On overview of Uto-Aztecan grammar.   Dallas: Summer Institute of
            Linguistics.
Langdon, Margaret
    1975   Boundaries and lenition in Yuman languages.   IJAL 41:218-33.
Langhoff, Stephan
    1979   Ganzheitliche Sprachbeschreibung am Beispiel modaler Infinitivkonstruk-
            tionen im Deutschen und Englischen.   University of Hamburg dissertation.
Lapointe, Steven G., and Mark H. Feinstein
    1982   The role of vowel deletion and epenthesis in the assignment of syllable
            structure.   Hulst & Smith 1982.I:69-120.
Laskowski, Roman
    1975   Studia nad morfonologią współeczesnego języka polskiego.   Wrocław:
            Ossolineum.
    1979   Polnische Grammatik.   Leipzig: Verlag Enzyklopädie.
    1980   Semiotyczna funkcja alternacji morfonologicznych.   Polonica 6:7-18.
    1981   Kakuju morfonologiju vybrat'?   Popova 1981:5-35.   [Cf. the Polish ver-
            sion: Czy alternacje morfonologiczne są zbędne?   Slavica Lundensia 7
            (1979), 21-34.]
Lass, Roger
    1971   Boundaries as obstruents.   Old English voicing assimilations and
            universal strength hierarchies.   JL 7:15-30.
    1974   Linguistic orthogenesis?   Scots vowel quantity and the English length
            conspiracy.   In Historical linguistics (ICHL 1, eds. J. M. Anderson &
            C. Jones).   Amsterdam: North Holland, II:311-52.

1975   How intrinsic is content? Goyvaerts § Pullum 1975:475-504.
1976   English phonology and phonological theory. Synchronic and diachronic
        studies. Cambridge University Press.
1980a   On explaining sound change. Cambridge University Press.
1980b   Paradigm coherence and the conditioning of sound change: Yiddish
        'schwa-deletion' again. Fisiak 1980:251-72.
1980c   On some possible weaknesses of 'strong naturalism'. TCLC 20:93-102.
1981   Explaining language change: the future of an illusion. Phonologica
        1980, 257-73.
1983   Velar /r/ and the history of English. In Current topics in English
        historical linguistics (eds. M. Davenport et al.). Odense University
        Press, 67-94.
Le Page, Robert
1977   Processes of pidginization and creolization. Valdman 1977a:222-55.
Leben, William, and Orrin W. Robinson
1977   'Upside-down' phonology. Lg 53:1-20.
Lee, Gregory, and Irwin Howard
1974   Another mouthful of divinity fudge. NatPhon, 220-32.
Lehiste, Ilse
1970   Suprasegmentals. Cambridge, MA: MIT Press.
1973   Phonetic disambiguation of syntactic ambiguity. Glossa 7:107-22.
1978   Einige Beobachten über Wortgrenzen im Deutschen. Wege der Worte,
        Festschrift Fleischhauer (ed. D. Riechel). Cologne: Böhlau, 70-5.
1983   The role of prosody in the internal structuring of a sentence. PICL
        13:220-31.
Lehiste, Ilse, et al.
1976   Role of duration in disambiguating syntactically ambiguous sentences.
        JASA 60:1199-202.
Lehmann, Christian
1974   Isomorphismus in sprachlichen Zeichen. Linguistic Workshop II (ed.
        H. Seiler). Munich: Fink, 98-123.
1981   Zur Universaliendiskussion in der italienischen Linguistik. Folia
        Linguistica 15:443-58.
Lehmann, Winfred P.
1952   Proto-Indo-European phonology. Austin: University of Texas Press.
1978   Syntactic typology. Austin: University of Texas Press.
Lehmann, Winfred P., and Yakov Malkiel, eds.
1968   Directions for historical linguistics. Austin: University of Texas
        Press.
Lehtonen, Jaako, and Matti Koponen
1977   Signalling of morphophonological boundaries by Finnish speakers of
        English. Jyväskylä Contrastive Studies 4:75-87.
Leinfellner, Elisabeth
1980   Kausalität und Sprache. Vienna: Österreichische Studiengesellschaft
        für Kybernetik.
Leinfellner, Werner
1965   Einführung in die Erkenntnis- und Wissenschaftstheorie. Mannheim:
        Bibliographisches Institut.
Lekomtseva, Margarita I.
1983   Towards a typology of phonological systems of Central and South-East
        European languages. MS. 10th Intern. Congress of Phonetic Sciences
        (Utrecht).
Leonard, Laurence, et al.
1980   Individual differences in early child phonology. Applied Psycholin-
        guistics 1:7-30.

Lepschy, Anna Laura, and Giulio Lepschy
  1981   La lingua italiana. Milan: Bompiani.
Lepschy, Giulio
  1965   K(i) e k(i̯). L'Italia Dialettale 28:181-99.
Lightner, Theodore
  1972a Problems in the theory of phonology. I: Russian phonology and Turkish
         phonology. Edmonton: Linguistic Research Inc.
  1972b Some remarks on exceptions and on coexistent systems in phonology. In
         The Slavic word (ed. D. S. Worth). The Hague: Mouton, 426-36.
Lindau, Mona
  1978   Vowel features. Lg 54:541-63.
  1980   The story of /r/. WPP (UCLA) 51:114-9.
Lindblom, Bjørn
  1972   Phonetics and the description of language. PICPhS 7:63-97.
  1983   On the teleological nature of speech processes. Speech Communication
         2:155-8.
  1984   Can the models of evolutionary biology be applied to phonetic problems?
         MS. Dept. of Linguistics, Stockholm.
Lindblom, Bjørn, and Johan Liljencrants
  1972   Numerical simulation of vowel quality systems: the role of perceptual
         contrast. Lg 48:839-62.
Lindblom, Bjørn, Peter MacNeilage, and Michael Studdert-Kennedy
  forthc. Self-organizing processes and the explanation of phonological univer-
         sals. In Explanations of linguistic universals (eds. B. Butterworth et
         al.). The Hague: Mouton.
Lindner, Gerhart
  1975   Der Sprechbewegungsablauf. Berlin: Akademie-Verlag.
Linell, Per
  1974   Problems of psychological reality in generative phonology. RUUL 4.
  1979a Evidence for a functionally-based typology of phonological rules.
         Communication and Cognition 12,1:53-106. [An earlier version appeared
         in Phonologica 1976, 9-20.]
  1979b Psychological reality in phonology. Cambridge University Press. [Com-
         pletely revised version of Linell 1974.]
  1980   The synchronic validity of linguistic constructs: comments on the
         treatment of 'psychological reality' in contemporary linguistics.
         Papers from the Institute of Linguistics, University of Stockholm.
  1981   The concept of phonological form and the activities of speech produc-
         tion and perception. RUUL 8:1-66. [Journal of Phonetics 10, 1982:37-
         72.]
  1983   How misperceptions arise. In From sounds to words, Festschrift C.-C.
         Elert. Umeå Studies in the Humanities 60:179-91.
Lipski, John M.
  1973   The surface structure of Portuguese: plurals and other things.
         Linguistics 111:67-82.
Locke, John
  1983   Phonological acquisition and change. New York: Academic Press.
Loos, Eugene E.
  1969   The phonology of Capanahua and its grammatical basis. Norman, OK:
         Summer Institute of Linguistics.
Lopatin, Vladimir V.
  1975   Tak nazyvaemaja interfiksacija i problemy struktury slova v russkom
         jazyka. VJa 1975,4:24-37.

Lovins, Julie Beth
    1973   Loanwords and the phonological structure of Japanese. University of
            Chicago dissertation. [Bloomington: Indiana University Linguisics
            Club, 1975.]
Lowenstamm, Jean
    1979   Topics in syllabic phonology. University of Massachusetts, Amherst,
            dissertation.
Lüdtke, Helmut
    1970   Sprache als kybernetisches Phänomen. In Theorie und Empirie in der
            Sprachforschung (eds. H. Pilch & H. Richter, Festschrift E. Zwirner),
            34-50.
    1980   (ed.) Kommunikationstheoretische Grundlagen des Sprachwandels.
            Berlin-New York: de Gruyter.
Luftig, Richard L.
    1983   Variables influencing the learnability of individual signs and sign
            lexicons: a review of the literature. Journal of Psycholinguistic
            Research 12:361-76.
Luick, Karl
    1914   Grammatik der englischen Sprache I. Leipzig: Tauchnitz.
Lupaş, Liana
    1972   Phonologie du grec attique. The Hague: Mouton.
Luschützky, Christian
    to appear Zur Natürlichen Phonologie der Affrikaten. Akten des 18. Linguis-
            tischen Kolloquiums. Tübingen: Niemeyer.
Lyche, Chantal
    1979   Glides in French: questions for Natural Generative Phonology. Lingua
            49:315-30.
Lyons, John
    1977   Semantics I. Cambridge University Press.
MacKay, Donald
    1973   Spoonerisms. Fromkin 1973:164-94.
    1978   Derivational rules and the internal lexicon. Journal of Verbal
            Learning and Verbal Behavior 77:61-71.
    1979   Lexical insertion and derivation: creative processes in word produc-
            tion. Journal of Psycholinguistic Research 8,8:477-83.
Macnamara, John, ed.
    1977   Language learning and thought. New York: Academic Press.
MacNeilage, Peter F.
    1979   Speech production. PICPhS 9,I:11-39.
MacWhinney, Brian
    1978   The acquisition of morphophonology. University of Chicago Press.
MacWhinney, Brian, and Csaba Pléh
    forthc. Competition between grammatical and morphophonological cues: a study
            of agreement in Hungarian. MS.
Magnus, G. B.
    1973   A case of rule reversal? PILUS 16:1-7.
Major, Roy C.
    1981   Stress-timing in Brazilian Portuguese. Journal of Phonetics 9:343-51.
Makkai, Valerie B., ed.
    1972   Phonological theory. New York: Holt.
Malécot, A., and G. Metz
    1972   Progressive nasal assimilation in French. Phonetica 26:193-209.

Malkiel, Yakov
 1958   Los interfijos hispánicos. In Miscelánea homenaje a A. Martinet II.
         Madrid: Gredos, 107-99.
 1964/1968 Some diachronic implications of fluid speech communities. American
         Anthropologist 66:177-86. [Reprinted in Essays on linguistic themes.
         Berkeley: University of California Press, 19-31.]
 1967   Multiple versus simple causation in linguistic change. In To honor
         Roman Jakobson II. The Hague: Mouton, 1228-46.
 1968   The inflectional paradigm as an occasional determinant of sound change.
         Lehmann & Malkiel 1968:21-64.
 1969a   Sound changes rooted in morphological conditions. Romance Philology
         23:188-200.
 1969b   Morphological analogy as a stimulus for sound change. Lingua e Stile
         4:305-27.
 1976   Multi-conditioned sound change and the impact of morphology on phonolo-
         gy. Lg 52:757-78.
Malmberg, Bertil
 1962   La notion de 'force' et les changements phonétiques. Studia Linguisti-
         ca 16:131-78.
Malone, Joseph
 1971   Systematic metathesis in Mandaic. Lg 47:394-415.
Malsheen, Bathsheba J.
 1980   Two hypotheses for phonetic clarification in the speech of mothers to
         children. Yeni-Komshian et al. 1980:173-84.
Manaster-Ramer, Alexis
 1984   How abstruse is phonology? Bloomington: Indiana University Linguistics
         Club.
Manessy, Gabriel
 1977   Processes of pidginization in African languages. Valdman 1977a:129-154.
Mansell, P.
 1973   Counter-feeding and rule reordering. FIPK Munich 1:163-83.
Marchand, Hans
 1964   A set of criteria for the establishing of derivational relationship
         between words unmarked by derivational morphemes. IF 69:10-19.
Mardirussian, Galust
 1975   Noun-incorporation in universal grammar. PCLS 11:383-9.
Markey, Thomas L.
 1981   Diffusion, fusion and creolization: a field guide to Developmental
         Linguistics. Papiere zur Linguistik 24:3-37.
Marstrander, Carl S. J.
 1942   Notes on alliteration. Serta Eitremiana. Oslo: Brøgger, 185-208.
Martin, Samuel E.
 1952   Morphophonemics of standard colloquial Japanese. Baltimore: LSA.
 1954   Korean morphophonemics. Baltimore: LSA.
Martinet, André
 1949   Phonology as functional phonetics. London: Oxford University Press.
 1955   Économie des changements phonétiques. Bern: Francke.
 1957   Substance phonique et traits distinctifs. BSLP 53:72-85.
 1965   De la morphonologie. La linguistique 1:15-30.
Mascaró, Joan
 1978   Catalan phonology and the phonological cycle. Bloomington: Indiana
         University Linguistics Club.
Maslov, Jurij S.
 1979   O tipologii čeredovanii. Avanesov 1979:195-201.

Mathesius, Vilém
  1934   Zur synchronischen Analyse fremden Sprachguts. Englische Studien 70: 21-35. [English translation in J. Vachek, ed., 1964, A Prague School reader in linguistics. Bloomington: Indiana University Press, 398-412.]

Matthews, Peter H.
  1972   Inflectional morphology. Cambridge University Press.
  1974   Morphology. Cambridge University Press.
  1981   Formalization. In Linguistic controversies, Festschrift F. R. Palmer (ed. D. Crystal). London: Arnold, 1-15.
  1982   Do languages obey general laws? Cambridge University Press.

Mauro, Tullio de
  1967   Corso di linguistica generale = [Commented Italian translation of de Saussure 1916.] Bari: Laterza.

Mayerthaler, Eva
  1981   Review of Klausenburger 1979. Kratylos 26:132-8.
  1982   Unbetonter Vokalismus und Silbenstruktur im Romanischen. Tübingen: Niemeyer.

Mayerthaler, Willi
  1977   Studien zur theoretischen und zur französischen Morphologie. Tübingen: Niemeyer.
  1980a   Ikonismus in der Morphologie. Zeitschrift für Semiotik 2:19-37.
  1980b   Aspekte der Analogietheorie. Lüdtke 1980:80-130.
  1981   Morphologische Natürlichkeit. Wiesbaden: Athenaion. [An English translation 'Morphological naturalness' is to appear. Ann Arbor: Karoma.]
  1982   Markiertheit in der Phonologie. In Silben, Segmente, Akzente (ed. Th. Vennemann). Tübingen: Niemeyer, 205-46.

McCalla, Kim
  1984   Entropy in natural languages. MS. for Folia Linguistica.

McCawley, James D.
  1971   On the role of notation in generative phonology. Bloomington: Indiana University Linguistics Club.
  1979   Remarks on Cena's vowel shift experiment. In The elements, parasession CLS (eds. P. R. Clyne et al.). Chicago Linguistic Society, 110-8.

McCormick, Susan
  1981   A metrical analysis of umlaut. Cornell University Working Papers in Linguistics 2:126-37.

McNeill, David
  1979   The conceptual basis of language. Hillsdale, NJ: Lawrence Erlbaum.
  1980   Iconic relationships between language and motor action. Rauch & Carr 1980:240-51.

Meara, Paul, and Andrew W. Ellis
  1981   The psychological reality of deep and surface phonological representations: evidence from speech errors in Welsh. Linguistics 19:797-804.

Mehmeti, Ismail
  1982   A morphological and semantic analysis of the adaptation of anglicisms in Albanian. Filipović 1982:28-56.

Meillet, Antoine
  1936   Esquisse d'une grammaire comparée de l'arménien classique. Vienna: Mekhitarists.

Mel'čuk, Igor
  1973   Model' sprjaženija v aljutorskom jazyke. Moscow: Institut Russkogo Jazyka ANSSR.

1974   Opyt teorii lingvističeskih modelej 'smysl ⟺ tekst'. Moscow: Nauka.
1976   On suppletion. Linguistics 170:45-90.
1982   Towards a language of linguistics: a system of formal notions for theoretical morphology. Munich: Fink.

Melikischwili, I. G. (= Melikišvili)
1970   Einige universale Gesetzmäßigkeiten in dem System der Affrikaten. In Theoretical problems of typology and the northern Eurasian languages (eds. L. Dezső & P. Hajdú). Budapest: Akadémia Kiadó, 65-73.

Meringer, Rudolf
1908   Aus dem Leben der Sprache. Berlin: Behr.

Meringer, Rudolf, and Karl Mayer
1895   Versprechen und Verlesen. Stuttgart: Göschen. [Reedited by A. Cutler & D. Fay, 1982. Amsterdam: Benjamins.]

Merlan, Francesca
1982   Mangarayi. Lingua Descriptive Series 4. Amsterdam: North Holland.

Metzing, Dieter, ed.
1980   Frame conceptions and text understanding. Berlin-New York: de Gruyter.

Meyer-Ingwersen, Johannes
1975   Deutschfehler bei türkischen Schülern. Zeitschrift für Literatur und Linguistik 5/18:68-77.

Michaels, David
1980   Spelling and the phonology of tense vowels. Lg&Sp 23:379-92.
1981   Upside-down rules, via-rules and derivational phonology. Goyvaerts 1981.

Michaels, David, and Howard Lasnik
1978   A reanalysis of English vowel alternations. PICL 12:808-11.

Migliorini, Bruno
1960   Storia della lingua italiana. Florence: Sansoni.

Mikoś, Michael J.
1979a   Phonological rules of consonants in Polish. IRSL 4:31-47.
1979b   Phonological rules of vowels in Polish. IRSL 4:183-92.

Miller, D. Gary
1973   On the motivation of phonological change. Kachru 1973:686-718.
1975   When are non-alternating surface features not lexicalized? MS, University of Florida, Gainesville.
1977   Language change and poetic options. Lg 53:21-38.

Miner, Kenneth L.
1981   Bloomfield's process phonology and Kiparsky's opacity. IJAL 47:310-22.

Minsky, Marvin
1980   A framework for representing knowledge. Metzing 1980:1-25.

Mioni, Alberto
1971a   Analisi binaria del sistema fonematico di una lingua bantu: il rundi. Lingua e Stile 6:67-96.
1971b   Sistema primario plurimo, sistema secondario italiano: fonematica contrastiva. In L'insegnamento dell' italiano (Atti di Società di Linguistica Italiana 4). Rome: Bulzoni, 549-77.

Mioni, Alberto, and John Trumper
1977   Per un'analisi del 'continuum' linguistico veneto. Aspetti Sociolinguistici dell' Italia contemporanea (eds. R. Simone & C. Ruggiero). Rome: Bulzoni, 329-72.

Miranda, Rocky
1973   The nature of rule loss. Battle & Schweitzer 1973:240-5.

Mithun, Marianne
1979   The consciousness of levels of phonological structure. IJAL 45:343-8.

Moessner, Lilo
    1978   Morphonologie. Anglistische Arbeitshefte 17. Tübingen: Niemeyer.
Mohanan, Karuvannur P.
    1982   Lexical Phonology. Bloomington: Indiana University Linguistics Club.
Moravcsik, Edith A.
    1977a   Necessary and possible universals about temporal constituent-relation
            in language. Bloomington: Indiana University Linguistics Club.
    1977b   Phonological metathesis and the invariant ordering constraint. In Pro-
            ceedings of the 1976 Mid-America Linguistics Conference (eds. R. L.
            Brown et al.). Minneapolis: University of Minnesota Press, 243-54.
    1977c   On rules of infixing. Bloomington: Indiana University Linguistics
            Club.
    1978   Reduplicative constructions. Greenberg 1978.III:297-334.
    1980   Some crosslinguistic generalizations about motivated symbolism. In
            Wege zur Universalienforschung, Festschrift H. Seiler (eds. G. Brett-
            schneider & C. Lehmann). Tübingen: Narr.
Moravcsik, Michael
    1977   The crisis in particle physics. Research Policy 6:78-107
Morin, Yves-Charles
    1970   Syntax and phonology meet at more than one point. University of
            Michigan Phonetics Lab Notes 6:6-18.
    1971   Computer experiments in generative phonology: low-level French phonolo-
            gy. Natural Language Studies 11. Ann Arbor: Department of Computer
            and Communication Sciences Phonetics Laboratory, University of Michigan.
            [Second edition, ed. K. C. Hill, 1979, Department of Linguistics, Uni-
            versity of Michigan.]
    1975a   La phonétique est-elle abstraite? Le cas du bourouchaskie. Recherches
            linguistiques à Montréal 5:175-9.
    1975b   Les contraintes phonotactiques et le lexique. Recherches à Montréal
            5:181f.
    1976   Naissance d'une contrainte de structure smophématique en bourouchaski.
            Recherches linguistiques à Montréal 7:157-62.
    1978   Morphological regularization in the verbal paradigm of French. In
            Contemporary studies in Romance linguistics (ed. M. Suñer). Washington:
            Georgetown University Press, 218-40.
    1979   La morphophonologie des pronoms clitiques en français populaire. MS
            for Cahier de linguistique 9. (UCAM)
    1980   Morphologisation de l'épenthèse en ancien français. Revue Canadienne
            de linguistique 25:204-25.
    1983   De la (dé)nasalisation et de la marque du genre en français. Lingua
            61:133-56.
Morin, Yves-Charles, and Jonathan D. Kaye
    1982   The syntactic bases for French liaison. JL 18:291-330.
Morpurgo-Davies, Anna
    1976   The -essi- datives, Aeolic -ss-, and the Lesbian poets. In Studies in
            Greek, Italic, and Indo-European linguistics, offered to L. R. Palmer
            (eds. A. Morpurgo-Davies & W. Meid). Innsbruck, 181-97.
    1978a   Analogy, segmentation, and the early Neogrammarians. TPS 1978:36-60.
    1978b   Thessalian eintessi and the participle of the verb 'to be'. In Etrennes
            de Septantaine, offerts à M. Lejeune. Paris: Klincksieck, 157-66.
Morris, Charles W.
    1938   Foundations of the theory of signs. University of Chicago Press.
    1971   Writings on the general theory of signs. The Hague: Mouton.
    1981   Zeichen, Sprache und Verhalten. Frankfurt: Ullstein.

Moses, Judith
  1982   The Swiss German case of vowel lowering and umlaut: rule reordering or
          rule restructuring. PCLS 18:367-76.
Moskowitz, Breyne A.
  1973   On the status of vowel shift in English. In Cognitive development and
          the acquisition of language (ed. T. Moore). New York: Academic Press,
          233-60.
Motsch, Wolfgang
  1981   Der kreative Aspekt in der Wortbildung. In Wortbildung (ed. L. Lipka).
          Darmstadt: Wissenschaftliche Buchgesellschaft, 94-118.
Moulton, William
  1960   The short vowel system of Northern Switzerland: a study in structural
          dialectology. Word 16:155-82.
Mugdan, Joachim
  1977   Flexionsmorphologie und Psycholinguistik. Tübingen: Narr.
Mühlhäusler, Peter
  1979   Growth and structure of the lexicon of New Guinea Pidgin. Canberra:
          Pacific Linguistics.
  1981   Structural expansion and the process of creolization. Highfield &
          Valdman 1981.
  1983   The development of word formation in Tok Pisin. FoL 17:463-87.
Mulder, Jan W. G., and Sándor G. J. Hervey
  1980   The strategy of linguistics: papers on the theory and methodology of
          axiomatic functionalism. Edinburg: Scottish Academic Press.
Muraki, Masatake
  1982   Two types of rule orderings. Annual Reports, International Christian
          University (Tokyo), 7:137-45.
Murphy, Gerard
  1961   Early Irish metrics. Dublin: Hodges.
Murray, Robert W.
  1982   Consonant cluster developments in Pali. FLH 3:163-84.
Murray, Robert W., and Theo Vennemann
  1983   Sound change and syllable structure in Germanic phonology. Lg 59:514-
          28.
Muysken, Pieter
  1981   (ed.) Generative studies in Creole languages. Dordrecht: Foris.
  1982   Parametrizing the notion head. Journal of Lg Research 2,3:57-75.
Myerson, Rosemarie F.
  1976   A study of children's knowledge of certain word formation rules and the
          relationship of this knowledge to various forms of reading achievement.
          Harvard University dissertation.
Narang, G. C., and D. A. Becker
  1971   Aspiration and nasalization in the generative phonology of Hindi-Urdu.
          Lg 47:646-67.
Nasálfest (1975), eds. C. A. Ferguson et al., Language Universals Project,
          Department of Linguistics, Stanford University.
Nater, H. F.
  1979   Bella Coola phonology. Lingua 49:169-187.
NatPhon = Papers from the parasession on Natural Phonology (1974), eds. A. Bruck
          et al. Chicago: Chicago Linguistics Society.
Neeld, Roland L.
  1973   Remarks on palatalization. WPL (Ohio State University) 14:37-49.
Németh, J.
  1965   Die Türken von Vidin. Budapest: Akadémiai Kiadó.

Neuhaus, H. Joachim
    1973   Zur Theorie der Produktivität von Wortbildungssystemen. In Linguisti-
            sche Perspektiven (eds. A. P. ten Cate & P. Jordens). Tübingen: Nie-
            meyer, 305-17.
    1975   Morphotaktische Zyklen. Rix 1975:220-31.
Neumann, Ursula, and Hans Reich
    1977   Türkische Kinder - deutsche Lehrer. Düsseldorf: Schwann.
Newell, Allan
    1969   Problem solving. Encyclopaedia of linguistics, information and control
            (ed. A. R. Meetham). New York: Pergamon Press, 413-26.
Newell, Allan, and Herbert Simon
    1972   Human problem solving. Englewood Cliffs, NJ: Prentice-Hall.
Newmeyer, Frederick J.
    1980   Linguistic theory in America. New York: Academic Press.
    1983   Grammatical theory: its limits and its possibilities. University of
            Chicago Press.
Nicole, Jacques
    1979   Phonologie et morphophonologie du Nawdm. Université de Benin, Dept.
            de linguistique.
Nida, Eugene A.
    1946   Morphology. Ann Arbor: University of Michigan Press.
Nigam, R. C., ed.
    1975   Grammatical sketches of Indian languages with comparative vocabulary
            and texts, I. Delhi: Civil Lines.
Nikolaeva, Tat'jana M.
    1983   Sintaksičeskaja akcentologija i/ili frazovaja intonacija. Fonetika 83:
            135-50.
Norman, Donald A., and David E. Rumelhart, eds.
    1975   Explorations in cognition. San Francisco: Freeman.
Norman, Linda Schwartz, and Gerald A. Sanders
    1977   Vocalic variation in Spanish verbs. Glossa 11:171-90.
Norrick, Neal R.
    1981   Semiotic principles in semantic theory. Amsterdam: Benjamins.
Noske, Roland, Jos Shinkel, and Norval Smith
    1982   The question of rule ordering: some counter-fallacies. JL 18:389-408.
Nöth, Winfried
    1976   Genese und Arbitraritätsgrade der Zeichentypen. Linguistische Be-
            richte 43:43-54.
    1979   Errors as a discovery procedure in linguistics. IRAL 17:61-76.
Nuhin, Vejsel
    1982   The English element in Albanian. Filipović 1982:1-27.
Nyman, Martti
    1979   Morphosyntactic motivation in reconstructed words: Latin tranquillus.
            IF 84:132-53.
    1980   Descriptive machinery as a non-source of theoretical insight: Modern
            Greek glide-formation and related matters. MS Helsinki. [Cf. Para-
            digms and transderivational constraints: stress and yod in Modern
            Greek. JL 17 (1981):231-46.]
    1984   On evaluation, causation, and validation: pre-Latin *-tl-. FLH 5,1.
Ó Dochartaigh, Cathair
    1980   Aspects of Celtic lenition. Ludwigsburg Studies in Language and
            Linguistics 4:103-37.
Odden, David
    1979   Review of Hooper 1976. Linguistic Analysis 5:439-60.

1980   The irrelevancy of the relevancy condition: evidence for the feature
        specification constraint. LAn 6:261-304.
1981   Assigned rule features in Shona. NELS 11:235-48.
Oeconomides, D. E.
1908   Lautlehre des Pontischen. Leipzig: Deichert.
Ogawa, Kunihiko
1981   A crosslinguistic study of voiceless vowels and some related phenomena.
        Annuan Reports, The Division of Languages, International Christian Uni-
        versity (Tokyo), 4:143-89.
Ohala, John J.
1974a   Experimental historical phonology. In Historical linguistics II (FICHL,
        eds. J. Anderson & C. Jones). Amsterdam: North Holland, 353-89.
1974b   Phonetic explanation in phonology. NatPhon, 251-74.
1975   Phonetic explanations for nasal sound patterns. Nasálfest, 289-316.
1979a   The phonetics of dissimilation: a hypothesis. MS for the 54th annual
        meeting of the Linguistic Society of America.
1979b   The contribution of acoustic phonetics to phonology. In Frontiers of
        speech communication research (eds. B. Lindblom & S. Öhman). New York:
        Academic Press, 355-62.
1980   The application of phonological universals in speech phonology. In
        Speech and language III (ed. N. J. Lass). New York: Academic Press,
        75-97.
1983   The phonological end justifies any means. PICL 13:232-43.
forthc. Consumer's guide to evidence in phonology. Rhodes, forthc.:1-34.
Ohala, Manjari
1972   Topics in Hindi-Urdu phonology. University of California, Los Angeles
        dissertation.
1974   The abstractness controversy: experimental input from Hindi. Lg 50:
        225-35.
1977   The treatment of phonological variation: an example from Hindi. Lingua
        42:161-76.
Ohlander, Sölve
1976   Phonology, meaning, morphology. Göteborg: Gothenburg Studies in En-
        glish 33.
Oller, John W.
1971   Coding information in natural languages. The Hague: Mouton.
Orešnik, Birgitta
1982   On the adaptation of English loanwords into Finnish. Filipović 1982:
        180-212.
Orešnik, Janez
1977   Modern Icelandic u-umlaut from the descriptive point of view. Gripla
        2:151-82.
1979   On the pronunciation of modern Icelandic röul(a) and slafneskur.
        Íslenskt mál 1:225-32.
Pačesova, Jaroslava
1978   Word-formation in children. PICL 12:450-2.
Panagl, Oswald
1975   Kasustheorie und Nomina agentis. Rix 1975:232-45.
1977a   Zum Verhältnis von Agens und Instrument in Wortbildung, Syntax und
        Pragmatik. wlg 16:3-17.
1977b   Aspekte der kindersprachlichen Wortbildung. L.A.U.T. b 24.
Papademetre, Leo
1982   Metrical structure and its interaction with vowel deletion in the
        Northern dialects of Modern Greek. NELS 12:199-208.

Papadopoulos, Anthimos A.
  1955   Istorikē grammatikē tēs Pontikēs diakéktou. Athens: Epitropē Pontikōn
         Maletōn.
Pape, Helmut
  1980   A Peircean theory of indexical signs and individuation. Semiotica 31:
         215-43.
Paris, Catherine
  1974   Système phonologique et phénomènes phonétiques dans le parler Besney de
         Zennun-köyü. Paris: Klincksieck.
Parker, Frank
  1981   A functional perceptual account of final devoicing. Journal of Phonet-
         ics 9:129-37.
Pateman, Trevor
  1982   Realism and language change. Language and Communication 2:161-78.
Paul, Hermann
  1880   Prinzipien der Sprachgeschichte. Halle: Niemeyer.
Paulson, Olof
  1969   Das Phonemsystem der modernen polonischen Literatursprache. Scando-
         Slavica 15:215-36.
Payne, David L.
  1981   The phonology and morphology of Axininca Campa. Dallas: SIL 66.
Peipmann, Rolf
  1976   Erkennen von Sturkturen und Mustern. Berlin: de Gruyter.
Peirce, Charles S.
  1965   Collected papers (eds. C. Hartshorne & P. Weiss). Cambridge, MA: Har-
         vard University Press.
Pelc, Jerzy
  1981   Prolegomena zu einer Definition des Zeichenbegriffs. Zeitschrift für
         Semiotik 3:1-9.
Pelletier, Francis J.
  1980   The generative power of rule orderings in formal grammars. Linguistics
         18:17-72.
Pennanen, Esko
  1980   Observations on word formation and syntax. L.A.U.T.
Penzl, Herbert
  1957   The evidence for phonemic changes. In Studies presented to J. Whatmough
         (ed. E. Pulgram). The Hague: Mouton, 193-208.
  1973   Orthography and phonology in the Old High German Ludwigslied. Kachru
         1973:759-65.
Perkell, J. S.
  1980   Phonetic features and the physiology of speech perception. In Language
         perception I (ed. B. Butterworth). New York: Academic Press, 271-96.
Pesot, Jürgen
  1980   Ikonismus in der Phonologie. Zeitschrift für Semiotik 2:7-18.
Peuser, G., and M. Fittschen
  1977   On the universality of language dissolution: the case of a Turkish
         aphasic. Brain & Language 4:196-207.
PhonGeg = Phonologie der Gegenwart (1967), ed. J. Hamm. Vienna: Böhlau.
Picard, Marc
  1977   Les règles morphophonémiques en diachronie. Montreal Working Papers
         in Linguistics 8:129-36.
  1981   Vowel harmony and morphophonemic rules. Vago 1981:237-44.
Picard, Marc, and Janet Nicol
  1982   Vers un modèle concret de la phonologie des emprunts. CJL 27:156-69.

Pike, Eunice K.
  1964   The phonology of New Guinea Highlands languages. American Anthropolo-
          gist 66:121-32.
Pike, Kenneth L.
  1947   Phonemics. Ann Arbor: University of Michigan Press.
Pilch, Herbert
  1965   Zentrale und periphere Lautsysteme. PICPhS 5:467-73.
  1974   Phonemtheorie I. Basel: Karger.
Plank, Frans
  1965   Rule inversion: Hermann Paul already had an idea-r-of it. York Papers
          in Linguistics 5:131-8.
  1978   Über Asymbolie und Ikonizität. In Brennpunkte der Patholinguistik (ed.
          G. Peuser). Munich: Fink, 243-73.
  1979   Ikonisierung und De-Ikonisierung als Prinzipien des Sprachwandels.
          Sprachwissenschaft 4:121-58.
  1981   Morphologische (Ir-)Regularitäten. Tübingen: Narr.
  n.d.   On the re-application of morphological rules after phonological rules.
          MS.
Plank, Sigrid, and Frans Plank.
  1979   Der Zusammenhang von Laut und Bedeutung als mögliche Konvergenzsphäre
          von Psychoanalyse und Linguistik. Linguistische Berichte 61:32-48.
Pohl, Alek
  1983   Morphonologie des Genativs im Russischen und Polonischen der Gegenwart.
          Studia alavica in honorem O. Horbatsch (eds. G. Freidhof et al.).
          Munich: Sagner, 109-30.
Poldauf, Ivan
  1982   Phonological aspects of English words by Czech. Filipović 1982:57-70.
Popova, T. V. et al., eds.
  1981   Slavjanskoe i balkanskoe jazykoznanije: problemy morfonologii. Moscow:
          Nauka.
Popper, Karl
  1959   The logic of scientific discovery. London: Hutchinson.
Poser, William J.
  1982   Phonological representations and action-at-a-distance. Hulst & Smith
          1982.II:121-58.
Postal, Paul
  1968   Aspects of phonological theory. New York: Harper and Row.
Prędota, Stanislaw
  1980   On vowel reduction in Dutch. In Studies in Dutch phonology (eds. W.
          Zonneveld et al.). The Hague: Nijhoff, 123-38.
Prince, Alan S.
  1983   Relating to the grid. LInq 14:19-100.
Prokosch, E.
  1939   A comparative Germanic grammar. Philadelphia: LSA.
Pulgram, Ernst
  1970   Syllable, word, nexus, cursus. The Hague: Mouton.
Pullum, Geoffrey K.
  1976   The Duke of York gambit. JL 12:83-102.
  1983   Morphophonemic rules, allophonic rules, and counterfeeding. LInq 13:
          179-84.
Pustejovsky, James, and Victoria Burke, eds.
  1981   Markedness and learnability. University of Massachusetts Occasional
          Papers in Linguistics 6.

Raible, Wolfgang
    1980   Regel und Ausnahme in der Sprache. Romanische Forschungen 92:199-222.
Ralph, Bo
    1977   Rule extension in historical phonology. Studia Linguistica 21:164-91.
    1981   Rule naturalness and rule diffusion. Phonologica 1980, 343-9.
Ransom, Jay E.
    1945   Notes on Duwamish phonology and morphology. IJAL 11:204-10.
Rauch, Irmengard, and C. Carr, eds.
    1980   The signifying animal. Bloomington: Indiana University Press.
Read, Charles
    1971   Pre-school children's knowledge of English phonology. Harvard Educa-
            tional Review 41:1-34.
Rédei, Károlyi
    1975   Phonologische Beschreibung des Syrjänischen. Linguistische Studien.
            A. Arbeitsberichte (Berlin) 22:103-16.
    1978   Syrjänische Chrestomathie. Vienna: Verband der wissenschaftlichen
            Gesellschaft Österreichs.
Redenbarger, Wayne J.
    1981   Articulatory features and Portuguese vowel height. Cambridge, MA:
            Harvard Studies in Romance Languages 37.
Reformatskij, Aleksandr A.
    1975   Ešče raz o statuse morfonologii: eё granicah i zadačah. Fonologičeskie
            Studi. Moscow: Nauka, 98-112.
    1979a   Kompressivno - allegrovaja reč'. Avanesov 1979:244-51. [Also in Re-
            formatskij 1979b:28-38.]
    1979b   Očerki po fonologii, morfonologii i morfologii. Moscow: Nauka.
Reider, Michael E.
    1981   Theoretical aspects of denasalization in Brazilian Portuguese. Glossa
            15:199-210.
Rennison, John
    1979   Synchronic phonological hierarchies and imaginary phonology: evidence
            from Salzburg German. ZDL 46:338-47.
    1981   What is schwa in Austrian German? The case for epenthesis and its
            consequences. Phonologica 1980, 351-6.
    1984   On the vowel harmonies of Koromfe. MS for Phonologica 1984 (eds. W. U.
            Dressler et al.). Cambridge University Press.
Rescher, Nicholas
    1978   Scientific progress. Oxford: Blackwell.
Resnick, Melvyn C.
    1975   Phonological variants and dialect identification in Latin American
            Spanish. The Hague: Mouton.
Reuse, Wilhelm J. de
    1981   Grassmann's law in Ofo. IJAL 47:243f.
Rheinfelder, Hans
    1968   Altfranzösische Grammatik I. Munich: Hueber.
Rhodes, Richard A.
    1972   Natural Phonology and MS conditions. PCLS 8:544-57.
    forthc. (ed.) Evidence in phonology. MS.
Rice, Karen
    1980   A rule ordering paradox in Hare. CJL 25:25-33.
Riedl, Rupert
    1981   Biologie der Erkenntnis. Die stammesgeschichtlichen Grundlagen der
            Vernunft. Berlin: Parey. [English translation: Biology of knowledge.
            The evolutionary basis of reason. New York: John Wiley & Sons, 1984.]

Ringen, Catherine
  1981   A concrete analysis of Hungarian vowel harmony.   Vago 1981:135-54.
  1983   Asymmetric vowel harmony in autosegmental phonology.   MS., Minnesota
         Regional Conference on Language and Linguistics (University of Minne-
         sota).   [Cf. her 1983 winter LSA paper: On autosegmental treatments
         of vowel harmony.]
Ringen, Jon, and Lyle Campbell
  1981   The explanation of linguistic change.   MS. for the Int. Conference of
         Historical Linguistics (Galway).
Rischel, Jørgen
  1974   Topics in West Greenlandic phonology.   Copenhagen: Akademisk Forlag.
Rix, Helmut, ed.
  1975   Flexion und Wortbildung.   Wiesbaden: Reichert.
Roberge, Paul T.
  1980   Morphologization of phonological alternations: a theoretical study
         based on the evidence from Germanic.   Ann Arbor: University of Michigan
         dissertation.
Robins, R. H., and N. Waterson
  1952   Notes on the phonetics of the Georgian word.   BSOAS 14:55-72.
Robinson, Kimball, et al.
  1977   Phonological ambiguity vs. the biuniqueness condition.   Journal of
         Phonetics 5:377-86.
Robinson, Orrin
  1972   Synchronic reflexes of diachronic phonological rules.   Ithaca, NY:
         Cornell University dissertation.
  1976   A 'scattered' rule in Swiss German.   Lg 52:148-62.
Rodríguez González, Félix
  1982   Variaciones fonotácticas en siglas: condicionamentos lingüísticos y
         sociolingüísticos.   Revista Española de Lingüística 12:357-74.
Rohlfs, Gerhard
  1966/1968   Grammatica storica della lengua italiana e dei suoi dialetti.
         Turin: Einandi, I 1966, II 1968.
Romaine, Suzanne
  1981   The status of variables in sociolinguistic theory.   JL 17:93-119.
  1983   On the productivity of word formation: rules and limits of variability
         in the lexicon.   Australian Journal of Linguistics 3:177-200.
  1984   On the problem of syntactic variation and pragmatic meaning in socio-
         linguistic theory.   Folia Linguistica 18.
Ronneberger-Sibold, Elke
  1980   Sprachverwendung - Sprachsystem: Ökonomie und Wandel.   Tübingen: Nie-
         meyer.
Rood, David S.
  1971   Wichita: an unusual phonology system.   Colorado Research in Linguis-
         tics 1.
  1975   The implications of Wichita phonology.   Lg 51:315-37.
Roux, Justus C.
  1981   On the notion 'phonologization': some experimental phonetic considera-
         tions from Sesotho.   Phonologica 1980, 373-8.
Rubach, Jerzy
  1976a Overkill in phonology.   Papers and Studies in Contrastive Linguistics
         5:39-46.
  1976b Surface phonetic constraints revisited.   Sprache 22:121-30.
  1977   Changes of consonants in English and Polish.   Wrocław: Ossolineum.
  1978   Non-uniqueness in phonology.   Lingua 44:49-66.

1980   Rule typology and phonological interference. MS. for Theoretical issues in contrastive phonology (ed. S. Eliasson).

1981   Cyclic phonology and palatalization in Polish and English. Wydanictwa Universytetu Warszawskiego.

1982   Analysis of phonological structures. Warsaw: Pañstwowe wydawnictwo naukowe.

1984   Soft stems and the problem of abstractness. PoL XVIII:28-63.

Rudes, Blair A.

1976   Lexical representation and variable rules in natural generative phonology. Glossa 10:111-50.

1977   Another look at syllable structure. Bloomington: Indiana University Linguistics Club.

1980   On the nature of verbal suppletion. Linguistics 18:655-76.

Ruhlen, Merritt

1975   A guide to the languages of the world. Stanford: Language Universals Project.

1978   Nasal vowels. Greenberg 1978.II:203-41.

Ruijgh, C. J.

1975-1976   Analyse morphopholonogique de l'attique classique. Mnemosyne 28: 225-9, 337-79, 29:1-25.

Russ, C. V. J.

1975   Umlaut in German: the development of a phonological rule. York Papers in Linguistics 5:51-65.

Saciuk, Bohdan

1969   The stratal division of the lexicon. Papers in Linguistics 1:464-532.

1974   Spanish stress and language change. Current studies in Romance languages (eds. R. J. Campbell et al.). Washington, DC: Georgetown University Press, 28-37.

Sadock, Jerrold M.

1983   The necessary overlapping of grammatical components. Interplay, 198-221.

Šahnarovič, A. M.

1973   Problemy motivirovannosti jazykovogo znaka v ontogeneze reči. In Obščaja i prikladnaja psiholingvistika (eds. A. A. Leon'tev & A. M. Šahnarovič). Moscow: Institut Jazykoznanija Akademii Nauk SSr, 81-7.

Saltarelli, Mario

1970   A phonology of Italian in a generative grammar. The Hague: Mouton.

Sampson, Geoffrey

1970   On the need for a phonological base. Lg 46:586-626.

Sanders, Gerald A.

1972   The simplex-feature hypothesis. Bloomington: Indiana University Linguistics Club. [= Glossa 8:141-92.]

1977   Functional constraints on grammars. Studies J. Greenberg (ed. Juilland). Saratoga: Anma Libri, I:161-78.

1979   Equational rules and rule function in phonology. Dinnsen 1979a:74-105.

Sapir, Edward

1921   Language. New York: Harcourt & Brace.

1922   Takelma. Handbook of American Indian languages II, 1-296.

1963[1933]   The psychological reality of phonemes. In Selected writings of Edward Sapir (ed. D. G. Mandelbaum). Berkeley: University of California Press, 46-60. [La réalité psychologique des phonèmes. Journal de Psychologie Normale et Pathologique 30 (1933):247-65.]

Saporta, Sol

1963   Phoneme distribution and language universals. In Universals of language (ed. J. Greenberg). Cambridge, MA: MIT Press, 61-72.

Sasse, Hans-Jürgen
  1976   Multikolumnale Segmente in der Phonologie. FIPK München 6:115-62.
  1979   Entlehnung morphophonemischer Regeln im Boni. Sprache und Geschichte
          in Afrika 1:93-108.
Sauer, Gert
  1975   Phonologische Analyse der ostjakischen Mundarten von Tremjugan. Lin-
          guistische Studien 22:130-55.
Saussure, Ferdinand de
  1916   Cours de linguistique générale. Paris: Payot. [Critical edition by
          R. Engler, Wiesbaden: Harrassowitz, 1968. Commented Italian transla-
          tion: Mauro 1967.]
Sawicka, Irena
  1974   Korelacija mekoče u poljskom književnom jeziku. Zbornik za filologiju
          i lingvistiku 17, 2 (Novi Sad), 31-6.
Schane, Sanford A.
  1968   French phonology and morphology. Cambridge, MA: MIT Press.
  1971   The phoneme revisited. Lg 47:503-21.
  1973   Generative phonology. Englewood Cliffs, NJ: Prentice-Hall.
Schenker, Alexander M.
  1964   Polish declension. The Hague: Mouton.
Scherfer, Peter
  1983   Natürliche Phonologie und Struktur des Französischen. Linguistische
          Berichte 86:14-26.
Schindler, Jochem
  1972   Wortbildungsregeln. wlg 1:39-52.
  1974   Fragen zum paradigmatischen Ausgleich. Sprache 20:1-9.
  1976   Diachronic and synchronic remarks on Bartholomae's and Grassmann's
          laws. LInq 7:622-37.
Schmitt, Rüdiger
  1967   Medisches und persisches Sprachgut bei Herodot. ZDMG 117:119-45.
Scholes, Robert J.
  1966   Phonotactic grammaticality. The Hague: Mouton.
Schourup, Lawrence
  1973   Unique New York unique New York unique New York. PCLS 9:587-96.
Schuh, Russell G.
  1978   Tone rules. In Tone (ed. V. A. Fromkin). New York: Academic Press,
          221-56.
Schütz, Albert J.
  1969   Nguna grammar. Honolulu: University of Hawaii Press.
Schwartz-Norman, Linda, and Gerald A. Sanders
  1977   Vocalic variations in Spanish verbs. Glossa 11:171-90.
Schwarze, Christoph
  1970   Suppletion und Alternanz im Französischen. Linguistische Berichte 6:
          21-34.
Scliar-Cabral, Leonor, et al.
  1979   Acquisition of rules of noun number and verbal metaphony in a Portu-
          guese dialect. PICL 12:617-20.
Scott, J. Robert
  1975   Morphological development in noun plurals in four Catalan dialects.
          Texas Linguistic Forum 2:142-51.
Sebeok, Thomas A.
  1977   (ed.) Perfusions of signs of signs. Bloomington: Indiana University
          Press.
  1979   The sign and its masters. Austin: University of Texas Press.

Seidler, Herbert
 1978   Grundfragen einer Wissenschaft von der Sprechkunst. Munich: Kindler.
Seifert, Katharina
 1984   Gibt es eine 'natürliche' Hierarchie der Pluralmorpheme auch in der
         psychologischen Realität? Sprache und Gesellschaft (eds. H. Krenn et
         al.). Tübingen: Niemeyer, 190-201.
Seiler, Hansjakob
 1965   Accent and morphophonemics in Cahuilla and in Uto-Aztecan. IJAL 31:50-
         9.
 1975   Die Prinzipien der deskriptiven und der etikettierenden Benennung. In
         Linguistic Workshop III (ed. H. Seiler). Munich: Fink, 2-57.
 1977   Cahuilla grammar. Banning, CA: Malki Muesum Press.
 1978a   (ed.) Language universals. Tübingen: Narr.
 1978b   The Cologne project on language universals. Seiler 1978a:11-25.
 1978c   Language as a mental operation. Leuvense Bijdragen 67:257-65.
 1979   Language universals research, language typology and individual grammar.
         Acta Ling. Hung. 29:353-67.
Seliger, Herbert W.
 1977   Biological analogs for language contact situations. International Jour-
         nal of Applied Linguistics 2.
Selkirk, Elisabeth O.
 1980a   Prosodic domains in phonology: Sanskrit revisited. Aronoff & Kean 1980:
         107-29.
 1980b   The role of prosodic categories in English word stress. LInq 11,3:
         563-605.
 1982   The syllable. Hulst & Smith 1982.II:337-83.
Semiloff-Zelasko, Holly
 1973   Glide metathesis. WPL (Ohio State University) 14:66-76.
Serebennikov, Boris A.
 1970   Jazyk kak obščestvennoe javlenie. In Obščee jazykovedenie. Moscow:
         Nauka, 417-50.
Ševeroškin, Vitalij V.
 1969   Zvukovye cepi v jazykah mira. Moscow: Nauka.
Sezer, Engin
 1981   The k/Ø alternation in Turkish. Harvard Studies in Phonology 2:354-82.
Sgall, Petr
 1971   On the notion 'type of language'. Traveaux linguistiques de Prague 4:
         75-87.
 1972   A note on typology and development of languages. Linguistics 85:67-71.
Sgall, Petr, et al.
 1969   A functional approach to syntax in a generative description of lan-
         guage. New York: American Elsevier.
 1975   = Prager Autorengruppe: Einführung in die generative Grammatik. Kron-
         berg: Scriptor.
Shapiro, Michael
 1967   Concatenators and Russian derivational morphology. General linguistics
         7:50-66.
 1969   Aspects of Russian morphology: a semiotic investigation. Cambridge,
         MA: Slavica Publishers, Inc.
 1974   Morphophonemics as semiotic. ALHaf 15:29-50.
 1976   Asymmetry: an inquiry into the linguistic structure of poetry. Amster-
         dam: North Holland.
 1980a   The structure of meaning in semiotic perspective. Papers 4th Intern.
         Conference on Historical Linguistics (eds. E. C. Traugott et al.). Am-
         sterdam: Benjamins, 53-9.

1980b   Russian conjugation: theory and hermeneutic.   Lg 56:67-93.
1983   The sense of grammar.   Language as semiotic.   Bloomington: Indiana University Press.

Sharpe, Margaret C.
1972   Alawa phonology and grammar.   Canberra: Australian Institute of Aboriginal Studies.

Sherzer, Joel
1970   Talking backwards in Cuna: the sociological reality of phonological descriptions.   Southwestern Journal of Anthropology 26,4:343-53.
1976   Play languages: implications for (socio)linguistics.   Kirshenblatt-Gimblett 1976:19-36.

Shevelov, G.
1965   A prehistory of Slavic.   New York: Columbia University Press.

Shibatani, Masayoshi
1973   The role of surface phonetic constraints in generative phonology.   Lg 49:87-106.

Shockey, Linda
1973   Phonetic and phonological properties of connected speech.   Ohio State University dissertation.

Sievers, Eduard
1893   Grundzüge der Phonetik.   4th ed.   Leipzig: Breitkopf & Härtel.

Sihler, Andrew L.
1977   Morphologically conditioned sound change and OE. past participles in -en.   General Linguistics 17:76-97.

Silva, Clare M.
1973   Metathesis of obstruent clusters.   WPL (Ohio State University) 14:77-84.

Singh, Rajendra
1981   The English plural.   Recherches linguistiques à Montréal 17:145-8.

Siptár, P.
1980   A note on initial clusters in English and Hungarian.   ALHung 30:327-43.

Skalička, Vladimír
1935   Zur ungarischen Grammatik.   Prague: Charles University.   [Reprinted in Skalička 1979.]
1979   Typologische Studien.   Braunschweig: Vieweg.

Skousen, Royal
1972   On capturing regularities.   PCLS 8:567-77.
1975   Substantive evidence in phonology.   The Hague: Mouton.
1979   Empirical interpretations of psychological reality.   PICPhSc 9.II:121-8.
1981   Analogical sources of abstractness.   Goyvaerts 1981:55-92.

Slagle, Uhlan V.
1974   A viable alternative to Chomskyan rationalism.   Lacus 1:177-93.

Slis, I.
1971   Articulatory effort and its duration and electromyographic correlates.   Phonetic 23:171-88.

Sloat, Clarence
1980   Vowel alternations in Coeur d'Alene.   IJAL 46:14-20.

Słoński, Stanisław
1947   Słownik polskich błędów językowych.   Warsaw: Czytelnik.

Smith, Jan R.
1978   Sri Lanka Creole Portuguese phonology.   Trivandrum: Dravidian Linguistics Association.

Smith, Neilson V.
1973   The acquisition of phonology.   Cambridge University Press.
1981   Consistency, markedness, and language change: on the notion 'consistent language'.   JL 17:39-54.

Smith, R. Edward
1980   Natural Phonology of Japanese. University of Hawaii dissertation.
Smoczyński, Paweł
1955   Przyswajanie przez dziecko podstaw systemu językowego. Łódź:
        Ossolineum.
Snow, Catherine E., and Charles A. Ferguson, eds.
1977   Talking to children: language input and acquisition. Cambridge Univer-
        sity Press.
Söderpalm, Ewa
1979   Speech errors in normal and pathological speech. Malmö: CWK Gleerup.
Sommerfelt, Alf
1921   Le Breton parlé à Saint-Pol-de-Léon. Paris: Champion. [New edition:
        Oslo: Universitetsforlaget, 1978.]
1949/1962 Le point de vue historique en linguistique. ALHafn.5. Reprinted
        in A. S., Diachronic and synchronic aspects of language. The Hague:
        Mouton, 72-80.
Sommerstein, Alan H.
1974   On phonotactically motivated rules. JL 10:71-94.
1977   Modern phonology. London: Arnold.
Stachowiak, Franz J.
1978   Some universal aspects of naming as a linguistic activity. Seiler
        1978a:207-28.
Stahlke, Herbert
1978   Segment sequences and segmental fusion. Studies in African Linguistics
        7:41-63.
Stampe, David
1969   The acquisition of phonetic representation. PCLS 5:443-54.
1972   On the natural history of diphthongs. PCLS 8:578-90.
1973   On Chapter nine. In Issues in phonological theory (eds. M. Kenstowicz
        & C. Kisseberth). The Hague: Mouton, 44-52.
1980   A dissertation on Natural Phonology. New York: Garland.
Stankiewicz, Edward
1955   The distribution of morphemic variants in the declension of Polish
        substantives. Word 11:554-74.
1960   The consonantal alternations in the Slavic declensions. Word 16:183-
        203.
1961   Opposition and hierarchy in morphophonemic alternations. In To honor
        Roman Jakobson III. The Hague: Mouton, 1895-905. [= Stankiewicz 1979:
        1-13.]
1972   (ed.) A Baudouin de Courtenay anthology. Bloomington: Indiana Univer-
        sity Press.
1976   Prague School morphophonemics. In Sound, sign and meaning: quinquage-
        nary of the Prague Linguistic Circle (ed. L. Matejka). Ann Arbor:
        Michigan Slavic Contributions 6:101-18. [= Stankiewicz 1979:14ff.]
1979   Studies in Slavic morphophonemics and accentology. Ann Arbor: Michigan
        Slavic Publications.
Stanley, Richard
1973   Boundaries in phonology. In A Festschrift for Morris Halle (eds. S. R.
        Anderson & P. Kiparsky). New York: Holt, 185-206.
Stark, Jacqueline
1974   Aphasiological evidence for the abstract analysis of the German velar
        /ŋ/. wlg 7:21-37.

Stegmüller, Wolfgang
    1969a/1979 Hauptströmungen der Gegenwartsphilosophie I (1969), II (1979).
        Stuttgart: Kröner.
    1969b Das ABC der modernen Logik und Semantik. Der Begriff der Erklärung und
        seine Spielarten. Berlin-New York: Springer.
Stein, Gabriele
    1970 Zur Typologie der Suffixentstehung. Idg. Forschungen 75:131-65.
Steinberg, Danny D.
    1973 Reading, phonology and Chomsky-Halle's optimal orthography. Journal
        of Psycholinguistic Research 2:239-58.
Steinberg, Danny D, and Robert K. Krohn
    1975 The psychological validity of Chomsky and Halle's vowel shift rule.
        In The transformational-generative paradigm and modern linguistic
        theory (ed. E. F. K. Koerner). Amsterdam: Benjamins, 233-59.
Stemberger, Joseph P.
    1981 Morphological haplology. Lg 57:791-817.
    1982 The nature of segments in the lexicon: evidence from speech errors.
        Lingua 56:235-59.
Stephany, Ursula
    1980 Zur psychischen Realität der Dimension der Deskriptivität. In Wege zur
        Universalienforschung, Festschrift H. Seiler. Tübingen: Narr, 549-55.
Stephens, Laurence D., and John S. Justeson
    1980 Some generalizations concerning glides. Proceedings of the 8th Annual
        Meeting of the Western Conference on Linguistics (eds. D. Malsch et
        al.). Edmonton: Linguistic Research Inc., 151-64.
Stevens, Alan M.
    1980 Formative boundary in phonological rules. Aronoff & Kean 1980:135-41.
Stieber, Ldzisław
    1973 A historical phonology of the Polish language. Heidelberg: Winter.
Stockwell, Robert, and Ronald Macauley, eds.
    1972 Linguistic change and generative theory. Bloomington: Indiana Univer-
        sity Press.
Straka, Georges
    1964 L'évolution phonétique du latin au français sous l'effet de l'énergie
        et de la faiblesse articulatoires. TraLiLi 2.17ff.
Strauss, Steven L.
    1982 Lexicalist Phonology of English and German. Dordrecht: Foris.
Sussex, Roland
    1976 Palatalization, liquidization and the description of maternal Polish.
        Talanya 3:93-106.
Swadesh, Morris
    1952 Salish phonologic geography. Lg 28:232-48.
Swanton, John R.
    1911 Haida. Handbook of American Indian languages I:205-82.
Swiggers, Pierre
    1983 The notation system of the Old Aramaic inscriptions. Archív Orientální
        51:378-81.
Szabó, Z.
    1970 Some characteristics of agglutinative type in derivation. In Theoreti-
        cal problems of typology and the northern Eurasian languages (eds. L.
        Dezső & P. Hajdú). Budapest: Akadémiai Kiadó, 157-63.
Tarte, Robert D., and Michael W. O'Boyle
    1982 Semantic judgments of compressed monosyllables: evidence for phonetic
        symbolism. Journal of Psycholinguistic Research 11:183-96.

Tauli, Valter
  1958   The structural tendencies of languages. I: General tendencies.
          Helsinki: Suomalainen Tiedeakatemia.
Tekavčić, Pavao
  1972   Grammatica storica dell' italiano. I-III. Bologna: Mulino.
Terbeek, Dale
  1973   Six dimensions of vowel quality. PCLS 9:672-8.
  1977a   A cross-language multidimensional scaling study of vowel perception.
          WPP (UCLA) 37.
  1977b   Some constraints on the principle of maximum perceptual contrast
          between vowels. PCLS 13:640-50.
Ternes, Elmar
  1970   Grammaire structurale du breton de l'île de Groix. Heidelberg: Winter.
  1974   The phonemic analysis of Scottish Gaelic. Hamburg: Buske.
Thelin, Nils B.
  1971   On stress assignment and vowel reduction in contemporary standard
          Russian. Uppsala.
Theophanopoulou-Kontou, Dimitra
  1973   Acquisition of noun morphology by children learning Greek as a native
          language. Ohio State University MA thesis.
Thomas, David
  1979   Centrifugal force and black holes in language. Lacus 6:30-5.
Thomason, Sarah G.
  1976   What else happens to opaque rules? Lg 52:370-88.
  1980   Review of Anttila 1974/1977. Lg 56:418-24.
Thomason, Sarah G., and Terrence S. Kaufman
  1976   Contact-induced language change: loanwords and the borrowing language's
          pre-borrowing phonology. In Current progress in historical linguistics
          (Proceedings ICHL 2, ed. Christie). Amsterdam: North Holland, 167-79.
Thráinsson, Höskoldur
  1978   On the phonology of Icelandic preaspiration. NJL 1:3-54.
Tillmann, H. G., and P. Mansell
  1980   Phonetik = Lautsprachliche Zeichen, Sprachsignale und lautsprachlicher
          Kommunikationsprozeß. Stuttgart: Klett-Cotta.
Timberlake, Alan
  1978   Uniform and alternating environments in phonological change. Folia
          Slavica 2:312-28.
Tinelli, Henri
  1981   Creole phonology. The Hague: Mouton.
Tokarski, Jan
  1978   Fleksja polska. Warsaw: Państwowe wydawnictwo naukowe.
Tolstaja, S.
  1971   O nekotoryh trudnostjah morfonologičeskogo opisanija. VJa 1971,1:37-43.
Tonelli, Livia
  1981   Überlegungen zur Natürlichen Phonologie: Eine kontrastive Analyse des
          Boznerischen und des Südtiroler Italienischen. University of Vienna
          dissertation. [Published by University of Trieste, 1984.]
Tranel, Bernard
  1978   The status of nasal vowels in Modern French. Studies in French
          Linguistics 1,2:27-70.
  1981   Concreteness in generative phonology. Evidence from French. Berkeley:
          University of California Press.
Trépos, Pierre
  1957   Le pluriel breton. Brest: Emgleo Breiz.

Trnka, Bohumil
    1931   General laws of phoneme combinations.   TCLP 4:57-61.
Trnka, Bohumil, et al.
    1958   Prague structural linguistics.   Philologica Pragensia 1:33-40.
Trubetzkoy, Nikolaj S.
    1929   Sur la morphonologie.   TCLP 1:85-8.
    1931   Gedanken über Morphonologie.   TCLP 4:160-3.   [French translation in the
            French version of Trubetzkoy 1939:337-42.]
    1932   Charakter und Methode der systematischen phonologischen Darstellung
            einer gesprochenen Sprache.   PICL 1:18-22.
    1934   Das morphonologische System der russischen Sprache.   TCLP 5,2.
    1939   Grundzüge der Phonologie.   Prague (= TCLP 7).   [Principles of phonology.
            Berkeley: University of California Press, 1969.]
Trudgill, Peter
    1974   The social differentiation of English.   Cambridge University Press.
Tuggy, David H.
    1979   Tetelcingo Nahuatl.   In Modern Aztec grammatical sketches (ed. R.
            Langacker).   Dallas: Summer Institute of Linguistics, 1-140.
Twaddell, W. Freeman
    1935   On defining the phoneme.   Lg Monograph 16.
Ułaszyn, Henryk
    1931   Laut, Phonema, Morphophonema.   TCLP 4:53-61.
Ultan, Russell
    1970   Some sources of consonant gradation.   Stanford: Working Papers on
            Language Universals 2.C1-30.
    1976   Descriptivity in the domain of body-part terms.   akup 21.
    1978a   A typological view of metathesis.   Greenberg 1978.II:367-402.
    1978b   Size-sound symbolism.   Greenberg 1978.II:525-68.
Uluhanov, Igor S.
    1975   O vidah usečenija osnov motivirujuščih slov v russkom slovoobrazovanii.
            Razvitie sovremennogo russkogo jazyka 1972 (ed. E. A. Zemskaja).
            Moscow: Nauka, 95-113.
Ungeheuer, Gerold
    1972   Sprache und Kommunikation.   Hamburg: Buske.
UNITYP-Forschergruppe
    1983   Beiträge zum Problembereich Skalen und Kontinua.   akup 53.
Vachek, Josef
    1968   The Linguistic School of Prague.   Bloomington: Indiana University Press.
    1981   Morphonological signals in linguistic typology.   FLH 2:99-114.
Vago, Robert, ed.
    1981   Issues in vowel harmony.   Amsterdam: Benjamins.
Vago, Robert, and Edwin Battistella
    1982   Rule application in phonology.   MS., Department of Linguistics, Queens
            College, CUNY.
Valdman, Albert
    1977a   (ed.) Pidgin and Creole linguistics.   Bloomington: Indiana University
            Press.
    1977b   Creolization: elaboration in the development of Creole French dialects.
            Valdman 1977a:155-89.
Valentin, Paul
    1978   The simplification of the unstressed vowel systems in Old High German.
            Fisiak 1978:373-89.
Valle, Maria V.
    1977   Interpretazione storica-fonetica dell' evoluzione 1 > u nelle lingue
            romanze.   Pisa: Giardini.

van den Broecke, Marcel, and Louis Goldstein
1980   Consonant features in speech errors.   Fromkin 1980:47-65.
van Lessen Kloeke, Wus
1982   Deutsche Phonologie und Morphologie.   Tübingen: Niemeyer.
van Marle, J.
1978   Review of Booij 1977.   Lingua 46:265-75.
van Parijs, Philippe
1981   Evolutionary explanation in the social sciences.   An emerging paradigm.
       London - New York: Tavistock.
van Wijk, Nicholas
1939   Phonologie.   The Hague: Nijhoff.
Vanecek, Erich, and W. U. Dressler
1977   Untersuchungen zur Sprechsorgfalt als Aufmerksamkeitsindikator.   Studia
       Psychologica 19:105-18.
Vennemann, Theo
1972a Phonetic detail in assimilation: problems in Germanic phonology.   Lg
       48:863-92.
1972b Phonetic analogy and conceptual analogy.   In Schuchardt, the Neogram-
       marians and the transformational theory of phonological change (eds.
       T. Vennemann & T. H. Wilbur).   Frankfurt: Athenäum, 181-204.
1972c Phonological concreteness in Natural Generative Grammar.   In Toward
       tomorrow's linguistics (eds. R. Shuy & C.-J. Bailey).   Washington:
       Georgetown University Press, 202-19.
1972d On the theory of syllabic phonology.   Linguistische Berichte 18:1-18.
1972e Rule inversion.   Lingua 29:209-42.
1974a Restructuring.   Lingua 33:137-56.
1974b Words and syllables in Natural Generative Grammar.   NatPhon 346-74.
1978   Universal syllabic phonology.   Theoretical Linguistics 5:175-215.
1981   Phonology as non-functional non-phonetics.   Phonologica 1980, 391-402.
Vértes, Edith
1977   Morphonematische Untersuchung der ostjakischen Vokalharmonie.
       Budapest: Akadémiai Kiadó.
Vijayakrishnan, K. G.
1981   The syllable in phonological theory: arguments from Tamil.   Studies in
       the Linguistic Sciences 11,2:101-5.
Viñas Urquiza, María Teresa
1970   Fonología de la lengua mataca.   Buenos Aires: Universidad.
Vincent, Nigel
1976   Three queries concerning one thesis concerning phonological representa-
       tions.   JL 12:75-82.
1977   The derivation of Italian *cresce*.   Linguistics 192:69-74.
1980   Words versus morphemes in morphological change: the case of Italian
       -iamo.   Fisiak 1980:383-98.
Vogt, Hans
1971   Grammaire de la langue georgienne.   Oslo: Universitetsforlaget.
Voorhoeve, Jan
1981   Multifunctionality as a derivational problem.   In Generative studies
       on Creole languages (ed. P. Muyskens).   Dordrecht: Foris, 25-34.
Voronin, S. V.
1983   Osnovy universal'noj klassifikacii onomatopov (onomatopeja i fonoseman-
       tika).   Fonetika - 83:45-54 (cf. 10).
Waight, Terence
1980   On the phonology of words of foreign origin.   Russian Linguistics 5:75-
       90.

Walker, Douglas C.
  1975   Lexical stratification in French phonology. Lingua 37:177-96.
  1979   On a morphophonemic innovation in Old French. CJL 24:52-4.
  1980   Review of Klausenburger 1979. Lg 56:879-82.
  1982   On a phonological innovation in French. Journal of the International
          Phonetic Association 12:72-7.
Walter, Henriette
  1984   Entre la phonologie et la morphologie. Variantes libres et fluctua-
          tions. FoL 18:65-72.
Wang, William S.-Y.
  1969   Competing changes as a cause of residue. Lg 45:9-25.
  1977   (ed.) The lexicon in phonological change. The Hague: Mouton.
Wanner, Dieter
  1972   The derivation of inflectional paradigms in Italian. In Generative
          studies in Romance languages (eds. J. Casagrande & B. Saciuk). Rowley,
          MA: Newberry House, 293-318.
Warburton, Irene
  1977   The function of inflectional paradigms in synchronic and diachronic
          linguistic descriptions. Phonologica 1976, 53-8.
Ward, Dennis
  1972   Softening in the morphophonemics of Russian. In The Slavic word (ed.
          D. S. Worth). The Hague: Mouton, 215-31.
Wares, Alan C.
  1968   A comparative study of Yuman consonantism. The Hague: Mouton.
Warren, D.
  1976   Aerodynamics of speech production. In Contemporary issues in experi-
          mental phonetics (ed. R. Lass). New York, 105-37.
Watt, W. C.
  1979   Iconic equilibrium. Semiotica 28:31-62.
Watzlawik, Paul, Janet H. Beavin, and Don. D. Jackson
  1967   Pragmatics of human communication. New York: Norton.
Waugh, Linda R.
  1976   Roman Jakobson's science of language. Lisse: de Ridder.
  1979   Remarks on markedness. Dinnsen 1979a:310-5.
Weinreich, Uriel
  1967   Languages in contact. The Hague: Mouton.
Weinreich, Uriel, William Labov, and Marvin Herzog
  1968   Empirical foundations for a theory of language change. Lehmann &
          Malkiel 1968:95-188.
Wells, C. G., and W. P. Robinson
  1982   The role of adult speech in language development. In Advances in the
          social psychology of language (eds. C. Fraser & K. R. Scherer).
          Cambridge University Press, 71-6.
Werner, Fritz
  1982   Die introflexive Wortbildung im Hebräischen. FoL 16:263-95.
  1983   Die Wortbildung der hebräischen Adjektiva. Wiesbaden: Harrassowitz.
Werner, Heinz, and Bernard Kaplan
  1967   Symbol formation. New York: Wiley.
Werner, Ottmar
  1977   Suppletivwesen durch Lautwandel. Salzburger Beiträge zur Linguistik
          3:269-83.
Wewiór, Barbara
  1978   Typowe błędy popłniane przez uczniców i kandydatów na studia w języku
          rosyjskim. Błędy grammatyczne i leksykalne. In Z problematyki błędów
          obcojęzycznych (ed. F. Grucza). Warsaw: Wydawnictwa Szkolne, 160-88.

Whorf, Benjamin L.
  1956   Language, thought, and reality. Cambridge, MA: MIT Press.
Wickman, Bo
  1975   Phonologische Analyse des Lulelappischen. Linguistische Studien 22:1-5.
Wierzchowska, Bożena
  1980   Fonetyka i fonologia języka polskiego. Wrocław: Ossolineum.
Wilbur, Ronnie B.
  1973   Reduplication and rule ordering. PCLS 9:679-87.
  1974   When is a phonological rule not a phonological rule? NatPhon 385-95.
  1975   Morphology and the rule ordering controversy. BLS 1:460-74.
Wilks, Yorick
  1979   Making preferences more active. In Associative networks (ed. N.
          Findler). New York: Academic Press, 239-66.
Williams, Edwin B.
  1962   From Latin to Portuguese. Philadelphia: University of Pennsylvania
          Press.
Wilson, Helen I.
  1972   The phonology and syntax of Palauan verb affixes. WPL (Hawaii) 4,5.
Wissemann, Heinz
  1954   Untersuchungen zur Onomatopoiie. Heidelberg: Winter.
Wodak, Ruth, and Wolfgang U. Dressler
  1978   Phonological variation in colloquial Viennese. Michigan Germanic
          Studies 4:30-66.
Wode, Henry
  1977   The L₂ acquisition of /r/. Phonetica 34:200-17.
  1978   The beginnings of non-schoolroom L₂ phonological acquisition. IRAL
          16:109-25.
Wojcik, Richard
  1976   The interaction of syllable and morpheme boundary in Natural Phonology.
          MS., Columbia University.
  1979   Borderline cases between rules and processes. Paper read at LSA Annual
          Meeting, Los Angeles.
  1981   Natural phonology and generative phonology. Goyvaerts 1981:635-47.
Woodfield, Andrew
  1976   Teleology. London: Cambridge University Press.
Wright, James
  1975   Nasal-stop assimilation: testing the psychological reality of an
          English MSC. Nasålfest 389-97.
Wright, Larry
  1976   Teleological explanations: an etiological analysis of goals and
          functions. Berkeley: University of California Press.
Wright, Georg H. von
  1974   Erklären und Verstehen. Frankfurt: Athenäum.
Wunderlich, Dieter, ed.
  1976   Wissenschaftstheorie der Linguistik. Frankfurt: Suhrkamp.
Wurzel, Wolfgang U.
  1970   Studien zur deutschen Lautstruktur. Studia Grammatica 8. Berlin:
          Akademie-Verlag.
  1980a   Some remarks on the relations between naturalness and typology. TCLC
          20:103-13.
  1980b   Der deutsche Wortakzent. Zeitschrift für Germanistik 3:299-318.
  1980c   Ways of morphologizing phonological rules. Fisiak 1980:443-62.
  1980d   Sprachsystem und Dialektik. ZPSK 33:165-75.
  1981a   Problems in morphonology. Phonologica 1980:413-34.

1981b   Dialektischer Determinismus und Sprachsystem. Deutsche Zeitschrift für
        Philosophie 29:1360-9.
1982   Phonologie - Morphonologie - Morphologie. Linguistische Studien 93A.
        Berlin: Akademie der Wissenschaften der DDR.
1984   Flexionsmorphologie und Natürlichkeit. Studia Grammatica.
Wüster, Eugen
1979   Einführung in die Allgemeine Terminologielehre und Terminologische
        Lexikographie. I, II. Vienna - New York: Springer.
Yakut, Attila
1981   Sprache der Familie. Tübingen: Narr.
Yartseva, Victoria, et al.
1977   Philosophical orientation of linguistic research. Social Sciences 8:
        147-57.
Yavas, Mehmet
1980   Vowel and consonant harmony in Turkish. Glossa 14:189-211.
1982   Natural phonology and borrowing assimilations. Linguistics 20:123-32.
Zabrocki, Ludwik
1951   Usilnenie i lenicja w językach indoeuropejskich i w ugrofińskim.
        Poznań: Poznańskie Towarzystwo Przyjaciół Nauk.
Zarębina, Maria
1965   Kształtowanie się systemu językowego dziecka. Wrocław: Ossolineum.
Zemskaja, Elena A.
1973   Sovremennyj russkij jazyk: Slovoobrazovanie. Moscow: Prosveščenie.
1978   Unités fondamentales du système synchronique de la formation des mots.
        PICL 12:78-83.
Zimmer, Karl E.
1969   Psychological correlates of some Turkish morpheme structure conditions.
        Lg 46:309-21.
1975   Some thoughts on likely phonologies for non-ideal speakers. Papers
        from the Parasession on Functionalism (CLS), 556-67.
Zimmer, Karl E., and Barbara Abbott
1978   The k/∅ alternation in Turkish: some experimental evidence for its
        productivity. Journal of Psycholinguistic Research 7:35-46.
Zipf, George K.
1935/1965 The psycho-biology of language. Cambridge, MA: MIT Press.
1949   Human behavior and the principle of least effort. New York: Hafner.
Zonneveld, Wim
1976   A phonological exchange rule in Flemish Brussels. LAn 2:109-14.
1978   A formal theory of exceptions in generative phonology. Dordrecht:
        Foris.
Zonneveld, Wim, et al., eds.
1980   Studies in Dutch phonology.
Zubin, David, and Klaus-M. Koepcke
1981   Gender: a less than arbitrary grammatical category. PCLS 17:439-49.
Žuravlëv, Vladimir K.
1967   Opyt fonologičeskoj interpretacii praslavjanskih gruppofonem. PhonGeg
        142-57.
Zwicky, Ann D., and Arnold M. Zwicky
1980   America's national dish: the style of restaurant menus. American
        Speech, 83-92.
Zwicky, Arnold M.
1972   On casual speech. PCLS 8:607-15.
1973   The analytic leap: from 'some Xs are Ys' to 'all Xs are Ys'. PCLS 9:
        700-9.

1974   Taking a false step. Lg 50:215-24.
1975a The strategy of generative phonology. Phonologica 1972 (eds. W.
       Dressler & F. Mareš). Munich: Fink, 151-68.
1975b Settling on an underlying form: the English inflectional endings.
       Cohen & Wirth 1975:129-85.
1976   Bibliography on cyclical segmental rules. IJAL 42:267f.
1977   On clitics. Phonologica 1976, 29-39.
1983   An expanded view of morphology in the syntax-phonology interface. PICL
       13:198-208.
1984   Autonomous components and limited interfacing: phonology-free syntax,
       the Hallean syllogism, and their kin. PCLS 20:365-86.
Zwicky, Arnold M., and Geoffrey Pullum
1983   Phonology in syntax: the Somali optional agreement rule. Natural
       Language and Linguistic Theory 1,3:385-402.
to appear The syntax-phonology interface.